AMERICAN ERAS

WESTWARD
EXPANSION

1 8 0 0 - 1 8 6 0

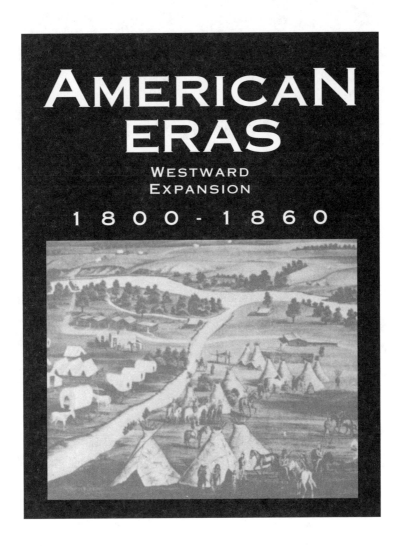

AMERICAN ERAS

WESTWARD EXPANSION

1 8 0 0 - 1 8 6 0

EDITED BY
PETER C. MANCALL

A MANLY, INC. BOOK

GALE

AMERICAN ERAS
1800-1860

Matthew J. Bruccoli and Richard Layman, Editorial Directors
Karen L. Rood, Senior Editor

ADVISORY BOARD

Copyright ©1999 by Gale Research
ISBN 0-7876-1483-1

CONTENTS

INTRODUCTION

Going West. In 1800 the United States population stood at 5,308,483, and virtually every man, woman, and child counted in the national census lived east of the crest of the Appalachian Mountains. By 1860 the population of the nation reached 31,443,321, and American citizens could be found from the Atlantic to the Pacific. Yet despite this almost 600 percent increase in the size of the population, the United States remained for the most part an agrarian nation: most people lived in small communities or on farms spread throughout the countryside. In an age of industrial revolution, massive emigration from Western Europe (especially from the German-speaking parts of the Continent and famine-struck Ireland), and epic conflict over the future course of American society, it could be argued that the most decisive development of the antebellum period was westward expansion. No other phenomenon played as significant a role as the mere fact that the United States during this period spread westward at a dizzying pace. When the nineteenth century began, the dominant population in most of the West was of Native American ancestry though there were large populations of Hispanic peoples in the areas that are now the Southwest. By 1860 the federal government had forced Indians out of the East, opened up lands in the Midwest for land-hungry white citizens, supported rebellion in Texas, and encouraged Easterners to keep moving west. When citizens of the eastern United States worried about their tragic move toward the Civil War, Americans in the West—at least those of European origin—were busy developing post–Gold Rush California, transforming Chicago into one of the nation's largest economic centers, and expanding their control over nonwhites.

News about the West. At the dawn of the nineteenth century few people living in the United States had a firm grasp on what lay west of the Appalachian Mountains. Although the West was already populated by American Indians and Hispanics, these people had little understanding of life along the Eastern seaboard. As a result the decades after 1800 were characterized by multiple discoveries. President Thomas Jefferson sent Meriwether Lewis and William Clark up the Missouri River to map out much of the territory the United States had acquired in the Louisiana Purchase of 1803. He also hoped that the Corps of Discovery would find a navigable water route to the Pacific. Other explorers (such as Zebulon Pike, John Colter, Manuel Lisa, Stephen Long, and Henry Schoolcraft) sent back vivid accounts of natural resources to an Eastern population that eagerly read them in newspapers. During the late 1840s those same newspapers carried word of what was one of the most dramatic moments of the age: the discovery of gold in northern California. The mad dash to profit from the West's natural resources signaled only one characteristic American response to what Easterners discovered in the West. In reality the process of discovery was always mutual. Native Americans in the Southwest and the Western plains discovered citizens from the United States and thought of them as trespassers; Mexicans and Hispanic Americans who lived in Texas discovered that Anglos would do everything in their power to gain control of the territory that had once demarcated the northern boundaries of Spain's American empire. For these native Western populations the discoveries of the antebellum period brought trouble, not opportunity.

Indian-White Relations. Perhaps no single arena of public life witnessed greater changes from 1800 to 1860 than the realm of Indian-white relations. In 1800 thousands of Native Americans remained east of the Appalachian Mountains. Many Indian communities had suffered for generations from contact with European colonists, especially since those newcomers had in the colonial period brought with them pathogens previously unknown in the Americas. As a result the native peoples of the Americas suffered a staggering demographic catastrophe when smallpox, measles, and other diseases raced through their communities. Historians now believe that the native population of North America in 1800 was perhaps only 10 percent of what it had been before 1492. Despite the loss of population and despite the fact that eastern Indians had to contend with Europeans who wanted their lands and their souls as well, many native peoples remained in the East. Most communities could be found in the Southeast in the Cherokee, Chickasaw, Creek, Choctaw, and Seminole nations though there were other Indians who lived in the Northeast as well. In the 1830s the federal government decided that the time had come to force Indians out of the East. In 1830 Congress passed the Indian Removal Act, a bill that encouraged Indians to sell their lands to the United States and take up new lands in what was then Indian Territory, located primarily in present-day Oklahoma. Some Indians agreed to move, but many thousands refused and tried to protect their lands by doing what all Americans had the right to do: take the government to court. But in the 1830s, in a series of crucial court decisions, the Supreme Court made it clear that Indians were not and could not be citizens of the United States. In the aftermath of those decisions the federal government decided to use its military power to move Indians off their lands and thus open up fertile farming areas for white citizens, many of whom hoped to establish plantations staffed by African American slaves. This forced population movement of Indians, referred to as the Trail of Tears by the Cherokees, led to the death of perhaps four thousand native men, women, and children who lacked adequate food and clothing for the overland march to Indian Territory.

A West for Whites. The federal government's actions in the Southeast in the 1830s were the most notable incidents in an age in which the West became home to thousands of American citizens of European extraction. Many of those people moved west because they believed that the West would be free of the disabling social and political tensions of the East that pivoted around the issue of slavery. In fact, the question of whether Western states would be open to slaves was among the most contentious issues of antebellum politics. Politicians in Congress struggled for decades to determine the future course of the West. As early as 1787, the year the founders drafted the Constitution in Philadelphia, Congress had created the Northwest Ordinance that forever banned slavery in what is now called the Old Northwest, territory that became the Midwestern states of Ohio, Indiana, Illinois, and Michigan. But Southerners eager to expand territory open to slavery sought lands west of the Appalachians that would be open to white farmers who had slaves, especially those who wanted to farm cotton, the most profitable crop of the industrial age. In a series of historic compromises, from the Missouri Compromise of 1820 to the Compromise of 1850 and the Kansas-Nebraska Act of 1854, Congress charted the westward course of the nation. Despite the well-intentioned goals of some politicians who despised slavery and wanted to eliminate it (as did many Americans, especially in the Northern states), there was little sense that the West would be a land of opportunity for all Americans. American Indians remained excluded from the benefits of citizenship; African Americans remained enslaved; most Northerners who moved to the West hoped to live in communities with no black residents; Anglo settlers in Texas and the Southwest treated Hispanics with cruelty; and the first migrants to the West from China found themselves in a land where they could obtain little recourse from the indignities and injustices they experienced in California. The famous New York City newspaper editor Horace Greeley might have told young Americans to "Go West" to find their future happiness, but the antebellum West was no place of equality for all Americans.

Opportunity. Thousands of Americans who moved to the West and were able to gain land found the opportunity advertised by Greeley. During the antebellum period a series of technological changes—from the invention of the cotton gin in 1793 to the plows manufactured by John Deere and his associates and the reapers produced by Cyrus McCormick—enabled American farmers to plant and harvest their crops with ever-increasing efficiency. Just as important, the federal government during this period supported what historians refer to as the transportation revolution, the creation of a commercial infrastructure of roads, canals, and railroad tracks that traversed much of the nation. Improved access to transportation routes allowed farmers who produced large harvests to move their goods to distant markets. In the 1810s the construction of the Erie Canal, which reduced the price of moving goods from the Great Lakes to New York City at the same time that it increased the speed of transit, demonstrated that the West could become a breadbasket for growing urban populations in the eastern United States and in Europe. By the late antebellum period farmers looking to market goods in the West could send them to regional cities, especially Chicago, which emerged as the most important urban center in the middle of the United States. Other cities—San Francisco, New Orleans, and St. Louis—also rose to prominence as regional trading entrepôts, further encouraging the development of Western lands.

Spiritual Encounters. At the same time that many citizens of the United States were spending time trying to find ways to harvest the natural resources of the West, some Americans were busy seeking a harvest of souls. Religious movements traveled rapidly in the antebellum West, and so, it seemed, did those involved in spiritual quests. At times revival movements focused on trying to reclaim core religious values of their respective people. The Shawnee Prophet Tenskwatawa and the evangelical preacher Charles Grandison Finney taught differing lessons to those who listened to them, but each hoped to cure the ills of their respective societies by awakening in their followers a sense of devotion to the true path of faith. The task for other religious leaders was far different. Missionaries from various Protestant denominations believed that the time had come to revive the centuries-long quest to convert American Indians to Christianity, a goal that some Indians refused to share; in specific places the conflict between missionaries and natives over the spiritual lives of Indians became so intense that some missionaries, most famously Marcus Whitman and his family, paid for their unyielding persistence (some would call it arrogance) with their lives. Perhaps the most notable religious movement in the West was also the least expected: the birth of the Church of Jesus Christ of Latter-Day Saints, the Mormons. Although the movement began in upstate New York, by the end of the antebellum period the followers of the patriarch Joseph Smith had migrated across much of the United States, suffering persecution in cities such as Nauvoo, Illinois, before creating their spiritual homeland in Salt Lake City in Utah Territory. No other spiritual movement from this age so shaped the future of religious practice in the United States.

An Empire for the Arts. Creativity flourished throughout the West, evident particularly in the emergence of distinctive regional art styles. In some places westward-moving Easterners transported their artistic culture and heritage with them; the opening of opera houses in New Orleans and then San Francisco testified to the commitment that settlers in these bustling cities were willing to make a place for what had always been one of the most expensive and extravagant forms of artistic expression imported from Europe. Even so, the West generated more than imitations of Eastern or European art. By 1860 Western writers had begun to express their ideas in a distinctive idiom. At times this literature emanated from ideas circulating in the East about the West; James Fenimore Cooper's Natty Bumppo became one archetype of the Western American—a man at home in undeveloped wilderness moving ever westward to escape the entangling social snares of a seemingly more civilized world. But the West and its people generated their own forms of literature as well. The author James Rollin Ridge, of mixed Anglo and Cherokee parentage, became one of the nation's most popular authors when he wrote about the exploits of the fabled Mexican bandit Joaquin Murieta, a figure cast in stark contrast to Cooper's characters. More distinctive still were the visual styles embraced by artists in the West. In native communities painting styles remained constant, mirroring the survival of a body of oral literature and folklore that enabled Indians to keep their particular cultures vibrant. When painters of European origin traveled to the West, the canvases they produced often dwelled on the grandeur of nature; the leading practitioners of the Hudson River School—notably Frederic Church and Albert Bierstadt—painted enormous canvases filled with the distinctive light and hues of the territory beyond the Appalachians. The painter Thomas Cole's series of history paintings called "The Course of Empire" might have suggested a bleak future for civilization in the United States, but that sense of pessimism was rare in the visual images generated by Easterners who traveled through the Great Plains or Rocky Mountains. George Catlin's portraits of Plains and Western Indians lacked the despair that Cole experienced even though Catlin believed he was leaving a permanent record of people he felt sure were destined for extinction.

Replicating the East. The citizens of the United States who moved westward during the antebellum period did not do so to escape American society. On the contrary, thousands hoped that they would be able to create in the West a better version of the life they had hoped to find in the East. Easterners thus spent an enormous amount of time, money, and effort to create schools and colleges in the West. Many of these schools had denominational affiliations, and those who organized them hoped to spread the benefits of their particular religions into new territories; but only in part did the move toward creating educational institutions stem from spiritual concerns. When the residents of the newly formed state of Indiana put into their constitution in 1816 provisions to establish a system of free education that would stretch from the primary grades through college, they were early proponents of educational impulses that found expression throughout the antebellum period. By 1860 some individuals involved in the business of schooling in the West realized that the benefits of formal education needed to spread to nonwhites as well as whites, a sentiment most famously evident in the founding of Oberlin Collegiate Institute in northern Ohio in the 1830s and carried on in the programs of John Swett, California's most influential educational policy proponent in the mid nineteenth century. In these same decades Westerners created state-supported educational institutions that instructed students in medicine and law and in some places—as in Cincinnati in 1840—mandated bilingual education for children of European immigrants. The growth of schools and colleges in the West mirrored another development as well: over time inhabitants of the West had ever-greater access to news from the East, carried in newspapers and by postal carriers. The invention of the telegraph in the late antebellum period might have signaled the end of the short-lived Pony Express, but that technological change was no doubt welcomed by Americans across the West who had learned to read and write in schools and colleges and were eager to keep abreast of news beyond their communities.

The American West. The territory that stretched from the Pacific Ocean in the West to the Appalachian Mountains in the East became, during the antebellum period, the American West. In some sense that designation, which is still used in the late twentieth century, is an ideal characterization of the region from 1800 to 1860, for what happened in this territory happened across the nation to some extent. In these years the federal government and the court system did little or nothing to improve the lives of nonwhites who resided within the political boundaries of the United States. Americans were busy defining their culture and system of politics, their economy, and their religious values. The conflicts in the West were starker than in the East, but for the most part any disputes in the region were not sui generis. Although the West has always had its distinctive attributes such as isolation and little rainfall, the human presence in the region during the early nineteenth century reflected the historical forces shaping the Western world, especially the United States. The West was a land of great bounty at the same time that it became a land of limited or diminishing fortune for many who lived there before 1800 or for those, such as Cherokees forced westward on the Trail of Tears, who were reluctant migrants to this purported land of opportunity.

ACKNOWLEDGMENTS

This book was produced by Manly, Inc. Anthony J. Scotti was the in-house editor.

Production and systems manager is Marie L. Parker.

Administrative support was provided by Ann M. Cheschi, Tenesha S. Lee, and Shawna Tillman.

Bookkeeper is Neil Senol.

Copyediting supervisor is Phyllis A. Avant. The copyediting staff includes Brenda Carol Blanton, Christine Copeland, Jannette L. Giles, Thom Harman, Melissa D. Hinton, and Raegan E. Quinn. Freelance copyeditors are Rebecca Mayo, Nicole M. Nichols, and Jennie Williamson.

Editorial associate is Jeff Miller.

Layout and graphics staff includes Janet E. Hill, Mark J. McEwan, and Alison Smith.

Office manager is Kathy Lawler Merlette.

Photography editors are Margo Dowling and Paul Talbot. Photographic copy work was performed by Joseph M. Bruccoli.

SGML supervisor is Cory McNair. The SGML staff includes Linda Drake, Frank Graham, Jennifer Harwell, and Alex Snead.

Database manager is Javed Nurani. Kim Kelly performed data entry.

Typesetting supervisor is Kathleen M. Flanagan. The typesetting staff includes Karla Corley Brown, Pamela D. Norton, and Patricia Flanagan Salisbury.

Walter W. Ross and Steven Gross did library research. They were assisted by the following librarians at the Thomas Cooper Library of the University of South Carolina: Linda Holderfield and the interlibrary-loan staff; reference-department head Virginia Weathers; reference librarians Marilee Birchfield, Stefanie Buck, Stefanie DuBose, Rebecca Feind, Karen Joseph, Donna Lehman, Charlene Loope, Anthony McKissick, Jean Rhyne, and Kwamine Simpson; circulation-department head Caroline Taylor; and acquisitions-searching supervisor David Haggard.

Peter C. Mancall wishes to thank Maril Hazlett for her research assistance and Lisa Bitel for her inspiration and wise counsel.

AMERICAN ERAS

WESTWARD EXPANSION
1800–1860

WORLD EVENTS:

SELECTED OCCURRENCES OUTSIDE THE UNITED STATES

by MARIL HAZLETT

MAJOR POWERS AND LEADERS

Austria (Habsburg Empire)—Emperor Francis (1804–1835); Ferdinand I (1835–1848); Francis Joseph (1848– 1916).

China—Emperor Jia-quing (1796–1820); Tao Kuang (1820–1850); Yi-Chu (1850–1861).

France—Napoleon Bonaparte, first consul (1799––1804), emperor (1804–1814; 1815); King Louis XVIII (1814– 1815; 1815–1824); Charles X (1824––1830); Louis Philippe (1830–1848); Louis Napoleon (later Emperor Napoleon III), president (1848–1852), emperor (1852– 1871).

Great Britain—King George III (1760–1820); George, Prince of Wales (later George IV), regent (1811–1820); King George IV (1820–1830); William IV (1830–1837); Queen Victoria (1837–1901). Prime Ministers: William Henry Cavendish Bentnick, third Duke of Portland (1783; 1807–1809); William Pitt the Younger (1783–1801; 1804–1806); Henry Addington (1801–1804); William Wyndham Grenville, first Baron Grenville (1806–1807); Spencer Perceval (1809–1812); Robert Banks Jenkinson, second Earl of Liverpool (1812–1827); George Canning (1827); Lord Goderich (1827–1828); second Earl Grey (1830– 1834); Lord Melbourne (1834; 1835–1839; 1839– 1841); Robert Peel (1834; 1841–1845; 1845––1846); Lord John Russell (1846–1852); Edward Geoffrey Stanley, fourteenth Earl of Derby (1852); George Hamilton-Gordon, fourth Earl of Aberdeen (1852–1855); Henry John Temple, Viscount Palmerston (1855–1858; 1859– 1866); Edward Geoffrey Stanley, fourteenth Earl of Derby (1858–1859).

Japan—Emperor Kokaku (1779–1816); Ninko (1817–1846); Komei (1846–1867). Shoguns: Ienari (1786– 1837); Ieyoshi (1837–1853); Iesada (1853–1858); Iemochi (1858–1866).

Ottoman Empire—Sultan Selim III (1789–1807); Mustafa IV (1807–1808); Mahmud II (1808–1839); Abdul Mejid I (1839–1861).

Prussia—King Frederick William III (1797–1840); Frederick William IV (1840–1861).

Russia—Czar Paul I (1796–1801); Alexander I (1801–1825); Nicholas I (1825–1855); Alexander II (1855–1881).

Spain—King Charles IV (1788–1808); Ferdinand VII (1808; 1813–1833); Joseph Bonaparte (brother of Napoleon I of France, 1808–1813); Ferdinand VII (1813– 1833); Queen Isabella II (1833–1868).

Zulu Kingdom—Senzagakona (1781–1816); Sigujana (1816); Shaka (1816–1828); Dingane (1828–1840); Mpande (1840–1872).

MAJOR CONFLICTS

1791–1802—Wars of the French Revolution: Britain and Austria versus France

1792–1804—War for Haitian Independence

1801–1805—Tripolitan War: United States versus Tripoli

1803–1805; 1817–1818—Mahratta Wars: Britain and allied Indian states versus Maharashtra

1803–1815—Napoleonic Wars: Britain, Austria, Prussia, and Russia versus France

1804–1810—West African Jihad (Holy War) of Moslem divine Usman dan Fodio

1809–1826—Wars for Latin American Independence: Spain versus Mexico, Paraguay, Ecuador, Bolivia, Venezuela, and Guatemala

1812–1815—War of 1812: United States versus Britain

1813–1814—Creek War: United States versus the Creek tribe

1821–1829—Greek War for Independence: Greece versus the Ottoman Empire

1822–1831—First Ashanti War: Britain versus Ashanti people of present-day Ghana

1824–1826—First Burmese War: Britain versus Burma

1826–1828—Russo-Persian War

1828–1829—Russo-Turkish War

1830–1832—Black Hawk War: United States versus the Sac and Fox tribes

1830–1847—French conquest of Algeria

1832–1833—Turko-Egyptian War

1834–1839—Carlist Wars: Spain versus the forces of the Royal Pretender Don Carlos

1835–1842—Seminole War: United States versus the Seminole tribe

1836—Texan War of Independence: Texas versus Mexico

1838–1842—First Afghan War: Britain versus Afghanistan

1839–1842—First Opium War: Britain versus China

1844–1848—New Zealand Wars: Britain versus the natives of New Zealand

1845–1849—Sikh Wars: British East India Company versus the Sikhs in India

1846–1848—Mexican War: United States versus Mexico

1848—Schleswig-Holstein War: Prussia versus Denmark

1848–1849—Austro-Sardinian War

1850–1863—Armed conflict between Britain and Siam on the Malayan frontier

1852–1853—Second Burmese War: Britain versus Burma

1853–1856—Crimean War: Great Britain, France, and the Ottoman Empire versus Russia

1856–1860—Second Opium War: Britain versus China

1857–1858—The Great Mutiny: Revolt of Sepoys (native troops) of the British East India Company

1858–1862—French invasion of Cochin China

1800

- Colonists in Freetown rebel against the Sierra Leone Company.

- Forces under Toussaint Louverture gain control of the French half of Hispaniola and then invade the Spanish area of the island.

- Italian physicist Allessandro Volta invents the voltaic cell, the prototype of the electric battery.

- The Romantic movement in literature, art, and music begins in Europe. Major contributors include William Wordsworth, Samuel Taylor Coleridge, Joseph Mallord William Turner, and Ludwig van Beethoven.

Feb.	France ratifies a new constitution.
13 Mar.	Gregorio Barnabo Chiaramonte becomes Pope Pius VII.
20 Mar.	The French defeat the Turks at Heliopolis.
20 Mar.–21 Apr.	The Pashas in Egypt lead a revolt against the French.
5 Apr.	The British capture the island of Goree (off Senegal) from France.
14 June	Napoleon Bonaparte defeats the Austrians at Marengo in Italy.
5 Sept.	The French garrison on Malta surrenders to the English.
1 Oct.	In the secret Treaty of San Ildefonso, Spain cedes the Louisiana Territory to France.
3 Dec.	French forces defeat the Austrians at Hohenlinden, Bavaria.

1801

Jan.	The Act of Union creates the United Kingdom of Great Britain; England and Ireland are to be governed by one parliament.
26 Jan.	Toussaint Louverture captures the Spanish capital of Santo Domingo on Hispaniola; France sends an army to recapture the colony.
9 Feb.	Austria and France sign the Treaty of Luneville in which France is to control Italy west of Venice.
11 Mar.	The insane Czar Paul I is murdered and replaced by his son, Alexander I; the new czar withdraws Russia from the war against France.
21 Mar.	At the Battle of Alexandria, Egypt, a British and Turkish force defeats the French.
2 Apr.	A British fleet defeats the Danish navy at the Battle of Copenhagen.
10 June	Tripoli declares war on the United States.
July	Louverture sends a constitution to France for Napoleon Bonaparte's approval.
15 July	Napoleon and Pius VII reach an agreement by which the French government will nominate bishops to be consecrated by the Pope.
Aug.	French forces in Egypt capitulate.
24 Dec.	Richard Trevithick in England uses a steam engine to power a carriage.

1802

- Portuguese traders begin the first successful crossing of the African continent from Angola to the Zambezi River, reaching Tete in 1811.

- Italian inventor Gian Domenico Romagnosi observes an electric current moving through a wire.

- Marie Grosholtz Tussaud, a Swiss wax modeler who had been commissioned in 1793 to make death masks of guillotine victims, opens a wax museum in London.

- The British Parliament passes the Factory Act to protect apprentices in textile mills.

- Nathaniel Bowditch of Salem, Massachusetts, publishes *The New American Practical Navigator*, correcting eight thousand errors in an earlier English text on navigation.

- Thomas Wedgwood, son of British potter Josiah Wedgwood, produces the first photographic image on paper coated with silver nitrate; however, the image fades quickly.

27 Mar.	England and France sign the Treaty of Amiens; England accepts France's conquests in Europe and gives up Malta, Elba, Minorca, and Cape Colony but keeps Ceylon and Trinidad.
11 Apr.	Freetown settlers repulse Temnes warriors.
1 June	Nguyen Phuc Anh proclaims himself Emperor Gia Long, changes the name of his country from Annam to Vietnam, and establishes the capital at Hue.
10 June	Toussaint Louverture is arrested and taken to France.
14 June	Napoleon Bonaparte orders slavery to be reestablished in Santo Domingo and other French colonies.
2 Aug.	A French plebiscite elects Napoleon consul for life.
1 Nov.	Gen. Victor-Emmanuel Leclerc, sent to Santo Domingo to restore slavery and French power, dies of yellow fever.

1803

- King Kamehaha I unites the eight islands of Hawaii.

- Wahhabi fundamentalists capture Mecca.

- English chemist John Dalton arranges a table of atomic weights.

- Cotton becomes the leading export of the United States.

20 Feb.	The British seize Kandy, Ceylon, and leave a small force to protect their puppet king.
7 Apr.	Toussaint Louverture dies in a French prison.
16 May	After refusing to surrender Malta, England resumes war on France.
23–24 June	British troops are massacred after an uprising in Kandy, Ceylon.
23 July	An uprising in Ireland fails.

| 23 Sept. | At the Battle of Assaye in India, British forces defeat the Mahrathas. |
| Dec. | The British capture Pondicherry from the Mahrathas. |

1804

- The Universities of Kazan and Kharkov in Russia are founded.
- The Code Napoleon, civil laws based on Roman statutes and egalitarian concepts of the French Revolution, spreads through France.
- The first vacuum-bottling factory, or cannery, opens near Paris.

Feb.	French authorities discover a Royalist plot to depose Napoleon Bonaparte.
21 Feb.	In West Africa, Usman dan Fodio accuses Hausa kings of laxity in Islamic observances and declares a jihad, or holy war. By 1810 he will control all of the Hausa territory and form the Sokoto Empire.
Oct.	The Russian warship *Nadezha* enters the harbor at Nagasaki, Japan, but local authorities order it to leave.
Oct.	The British seize the Spanish treasure fleet carrying gold valued at $3 million.
8 Oct.	Jean-Jacques Dessalines proclaims himself Emperor Jaques I of Santo Domingo.
2 Dec.	The Pope crowns Napoleon emperor of France.

1805

- In West Africa, Kebbi and Zaria fall to Usman's forces.
- The British House of Lords defeats a bill to abolish the slave trade.
- In Arabia, Wahhabi fundamentalists capture Medina.

11 Apr.	Russia forms an alliance with Italy.
26 May	Napoleon Bonaparte crowns himself king of Italy in order to legitimize French claims to northern Italy.
4 June	The United States and Tripoli sign a peace treaty.
9 Aug.	Austria and England sign a treaty of alliance.
9 Oct.	France and Naples agree to neutrality.
15–20 Oct.	A French army defeats and captures an Austrian force at Ulm in western Germany.
21 Oct.	At Cape Trafalgar off the coast of Spain, the Royal Navy under Horatio, Lord Nelson, destroys two-thirds of the French and Spanish fleets; Nelson is mortally wounded.
13 Nov.	Napoleon occupies Vienna.
2 Dec.	Napoleon defeats the Russians and Austrians at Austerlitz in present-day Czechoslovakia.
26 Dec.	Francis II of Austria cedes Venetia, Istria, and Dalmatia to France.

1806

- French inventor Joseph Marie Jacquard introduces a new attachment for weaving looms that will revolutionize the industry.

- The fur trade between America and China now exceeds $5 million annually. The Americans send ginseng and furs to China, and the Chinese send back teas, spices, and other goods. American vessels are also establishing trade contacts with the West and East Indies and the Philippines.

- African American boxer Bill Richmond is defeated in a match with the Englishman Tom Cribb.

12 Jan.	French forces leave Vienna.
19 Jan.	British forces arrive in South Africa to take Cape Colony.
23 Jan.	A French army forces King Ferdinand of Naples to flee; Joseph Bonaparte becomes king of Naples the following month.
16 May	British foreign minister Charles James Fox orders a naval blockade of the European continent.
27 June	A British force from the Cape of Good Hope captures Buenos Aires.
July	A Sepoy mutiny occurs at Velore, India, and one thousand people are killed or wounded.
Aug.	A Spanish force from Montevideo recaptures Buenos Aires.
6 Aug.	Napoleon Bonaparte has German states withdraw from the Holy Roman Empire and form the Confederation of the Rhine. In addition he forces Francis II of Austria to abdicate the title of Roman emperor.
13 Sept.	A Prussian army moves into Thuringia.
17 Oct.	Jacques I of Santo Domingo is assassinated; Henri Christophe takes control of the northern part of the island while Alexander Petion captures the southern area.
14 Oct.	The French severely defeat the Prussians at Jena and Auerstädt in central Germany.
27 Oct.	Napoleon occupies Berlin.
21 Nov.	Napoleon's Berlin Decree closes Europe to British trade and citizens by declaring that any neutral ship entering a British port would be denied access to any European port under French control.
Dec.	Russia and the Ottoman Empire go to war.
Dec.	Russian troops capture Bucharest.

1807

- Katsina in West Africa falls to forces under Usman dan Fodio.

- Russians attack Japanese settlements on Sakhalin Island and Hokkaido.

- Great Britain retaliates against Napoleon Bonaparte's Berlin Decree by requiring all neutral ships trading within the blockaded zones to get a special license.

•	Off of Norfolk, Virginia, HMS *Leopard* fires on USS *Chesapeake*. The *Chesapeake* undergoes a search, and four members of the crew are impressed into the British Navy.
•	The U.S. Congress passes the Embargo Act, forbidding all shipping with Europe.
7 Jan.	Great Britain declares war on the Ottoman Empire.
7–8 Feb.	Russian and Prussian forces halt Napoleon at Eylau in East Prussia.
19 Feb.	A British fleet breaks through Turkish defenses at the Dardanelles.
25 Mar.	Parliament bars British subjects from participating in the slave trade.
31 Mar.	Great Britain attempts to invade Egypt but is defeated at Rosetta.
29 May	Janissaries in the Ottoman Empire depose and kill Selim III, installing Mustapha IV as sultan.
14 June	The French defeat the Russians at Friedland, East Prussia.
7–9 July	Prussia cedes its west Elbean possessions to France's German satellites and yields Polish territories to the grand duchy of Warsaw; Frederick August of Saxony becomes grand duke of Warsaw; Prussia joins the Continental System and remains garrisoned by Napoleon; and Czar Alexander I recognizes French conquests.
Aug.	A truce is declared between Russia and the Ottoman Empire.
7 Sept.	The Danish fleet surrenders to the British after the bombardment of Copenhagen.
17 Dec.	Napoleon issues the Milan Decree, which declares that all neutral ships that submitted to British search would be confiscated by the French.

1808

•	The United States bans the transatlantic slave trade.
1 Jan.	Sierra Leone becomes a royal British colony, and the Royal Navy enforces the ban on the slave trade. By 1815 British officials capture six thousand slaves at sea and release them in the colony.
19 Mar.	Charles IV of Spain abdicates in favor of Ferdinand VII, who turns the Spanish crown over to Napoleon Bonaparte in May.
Apr.	In the Bayonne Decree, Napoleon orders the seizure of U.S. ships entering French, Italian, or Hanseatic ports. The French will eventually seize $10 million in U.S. ships and cargo. However, the British also are plundering approximately one in eight U.S. vessels at sea as well as impressing U.S. sailors into the Royal Navy.
2 May	A Spanish uprising starts against the French.
June	Muhammad 'Ali begins the conquest of Upper Egypt.
15 July	Joachim Murat becomes king of Naples after Joseph Bonaparte abdicates to become king of Spain.
20 July	French troops occupy Madrid, but the Spanish drive them out.

28 July	Mahmud II becomes sultan of the Ottoman Empire.
Sept.–Oct.	At Erfurt in central Germany the French and Russians affirm their alliance.
Nov.	Napoleon leads two hundred thousand men into Spain.
2 Dec.	Napoleon occupies Madrid and imprisons the royal family three days later.

1809

•	Usman dan Fodio takes over Kano in northern Nigeria. He founds the city of Sokoto and establishes control of the Islamic movement over the entire Hausa region.
•	Finland becomes an autonomous grand duchy of the Russian Empire.
•	Samuel Somering invents the electric telegraph.
Jan.	Parliament learns that the mistress of the duke of York is selling army commissions.
12 Mar.	England and Persia form an alliance.
12 Mar.	A coup d'etat in Sweden deposes King Gustavus IV.
Apr.	The Austrians invade Bavaria, but Napoleon Bonaparte defeats them.
25 Apr.	The British East India Company signs a treaty with Ranjot Singh, ruler of Lahore.
1 May	Napoleon annexes the papal states to France.
3 May	Russia declares war on Austria.
12 May	Napoleon captures Vienna.
21–22 May	Napoleon is defeated by the Austrians at Aspern, Austria.
5 June	The duke of Sudermania becomes King Charles XIII of Sweden.
12 June	The Catholic Church excommunicates Napoleon.
5–6 July	The French army defeats the Austrians at Wagram near Vienna.
5 July	Napoleon orders the imprisonment of Pope Pius VII.
14 July	The British seize Saint-Louis, Senegal, from France.
27–28 July	A British army under Sir Arthur Wellesley defeats Joseph Bonaparte's Spanish army at Talavera de Reina, and as a result Wellesley becomes Viscount Wellington of Talavera.
26 Sept.	The Turks defeat the Russians at Silistria in present-day Bulgaria.
14 Oct.	Austria and France sign a peace treaty.
16 Dec.	Napoleon divorces Josephine.

1810

•	Miguel Hidalgo y Costilla launches the eleven-year Mexican War for Independence with the cry "viva religion, viva America, death to bad government!"

- Portugal agrees to a gradual abolition of the slave trade.

- French chemist Louis-Nicolas Vaquelin identifies nicotine as the active chemical in tobacco.

6 Jan.   France and Sweden declare peace.

11 Mar.   Napoleon marries Maria Luisa, an eighteen-year-old Austrian archduchess.

9 July   Napoleon annexes Holland.

25 Aug.   Muhammad 'Ali Pasha requests that the Ottoman Empire grant Egypt autonomy.

27 Oct.   U.S. president James Madison orders the occupation and annexation of West Florida, currently occupied by Spain. Congress officially annexes West Florida to the Mississippi Territory on 14 May 1812.

16 Dec.   Representatives of New Spain present grievances to the Spanish Cortes.

31 Dec.   Czar Alexander I withdraws from the Continental System.

1811

- Spain debates abolishing the slave trade; Cuban planters object and defeat the move.

- English engineer John Blenkinsop invents a two-cylinder steam locomotive.

- English novelist Jane Austen publishes *Sense and Sensibility*.

- Earthquake tremors rock the Ohio and Mississippi River valleys, rising and sinking the earth's crust between five and twenty-five feet.

- From their capital in Riyadh, the Wahabis rule all of Arabia, except present-day Yemen.

- The Estados Unidos of Venezuela, led by Francisco de Miranda and Simon Bolívar, declare independence from Spain, initiating a decade-long civil war with Spanish general Pablo Morillo.

5 Feb.   Parliament appoints the prince of Wales as regent for King George III, who has gone mad.

Mar.   Riots occur in Nottingham, England, as unemployed workers destroy the textile machinery that put them out of work.

1 Mar.   Muhammad 'Ali Pasha, Ottoman viceroy in Egypt, massacres rebellious Mamluks.

21 Mar.   Father Migeul Hidalgo y Costilla is captured in Mexico.

7 July   A general congress in Venezuela declares independence.

31 July   Father Migeul Hidalgo is executed at Chihuahua.

14 Aug.   Paraguay declares independence.

18 Sept. The Dutch surrender Java to the British.

1812

- Russia and Sweden sign a secret alliance.

- Swiss orientalist Johann Ludwig Burckhardt begins an ascent of the Nile River to Korosko, then travels across the Red Sea and eventually to Mecca.

- Dingiswayo, Zulu chief, begins consolidating military forces in southern Africa.

- In order to exploit the sea otter trade, the Russians establish Fort Rossiya on the Pacific Coast, just north of Bodega Bay in present-day California.

- The United States declares war on Great Britain as a result of the disputes over the shipping rights of nations neutral in the European conflict.

1813

- Swiss novelist Johann Rudolph Wyss publishes the *Swiss Family Robinson*, a collection of stories told by his father.

- English novelist Jane Austen publishes *Pride and Prejudice*.

13 Aug. The Creeks, who allied with the British in the War of 1812, massacre settlers at Fort Mims in present-day Alabama, under the leadership of Red Eagle (William Weatherford). This act initiates the Creek Indian War.

5 Oct. In southeastern Ontario, U.S. forces led by Gen. William Henry Harrison defeat a British army under Gen. Henry Proctor. Shawnee chief Tecumseh is slain, and U.S. forces burn Fairfield, an Indian mission village. This victory secures the Old Northwest territories for the United States.

1814

9 Mar. Great Britain, Russia, Prussia, and Austria sign the Quadruple Alliance against France.

29 Mar. Militia forces under Andrew Jackson defeat the Creeks at Horseshoe Bend on the Tallapoosa River. The Creeks cede two-thirds of their land to the United States, which will form the present-day state of Alabama.

30 May The First Treaty of Paris, signed by France, Britain, Austria, Prussia, and Russia, establishes a preliminary peace in Europe.

4 June Louis XVII, in exile since 1795, is restored to the French throne.

24–25 Aug. British troops burn Washington, D.C. in retaliation for the American sacking of York (present-day Toronto), Canada, in 1813.

24 Dec. The Treaty of Ghent ends the War of 1812 between the United States and Great Britain; territories are returned to their prewar status.

25 Dec. Australian Anglican missionary Samuel Marsden is the first to preach the Christian gospel to the Maoris in New Zealand.

1815

- African American sailor and businessman Paul Cuffe tries to establish a colony of freed American slaves in Africa, near Sierra Leone.

	Because of increasing repression in Spain, Italy, and especially Germany, European Jews lose gains made during the Napoleonic era.
8 Jan.	American troops led by Andrew Jackson defeat a British army at the Battle of New Orleans two weeks after Great Britain and the United States sign the Treaty of Ghent, ending the war.
27 Feb.	Napoleon Bonaparte escapes from exile on the Mediterranean island of Elba.
20 Mar.	Louis XVIII flees Paris, and the Hundred Days begins as Napoleon assumes control of France.
18 June	The British and the Prussians defeat Napoleon at the Battle of Waterloo in Belgium.
22 June	Napoleon abdicates, and Louis XVIII is returned to the throne. Napoleon is exiled to St. Helena, a British island in the South Atlantic, and dies there on 5 May 1821.
20 Nov.	The Treaty of Paris allows the military occupation of France by allied troops.

1816

- British poet Samuel Taylor Coleridge publishes *Kubla Khan*.
- After the death of Senzangakoma, chief of the Zulu people scattered along the Tugelo River, another chief, Shaka, begins to gain control.
- Because of a volcanic explosion in the East Indies a year earlier, the resulting dust left in the atmosphere causes much of the world to experience a cold summer.

16 Jan.	Brazil declares itself an empire, led by the prince regent of Portugal.
5 May	Carl August of Saxe-Weimar declares the first German state constitution.
9 July	Argentina (the United Provinces of La Plata) declares independence.
July	Andrew Jackson initiates the Seminole War after he sends troops to Florida to destroy Negro Fort, a refuge for Indians and escaped slaves.

1817

- Swami Bhikkanaji Maharaja and his followers in India split from the Sthanakavasis and form the Jain sect of Terapathis.
- Georg Wilhelm Friedrich Hegel publishes the *Encyclopedia of Philosophy*.
- Elizabeth Fry, a Quaker woman in England, founds the Society for the Reformation of Prison Discipline. Her goals are to reform the notorious London penitentiary known as Newgate and to draw attention to the plight of female prisoners everywhere.

| 28 Apr. | The United States and Great Britain sign the Rush-Bagot Treaty, which limits the warships on the Great Lakes to four for each nation. |
| 14 July | French writer Madame de Stael dies; her salon was of international importance to politics and culture. |

1818

- Shaka establishes the Zulu Empire.

- British novelist Mary Wollstonecraft Shelley publishes *Frankenstein*.

6 Jan. Through the Treaty of Mundoseer the British gain control of the dominion of the Hoplkar of Indore and the Rajputana states in India.

12 Feb. Dictator Bernardo O'Higgins proclaims the Republic of Chile independent from Spain. In April the Spanish make their last unsuccessful attempt to reclaim Chile at the Battle of Maipo.

20 Oct. The Canadian-U.S. boundary is extended westward along the 49th parallel from the Lake of the Woods (present-day boundary of Manitoba, Ontario, and Minnesota) to the Rocky Mountains.

21 Nov. At the Congress of Aix-la-Chapelle, France joins the four Great Powers in the Quintuple Alliance, and allied troops leave France.

20 Nov. Simon Bolívar declares independence for Venezuela.

1819

- The *Savannah* completes the first steamship journey across the Atlantic in twenty-six days.

- Sikh leader Ranjit Singh conquers Kashmir.

- After the long delay caused by the Napoleonic Wars, the Spanish national art gallery, the Prado Museum, opens in Madrid.

6 Feb. Sir Stamford Raffles of the British East India Company founds Singapore.

22 Feb. According to the terms of the Transcontinental Treaty between Spain and the United States, Spain rescinds land claims east of the Mississippi River and gains Texas. Spain does not ratify the treaty until 1820.

7 Aug. Revolutionary leader Simon Bolívar wins a decisive battle with the Spanish Royalists at Boyaca.

16 Aug. In response to a large rally for broader representation in Parliament, the British government sends the cavalry to St. Peter's Field in Manchester. The ensuing confrontation results in eleven deaths at what later will be called the Peterloo Massacre.

20 Sept. The Frankfurt Diet issues the Carlsbad Decrees, measures that suppress political freedom in order to control revolutionary tendencies in Germany.

17 Dec. Simon Bolívar becomes president of an independent Colombia.

1820

- French chemists Pierre Joseph Pelletier and Joseph Bienaime Caventou isolate quinine.

- Thomas Robert Malthaus publishes *Principles of Political Economy*.

- For the first time the ancient Assyrian city of Nineveh is surveyed on the southern banks of the Tigris River. Later excavations will reveal artifacts from 6,000 B.C.

- Egypt begins a two-year campaign to conquer the Sudan.

- Football first appears on American college campuses, primarily as a way for up-perclassmen to haze freshmen.

- Jules Sebastian Cesar Dumont d'Urville discovers the statue of Venus de Milo on the Greek island of Melos.

1 Jan.–
7 Mar.   A revolution in Spain forces King Ferdinand VII to restore the 1812 constitution.

27 Jan.   Russian naval officer Fabian Gottlieb von Bellinghausen sails completely around the continent of Antarctica, describing it as an enormous, boundless field of ice.

29 Jan.   George III, king of Great Britain, dies after years of insanity, and George IV assumes the throne.

13 Feb.   French revolutionaries assassinate Charles Ferdinand de Bourbon, presumably the last of the Bourbons.

24 Aug.   In Oporto, Portugal, the Portuguese army supports a rebellion against the Spanish-supported regency. The revolution gains popular support and results in a liberal constitution.

1821

- Spain recognizes Mexico's independence.

- Ireland's population has reached nearly seven million, nearly one-half the combined population of England, Wales, and Scotland.

6 Mar.   A Greek from Constantinople, Alexander Ypsilanti, initiates an uprising at Iasi in Moldavia, resulting in the Greek War for Independence from the Ottoman Empire.

14 June   With the help from Turkish and Albanian forces, Egyptian soldiers take over Sennar, in the eastern Sudan, and capital of the Funj Sultanate. They depose Badi VI, and Muhammad 'Ali Pasha, the Ottoman pasha of Egypt, furthers his empire through the eastern Sudan.

24 June   In the final battle of the Venezuelan War for Independence, Simon de Bolívar defeats Spanish royal forces at Carabobo.

2 July   The British government recognizes the Hudson Bay Company, which controls Prince Rupert's Land, the Yukon Territory, British Columbia, Alberta, and western parts of Saskatchewan and the Northwest Territories.

28 July   José Francisco de San Martín declares Peru's independence after driving the Spanish out of Lima.

15 Sept.   Guatemala declares independence from Spain.

28 Nov.   Panama declares independence from Spain.

1 Dec.   The Republic of Santo Domingo is founded, independent of Spain.

1822

- Muhammed 'Ali, Ottoman pasha of Egypt, directs his empire on a program of economic development based around the export of cotton to Europe.

- Liberia is founded as a colony for freed slaves.

27 Jan. Greece declares independence from the Ottoman Empire.

7 Sept. Dom Pedro I declares Brazil independent of Portugal and later proclaims himself emperor of Brazil.

16 Sept. Robert Stewart, Viscount Castlereagh and British foreign secretary, commits suicide for no apparent reason; George Canning takes his office.

20 Oct. Under provisions of the Quadruple Alliance the Congress of Verona agrees to a French invasion of Spain.

14 Dec. At the Congress of Vienna, Great Britain refuses to intervene in the Spanish revolution while other nations refuse to interfere in the Greek War for Independence. These developments mark the end of the congress system of European diplomacy.

1823

- Charles Babbage begins work on a calculating machine.

19 Mar. Internal tensions force Emperor Augustus de Iturbide of Mexico to abdicate.

7 Apr. France invades Spain and removes Ferdinand VII from the Spanish throne.

31 Aug. France returns Ferdinand VII to the throne after crushing the Spanish rebels.

2 Dec. U.S. president James Monroe issues the Monroe Doctrine, which warns world powers to stay out of the Western Hemisphere.

1824

- Ludwig van Beethoven composes the *Ninth Symphony*.

- English inventor William Sturgeon develops the first electromagnet.

- The United States establishes the Bureau of Indian Affairs in order to negotiate treaties and to provide health care.

17 Mar. The United Kingdom of the Netherlands and Great Britain signs the Treaty of London. The Dutch cede Malacca and abandon claims to Singapore in return for Benkulen in Sumatra.

11 May In war with Burma, Great Britain takes Rangoon.

16 Sept. Louis XVIII dies, and Charles X becomes king of France.

12 Dec. The last Spanish army in South America surrenders.

1825

- Great Britain allows trade unions to form.

- Over the course of the next two years English explorer John Franklin maps approximately eight hundred miles of the Canadian Arctic Coast in an effort to find the Northwest Passage.

6 Aug.	The Republic of Bolivia declares independence from Peru.
25 Aug.	Uruguay declares independence from Brazil.
29 Aug.	Portugal recognizes Brazilian independence.
Nov.	Stocks and bonds prices drop precipitously in Europe, forcing many bankruptcies; in part, bad harvests during the French Revolution and Napoleonic Wars cause the crisis.
26 Dec.	In St. Petersburg the Decembrist uprising breaks out over who will succeed Czar Alexander I. Alexander had named his younger brother, Nicholas, as his successor, but his older brother, Constantine, challenged the succession. After the uprising was quelled Nicholas I ruled for thirty years.

1826

•	Scottish explorer Alexander Gordon Laing is murdered two days after leaving Timbuktu on the Niger River in Mali. He was the first European to reach this city from the north, crossing the Sahara Desert.
•	Persia declares war on Russia after its military forces occupy the Causcaus.
•	Nguan Nguan edits Confucius's writings.
•	A global cholera epidemic begins in India.
24 Feb.	The Treaty of Yandabu ends the First Burmese War.
15–16 June	At the orders of Ottoman sultan Mahmud II the Turks' standing army, the Janissaries, are massacred in their barracks.

1827

•	The Church Missionary Society founds Fourah Bay College in Sierra Leone, the first institution of higher education in West Africa.
•	Russian czar Nicholas I issues harsh anti-Jewish conscription laws, which use compulsory military service to force conversions.
26 Jan.	Peru secedes from Colombia.
26 Mar.	German composer Ludwig van Beethoven dies. He had been deaf since 1817 but still completed nine symphonies, an opera, and various concertos and sonatas.
Apr.	After serving in the Greek cause for independence Ioannes Antonios Kapodistras is elected ruler of Greece.
6 July	Great Britain, France, and Russia guarantee Greek independence in the Treaty of London.
15 Nov.	The Creek Indians cede to the federal government their remaining lands in what is now the southeastern United States.

1828

- King Radama I of Madagascar dies, and his queen, Ranavalona I, succeeds him. The queen pursues policies of avoiding foreign influences and entanglements while the British and the French launch unsuccessful naval and military campaigns in retaliation.

- Haiku poetry master Issa, who revived the Japanese art form, dies.

26 Apr. Nicholas I, Russian czar, declares war on the Ottoman Empire to serve national interests and aid Greek patriots.

9 May The British Parliament repeals the Test Act of 1673, which had forbidden Roman Catholics and Protestant nonconformists from holding public office. This act had been an attempt to marginalize the Irish threat of civil uprisings.

22 Sept. Zulu king Shaka is assassinated; his rule had established the Zulus as the dominant military power in southern Africa.

1829

- David Walker publishes *Walker's Appeal . . . with a Preamble to the Coloured Citizens of the World, but in Particular and Very Expressly to Those of the United States of America,* a plea for blacks to rise up against slavery. States in the southern United States try to prevent its printing and sale.

- French inventor Louis Braille, blind from an accident at age three, publishes his alphabet for the blind.

14 Sept. The Russo-Turkish War ends with the Treaty of Adrianople. Serbia and Greece gain autonomy; the Ottomans lose influence in the Balkans; and Russia gains strategic outposts at the mouth of the Danube River and along the Black Sea.

4 Dec. The British government in India outlaws the practice of suttee in which widows throw themselves on their husbands' funeral pyres as a mark of devotion.

1830

- In a climate of social reforms, such as abolition and an ascending middle class, the Chartism Movement gains strength in Great Britain. Its leaders believe in universal suffrage for men, secret balloting, no property requirements for Parliament members, and annual elections. Over the course of the next twenty years Chartists present petitions backing these demands, totaling more than one million signatures. Their movement declines after 1848, but by the end of the century most of their demands have been codified in British law.

- The U.S. Congress passes the Indian Removal Act, which authorizes the president to relocate American Indians west of the Mississippi River into the rather loosely defined Indian Territory. Over the next ten years, the federal government forces approximately sixty thousand Indians westward.

- Ferdinand VII repeals the Salic Law in order to name his heir, Isabella, to the throne of Spain; civil uprisings follow.

July Charles X attempts to suspend the French constitution by decreeing the Five Ordinances; Paris citizens riot and begin the July Revolution.

2 Aug.   Charles X abdicates, ending the line of Bourbon rulers in France.

17 Dec.   Simon de Bolívar dies. A leader in the Venezuelan Revolution, he also assisted independence movements in Colombia, Peru, Bolivia, and other South American countries.

1831

- Hunters bring in a record haul of more than 687,000 seals from the North Atlantic Ocean, dealing a horrible blow to seal populations.

- James Clark Ross, Scottish explorer, plots the position of the magnetic North Pole.

- The Indian state of Mysore, a former center of rebellion against European policies, comes under British control.

- Prussia makes a major attempt, the first of its kind, to reforest its lands in Europe.

1832

- An epidemic of Asiatic cholera strikes North America, killing more than fifteen thousand people in New Orleans, Quebec, and Montreal. The disease spreads westward, decimating Indian populations.

- U.S. Supreme Court Chief Justice John Marshall hands down his decision in *Worcester* v. *Georgia*, declaring the Cherokees had sovereignty over their own lands and those people within them.

2 Aug.   The U.S. Army forces defeat Black Hawk, leader of the Sac and Fox Indians, in Wisconsin.

21 Sept.   Scottish poet and novelist Sir Walter Scott dies. One of his better-known works is *Ivanhoe*, first published in the United States in 1819.

1833

- Antonio López de Santa Anna becomes president of Mexico, eventually declaring himself dictator.

- Charles Lyell publishes the *Principles of Geography*.

- Stephen Fuller Austin, American settler in Texas, travels to Mexico City to negotiate with Santa Anna on behalf of other white Texans. Mexican officials accuse him of treason and throw him in jail for eighteen months. After he is released and returns to Texas he agitates against Santa Anna's repressive policies.

25 May   Chile adopts a constitution.

8 July   In the Treaty of Unkiar, Russia and the Ottoman Empire agree to a mutual aid pact.

29 Aug.   Thomas Fowell Buxton founds the Antislavery Society of Great Britain.

1834

- Great Britain, France, Spain, and Portugal enter into the Quadruple Alliance.

- Bantu peoples and whites on the eastern frontier of Cape Colony clash in the Sixth Kafir War.

- The Carlist Wars begin in Spain.

- Victor Hugo publishes *The Hunchback of Notre Dame* in France.

15 July   Maria Cristina de Bourbon, queen regent for the infant Queen Isabella of Spain, declares an end to the Spanish Inquisition, which had been in operation for nearly 350 years.

1835

- Dutch settlers in South Africa, known as the Boers, begin the Great Trek, calling themselves the Voortrekkers. Twelve thousand Voortrekkers leave Cape Colony to escape British oppression. By the next year they establish the Republics of Natal, Transvaal (later the South African Republic), and the Orange Free State.

- Ferdinand I becomes emperor of Austria.

- Prince Matsukata of Japan is born.

Dec.   Texas revolutionary forces seize San Antonio in the first battle of their war of independence.

1836

- American inventor Samuel Colt patents the Colt revolver in England.

- Charles Louis Bonaparte tries to incite a revolt in Strasbourg and is exiled to America.

- Novelist Fritz Reuter is condemned to death for treason, but his sentence is reduced to thirty years in a Prussian prison.

24 Feb.   At the Alamo, a fortified mission in San Antonio, a force of fewer than two hundred Texans refuses to surrender to a Mexican army of three thousand.

2 Mar.   Texas declares its independence from Mexico and adopts a constitution that allows for slavery within its territory.

6 Mar.   The Alamo falls to Mexican troops; the entire garrison except for a woman, child, and servant are killed.

21 Apr.   At San Jacinto, Sam Houston leads Texan troops in a victory over the Mexican army, forcing Santa Anna to acknowledge the independent Republic of Texas.

1837

- William IV, king of Great Britain, dies, and Queen Victoria ascends the throne; her reign extends until 1901.

- Ole Rynning, a Scandinavian immigrant in America, publishes *A True Account of America for the Information and Help of Peasants and Commoners,* a text that encourages a large influx of immigrants to the United States from Scandinavia.

•	Canadian troops set fire to the *Caroline,* an American ship transporting supplies to Canadian insurgents.
•	Sioux Indian chief Sitting Bull is born.
29 Jan.	Russian poet Aleksander Sergeevich Pushkin dies after fighting a duel over his wife.
30 May	In the Treaty of Tafna, France agrees to respect the boundaries of Algerian territory held by Abd-el-Kader, emir of Mascara.
5 Dec.	Radical Canadian reformer William Lyon Mackenzie leads an abortive attack against Toronto in the Canadian Rebellion of 1837.

1838

•	Uruguay declares war against Argentina.
•	Christian VII succeeds his uncle Frederick IV, king of Denmark.
•	Abdul Mejid I becomes the sultan of the Ottoman Empire.
1 Oct.	George Eden, British governor general of India, instigates the First Anglo-Afghan War in order to close off Afghanistan to other foreign powers.
1 Oct.	U.S. Army forces the Cherokee Indians on the Trail of Tears, a forced migration from their homelands in the Southeast to the Great Plains. More than four thousand Indians die, and more than twenty other Indian nations are also exiled.

1839

•	Western powers recognize Belgium as an independent, neutral state.
•	John Lloyd Stephens and Frederick Catherwood enter the jungles at the Guatemala-Honduras borders and discover ancient Mayan ruins.
•	A Danish journal called *Light Reading for the Danish People* describes the discovery of a prehistoric woman's body at the bottom of a peat bog.
27 June	Sikh ruler Ranjit Singh dies, and within ten years the British will rule most of his former holdings in Punjab.
25 Sept.	France recognizes the Republic of Texas.
4 Nov.	The First Opium War begins between China and Great Britain.

1840

•	Frenchman Alexis de Tocqueville publishes the last two volumes of *La Democratie en Amerique,* a sociopolitical study of American life.
•	Queen Victoria of England marries Prince Albert.
•	King of Prussia Frederick William III dies, and Frederick William IV ascends the throne.
•	The Protocol de Droits is signed at the London Conference on the Turko-English conflict, closing the Black Sea to Russian warships.

- An act of Parliament unites Upper and Lower Canada.
- Fritz Reuter, a German poet imprisoned in 1836 for treason, is set free by general amnesty.

1841

- English colonist Edward John Eyre crosses the Australian continent through its interior deserts, traveling from Adelaide to Albany.
- British manufacturers in the Niger Delta begin producing palm oil.
- Charles Seafield, an Australian writer, publishes *Das Kajutenbuch,* an adventure novel about Texas.
- Slaves carried on board the American vessel *Creole* seize the ship and sail to Nassau, where the local government sets them free.
- Great Britain establishes the colony of New Zealand.
- Lajos Kossuth becomes the nationalist leader in Hungary.
- Victor Hugo is elected to the Academie Francaise.

1842

- The British Parliament passes the Constitution Act, granting limited self-government to the Australian colony of New South Wales.
- Sports lovers establish the Olympic Club in Montreal, Canada, and make plans to have competitive gatherings whenever they meet.

6 Jan.	British Anglo-Indian forces evacuate Kabul after a revolt led by Shah Suja. The local Afghan tribes massacre nearly seventeen thousand en route, and this event ends the First Afghan War.
5 May	The first railroad disaster occurs when a heavily loaded train derails on its return from Louis-Philippe's public birthday celebration at Versailles. Fifty-three passengers die from injuries and fire, which rages through the locked wooden carriages.
9 Aug.	The United States and Great Britain sign the Webster-Ashburton Treaty, establishing the northeastern Canadian border.
29 Aug.	The First Opium War ends with the Treaty of Nanking; China cedes Hong Kong to the British.

1843

- The British agree to respect Maori land rights in New Zealand, but disputes follow and lead to a five-year period of uprisings.
- Queen Isabella becomes ruler of Spain after a military revolt.

12 Feb.	The British annex the Sind, a region in present-day Pakistan.
11 Apr.	Gambia is separated from Sierra Leone and becomes a British colony.

Aug.	Cherokee Indian Sequoya dies; he was responsible for developing the Cherokee alphabet and helping the tribe establish a republican form of government.
Oct.	The Young Ireland movement plans a rally for more than one million, but British troops break up the operation.

1844

- Charles XIV of Sweden dies, and his son succeeds to the throne.
- Karl Marx and Friedrich Engels meet in Paris.
- China and the United States sign a treaty of peace and commerce.
- The U.S. Senate rejects the annexation of Texas.
- A British court finds Irishman Daniel O'Connell, an advocate of Irish independence, guilty of political conspiracy.

1845

- The potato crop fails in Ireland, and famine strikes the country. By 1851 nearly one-third of the Irish population will either die from starvation and typhoid or emigrate.
- Ramon Costilla is elected President of Peru and establishes a strong central government.
- British citizen Sir Austen Layard begins excavations of Nineveh.

1846

- Revolts break out in Poland, and Austria annexes Cracow.
- Wheat and potato crops fail in France, leading to an economic slump.
- Louis Napoleon flees to London.
- German astronomer Johann Gottfried Galle is the first to observe the planet Neptune.
- Norbert Rillieux, New Orleans resident and freed slave, invents a vacuum pan that revolutionizes the sugar refining process.

10 Feb.	The British win the First Sikh War in India and annex Kashmir.
13 May	The United States declares war on Mexico.
26 May	Britain repeals the Corn Laws, partially in response to the Irish famine and the need to lower the price of bread.
14 June	The Bear Flag Revolt in California topples the Mexican government in the area.
7 July	California becomes a U.S. Territory.

1847

- Karl Marx and Friedrich Engels issue the first edition of the *Communist Manifesto.*

- Black military leader Faustin Elie Soulouque becomes president of Haiti.

- U.S. forces capture Mexico City.

- English novelist Emily Brontë completes *Wuthering Heights,* a tragic tale of embittered love, while her sister Charlotte Brontë publishes *Jane Eyre.*

24 Aug. Liberia becomes the first independent republic under a constitutional government in Africa. Joseph Jenkins Roberts becomes its first president.

Oct.–Nov. The Sonderbund War begins in Switzerland.

1848

- France ends slavery in all its possessions.

- The U.S. Senate approves a treaty with New Grenada allowing travel rights across the isthmus of Panama.

- After the failure of the liberal revolutions in Europe many well-educated European Jews, particularly from the Reform branch, migrate to the United States.

- Nasr-ed-Din becomes the new shah of Persia.

Jan. A revolution occurs in Sicily.

2 Feb. The Treaty of Guadalupe Hidalgo ends the Mexican War and cedes to the United States territories that will eventually become parts of California, Nevada, Colorado, New Mexico, Utah, and Arizona. It also sets the southern border of Texas at the Rio Grande and grants $15 million to Mexico for compensation.

24 Feb. The February Revolution breaks out in France, and the king of France, Louis-Philippe, abdicates the throne. Students, workers, and the middle class form the Second Republic and advocate liberal reform.

Mar. King Charles Albert of Sardinia sets up a limited parliamentary government for his people, declares war on the Austrians occupying the richest regions of Italy, and then abdicates after suffering a military defeat.

20 Mar. The Second Sikh War begins.

23 Apr. A Polish revolt in Warsaw is suppressed.

June The French minister of war of the Second Republic brutally suppresses the June insurrection of unemployed workers in Paris.

Aug. Austrian troops suppress the Viennese Revolution.

29 Aug. The British defeat the Boers at Boomplatz in South Africa. The Boers retreat across the Vaal River to Transvaal.

24 Nov. Pope Pius IX flees Rome.

2 Dec. Hapsburg emperor Ferdinand I abdicates in favor of his nephew, Francis Joseph.

10 Dec. Louis-Napoleon Bonaparte, the nephew of Napoleon Bonaparte, is elected president of France's Second Republic.

1849

- Tories in Canada riot against the passage of the Rebellion Losses Bill, setting fire to and destroying the Montreal Parliament buildings.

- Charles Dickens publishes *David Copperfield.*

- Celebrated Japanese artist, painter, and wood engraver Hokusai dies.

Jan.	British forces win the Battle of Chilianwala in the Second Sikh War.
12 Mar.	Sikh forces surrender to the British at Rawalpindi, ending the Second Sikh War.
23 Mar.	At Novara, Austrian forces defeat a Sardinian army. Afterward Sardinian king Charles Albert abdicates in favor of Victor Emmanuel II.
28 Mar.	Frederick William IV of Prussia is elected "Emperor of the Germans" in an attempt to unify Germany.
30 Mar.	In a treaty with Maharajah of Lahore, Great Britain annexes Punjab.
14 Apr.	Hungary declares independence with Lajos Kossuth as president.
25 Apr.	French troops intervene in the papal states.
11 May	Guiseppe Garibaldi's forces enter Rome.
5 June	Denmark establishes its first constitution.
18 June	The German National Assembly is forcibly dispersed.
3 July	French troops restore Pius IX and crush the Roman Republic.
6 Aug.	The war between Austria and Sardinia ends with the Peace of Milan.

1850

- A movement toward "realism" begins in Western literature; major contributors include Charles Dickens, Leo Tolstoy, Fyodor Mikhaylovich Dostoyevsky, and Anton Pavlovich Chekhov.

- An epidemic of Asiatic cholera sweeps through the midwestern United States, after having struck the South in 1849.

- Alfred Tennyson publishes *In Memoriam.*

- Austrian monk and budding geneticist Gregor Mendel discovers the principles of heredity.

- Scottish chemist James Young finds a method to produce oil from cannel coal and shale.

- Hung Hsiu-ch'uan leads the Taiping Rebellion by organizing a revolt of native Chinese against the Ch'ing emperor and overlords. More than twenty million Chinese peasants lose their lives before the rebellion ends in 1854.

- Arab caravans from the eastern coast of Africa have established regular trade routes into the interior.

- The Xhosa, a Bantu tribe, and the British fight the Eighth Kafir War in the southeastern Cape of Good Hope colony. The Xhosa, their pastoral lives threatened by British and Boer settlements, commit a near mass social suicide by destroying their own corn and cattle.

Jan.–Mar.	The British blockade Greece in order to force Greece to pay the interest on an international loan.
2 Mar.	Rent banks are established in Prussia, allowing peasants to purchase the land they had been renting.
20 Mar.	Frederick William IV of Prussia summons a German parliament to form an anti-Austrian coalition.
12 Apr.	Pius IX returns to Rome.
19 Apr.	Great Britain and the United States sign the Clayton-Bulwer Treaty in which both countries renounce exclusive control of the Isthmus of Panama.
9 July	Controversial leader of the Muslim sect of Babism, the Bab, is executed in the public square of Tabriz, Persia, on charges of heresy. His followers rebel, and as many as twenty thousand die in the resulting conflict.
16 July	The French Assembly passes the Loi Tingey, which requires authors of newspaper articles to sign their names.
18 Aug.	French novelist Honoré de Balzac dies.

1851

- The Landlord and Tenant Act in Great Britain initiates reform in land leasing practices.

- American millionaire Cornelius Vanderbilt establishes a steamship route from New York City to California through Nicaragua.

- French physicist Jean Bernard Leon Foucault conducts pendulum experiments to show that the earth rotates on its axis.

- The French establish a trading port at Cotonau, in present-day Benin, West Africa.

- The St. Petersburg-Moscow line, the first major railroad in Russia, opens.

- Frederick Scott Archer, an English artist, invents the wet plate method of photography, which is used for the next twenty years.

- In New South Wales sheep rancher Edward Hammond Hargraves discovers gold. Over the next ten years Australia's population nearly triples from the immigration of gold-seeking British, Germans, and Americans.

2 Dec.	Louis Napoleon, president of the French Republic, proclaims himself dictator after a coup d'etat.

1852

- Omar Pasha and his Turkish army invade Montenegro, and the forces of Prince Danilo II defeat them near Ostrag. The Turks withdraw, but the international world does not recognize Montenegro's independence.

- In South Africa, Great Britain renounces sovereignty over the Transvaal area, and the Boer Republic and the Orange Free State Republic establish themselves.

- Catastrophic flooding dramatically alters the course of the Yellow River in China. Hereafter it enters the Yellow Sea, hundreds of miles north of its original riverbed.

- The Boers of Transvaal raid Dimawe, capital of the Kwena tribe, ruled by the Christian king Sechele.

- Al-Haij Umar, leader of the Muslim Tijaniyya brotherhood, launches a holy war against the non-Muslim Mandingo and Bambara kingdoms in western Sudan.

- Hungary's provisional government becomes permanent, and Austrian rule separates Transylvania and Serbian Voivodina from Hungary.

- France establishes a convict settlement at Île du Diable (Devil's Island) off the north coast of French Guiana in order to replace the colonial labor forces lost by the abolition of slavery. Most prisoners sent there die from disease and neglect.

17 Jan. According to the terms of the Sand River Convention, the British recognize the independence of the Boer Republic of Transvaal, which in 1856 reorganized as the South African Republic.

24 Sept. Henri Giffard, French balloonist, pilots a steam-engine-powered balloon on a trip over Paris.

2 Dec. Louis Napoleon, president and dictator of the French Republic, has himself crowned emperor as Napoleon III.

20 Dec. The British government, at the urging of the East India Company, annexes Pegu Province in South Burma.

1853

- In the Gadsden Purchase the United States acquires parts of southern Arizona and New Mexico from Mexico.

- In a prelude to the Crimean War, France and Russia both intervene in a boundary dispute in Turkish-ruled Jerusalem. Russia uses this opportunity to bring in more troops in order to dominate the Turks.

- Nicholas Pike introduces the house sparrow to New York City in order to control cankerworms. The sparrows eventually spread through most of North America.

27 Sept. The American mail ship *Arctic* and French steamer *Vesta* collide in a fog east of Newfoundland. Separate westbound and eastbound steamer lanes are then established in the Atlantic.

2 Oct. Dominique Arago, the French physicist responsible for investigating electro-magnetism, dies.

1854

- In Ethiopia, Lij Kassa defeats the alliance of Ras Ali and Ras Ubie, gains control over the northern and central regions, and crowns himself Emperor Tewodoros.

	27 Mar.	The Crimean War begins pitting the Ottoman Empire, France, and Great Britain against Russia.
	31 Mar.	Japan and the United States sign the Treaty of Kanagawa after four American warships appear in Tokyo Bay. The treaty establishes diplomatic and trade relations and breaks Japan's isolation from the outside world.
	July	A fourteen-year revolution breaks out in Spain, and Queen Mother Christina flees Spain.
	21 Oct.	Florence Nightingale travels to the Crimea, where her nursing work sets important foundations for modern nursing and public health. She introduces sanitary measures to curb the diseases that kill more soldiers than combat.
	5 Nov.	At the Battle of Inkerman, Anglo-French forces win a decisive victory in the Crimean War.
	30 Nov.	Egyptian viceroy Said Pasha grants the concession for the Suez Canal to French engineer Ferdinand Marie de Lesseps. Work begins in 1859, and the canal opens ten years later.
	8 Dec.	Pope Pius IX defines what has become the prevailing doctrine of the Immaculate Conception of Mary, the mother of Jesus Christ.

1855

	•	The Ayulta Revolt in Mexico unseats Antonio López de Santa Anna, in part through the liberal reforms urged by Benito Pablo Juarez.
	•	The Australian Provincial Parliament adopts a White Australia policy, excluding Chinese immigrants.
	2 Mar.	Alexander II succeeds his father, Nicholas I, as czar of Russia. He attempts to lift some of his father's harsh legislation targeting Jews, but no significant reform takes place.
	11 Sept.	In the Crimean War, British and French forces take Sevastopol, the main Russian port on the Black Sea.
	11 Nov.	Danish philosopher and theologian Soren Kierkegaard dies. His ideas emphasized the relationship of the individual to objective fact rather than importance of the fact itself.

1856

	•	When lightning strikes a church on the island of Rhodes, off the coast of present-day Turkey, gunpowder stored in the vault explodes and kills approximately four thousand people.
	•	Civil war breaks out in Zululand over the disputed succession between the sons of Mpande.
	•	French novelist Gustave Flaubert publishes *Madame Bovary*.
	•	English inventor Henry Bessemer invents a process for refining steel.
	•	Workers discover the fossils of a Neanderthal man near present-day Dusseldorf, Germany.

30 Mar.	Great Britain, France, the Ottoman Empire, Sardinia, and Russia sign the Treaty of Paris and end the Crimean War.
8 Oct.	The Second Anglo-Chinese War breaks out after Chinese officials search the vessel *Arrow* and lower its British flag.
19 Oct.	Sayyid II of the Al-Busayyid Dynasty, who ruled almost seven miles of coastline in East Africa, dies.

1857

- Gold is discovered near Melbourne, Australia. The population of Victoria province doubles in one year, in large part from British migration.

- French engineer Germain Sommeillier invents the compressed air drill.

- Great Britain's Queen Victoria declares Ottawa to be the capital of Canada.

- Russian writer Alexander Herzen smuggles the journal *Kolokol* into Russia. It urges the freedom of the serfs and makes appeals to Russian revolutionaries.

- The Dutch Reformed Church in South Africa holds synod and decides to separate white and non-white worshippers.

10 May	The Sepoy Mutiny breaks out in India, and evolves into a popular uprising against the British. The British and their allies, the Sikhs of Punjab, put down the revolt by July.
1 Aug.	Giuseppe Garibaldi establishes an agenda for the unification of Italy.
5 Sept.	French philosopher Auguste Comte, founder of sociology, dies.

1858

- A gold rush in western Canada, along the Fraser River, draws nearly twenty-five thousand people.

- Scottish botanist Robert Brown, who identified the nucleus as an essential element to a living cell, dies.

- Basuto warriors defeat an invading force of Boers from the Orange Free State.

- The French begin the conquest of the Amnan Empire in present-day Vietnam.

- In India, British forces besiege Jhansi, massacre approximately five thousand inhabitants, and then carry out a reign of terror.

1859

- Thomas Austin introduces rabbits into Australia, and they soon decimate sheep grazing areas.

- Ivan Aleksandrovich Goncherov, a Russian author, publishes *Oblomov*, a social analysis of the stagnating Russian nobility.

Oct.	Spain declares war on Morocco after a series of frontier incidents. Peace is restored the following April.

17 Feb.   The French capture the southern city of Saigon, and Vietnam becomes a French colony. The religious persecution of the Amnamese regime put to death nearly 150,000 Christians since 1827.

19 Apr.   The Italian War breaks out as a result of Austria's demand that the Piedmont, part of the kingdom of Sardinia, be disarmed.

28–29 June   The first dog show is held at Newcastle upon Tyne, England.

24 Nov.   Charles Darwin publishes *On the Origin of Species by Means of Natural Selection*. His argument proposes that natural selection within the species is the main engine of evolution. Much of his data comes from his observations in the Galapagos Islands, and his theory challenges traditional Christian beliefs of creation.

28 Dec.   Thomas Babington Macauley, English poet and historian, dies. His best-known work is the *History of England from the Accession of James II*.

1860

•   British colonists and several Maori tribes fight in the New Zealand Wars.

23 Jan.   Great Britain and France sign a treaty making it easier to trade between the two countries. This agreement moves Europe toward a policy of free trade and away from the mercantilist tradition.

24 Mar.   French leader Napoleon III and Camillo Benso, prime minister of Sardinia, sign the Treaty of Turin, which forces Sardinia to relinquish the provinces of Savoy and Nice to France.

29 June   English physician Thomas Addison dies. He is famous for recognizing Addison's disease, atrophy of the outer layer of the adrenal gland.

14 Sept.   French tightrope walker Charles Blondin crosses Niagara Falls on stilts on a cable stretched 160 feet above the falls.

21 Sept.   German philosopher and professional pessimist Arthur Schoepenauer dies. Some of his works include *On the Will in Nature* and *The Basis of Morality*.

THE ARTS

by JAMES MANCALL

CONTENTS

Sidebars and tables are listed in italics.

1800

- Itinerant artist Ralph Earl is one of the first American painters to show a great passion for nature, as evidenced in his painting *Looking East From Leicester Hills.*

24 Apr. Congress establishes the Library of Congress.

1801

- François René de Chateaubriand paints *Atala,* a romantic rendering of the North American landscape and Native Americans based on his six-month visit.

1802

29 Jan. Thomas Jefferson appoints John James Beckley, former clerk of the House of Representatives, to the position of librarian of Congress.

Apr. The Library of Congress issues the first catalogue of books in the United States.

1803

- Daniel Bradford publishes *The Medley, or Monthly Miscellany,* the first magazine in the West, in Lexington, Kentucky.

1804

- Charles Balthazer Julien Févret de Saint-Mémin paints portraits of five Osage chiefs visiting Washington, D.C.

29 Nov. New York City mayor DeWitt Clinton, Judge Egbert Benson, merchant John Pintard, and botanist David Hosack found the New-York Historical Society.

1806

Jan. Connecticut journalist Noah Webster publishes his *Compendious Dictionary of the English Language,* a book that attempts to standardize the use of English in the United States.

1807

Jan. Washington Irving, James Kirk Paulding, and William Irving begin to publish a series of satirical essays under the title *Salmagundi; of the Whim-Whams and Opinions of Launcelot Longstuff, Esq., and Others;* the magazine encourages the formation of a group of writers known as the Knickerbocker School, most of them living in New York, who focus their realistic accounts on American subjects.

1808

- The Theatre d'Orleans, a one-hundred-thousand-dollar opera house, opens in New Orleans.
- James N. Becker's play, *The Indian Princess, or La Belle Sauvage,* is performed in Philadelphia.

12 July The *Missouri Gazette* is founded in St. Louis, the first newspaper published west of the Mississippi River.

1809

- Under the pseudonym Diedrich Knickerbocker, Washington Irving publishes *History of New York,* a satirical account of colonial New Amsterdam. The book makes Irving famous in the United States and Europe.

1810

- Zebulon Pike publishes *Account of Expeditions to the Sources of the Mississippi and Through the Western Parts.*

1813

- Daniel Bryan, Daniel Boone's nephew, publishes *The Mountain Muse,* an epic poem about his uncle.

1814

- Nicholas Biddle edits and publishes the first edition of the journals of Meriwether Lewis and William Clark, who explored the Trans-Mississippi West between 1804 and 1806.
- The Library of Congress purchases the seven-thousand-volume library of Thomas Jefferson, which becomes the heart of the national library in its formative period.

1816

- John Pickering's *Vocabulary,* a collection of five hundred words and phrases native to the United States, marks an attempt to define a distinct American idiom separate from British English.

1819

- Samuel Seymour and Titian Peale join the Stephen Long expedition to the Rocky Mountains as painters and naturalists.
- William Gibbes Hunt publishes *The Western Review and Miscellaneous Magazine* in Lexington, Kentucky.

1820

- James Fenimore Cooper publishes his first novel, *Precaution.*

- Outside of St. Louis, Chester Harding meets and paints two pictures of Daniel Boone, the only portraits known to be done from life.

26 Sept. Boone dies in Missouri at age eighty-five.

1821

- Charles Bird King paints the portraits of prominent Kansas, Otos, Missouris, Omahas, and Pawnees who visit Washington, D.C.
- James Fenimore Cooper publishes *The Spy*.

1822

- James Hall publishes *Letters from the West*, a collection of pioneer legends and sketches.
- Edwin James publishes *An Account of an Expedition from Pittsburgh to the Rocky Mountains*, a record of the journey of Stephen Long.

1823

- James Fenimore Cooper publishes *The Pioneers*, the first of the Leatherstocking tales that pit the frontiersman Natty Bumppo against the forces of a developing, westward-moving American society.

1826

- James Fenimore Cooper publishes *The Last of the Mohicans*.
- Timothy Flint publishes *Frances Berrian*, generally regarded as the first Southwestern novel.
- Thomas Cole paints *Daniel Boone Seated Outside His Cabin*.
- Enrico Causcici's relief sculpture for the Rotunda of the Capitol Building in Washington, D.C., *The Conflict Between Daniel Boone and the Indians*, depicts Boone defeating two Indians in hand-to-hand combat.

1827

- Timothy Flint begins publication of *The Western Monthly Review*, the first magazine to be published west of the Alleghenies.
- James Fenimore Cooper publishes *The Prairie*.

1828

- Charles Sealsfield, a German American writer, records his impressions of the United States in *Americans as They Are*.

21 Apr.   Noah Webster includes seventy thousand entries in his *Dictionary of the American Language,* a prodigious work that reflects twenty years' work and includes twelve thousand more definitions than any other dictionary of the English language.

1829

- Charles Sealsfield publishes the novel *Tokeah, or, the White Rose.*

1830

- Timothy Flint publishes the novel *The Shoshonee Valley.*

1831

- James Ohio Pattie publishes *The Personal Narrative of James O. Pattie,* an early document of travel in the Southwest and California.

1832

- Albert Pike writes "The Fall of Poland," the first published poem in English composed in the West.

- George Catlin paints *Buffalo Bull's Back Fat, Head Chief of the Blood Tribe of Blackfeet,* a picture that highlights Catlin's desire to show the American public what Western Indians looked like.

1833

- Mary Holly publishes the novel *Texas.*

- Timothy Flint publishes *Biographical Memoir of Daniel Boone,* one of the most widely read books about a Western character published in the first half of the nineteenth century.

- Carl Bodmer witnesses a battle between some six hundred Assiniboines, Crees, and Piegans, and paints *Assiniboine-Cree Attack.*

1834

- William Gilmore Simms publishes *Life of David Crockett.*

1835

- Augustus Baldwin Longstreet publishes the collection of sketches, *Georgia Scenes.*

- Washington Irving reports on his frontier experience in *A Tour of the Prairies.*

- James Freeman Clarke publishes the *The Western Messenger.*

1836

- Washington Irving's *Astoria* documents John Jacob Astor's failed attempt to establish a Northwest trading post and argues for strong federal support of Northwestern claims.

- Thomas Cole paints *The Oxbow,* a natural formation along the Connecticut River in western Massachusetts; the landscape reveals Cole's ambivalence about the progress of American society.

- Cole begins work on his series, *The Course of Empire;* the last work in the group, *Desolation,* calls into question the promises of Manifest Destiny.

- Davy Crockett, scout, hunter, politician, and subject of various tall tales, dies at the siege of the Alamo in San Antonio, Texas.

1837

- In *The Adventures of Captain Bonneville* Washington Irving recounts the travails of Capt. Benjamin Louis Eulalie de Bonneville in the Northwest.

- George Catlin's Indian Gallery, a collection of his portraits of Plains Indians, opens in New York.

1838

- After eighteen years of research John James Audubon, naturalist and painter, publishes his *Birds of America,* containing 485 plates.

1839

- Caroline Kirkland publishes her novel *A New Home—Who'll Follow?*

1840

- James Fenimore Cooper publishes *The Pathfinder.*

- Richard Henry Dana Jr. publishes *Two Years Before the Mast,* the record of his trip around Cape Horn, of South America, and to Spanish California.

- Carl Bodmer, after attending the Mountain Man Rendezvous, paints *The Trapper's Bride,* an idyllic vision of interracial marriage.

1841

- James Fenimore Cooper publishes *The Deerslayer.*

- Charles Sealsfield publishes *The Cabin Book.*

- Thomas Bangs Thorpe writes "Big Bear of Arkansas."

- George Catlin publishes his *Letters and Notes on the Manners, Customs and Conditions of the North American Indians.* Beyond documenting Native American cultures, Catlin also calls attention to the devastating effects of American expansionism.

1842

Dec.   P. T. Barnum opens the American Museum in New York City.

1843

- Daniel Decatur Emmett composes "Old Dan Tucker" and "My Old Sally."
- Catherine Stewart publishes *New Homes in the West*, describing life on the Western prairie.

1844

- Charles Sealsfield publishes the novel *Life in the New World.*
- Two influential accounts of Western exploration are published: George Wilkins Kendall's *Narrative of the Texan-Santa Fé Expedition* and Josiah Gregg's *Commerce of the Prairies.*
- Charles Deas paints *The Death Struggle,* a romantic vision of hand-to-hand combat between a trapper and an Indian.
- Margaret Fuller's *Summer on the Lakes* examines the lives of women in the Midwest.

1845

- Johnson Jones Hooper publishes his novel *Some Adventures of Simon Suggs.*
- With *Fur Traders Descending the Missouri* George Caleb Bingham begins a series of river scenes.

1846

- Daniel Decatur Emmett composes "Jimmy Crack Corn."
- Stephen Foster composes "My Old Kentucky Home."
- John C. Frémont publishes *Narrative of the Exploring Expedition to the Rocky Mountains in the Year, 1842.*

1847

- David Coyner publishes his novel *The Lost Trappers.*
- George Copway, an Ojibwa, publishes his autobiography, *The Life, History, and Travels of Kah-ge-ga-gah-bowh.*
- George Catlin begins his painting *La Salle Claiming Louisiana for France, April 9, 1682,* a grand tableau depicting an historic moment in the European colonization of the American West; he completes the picture the next year.

1848

- Stephen Foster composes "Oh, Susanna!"
- John Nichols composes "Oh, California."

- Rebecca Burlend publishes *True Picture of Emigration,* a narrative of her fourteen years in Illinois.
- Thomas Cole, the founder of the Hudson River School of painting, dies.

24 Jan.   James Marshall and John Sutter discover gold particles at a sawmill in Coloma, California, inspiring the gold rush.

1849

- Charles Averill publishes his novel *Kit Carson, The Prince of the Gold Hunters.*
- Francis Parkman publishes *The California and Oregon Trail,* a record of his travels beyond the Missouri River.
- George Frederick Ruxton publishes *Life in the Far West,* an Englishman's perspective on Western America.
- In New York City a panorama featuring a voyage around Cape Horn opens to the public.

1850

- Opera debuts in San Francisco with an aria from Verdi's *Ernani.*
- David G. Robinson publishes "Seeing the Elephant."
- Bayard Taylor, the San Francisco correspondent for the *New York Tribune,* collects his letters in *Eldorado.*
- Josiah Gregg, explorer and author of *Commerce of the Prairies,* dies.
- James Wilkins creates intense excitement when he exhibits his *Moving Mirror of the Overland Trail* in Peoria, Illinois.
- Frederic Church paints *Twilight, Short Arbiter 'Twixt Day and Night,* an epic landscape suggesting the grandeur of the American West.

1851

- Dame Shirley (Louise Amelia Knapp Smith Clappe) begins publishing *The Shirley Letters,* vivid accounts of life amongst the miners.
- Mayne Reid publishes the novel *The Scalp Hunters.*
- Stephen Foster composes "Old Folks at Home."
- Henry Rowe Schoolcraft, ethnographer, geologist, and Indian agent, publishes the first volume of his *History, Condition and Prospects of the Indian Tribes of the United States.* Schoolcraft's work becomes a resource for writers such as Henry Wadsworth Longfellow.
- George Caleb Bingham depicts Daniel Boone as a Moses-like figure in *The Emigration of Daniel Boone into Kentucky.*
- With the *Country Election* Bingham begins his "Election" series, three paintings depicting the democratic process in the West.

- James Fenimore Cooper, author of the Leatherstocking novels, dies in his home in Cooperstown, New York, the basis for the fictional settlement in Cooper's *The Pioneers*.

- George Copway briefly publishes a newspaper devoted to Native Americans, *Copway's American Indian*.

- John James Audubon, naturalist, painter, and author of *Birds of America*, dies.

1852

- Harriet Beecher Stowe publishes *Uncle Tom's Cabin*.

- San Francisco's *Golden Era*, a literary journal, begins publication.

1853

- Augustus Baldwin Longstreet publishes his novel, *Flush Times*.

- Old Block (Alonzo Delano) collects his *Pacific News* articles, humorous sketches of life in gold-rush San Francisco, in *Pen Knife Sketches; or, Chips of the Old Block*, illustrated by Charles Christian Nahl, well known as the premier artist of the gold rush.

- For the first time San Francisco has its own resident opera company, The Pacific Musical Troupe.

- Asher B. Durand paints *Progress (The Advance of Civilization)*, commissioned by railroad baron Charles Gould.

1854

- Margaret Jewell Bailey publishes *The Grains*, and John Rollin Ridge publishes *The Life and Adventures of Joaquin Murieta, the Celebrated California Bandit*.

- Henry David Thoreau publishes *Walden, Or Life in the Woods*, a work that would soon have an enormous impact on that way that American writers viewed nature.

1855

- Augusta J. Evans publishes the novel *Inez, A Tale of the Alamo*.

- Henry Wadsworth Longfellow publishes the poem *Song of Hiawatha*.

- Walt Whitman anonymously publishes a collection of poems titled *Leaves of Grass*.

- John Phoenix (George Horatio Derby), one of the first Far Western humorists, publishes a collection of his sketches, *Phoenixiana*.

- Maria Ward publishes *Female Life Among the Mormons*.

1857

- Alonzo Delano presents his play, *A Live Woman in the Mines*, one of the earliest dramas written in the West.

- Frederick Church paints *Niagara*, one of the great achievements of nineteenth-century landscape painting in the United States.

1858

- Dewitt C. Peters publishes *The Life and Adventures of Kit Carson*, portraying Carson as a gentleman with "no bad habits."
- Currier and Ives, in a series popularizing the image of the mountain men, print a lithograph of Louis Maurer's *The Last Shot*.

1859

- Washington Irving, best known as the author of "The Legend of Sleepy Hollow" and "Rip Van Winkle" as well as three books on the West, dies.

1860

- Catherine Soule publishes her novel *Pet of the Settlement: A Story of Prairie-Land.*
- Horace Greeley, editor of the *New York Tribune,* reports on San Francisco in *Overland Journey, from New York to San Francisco.*
- Frederick Church paints *Twighlight in the Wilderness,* a painting that echoes the ambivalence that Thomas Colt felt about the future of the United States.

Oct.
- Thomas Maguire's lavish Opera House opens the season with a festival of twelve successive nights of opera, each featuring a different production.

A circa 1837 painting of an Indian village with women dressing a hide and buffalo meat drying on racks (Buffalo Bill Historical Center, Cody, Wyoming)

OVERVIEW

The Rise of Empire and the Arts. "There shall be sung another golden age," prophesied the poet George Berkeley in 1752, "westward the course of empire takes its way." With the Louisiana Purchase of 1803, and subsequent explorations by Meriwether Lewis, William Clark, Stephen Long, and John C. Frémont, the West captured the American public's imagination. To many Americans, the new territories and the lands beyond stretching to the Pacific Ocean held great promise. No longer would America be subordinate to England and Europe. The new lands heralded, as Berkeley's verses put it, "the rise of empire and of arts." The golden age seemed on the verge of realization. As the American empire spread West, the arts followed; artists and writers such as George Catlin, a Philadelphia portraitist who traveled the interior for eight years, began to explore and report on the new frontier. Others, such as the Eastern novelist James Fenimore Cooper, never went West but did much to shape the image of the West in the American imagination. Some of these artists, in the tradition of Berkeley, sang a new golden age, celebrating the spirit of progress and national fulfillment. Others questioned the greed, racism, and violence that seemed to fuel the Westward expansion. Nevertheless, each of these artists, in their own ways, sought to answer the same fundamental question: What was the West? Was it, as many promotional tracts promised, a new garden of plenty, a land of untapped beauty and wealth? Or was it a desolate wasteland, demanding hard labor in crude, harsh conditions? What of the Indians who lived in the West? Were they hostile "savages," children of nature, or sovereign nations victimized by American imperialism? And what of the first hunters and trappers who ventured into the wilderness? Were they the virtuous and brave builders of a new civilization? Or were they men debased by the freedom and liberty of the wilderness? Each of the artists who documented the West in the first half of the nineteenth century struggled with these questions, questions that would shape—and continue to shape—America's vision of itself.

American Icons. The arts of the West produced some of the most enduring icons in American culture. Daniel Boone, the famed backwoodsman and settler of the state of Kentucky, became a legendary figure as the subject of countless biographies, poems, and paintings. The various interpretations of the Boone legend suggested different visions of the West. To some, Boone was a heroic man of action; to others, a romantic figure of solitude and freedom. Still others portrayed Boone as a threatening figure of radical democracy. Influenced by the Boone legend, Cooper, the Eastern novelist, created one of the most enduring of Western characters, Leatherstocking. In Cooper's novels Leatherstocking appeared as a humble and skilled man of nature, free but disciplined in the arts of the wilderness. Cooper contrasted Leatherstocking's wisdom and virtue with the laws and excesses of American "civilization" as it advanced westward. Kit Carson, who served as a scout and soldier under Frémont, also became a legendary figure. In popular accounts Carson appears as a gentleman-hunter, skilled as a horseback-rider and marksman. Novelists such as Charles Averill exaggerated the Carson legend ever further, claiming that it was Carson, prince of the wilderness, who discovered gold in California. Recently, however, some historians have called into question the heroic image of Carson, suggesting that he may have been responsible for the needless and indiscriminate slaughter of Navajo Indians.

New Lands, New Voices. The West inspired not only new American icons but also new American voices. German American writers, led by Charles Sealsfield, immigrated to the Midwest and, in novels and travel books, documented the life they found there. Some found Americans to be crude philistines; others, such as Sealsfield, saw America as the herald of a new global democracy. Women who traveled west also found new opportunities for self-expression. Authors Catherine Stewart, Rebecca Burlend, and Catherine Soule celebrated the beauty they found in the prairies. Many women who did not have the opportunity to write documented their experiences in the quilts they painstakingly crafted. Native Americans also began to address American audiences; George Copway, an Ojibwa who converted to Methodism, recorded the history of the Ojibwa and critiqued American attitudes toward Indians. John Rollin Ridge, a Cherokee exiled to California, wrote essays advocating Indian rights, and in 1854 he published *The Life and Adventures of Joaquin Murieta,* a novel depicting American racism against Mexicans.

Gold Rush. In 1848 James Marshall and his employer, John Sutter, discovered gold particles in the tailrace of a sawmill. As news of the discovery spread, the gold rush lured thousands of fortune hunters to California. San Francisco, a popular port of entry, was transformed virtually overnight. By the mid 1850s the city supported newspapers, prestigious literary journals, public libraries, and an opera. While newspapers trumpeted sensational stories of fortunes made overnight, for most miners it was only a matter of time before they, as the popular song put it, "saw the elephant." Seeing the elephant meant recognizing that one was never going to strike it rich and deciding to pack up to return home. Popular newspaper writers, such as Dame Shirley and Old Block, wrote with sympathy and humor of the hunger, exhaustion, backbreaking labor, and chronic disappointment endured by most miners. The San Francisco newspapers also nurtured other talents. John Phoenix, with his satirical sketches and mock news items, became the first of the Far Western humorists, setting the stage for later authors such as Bret Harte and Mark Twain. Phoenix's sardonic sense of humor and the spirit of laughter amongst despair and hardship became trademarks of Western culture.

East v. West. Not everyone, however, found humor in the sometimes difficult and crude conditions of the frontier. Some Easterners looked with disdain upon the West. Francis Parkman, a Harvard student who traveled West, found some of the backwoodsmen he met "uncouth, mean and stupid." In her novel *A New Home—Who'll Follow?* (1839), Caroline Kirkland, a New Yorker transplanted to Michigan, portrayed the residents of a Michigan frontier village as boorish degenerates. In response some Westerners mocked Eastern standards of propriety. Tall tales, featuring superhuman heroes such as the "helliferocious fellow" Mike Fink, celebrated rather than censured the aspects of Western life Easterners found so objectionable. Fink vowed that he could outshoot, outfight, and outdrink any and all, especially effete Easterners. Sut Lovingood, the hero of George Washington Harris's humorous sketches, proclaimed himself "a nat'ral born durn'd fool" and delighted in exposing the empty authority of parsons, circuit riders, sheriffs, and prudes. Other Westerners responded to Eastern disdain by affirming the respectability of Western culture. In the 1850s San Francisco devoted itself to becoming a capitol of grand opera. Lavish productions, luxuriously decorated opera houses, and full audiences attested to the cultural status of the West.

A Question of National Destiny. At its core the questions surrounding the status and nature of the West were really questions about America as a whole. In 1845 John L. O'Sullivan, editor of *United States Magazine and Democratic Review,* declared that it was "our manifest destiny . . . to overspread the continent allotted by Providence for the free development of our yearly multiplying millions." Many others echoed O'Sullivan's sentiments. Hudson River School painters such as William Sontag and Asher B. Durand celebrated the spirit of progress embodied by expansion. Thomas Cole, the founder of the Hudson River School, was much more skeptical. He found the Mexican War "vile," and warned, in his series of paintings called *The Course of Empire,* that empires ended in ruin. George Catlin, in his travels, discovered that American policy toward Native Americans was often brutal and ruthless. He found Indians' "rights invaded, their morals corrupted, their land wrested from them, their customs changed." In his view such injustice called for "national retribution." For these and many other artists there was much at stake in the Western images they created. Their visions of the West reflected larger debates about national character and values. As the course of empire took its way, the arts followed, not only westward but also to the heart of America.

TOPICS IN THE NEWS

AMONG THE MOUNTAIN MEN

Liberty or Savagery? With the explosive growth of the Rocky Mountain fur trade in the 1830s, mountain men, who lived in the wilderness trapping and selling animal pelts, captured the American imagination. To some they symbolized the rugged freedom of the frontier, to others, anarchy and degradation. In *The Prairie* (1827) James Fenimore Cooper's trapper hero, Leatherstocking, possessed natural virtue. Lewis H. Garrard, who traveled along the Sante Fe Trail in 1846 at the age of seventeen, admired the trapper's independence. His *Wah-To-Yah and the Taos Trail* (1850) celebrated the "grand sensation of liberty and a total absence of fear" he found in the trappers' camps. Other commentators, how-

Kit Carson

ters's *The Life and Adventures of Kit Carson* (1858), Carson mingles with the crude mountain men, but he rises above them: he "contracted no bad habits, but learned the usefulness and happiness of resisting temptation." Charles Burdett, in an 1862 biography, depicted Carson as a man who never drank liquor and carefully saved his money. At the same time Carson also appeared in popular literature as the self-reliant man of action. In Charles Averill's *Kit Carson, The Prince of the Gold Hunters* (1849) Carson is a man of daring and skill, "the noble figure of the hunter-horseman," possessing "a look of proud indifference to all, and the conscious confidence of ennobling self-reliance." Averill even went so far as to claim that it was Carson who first discovered gold at Sutter's Mill in California. The real-life Carson went on to serve as a Civil War general and federal administrator in New Mexico. In the popular imagination his daring and skill became the model for many Western heroes to come. Some historians have recently challenged this heroic image of Carson, arguing that he took part in atrocities committed against the Navajo.

ever, saw the mountain men as corrupt renegades. Timothy Flint's *The Shoshonee Valley* (1830), the first novel to feature mountain men as characters, suggested that they had "an instinctive fondness for the reckless savage life . . . interdicted by no laws, or difficult morals, or any restraints." Charles Sealsfield, the popular German American novelist and travel writer, agreed with Flint; his *Life in the New World* (1844) represented mountain men as violent, cunning monsters who killed with "a real fiendish joy." The debate surrounding the character of mountain men was, at its core, really a debate about the nature of the West: was the frontier the site of healthy independence or dangerous dissolution?

Kit Carson. The most legendary of mountain men was Christopher (Kit) Carson, who gained fame first as John Frémont's scout during his expeditions into the Far West and then as Frémont's dispatch bearer in the Mexican War. In Frémont's reports of his expeditions into the Rocky Mountains, Oregon, and Northern California (reports skillfully edited by his wife, Jessie Benton Frémont), published in the 1840s, Carson appears as a real-life Leatherstocking figure, a brave but humble man of the wilderness. Carson soon became the subject of a number of biographies, novels, and sketches. As with the popular figure of Daniel Boone, Carson's character reflected varied interpretations of the West. On the one hand, Carson appeared as a refined man of virtue, an agent of civilization in the open West. In DeWitt C. Pe-

The cover of a dime novel relating the adventures of an early American hero

The Trapper's Last Shot (1850); oil painting by William Ranney
(W. Graham Arader III Collection)

Alfred Jacob Miller. Visual artists also popularized the image of the mountain man. The first professional painter to document the lives of the mountain men was Alfred Jacob Miller. He studied under the portraitist Thomas Sully and then traveled to Europe to study at the famed Ecole des Beaux-Arts. Miller returned to Baltimore in 1834, and in the fall of 1836 he set up a studio in New Orleans. His career took a dramatic turn when he was visited by Capt. William Drummond Stewart of the British army. Stewart had served under Sir Arthur Wellesley, Duke of Wellington, at Waterloo in 1815, and after his retirement from the military he sought adventure and fortune among the mountain men of the Far West. Impressed by Miller's landscapes and portraits, he asked Miller to accompany him on his next expedition; Stewart wanted Miller to document the upcoming Mountain Man Rendezvous. The Rendezvous was the most significant social and business event of the American fur trade during the 1820s and 1830s. Rocky Mountain fur trappers and their Indian allies met with the trading companies in order to purchase supplies and exchange the year's pelts. The Rendezvous was also a raucous holiday, a celebration of surviving the year's hardship, isolation, and danger. The mountain men drank, gambled and fought, exchanged tall tales, challenged each other in athletic contests, and bartered for wives. Miller made field sketches during his travels with Stewart and, once he returned to New Orleans, painted finished canvases. Compared to Catlin and Bodmer before him, Miller's work was informed by a romantic vision; his paintings celebrated the mountain man's unfettered life in an idyllic landscape. "Only in savage life [does] real and absolute liberty exist," he would write. In *Trappers Starting for the Beaver Hunt* (1857–1860), completed long after his journey with Stewart, two mounted trappers, their backs to the viewer (and by extension, Eastern culture), move across an open plain and toward the distant horizon. Miller described these trappers as leading "the van in the march of civilization" and as "adventurous, hardy, and self-reliant—always exposed to constant danger from hostile Indians, and extremes of hunger and cold."

The Trapper's Bride. First painted in 1840 and painted again from 1858 to 1860, *The Trapper's Bride* is one of Miller's most popular works and depicts the wedding ceremony between a trapper and an Indian woman. This interracial marriage, painted at a time when the issue of race and slavery was dividing the Union, spoke to a romantic vision of universal brotherhood and displayed a hope for the peaceful reconciliation of nature and civilization. In fact, *The Trapper's Bride* borrowed its imagery from European renditions of the marriage of the Virgin, lending an idealized air of sanctity to the union of white and Indian. At the same time it represented the mountain man's escape from the confines of Eastern society and sexual mores; indeed, marriages between whites and Indians were forbidden by law in Miller's home state and many other states of the Union. If Catlin's work documented a "doomed" race's fall from innocence, Miller's celebrated the West as an escape from civilization, a West where the white man realized a rugged and ennobling freedom.

Deas and Others. Many other painters of the period also celebrated a romantic vision of the mountain man. In the 1840s Charles Deas's paintings represented the trapper as a daring hero; his *Death Struggle* (1844) depicts, in sensational fashion, a fight to the finish between an Indian and a lone trapper. Deas made periodic excursions into the frontier, adopting the customs and aura of the trapper himself. Dressing in a "broad white hat," he was called "Rocky Mountains" because, as one observer put it, "he had a Rocky Mountain way of getting along; for, being under no military constraint, he could go where he pleased, and come back when he had a mind to." William Ranney's mountain men, in such works as *The Trapper's Last Shot* (1850), are more understated than Deas's, highlighting the trapper's vulnerable isolation in a wilderness that is both barren and dangerous. In the 1850s and 1860s Nathaniel Currier and James Merrit Ives popularized the images of the trapper through a series of lithographs done after paintings by Arthur Fitzwilliam Tait. Although he never traveled further West than the Adirondacks, Tait reached the widest audience of any of the midcentury painters. His works celebrated—often in violent terms—the mountain man's triumph over "savage" Indians. *The Prairie Hunter/One Rubbed Out* (1852), depicts a trapper escaping distant Indian pursuers after "rubbing one out" with his rifle. Another Currier and Ives print, done after Louis Maurer's *The Last Shot* (1858), depicts a fallen hunter about to be dispatched by his Indian enemy's tomahawk. The hunter surprises the Indian, however, with the "last shot" from his revolver. Maurer confessed that both he and Tait learned about the Plains Indians from reproductions of Catlin's and Bodmer's work; nevertheless, such lithographs fostered the myth that Indians were savages wielding primitive weapons while white Americans possessed superior technology, industry, and character.

Sources:

Dawn Glanz, *How the West Was Drawn: American Art and the Settling of the Frontier* (Ann Arbor: UMI Research Press, 1978);

R. C. Gordon-McCutchan, ed., *Kit Carson: Indian Fighter or Indian Killer?* (Niwot: University Press of Colorado, 1996);

Jules David Prown and others, *Discovered Lands, Invented Pasts: Transforming Visions of the American West* (New Haven: Yale University Press, 1992);

Richard Slotkin, *The Fatal Environment: The Myth of the Frontier in the Age of Industrialization, 1800–1860* (New York: Atheneum, 1985);

Henry Nash Smith, *Virgin Land: The American West as Symbol and Myth* (Cambridge, Mass.: Harvard University Press, 1950).

CHARLES SEALSFIELD AND GERMAN AMERICAN LITERATURE

A New Country, A New Literature. With an increase in German immigration during the second and third decades of the nineteenth century, especially to the Midwest territories, a stream of German American travel literature began. Some accounts celebrated the democratic ideals of the new country, but others found Americans to be "philistines . . . scoundrels all, who in their horrible vacuity cannot conceive that there can be any gods higher than those struck in mint." Travel accounts eventually gave way to fiction. Friedrich Armand Strubberg, hunter, soldier, rancher, and physician, published sensational novels including *Sklaverei in Amerika* (1862). During the 1850s Friedrich Gerstacker became the most popular German American novelist. His best-known work is *Nach Amerika!* (1855), a realistic account of a group of German Americans traveling up the Mississippi. Otto Ruppius worked as a journalist in New York City and St. Louis. Heinrich Balduin Mollhausen, sometimes called the "German Cooper," served as artist and topographer on expeditions charting trans-continental railway routes; he recorded his adventures in more than fifty novels and travel books.

Sealsfield. The first significant German American writer to devote himself to fiction was Charles Sealsfield. Sealsfield's great theme was the movement of American civilization from the East to the West. Western literary scholars regard him as one of the earliest of Western writers. Sealsfield was born Karl Anton Postl in 1793 in Popitz, a small village in Moravia, then part of the Austro-Hungarian Empire. He had taken his vows as a monk and was serving in a Bohemian monastery when, in 1823, he immigrated to America, escaping an increasingly repressive political atmosphere. His 1828 travel book, *Americans as They Are,* describes his travels through Pennsylvania, Ohio, Kentucky, Indiana, Illinois, Missouri, Mississippi, Tennessee, Louisiana, and Arkansas. Sealsfield's first novel, *Tokeah; or the White Rose* (1829), is set against the backdrop of the War of 1812 and traces the adventures of a young white girl raised by Tokeah, chief of the Oconee Indians. Reviewers compared the novel to James Fenimore Cooper's most successful work, and indeed, both *Tokeah* and Cooper's *Last of the Mohicans* (1826) deal with Indians' fight for survival against the tide of American civilization. Some twentieth-century readers have seen Sealsfield as a sympathetic observer and early champion of Indian rights; others have read this sensitivity as a sentimental lament for the "Vanishing American," a stock character in novels that often celebrated American expansion.

The Cabin Book. Sealsfield's most famous novel is *The Cabin Book,* among the first "Texas" novels in American literature. Written in 1841 but first published in America in 1844, the novel consists of five different stories told at a dinner party. The stories revolve around the fictional history of Edward N. Morse, Texan settler and independence fighter. Sealsfield's storytellers see the fight for Texan independence as fulfilling the spirit of the American Revolution. The East, in their view, has become corrupt, but "in the prairie . . . a different light starts shining inside you than in your big cities; after all, your cities are constructed by humans, are polluted by human breath; the prairie, however, is made by God." Sealsfield's vision of Western regeneration extended globally; other stories in the novel concern Irish and Latin American struggles for independence. Sealsfield's

Daniel Boone Escorting Settlers through the Cumberland Gap (1851–1852); oil painting by George Caleb Bingham (Washington University Gallery of Art, St. Louis, Missouri)

other major work was *Life in the New World* (first American edition, 1844), a cycle of five novels narrated by George Howard and a variety of Western storytellers. The cycle follows Howard as he moves from New York City into the frontier, surveying all strata of Western and Southwestern society. Howard finds that life in the West is perhaps more simple and primitive than in the East, but at the same time, more egalitarian and honest. On the frontier, Howard claims, "the points of social position touch each other; and, by continual contact, smooth each other's harsh and rough corners." Such egalitarianism did not extend to African American slaves, however. Two of the five volumes of *Life in the New World* deal with the issue of slavery, and while Sealsfield acknowledges that the frontier could not have been won without the help of slaves, slavery is portrayed as a positive good; he depicts bondsmen as ignorant and in need of care by their paternal masters.

"America's Most Famous Author." Sealsfield's work is unfamiliar to most contemporary students of American and Western literature, but in the nineteenth century he was quite popular. Like Cooper, he celebrated a frontier that was, in the 1840s (the height of Sealsfield's popularity), already receding. His voice contributed to the heated debate surrounding Texan independence, sometimes tapping into anti-Catholic and anti-Mexican feelings that were prevalent at the time. Henry Wadsworth Longfellow spent entire evenings reading "our favorite Sealsfield" and reread the Louisiana portions of *Life in the New World* while working on *Evangeline*. Both

Nathaniel Hawthorne and Edgar Allan Poe acknowledged (and resented) Sealsfield's popular success, and later writers such as William Gilmore Simms, Helen Hunt Jackson, and Mayne Reid were influenced by Sealsfield's work. It was with some justification that Sealsfield, till the end of his life, claimed to be "America's Most Famous Author."

Sources:

Walter Grunzweig, *Charles Sealsfield* (Boise, Idaho: Boise State University Western Writers Series, 1985);

Robert E. Spiller and others, *Literary History of the United States,* third edition (New York: Macmillan, 1973).

DANIEL BOONE AS AN ICON

Many Boones. One of the most popular frontier figures was Daniel Boone, famous backswoodsman, foe of Indians, and one of the first settlers of the state of Kentucky. Boone's legend grew in the first half of the nineteenth century; he became the subject of many biographies, poems, adventure tales, paintings, and sculptures. Each of these works emphasized different elements of the Boone legend, and in doing so, affirmed different visions of the frontier. For Westerners, Boone was a hero, a solitary, courageous man of action. For some Easterners he became either a gentleman-hunter or an emblem of unrestrained, degenerate, radical democracy. In the South, Boone was a chivalric "knight-errant."

Filson. Boone's first literary appearance was in John Filson's *Discovery, Settlement and Present State of Kentucke* (1784). Filson was a Pennsylvannia schoolteacher and speculator who traveled through the Kentucky frontier with Boone as his guide. His narrative blends elements of the Puritan "errand into the wilderness," captivity narratives, and a romantic vision of man redeemed by nature. Filson's Boone escapes the corrupt elements of Eastern and European civilization but never succumbs to the savage temptations of the wilderness. He is ever mindful of his role as the vanguard of civilization. In the conclusion to his narrative he admits that "my footsteps have often been marked with blood," but he nevertheless gives thanks that the "all superintending providence" has "turned cruel war into peace" and "brought order out of confusion." Filson's narrative was followed by *The Mountain Muse* (1813), a Miltonic epic published by Boone's nephew, Daniel Bryan. In Bryan's vision a gentlemanly Boone is chosen by the Spirit of Enterprise to bring civilization, knowledge, and philanthropy to the heathen of the trans-Allegheny. Boone himself found this grand treatment distasteful; he is reported to have wished he could sue Bryan "for slander."

Midcentury Boones. James Hall's *Letters from the West* (1822–1828) suggested a more Western perspective. His Boone appears as a common man who rejects the riches of the East for the open wilderness. Similarly, in John McClung's *Sketches of Western Adventure* (1832) Boone is a simple man of action, a hunter who enjoys the hardship, adventure, and danger of the frontier with little regard for the values of civilization. John Peck's *Life of Daniel Boone* (1847), on the other hand, appearing in the *Library of American Biography,* a popular encyclopedia of famous American lives, presented Boone as a family man affirming American domestic and Christian values. The Southern writer William Gilmore Simms depicted Boone as a chivalrous and aristocratic rescuer of beautiful damsels in distress. The most popular Boone narrative was Timothy Flint's *Biographical Memoir of Daniel Boone* (1833), which the historian Henry Nash Smith calls "perhaps the most widely read book about a Western character published during the first half of the nineteenth-century." Flint's Boone was a blend of Eastern and Western characteristics. He is an instinctive hunter, a lover of nature, and emulator of Indians fleeing "the tide of emigration." He is also a gentlemanly agent of civilization; his patriotic heart swells "with joy" at the vision of a settled Kentucky. Still, not all writers saw Boone as a hero; C. Wilder, an Eastern publisher, critiqued Boone as a barbarian in an 1823 reprint of Filson's chapter on Boone.

Boone and the Visual Arts. Visual representations of Boone are equally varied. In 1820, a few months before Boone's death, Chester Harding sought out and met the backwoodsman more than a hundred miles outside of St. Louis. Harding is the only artist known to paint a portrait of Boone from life. From this original, Harding made two variants, a half-length and full-length portrait. The half-length, *Boone in a Fur Collar* (circa 1820), borrowed from familiar portraits of Rousseau, Benjamin

Franklin, and Thomas Jefferson. Such allusions placed Boone among the young country's most revered statesmen and suggested that he was both a yeomanlike child of nature and an Enlightenment figure of progress and civilization. The full-length portrait, *Col. Daniel Boone* (1820), placed the aged Boone in a landscape setting, holding his rifle and accompanied by his hunting dog. This work follows in the tradition of eighteenth-century English hunting portraits, but Boone's buckskin clothes and Kentucky rifle suggest a democratic frontiersman rather than an aristocratic man of leisure. In this painting Boone is the Jacksonian common man doing his part to open the West. Boone's image was put to use by a number of other artists. Sometime after Texas applied for and was denied statehood in 1836, Boone's image was incorporated into the design of Texan banknotes. Though Boone never actually set foot in Texas, his appearance on the state's currency served to affirm Texans' view of themselves as true American pioneers. The Hudson River School painter Thomas Cole suggested a different Boone in his *Daniel Boone Seated Outside His Cabin* (1826). Among a romantic American landscape of forest, rock formations, and lake, the aged Boone is seated on a rock outside his cabin, with his dog nearby. The inspiration for this portrait was Lord Bryon's description of Boone in *Don Juan* (1819–1824), but Cole also drew upon Christian iconographic traditions. Immersed in an immense and sublime landscape, Cole's Boone is a wilderness saint, epitomizing the romantic notion of moral enlightenment achieved in nature. Contemporary with, but in contrast to, Cole's painting is Enrico Causcici's relief sculpture for the Rotunda of the Capitol Building in Washington, D.C. Titled *The Conflict Between Daniel Boone and the Indians* (1826–1827), Causcici's sculpture depicts Boone defeating two Indians in hand-to-hand combat, an image celebrating the victory of American civilization and superiority over alleged savages.

Boone and Manifest Destiny. This vision of Boone as active conqueror became more popular as Americans began to believe it was their Manifest Destiny to occupy the entire North American continent. In 1840 the state of Kentucky purchased William Allen's portrait of Boone as a replacement for Harding's. Allen's Boone is more active and dynamic than Harding's; this Boone is a vigilant guardian, hand on his rifle and ready for action. By the time George Caleb Bingham painted *The Emigration of Daniel Boone into Kentucky* (1851), Boone had come to be regarded as a mythical figure in the Western history of the United States. Bingham's Boone is, in one critic's words, "a modern-day Moses leading the American Chosen People into the new Promised Land." Perhaps the culmination of this canonization of Boone is Emanuel Leutze's mural, *Westward the Course of Empire Takes its Way* (1861–1862). Painted during the Civil War and adorning the west wall of the House of Representatives in the Capitol in Washington, D.C., Leutze's mural depicts "the grand-peaceful conquest of the great west." In rondels on side panels, Boone's portrait, along with that of the explorer William Clark, hangs near depictions of Moses, Hercules, the Argonauts, and the Magi.

Sources:

Dawn Glanz, *How the West Was Drawn: American Art and the Settling of the Frontier* (Ann Arbor: UMI Research Press, 1978);

Henry Nash Smith, *Virgin Land: The American West as Symbol and Myth* (Cambridge, Mass: Harvard University Press, 1950);

Richard Slotkin, *Regeneration Through Violence: The Mythology of the American Frontier, 1600–1860* (Middletown, Conn.: Wesleyan University Press, 1973).

EARLY WOMEN WRITERS OF THE WEST

Freedom in the West? The early women writers of the West, like their male counterparts, grappled with the question of how to represent the frontier—was the West a blissful garden or a barren, crude wasteland? Did the West represent new freedom and new opportunities or hardscrabble labor and stifling isolation?

Life on the Prairies. Many Midwestern women writers, including Catherine Stewart, Rebecca Burlend, and Catherine Soule, found the prairies as beautiful and joyful as they had hoped. In 1843 Stewart published *New Homes in the West*, describing her travels and the "fine farms, with substantial houses and barns, good fences" she found there. For Stewart the West had "all the indications of comfortable living." Burlend, an immigrant to Illinois, recorded her impressions of life there in her *True Picture of Emigration, or Fourteen Years in the Interior of North America* (1848). Though acknowledging the hard labor required to cultivate a farm, she painted a glowing picture of her adopted land, a land where "nothing can surpass in richness of colour, or beauty of formation many of the flowers." Soule, in her novel *Pet of the Settlement: A Story of Prairie-Land* (1860), was equally enthusiastic. She described life on the prairie as one of "tranquil joy" and "beautiful health." Yet other women discovered life on the frontier to be harsh and joyless. In *Summer on the Lakes* (1844) Margaret Fuller, the New En-

---

A NEW HOME—WHO'LL FOLLOW?

How was I surprised some two months after at being called out of bed by a most urgent message from Mrs. Newland, that Amelia, her eldest daughter, was dying! The messenger could give no account of her condition, but that she was now in convulsions, and her mother despairing of her life.

I lost not a moment, but the way was long, and ere I entered the house, the shrieks of the mother and her children, told me I had come too late. Struck with horror I almost hesitated whether to proceed, but the door was opened, and I went in. Two or three neighbors with terrified countenances stood near the bed, and on it lay the remains of the poor girl, swollen and discoloured, and already so changed in appearance that I should not have recognized it elsewhere.

I asked for particulars, but the person whom I addressed, shook her head and declined answering; and there was altogether an air of horror and mystery which I was entirely unable to understand. Mrs. Newland, in her lamentations, alluded to the suddenness of the blow, and when I saw her a little calmed, I begged to know how long Amelia had been ill, expressing my surprise that I had heard nothing of it. She turned upon me as if I had stung her.

"What, you've heard their lies too, have ye!" she exclaimed fiercely, and she cursed in no measured terms those who meddled with what did not concern them. I felt much shocked: and disclaiming all intention of wounding her feelings, I offered the needful aid, and when all was finished, returned home uninformed as to the manner of Amelia Newland's death.

Yet I could not avoid noticing that all was not right.

Oft have I seen a timely-parted ghost

Oft ashy semblance, meagre, pale and bloodless—

but the whole appearance of this sad wreck was quite different from that of any corpse I had ever viewed before. Nothing was done, but much said or hinted on all sides. Rumour was busy as usual; and I have been assured by those who ought to have warrant for their assertions, that this was but one fatal instance out of *many cases,* wherein life was perilled in the desperate effort to elude the "slow unmoving finger" of public scorn.

That the class of settlers to which the Newlands belong, a class but too numerous in Michigan, is a vicious and degraded one, I cannot doubt: but whether the charge to which I have but alluded, is in any degree just, I am unable to determine. I can only repeat, "I say the tale as 't was said to me," and I may add that more than one instance of a similar kind, though with results less evidently fatal, has since come under my knowledge.

The Newlands have since left this part of the country, driving off with their own, as many of their neighbours' cattle and hogs as they could persuade to accompany them; and not forgetting one of the train of fierce dogs which have not only shown ample sagacity in getting their own living, but "gin a' tales be true," assisted in supporting the family by their habits of nightly prowling.

I passed by their deserted dwelling. They had carried off the door and window, and some boys were busy pulling the shingles from the roof to make quail-traps. I trust we have few such neighbours left. Texas and the Canada war have done much for us in this way; and the wide west is rapidly drafting off those whom we shall regret as little as the Newlands.

Source: Caroline Kirkland, *A New Home—Who'll Follow?, or, Glimpses of Western Life* (New York: C. S. Francis, 1839).

gland Transcendentalist and feminist, found a beautiful landscape, but one which prairie women could hardly enjoy. "While their husbands and brothers enjoyed the country in hunting and fishing," Fuller wrote, women "found themselves confined to a comfortless and laborious indoor life." In *Went to Kansas* (1862) Miriam Colt also found the promises of the West to be empty. Colt and her husband joined the Vegetarian Settlement Company, leaving the East for Kansas. Once they arrived, however, they found that they had been swindled; no settlement actually existed. Colt's husband and son died shortly thereafter, and Colt, defeated and disillusioned, returned home with her daughter.

Caroline Kirkland. Perhaps the most famous woman writer to debunk the myth of the West was Caroline Kirkland, author of the Northwestern novel, *A New Home—Who'll Follow?, or, Glimpses of Western Life* (1839). Born in 1801, Caroline Stansbury moved west after her marriage to William Kirkland in 1828. In 1835 they moved to Michigan in order to jointly head the new Detroit Female Seminary. In 1837 they moved to the frontier village of Pinckney. There, "the strange things [she] saw and heard" prompted Kirkland to write her novel, which she intended as a correction to the overly romantic or sentimental portraits of the West in popular fiction. Narrated by the witty Mrs. Mary Clavers, *A New Home* describes daily life on the frontier, portraying the fictional villagers of Montacute as corrupt, lazy, vulgar, and opportunistic. Pinckney residents were angered by the satire; Kirkland's neighbors reportedly warned her to "attend to her own family and let other people's alone." The Kirklands returned East in 1843, where, after William died unexpectedly, Caroline continued a career in writing and publishing. She became an editor at the *Union Magazine,* a literary and art journal, and became an active member of the midcentury New York literary circle. Her later publications include further (and somewhat less satiric) sketches of Western life in *Forest Life* (1842) and *Western Clearings* (1845), three book-length memoirs of her travels in Europe, and *Personal Memoirs of Washington* (1856), a biography of George Washington that emphasized Washington's personal life as well as his political and military concerns. The biography also spoke to Kirkland's concerns with feminism and abolition.

Gold Rush Women. It was perhaps around booming San Francisco that women writers enjoyed the most freedom. Francis Fuller Victor made her living as an assistant to the California historian Hubert Howe Bancroft. She also produced short stories, novels, and poetry. Most famous is her *New Penelope and Other Stories and Poems* (1877). *New Penelope* is a Western retelling of Homer's *Odyssey* from the point of view of the matron of an Oregon boardinghouse. The work is a critique of frontier social standards that limited opportunity for women. Beginning in 1852, Georgiana Kirby penned short fiction that realistically described the prolonged and sometimes stifling seclusion of life on the frontier outside a Santa Cruz mission. Her *Tale of the Redwoods* (1852), the story of a man with two wives, one west and one east of the Rockies, suggests the style of both Margaret Fuller and Nathaniel Hawthorne. Jesse Benton Frémont, the wife of Col. John C. Frémont, also wrote tales of life around Yosemite, noting the displacement of native peoples and the foibles of "civilization." Frémont's work was generally realistic, though, perhaps in deference to social prescriptions against women as professional writers, she referred to her work as "harmless puddings." These writers paved the way for the flourishing of Far Western women writers in the latter part of the century, including the poet Ina Coolbrith, Ada Clare, Adah Menken, Josephine Clifford, Helen McCowen Carpenter, and Ella Sterling (Clark) Cummins Mighels.

North and Southwest. Beyond the borders of California, other women were beginning to write literary pieces in other regions of the West as well. In the Northwest, Margaret Jewett Bailey published her novel, *The Grains* (1854), depicting her voyage around the Horn of South America to Oregon. *The Grains* is also a protofeminist work on the lack of legal protection for women on the frontier. In the Southwest, women writers were also beginning to flourish. In 1833 Mary Holly published *Texas,* an epistolary travel and pioneering log intended to entice other emigrants westward. In 1846 Susan Shelby Magoffin recorded her impressions as the first woman to travel the Santa Fe Trail full circle, later published as *Down the Santa Fe Trail and Into Mexico: 1846–1847* (1926). Augusta J. Evans, in Texas, also published her novel, *Inez, a Tale of the Alamo* (1855).

Sources:

Carol Fairbanks, *Prairie Women: Images in American and Canadian Fiction* (New Haven: Yale University Press, 1986);

Caroline M. Kirkland, *A New Home—Who'll Follow?, or, Glimpses of Western Life,* edited by Sandra A. Zagarell (New Brunswick, N.J.: Rutgers University Press, 1990);

Thomas J. Lyon and others, *Updating the Literary West* (Fort Worth: Texas Christian University Press, 1997).

GENRE PAINTING AND GEORGE CALEB BINGHAM

Origins. Genre painting emerged in the 1820s and 1830s as American artists searched for uniquely American subject matter. Turning from formal portraits and history painting, genre painters such as John Quidor, William Sidney Mount, and George Caleb Bingham painted scenes from everyday life and popular American literature. Genre painting, in its embrace of the everyday, lent symbolic importance to the common experiences of ordinary American citizens. In the late 1820s Quidor began painting subjects from the works of Washington Irving and James Fenimore Cooper, producing such works as *The Return of Rip Van Winkle* (1829) and *The Money Diggers* (1832). Mount documented rural life on the farms of his native Long Island, New York. In paintings such as *Farmers Nooning* (1836), *Cider Making*

(1840–1841), and *Eel Spearing at Setauket* (1845), Mount created an optimistic mood of harmony, serenity, and abundance.

Bingham's Early Career. George Caleb Bingham, born in Virginia in 1811, spent most of his childhood in Missouri. At the age of nine, Bingham met and observed Chester Harding as he was completing a portrait of Daniel Boone. Bingham began to assist Harding in his studio and was so impressed by Harding's work that he decided to become a painter himself. In fact, art historians believe that Bingham's first work, possibly completed in the 1820s, was a signboard for a hotel featuring the image of Boone. Aided by his study of composition books, but without formal training, Bingham began a career as a portraitist. He enjoyed some measure of success; the Columbia *Missouri Intelligencer* boasted proudly that Bingham was a "Western 'meteor of the arts'" whose work heralded the development of Western culture and refinement. Despite this acclaim, Bingham felt the need for further study and training. In 1835 he went to St. Louis, and in 1838 he traveled to Philadelphia, where he visited the Pennsylvania Academy of Fine Arts. Visiting New York's National Academy of Design, he may have seen Mount's work on exhibition.

Life on the River. After returning to Missouri in the fall of 1838, Bingham turned to regional subjects, attempting to create works that were authentic records of life in Missouri and at the same time appealed to Eastern curiosity about the West. His most famous paintings of this period are river scenes, depicting the lives of trappers and raftsmen along the Missouri. In contrast to the boastful, crude, and often violent depiction of rivermen in tall tales, Bingham's *Fur Traders Descending the Missouri* (1845), *Boatmen on the Missouri* (1846), *The Jolly Flatboatmen* (1846), and *Raftsmen Playing Cards* (1847) are golden scenes of harmony and rural virtue. Bingham's boatmen are not, like tall-tale hero Mike Fink, "half-horse, half-alligator." They are, as one critic has put it, "hearty men in tune with themselves and their place in creating the nation's future." In his first history painting, *The Emigration of Daniel Boone* (1851), Bingham mythologized the frontier experience more explicitly. The painting borrows from classical and religious sources; Bingham's Boone is a statuesque pioneer, leading his family from a dark, foreboding landscape into the promised land.

Bingham and Democracy. Bingham was not only an artist; he was also active in the Whig party during the 1840s and 1850s, a period of intense debate over the expansion of slavery in the West. Bingham had a fervent belief in democracy, but his own experience as an elected official tempered this faith. In 1846 he ran as a Whig candidate for the Missouri state legislature. After initially being declared the winner by a margin of three votes, Bingham lost in a recount. He wrote to a friend, "as soon as I get through with this affair, and its consequences, I intend to strip off my clothes and bury them,

scour my body all over with sand and water, put on a clean suit, and keep out of the mire of politics *forever*." Bingham's election scenes reflect both his idealism and his skepticism; paintings such as *The Stump Orator* (1847), *Country Politician* (1849), and *Canvassing for a Vote* (1851–1852) document a Western electoral process that is at once rambunctious and serious, flawed and heroic. In *The Country Election* (1851–1852), a panoramic view of the electoral process, a range of activities and figures appear: a drunken voter, two men engaged in a serious debate, children playing games, and a knife-throwing contest. Above all of these figures, a banner proclaims "The Will of the People The Supreme Law," ultimately affirming Bingham's faith in the popular voice. *The Country Election* became part of a trilogy of paintings including *Stump Speaking* (1853–1854) and *The Verdict of the People* (1854–1855). Painted as the Union was heading toward crisis, the Election Series trilogy affirms Bingham's hope for a democratic resolution to sectional differences. Some art historians also see evidence of Bingham's antislavery views in these works, as well as his support for the temperance movement.

Rediscovery. After his death in 1879, Bingham's work as a painter was largely forgotten; he was "rediscovered" when Regionalist painters of the 1930s, such as Thomas Hart Benton, claimed Bingham as an influence. The recognition of Bingham's national importance grew with exhibitions devoted to his work, first in 1934 at the St. Louis Art Musuem, and then in 1935 at the Musuem of Modern Art in New York.

Sources:

Nancy Rash, *The Paintings and Politics of George Caleb Bingham* (New Haven: Yale University Press, 1991);

Michael Edward Shapiro, *George Caleb Bingham* (New York: Harry N. Abrams, 1993);

John Wilmerding, *American Art* (New York: Penguin, 1976).

GOLD RUSH SAN FRANCISCO

Dreams of Gold. Before the Spanish explorer Juan Rodríguez Cabrillo identified the West Coast, and before Hernando Cortez set foot on lower California, the allure and adventure of California was imagined in a Spanish romance written by Garcia Ordonez de Montalvo. In *The Adventures of Esplandian* (1510) Montalvo wrote: "Know then, that on the right hand of the Indies, there is an island called California, very close to the side of the Terrestrial Paradise." Montalvo's California was peopled by Amazonian women warriors. Perhaps most telling of all, Montalvo imagined that "in the whole island, there was no metal but gold."

An Overnight Metropolis. In 1840 Richard Henry Dana published his *Two Years Before the Mast*, a vivid recounting of his journey to California around Cape Horn and his life as a merchant sailor. Dana found California sparsely settled, and the Spaniards, in Dana's view, led a primitive life. All that would change on 24 January 1848, when James Marshall and his employer, John A. Sutter,

I came from Salem City,

With my washbowl on my knee,

I'm going to California,

The gold dust for to see.

It rained all night the day I left,

The weather it was dry,

The sun so hot I froze to death

Oh, brothers, don't you cry!

Chorus:

Oh, California,

That's the land for me!

I'm bound for San Francisco

With my washbowl on my knee.

I jumped aboard the 'Liza ship

And traveled on the sea,

And everytime I thought of home

I wished it wasn't me!

The vessel reared like any horse

That had of oats a wealth;

I found it wouldn't throw me, so

I thought I'd throw myself!

I thought of all the pleasant times

We've had together here,

I thought I ought to cry a bit,

But couldn't find a tear.

The pilot's bread was in my mouth,

The gold dust in my eye,

And though I'm going far away,

Dear brothers don't you cry!

I soon shall be in Frisco,

And there I'll look around,

And when I see the gold lumps there,

I'll pick them off the ground.

I'll scrape the mountains clean, my boys,

I'll drain the rivers dry,

A pocketful of rocks bring home—

So brothers don't you cry!

Source: Richard E. Lingenteller, Richard A. Dwyer, and David Cohen, *Songs of the American West* (Berkeley: University of California Press, 1968), pp. 26–27.

discovered gold particles in the tailrace of a sawmill at Coloma on the American River. Despite the efforts of both men to keep their discovery a secret, word leaked out, and by 1849 the "gold rush" lured thousands of fortune hunters to California. San Francisco, the port of entry, was transformed practically overnight. The influx of a new population and new wealth fostered San Francisco's development as a cultural capital. By the mid 1850s San Francisco boasted that it published more newspapers than London and more books than all the areas west of the Mississippi put together. Aside from English language papers such as the *Alta,* the *Evening Bulletin,* and the *Pacific News,* newspapers were published in German, Italian, French, Swedish, Spanish, and Chinese. Literary journals also flourished: the *Pioneer,* the *Golden Era,* the *Hesperian,* and the *Californian* all compared favorably with the Eastern literary journals. San Francisco had also established three public libraries. The change was so marked that when Dana returned to California twenty years later, he was astonished at the thriving metropolis he found there. Of course, with such rapid growth and so much wealth the city did not completely lose its rough-and-tumble frontier atmosphere. Edward Gilbert, editor of the *Alta,* was killed in a duel, and James Casey, a local politician, shot the editor of the *Bulletin* after the newspaper exposed him as corrupt. A vigilante committee was organized and shortly thereafter hung Casey.

Early Literary Figures. Most of the literary writing of the period came from the newspapers. Bayard Taylor, a writer for the *New York Tribune,* was sent by his editor, Horace Greeley, to cover the height of the gold rush. His letters back East were collected as *Eldorado, or Adventures in the Path of Empire* (1850). Greeley himself reported on San Francisco for his Eastern readers in *An Overland Journey, from New York to San Francisco* (1860). While Taylor and Greeley returned east, three other important literary figures of the fifties fostered a local literary culture: Dame Shirley (Louise Amelia Knapp Smith Clappe), Old Block (Alonzo Delano), and John Phoenix (George Horatio Derby).

Dame Shirley. Dame Shirley emigrated from New England to San Francisco with her husband in 1849 and recounted, in vivid and elegant letters to her sister, her experience of living in the gold camps of Rich Bar and Indian Bar. She wrote of "the darker side of mountain life," including "murders, fearful accidents, bloody deaths, a mob, whippings, a hanging, an attempt at suicide, and a fatal duel." Yet by the end of her stay, Clappe found herself reluctant to leave Indian Bar. "I like this wild and barbarous life," she wrote to her sister, "I look kindly to this existence, which to you seems so sordid and mean. Here, at least, I have been contented." The *Shirley Letters* (1851–1852), as they came to be called, so impressed *Pioneer* publisher Ferdinand Ewer that when Clappe brought them to him, he decided to print them as they were.

Old Block. Daily life among the miners was also the subject of Alonzo Delano's articles in the *Pacific News*. Delano described greenhorns, gamblers, miners, traders, and others with a combination of realism, pathos, and humor. While newspapers and guidebooks trumpeted "big strikes" and "rich leads," most miners, as Old Block learned firsthand, worked with little success and under miserable conditions. The hardship and black humor of the miner's life was vividly symbolized by a stuffed dummy Old Block reported finding in an abandoned mining camp. Tacked to the dummy's chest was an epitaph containing a parody of the popular song, "O, Susannah:" "O, Califony! this is the land for me / A pick and a shovel, and lots of bones, / Who would not come, this sight to see? / The golden land of dross and stones! / O, Susannah! don't you cry for me, / I'm *living dead* in Californ—ee!" Block's articles were collected into two books, *Pen Knife Sketches; or, Chips of the Old Block* (1853), which sold more than fifteen thousand copies in California, and *Old Block's Sketch Book* (1856), which was nearly as popular. For Eastern audiences he adopted a more realistic and restrained manner in *Life Among the Plains and among the Diggings* (1853). He also wrote one of the earliest Western dramas, *A Live Woman in the Mines*, blending conventional melodrama with local color and Western humor.

John Phoenix. George Horatio Derby was born in Massachusetts but became one of the first of the Far Western humorists. He arrived in San Francisco in 1849, met Jessie Benton Frémont, performed in theatrical productions and wrote satiric sketches. Phoenix created a stir when he temporarily took over editorship of the Democratic newspaper the *San Diego Herald*. During his brief tenure Phoenix published mock news items, editorials, and advertisements. To make things worse, he then switched the political allegiance of the paper, supporting the Whig candidate for governor. The joke became known all over California, and when the regular editor returned, Phoenix fled back to San Francisco, where he contributed satiric articles to the *Pioneer* and local newspapers. Phoenix, like Mark Twain after him, became known as both the subject and author of humorous tall tales. One oft-told story recounted the time he stopped a driver of the Golden Eagle Bakery wagon with an order for "three golden eagles, baked brown and crisp." In another he asked if he could leave his wife at the Delaware Women's Depository, even though she was from Maryland. His collected sketches were published as the *Phoenixiana* (1855). While the works of Dame Shirley, Old Block, and John Phoenix are little known today, these pioneer literary figures set the stage for the later flourishing of the San Francisco Circle, a renowned group of writers centered around the increasingly cosmopolitan city: Twain, Bret Harte, Ina Coolbrith, Charles Warren Stoddard, Joaquin Miller, and Ambrose Bierce.

Painting the Gold Rush. Writers were not the only ones to follow the gold trail; painters came too, some hoping to strike it rich, some hoping for commissions and fame in the new city. Most of the painters were not "stickers," and after a brief and often rough fling at mining, they would return to the more congenial East; but a few, including George Holbrook Baker, Harrison Eastman, and Charles Christian Nahl, settled and made careers in San Francisco. Baker arrived in the winter of 1849, and after trying his hand at mining, storekeeping, and other commercial ventures, found employment as an illustrator for local periodicals. Eventually he published his own, *The Spirit of the Times*. Through *The Spirit* and other journals Baker's illustrations of mining camps and towns did much to shape the national image of the California Gold Rush. Harrison Eastman also had success documenting San Francisco's growth. Arriving in San Francisco in February 1849 he began work as a clerk in the post office. Eastman supplemented his postal salary with earnings from wood engravings and lithographs, illustrating a number of local periodicals. His reputation grew, and he was commissioned to do a wide range of work, from lithographs to portraits to panoramic views of the docks of the city.

Charles Christian Nahl. The most important of the San Francisco pioneer artists was Charles Christian Nahl, a German-born artist who followed the gold fever to San Francisco in 1851. He worked in the mines at the Rough and Ready Camp, northeast of Sacramento, and sketched the lives of the miners. In 1852 he moved to San Francisco, where he found a market for his gold-rush drawings in newspapers, magazines, and books. He illustrated Delano's *Pen Knife Sketches; or, Chips of the Old Block* and also painted his impressions of gold-camp life. His *Saturday Evening in the Mines* (circa 1850s) hung in the California State Capitol before being acquired by Stanford University. Nahl's masterpiece is *Sunday Morning in the Mines* (1872), a six-by-nine-foot canvas depicting a drunken brawl, a horserace, the weekly wash, and a small group of miners reading from the Bible. Nahl eventually designed the bear on the California State flag, and when he died in 1878, the *San Francisco Evening Bulletin* mourned the "man of genius" whose "mining scenes were probably as good as any ever executed here."

Sources:
Robert E. Spiller and others, *Literary History of the United States*, third edition (New York: Macmillan, 1973);

J. Golden Taylor and others, *A Literary History of the American West* (Fort Worth: Texas Christian University Press, 1987);

Jeanne Van Nostrand, *The First Hundred Years of Painting in California, 1775–1875* (San Francisco: John Howell Books, 1980);

Franklin Walker, *San Francisco's Literary Frontier* (New York: Knopf, 1939).

GRAND OPERA IN SAN FRANCISCO

Mad for Opera. While tall tales and the Davy Crockett almanacs celebrated the rough-hewn culture of the frontier, the West was not without pretensions to elite art. In San Francisco during the gold-rush years grand opera grew into a popular entertainment. Opera had its devotees in Chicago and New Orleans, but it was San Francisco that, as one historian has put it, went "mad for opera." Some scholars have explained this as the city's attempt to emulate the East, an assertion that San Francisco could be as cultured and sophisticated as the East and even Europe. Another view is that the melodrama of opera—with its heroic striving, pledges and betrayals, and shifting fortunes—mirrored the volatile and sometimes violent nature of life during the gold boom.

Opera's Debut. Opera's probable debut in San Francisco was in 1850, when Mathilda Korsinsky, a German-born singer, sang an aria from Verdi's *Ernani* during the intermission between a drama and a farce at the Jenny Lind Theatre. According to a review in the *Evening Picayune*, Korsinsky was "rapturously encored," and other operatic performances followed. In early 1851 Italian singer Innocenzo Pellegrini presented the first complete opera in San Francisco, Bellini's *La sonnambula*. The *Alta California* reported that a "crowded house greeted the opening" and "torrents of applause . . . continually broke forth." Sometimes, in fact, audiences could be a bit *too* enthusiastic. It was not uncommon for audiences to yell, groan, or hiss during performances; fist fights occasionally broke out, sometimes to be settled as armed duels outside the theatre. Nevertheless, by 1853 San Francisco had its first resident company, The Pacific Musical Troupe, and by 1854 city audiences supported performances by four different operatic sopranos: Anna Bishop, Catherine Hayes, Clarissa Cailly, and Anna Thillon. In the spring of 1855 Bishop and the Italian prima donna Clotilda Barili-Thorn appeared together in three sold-out performances of *Don Giovanni*. Despite its popularity, opera, because it was expensive to produce, was not very profitable, and as a depression hit San Francisco in 1855, performances virtually disappeared. Reviewing a poorly attended performance of Meyerbeer's *Rober le diable*, the *Alta California* noted that "these are hard times, and of that there can be no better evidence than the Metropolitan . . . the house was thin last evening." Staged opera would not return to San Francisco until 1859.

Maguire's Revival. The revival, when it came, was brought about mainly through the efforts of Thomas Maguire. Maguire came to San Francisco from New York, where, it was said, he was nothing more than an illiterate hack driver and bartender. Whatever the truth, in San Francisco Maguire was a gentlemanly cultural impresario, opening lavishly decorated opera houses not only in San Francisco but also in Virginia City, Nevada. In 1858 Maguire and an Italian tenor, Eugenio Bianchi, staged a series of concerts. Bianchi and his wife, Gio-

vanna, a soprano, sang arias and duets from Verdi operas. The programs proved "vastly popular," according to the *Alta,* drawing the largest crowds "ever seen in the opera house." In the spring of 1859 the Bianchis performed in a staged production of an entire opera, Verdi's *Il trovatore.* The opera quickly became a favorite in San Francisco, selling roughly twenty thousand tickets over five months—in a city with a population estimated at fifty-five thousand. Despite a dispute between Maguire and the Bianchis, and occasional downturns in attendance, other operatic performances followed. For the October 1860 season Maguire's Opera House opened with a festival of twelve successive nights of opera, each featuring a different production. The Civil War would soon dampen interest in the arts, and Maguire would ultimately face bankruptcy, but for this brief moment San Francisco was at the forefront of opera in the United States. The music critic for the *Alta* proclaimed, "the opera has become a regular institution among us," or as Maguire is reported to have said, "I lost thirty thousand dollars; but didn't I give them opera—eh?"

Sources:

Ronald L. Davis, *A History of Music in American Life: Volume I: The Formative Years, 1620–1865* (Malabar, Fla.: Robert Krieger, 1982);

George Martin, *Verdi at the Golden Gate: Opera and San Francisco in the Gold Rush Years* (Berkeley: University of California Press, 1993).

THE HUDSON RIVER SCHOOL AND WESTERN EXPANSION

Expansion and Debate. American painting in the first half of the nineteenth century was dominated by the artists of the Hudson River School: Thomas Cole, Asher B. Durand, Jasper Cropsey, Frederick Church, and others who found in the American landscape a distinctly American subject. Cole wrote that "the most distinctive, and perhaps the most impressive, characteristic of American scenery is its wildness." The painters of the Hudson River School celebrated this "wildness" in romantic terms; they infused their landscapes with transcendent truths and moral beauty. As the United States expanded westward, displacing Indian nations and intensifying sectional rivalries, the landscapes of the Hudson River School were shaped by (and helped shape) the national debate. Their panoramic views engaged American optimism, beckoning the observer's eye and imagination to the horizon, and by extension, the frontier. Yet even amid this celebration some of the works of the Hudson River School expressed skepticism about the advances of the American empire.

Cole's Skepticism. It was in the works of Cole, the founder of the Hudson River School, that such skepticism was most clearly present. Cole was committed to American democracy, but at the same time he questioned the nation's ability to fulfill its ideals. Cole's work reflected this ambiguity; while his paintings often celebrated the beauty and grandeur of the American landscape, some expressed an uneasy pessimism. In *View from Mount Holyoke, Northampton, Massachusetts, or The Ox-*

bow (1836), a view of the Connecticut River and a nearby settlement from the peaks of Mount Holyoke, a dark storm cloud appears in the upper left corner of the painting. Is the storm entering or exiting the plane of the painting? Does it portend a sunny future for the settlement or strife ahead? The question-mark appearance of the oxbow heightens the sense of ambiguity. While the immediate subject of *The Oxbow* is Eastern, the painting also suggested, by analogy, the tenuous survival of settlements in the West.

The Course of Empire. In his series of canvases titled *The Course of Empire* (1836), Cole quite literally questioned the promises of Manifest Destiny. The series, depicting the rise and fall of an allegorical empire, begins with the primordial *Savage State*, continues through *The Arcadian or Pastoral State*, reaches its zenith with *The Consummation of Empire*, and from there declines into the war-torn *Destruction* and ends in *Desolation*. While some Americans viewed the United States as the New World fulfillment of the great Greek and Roman empires of the Old World, Cole's *Course of Empire* series asked them to also consider the fates of those empires. He considered the Mexican-American War "vile," and the year before completing *The Course of Empire* he wrote in his journal, "it appears to me that the moral principle of the nation is much lower than formerly . . . It is with sorrow that I anticipated the downfall of the pure republican government—its destruction will be a death blow to Freedom."

Cole's Followers. Cole's uncertainty was recast into optimism by his Hudson River followers in the 1840s and 1850s. William Sonntag's *Progress of Civilization* series (1847), now lost, echoed Cole's *Course of Empire* but ended with a scene of progressive urbanization paralleling Cole's *Consummation*. Cropsey reversed Cole's *Course of Empire* with a pair of paintings, moving from *The Spirit of War* to the idyllic *Spirit of Peace* (1851). Durand's *Progress (The Advance of Civilization)* (1853), commissioned by Charles Gould, broker and treasurer of the Ohio and Mississippi Railroad, celebrated the advances of American civilization and technology. In the left foreground a group of Indians on a dark and craggy outcropping peer out over a light-filled settlement in which they view a wagon, steamboat, and train. Such a vision suggested an evolution from an allegedly unenlightened culture to a sunny blend of pastoralism and technology. If Cole's work expressed doubts about American expansion into the West, Durand's vision was one of optimism and peaceful progress.

Church's Ambiguity. Cole's only pupil, Frederick Church, expressed both his optimism and his skepticism. Vast panoramas such as *Niagara* (1857) combined scientific precision and botanical detail with a sense of grandeur and promise. Church's South American landscapes, such as his spectacular *Cotopaxi* (1862), beckon Americans beyond regional differences; Church's global vision suggested that the nation could fulfill its promise, not only over the North American continent but also over the entire hemisphere. Yet at the same time ambiguity lurked in some of these landscapes. Church's *Twilight in the Wilderness* (1860) depicts an intense, tropical sunset. It might be seen, as many saw the approaching Civil War, as a baptism by fire, the dawn of a new millennium, or as an apocalyptic ending similar to Cole's *Desolation*. As the nation headed toward a war provoked in part by tensions surrounding westward expansion, Church's *Twilight in the Wilderness* returned to the ambiguity of Cole's *The Oxbow*, questioning the future of the American empire.

Sources:

Angela Miller, *Empire of the Eye: Landscape, Representation and American Cultural Politics, 1825–1875* (Ithaca, N.Y.: Cornell University Press, 1993);

John Wilmerding, *American Art* (New York: Penguin, 1976).

MOVING PANORAMA

Early Panoramas. Invented in Edinburgh in 1787 by Robert Barker, panoramas—an early version of "motion pictures"—became a popular form of entertainment in nineteenth-century America. In the first panorama theaters viewers entered a darkened corridor, then climbed a flight of stairs to arrive at a raised platform in the center of a large exhibition space. Surrounding the viewer was a detailed, brightly lit, 360-degree landscape scene, perhaps of Naples, London, or Niagara Falls. The audience could read about the scene in an accompanying pamphlet that explained important details and figures. One patron, writing in the *New York Mirror*, found the illusion "so complete" that "the spectator might be justified in forgetting his locality, and imagining himself transposed to a scene of tangible realities!" The first American exhibition of a panorama, a view of Westminster and London painted by the English artist William Winstanley, was in New York in 1795. American artists such as Robert Fulton, John Trumbull, and John Vanderlyn all became interested in panoramas. Thomas Cole planned, though he never executed, a panoramic view of Naples. In 1819 Vanderlyn exhibited his *Panorama of the Palace and Gardens of Versailles* in New York City. The exhibition did not do as well as Vanderlyn hoped, and he believed American audiences wanted American subjects: "Had I bestowed my time and attention in painting a view of New York instead of Versailles," he wrote, "I should I am now convinced have reaped more profits."

The West. A technological innovation and the opening of the West provided just the right combination to lure Eastern audiences. British landscape painters had moved from stationary panoramas to moving panoramas: landscape scenes that, instead of enveloping the viewer, scrolled by on tremendous rollers. Moving panoramas had the advantage of unfolding over time; they could portray dramatic stories and changes in scenery. Soon American artists began to adopt this new stage device.

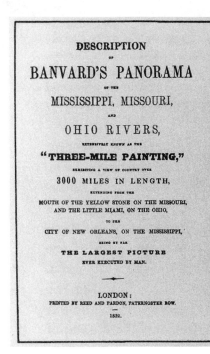

Title page and pages for a catalogue of a popular nineteenth-century art form

While audiences sat for two to three hours, scenes unfolded before their eyes. A lecturer would comment on particular details while a pianist played accompanying music. Popular subjects were the funeral of Napoleon in Paris, the burning of Moscow, Zachary Taylor's campaigns in Mexico, whaling voyages, and journeys through New York City. In the 1840s one of the most famous panoramas was John Banvard's *Panorama of the Mississippi River,* which he claimed—probably with a showman's exaggeration—was "painted on Three Miles of Canvas." Banvard's panorama exhibited a view from the mouth of the Missouri down to New Orleans, treating amazed audiences "to every detail of life on these river banks." In a show that lasted more than two hours, dramatic landscape scenes alternated with exotic views of Indian life. Banvard's view of the West was a thoroughly romantic one. According to his pamphlet, "the scenery in these remote regions has an aspect of majestic grandeur rarely witnessed upon the globe." The canvas was so large that it was impractical to rewind after each performance; instead Banvard encouraged audiences to stay for the next show and read their descriptive pamphlets in reverse order. Banvard's panorama was such a hit in cities such as Louisville, Boston, and New York that, according to his estimates, more than four hundred thousand Americans saw it. Imitators followed, with at least five panoramas touring the country. Blanvard took his original to Europe, where he became an international celebrity and a wealthy man.

Gold Rush Panoramas. The gold rush provided a new stimulus to the artists who laboriously created the moving panoramas. As tales of "striking it rich" spread, Eastern audiences flocked to find out more about the West and life in the gold mines. In 1849 a panorama featuring a voyage around Cape Horn was exhibited in New York. Other panoramas at this time included *Gold Mines of California, Voyage to California and Return,* and *Land Route to California.*

Moving Mirror. Another well-known panorama was James Wilkins's *Moving Mirror of the Overland Trail.* Wilkins was a British-born painter who had settled in St. Louis in 1844. In 1849 he traveled West to California; along the way he sketched "every remarkable object he met with, whether in scenery or the numberless caravans of emigrants, along the whole route." He returned in 1850 and began working from his sketches to assemble the *Moving Mirror,* which opened in Peoria, Illinois, in September of that year. Estimated to be about ten feet high and seven hundred feet long, the *Moving Mirror* re-created Wilkins's journey from the Missouri River to San Francisco. In its first six nights it created so much excitement, according to the *Democratic Press* review, that "every night numbers had to be turned away." The reviewer found himself transported by Wilkins's work: "Mind, sense, all seemed wrapped up in the great Panorama before us; and anyone with a little imagination, would actually believe that he was on his way to California, instead of viewing the route." Wilkins's work, like Blanvard's, also played to romantic notions of the West. In the *Moving Mirror* the reviewer found "all that Byron or Coleridge have written or sung of the far famed Alpine scenery."

Pantoscope. J. Wesley Jones's *Pantoscope of California* presented a West that was both romantic and rugged. Working from the fifteen hundred daguerreotypes and sketches he made while traveling the Overland Trail in

A drawing of the machinery for a moving panorama (in *Scientific American,* 16 December 1848)

1851, his panorama depicted the Sierra Nevadas as comparable, in their sublimity and grandeur, to the "mountain paths of the Alps." Nebraska and Kansas, however, were "desert wastes . . . fit only for the wandering tribes to whom it has hitherto been devoted by nature." Jones and his promoter, John Dix, found that regions "of dreariness" also had selling points to an Eastern audience. The Humboldt River, in the deserts of Utah and Nevada, "zig-zaged [*sic*] through a desert of ashes and lime," Dix pronounced; "all the horrors of the desert follow. Broken wagons, dying animals, and men feeding on their carcasses, groaning in agonies of despair and death." Such melodrama proved popular, and the *Pantoscope* met with great success. In Boston, according to one reviewer, the show "played to overflowing houses, where it met with the most triumphant success. Extra railway trains brought in large parties on excursions from neighboring towns."

A Vanishing Vision. Unfortunately none of these panoramas exist today. Some may have simply worn out as they moved on their rollers, and the development of photographic processes, such as the stereoscope, made them obsolete. However, they did make an impact on the nineteenth-century vision of the Western landscape. While Cole may have abandoned his own plans for a panorama, some art historians have suggested that his *The Oxbow* and the *Course of Empire* series were influenced by the popularity of panoramas. Further, these panoramas helped shape the Eastern view of the West. As the minister Henry Ward Beecher commented about the *Pantoscope,* "It communicates important knowledge about a large tract of our own territory, the like of which

for its peculiar, wild, and original features, is nowhere else to be seen on earth."

Sources:

Anne Hyde, *An American Vision: Far Western Landscape and National Culture, 1820–1920* (New York: New York University Press, 1990);

John Francis McDermott, "Gold Rush Movies," *California Historical Society Quarterly,* 33 (March 1954): 29–38;

Lee Parry, "Landscape Theater in America," *Art in America,* 53 (November–December 1971): 52–61.

NATIVE ORAL TRADITIONS

Orality and Community. Most contemporary readers who are trained in the European tradition are likely to think of the literature of the early nineteenth century as something written, as poetry or fiction appearing in books. Among Native Americans, oral literature, still prevalent, enjoyed an exalted status in the nineteenth century. Those who performed stories, songs, and rituals were some of the most valued members of a community. Their performances served to remind the members of a community of their origin, how they came to be in a particular place, and how they should continue to live. Most native traditions distinguished between three oral genres: narrative, song, and ritual drama. In all these genres the oral tradition was informed by a central belief that human beings should strive for harmony with the universe. Because Native oral traditions were inherited and at times evolving, it is difficult and inaccurate to label particular songs and performances as belonging to a certain period. Thus the twentieth-century student of nineteenth-century Native American literature should proceed with caution: in addition to the difficulties that arise with the written translation of a verbal text, one

Young Omahaw, War Eagle, Little Missouri, and Pawnees (1822); oil painting by Charles Bird King
(National Museum of American Art, Smithsonian Institution, Washington, D.C.)

must keep in mind the timeless nature of the oral tradition.

Narratives. Oral narratives tended to be divided into "true" and "fictional" categories. True narratives often served a kind of Biblical function, a collection of central texts that defined communal values and from which other narratives branched off. The core story was the origin tale, a narrative that explained the creation of the world and the tribe. Among many nations of the Southwest the world was created by the Sky Father and the Earth Mother. The Papago origin tale celebrated the powers of the First Born, who "finished the earth and then made all animal and plant life":

Long ago, they say, when the earth was not yet finished, darkness lay upon the water and they rubbed each other. The sound they made was like the sound at the edge of a pond. There, on the water, in the darkness, in the noise, and in a very strong wind, a child was born.

Other narratives told of ancestral migration, the adventures of cultural heroes, or accounted for the origins of specific rituals and ceremonies. Stylistically, narratives varied widely from group to group. A Papago narrative might have been broken into lengthy stanzas and told over a succession of nights. An Apache narrative, on the other hand, was often spare, compact, repetitive, and would have been told in less than an hour. Additionally, narrative songs might vary with each performance; while Papago storytellers worked for years to memorize the canon of verse and song that constituted their bible, Cherokee storytellers were free to improvise if the spirit moved them do so.

Trickster Tales. The second type of narrative was often told at night by grandparents to amuse and instruct children. They were analagous to Western fairy tales but were often episodic, cyclical, and revolved around the adventures of a conventional character. The most popular character was the "trickster" character, so-called because of his mischievous and deceptive antics. Often appearing as a raven, rabbit, fox, or most commonly a coyote, the trickster was a humorous figure who sometimes outwitted others and sometimes outwitted himself. He typically embodied qualities such as lust, greed, and avarice. His tales entertained but also taught listeners the consequences of such foibles.

Songs. Songs were, and continue to be, a significant component of Native American culture, accompanying both ceremonial and everyday activities. Like narratives, ceremonial songs varied widely from group to group.

The Navajo Nightway Ceremony, composed of about four hundred songs, filled nine days and eight nights:

May it be beautiful before me.
May it be beautiful behind me.
May it be beautiful below me.
May it be beautiful all around me.
It beauty it is finished.
In beauty it is finished.

In contrast, a Yaqui fiesta consisted of a dozen compressed, imagistic songs, such as the following:

These three like enchanted night buzzards
Hover above me.
These three like enchanted night buzzards
Hover above me.
As they are coming with the light before dawn,
Here from the enchanted light before dawn,
On top, on the highest point where the mountain sits,
They are swinging.
These three like enchanted night buzzards
Hover above me.

Nonceremonial songs accompanied nearly all aspects of daily life. There were songs for traveling, housework, lullabies, or social occasions. Some ceremonial songs also had a nonceremonial function. The Navajo Nightway Chant, for example, might also have been used as a traveling song.

Ritual Drama. Ritual drama was a sacred form of oral literature that often combined song and narrative. These performances were ritualized attempts to communicate with natural and supernatural forces, to use the power of the word to achieve order in the spiritual and physical worlds. They might have been performed seasonally to celebrate the renewal of the earth, they might have marked communal events, or pertained to important personal events, such as birth, death, and marriage. Others may have functioned as purification ceremonies. Ritual dramas were performed by priests, respected singers, or shamans. Priests and shamans inherited ritual forms and songs from their family or, alternatively, underwent rites of initiation. In some cases certain rites were the responsibility of specially empowered societies. Among the Ojibwas, Menominees, and Winnebagos, for example, healing ceremonies were performed by the Grand Medicine Society.

Themes. Underlying the diversity of forms and language in the oral tradition were a number of common themes: the sense of the sacred, the sense of the beautiful, the sense of place, and the sense of community. To many Native Americans in the nineteenth century, all things were sacred; this sacred power created a sense of balance throughout the universe. The patterns within songs and narratives, such as repetition and symmetry, reflected that balance. For each tribe, however, the sacred was often located in a specific place, sometimes described as a mythical dwelling place or the site of origin.

For example, the Navajos and Hopis viewed some southwestern mountains as sacred dwelling places. As the tradition celebrated sacred places, it also reminded the individual that he or she was part of a larger whole, a whole that included not only the community but also all of creation. Spirit and harmony informed all life. The power of the word, given by and reflecting the sacred, affirmed and celebrated this unity, as in this Yokuts prayer:

My words are tied in one
With the great mountains,
With the great rocks,
With the great trees,
In one with my body,
And my heart.
Do you all help me
With supernatural power,
And you, Day
And you, Night!
All of you see me
One with this world!

Sources:
A. LaVonne Brown Ruoff, *American Indian Literatures* (New York: Modern Language Association, 1990);

Andrew Wiget, *Native American Literatures* (Boston: Twayne, 1985).

NATIVE AMERICAN WRITTEN LANGUAGE

Early Writers. The first Indian author to publish in English was Samson Occom, a Methodist missionary and author of *Sermon Preached at the Execution of Moses Paul, an Indian* (1772). In 1829 William Apess, a Pequot, published his autobiography, *A Son of the Forest.* He later published a brief autobiography in his *Experience of Five Christian Indians of the Pequot Tribe* (1833). Both autobiographies, similar to many spiritual confessions of the period, follow Apess's life history from a period of ignorance to Christian redemption. Apess, who became ordained as a Methodist, also became one of the most influential native protest writers in the nineteenth century. He saw alcohol abuse as one of the "fatal and exterminating diseases" introduced to the Indians by white civilization. In his *Eulogy on King Philip* (1836), a sermon preached in Boston, he criticized the Pilgrims for their hostile and duplicitous treatment of the Indians, even as they "came to these Indians for support" and received many "acts of kindness" from them.

Copway. George Copway, an Ojibwa who converted to Methodism in 1827, was also a popular Indian lecturer and writer. In 1847 he published his autobiography, *The Life, History, and Travels of Kah-ge-ga-gah-bowh.* Like Apess's autobiography, Copway's work is a tale of Christian salvation, but it also critiques American attitudes toward Indians. His warm portrayals of Ojibwa domestic life counteract stereotypes of Indians as "savage" or "primitive." He also questioned the value of the federal government's payments for Indian land: "I would now ask, what are millions of money without education?" In itself, Copway believed, money would be of little value to

A front page of the first Native American newspaper

Indians. He also published the first full-length travel book by an Indian, *Running Sketches of Men and Places, in England, France, Germany, Belgium, and Scotland* (1851), and briefly published a newspaper, *Copway's American Indian* in the summer and fall of 1851.

Tribal Histories. As the federal government continued to pressure Indians to leave their lands, tribal histories reminded white audiences of the human costs of such policies. Many Indian authors of the period wrote histories of their tribes based on oral traditions. David Cusick, a Tuscarora, published his *Sketches of Ancient History of the Six Nations* in 1827. Copway published his *Traditional History and Characteristic Sketches of the Ojibway Nation* in 1850, describing Ojibwa culture, their migrations and hostilities with the Iroquois, Huron, and Sioux. Peter Jones also wrote a history of the Ojibwa, published posthumously in 1861 as *History of the Ojibway Indians*. The most accomplished account of the Ojibwa is

William Wipple Warren's *History of the Ojibway, Based Upon Traditions and Oral Statements,* which he completed in 1852 but was not published until 1885.

John Rollin Ridge. John Rollin Ridge, the son of a Cherokee father and white mother, published poetry, journalism, and fiction under the name of "Yellow Bird," a translation of his Cherokee name. Ridge was the first Native American to publish a novel, *The Life and Adventures of Joaquin Murieta, the Celebrated California Bandit* (1854). As a child in Georgia, Ridge witnessed the assassination of his grandfather, the respected Cherokee chief Major Ridge, and his father, John, for their role in the sale of tribal lands. Ridge eventually fled to gold rush California, where he contributed to the San Francisco journals the *Golden Era, Hesperian,* and the *Pioneer.* Most of Ridge's poems (written mainly before he was twenty and published posthumously as *Poems* in 1868) reflect

The Cherokee people have, more than any other Indians perhaps, engaged the attention of the citizens and government of the United States. So many associations have existed between the whites and them; so many noble and thrilling incidents have filled up their history; so many tragical events have occurred amongst them, and finally, their doom, for the last twelve or thirteen years, has been so unfortunately dark, that philanthropists and statesmen could not but look upon them with the intensest interest. To behold a branch of the aborigines of this continent, quietly seated in their acknowledged territory; having abandoned their savage customs and habits for the condition of civilized life; creating for themselves a simple but a wise form of government, and gathering around them all those circumstances which were favorable to their advancement in human knowledge and human happiness, was indeed a lovely and beautiful vision. But, to see them, while thus prosperous and happy, rudely thrown, by the iron arm of cold State policy, from the proud elevation which they had attained by the work of long and painful years; to see the fire-brands of discord and contention hurled in their midst, to blast and wither their energies, and almost effectually to cancel all the good which they had wrought themselves, was truly a painful contrast, and a heart-rending sight. [Ah, well may the intelligent Cherokee weep over the fallen condition of his tribe, and curse, deeply, and bitterly curse, the hand which placed it there.]

Source: John Rollin Ridge, "The Cherokees: Their History—Present Condition and Future Prospects (1849)," in *A Trumpet of Our Own: Yellow Bird's Essays on the North American Indian*, edited by David Farmer and Rennard Strickland (San Francisco: Book Club of California, 1981), p. 49.

the popular sentimentality of the period, but some also suggested an enduring sense of isolation and exile.

The Legend of Murieta. Ridge's novel was based on the legend of Joaquin Murieta, known to some as a ruthless Mexican bandit and to others as a romantic Robin Hood–type figure. Ridge's *Life* presents Murieta as a wronged man, a gallant gentleman-bandit who seeks justice after a band of Anglo-Saxons rape his wife and hang his half brother. It is this "wanton cruelty and the tyranny of prejudice" that force Murieta to become an outlaw. He vows "that he [will] live henceforth for revenge and that his path [will] be marked with blood." As he coolly avenges his wife and half brother, Murietta also makes plans to lead the Mexican people in an uprising against the Anglo invaders of California. Ridge's novel is remarkable not only because it vividly portrays anti-Mexican prejudice among the Anglos but also because it suggests, by analogy, the injustice with which the Cherokees were displaced from their own land. While Ridge's novel was not immediately successful, the legendary Murieta began to appear in the works of other writers. Murieta was the subject of a number of novels, plays, "biographies," and eventually a film. Some contemporary historians, such as Hubert Howe Bancroft, were so swayed by Ridge's novel that they accepted it as factual, thus perpetuating the legend even further.

Sources:
A. LaVonne Brown Ruoff, *American Indian Literatures* (New York: Modern Language Association, 1990);

Franklin Walker, *San Francisco's Literary Frontier* (New York: Knopf, 1939);

Andrew Wiget, *Native American Literatures* (Boston: Twayne, 1985).

PAINTING THE FIRST ENCOUNTER

Curiosities. Early in the spring of 1804, as Meriwether Lewis and William Clark were exploring the newly acquired Louisiana Territory, a party of Osage chiefs traveled from St. Louis to Washington, D.C. They were welcomed by President Thomas Jefferson, and as they toured Eastern American cities they became objects of great curiosity. In Washington at least five of the Osage Chiefs sat for portraits by Charles Balthazar Julien Févret de Saint-Mémin, a successful painter who had fled to America to escape the French Revolution. Saint-Mémin's works, drafted with the aid of the mechanical "physiognotrace," a wooden-framed drawing aid, are the earliest known portraits of Plains Indians. Another delegation of Plains Indians came East in 1805. While in Philadelphia they visited Charles Wilson Peale's natural history museum; Peale, also using the physiognotrace, cut silhouettes of a group of the Indians and later sent them to Jefferson, remarking that "some of these savages have interesting characters in the line of their faces." By October 1805 Lewis and Clark sent back East their first collection of scientific specimens. Among this shipment were some magpies, a prairie dog, animal skins, and a buffalo robe on which a Mandan Indian artist documented a battle around 1797.

Charles Bird King. In 1821 Maj. Benjamin O'Fallon, Indian agent for the Missouri River nations, persuaded prominent members of the Kansa, Oto and Missouri, Omaha, and Pawnee Nations to visit Washington. Thomas L. McKenney, superintendent of Indian trade, commissioned Charles Bird King, a gentleman-artist who had studied under Benjamin West, to paint portraits of the Indian delegation. These works were the first series of oil paintings of prominent Western Indians. King's *Petalesharo, Skidi Pawnwee Chief* (1821) depicted a young chief who had become something of a popular hero during the tour; he was lauded for his heroic rescue of a Comanche maiden about to be sacrificed by the Pawnees. *Petalesharo* and other portraits, including *White Plume, Head Chief of the Kansa,* and *Eagle of Delight, Wife*

Buffalo Bull's Back Fat, Head Chief of the Blood Tribe of Blackfeet (1832); oil painting by George Catlin (Smithsonian Institution, Washington, D.C.)

of *Prairie Wolf* (both 1821), became part of the National Indian Portrait Gallery in Washington, D.C. In 1858 the Portrait Gallery was transferred to the Smithsonian Institution, where it remained until a fire destroyed many of the portraits in 1865. Fortunately King's work survives in replicas, as well as in lithographs illustrating McKenney and James Hall's three-volume work titled *History of the Indian Tribes of North America* (1836–1844).

THE NATIVE AMERICANS

I have closely studied the Indian character in its native state, and also in its secondary form along our Frontiers; civilized, as it is often (but incorrectly) called. I have seen it in every phase, and although there are many noble instances to the contrary, and with many of whom I am personally acquainted; yet the greater part of those who have lingered along the Frontiers, and been kicked about like dogs, by white men, and beaten into a sort of a civilization, are very far from being what I would be glad to see them, and proud to call them, civilized by the aids and examples of good and moral people. . . .

Such are the results to which the present system of civilization brings that small part of these poor unfortunate people, who outlive the first calamities of their country; and in this degraded and pitiable condition, the most of them end their days in poverty and wretchedness, without the power of rising above it. Standing on the soil which they have occupied from their childhood, and inherited from their fathers; with the dread of "pale faces," and the deadly prejudices that have been reared in their breasts against them, for the destructive influences which they have introduced into their country, which have thrown the greater part of their friends and connexions into the grave, and are now promising the remainder of them no better prospect than the dreary one of living a few years longer, and then to sink into the ground themselves; surrendering their lands and their fair hunting grounds to the enjoyment of their enemies, and their bones to be dug up and strewed about the fields, or to be labelled in our Museums.

For the Christian and philanthropist, in any part of the world, there is enough, I am sure, in the character, condition, and history of these unfortunate people, to engage his sympathies—for the Nation, there is an unrequited account of sin and injustice that sooner or later will call for *national retribution*—and for the American citizens, who live, every where proud of their growing wealth and their luxuries, over the bones of these poor fellows, who have surrendered their hunting-grounds and their lives, to the enjoyment of their cruel dispossessors, there is a lingering terror yet, I fear, for the reflecting minds, whose mortal bodies must soon take their humble places with their red, but injured brethren, under the same glebe; to appear and stand, at last, with guilt's shivering conviction, amidst the myriad ranks of accusing spirits, that are to rise in their own fields, at the final day of resurrection!

Source: George Catlin, *Letters and Notes on the Manners, Customs, and Conditions of the North American Indians* (New York: Dover, 1973), pp. 255–256.

Audubon. In the meantime, as Plains Indians traveled East, some American artists began to explore the West. One of the first artists to document the wildlife of the West was John James Audubon. Born in Haiti and working as a portraitist in Philadelphia, Audubon became interested in documenting birds in their natural settings. In 1820 he set out to provide a comprehensive pictorial record of every bird species in North America. It was a massive project that took eighteen years of traveling, sketching and studying to complete. When Audubon's *Birds of America* was published in 1838, it contained 435 plates, portraits of birds that are rich in detail and crisp in color and scale. Audubon's work was scientific in impulse, but he would become a romantic figure. Charles W. Webber, a popular nineteenth-century interpreter of the West, would later compare Audubon to Daniel Boone. Audubon, who had met and painted Boone, was, according to Webber, a model of the "Hunter-Naturalist," ruggedly enduring danger, exposure, and solitude in the wilderness.

The Long Expedition. Lewis and Clark were not accompanied by formally trained artists, but in 1818 Titian Ramsay Peale and Samuel Seymour joined an expedition up the Missouri River led by Maj. Stephen H. Long. Peale was Charles Wilson Peale's son, and although not formally trained as an artist, he had grown up in his father's museum and become remarkably adept at depicting the animals there. His skill was recognized by Thomas Say, the naturalist appointed to the Long Expedition, and Say chose Peale as his assistant. Samuel Seymour, a Philadelphia-based painter and engraver, also joined the expedition. Seymour's duties, as described by Long, were to "furnish sketches of landscapes, wherever we meet with any distinguished for their beauty or grandeur" and to paint likenesses "of distinguished Indians, and exhibit groups of savages engaged in celebrating their festivals, or sitting in council." In June 1819, fifteen years after Lewis and Clark's expedition, the Long expedition began its ascent up the Missouri, following the south fork of the Platte River into present-day Colorado. They went as far west as to come in sight of the Rockies. Along the way Peale collected specimens and hunted; he completed more than 120 drawings of mammals, birds, fish, reptiles, insects, shells, and plants. Together, he and Seymour were the first known white artists to make field sketches documenting the lives of the Plains Indians. Peale's *Bulls* (1820) is the earliest known picture of buffalo grazing on the Great Plains, and his *Sioux Lodges* (1819) is the earliest known picture of a Plains tipi.

George Catlin. George Catlin was the first painter who devoted his entire career to the West. In 1832, while working as a portraitist in Philadelphia, Catlin witnessed a delegation of Indians passing through Philadelphia on their way to Washington. Struck by this vision, he resolved that "nothing short of the loss of my life, shall prevent me from visiting their country, and of becoming their historian." He spent the next eight years traveling

The Light, an Assiniboine Indian, on his Way to and Return from Washington (1832); oil painting by George Catlin
(Smithsonian Institution, Washington, D.C.)

THE ARTS   63

the frontier and painting as many as 146 Indian nations. Catlin worked from sketches to paint in a number of genres. His portraits, such as *Buffalo Bull's Back Fat, Head Chief of the Blood Tribe of Blackfeet* (1832), were among the first by an American artist to portray Indians as unique individuals. He also painted hunting and ceremonial scenes, such as the *Mandan Okipa Ceremony* (1832), as well as landscapes, such as his panoramic view of *The Pipestone Quarry* (1848), a Santee Sioux site Catlin described as "great . . . in traditions, and stories, of which this Western world is full and rich." In addition to his paintings, in 1841 Catlin published his *Letters and Notes on the Manners, Customs, and Conditions of the North American Indians*. *Letters* recounts Catlin's adventures in the West and his encounters with Indians. Catlin's travels left him with a keen empathy for the Indians as he witnessed the often brutal and ruthless Indian removal policies of the United States government. The last chapter of *Letters* is a scathing critique of the American exploitation and destruction of "the noble races of red men."

Carl Bodmer. In 1832 Alexander Phillipp Maximilian, a former general in the Prussian army during the Napoleonic Wars and the prince of a small German principality, was planning an expedition into Western North America. Aside from being a soldier, Maximilian was a scholar and natural historian who had gained wide recognition for his research in Brazil from 1815 to 1817. On that expedition he had executed his own field sketches, but now he felt he needed a full-time artist. To record his North American findings he engaged Carl Bodmer, a twenty-three-year-old Swiss artist who was formally trained in drawing and watercolors.

In the West. To prepare for their journey Maximilian and Bodmer visited bookshops and museums with materials on the West. In Philadelphia they talked with Titian Peale and studied Indian artifacts gathered by Lewis and Clark. Near St. Louis they examined a small collection of Catlin's oil paintings. They left St. Louis on *The Yellowstone*, the same American Fur Company steamer on which Catlin traveled, proceeding up the Missouri to Fort Lookout, near the mouth of the White River. There Bodmer drew his first full-length portrait of a Plains Indian, *Big Soldier, Teton Sioux Chief* (1833). After reaching Fort Union, at the mouth of the Yellowstone River, Maximilian and Bodmer followed the 1805 trail of Lewis and Clark and arrived at Fort McKenzie, near the mouth of the Marias River, in the heart of Blackfoot country. There they witnessed a daybreak attack by some six hundred Assinboines and Crees on the Piegans living outside the Fort. Bodmer recorded the event in his *Assinboine-Cree Attack* (1833). Maximilian and Bodmer spent a cold winter at Fort Clark, where Bodmer documented Mandan and Hidatsa culture, including his *Interior of a Mandan Earth Lodge* (1833) and *Bison Dance of the Mandan Indians* (circa 1834). Bodmer's technique was to make quick sketches of ceremonial scenes and then later fill in details, after making watercolors of the principal performers wearing the ceremonial dress. Bodmer used this technique throughout much of the expedition; in fact, many of his paintings were finished only after he returned to Europe.

Legacy of the First Encounter. Compared to Catlin's broad brushstrokes and bold colors, Bodmer's work was much more precise. Spurred by Maximilian's scientific agenda, he took great pains to render lodgings, clothing, and landscapes in nearly photographic detail. In addition, whereas Catlin's work frequently portrayed individual Indians in isolation, Bodmer's work reflected a stronger sense of environment. His *Assiniboine Medicine Sign* (1833), for example, quietly suggests a uniquely Indian landscape, one in which spirits, nature, and the living coexisted. Maximilian's expedition was Bodmer's only trip to North America. He returned to Europe and spent the rest of his life in Paris, successfully exhibiting wildlife and forest scenes and eventually being named a chevalier of the Legion of Honor. Together, Bodmer and Catlin's work helped to document nations that were in flux. Their paintings established the Plains Indian as the dominant image of the American Indian in both America and Europe.

Sources:

Chris Bruce and others, *The Myth of the West* (Seattle: Rizzoli, 1990);

John C. Ewers, *Artists of the Old West* (Garden City, N.Y.: Doubleday, 1965);

Dawn Glanz, *How the West Was Drawn: American Art and the Settling of the Frontier* (Ann Arbor: UMI Research Press, 1978);

Jules David Prown and others, *Discovered Lands, Invented Pasts: Transforming Visions of the American West* (New Haven: Yale University Press, 1992);

John Wilmerding, *American Art* (New York: Penguin, 1976).

PERIODICALS OF THE OLD WEST

Newspapers. In 1784, when John Filson finished his manuscript on the history of Kentucky, he had to travel back to Delaware in order to get it published; at that time there were no printing presses in the West. Two years later the *Pittsburgh Gazette* was published, the first newspaper printed in the trans-Allegheny territories. John Scull, the publisher of the *Gazette*, also printed the first book west of the Alleghenies, the third volume of Hugh Henry Brackenridge's novel, *Modern Chivalry* (1793). In the meantime, using a printing press carried from Philadelphia by wagon and boat, John Bradford, in 1787, started the second Western newspaper, the *Kentucke Gazette*. Since these newspapers often lacked up-to-date national and international news, the editor often published articles with a literary bent. Essays in the style of the English eighteenth-century essayists Joseph Addison and Richard Steele and the local "poets corner" were popular features; frontier politics and religion were common subjects for verse. Despite any limitations, newspapers continued to grow in the West. By 1840 they comprised more than a quarter of the total newspapers published in the nation.

Western Magazines. The first magazine in the West was Daniel Bradford's *The Medley, or Monthly Miscellany*, published only for one year, in 1803, in Lexington, Kentucky. In 1813 Zadoc Cramer briefly published Pittsburgh's *Western Gleaner*. From 1819 to 1821 William Gibbes Hunt, again in Lexington, published the *Western Review and Miscellaneous Magazine*. *Western Review* featured history, biography, poetry, synopses of British novels, and natural science. In two years Hunt's magazine also collapsed for lack of contributors. Yet the next two decades witnessed sustained growth by Western magazines. Lexington and Cincinnati became cultural rivals, and in 1824 the Cincinnati *Literary Gazette* (1824–1825) declared: "This is the Age of Magazines—/ Even skeptics must confess it: / Where is the town of much renown / That has not one to bless it?"

Flint and the Western Review. Timothy Flint, a New England missionary, teacher, historian, and novelist, began publishing his *Western Review* in 1827. Flint had already published *Frances Berrian, or the Mexican Patriot* (1826), which many consider to be the first "Westerns" ever written, the tale of a New Englander who finds a new life on the frontier. Flint envisioned the *Review* as a journal devoted to developing and celebrating Western culture. "It is high time," Flint wrote in the "Editor's Address" in the first volume, "amidst our improvements of every sort, that some effort should be made, to foster polite literature among us." Flint had a romantic faith in Western, rural virtue; he believed that great writing would come out of the "freshness of our unspoiled nature, beneath the shade of the huge sycamores of the Miami, or . . . in the breeze of the beautiful Ohio" just as it now came out of "the dark dens" of the cities in the East. Unfortunately, Flint's optimism was not entirely justified; he himself wrote three-quarters of the material in the *Review*, with his son, Micah, contributing poetry. Most of the material was historical or factual, but Flint also contributed his own tales and reviews. In 1830, unable to continue editing and writing most of the magazine, Flint ceased publication; but Flint had made his mark. In her *Domestic Manners of the Americans* (1832) the English traveler Francis Trollope deplored the volume and quality of America's "periodical trash" but singled out Flint as an exception. "In some of his critical notices," she wrote, "there is strength and keenness second to nothing of the kind I have ever read." Nathaniel P. Willis, New York publisher and writer, praised the *Review* to Eastern audiences, though he reassured incredulous readers that the journal's success was understandable because, after all, Flint was originally "a New-England man."

Western Monthly Magazine. James Hall, lawyer and politician, started the first literary periodical west of Ohio, *The Illinois Monthly Magazine* (1830), which later became the *Cincinnati Western Monthly Magazine*. Like Flint, Hall was a champion of western virtue, and he criticized James Fenimore Cooper and others for their unrealistic view of the West. This same realistic impulse informed Hall's own work, published as *Letters from the West* (1828), *The Soldier's Bride & Other Tales* (1833), and *Tales of the Border* (1833). Hall's style was somewhat sentimental, but he aimed at realism. Genteel readers critiqued his use of "vulgar backwoods expressions" and his portraits of the sometimes crude living conditions on the frontier.

Western Messenger. Perhaps the most significant Western journal to come out of this era was the *Western Messenger*, begun in 1835 by the Unitarian reverend James Freeman Clarke. The *Messenger* had strong New England, Transcendentalist ties. It was the first periodical to publish Ralph Waldo Emerson's poetry, and John Keats's "Ode to Apollo" was first published posthumously in the *Messenger*—in part due to the efforts of George Keats, the poet's brother, who lived in Louisville. The *Messenger* struggled against anti-Unitarian prejudice and stopped publication in 1841. In the 1850s, however, with the growth of San Francisco as a cultural center, magazines flourished in the Far West. Journals such as *The Pioneer, Golden Era, The Hyperion, The Californian*, and *The Overland Monthly*, centered around San Francisco, Monterey, and Sacramento, sprouted up around the gold rush. Bolstered by the success of these journals, Edward Pollock, a popular California poet of the 1850s, predicted a great future for Western literature. Writing in *The Pioneer*, he boldly predicted that "this is the country" that will produce the "New Epic." Where else, Pollock asked, "could exist the land of liberty and of change . . . [this] land should grow giants and will."

Sources:

James K. Folsom, *Timothy Flint* (New York: Twayne, 1965);

Thomas J. Lyon and others, *Updating the Literary West* (Fort Worth: Texas Christian University Press, 1997);

Robert Spiller and others, *Literary History of the United States*, third edtion (New York: Macmillan, 1963).

POPULAR MUSIC IN THE WEST

Fiddles and Dances. In the late fall of 1804, as Meriwether Lewis and William Clark reached the Mandans and Minitaris in what is now North Dakota, the expedition paused to build winter quarters. While passing the winter months, the men of the expedition traded with the Indians, hunted, gathered wood, and repaired their equipment. They also spent many evenings enjoying music. On Christmas Day 1804 Clark's journal records that one of the rooms of the winter fort was "prepared for dancing, which was kept up until 8 p.m." The explorers celebrated New Year's Day with dancing, joined by the Mandans and accompanied by fiddles and tambourines. Indeed, Pierre Cruzatte, a fiddler and trader on the Missouri River, joined the expedition for the sole purpose of providing entertainment. According to the journals, the men of the expedition, no matter how fatigued, always enjoyed square dancing to Cruzatte's fiddle.

Lonesome Tunes. Music was an important aspect of the Western experience; from the Mountain Men's Rendezvous to military posts to the gold camps, singing and dancing were popular pastimes. Music was often supplied by fiddles, tambourines, accordions, banjos, and harmonicas, instruments small enough to be transported across the westward trails. Some of the songs were "lonesome tunes," emphasizing isolation and homes left behind. Other songs recalled the spirit of the tall tale, exaggerating and laughing at the dangers of the wilderness and parodying the foibles of greenhorns and conventional culture. Some campfires resonated with both kinds of music. One traveler along the Oregon Trail, recalling evening camp life, contrasted the improvised dances accompanied by the "lively music" of the violin to the "mellow and melancholy notes" of the flute, which seemed "a lament for the past rather than a hope for the future." G. W. Thissell, who traveled to California from Iowa, recorded in his diary the pleasures of sitting around the campfire, telling stories, and singing songs, including Stephen Foster's popular "Oh! Susanna": "It rained all night, the day I left, / The weather, it was dry. / The sun so hot, I froze to death / Susanna, don't you cry. / O Susanna, / Don't you cry for me, / I'm going to California / Some gold dust to see." Emigrants brought other popular songs along with them on the Oregon Trail, including Daniel Decatur Emmett's "Old Dan Tucker" (1843), "My Old Sally" (1843), "The Blue Tail Fly" and "Jimmy Crack Corn" (1846); Foster's "Old Folks at Home" (sometimes called "Swanee River"); and M. A. Richter's "The California Pioneers." Popular folk songs included "Skip to My Lou," "Swing on the Corner," "Old Joe Clark," and "Sourwood Mountains." Many of the melodies were borrowed from Irish reels or Eastern popular songs but were transformed by frontier fiddlers, becoming more rhythmic, energetic, and idiosyncratic.

Songs of the Gold Camps. Music was also often heard around the camp fires of Forty-Niners. Some songs recalled the pleasures and comforts of their distant homes, such as "Carry Me Back to Old Virginny," which one Eastern emigrant called an "especial favorite" of the miners: "party after party joined in the chorus, and the melody would come pealing round odd corners and from distant tents, in heartfelt strains." Miners rewrote or parodied familiar tunes, such as John Nichols's "Oh, California" (1848), a parody of Foster's "Oh! Susanna." Another boomtown songwriter borrowed the tune of "New York Gals" to warn greenhorns about "Hangtown Gals," who were, according to the song, "plump and rosy, / Hair in ringlets mighty cozy; / Painted cheeks and gassy bonnets" but "Touch them and they'll sting like hornets." The first gold rush song actually written in California is believed to be David G. Robinson's "Seeing the Elephant" (1850), a song documenting the high hopes and disappointments of life among the miners. Newpaper editor George W. Kendall, in his *Santa Fe Expedition* (1844), defined "seeing the elephant" as "when a man is disappointed in anything he undertakes, when he has seen enough, when he gets sick and tired of any job he may have set himself about, he has seen the elephant." The phrase became a popular one to describe the harsh realities of camp life, as Robinson's song makes clear: "When the elephant I had seen, / I'm damned if I thought I was green; / And others say, both night and morn, / They saw him coming round the Horn." Music was such a popular pastime among the miners that between 1852 and 1861 twelve songbooks, or "songsters," were published and sold around the camps.

Sources:

David Dary, *Seeking Pleasure in the Old West* (New York: Knopf, 1995);

Ronald L. Davis, *A History of Music in American Life: Volume I: The Formative Years, 1620–1865* (Malabar, Fla.: Robert Krieger, 1982);

Richard E. Lingenfelter, Richard A. Dwyer, and David Cohen, *Songs of the American West* (Berkeley: University of California Press, 1968).

QUILTS OF THE OLD WEST

Quilting Women's Lives. While books, paintings, and almanacs often portrayed the West as a realm of masculine adventure, a contest between men and nature or between white men and Indians, women, of course, played vital roles in the migration to and settling of the West. The demands of frontier life, however, as well as cultural norms, limited opportunities for artistic expression by women; but recently scholars have discovered that the important contributions of women in the West did not go undocumented. Aside from diaries and journals, Western women also recorded their daily lives in their quilts. Quilts were the most popular form of needlework produced in the nineteenth century; on the westward trail or the frontier settlements, quilts were a means of both physical and emotional comfort. Thick quilts lined and covered wagons, padded fragile china, or became window covers or primitive shelters such as tents. Quilts were even used in the place of coffins. One 1849 diary records the bodies of a mother and infant "wrapped together in a bed comforter and wound . . . with a few yards of string that we made by tying together torn strips of a cotton dress shirt."

Patterns and Themes. Quilts made by pioneer women often reflected the flora and fauna encountered in the West. Hawks, honeysuckle, peonies, and stars appear on a number of quilts of the period. Migration was also a prominent theme. The pattern of Sarah Koontz Glover's "Pinwheel" quilt, made while crossing the Oregon Trail in 1849, suggests both movement and wind. Wheel patterns were popular, as well as patterns that have come to be known as "wandering foot" and "log cabin." Other quilts or pieces of quilts commemorated births, arrivals, weddings, or accomplishments. Despite their celebratory themes, the process of making quilts was not easy. Quilting demanded long hours and painstaking skill, often in extremely difficult conditions. In the early 1820s, for example, Mary Rabb, an early settler of Texas, described the arduous labor of life on the frontier, even with the advantage of a spinning wheel: "The mosquitoes and sand gnats was so bad that it was impossible to get any sleep . . . I would pick the cotton with my fingers and spin six hundred thread around the wheel every day and milk my cows and pound my meal in a mortar and churn and mind my children."

Bees and Friendship. In the often harsh and isolated conditions on the frontier, quilts also became a means of building community. Prior to departing for the West, quilting bees were held, bringing together female friends to work cooperatively. These bees became farewell ceremonies, or as Miriam Davis Colt put it in 1856 as she left New York for Kansas, they "unit[ed] pleasure with business." "Friendship quilts," inscribed with the names and best wishes of old friends, were also popular, treasured remembrances of the life left behind. The quilts themselves could become records of the journey West. Blocks of one existing quilt, made by members of the Hezlep and Shuey families as they journeyed from Illinois to California in 1858–1859, record: "Piec[e]s cut in the winter of 1858," "Left Illinois for California—April 15th, 1859," "Crossed the Plains," "Seven months on the road," and "Ho for California!" Once a group of settlers arrived, quilts often became the means of joining the community. In 1853 Rebecca H. N. Woodson, just turned eighteen and newly arrived in Sonoma City, California, derived "great comfort" from the company of her neighbors. "There was scarcely ever a day we was not togeather [*sic*]. We did not think we could start to make a dress or start piecing a new quilt without consulting each other." A Swedish woman who came to Kansas in the early 1850s recalled an invitation to a sewing circle as a signal of friendship and acceptance. She returned the favor by inviting her neighbors to an all-day quilting at her home. In conditions that were often harsh and performing labor that was often draining, women found both relief and a means of expression in quilting. As one female settler recalled, writing of life in Texas in the 1830s, "quiltin' bees" were occasions for the attending women to help "each other in every way . . . *they helped each other.* Perhaps this thought justifies the whole of pioneer woman's suffering."

Sources:

Caroline Patterson Bresenhan and Nancy O'Bryant Puentes, *Lone Stars: A Legacy of Texas Quilts, 1836–1936* (Austin: University of Texas Press, 1986);

Mary Bywater Cross, *Treasures in the Trunk: Quilts of the Oregon Trail* (Nashville, Tenn.: Rutledge Hill Press, 1993);

Elaine Hedges and others, *Hearts and Hands: Women, Quilts and American Society* (Nashville, Tenn.: Rutledge Hill Press, 1987).

TALL TALES AND SKETCHES OF THE OLD SOUTHWEST

American Humor. Tall tales and humorous sketches depicting life along the frontier of the Old Southwest flourished from the 1820s until the Civil War. Characterized by comic exaggeration and vernacular language, reveling in superhuman feats and hoaxes, these tales

A windmill-pattern quilt circa 1850 (Colorado Historical Society, Denver)

popularized a uniquely American brand of literary humor. In response to European and Eastern travelers who depicted Westerners as crude illiterates living in squalor, these humorists celebrated the rugged frontier with flourish and extravagance. At the same time, they often parodied the naïveté of greenhorns and the hypocrisy of authority figures. In this way tall tales became expressions of regional and national identity.

The Tall Tales. The tall tale, according to the literary scholar Carolyn S. Brown, is a "comic fiction disguised as fact, deliberately exaggerated to the limits of credibility." Or, as the scholar Walter Hill puts it, the tall tale is "a beautiful lie." Two of the most popular tall-tale figures of the nineteenth century were Mike Fink and Davy Crockett. The real Fink was a famed scout, hunter, keelboatman, and storyteller. His adventures were enlarged and embroidered by oral storytellers, folk journalists, and even playwrights. He was a "helliferocious fellow" who epitomized a rough-and-tumble vision of the frontier. Fink, it was said, could outshoot, outfight, and outdrink any and all comers. "I'm a regular tornado," Fink boasts in an 1842 story by Thomas Bangs Thorpe, "tough as a hickory withe, long-winded as a nor'-wester. I can strike a blow like a falling tree." Davy Crockett, like Fink, was

That Colonel Crockett could avail himself, in election-eering, of the advantages which well applied satire ensures, the following anecdote will sufficiently prove:

In the canvass of the Congressional election of 18—, Mr.— was the Colonel's opponent—a gentleman of the most pleasing and conciliating manners—who seldom addressed a person or a company without wearing upon his countenance a peculiarly good humoured smile. The colonel, to counteract the influence of this winning attribute, thus alluded to it a stump speech:

"Yes, gentlemen, he may get some votes by *grinning*, for he can *outgrin me*—and you know I ain't slow—and to prove to you that I am not, I will tell you an anecdote. I was concerned myself—and I was fooled a little of the wickedest. You all know I love hunting. Well, I discovered a long time ago that a 'coon couldn't stand my grin. I could bring one tumbling down from the highest tree. I never wasted powder and lead, when I wanted one of the creatures. Well, as I was walking out one night, a few hundred yards from my house, looking carelessly about me, I saw a 'coon planted upon one of the highest limbs of an old tree. The night was very *moony* and clear, and old Ratler was with me; but Ratler won't bark at a 'coon—he's a queer dog in that way. So, I thought I'd bring the lark down in the usual way, *by a grin*. I set myself—and, after grinning at the 'coon a reasonable time, found that he didn't come down. I wondered what was the reason—and I took another steady grin at him. Still he was *there*. It made me a little mad; so I felt around and got an old limb about five feet long, and, planting one end upon the ground, I placed my chin upon the other, and took *a rest*. I then grinned my best for about five minutes; but the cursed 'coon hung on. So, finding I could not bring him down by grinning, I determined to have him—for I thought he must be a droll chap. I went over to the house, got my axe, returned to the tree, saw the 'coon still there, and to cut away. Down it come, and I ran forward; but d—n the 'coon was there to be seen. I found that what I had taken for one, was a large knot upon the branch of the tree and, upon looking at it closely, I saw *I had grinned all the bark off, and left the knot perfectly smooth.*

"Now, fellow-citizens," continued the Colonel, "you must be convinced that, in the *grinning line*, I myself am not slow—yet, when I look upon my opponent's countenance, I must admit that he is my superior. You must all admit it. Therefore, be wide awake—look sharp—and do not let him grin you out of your votes."

Source: *Sketches and Eccentricities of Col. David Crockett of West Tennessee* (London: O. Rich, 1834).

elected to Congress in 1827 and again in 1833. As a politician Crockett made a virtue out of his lack of schooling and polish. "I ain't used to oily words; I am used to speak what I think, of men, and to men," he told an audience in Boston. After his political career ended, Crockett moved to Texas, where he fought and died in the battle of the Alamo. During his lifetime tall tales were told about his adventures, and after his death they appeared in "Crockett almanacs," popular collections of tall tales and comic anecdotes. Crockett was, in these tales, comic storyteller, frontier politician, hunter, and fighter extraordinaire. "I'm the same David Crockett," he tells a tavern audience, "fresh from the backwoods . . . can wade the Mississippi, leap the Ohio, ride upon a streak of lightning . . . whip my weight in wildcats . . . and whip any man opposed to Jackson."

Lincoln. Perhaps the most famous frontier politician and storyteller was Abraham Lincoln. Like Crockett, Lincoln often played on his image as a simple bumpkin from the Western plains, and he had a reputation as a "backwoods humorist." Nathaniel Hawthorne, during an 1862 visit to Washington, met Lincoln and remarked on his yarnspinning. Hawthorne reports laughing heartily at a story Lincoln told, a story that Hawthorne could not, however, repeat for the pages of *The Atlantic.*

Humor. Along with tall tales, sketches depicting backwoods comics and con men also flourished. Some of the important collections of these sketches are Augustus Baldwin Longstreet's *Georgia Scenes* (1835), William Tappan Thompson's *Major Jones Courtship* (1843), Johnson Jones Hooper's *Some Adventures of Simon Suggs* (1845), Thomas Bang Thorpe's *Mysteries of the Backwoods* (1846), John S. Robb's *Streaks of Squatter Life* (1847), Joseph M. Field's *The Drama in Pokerville* (1847), Henry Clay Lewis's *Odd Leaves from the Life of a Louisiana "Swamp Doctor"* (1850), Joseph B. Cobb's *Mississippi Scenes* (1851), Joseph B. Baldwin's *The Flush Times of Alabama and Mississippi* (1853), and George Washington Harris's *Sut Lovingood's Yarns* (1867). Many of the sketches in these collections were first printed and popularized by the New York humor and sporting magazine, the *Spirit of the Times,* edited by William T. Porter.

"Durn'd fools" and Con Men. While these tales were often introduced by the cultured voices of upper-class frame narrators, the heroes of these tales are just as often subversive backwoodsmen. Sut Lovingood, who admits to being a "nat'ral born durn'd fool," takes great joy in exposing the foolishness of circuit riders, ministers, sheriffs, and prudes. Illiterate con men such as Simon Suggs make no bones about the fact that the world is an amoral place where survival and laughter are more important than ethical niceties. His motto is, "it is good to be shifty in a new country." The earthy spirit and dark humor of these sketches contrast sharply with the more refined sensibility of New England literature. And to some readers, that was just the point—to make fun of, dupe, or offend genteel outsiders, or as Sut puts it when a pedantic

also an historical figure. Born into poverty in Tennessee, and with little schooling, Crockett served in the Creek War under Gen. Andrew Jackson, where he became renowned as a hunter, soldier, and storyteller. He was

listener interrupts one of his narratives to offer a correction, "yu go to hell, mistofer; you bothers me." Nevertheless, for twentieth-century audiences there is much to take offense at in both the sketches and the tall tales; many reveal the pervasiveness of nineteenth-century racism and sexism.

Influence. In many ways these sketches anticipated the local color movement of the late nineteenth century. Though sometimes he did so with exaggeration and disdain, the Southwestern humorist attempted to realistically record local manners and customs. In their use of frontier metaphors and language ("I ladles out my words at random, like a calf kickin at yaller-jackids," claims Sut), they popularized a rich, earthy, boasting vernacular. The Civil War brought an end to the genre, but the tall tale and the Southwestern sketch would have an influence on authors ranging from humorists such as Mark Twain and John Phoenix to William Faulkner. Faulkner's novella *The Bear* (1958) was influenced by Thorpe's "The Big Bear of Arkansas" (1841). Faulkner, who owned a copy of Harris's *Sut Lovingood's Yarns,* once praised Sut's honest character: "He had no illusions about himself, did the best he could; at certain times he was a coward and knew it and wasn't ashamed; he never blamed his misfortunes on anyone and never cursed God for them."

Sources:

Walter Blair and Hamlin Hill, *America's Humor from Poor Richard to Doonesbury* (New York: Oxford University Press, 1978);

Carolyn S. Brown, *The Tall Tale in American Folklore and Literature* (Knoxville: University of Tennessee Press, 1987);

Hennig Cohen and William B. Dillingham, *Humor of the Old Southwest* (Athens: University of Georgia Press, 1975).

THE WEST AS SEEN FROM THE EAST

Literary Explorations. With the Louisiana Purchase of 1803, Eastern newspapers, magazines, and books began to carry the accounts of official explorers, such as Lewis and Clark, Zebulon Pike, Stephen Long, and John Frémont. The adventures of unofficial explorers, such as painter George Catlin and trader Josiah Gregg, also became popular. This new interest in the West inspired Eastern literary figures such as James Fenimore Cooper, Washington Irving, and Henry Wadsworth Longfellow to produce their own impressions of the frontier. While such literary accounts were often shaped by reading rather than firsthand experience, they had a tremendous influence upon future visions of the West.

Cooper. James Fenimore Cooper created an immensely influential vision of the West in his Leatherstocking novels, the first of which was *The Pioneers* (1823), set near Otsego Lake, New York, in the late eighteenth century. The novel's fundamental conflict is played out between Judge Temple, a Christian gentleman and proprietor of a large tract of land, and Natty Bumppo, also known as Leatherstocking, a hunter and trapper who has lived for forty years on the judge's land.

Cooper depicts Leatherstocking as a man "form'd for the wilderness," "kindred [to] the beasts of the forest," and steeped in Indian lore and the moral code of nature. After being arrested for killing a single deer out of season, Leatherstocking chooses to leave the settlement, disappearing into the woods, "towards the setting sun." *The Pioneers,* like the other novels in the Leatherstocking series, is driven by conflicts between civilization and freedom, law and nature, conflicts that would be played out again and again in Western literature. Cooper himself continued to explore these questions through the character of Leatherstocking in *The Last of the Mohicans* (1826), *The Prairie* (1827), *The Pathfinder* (1840), and *The Deerslayer* (1841). Cooper never actually visited the West, and his novels remained unconvincing to his critics. Nevertheless, the character of Leatherstocking, blending the man of action with the man of natural philosophy, became one of the most influential and enduring characters of American literature.

Irving's Tours. Washington Irving, widely regarded as the first professional American author and best known today as the author of "Rip Van Winkle" and "The Legend of Sleepy Hollow," also wrote of the West. In 1832, after a seventeen-year sojourn in Europe, Irving returned home to New York, anxious to again take up American subject matter. In the next few years he published three Western volumes, *A Tour of the Prairies* (1835), *Astoria* (1836), and *The Adventures of Captain Bonneville* (1837). *A Tour of the Prairies* records Irving's experience as a member of a federal government expedition across what is now Oklahoma. Irving considered *A Tour of the Prairies* a "light" work, a miscellaneous collection of sketches varied in their range and tone. *Astoria* and *Captain Bonneville* were intended as more "serious" works. *Astoria,* written at the behest of business magnate John Jacob Astor, documented Astor's "grand enterprise" in the Northwest—his attempt, between 1809 and 1813, to establish a fur-trading colony at the mouth of the Columbia River. The colony failed, in part because of confusion created by the outbreak of hostilities with the British. The lesson of *Astoria,* according to Irving, is that the growth of the American empire will depend upon bold entrepreneurs such as Astor, entrepreneurs who deserve recognition and support from the federal government. *Captain Bonneville* was based on the journals of Benjamin Bonneville, a gentleman-soldier who in 1831 was granted leave from the U.S. Army to explore the Rocky Mountains. The mountain region was, in Irving's view, "an irreclaimable wilderness," populated by mountain men and Indians of "savage habitudes." In contrast to Cooper's pastoral vision of the frontier as home to yeomanlike virtue, Irving's wilderness tests and nearly exhausts the resources of both empire builders, such as Astor, and experienced soldiers, such as Bonneville.

New Englanders Look West. In 1834 Richard Henry Dana, a Boston Brahmin and Harvard undergraduate, sailed around Cape Horn on the *Pilgrim.* His *Two Years*

A Reconnoitre, an 1838 painting by Alfred Jacob Miller (Public Archives of Canada, Ottawa)

An 1820 painting of a buffalo herd by Titan Ramsay Peale (Amon Carter Museum, Fort Worth, Texas)

Before the Mast (1840) vividly recounts his experiences as a merchant sailor and in pre-gold-rush California. In 1842 Francis Parkman, also a Harvard student, followed Dana westward, leaving his studies for a "tour of curiosity and amusement" beyond the Missouri River. His *Oregon Trail* (1846), the record of his journey, reveals an Easterner's paradoxical disdain for and romantic vision of the West. He found some backwoodsmen to be "uncouth, mean and stupid"; yet his guide, Henry Chatillon, appears as a heroic figure, brave, true, and possessing "a natural refinement." Another group of prominent New England literary figures, the Transcendentalists, were more concerned with the Far East than the Far West. Ralph Waldo Emerson had little to say about the West, and while we might expect Henry David Thoreau to have a great interest in the frontier, in fact he decried the base economic motivations of those who went West. The mountain men were, according to Thoreau, a "loafing class tempted by rum and money." He thought the gold rush marked "the greatest-disgrace on mankind." Henry Wadsworth Longfellow, the most famous American poet of his day, created a popular, if sentimentalized, vision of Indian life in his epic poem, *The Song of Hiawatha* (1855). Whatever the attitude of literary Easterners toward the West, by 1850 references to the West were commonplace in Eastern literature. Herman Melville's *Moby-Dick* (1851) is dotted with Western allusions, and Hawthorne, in *The Scarlet Letter* (1850), described the fiendish Chillingworth as probing his enemy's secret "like a miner searching for gold."

Sources:

Ralph M. Aderman, ed., *Critical Essays on Washington Irving* (Boston: G. K. Hall, 1990);

Donald A. Ringe, *James Fenimore Cooper* (Boston: Twayne, 1988);

Richard Slotkin, *The Fatal Environment: The Myth of the Frontier in the Age of Industrialization, 1800–1890* (New York: Atheneum, 1985);

Robert E. Spiller and others, *The Literary History of the United States* (New York: Macmillan, 1973);

J. Golden Taylor, *A Literary History of the American West* (Fort Worth: Texas Christian University Press, 1987).

GEORGE CATLIN

1796–1872
PAINTER

Innate Talent. George Catlin became the first painter to devote his career to the West. Born in Wilkes-Barre, Pennsylvania, Catlin studied law and practiced as a lawyer for a few years before, as he put it, selling his "law library" and "converting their proceeds into brushes and paint pots." Without benefit of either a teacher or formal art training, he began his career as a painter of portrait miniatures in Philadelphia. In 1824 Catlin was elected to the Pennsylvania Academy of the Fine Arts. In 1832 Catlin's career changed when he witnessed a delegation of Indians passing through Philadelphia on their way to Washington. These Indians appeared to Catlin as "lords of the forest" who walked with "silent and stoic dignity." He resolved that "nothing short of the loss of my life, shall prevent me from visiting their country, and of becoming their historian." Ignoring the objections of friends and relatives, Catlin boarded the American Fur Company's steamer *Yellowstone* on its maiden voyage to the Upper Missouri River. Over the next eight years he traveled in the West, painting as many as 146 Indian nations. In his effort to document what he believed was a "doomed" race, Catlin worked from sketches to paint in a number of genres. His portraits, such as *Buffalo Bull's Back Fat, Head Chief of the Blood Tribe of Blackfeet* (1832), were among the first by an American artist to portray Indians as unique individuals. He also painted hunting scenes, ceremonial scenes, and landscapes, such as his panoramic view of *The Pipestone Quarry* (1848), a Santee Sioux site Catlin described as "great . . . in traditions, and stories, of which this Western world is full and rich."

The Indian Gallery. In September 1837 Catlin returned East to open his Indian Gallery in New York. Initially, Eastern audiences did not know what to make of the brilliant face paint and the strange customs Catlin depicted; but Catlin had a flair for showmanship, and soon the tour became a popular success. The Indian Gallery traveled throughout the Eastern seaboard, garnering critical acclaim and large audiences. Despite this success, in 1839 the U.S. Senate voted not to purchase Catlin's gallery and thereby support his project. Stung by this rejection, Catlin packed up the Indian Gallery and sailed for England. Here, too, the gallery was a tremendous success, and he was commanded to give a private showing to both England's Queen Victoria and King Louis Philippe of France. In 1852, however, Catlin suffered bankruptcy, and he offered the Indian Gallery as collateral toward a loan that allowed him to pay off some of his creditors. He was never able to reclaim the original works, and he was forced to hastily produce a second, inferior group of paintings. Never fully escaping poverty, Catlin remained in Europe until 1870, returning to the United States only two years before his death.

Letters and Notes. In addition to his Indian Gallery, Catlin published *Letters and Notes on the Manners, Customs, and Conditions of the North American Indians* in 1841. *Letters* recounted Catlin's adventures traveling in the West and his encounters with Native Americans. Catlin's travels left him with a keen sense of the brutal and ruthless nature of advances of white "civilization." The last chapter of *Letters* is a scathing critique of American expansionism. In Catlin's view "the noble races of red men" were being eradicated by the advances of pioneers, fur traders, and American government policy. They had been "kicked about like dogs, by white men, and beaten into a sort of civilization." He found Indians' "rights invaded, their morals corrupted, their lands wrested from them, their customs changed." Such injustice called for "national retribution," a retribution that would be served, Catlin warned, if not in the present, then surely "at the final day of resurrection!"

A Powerful and Ambiguous Influence. Catlin's legacy is complex. His paintings made an indispensable contribution to our understanding of the Plains Indians of the early nineteenth century, yet at the same time they are sometimes primitive in execution and, for all his ethnographic care, inaccurate. *Letters* railed against social injustice, but his portraits rarely speak with the same force. Very few of Catlin's paintings comment on the ramifications of the Euramerican-Indian encounter. Indeed, one recent critic has suggested that his work fostered nineteenth-century America's romanticization of the Vanishing American, the sentimentalized lament—albeit from a safe distance since many of the Eastern and Midwestern Indians had already been displaced—for disappearing Indians and North American wilderness. Nevertheless, Catlin's influence was and continues to be immense. He visualized the West and depicted Indians for a vast national and international audience. Further, his emphasis on firsthand observation and experience became part of the ethos of Western art.

Sources:

Chris Bruce and others, *The Myth of the West* (Seattle: Rizzoli, 1990);

George Catlin, *Letters and Notes on the Manners, Customs, and Conditions of the North American Indians,* 2 volumes (New York: Dover Publications, 1973);

Anne Farrar Hyde, *An American Vision: Far Western Landscape and National Culture, 1820–1920* (New York: New York University Press, 1990);

Jules David Prown, *Discovered Lands, Invented Pasts: Transforming Visions of the American West* (New Haven: Yale University Press, 1992);

Joan Carpenter Troccoli, *First Artist of the West* (Tulsa, Okla.: Gilcrease Museum, 1993).

JAMES FENIMORE COOPER

1789-1851

NOVELIST

Novelist by Chance. James Cooper (he added Fenimore, his mother's name, in 1826) was born in Burlington, New Jersey, on 15 September 1789. He grew up in Cooperstown, New York, a settlement founded on Otsego Lake by his father, William, a prominent land speculator, judge, and Federalist politician. At the age of thirteen James attended Yale, but he was expelled in his third year, apparently for a prank. He then served in the U.S. Navy for several years. In January 1811, Cooper resigned his commission and married Susan DeLancey, heiress to what Cooper called "a handsome fortune." With his new wife, Cooper settled down as a gentleman-farmer. There was nothing in Cooper's experience to suggest that he would become a man of letters, much less a professional novelist, and nothing to suggest that he would go on to create one of the most influential Western characters in American literature. It was said that he could not bear to even write a letter. However, as Cooper's daughter later recalled, in 1820 Cooper was reading aloud a new British novel to his wife when he suddenly flung it down in disgust. He found it tedious and proclaimed, "I can write you a better novel than that, myself!" His wife challenged him to do so, and he quickly wrote and published *Precaution* (1820). *Precaution* was well received in England and America, and in 1821 Cooper followed it with another novel, *The Spy*, an adventure tale set during the American Revolution. A literary career was launched.

The Creation of Leatherstocking. It was Cooper's next novel, *The Pioneers* (1823), that established him as a successful American author. *The Pioneers* is set in Templeton, on the shores of Lake Otsego, in the late eighteenth century. Cooper describes the areas as a onetime primeval forest being developed into a village. The novel's fundamental conflict is played out between the town's founder, Judge Temple, a Christian gentleman and proprietor of a large tract of land, and Natty Bumppo, also known as Leatherstocking, a hunter and trapper who has lived peacefully with his Indian companion, Chingachgook, on the judge's land. Leatherstocking is a man of the forest, a kindred spirit of its wildlife. He is steeped in Indian lore and the moral code of nature and is disgusted by the sometimes senseless and destructive acts of the settlers. Judge Temple is also disgusted, but as a representative of refined society he sees the law as the solution to the excesses of civilization. Thus, when Natty is arrested for killing a single deer out of season, the Judge is forced to sentence him to jail. Leatherstocking chooses to leave the settlement, disappearing into the woods. The novel suggests that Judge Temple is right to apply the law and it also warns that the wilderness must not be sacrificed in the westward march of American civilization.

Natty's Youth and Death. After writing a novel of the sea, *The Pilot* (1824), and a second American Revolution novel, *Lionel Lincoln* (1825), Cooper returned to the adventures of Leatherstocking in *The Last of the Mohicans* (1826) and *The Prairie* (1827). Both novels examine the moral implications of Westward expansion. *The Last of the Mohicans* is set in 1757, when Leatherstocking, here known as Hawkeye, is a young man. The novel is primarily an adventure tale set in the wilderness during the French and Indian War. Hawkeye, more so than any of the white characters in the book, respects the wilderness and understands the Indians who live there. He warns the white characters (and by extension, Cooper's white readers) of their arrogance: "If you judge of Indian cunning by the rules you find in books, or by white sagacity, they will lead you astray, if not to your death." Hawkeye's humility and virtue allow him to survive in the wilderness. However, as we know from the end of *The Pioneers,* neither Natty nor the Indians will flourish for long. *The Prairie*, which portrays Leatherstocking at eighty, completes the cycle begun by the first two novels. The process of expansion has continued into the Great Plains, and the squatters and trappers who lead the way are lawless and reckless, possessing little regard for either law or nature. In his old age Leatherstocking has achieved the necessary virtue and discipline to live free, but he is pursued into the wilderness by those who, as Judge Temple once feared, abuse freedom. At the end of the novel

Leatherstocking dies quietly, standing upright and calling out to his maker, "Here!" His grave is guarded by Pawnee Indians as the "spot where a just White-man sleeps."

Europe and America. With the publication of *The Last of the Mohicans* and *The Prairie,* Cooper enjoyed great success. He was called the "American Scott," after the popular British novelist Sir Walter Scott. In 1826 he sailed for Europe, where he visited England, France, Switzerland, Italy, Germany, and Belgium. During his seven-year stay in Europe, Cooper found that many Europeans looked down upon or simply misunderstood America. In addition, he found that many Americans admired Europe, ignoring, he felt, the dangers of aristocracy and monarchy. He wrote *Notions of the Americans* (1827) in order to correct European misconceptions of America, and a series of novels, most notably, *The Bravo* (1831), in which he attempted to realistically document European society; but when Cooper returned to America in 1833, he found that America had changed. The rise of Jacksonian democracy, emphasizing, in Cooper's view, individualism and commercial gain, threatened the values America had been founded on. In the novels *Homeward Bound* (1838) and *Home as Found* (1838) Cooper commented on what he saw as the decay of democratic virtue.

Return to Leatherstocking. Cooper's critiques of America were not well received, and his difficulties increased as he found himself embroiled in a series of libel suits and a dispute between New York tenant farmers and landlords. Despite these distractions, Cooper was able to return to the saga of Leatherstocking. In 1840 he published *The Pathfinder,* and in 1841, *The Deerslayer,* which echoed Cooper's earlier critiques of American democracy. Set again near Lake Otsego at the time of Natty's youth, before the settlement of Judge Temple, the "soothing . . . holy calm" of nature is threatened by lawless and economically motivated settlers. Again, Natty embodies simple competence and virtue. As we know from the other novels, Lake Otsego will continue to develop, and Natty and his Indian companion, Chingachgook, will be pushed further and further into the wilderness. As one critic has put it, the character of Natty Bumppo remains, "an embodied conscience for America." Cooper died in 1851, but his explorations of the conflicts between civilization and freedom, law and nature, would be played out repeatedly in Western literature. His novels would be criticized by Timothy Flint, Bret Harte, and Mark Twain (in his famous essay "Fenimore Cooper's Literary Offenses") as unrealistic and inaccurate. Nevertheless, the character of Leatherstocking, blending the man of action with the man of natural philosophy, was tremendously influential. As the literary historian Richard Slotkin has pointed out, the figure of the white hunter accompanied by an Indian companion became an essential pairing in American literature and popular culture, from Herman Melville's *Moby-Dick* (1851) to Mark Twain's *Adventures of Huckleberry Finn* (1884) to the Lone Ranger and Tonto. Further, as Slotkin writes, "the image of the American hero as a man armed and solitary, plebian but worthy somehow of nobility . . . seeking in action his heart's desire" continues through Melville's Ahab, Hemingway's Robert Jordan, and the hard-boiled detective, such as Ross MacDonald's Lew Archer, who tells a woman in *The Zebra-Striped Hearse* (1969), "My real name is Natty Bumppo. . . . He's a character in a book. He was a great man and a great tracker . . . I can shoot a rifle, but as for tracking, I do my best work in cities."

Sources:

Donald Ringe, *James Fenimore Cooper* (Boston: Twayne, 1988);

Richard Slotkin, *The Fatal Environment: The Myth of the Frontier in the Age of Industrialization, 1800–1890* (New York: Atheneum, 1985);

Slotkin, *Regeneration Through Violence: The Mythology of the American Frontier* (Middletown, Conn.: Wesleyan University Press, 1973).

CAROLINE KIRKLAND

1801-1864
WRITER AND EDITOR

New York to the Frontier. Caroline Matilda Stansbury, who would become a pioneering literary realist, was born on 11 January 1801 in New York City. Her literary career had its roots in her family upbringing. Her parents nurtured a love of reading, and she was also influenced by the satiric verses of her grandfather Joseph Stansbury, an ardent Loyalist during the American Revolution. In 1828 Caroline married William Kirkland, a bright young tutor at Hamilton College. In 1835 the couple moved west to Detroit, and then, in 1837, as Michigan boomed and the Western frontier expanded, William purchased land in the new settlement of Pinckney, Michigan. Here, as Caroline later recalled, the Kirklands believed hard work and perseverance would be rewarded with "boundless treasures," but life in Pinckney turned out to be less rewarding than the Kirklands hoped. William, like many of his neighbors, was swindled by dishonest land agents. Wildcat banks issued paper notes that turned out to be worthless and then closed, virtually overnight. The Kirklands, along with others who joined them in Pinckney, became poorer, rather than richer in the new settlement.

A New Home. Through her misfortunes Caroline did find material for a novel in Pinckney. Setting out to debunk the popular notion of the West as a bounteous garden, a land of untapped wealth, in 1839 she published *A New Home—Who'll Follow? or, Glimpses of Western Life* (1839). Narrated by her fictional counterpart, Mrs. Mary Clavers, *A New Home* described daily life on the frontier in realistic (and sometimes hilarious) terms. As she wrote in the opening of her book, *A New Home* was to be an honest account of the frontier, not a romantic adventure. "I have never seen a cougar—nor been bitten by a rattlesnake," she warned her readers; "in short," her book was "valuable only for its truth." Writing from her cultured Eastern background, Kirkland found that the "savage state" was not always a noble one. She laughed at her own misadventures, but she also portrayed some of the villagers of "Montacute" as greedy and crude vulgarians. In one grim episode Amelia Newland, a young neighbor from an impoverished, "wretched" family, dies, apparently the victim of a beating. Kirkland comments that "the class of settlers to which the Newlands belong, a class but too numerous in Michigan, is a vicious and degraded one," and she notes that when the Newlands left Montacute, they took "as many of their neighbors' cattle and hogs as they could persuade to accompany them." *A New Home* was a departure from conventional Western narratives in several respects. In substituting experience for popular myth, the novel's realism offered a corrective to the "romance of rustic life." Second, Kirkland emphasized what other Western writers overlooked or omitted: frontier life could be most difficult for women, who suffered isolation and other "sacrifices for which they were not at all prepared." Finally, the novel's satirical tone was unusual; popular women writers of the antebellum period were generally much more circumspect in their social critiques. While the novel was generally well received by Eastern critics, Pinckney residents were not amused by Kirkland's satire. They felt, according to one visitor, that Kirkland had "slander[ed] them most scandously" and suggested that "she should be more usefully employed. There is not the least benefit to mind or mortals in her writings." Kirkland returned to her Western experiences in *Forest Life* (1842) and *Western Clearings* (1845), later collections of sketches. Perhaps stung by the response to *A New Home*, these works were less pointedly satirical.

Return to New York. In 1843, disappointed by their western experiment, the Kirklands returned to New York City. William became active as a writer and newspaper editor, but in 1846 he apparently drowned after falling from a dock as he tried to board a steamer. Caroline was determined to take responsibility for supporting herself and her children. She was already publishing educational pieces, sketches, and essays; she now joined the new literary journal *The Union Magazine of Literature and Art*, which she edited and contributed to from 1847 to 1851. An editorial position was unusual for a woman of her day, and Kirkland's career in New York is notable for her ability to successfully negotiate and flourish in a business world dominated by men. In addition to her duties at the *Union*, Kirkland also supported the abolition of slavery, wrote on behalf of female convicts, and opposed capital punishment. Her last significant work was *Personal Memoirs of Washington* (1856), a biography of George

Washington in which Kirkland returned to writing social commentary. Devoting several sections to Mary Washington, George's mother, Kirkland argued for the important role played by women in the nation's history. Further, Kirkland's biography emphasized Washington's opposition to slavery, suggesting that Washington "would have been slow to believe" that good people would "refuse to condemn slavery." When Kirkland died in 1864, Bayard Taylor, author and Western correspondent, remembered her as "the possessor of more genius than any woman in America." Yet later literary critics overlooked Kirkland's work for nearly a century until the 1970s, when several scholars sought to reestablish her reputation as both social critic and pioneering literary realist.

Sources:

Caroline Kirkland, *A New Home—Who'll Follow?, or, Glimpses of Western Life*, edited by Sandra A. Zagarell (New Brunswick, N.J.: Rutgers University Press, 1990);

Annette Kolodny, *The Land Before Her: Fantasy and Experience of the American Frontiers, 1630–1860* (Chapel Hill: University of North Carolina Press, 1970);

William S. Osborne, *Caroline M. Kirkland* (New York: Twayne, 1972).

JOHN ROLLIN RIDGE

1827-1867
NEWSPAPERMAN AND NOVELIST

Idylls and The Trail of Tears. John Rollin Ridge was born in the Cherokee Nation in Georgia to a Cherokee father, John Ridge, and a white mother, Sara Bird Northrup. He recalled his early childhood years as a pleasant idyll, straying along the "summershaded shores" of the Oostanaula River near his grandfather's home in Rome, Georgia, gliding along "in a light canoe" and lolling beneath the river's "overhanging willows." His life changed when the federal government passed the Indian Removal Act in 1830, legislation that allowed the federal government to resettle Indians in lands west of the Mississippi River. Ridge's grandfather, Major Ridge; his father; and other Cherokees challenged the legality of the Indian Removal Act. When their protests failed, the Ridges came to terms with the federal government and voluntarily moved to Indian Country (Oklahoma). During the late 1830s the Cherokees who did not acquiesce to the government's plans were forcibly removed by federal troops from their own nation and pushed westward along what became known as the Trail of Tears. Along the way four thousand Cherokees died from starvation, exposure, and exhaustion. Followers of the Cherokee leader John Ross who wanted to remain in their homeland viewed the acquiescence of the Ridges as despicable and were determined to punish them. In the summer of

1839 members of the Ross party assassinated both Major Ridge and John Ridge. Twelve-year-old John Rollin Ridge witnessed the murder of his father, an event he could never forget or forgive. As he wrote to his uncle in 1849, "there is a deep-seated principle of revenge in me which will never be satisfied until it reaches its object. It is my firm determination to do all that I can to bring it about."

Miner and Poet. After the assassinations the Ridge family fled to Arkansas, and the young John Rollin Ridge was sent to school in Great Barrington, Massachusetts. He eventually returned to Arkansas and is said to have killed David Kell, a pro-Ross partisan in 1849. Fearing a trial, Ridge fled first to Missouri and then, in 1850, to California. In California, Ridge tried his hand at prospecting, trapping, and trading, but without much success. He had more success as a correspondent for the *New Orleans True Delta,* sending back letters, printed under the title, "Letter from Yellow Bird—Our California Correspondent." ("Yellow Bird" was the English translation of Ridge's Cherokee name.) Ridge's *True Delta* letters vividly conveyed the frustrations and hard-fought rewards of life in the mining camps. "Two or three months have placed me on the list of acknowledged miners," he wrote in 1851, "giving me the miner's experience, with its sweet and bitter fruits." At the same time Ridge was publishing poetry in respected California literary journals such as the San Francisco-based *Golden Era.* Ridge's poetry, like much of the poetry in this period, was modeled after the works of European Romantics such as John Keats and Percy Bysshe Shelley. "Mount Shasta," the best known of Ridge's poems, echoes Shelley's "Mont Blanc." In both cases the mountain's grandeur suggests permanence amidst change; Mount Shasta is, in Ridge's words, "the great material symbol of eternal / Things." Isolation and exile were major themes of Ridge's poetry. At times he portrayed himself as a darkly fated Cain figure. In "To Lizzie," addressed to his absent wife who remained in Arkansas, he appears as "a wanderer from my distant home . . . I look around me sternly here, / And smother feelings strong and deep." In other poems he pines after "the beauteous one" and her "pure spirit." His collected poems were gathered and published posthumously in 1868.

The California Bandit. In 1854 Ridge published *The Life and Adventures of Joaquin Murieta, the Celebrated California Bandit,* the first novel in English published by an Indian author. Ridge based the story on California newspaper reports of Mexican bandits who stole livestock and robbed businesses and travelers. The leader of many of these bands was said to be a dashing, mysterious figure named Joaquin "Murieta" or "Murreitta." According to newspaper accounts and interviews, Murieta turned to crime in order to avenge the abuse he suffered at the hands of racist Americans. They drove him from the Shaw's Flat mining area, beat and flogged him, and, in some versions, raped his wife and hung his half brother. In 1853 Harry Love, a Texan scout and soldier, claimed to have captured and killed the elusive Murieta, though some Californians believed the outlaw still lived. Whatever the facts of the story, Murieta's legend held fascination for Ridge. Like Ridge himself, Murieta was driven to desperate acts by crimes against his family. And like Ridge, Murieta was forced into exile by the forces of American racism. While *The Life and Adventures of Joaquin Murieta* was not, as Ridge hoped, financially successful, it did secure him a place in the literary history of California. Murieta became a popular icon; pirated versions of Ridge's book began to appear, and Murieta appeared as a character in plays and novels. In 1936 a film version of the Murieta legend was produced, and in 1967, the Chilean poet Pablo Neruda wrote a play depicting Murieta as a victim of American racism and expansionist policy.

Newspapers and Politics. After the financial disappointment of *The Life and Adventures of Joaquin Murieta,* Ridge took a series of jobs editing California newspapers. He was known for his quick wit and equally quick temper. His columns railed against Lincoln, abolitionists, and the Republican party, forces he felt were destroying the Union. At the same time he did not lose sight of the Cherokee cause; his greatest hope, as he wrote to his uncle in 1855, was to publish "a newspaper devoted to the advocacy of Indian rights and interests," but this plan was never realized. In 1867, shortly after a failed attempt at gaining federal recognition of the Southern Cherokees, the group still opposed to the Ross faction, he became ill and died of "brain fever." Ridge's life was one of contradiction: he was the author of sentimental love poetry, but he was also obsessed with violent revenge. He studied and worked in white society, yet clung strongly to his Cherokee heritage. He deeply lamented the suffering endured by Cherokees, yet defended slavery and became involved with the Know-Nothing Party, an anti-immigration political party. As one biographer, James W. Parins, has suggested, it would have been difficult for Ridge, given the circumstances of his life, to resolve these conflicts. As one of the first modern American Indian writers he "found himself caught between two worlds, discovering sympathy and hostility in both."

Sources:
James W. Parins, *John Rollin Ridge: His Life and Works* (Lincoln: University of Nebraska Press, 1991);

John Rollin Ridge, *A Trumpet of Our Own: Yellow Bird's Essays on the North American Indian,* edited by David Farmer and Rennard Strickland (San Francisco: Book Club of California, 1981).

PUBLICATIONS

William Apess, *A Son of the Forest* (New York: Author, 1829)—the autobiography of a Pequot who converted to Christianity, fought for the Americans in the War of 1812, and championed the rights of Native Americans;

Charles Averill, *Kit Carson, The Prince of the Gold Hunters* (Boston: G. H. Williams, 1849)—adventure novels such as Averill's helped establish (and exaggerate) the legend of Kit Carson, famed scout and soldier;

George Catlin, *Letters and Notes on the Manners, Customs and Conditions of the North American Indians*, 2 volumes (London: Published by the author, 1841)—Catlin's account of his travels into the West; especially noteworthy for his documentation of the lives of Native Americans;

James Fenimore Cooper, *The Deerslayer*, 2 volumes (Philadelphia: Lea & Blanchard, 1841)—the last novel in the Leatherstocking series demonstrates Cooper's maturity as a novelist and growing religious vision;

Cooper, *The Last of the Mohicans: A Narrative of 1757*, 2 volumes (Philadelphia: H. C. Carey & I. Lea, 1826)—the second in the Leatherstocking series; a thrilling adventure featuring Natty Bumppo as the young Hawkeye;

Cooper, *The Pioneers*, 2 volumes (New York: Charles Wiley, 1823)—the first in the Leatherstocking series. Set in the new settlement of Templeton, the novel establishes the moral conflicts that will inform the entire series: civilization v. nature; law v. virtue; individual v. society;

Cooper, *The Prairie*, 2 volumes (Philadelphia: Carey, Lea & Carey, 1827)—the third in the Leatherstocking series. Featuring Natty as an older man, the novel suggests that the wilderness and Natty's natural virtue are being overrun by the advances of American civilization;

George Copway, *The Life, History, and Travels of Kahjge-ga-gah-bowh* (Albany: Weed & Parsons, 1847)—like the Apess autobiography, this Ojibwa autobiography is a tale of Christian salvation, but also critiques American racism and documents life among the Ojibwa;

Richard Henry Dana Jr., *Two Years Before the Mast* (New York: Harper, 1840)—a vivid and exciting recounting of Dana's experiences sailing around Cape Horn, of South America, and in Spanish California. Dana's book continues to influence American literature of the sea and is considered a minor masterpiece;

Alonzo Delano, *Pen Knife Sketches; or, Chips of the Old Block* (Sacramento: Published at the Union Office, 1853)—a collection of "Old Block's" articles for the *Pacific News* that sold more than fifteen thousand copies in California. Old Block drew a sympathetic, rueful portrait of life in the gold mines;

Timothy Flint, *Biographical Memoir of Daniel Boone* (Cincinnati: N. & G. Guilford, 1833)—Flint's immensely influential biography of Daniel Boone established Boone as an icon within popular literature;

Margaret Fuller, *Summer on the Lakes* (Boston: Charles C. Little & James Brown; New York: Charles S. Francis, 1844)—influenced by Caroline Kirkland's novel, *A New Home—Who'll Follow* (1839), Fuller, New England transcendentalist and feminist, describes the beautiful but often harsh, isolated conditions of the Midwest frontier;

Caroline Kirkland, *A New Home—Who'll Follow?* (New York: C. S. Francis; Boston: J. H. Francis, 1839)—Kirkland's realistic and satirical account of life on the Midwestern frontier;

Francis Parkman, *The California and Oregon Trail* (New York: Putnam, 1849)—the young Parkman's account of his exploration beyond the Missouri River reveals much about Eastern attitudes toward the West;

John Rollin Ridge, *The Life and Adventures of Joaquin Murieta, the Celebrated California Bandit* (San Francisco: F. MacCrellish, 1854)—the first novel in English by a Native American. Ridge recounts the popular legend of Joaquin Murieta, a Mexican bandit who avenges abuse suffered at the hands of Americans;

Charles Sealsfield, *The Cabin Book*, translated by C. F. Mersch (New York: J. Winchester, 1844)—Sealsfield's epic narrative of the movement of American civilization from the East to the West. The novel centers on the struggle for Texan independence;

Catherine Soule, *Pet of the Settlement: A Story of Prairie-Land* (Boston: A. Tompkins, 1860)—Soule's optimistic and colorful vision of life on the prairies. The novel is notable for transferring literary domesticity to a Western setting.

Samuel Finley Breese Morse's 1822 oil painting *The Old House of Representatives* (Corcoran Gallery of Art, Washington, D.C.)

John Banvard's 1852 drawing *Cottonwood Tree in Grandview Reach* (Minnesota Historical Society, St. Paul)

BUSINESS AND THE ECONOMY

by MARK C. FREDERICK

CONTENTS

Sidebars and tables are listed in italics.

1800

- The Santee Canal in South Carolina is completed; it is the country's first significant canal.

4 Apr. Congress passes the first federal bankruptcy law. It is repealed on 19 December 1803.

10 May Congress revises the national land policy. No longer needing to acquire public lands in 640-acre blocks, purchasers can now buy public land in 320-acre sections (at two dollars an acre) on credit. Obtaining land becomes easier for more people.

1801

- One hundred thousand bales of cotton are picked in the United States this year. Production will later skyrocket with the expansion of the cotton frontier.

1 Nov. With the revision in the public land laws in 1800, an additional 398,000 acres have been purchased by this date.

1802

- Congress authorizes the National Road to cross the Appalachian Mountains.

- Merino sheep, a breed with high-quality wool, are imported into the United States from Spain.

1803

- Spanish colonists in New Mexico send about twenty-five thousand sheep south to Chihuahua, Mexico, as part of an established north-south trading network.

30 Apr. The United States buys the Louisiana Purchase from France; New Orleans and St. Louis come under American control.

1804

- The nation's first agricultural fair is held in Washington, D.C.

26 Mar. Congress again modifies the land law so that settlers and speculators can buy public land in 160-acre parcels.

1805

- As a result of the booming international trade with the Caribbean and Asia, the United States imports more than seven million pounds of pepper.

1806

- The American fur trade with China surpasses $5 million annually. In exchange for furs merchants, such as John Jacob Astor, acquire tea, silk, and spices.

1807

•	Approximately $5 million worth of goods are sold in the newly acquired port of New Orleans.
11 Aug.	Robert Fulton's steamboat, the *Clermont*, travels up the Hudson River from New York City to Albany.
Nov.	Manuel Lisa completes Fort Raymond in Montana. It is the first U.S. trading post on the Upper Missouri River.
22 Dec.	President Thomas Jefferson signs the Embargo Act, which bans U.S. exports to Great Britain and France. Although designed to enforce the United States' neutrality in the Napoleonic Wars, it fails and hurts the American economy.

1808

•	Secretary of the Treasury Albert Gallatin submits his report on a national transportation system to Congress. Although his plan is rejected, Gallatin predicts many features of the upcoming transportation revolution.
1 Jan.	The importation of slaves from Africa is forbidden after this date, but an illegal slave trade continues, with perhaps as many as 250,000 slaves illicitly imported before 1861. Meanwhile the domestic slave trade flourishes.
4 Apr.	John Jacob Astor obtains a charter for the American Fur Company, later to become the nation's largest company in the vast fur trade.
16 July	Manuel Lisa and partners form the Missouri Fur Company, which emerges as the largest firm in the Upper Missouri and Rocky Mountain fur trade for the next six years.

1809

1 Mar.	Congress repeals the Embargo Act.
23 May	William Bent is born in St. Louis, Missouri. Bent will become one of the most important American merchants in the Indian trade on the Southern Plains.

1810

•	There are 171,000 bales of cotton picked in the United States.
1 Oct.	The Berkshire Cattle Show opens in Pittsfield, Massachusetts. This is an early county fair demonstrating agricultural improvements. Such a fair will become common throughout much of the West in the years to come.

1811

•	The charter for the First Bank of the United States expires and is not renewed. In 1791 Alexander Hamilton had convinced Congress to establish this bank to stabilize the new U.S. economy and encourage capital investments.
12 Apr.	John Jacob Astor's men arrive in Oregon to establish the trading post Astoria.

1812

- The War of 1812 begins, and the federal government has trouble funding the war without the First Bank of the United States. A lack of adequate transportation routes also hinders the war effort. American manufacturing receives a boost because of the lack of British goods.

- William Monroe of Massachusetts manufactures the first lead pencils, which will later become common in business offices.

12 Jan. The steamboat *New Orleans* travels from Pittsburgh to New Orleans, thus initiating the age of steam on the Ohio and Mississippi Rivers.

1813

- Robert Stuart, a fur trader, completes his expedition from Astoria to St. Louis. On this trip he discovers the South Pass through the Rocky Mountains, which will later provide a route for settlers immigrating to the West Coast.

1814

- David Melville produces the first circular saw, making the future timber industry more efficient.

9 Aug. The Creek Indians, residing in what will later become Alabama, yield large tracts of land in the Treaty of Fort Jackson, thereby opening a considerable area to white settlement.

1815

- The availability of credit expands in a postwar economic boom. In the next two years the number of state banks grows from 88 to 208.

- Settlement of the West increases with the end of the War of 1812.

- The steamboat *Enterprise* travels from Brownsville, Pennsylvania, to New Orleans, Louisiana, and back again. This is the first steamboat to come back up the Mississippi and Ohio Rivers. Keel boats soon become obsolete.

- With the treaties of Portage des Sioux much of the resistance of Native Americans north of the Ohio River ends. White settlers begin to pour into the region.

1816

- Approximately $10 million of goods are sold in New Orleans—twice the amount from nine years earlier.

6 Feb. The New Jersey State legislature gives the first charter for a railroad in the United States to John Stevens.

10 Apr. The Second Bank of the United States is chartered in order to curb the inflation stemming from unregulated banknotes issued by state banks.

1817

3 Mar. President James Madison vetoes the Bonus Bill, which would have appropriated federal funds for transportation routes.

Apr. The New York state legislature approves the building of the Erie Canal, which will stretch from Albany to Buffalo.

4 July Construction begins on the Erie Canal.

1818

- The National Road reaches Wheeling in what will become West Virginia.

- Cincinnati, Ohio, establishes its famous meatpacking industry. Eighty-five thousand hogs are butchered in 1833 and five hundred thousand in 1848. Only in 1860 does Chicago surpass Cincinnati as the nation's center for meatpacking.

1819

- Jethro Wood patents the first moldboard for a plow to help turn the soil.

- Cotton prices plummet and, combined with land and bank speculation, create a financial panic. Demand for American goods declines; businesses fail; and banks collapse. The resulting depression lasts until 1823.

2 Apr. John Skinner begins the publication of *American Farmer,* the first of many agricultural journals.

1820

24 Apr. The federal government modifies the public land law to enable settlers to purchase land in eighty-acre parcels at $1.25 an acre. The credit system, which primarily benefited speculators, is canceled.

1821

- Kentucky becomes the first state to abolish incarceration for debt.

24 Feb. Mexico achieves independence from Spain.

1 Sept. William Becknell leaves Missouri for a successful trading venture to New Mexico, thereby opening the Santa Fe Trail.

1822

4 May President James Monroe vetoes a bill to repair and collect tolls on the National Road.

1823

- Nicholas Biddle of Philadelphia is appointed president of the Second Bank of the United States. Confidence in the bank increases, but many in the West resent his growing power over the economy.

- William Ashley creates the rendezvous system for American fur trappers in the Rocky Mountains.

1824

- Twenty-five American wagons with $30,000 worth of merchandise traverse the Santa Fe Trail and return from New Mexico with $190,000 worth of silver and furs.

- Fur trader and scout Jedediah Smith rediscovers the South Pass through the Rocky Mountains.

2 Mar.   The U.S. Supreme Court hands down the *Gibbons* v. *Ogden* decision, which establishes the federal government's power over interstate commerce.

1825

- Steamboats represent about one-half of the traffic on Western waterways.

3 Jan.   The British cotton industrialist Robert Owen attempts to set up a utopian society in the United States with the establishment of New Harmony, Indiana, a community based on the equal ownership of property.

26 Oct.   The state of New York completes the 364-mile Erie Canal, connecting Lake Erie to the Hudson River; the commerce between East and West accelerates.

1826

- John Stevens maneuvers the first steam locomotive on tracks in Hoboken, New Jersey.

1827

- Baltimore businessmen plan the Baltimore and Ohio Railroad in order to connect their city with the Ohio River. Although not completed until 1852, this railroad trunk line becomes the prototype for future westward railroads.

- Through buying out or merging with its competitors, the American Fur Company gains a dominant position among U.S. firms in the Upper Missouri fur trade.

1828

- The Georgia state legislature passes a law claiming that it will have jurisdiction over Cherokee lands in two years. Although struck down as unconstitutional in 1831, Georgia, with the support of President Andrew Jackson, ignores the ruling.

- Robert Owen's New Harmony community in Indiana fails.

4 July   Construction begins on the Baltimore and Ohio Railroad.

1829

- The demand for U.S. cotton in British factories fuels the expansion of the cotton frontier in the American South.

1830

- An estimated $22 million worth of goods are sold in New Orleans, more than twice the amount from fourteen years earlier.

- Approximately 731,000 bales of cotton are picked in the United States, more than four times the amount from twenty years earlier.

- Surveyors plot the city lots for Chicago, Illinois; in sixty years it will become the nation's second-largest city.

27 May President Andrew Jackson vetoes the Maysville Road Bill because the road is to be built within only one state, Kentucky.

28 May President Jackson signs the Indian Removal Act to facilitate the migration of the major Indian nations from east of the Mississippi River to "Indian Country," a region in present-day Oklahoma and Kansas.

1831

- The federal government removes the Choctaw Indians from Mississippi and settles them in Indian Territory.

- Edmund Ruffin of Virginia publishes *Essay on Calcareous Manures* to encourage the use of fertilizers such as lime and gypsum in depleted Southern soils.

1832

- President Jackson vetoes Nicholas Biddle's attempt to recharter the Second Bank of the United States. Jackson claims, with some legitimacy, that the bank is too powerful and primarily benefits the rich. Federal funds are placed in various state banks. "Wildcat" banks lend paper money, not supported by gold and silver, to Westerners. The amount of currency in circulation expands from $59 million to $140 million in the next four years.

1833

- The National Road reaches Columbus, Ohio.

- The Ohio and Erie Canal opens, connecting the Ohio River with Lake Erie.

1 Oct. President Andrew Jackson withdraws federal funds from the Second Bank of the United States.

1834

- Cyrus McCormick patents his first mechanical reaper. McCormick's machines and others similar to them transform American agriculture in the decades ahead.

- Jesse Buel of Albany, New York, begins publication of the *Cultivator*, which will become the first nationwide farm journal.

1835

- Land speculation reaches feverish heights. In this year and the next, speculators buy as much as 22 to 25 million acres of public land.

- Wheat farmers suffer a crop failure in the West, which in turn creates economic hardship.

1836

4 July   The federal government revises and significantly improves the system for patenting inventions.

11 July   President Andrew Jackson issues the Species Circular, demanding that public lands be bought with gold and silver. The circular curbs land speculation with questionable banknotes, but it also destabilizes the Western economy.

1837

- Wildcat banking and land speculation are matched by a fall in cotton prices, and the tightening of British credit brings the overheated economy to a screeching halt. The ensuing depression lasts until the mid 1840s. Banks collapse throughout the West. Western states repudiate debts for roads, canals, and railroads—temporarily slowing the transportation revolution.

- American economist Henry Carey publishes the first volume of *Principles of Political Economy*. In it he defends tariffs but argues against most forms of governmental interference in the economy.

- John Deere manufactures the first steel-blade plow.

29 Dec.   Hiram Avery and John Avery Pitts of Maine patent and later produce a more efficient machine for the threshing of grain.

1838

- The National Road reaches Vandalia, Illinois; the federal government ends construction of the road there.

25 Apr.   The steamboat *Moselle* explodes on the Ohio River, killing one hundred people; this is only one of many accidents occurring on Western steamboats.

1839

7 Jan.   Washington Mining Company is chartered; it is the first silver-mining company in the nation.

1840

- The beaver fur-trapping systems of the West finally collapse because of the depletion of beaver populations and the shift in fashion to silk hats.

- More than twenty-eight hundred miles of railroad tracks have been built in the United States.

- Approximately $50 million worth of goods are sold at New Orleans—more than twice the amount from ten years earlier.

1841

16 Aug. President John Tyler vetoes the first of two attempts to create another national bank, called the Fiscal Bank of the United States.

19 Aug. A new federal bankruptcy law is enacted; it is repealed on 3 March 1843.

4 Sept. The U.S. Congress passes the Preemption Act, allowing squatters the right to purchase the land on which they had settled for $1.25 an acre.

1842

16 May The migration to Oregon commences when 112 men and women leave Independence, Missouri; they arrive in the Oregon territory in December.

1843

22 May One thousand emigrants herding five thousand head of cattle leave Independence, Missouri, to settle in the Oregon territory; most reach the area in October.

1844

24 May Samuel Morse sends his first telegraph message. It travels between Washington, D.C., and Baltimore, Maryland, and reads "What Hath God Wrought." Later, telegraph lines, which become central to the business community, stretch across the West.

19 Sept. Federal surveyor William Burt discovers iron on the upper peninsula of Michigan. Iron mining later becomes one of the region's chief industries.

1845

• Missouri is the fourth Western state to abolish incarceration for debt.

1 Mar. The United States annexes the Republic of Texas. The state becomes a leading exporter of cotton and cattle in the decades to come.

1846

Aug. U.S. forces under Stephen Kearny take New Mexico in the Mexican War. The sheep trade south to Chihuahua, Mexico, declines.

Summer England repeals its Corn Laws. American farmers can now export their grain to the British Isles; demand for American grain increases 170 percent in the next decade.

1847

16 Apr. Samuel Morse forms the first telegraph company in the United States, named the Magnetic Telegraph Company.

1848

24 Jan.   James Marshall discovers gold at John Sutter's Mill, and the California Gold Rush begins. Later in the year New Mexicans begin herding sheep to California to feed the miners.

2 Feb.   In the Treaty of Guadalupe Hidalgo, Mexico cedes most of what is now the American Southwest to the United States. This region will form an economy based on mining and livestock through the rest of the nineteenth century.

1849

•   Eighty thousand people arrive in California for the Gold Rush. In this year miners extract approximately $10 million in gold.

1850

•   John Heath invents a binder to tie grains, further mechanizing U.S. agriculture.

•   In the last six decades the center of population for the United States shifted westward from near Baltimore, Maryland, to near Parkersburg, in what will become West Virginia, on the Ohio River.

•   Approximately 2,133,000 bales of cotton are picked in the United States—nearly three times the amount from twenty years earlier.

9 Sept.   Only two years after gold is discovered, California achieves statehood.

20 Sept.   Congress grants the first federal land to states for the construction of a railroad between Chicago, Illinois, and Mobile, Alabama. The federal government awards more than 27 million acres for 7,500 miles of track in the next six years.

1851

•   The 483-mile Erie Railroad, linking the Hudson River to Lake Erie, is completed.

•   The Pacific Railroad Company, later called the Missouri Pacific Railroad, begins construction across the state of Missouri to connect St. Louis with Kansas City.

1852

•   Two railroad lines connect Chicago, Illinois, with eastern ports. The new city begins its rise to dominance as the great metropolis of the West.

•   In this year alone, $81 million worth of gold is mined in California.

Dec.   The Baltimore and Ohio Railroad is finally completed when it reaches Wheeling in what will become West Virginia.

1853

•   Seven railroad trunk lines connect eastern ports with the Trans-Appalachian West.

3 Mar.   Congress authorizes the War Department to conduct a survey for a future transcontinental railroad.

	30 Dec.	The United States buys the Gadsden Purchase from Mexico. This stretch of land in southern Arizona and New Mexico completes the boundaries of the continental United States.

1854

- By this year three hundred thousand people have arrived in California for the Gold Rush.

- The nation's first commercial flour mill opens in Minneapolis, Minnesota, a city that will become a major wheat-processing center.

30 May The Kansas-Nebraska Act commences the white settlements of Kansas and Nebraska. It also helps push the country toward civil war over the issue of slavery in the territories, including Kansas.

3 Aug. The Graduation Act is passed to reduce the price of federal land. The price per acre varies from 12.5¢ to $1.25, depending on the length of time it has been on the market.

30 Dec. George Bissell and Jonathan Eveleth create the nation's first oil corporation, called the Pennsylvania Rock Oil Company.

1855

- Chicago, Illinois, surpasses St. Louis, Missouri, as the center for the Western grain trade.

- David Christy publishes his book *Cotton is King, or the Economical Relations of Slavery,* coining the phrase "Cotton is King" for the South.

1856

- The Illinois Central Railroad between Chicago and Cairo, Illinois, is completed; it receives more than 2.5 million acres of federal land to help finance its construction.

21 Apr. The first railroad bridge across the Mississippi River is constructed between Rock Island, Illinois, and Davenport, Iowa.

1857

24 Aug. A drop in grain prices and the over-production of U.S. manufactured goods in an atmosphere of renewed land speculation and wildcat banking set off another panic. The resulting depression lasts two years.

1858

- The Butterfield Overland Mail begins service to California.

30 Mar. Hyman Lipman patents the first pencil with an eraser, which will later become common in the business office.

July Gold is discovered near present-day Denver, Colorado, thus initiating the Pikes Peak Gold Rush and the white settlement of Colorado.

1859

- Vast quantities of silver are discovered near what will become Virginia City, Nevada. The Comstock Lode will yield $300 million worth of silver and gold in the next twenty years.

- For the first time in U.S. history the value of manufactured items (almost $2 billion worth) surpasses the value of agricultural goods.

- Approximately 5,387,000 bales of cotton are picked in the United States—more than twice the amount from nine years earlier.

1860

- Thirty thousand miles of railroad tracks have been laid in the United States. Almost $1 billion has been invested in railroads in the last twenty years.

- Approximately 16 percent of the nation now lives in cities with more than eight thousand residents; in 1790 the percentage stood at just over 3 percent.

- An estimated $185 million worth of goods are sold in New Orleans—three times the amount from twenty years earlier.

- Illinois, Indiana, and Wisconsin are the top wheat producing states in the United States. Illinois, Ohio, Missouri, and Indiana are the top corn producing states in the nation.

3 Apr. Pony Express mail service between St. Joseph, Missouri, and San Francisco, California, commences.

16 June The federal government passes the Pacific Telegraph Act to build a telegraph line between Missouri and California.

An 1833 cartoon of President Andrew Jackson and a supporter watching the Second Bank of the United States collapse on Whig politicians (American Antiquarian Society, Worcester, Massachusetts)

OVERVIEW

Westward Migration. Following the American Revolution, Americans swarmed to the West. Kentucky and Tennessee provided the beachhead for the vanguard of land-hungry settlers. After the War of 1812 subsequent waves of pioneers flowed into the Ohio River valley, the Great Lake states, the Gulf Plain, and the Mississippi River valley. Still more moved to Oregon and California in the 1840s and into Kansas by the 1850s. By the Civil War much of the territory between the Mississippi River and the Atlantic, as well as areas along the Pacific coast and in the Southwest, had been settled by the descendants of Europeans.

Economic Revolutions. This mass migration produced a series of economic revolutions. The Trans-Appalachian West contained hundreds of Indian nations, each with their own economies based on the local geography. Even before large numbers of Americans settled the West, the economic structures of the native peoples changed. The trade in furs and hides with the whites and the arrival of Old World animals (such as the horse) drove Indians to accommodate and take advantage of the new opportunities before them; but sooner or later, opportunities turned into conquest. Already weakened by European diseases, many native nations found themselves unable to resist the economic and military power of the invaders.

Land and Agriculture. When most American settlers entered a new area, they sought land. Whether for cotton, wheat, or livestock, land ownership often determined one's economic standing. Although commercial and industrial wealth assumed a growing importance in the first six decades of the nineteenth century, the United States remained an agricultural nation. Individuals such as John Jacob Astor were able to make a fortune from the fur trade, and other merchants grew rich from selling different commodities in the West. Nevertheless, the soil remained fundamental.

The Market Revolution. Despite the continued dominance of agriculture, far-reaching changes made the United States of 1860 different from the nation of 1800. Some historians have described the development of long-distance domestic trade as a market revolution, in which thousands of Americans participated in the rapidly expanding cash economy. Growing crops or producing goods for the market became increasingly common. Although colonists before the Revolution sold commodities to merchants in exchange for cash or goods, the early nineteenth century had fewer self-sufficient farmers. Tools fashioned by the local blacksmith and hand-spun clothing increasingly gave way to factory-made farm equipment and cloth. Americans reoriented their businesses and farms in order to acquire manufactured goods of all kinds.

Transportation Revolution. Still, though the economy grew and became more diverse, especially as a result of industrialization, most early settlers in the Trans-Appalachian West initially had limited access to profitable markets. Another revolution, this time in transportation, served as a catalyst for the new economic landscape. The construction of paved roads, new canals, and railroads allowed, or forced, more Americans into the larger economy. East and West, and to a lesser extent North and South, were joined by transportation routes that carried commodities to national and foreign markets. These paths of commerce accelerated American settlement by spurring migration to new lands.

Gateway Cities. From 1800 to 1860 men and women moved into western cities to find new opportunities and new profits. Exchanging raw materials such as crops, minerals, and animal skins for manufactured goods, or providing services to outlying communities, became the primary economic roles of these urban areas. The early nineteenth century saw the birth of new cities when trading posts or small towns blossomed into Cincinnati, St. Louis, Chicago, and San Francisco. These cities functioned as gateways between the rural hinterland and markets on the East coast or in Europe.

Economic Instability. U.S. cities during the first half of the nineteenth century also became banking centers that financed the commercial development of the West. Although New York remained the principal financial center for the nation, capital flowed in and out of every city. As a result the number of banks multiplied spectacularly. An inconsistent federal banking policy generated many shaky banks and periods of intense inflation. Land speculation, a longtime staple of American business, further fueled chronic instability, even when the federal government directed its course. Panics that produced economic depressions occurred in 1819, 1837, and 1857. The West was far from immune to these economic slumps; in fact, with land speculation and poor banking, the region helped produce them.

Hispanic Influences. When the United States expanded westward, it encountered the Spanish Empire, and, later, the Republic of Mexico. The Spanish had established colonies within the present boundaries of the United States before the English even gained their weak foothold in Virginia in 1607. In 1598 Spaniards led by Juan de Oñate formed the colony of New Mexico. Although it never possessed a large population or a dynamic economy (by European standards at least), New Mexico, and later Texas and California, developed distinct economies based on livestock production. Aided by the American penetration of Mexican markets in the 1820s through the 1840s, most of what is now the

Southwest came under American control by 1848. As with the Indians, the Hispanics of New Mexico witnessed an economic revolution. Anglos came to legally and illegally acquire much of their land, and more Mexican-Americans entered the cash economy.

The Western Economy. From Kentucky corn fields to California gold mines, the United States expanded its boundaries and its economy over much of the American West before 1860. Americans brought themselves, their animals, their seeds, and their tools to transform the landscape beyond the Appalachian Mountains. By the time of the Civil War, they had accomplished much of their goal east of the Missouri River and had tendrils into the Great Plains and along the Pacific Ocean. Although during the fifty years after 1860 there was further expansion into the West, the economic revolutions from 1800 to 1860 established patterns of commerce that would remain influential for generations to come.

TOPICS IN THE NEWS

FRONTIERS OF COTTON AND GRAIN

Clearing the Land. When Americans first moved west of the Appalachians, they found trees—mile after mile of vast forests stretching all the way to the Great Plains. If they had been in North America long, they were used to felling trees; it was the first thing they did when they settled a new piece of western land. Farmers cleared an area for fields by cutting, burning, and girdling (cutting a large ring around a tree trunk so it would later die). Most farmers then planted corn, the staple crop of the first settlers because of its high yield. Like the Indians, pioneers fished and hunted and sometimes planted beans and squash. White settlers arrived with their livestock and preferred pigs because free-range swine required little labor and provided a wide variety of meat products.

Agricultural Improvements. After clearing and planting a field, pioneers built a log cabin and moved out of the hastily constructed lean-to that had served as their first house. The construction of wooden fences, often built in a zigzag pattern, followed. Subsistence was often the main goal of these early settlers, who possessed few ties to the outside market, but in the antebellum West a second surge of farmers further transformed the land by

bringing down even more trees and plowing acre after acre. These new farmers were more likely to produce surplus for the market. The newly plowed fields could be planted with a variety of crops, though geography often determined what could be grown. Northerners planted wheat and corn while Southerners focused on corn and cotton.

Across the Appalachians. Americans crossed the Appalachians in large numbers after the War of 1812. By wagon, handcart, and flatboat they descended on the area of the Ohio River. Moving north out of Kentucky and Tennessee, they planted fields of corn in the southern parts of what would become Ohio, Indiana, and Illinois. Abraham Lincoln's parents followed this route. More pioneers came out of the northeastern states and settled nearer to the Great Lakes. Here wheat emerged as the dominant commercial crop. After the American government forced the Indians westward in the 1830s, native-born whites, along with thousands of immigrants from Europe, especially Germans, moved into southern Wisconsin and Minnesota. Once there, they created a timber industry, harvesting the great forests of the region. After they cut the most desirable trees, the settlers turned their attention to farming. Iowa became a favorite destination in the 1840s; farmers there planted large fields of corn in its rich soil. The cultivation of wheat continued when Americans settled Oregon and California in the 1840s and 1850s. Only later did Americans plant wheat in the more arid Great Plains.

Reasons for Moving West. Motivations for moving west varied according to circumstance, but certain economic patterns prevailed. New Englanders faced a land shortage in the nineteenth century. With a rapidly growing population, even the marginal lands had been settled. After 1800 the quest for land sent New England sons and daughters westward. Land scarcity likewise pushed Southerners westward. As slave plantations became larger and more cost-efficient, smaller farmers became economically marginalized. Further, Southern cash crops, such as tobacco and cotton, habitually exhausted the soil, leaving less productive acreage throughout the South Atlantic states.

Cotton. More than any other crop, cotton came to dominate the South. Planters had been growing Sea Island (or long-staple) cotton on the islands off South Carolina since the late seventeenth century, but it failed to grow far from the coast. Another type, upland (or short-staple) cotton, could be raised in most areas of the South, but picking the seeds out of the fiber proved too labor-intensive to be profitable. When Eli Whitney invented a new machine that separated and discarded the seeds in 1793, his cotton gin spread swiftly. Upland cotton became enormously profitable. The expanding textile factories of Britain and New England spurred the demand for this precious cash crop.

The Cotton Frontier. Cotton farmers, who in their quest for good land had moved westward even before the yeoman farmer so famous in American lore, pushed the cotton frontier into the Gulf Plains and the lower Mississippi River valley after 1812. Though yeomen and their families were often the first cotton producers in some western areas, wealthier Southerners moved in with their slaves. Relying on slave labor, these planters soon controlled extensive cotton plantations. By the 1820s planters in the Gulf Plains region grew one-half of the cotton in the United States. By 1850 it produced three-fourths of the national supply.

Inequality in the South. The Cotton Kingdom made some Southerners rich, but the social costs were high. Americans in the Old South lived in a highly stratified society. The richest planters controlled around three-quarters of the region's wealth. Farther down the hierarchy were smaller planters who possessed between one and twenty slaves and then other farmers (who comprised 77 percent of the white population) who worked the poorer soils on their own. African American slaves labored on the cotton plantations and remained a substantial part of the population. By 1850 the lower South had 1.8 million black slaves and 2.1 million whites. Dur-

ing the period of westward expansion, both black and white Americans migrated to the cotton frontier.

A Troubled Business. Though cotton seemed at first an ideal crop in the West, year after year of planting steadily decreased the productivity of the soils. Still, most farmers, in a mad rush to make a profit as quickly as possible from the high price of cotton, put off an agricultural system that would have enabled them to maintain the fertility of their fields longer by employing a scheme of crop rotation. The South became stuck in an economic system detrimental to all but a few elites. Though some cotton farmers used bat guano and other fertilizers, one Southern editor calculated in 1858 that soil exhaustion had struck two-fifths of the land used for growing cotton. The practice of plowing in straight lines up and down slopes also invited soil erosion, further diminishing yields over time. Soil exhaustion became a motivation for finding more lands in the West. The long-term consequences of cotton farming often included poverty and a growing reliance on fertilizers. By 1860 the cotton frontier had pushed into Texas, and the Deep South had become a Cotton Kingdom that would face troubles in the years ahead.

Sources:

Ray Allen Billington and Martin Ridge, *Westward Expansion: A History of the American Frontier*, fifth edition (New York: Macmillan, 1982);

Carolyn Merchant, ed., "The Cotton South Before and After the Civil War," in *Major Problems in American Environmental History* (Lexington, Mass.: D.C. Heath, 1993), pp. 209–246;

Elliot West, "American Frontier," in *The Oxford History of the American West*, edited by Clyde Milner and others (New York: Oxford University Press, 1994), pp. 115–149.

GOLD RUSH

Sutter's Mill. On 24 January 1848 the American James Marshall discovered gold at John Sutter's mill in northern California. This strike set off one of the most dramatic economic events of the nineteenth century. When word got out concerning the gold's location, people soon began scurrying into the hills seeking even more of the precious yellow metal—and many found it, at least at first. Word of the placer (or surface) gold spread throughout the world. In 1849 alone, about eighty thousand people came to California; by 1854 three hundred thousand had arrived. Vast amounts of gold came out of California. Historians have estimated that miners extracted $10 million of gold in 1849, $41 million more of gold the following year, and another $81 million of gold in 1852. The amount declined thereafter, but miners still mined $45 million of gold from California in 1857.

Forty-Niners. The miners were mostly young males. Forty-Niners (as these miners were called) came from the American East, Chile, China, France, Mexico, and elsewhere. Newspapers throughout the United States—in big cities and small towns—proclaimed the newfound riches. Different visions of what could be accomplished in California appeared among the various groups, but many Americans felt that the gold strike represented an equality of opportunity, an optimistic idea that had long been the hallmark of their culture. Easterners came by ship around South America or by way of Panama. Other Americans crossed the Great Plains, Rocky Mountains, Great Basin Desert, and Sierra Nevada Mountains to reach the land of gold.

Early Success. The early days of the Gold Rush provided the greatest opportunity for the miners. Placer gold was fairly abundant. In fact, gold dust soon emerged as the currency of California. A shovel, pan, and maybe a pick were the common tools of the early miner. Many men labored with partners. Forty-Niners believed that if they worked hard, they could get rich. Few actually struck it big in the gold fields, but 1849 and 1850 were years of success for a significant number of miners.

Increasing Costs of Mining. Yet however much gold came out of California's hills, life was never easy for the Forty-Niners. When the placer gold gave out around 1851, conditions became even more difficult, but people kept coming. Nevertheless, mining gold in northern California became increasingly expensive. The possession of capital became a necessity because new mining techniques demanded larger operations. With the scarcity of easy gold, quartz mining (digging underground in search of ore) developed; this system, too, required more capital and organization. Flocks of miners arrived, and more companies with greater resources formed. Claims,

which could be sold, became costlier. By 1853 hydraulic mining appeared. In this expensive process, workers redirected water into hillsides to break up the soil and more easily extract the gold. Hydraulic mining permanently scarred the landscape of northern California. These commercial innovations led to a change in the use of water that was crucial to the large-scale operations. Water became a precious commodity, adding further to the cost of the newer, more industrial, gold mining.

The California Economy. Even before the arrival of these large-scale operations, prices for food and clothing in California were extremely high. Though an early miner could make more than ten times as much money mining gold than working in the East, the inflated economy and the shortage of goods diminished the Forty-Niners' purchasing power. Sarah Royce, who went to northern California in 1849 with her husband and small daughter, found that an onion cost one dollar in the boom town of Sacramento. In fact, some migrants came to California not so much to mine gold but to mine the miners. They brought goods and services that fetched high prices in a booming economy based on gold dust. Since the scramble for gold brought conflict, it comes as no surprise that lawyers prospered. As Royce noted, some Americans came with, or developed, highly questionable schemes in order to get rich through the miners. These budding and impatient entrepreneurs tried their hand at such ventures as cattle or land speculation, but most failed. Yet some new migrants, including frustrated miners, went into other lines of work and invested in businesses that succeeded. The Royces, for example,

Sutter's Mill, a lumber mill on the American River in California, at about the time gold was discovered on the mill property, initiating the California Gold Rush (Bancroft Library, University of California, Berkeley)

A circa 1850 daguerreotype of gold prospectors in California (Matthew R. Isenburg Collection)

gave up mining and settled down and established a farm near Grass Valley, California.

The Ascendancy of the Anglos. The rush of Americans into California proved beneficial primarily for the native English-speaking people. Attacks by Anglos and the erosion of native subsistence economies in the face of the new mining regime drastically reduced the Indian population. By using law and force of arms, Americans drove Mexicans from the mines. Many Chinese men who had emigrated hoping to become rich found themselves driven out of the gold fields by racist Americans. Violence and discrimination were particularly pronounced after the placer gold diminished. White Americans believed California to be theirs alone even though the United States had only recently acquired it from Mexico.

The Golden State. The Gold Rush created the state of California. California had been part of the Spanish Empire since the late 1700s, but Mexico ceded it to the United States in 1848. It reached statehood in 1850—only two years after gold had been discovered at Sutter's Mill. Entire cities materialized throughout the state. San Francisco surfaced as the great city of the nineteenth-century Far West. In 1848 the city had only eight hundred inhabitants; two years later, twenty thousand people lived there. By 1860 it held fifty thousand residents. In short, the precious yellow metal created not

only big dreams, big disappointments, and a few big fortunes, but it also gave birth to the nation's richest and most populous state.

Sources:

Malcolm J. Rohrbough, *Days of Gold: The California Gold Rush and the American Nation* (Berkeley: University of California Press, 1997);

Sarah Royce, *A Frontier Lady: Recollections of the Gold Rush and Early California* (New Haven: Yale University Press, 1932).

LAND LAW AND LAND SPECULATION OVER THE APPALACHIANS

Dividing Up the West. American colonists moved into the land west of the Appalachian Mountains in the eighteenth century. After achieving independence in 1783, Americans crossed these mountains in greater numbers. The Land Ordinance of 1785 made the process of Western land ownership easier. Federal surveyors divided the land into six-mile-square townships, which were further sorted into 36 sections of 640 acres each. These sections, in turn, could be further subdivided into 320-, 160-, 80-, and 40-acre units. The end result was the partitioning of large sections of the Trans-Appalachian West into neat squares. Dividing land into orderly squares facilitated sales and, later, ownership. However, the system ignored the topography of the land. As a result some farmers were stuck with uplands without access to waterways. Further, because the surveyed lines ig-

The expansion of the United States over the Appalachian Mountains raised questions about who should benefit from the new lands. Thomas Jefferson, author of the Declaration of Independence and later president of the United States, believed that the country, including the West, should be composed primarily of independent yeomen farmers. Although his vision never became a reality, he nonetheless offered perhaps the most eloquent defense of American farming. "Those who labour in the earth are the chosen people of God, if ever he had a chosen people, whose breasts he has made his peculiar deposit for substantial and genuine virtue. It is the focus in which he keeps alive that sacred fire, which otherwise might escape from the face of the earth. Corruption of morals in the mass of cultivators is a phenomenon of which no age nor nation has furnished an example."

Source: Thomas Jefferson, "Manufactures," in *Notes on the State of Virginia*, edited by William Penden (Chapel Hill: University of North Carolina Press, 1982), pp. 164–165.

nored the contours of western watersheds, erosion led to land degradation in some parts of the country.

Government Support. Yet however ill-suited to the terrain, the arrangement of the land into sections nonetheless promoted American expansion in the West. Three conflicting groups determined the distribution of Western land: the newly created federal government, farmers, and land speculators. The federal government's goal was straightforward: sell public lands to provide funds to finance the national debt. Of course, government officials also saw the benefit of peopling the West with citizens loyal to the new republic.

Yeoman Farmers. Independent farmers and their supporters comprised the second group. While hoping to make a living, some farmers also believed, along with Thomas Jefferson, that a republic could survive only if it were composed of virtuous farmers; but farmers could not easily move West on their own. They needed new lands to be acquired, explored, and surveyed by the government. Jefferson thought the Louisiana Purchase of 1803 would solve any problems of land shortage. American explorers, starting with Meriwether Lewis and William Clark in 1804, investigated the new lands of the Far West. Federal surveyors slowly moved west from the Appalachian Mountains (sometimes at a pace slower than settlers), but even this was not enough. For farmers to thrive as virtuous Americans, the land had to be available and cheap so that they, not land speculators, received the best, most productive lands. Arguing that they were the bedrock of the new nation, small farmers repeatedly fought for new legislation to support their move westward.

Land Speculation. Businessmen who participated in one of America's oldest activities—land speculation—made up the third group. The 1785 Ordinance benefited these men more than the federal government or the small farmer. The government sold some land in huge blocks at small prices to large speculators. Federal officials sold other lands at public auctions in 640-acre sections for a minimum of one dollar per acre. Accumulating at least $640 (and the bids could go higher) was beyond the means of most farmers. As a result less-prosperous farmers often had to purchase land from wealthy speculators.

Changes in the Land Laws. The perpetual conflict between farmer, government, and speculator became a fundamental feature of western settlement. The federal government, for its part, was inconsistent. Wooed by speculators on the one hand and pressured by farmers (who were gaining a stronger voice in the nineteenth century) on the other, Congress revised the land laws time and time again. Gradually the federal government sold land in smaller blocks: from 640 acres in 1785 to 320 in 1800, 160 in 1804, and 80 acres in 1820. The price per acre for public land fluctuated: from $1 in 1785, $2 in 1796, $1.25 in 1820, and a variable rate (from $1.25 to 12.5¢ an acre) in 1854. Recognizing that many farmers lacked sufficient capital to purchase even small tracts, the federal government offered credit to buyers in 1796. The policy (canceled in 1820) was ostensibly created to encourage investment by actual farmers, but it tended to benefit land speculators instead.

Squatters. Settlers without a title to their land (called squatters) constituted another source of conflict in the West. A farmer who found a desired piece of land became a squatter by clearing and planting it with the hope of one day purchasing the acres he had improved. However, when the cleared lands went up for auction, a speculator could out-bid the squatter, gain control of the small farm, and later sell it for a profit. Profiting from the toil of one's fellow citizens was anathema to those who thought that virtue sprang from working the land. It was not until 1841, with the passing of the Preemption Act, that the squatter was able to be the sole purchaser (for $1.25 an acre) of 160 acres of his improved land. Theoretically, the small farmer benefited even more when in 1862 Congress passed the Homestead Act. A citizen, or an individual who planned to become one, was then able to acquire 160 acres of public land for virtually no cost—paying only a small filing fee. Although many small farmers in the West benefited from this policy, Americans frequently, sometimes flagrantly, abused the Homestead Act.

A Mixed Legacy. It would be a mistake to make rigid distinctions between the small farmer (whether squatter or landowner), the speculator, and the government in the West. Congressmen often purchased large sections of

Examples of the paper money circulated in the West during the 1850s (top: Chase Manhattan Bank Museum of Moneys of the World, New York; bottom: New-York Historical Society)

land to be sold; in fact, some of the founding fathers actively speculated in land. Further, many farmers came to the West with an eye to future land sales. Some squatters moved in, improved and claimed a small area, and then sold it to another person before it was even officially available for sale. Other farmers bought a parcel, accumulated the adjacent acreage, and then sold all or parts of the large holding to incoming settlers. These small-time speculators either stayed in the area or moved on and repeated the process elsewhere. As the historian Paul Gates reminds us, financiers living in the East profited most by American land policies. Although these big-time speculators sometimes got stung by a bad purchase or a depression, they were also able to obtain larger sections and lend money to land-hungry farmers at high interest rates. Conflicting goals and the quest for wealth prevented a fair distribution of public land in the United States.

Sources:

Paul Gates, *The Jeffersonian Dream: Studies in the History of American Land Policy and Development,* edited by Allan G. and Margaret Beattie Bogue (Albuquerque: University of New Mexico Press, 1996);

Howard R. Lamar, ed., *The Readers Encyclopedia of the American West* (New York: Crowell, 1977);

Elliot West, "American Frontier," in *The Oxford History of the American West,* edited by Clyde Milner and others (New York: Oxford University Press, 1994), pp. 115–149.

NATIVE AMERICAN ECONOMIES: ADAPTATION AND SECURITY

Diversity in Indian Country. Many modern Americans fail to realize the diversity of native economies in pre-Columbian North America. Some may think only of Squanto helping the Pilgrims or Plains Indians hunting bison on horseback. On the contrary, before and after contact with Europeans and Anglo-Americans, Indians throughout the Trans-Appalachian West subsisted on a wide variety of resources. Despite the differences, though, indigenous nations tended to adapt to the local environment to provide subsistence security. They used the land in order to survive, and many refused to rely too heavily on any one resource because such actions often led to starvation.

Agriculture. Because the geography of the Trans-Appalachian West is so varied, Indian economies differed dramatically according to local soils and climate. Still, about one-half of all groups relied regularly on farming, which provided from one quarter to three quarters of a typical community's dietary needs. Often Indians cleared a certain area in order to plant fields and then later cultivated another stretch to allow the first tract to regain its nutrients. Further, a family would generally have usufruct rights (giving them the right to use, not possess, the land) over a given patch of land to allow them to grow their own crops. Among those groups engaged in agriculture (except some of those in the Southwest), the women usually did much of the farming, to the disgust of Anglos who saw it as a man's job. All told, American Indians grew at least eighty-six different kinds of plants, with maize, beans, and squash being the most important.

Women's and Men's Roles. If not all groups cared for crops, virtually all gathered wild plants, and women were usually responsible for this task as well. Moreover, native economies usually involved hunting (with deer and bison being among the favorite species), and many Indians fished if they had access to bodies of water. Hunting was predominantly a male activity; some Europeans again scorned this practice because chasing game was seen more as leisure sport than as an occupation for civilized, hardworking men.

The Ute Economy. Native Americans of the West developed successful economic strategies that had little impact on the landscape when compared to the practices of peoples from Europe. For example, the Ute Indians of Utah and Colorado lived in what many would consider to be a harsh, arid environment of mountains and basins. Yet some Ute groups were able to adjust to the land by moving up and down the mountains according to the seasons. They did not practice agriculture, but they did encourage the growth of some plants by using fire. For food, hides, and furs the Ute men would hunt large game such as bison and deer as well as smaller animals. Both men and women fished and captured birds and edible insects, and women gathered a variety of plants, seeds, and roots. This diversified economy ensured a certain amount of security because the Utes refused to depend too heavily on any one resource.

The Hupa Economy. By contrast to the widely dispersed Utes, the Hupa Indians of northern California lived primarily in a valley on the Trinity River for centuries. The Hupas fished, gathered plants and nuts, and hunted. Depending on the season, they took different resources from the river, the foothills, or the mountains. Fish provided food for the Hupas and many other groups who lived on or near the Pacific Ocean. Employing traps, spears, nets, and dams, Hupa men caught salmon, eels, and trout. Acorns—a staple for many California Indians—formed a central part of their diet. Families gathered these valuable nuts at private groves; Hupa women then processed the acorns into flour. Like many West Coast nations, the Hupas arranged themselves hierarchically according to wealth and property. They possessed both private and communal land rights. By relying on numerous food sources to meet their needs, and by modifying, but not destroying, their valley, the Hupas lived well for centuries.

Desert Economy of the Tohono O'Odham. The Sonoran desert of southern Arizona and northern Mexico receives very little rainfall. Yet the Tohono O'Odham (or Papagos) managed to ensure a level of economic security by adopting a semisedentary lifestyle adjusted to the harsh desert landscape. Depending on the time of year, the Tohono O'Odham hunted, gathered, and grew a wide variety of food. Women harvested such important wild foods as mesquite beans and the fruit of the imposing saguaro cactus. The men hunted game, but unlike most Indians outside the Southwest, they also farmed. The Tohono O'Odham men planted maize, beans, squash, and cotton in or around the mouths of arroyos (desert creeks which run dry for part of the year). They had effective but small-scale water diversion projects to quench their thirsty fields. These natives lived for centuries in this arid environment by creating a flexible and ingenious economy.

Sources:

R. Douglas Hurt, *Indian Agriculture in America: Prehistory to the Present* (Lawrence: University Press of Kansas, 1987);

David Rich Lewis, *Neither Wolf Nor Dog: American Indians, Environment, and Agrarian Change* (New York: Oxford University Press, 1994).

NATIVE AMERICAN ECONOMIES: ADOPTION AND DEPENDENCY

A New World. The arrival of Europeans meant the eventual destruction of most traditional Indian economies, but the devastation was not inevitable or immediate. Natives adopted certain European plants, animals, and technologies into their older economic structures; in fact, some nations flourished for a time by embracing such Old World animals as the horse. Indeed, adjustment to the natural world and to European invasion was common throughout the continent. Yet, for those groups that survived the European onslaught, the shift from economic self-sufficiency to reliance on outsiders, including the federal government, ultimately undermined both their traditional and newly adopted economies.

Technology. Native Americans had dynamic economies even before the Europeans arrived, but the pace of change quickened after 1500. The introduction and selective adoption of plants, animals, and technology from the Europeans played an important role in their ability to survive and even prosper—at least for a while. Technological differences between Europeans and Indians were considerable at the time of contact; for example, natives used tools and weapons made of stone. Accordingly, European metal goods, such as cooking pots, knives, and guns, remained in high demand among Native Americans who obtained these valuable tools by trading commodities such as furs and hides.

Livestock. Many natives initially rejected Old World plants (including weeds) and animals brought across the ocean. Some groups did eventually accept livestock such as cattle, hogs, and sheep as well as plants such as wheat and peach trees. The horse, however, proved especially desirable; this is particularly true for some tribes on the Great Plains.

The Horse. The introduction of the horse on the Plains altered most native economies in the region. It allowed some Indian nations to expand across the wide grasslands and pursue more bison and new trade opportunities. The Cheyennes, among others, adopted (at least for a while) the Old World horse. Starting in Canada north of Lake Superior, the Cheyennes moved first down into Minnesota (where the first written records of them appear in 1680), then westward into the Dakotas. During these early movements their economy was based on farming and hunting. Then, in the 1700s, they slowly abandoned the practice of raising crops, and in the 1800s they turned into full-fledged nomads when they moved into territories that became modern-day Nebraska, Wyoming, Colorado, and Kansas. As horse nomads their economy was based on bison hunting and trade. Historians and anthropologists remain unsure why the Cheyennes decided to give up farming, but the adoption of the horse surely allowed them to carry more possessions greater distances, as well as more effectively hunt the buffalo.

New Cheyenne Economy. Cheyenne trade networks expanded when they emerged as middlemen between native groups on the northern and southern Plains. The primary role of Cheyenne chiefs was obtaining trade goods. Some of these leaders specialized in certain commodities, including horses. By the 1820s the Cheyennes had entered the bison robe market. They killed these large beasts and exchanged the skins for American manufactured goods. The increased economic activity, made possible by the acquisition of the horse, also had its price. Acquiring grass for new steeds became a major priority for the Cheyenne. Although the Plains were full of grasses, horses needed good forage grass, and they needed it throughout the year. As a result the Cheyenne had to move to new campsites whenever their horses had eaten the good forage in a particular area. Furthermore, they had to break into small camps in the winter to ensure adequate food for themselves and their mounts. Suitable campsites also had to have enough water and wood; valleys along the rivers proved ideal for the grass-wood-water combination.

Decline. When white settlers began moving onto and through the Plains in the middle decades of the nineteenth century, the Cheyenne economy began to crumble. Anglo migrants to the West and later farmers found the traditional Cheyenne campsites ideal for wagon trails and settlement. Grass and wood became scarce. To make matters worse, the bison—the primary food source of the Cheyenne and one of their most important items of trade—began to vanish because of, among other things, the Cheyenne quest for buffalo robes. Finally, since the prestige of the chiefs was based on their ability to gain trade goods from the Americans, these leaders often proved reluctant to go to war; this hesitation caused rifts in Cheyenne society. Some warriors broke off from their

---

PAWNEE HORTICULTURE

The Pawnee Indians of modern-day Nebraska survived on the Great Plains for centuries by mixing a sophisticated agriculture with the hunting of bison. Anthropologist Gene Weltfish describes their ingenious economy: "Pawnee life, like our own, was strongly molded by the four seasons. . . . The spring and the fall of the year were the times of planting and harvesting the crops of corn, beans, and squash. . . . During the summer and again in winter, the whole tribe left their villages behind and set out on a long expedition to the southwest part of the state [Nebraska] where large herds of buffalo followed their accustomed paths of migration."

Source: Gene Weltfish, *The Lost Universe: The Way of Life of the Pawnee* (New York: Ballantine, 1965), p. 9.

---

traditional groups in order to fight the intruders who were destroying their horse-based economy.

Pawnee Experience. Not all Plains Indians who adopted the horse became full-fledged nomads like the Cheyennes. Village Indians, many of whom had lived along the rivers for many years, were dispersed throughout the Great Plains. The Pawnees of modern-day Nebraska were a horticultural village people who continued to farm river bottoms and to hunt bison as they had for centuries. Although resisting the nomadic lifestyle, the Pawnee acquisition of the horse did produce important social and economic effects. The men who possessed these mounts were more successful in the hunt. Greater divisions between rich and poor appeared. Like the Cheyennes, the Pawnees also had problems obtaining sufficient grass for their mounts. When they hunted in the winter, they sought both grass and bison. Still, even with the acquisition of a limited number of horses, the Pawnees managed to continue much of their traditional way of life well into the middle of the nineteenth century. Disease, drought, constant attacks by the Sioux Indians, a growing dependency on the Americans for basic supplies, and the disappearance of bison finally undermined their economy. Only then did the Pawnees finally move. In the 1870s they left Nebraska and moved south into Indian Territory, in the current state of Oklahoma.

Debt. Many nineteenth-century Indians faced an erosion of their economies in the face of American expansion. Removal from their lands or a corrosive reliance on the Anglo-dominated market (or both) was a common outcome. The natives of the Eastern seaboard had faced these problems in the colonial period. As Americans moved westward, growing numbers of Indian nations who were once self-sufficient became indebted to Anglo traders, making them vulnerable to the seizure of their lands and to the whims of the U.S. government.

A drawing of Denver in late 1858 attributed to John Glendenin (Colorado State Historical Society, Denver)

Choctaw Economy. The Choctaws, who mostly lived in what is now the state of Mississippi, were one group that became integrated into the world market. As a result their independence was slowly undermined, and whites gained increasing control over their fate. The Choctaw economy of the 1700s was based on farming and hunting. Although around two-thirds of their food came from farming, deer hunting was critical in the winter months, as well as in those years when their crops failed. Choctaws traded deerskins with the Europeans but managed to do so on favorable terms. The chiefs controlled the distribution of European goods and were able to maintain much of the Choctaw way of life.

Threats to Communities. When growing numbers of traders entered their lands, the Choctaws began supplying even more deerskins in order to acquire liquor. Earlier these natives were able to keep their demand for European products down by limiting their desires to certain goods, such as metal pots, which only occasionally needed to be replaced. When more English, and later American, merchants traveled inland, alcohol flowed in much greater quantities. Choctaw leaders were no longer able to control the terms of trade as hunters circumvented their authority. Consequently, the Choctaws killed more deer, consumed more alcohol, and became increasingly indebted to outsiders.

Removal. When the deer started to disappear, starvation became a real possibility. Whenever the crops failed, these natives had to turn to the Americans for food. Americans also used the debts the Choctaws had incurred as leverage for land. The Americans acquired their first part of Choctaw territory in 1805. Some Choc-taws tried to adjust to the new economy by adopting American-style agriculture, raising livestock, and espousing values that put more emphasis on the individual and less on the group. Those who were more willing to assimilate fought with the traditionalists. Economic decline and rampant conflict undermined any chance for these Indians to resist whites' demands for removal. In 1831 the federal government removed the Choctaws from Mississippi and forced them to resettle in Indian Territory. Many other Indian groups whose economies were weakened by the fur or deerskin trade faced a similar fate in the first half of the nineteenth century.

Sources:

John H. Moore, *The Cheyenne Nation: A Social and Demographic History* (Lincoln: University of Nebraska Press, 1987);

Richard White, *Roots of Dependency: Subsistence, Environment, and Social Change among the Choctaws, Pawnees, and Navajos* (Lincoln: University of Nebraska Press, 1983).

NEW GATEWAY CITIES

The Role of the City. As Americans moved westward, new town sites fueled by land speculation appeared on the nation's map. A few of them became what were later called "gateway cities"—centers of commerce where manufactured goods flowed one way (often west or north) and raw materials and agricultural products flowed the other. These urban areas tied the West to the Atlantic market. With Western fields, forests, plains, and deserts at one end and New York and other Eastern ports on the other, the gateway cities brought the two sections of the country together in a vast economic network. New York City evolved into the main center of transcontinental commerce in the nineteenth century. By

A daguerreotype of Cincinnati, 1848 (Cincinnati Historical Society, Ohio)

1860 New York had one million residents and functioned as the country's foremost port. It likewise served as the center of finance for many Western ventures. New York financiers, and similar-minded developers located in Philadelphia, Boston, and Baltimore, directed much of the economic development of the West.

New Orleans. In the American West various cities dominated the region at different times. Once established, these centers of commerce were difficult to displace, but in the first half of the nineteenth century there always seemed to be a competitive city growing just around the corner. New Orleans originally served as a depot for French furs and deerskins. Located at the mouth of the Mississippi River, it soon expanded into a booming center of trade for pelts, cotton, and grain. New Orleans continued to grow, and by 1860 it was the only Southern city to reach any significant size.

Cincinnati. In the Northeast, Buffalo, sitting astride one end of the Erie Canal, and Pittsburgh, at the head of the Ohio River, functioned as meeting places between the East coast and the Trans-Appalachian West. Soon Cincinnati, Ohio, emerged as the great urban area of the Midwest; it held twice the population of any other city in

the region in 1820. As a river city, and later as a center for processing meat (especially hogs), Cincinnati kept growing into an even larger commercial center through the rest of the nineteenth century.

St. Louis. Further west, St. Louis, Missouri, rose to prominence as the center for the fur trade and the growing commerce between the United States and the Hispanic Southwest. St. Louis also became a depot for the flourishing grain trade of the Mississippi River valley. At the confluence of two major rivers, the city emerged as a thriving hub of waterborne transportation. Because of all this trade, St. Louis prospered in the 1830s, 1840s, and 1850s; it even became an industrial site for iron works in the decade before the Civil War. By 1860 St. Louis had matched Cincinnati in population with 160,000 residents. Today, its famous arch demonstrates the prominence of this gateway city to the West.

Chicago. For all its success, St. Louis was not destined to become the foremost metropolis of the nineteenth-century West. Instead, a small town on the edge of Lake Michigan arose as the dominant nexus of commerce in the region. Chicago, Illinois, lacked easy access to the rivers of the West, so it was far from prede-

Buffalo pelts drying at a skinners' camp, circa 1860 (National Anthropological Archives, Smithsonian Institution, Washington, D.C.)

termined that it would become the second largest city in the nation. Yet Chicago acquired two key resources that left its competitors behind. First, it secured a large influx of capital from the East, thus ensuring heavy and stable investment. Second, Chicago became the major railroad center of the country. Although other gateway cities attracted railroads, none ever matched Chicago. By 1852 two trunk lines reached it from the East. From there the lines fanned out into the West. Increasing numbers of cities, towns, and farms were brought within the long grasp of Chicago.

The Nation's Second City. Railroads transported heavier commodities such as grains into Chicago, where they were loaded onto ships traveling the Great Lakes. Lighter items went directly east. Manufactured goods returned west, and the city became a wholesale center for the region. Chicago also developed its own industries, such as the making of agricultural machinery. Much of Chicago's fame and fortune became apparent in the last half of the nineteenth century. Still, it was already clear by 1860 that this was the new gateway city of the West. In 1855 Chicago surpassed St. Louis in the grain trade. As Americans plowed up acre after acre of the prairie, corn and wheat flowed into the city's new grain elevators. For a time, Chicago also became the center of the Western lumber trade. Timber companies cleared vast stretches of Michigan, Wisconsin, and Minnesota forests and shipped the newly cut pines to the southern tip of Lake Michigan. By 1860, 220 million board feet of

timber came through Chicago; only after the Civil War did the city lose its dominance in the lumber trade.

Commercial Centers. New York City grew to be the country's premier metropolis with its capital and culture, and Chicago, with its railroads, grain, timber, and meat, rose to become America's second largest city by 1890. Even if Chicago became the most famous of the gateway cities, New Orleans, Buffalo, Pittsburgh, Cincinnati, and St. Louis all contributed to the settlement of the Trans-Appalachian West. From 1800 to 1860 much of the economic activity that accompanied and fed westward expansion focused on these commercial centers.

Sources:
William Cronon, *Nature's Metropolis: Chicago and the Great West* (New York: Norton, 1992);

D. W. Meinig, *The Shaping of America: A Geographic Perspective on 1500 Years of History, Volume 2: Continental America, 1800–1867* (New Haven: Yale University Press, 1993).

THE PRAIRIE AGRICULTURAL ECONOMY

Sugar Creek, Illinois. After the War of 1812 many American farmers settled the region of grasslands and woods in central Illinois, especially along Sugar Creek. Most of these settlers came from Kentucky and other areas of the Upper South. (As so often happened in the expanding Southern economy, plantation slavery so restricted the opportunities of smaller farmers that many moved West and Northwest.) Some of the settlers on Sugar Creek quickly bought land, and others became squatters.

Moving onto the Prairie. Corn, hogs, and hunting formed the initial subsistence-based economy for those who lived on the Illinois prairie. Most families initially settled in the timberlands bordering creeks and rivers because they found open grassland daunting. Although farmers eventually discovered that the prairie possessed incredibly rich soil, early Illinois pioneers saw it otherwise. They believed that trees represented fertile soil and thought that land without trees was best suited for pasturage. Some did try to cultivate the grassland, but it was difficult to cut through the tough prairie sod until the 1830s, when a new plow made it possible to farm with more success. Only when farmers adopted the steel plow in the 1840s and 1850s could they cultivate large sections of prairie.

Economy of a Prairie Community. Early farmers on the Illinois prairie had little access to outside markets before 1840; they produced largely for themselves. Whatever they could not make themselves came from local stores where barter was common. They exchanged pork, whiskey, furs, butter, handspun clothing, and timber for iron products, gunpowder, salt, and coffee. The family served as the basic economic unit. A successful household depended on both men and women working together. Still, economic networks existed outside the home. Frequent sharing among kin and neighbors produced bonds of reciprocity. Early pioneers often borrowed from each other, and extensive ties of credit held farmers together. Exchanging labor and participating in community activities such as cabin raising made the many difficulties of early settlement easier. This mutual support allowed even the poor squatter a sufficient living.

A Maturing Economy. Communities on the Illinois prairie changed in the 1840s and 1850s. In the area of Sugar Creek, for instance, some local farmers, especially those with abundant land, pressed for better transportation routes, such as roads, so they would have better access to eastern markets. Full entrance into the larger economy became a fact in 1852 when the railroad reached the Sugar Creek community. Thereafter, residents sold grain and livestock to distant customers. Exchange, of course, went both ways; manufactured goods from the East became more familiar in prairie stores. Closer ties to the outside world encouraged farmers to transform even larger parcels of prairie; they fenced off and plowed up more and more of the land. Like most modern economic change, the growth of market-oriented agriculture benefited some people more than others.

Inequality on the Prairie. Tenancy increased as poorer families who could no longer be squatters farmed someone else's land. In turn tenants gave a percentage of their crops to the landowner. Wage work also increased dramatically. Poorer men performed agricultural work for wages instead of developing their own farms. Similarly, wealthier cultivators gained a larger proportion of the region's acreage. In the Sugar Creek area, for example, the richest 10 percent of the population possessed 25 percent of the land in 1838; the top tenth held 35 percent two decades later. Likewise, in 1838 the poorest 20 percent of the population controlled only 10 percent of the land, but in 1858 this same share of the population owned a mere 5 percent. The rich not only obtained more property; they also employed many of the new tools and farming techniques that made their land even more productive, creating an even greater surplus of crops. In less than a generation central Illinois went from subsistence agriculture to market-oriented farming.

Changing the Landscape. This economic transformation also altered the landscape. Early settlers tended to set up their farms in wooded areas along waterways. Although they might purchase the surrounding acreage, they laid out their homesteads more according to the natural formation of the land than the square lines drawn by federal surveyors. Moreover, many early pioneers used the adjacent grasslands as a common (shared) pasture where cattle and hogs grazed freely. As farmers became more intertwined in the market system, they changed their ways of using land; they fenced in pasturage to keep out the livestock of competitors. Property boundaries and roads eventually followed section lines, thereby imposing a grid on the land even though this new system of demarcating property ignored the natural topography. By 1860 the Midwestern landscape began to take its modern form: square fields, gridlike roads, and productive farms could be found across the prairie.

Source:
John Mack Faragher, *Sugar Creek: Life on the Illinois Prairie* (New Haven: Yale University Press, 1986).

A REVOLUTION IN TRANSPORTATION

Early Hopes. In 1808 Secretary of the Treasury Albert Gallatin called for a federally supported national transportation system. He suggested that roads, turnpikes, and canals be constructed to bring the new nation together, but Gallatin's plan, however appealing, never materialized. The questionable constitutionality of a federally funded transportation program; the constant bickering among cities, states, and regions; and the rapid changes in technology and population densities rendered such ideas impossible to implement. During the antebellum period a national transportation structure emerged, and by 1860 almost anyone living east of Texas could reach New York City within six days.

Steamboats. The eastern half of North America is blessed with many navigable bodies of water. The Mississippi-Missouri-Ohio River systems and the Great Lakes make for comparatively easy internal travel and shipping. In 1807 Robert Fulton's steamboat, the *Clermont*, chugged up the Hudson River from New York City to Albany. Soon, steam-powered river craft were carrying people and goods along many of the nation's arteries. In 1812 a steamboat went from Pittsburgh to New Orleans; even more important, in 1815 a steamboat left

New Orleans and ascended the Mississippi River to Louisville, Kentucky. The success of these new steam-powered crafts led to the disappearance of the slower keelboats, but flatboats, another familiar form of river transportation, continued to carry people and goods down river. The Ohio and Mississippi River systems bore seventy steamboats by the early 1820s and five hundred by 1840.

Roads. These new boats allowed Americans in the East and West to trade regionally, but the Appalachian Mountains remained a barrier to a nationwide transportation structure. Rutted, often muddy, roads through mountain passes were an early answer to the problem. In 1802 the federal government authorized the construction of the paved National Road, which reached from the Potomac River to the Ohio River.

Canals. The answer to east-west transportation came not with roads but instead through the development of a system of canals that captured the imagination of thousands of entrepreneurs and lawmakers. Private and public capital financed the building of smaller canals in the first two decades of the 1800s. However, 1825 marked a new age in transportation and commerce. That year the Erie Canal—connecting the Great Lakes to the Hudson River (and, thus, to New York City)—was finally completed. New York's accomplishment became a huge and immediate success for the state. For two decades the United States went through a "canal-mania." State gov-

A Forty-Niner Going Prospecting (circa 1850), painted by Henry Walton from a lithograph by Charles Nahl (courtesy of Dr. A. Shumate)

ernments rushed to connect cities and regions with rivers and lakes. No other man-made American water channel ever witnessed the transportation of goods that travelled the Erie Canal, which carried more than one million tons of cargo in 1845, but other canals appeared throughout the Northeast and Midwest.

Railroads. Nevertheless, the age of canals turned out to be short-lived when many Americans realized that railroads could better accomplish their goal of connecting the East with the West. In the 1830s most railroads simply joined major waterways, demonstrating again the power of water transportation. However, investors with large government subsidies in hand soon began to develop new routes known as trunk lines. As early as 1827 Baltimore businessmen, who feared that trade in their city would be damaged by the success of the Erie Canal, proposed laying tracks westward to connect their port with the Ohio River. Because of various delays, the Baltimore and Ohio Railroad was not finished until 1852, but railroad companies were hard at work constructing other trunk lines. By 1853 seven routes connected the eastern seaboard with the interior West. Private companies and state governments erected local and state rail lines within the West, so when the trunk lines reached over the mountains, the United States had its first integrated railroad system. Although no railroad connected the East Coast with California until 1869, by 1860 the United States possessed thirty thousand miles of rails, most of it east of the Missouri River.

Emergence of a National System. Since different and competing companies funded these railroads, not all the tracks were of the same width, and few tracks crossed major rivers due to the high cost of bridge construction.

SAMUEL CLEMENS REPORTS THE DANGERS OF RIVER TRAVEL

The steamboats that plied the western rivers were crucial to the hauling of goods and people throughout the region from the 1820s onward, but river travel could be dangerous before the Civil War. Explosions, accidents, and dangers from the rivers themselves were relatively common. Samuel Clemens, better known as Mark Twain, recalled the hazards faced by early Mississippi River steamboat pilots. "Fully to realise the marvellous precision required in laying the great steamer in her marks in that murky waste of water, one should know that not only must she pick her intricate way through snags and blind reefs, and then shave the head of the island so closely as to brush the overhanging foliage with her stern, but at one place she must pass almost within arm's reach of a sunken and invisible wreck that would snatch the hull timbers from under her if she should strike it, and destroy a quarter of a million dollars' worth of steam-boat and cargo in five minutes, and maybe a hundred and fifty human lives into the bargain."

Source: Mark Twain, *Old Times on the Mississippi* (Toronto: Belford, 1876).

Moreover, the railroads were not evenly distributed within the United States. Most joined the Northeast with the Midwest while the South rapidly fell behind because planters involved in the cotton-based economy still favored rivers over railroads. So, despite the phenomenal success and eventual dominance of the railroad, the waterborne traffic of steamboats and canals continued to play a crucial economic role in the antebellum period. Whether by land, water, or rail, Americans and their goods moved farther and faster in 1860 than they had half a century before.

Sources:

D. W. Meinig, *The Shaping of America: A Geographical Perspective on 500 Years of History, Volume 2: Continental America, 1800–1867* (New Haven: Yale University Press, 1993);

George Rogers Taylor, *The Transportation Revolution: 1815–1860* (White Plains, N.Y.: M. E. Sharpe, 1951).

SHEEP IN HISPANIC NEW MEXICO

Spain's Search for Wealth. Spain's far northern frontier in North America had few commodities to offer the outside world. The Spanish search for gold had failed, but for religious and military reasons the Spanish Empire still maintained the colony of New Mexico. In the first half of the nineteenth century small-scale irrigated agriculture and livestock formed the basis of the economy. Although residents bred and used cattle and horses, sheep became the dominant domesticated animal in the region. Unlike some sheep breeds, the small *churros*, which were more valuable for meat than wool, survived in the harsh, arid environment of New Mexico.

Churros. With the arrival of Juan de Oñate and his party of colonists in 1598, sheep became a part of the New Mexican economy. When the Pueblo Indians revolted in 1680, they ejected the Spanish and their religion but kept their sheep. At the end of the 1700s, a century after the Spanish reconquered the colony, sheep raising had developed into a major regional industry. Though New Mexico remained peripheral to the rest of New Spain, it helped feed the communities centered around the valuable silver mines of north-central Mexico. Hispanics of the northern Rio Grande started herding flocks of sheep southward into Chihuahua, Mexico, along a well-established route that connected the colony to the rest of the Spanish Empire. In 1803 perhaps as many as twenty-five thousand churros were driven south. The numbers exported from New Mexico fluctuated in the following years, but sheep remained important to the region's economy.

The *Partido* System. In the early nineteenth century the New Mexican sheep industry benefited the wealthier colonists. New Mexicans had developed the *partido* system in the mid eighteenth century. Under this system an owner of a flock lent a specific quantity of sheep to an individual and expected an equal number to be returned in three to five years. Each year the renter paid around 20 percent of the flock to the owner. If the sheep reproduced in sufficient numbers, the system worked well for both parties. The owners received annual payments while someone else watched over his livestock. The renter could build his own flock and eventually lend out some sheep of his own. Such arrangements in a cash-poor province functioned as a transfer of capital, but if the flock did not reproduce as planned, the renter remained in debt to the owner. Although the partido system resulted in economic opportunity for some, it worked to the advantage of the rich.

Ricos. By the early 1800s sheep were the most important asset of nearly all well-off New Mexicans. Moreover, a small cadre of families dominated the export trade. In 1835, when herders sent eighty thousand sheep south, a single family—the Chavez brothers—possessed almost half of these animals. The *ricos,* economic elites, dominated the New Mexican economy through much of the early nineteenth century.

Village Economies. Despite the wealth of the ricos and the larger economy of the sheep trade, villagers on the local level lived a more communal existence. In northern Hispanic settlements such as Las Trampas, certain social values discouraged an individual who was not a rico from profiting at an endeavor that hurt others. Also, most sheep grazed on communal pastures called *ejidos.* Though these villagers were poor by later standards, and divisions of wealth existed, few people starved because community members took care of each other in times of dearth. Northern New Mexico village econo-

JOSIAH GREGG DESCRIBES THE NEW MEXICAN SHEEP INDUSTRY

The American merchant Josiah Gregg participated in the trade along the Santa Fe Trail in the 1830s. In 1844 he published his famous book, *Commerce of the Prairies.* In his chapter titled "Domestic Animals" he describes the importance of sheep in the economy of Hispanic New Mexico: "Sheep may be reckoned the staple production of New Mexico, and the principle article of exportation. . . . This trade has constituted profitable business to some of the ricos of the country. They would buy sheep of the poor rancheros at from fifty to seventy-five cents per head, and sell them at from one to two hundred per cent advance in southern markets. . . . The sheep of New Mexico are exceedingly small, with very coarse wool, and scarcely fit for anything else than mutton, for which, indeed, they are justly celebrated. . . . The flesh of the sheep is to the New Mexicans what that of the hog is to the people of our Western States—while pork is but seldom met with in northern Mexico."

Source: Josiah Gregg, *Commerce of the Prairies: A Selection* (Indianapolis: Bobbs-Merrill, 1970), pp. 62–63.

mies remained largely self-sufficient; these Spanish-speaking villagers had only limited contact with the outside market until the last decades of the nineteenth century.

The Sheep Trade. The sheep trade south along the Rio Grande continued until 1846—the year the United States acquired New Mexico. After the California Gold Rush began in 1848, Hispanics sent thousands of churros to miners further west. Anglos intruded on this enterprise and began shipping their own flocks from New Mexico. However, in the early 1850s the profitability of the commerce diminished, although the Hispanic herders continued moving their stock to California for another five years. Still, sheep remained a fundamental part of the economy of northern New Mexico. The second half of the century witnessed improvements in breeding due to the expanding market in wool.

Overgrazing. The actual number of sheep in New Mexico during any given year remains in dispute. By the 1820s as many as two million of these woolly animals roamed the region. The dramatic nineteenth-century increase in sheep proved hard on the New Mexican range. Overgrazing had long been a part of the sheep industry, and it was particularly bad in long-settled areas. When sheep nibbled away pastures near the Rio Grande, New Mexicans pushed their flocks outward from the river. Still, overgrazing in the first half of the nineteenth century paled in comparison to the damage inflicted later because in the early 1800s the New Mexican economy remained relatively isolated, despite the Chihuahuan trade. With the arrival of the Anglo-American market, and with the villagers' growing participation in the cash economy, the number of livestock skyrocketed. Cattle also arrived in larger numbers. Overgrazing in New Mexico became a hotly debated issue that persists to this day.

Sources:

John O. Baxter, *Las Carneradas: Sheep Trade in New Mexico, 1700–1860* (Albuquerque: University of New Mexico Press, 1987);

William DeBuys, *Enchantment and Exploitation: The Life and Times of a New Mexico Mountain Range* (Albuquerque: University of New Mexico Press, 1985).

THE TRANS-MISSISSIPPI FUR TRADE

Desire for Peltry. The Trans-Mississippi commerce in animal pelts took three basic forms: the Upper Missouri River fur trade, the Rocky Mountain trapping system, and the independent trappers of the southern Rockies. Sent by President Thomas Jefferson, Meriwether Lewis and William Clark journeyed up the Missouri River to, among other things, discover the potential for an American fur trade in the recently acquired Louisiana Purchase. Reports of their expedition set off a flurry of American-based excursions into the northern plains. In 1807 Manuel Lisa established the first American trading post in Montana. There, Lisa and his men traded supplies for furs with natives.

American Fur Company. By 1822 five leading fur companies worked the upper Missouri in hopes of profiting from sales in beaver skins. Only five years later John Jacob Astor's American Fur Company developed a virtual monopoly among American firms on the northern plains. It was seriously challenged only by the British-owned Hudson's Bay Company operating out of Canada. Astor's company set up three main posts along the Missouri River. The men at these posts shuttled supplies to subsidiary depots where goods could then be transferred to temporary camps. At all of these stations the Americans exchanged manufactured goods for the furs brought in by the Indians.

Transatlantic Business. The Upper Missouri fur trade extended from the northern plains to St. Louis, Missouri, and from there to eastern cities and Europe. St. Louis was the linchpin of the system. Merchants shipped trade goods such as woolen cloth, metal items,

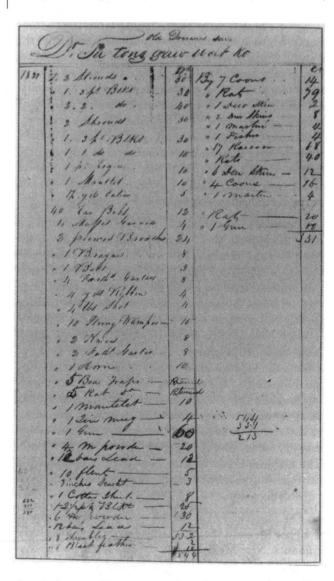

A page from the 1831 ledger of Alexis Bailly, a trader for the American Fur Company at Mendota, Minnesota; the standard of currency is the muskrat skin (Minnesota Historical Society, St. Paul)

and guns to this city from the east. From St. Louis the Americans brought the merchandise up river, first by keelboat, and then after 1831, by steamboat to the various trading posts. Traders and their employees loaded the furs and hides obtained from the Indians onto a variety of boats and floated their parcels downriver. After reaching St. Louis, merchants shipped the beaver pelts to New York City by way of New Orleans or eastward along the Ohio River. The final destination of many pelts was in Europe, often markets in England or Germany. Trading companies transported bison hides to eastern cities in the United States, such as New York and Boston, where manufacturers turned these skins into clothing and blankets. As the number of Western beaver dwindled in the 1830s, bison robes became increasingly important to the survival of the Upper Missouri trade.

Rocky Mountain Trading System. From the point of view of the people in charge of the fur companies, the limitation of the trading post system was its reliance on Native Americans. If the Indians refused to accumulate as many furs as the Americans wanted, or if they chose to sell to the British, there was little that the St. Louis-based merchants could do. So in 1823 William Ashley created the Rocky Mountain trapping system by sending out groups of Americans to trap beavers on their own—thereby bypassing the Indians altogether. After a successful season of trapping, these mountain men gathered in a river valley during the summer, at a place called the Rendezvous, to exchange furs for supplies that Ashley, and later others, had brought upriver.

Workers. Famous mountain men such as Jedediah Smith and Jim Bridger helped build and extend the Rocky Mountain trapping system. Myths and legends built around these and other men placed a thick layer of romance over a brutally exploitative economic arrangement. Profit at almost any cost was the goal for many Americans involved in the fur trade. The "free trappers" gathered pelts and sold them at the Rendezvous while others, called *engagés,* worked directly as salaried employees for one of the fur companies. Another group, "skin trappers," went out after obtaining credit from a company for their supplies. These men could easily fall into debt. In fact, most trappers made very little money; in the end the profits in this enterprise went almost ex-

A beaver hat (Missouri Historical Society, St. Louis)

clusively to the companies who supplied the trade goods from St. Louis.

Southwestern Fur Trade. The mountain men of the southern Rockies worked largely as free trappers. They began to rove the Southwest after Mexico declared its independence in 1821. Based in Taos and Santa Fe, men such as Kit Carson would scour the mountain streams for beaver. Less organized than the companies to the north, these trappers sold their goods (often illegally) to the merchants traveling the new Santa Fe Trail. What ended the trapping in the southern Rockies was a problem endemic to the whole trade: the depletion of resources—in this case the animals themselves.

Decline of the Trade. The entire fur trade was inherently temporary. The reckless quest for profit by competing trappers and companies ensured the rapid exhaustion of the slow-breeding furbearers. American and Indian trappers stripped streams and rivers of beavers throughout the West. As a result each year those involved in this commerce had to look harder and farther in order to gain any pelts. In the long run, the system collapsed. Prices for beaver plummeted in the 1830s, and they were saved from extinction. Changing fashions encouraged the well-dressed in America and Europe to wear silk hats. The beaver hat became a thing of the past. By 1840 the Rocky Mountain and Southwestern trapping systems had disappeared. The Upper Missouri trade only survived because entrepreneurs relied more heavily on the bison trade. Again, it was largely the Native American Indians, such as the Cheyenne, who supplied the skins to the Americans. Before 1860 the whole structure depended on Indian women to prepare the bison robes for sale to the Americans. Since these women only processed so many hides in any given year, the trade remained limited. Still, with the gradual reduction of habitat by the arrival on the Plains of settlers, the extension of the rail-

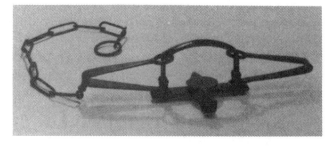

A hand-forged beaver trap, circa 1850 (Minnesota Historical Society, St. Paul)

roads westward, drought, diseases, and overhunting by Indian and American hunters, the vast bison herds of the Great Plains (numbering at least 25 million at one time) virtually vanished by the early 1880s.

Sources:

Richard White, "Animals and Enterprise," in *The Oxford History of the American West*, edited by Clyde Milner and others (New York: Oxford University Press, 1994), pp. 237–273;

David J. Wishart, *The Fur Trade of the American West, 1807–1840* (Lincoln: University of Nebraska Press, 1979).

WAGON TRAILS TO NEW MEXICO

A Remote Economy. With comparatively few desirable commodities, and lacking precious metals, the New Mexican economy in the period from 1800 to 1860 remained fairly stagnant. The colony's population grew but stayed quite low. Nevertheless, trade networks did exist on a North-South axis. The Spanish crown's policy of tightly controlling commerce did little to help the economy of the northern frontier. By the time Chihuahuan traders transported manufactured goods north to distant New Mexico, the prices were extremely high. Before 1821 it was illegal for New Mexicans to trade with the Americans, English, or French. Not surprising, smuggling existed throughout Spain's northern frontier; nevertheless, because of its isolation New Mexico generally remained distant from this black market despite the attempts of a few French traders. Overall, Spanish crown policies tended to discourage the formation of the kind of economic changes occurring in the English-speaking world. Thus, though the American economy boomed in the late 1700s and early 1800s, when Mexico declared its independence from Spain in 1821, its economy was already weaker than that of the United States.

The Santa Fe Trail. Independence for Mexico meant the legal opening of New Mexican markets to outsiders. In 1821 William Becknell, a Missouri merchant, reached Santa Fe with American goods. By the end of the year two other wagon trains owned by American merchants entered the city. The famous Santa Fe Trail was born. It ran from eastern Missouri through Kansas and south into New Mexico. At first the Hispanics of New Mexico appreciated the Anglo merchants since these newcomers sold many desirable items; local customers particularly wanted clothing and household goods. The American wares were more numerous, more varied, and less expensive than those coming north from Chihuahua. As a result the route from Missouri to Santa Fe, traveled largely by Anglo entrepreneurs, thrived; but the good times failed to last. Declining profitability led Americans to travel south out of Santa Fe to trade with Chihuahua.

Tensions in the Region. Still, from the 1820s to the 1840s citizens of Mexico's northern frontier relied heavily on U.S. goods. Soon northern Mexico entered the economic orbit of the United States. The Americans brought badly needed capital into the region. They financed and, in the end, largely benefited from the development of the fur trade and most new mining ventures. Yet the Anglos who brought all these wonderful goods did little to hide their racist sense of superiority, thereby creating tensions with longtime residents of the region.

American Dominance. In response to both the growing dependence on and the crude behavior of the Anglo merchants, the Mexican government passed restrictions and tariffs to encourage national economic strength. These laws tended to be piecemeal and far from enforceable. Anglos and New Mexicans alike often evaded them. The officials in Santa Fe were torn because they wanted a stronger territorial economy free from the Anglos, but they also desired goods that failed to arrive from Mexico; widespread smuggling and corruption resulted. Although Mexicans had a role in at least most aspects of the changing economy, American dominance continued into the 1840s.

The Threat to Mexico. In the long run, Mexico suffered from the Santa Fe Trail trade since this commerce discouraged economic development on its northern frontier. The presence of Americans in the Southwest boded ill for the Mexicans. Anglos moved into and eventually took Texas. Although New Mexico remained a part of Mexico until 1846, the many commercial ties between Missouri and Santa Fe facilitated the conquest of the region by the United States in the Mexican-American War.

Sources:

David Weber, *The Mexican Frontier: The American Southwest under Mexico* (Albuquerque: University of New Mexico Press, 1982);

Weber, *The Spanish Frontier in North America* (New Haven: Yale University Press, 1992).

HEADLINE MAKERS

JOHN JACOB ASTOR

1763-1848

FUR TRADE MAGNATE

Corporate Pioneer. Considered one of the richest and most powerful men of his time, John Jacob Astor was an entrepreneurial wizard who made his fortune from the western fur trade and urban real estate. Astor was a key part of many of the economic changes that propelled westward expansion in the nineteenth century. He created a corporate structure that spanned the continent and reached out to markets in Europe, South America, and Asia. In many ways his business practices anticipated the creation of the large corporations in the late nineteenth century made famous by John D. Rockefeller and Andrew Carnegie.

Millionaire Fur Trader. Born on 17 July 1763 in the city of Walldorf in what is now Germany, Astor left for London, England, at the age of sixteen to help his brother market musical instruments. At age twenty he arrived in Baltimore, Maryland; he soon moved to New York City, where he established a prosperous business purchasing furs in Canada for resale in Europe and the United States. He expanded his interest in furs and entered the profitable China trade, where Astor and his agents traded furs for tea and silk. Because of his extraordinary success, the forty-four-year-old Astor was a millionaire by 1807. With business connections in Europe, Asia, and North America, he had reached the peak of the American fur industry by 1811.

The American Fur Company. In 1808 Astor decided he wanted to command the fur trade from the Great Lakes to the Pacific and thus challenge the powerful British fur companies in the West. His men set up a trading post in Oregon, named Astoria, in 1811, from which they were to obtain furs from the Indians and then ship the pelts directly to China. Promising as the scheme first seemed, Astor's timing was poor. In 1812 the United States went to war with Great Britain. In 1813 the British Northwest Company surrounded Astoria and forced Astor's agent to liquidate the entire post for a paltry $44,000. Astor was furious, especially when the American government refused to help. Astor then opted to abandon Oregon and turn his attention elsewhere. Though the American Fur Company, which he established in 1808, was unable to capture the Pacific trade, it nonetheless became the largest American fur trading firm in the West.

Monopoly. In the 1810s Astor expanded his interest in the Great Lakes region. By 1819 he had secured the largest share of the area's fur market. In the same year his grandson accidentally drowned, and the depressed Astor began to withdraw from the business, leaving daily affairs under the control of others. In the next fifteen years Astor traveled to and from Europe but remained the principal company decision maker. In 1821 the American Fur Company invaded the Upper Missouri fur trade; by merging with and buying out its competitors, Astor's company managed to capture much of that market as well. Nevertheless, even the best-prepared company could not avoid the long-term problems of animal depletion or changing fashions. Recognizing these limitations, Astor sold the American Fur Company in 1834 before the market dried up.

Land Speculation. Astor had long invested his profits from furs into real estate in New York City. After 1834 and until his death fourteen years later, he continued to buy, improve, and sell land on Manhattan Island. In fact, from 1800 to 1848 Astor had invested $2 million in real estate; he owned at least $5 million in land when he died. Astor speculated in land elsewhere, including in the West, where the town of Astor, Wisconsin, was to later become Green Bay. He bought stock in railroads and canals, purchased government bonds, and was involved in various banks. When Astor died in 1848, his estimated worth was at least $8 million, a vast fortune at the time.

Reasons for Success. Astor succeeded where many failed for several reasons. He recognized the profits to be made in the West. He acquired his fortune because he tended to be attentive to and careful about his commercial ventures. He integrated his fur business horizontally through cutting deals with his competitors whenever possible. Astor watched, and successfully predicted, the market and kept tabs on company expenditures. Astor likewise attempted to integrate vertically; he worked to have the highly organized American Fur Company obtain furs at the source and control sales all the way to Europe or China. Lastly, he possessed many friends and acquaintances in political office. John Jacob Astor's business strategies, remarkably similar to those developed by later corporations, enabled him to become one of the richest men of his time while serving as a major component in America's westward expansion.

Sources:

John D. Haeger, "Business Strategy and Practice in the Early Republic: John Jacob Astor and the American Fur Trade," *Western Historical Quarterly,* 19 (May 1988): 183–202;

Haeger, *John Jacob Astor: Business and Finance in the Early Republic* (Detroit: Wayne State University Press, 1991).

WILLIAM BENT

1809-1869
TRADER

Trade in the Southwest. The trade between Anglos and Native Americans proved crucial to westward expansion in the nineteenth century. Few people were as central to that trade on the southern Great Plains as William Bent. Born into a large family on 23 May 1809 in St. Louis, Bent joined his older brother Charles in a Missouri River trading expedition in 1827. William and Charles then took a caravan of American goods along the Santa Fe Trail in 1829. Though proving profitable, William temporarily left the Santa Fe trade and began trapping. In the winter of 1829–1830 he saved the lives of two Cheyenne, thus inaugurating his long bond with these Indians. After an unsuccessful trapping excursion into Arizona, Bent resumed his commercial ventures by joining the company established by Charles and his partner, Ceran St. Vrain.

Ties to the Cheyennes. In 1831 the Bent brothers and some southern Cheyenne Indians agreed that the Bents would establish a trading post in eastern Colorado. After a competitor moved in, the Bents relocated their fort twice before establishing themselves in southeastern Colorado at Ft. William, or Bent's Fort. In the late 1830s and early 1840s the site became a thriving center of trade between Anglos, southern Plains Indians, and Hispanics from New Mexico. Bent exchanged American manufactured goods for bison hides, horses, and mules. He married a Cheyenne named Owl Woman, which strengthened his relationship with that nation. Their offspring included two famous sons, Charles and George, both of whom later came to live and fight with the Cheyenne in their struggle to maintain their independence. When Owl Woman died around 1847, Bent married her sister Yellow Woman. These marriages not only assisted his commercial venture but also drew Bent closer to the Cheyenne, with whom he occasionally lived.

Peacekeeper. The Mexican War, and the struggles between the natives and the army that followed, helped bring an end to trade at Bent's Fort. For unknown reasons the fort burned in 1849. Bent continued to participate in a number of profitable enterprises. During these years Bent strove to maintain peace between the Cheyenne, other native groups, and the American government. Although he did not always succeed at this largely hopeless task, he remained a powerful presence in the region until his death in 1869. William Bent was not only crucial in the expansion of the American market onto the Great Plains, but he also represents a transitional figure between the bison-based economy of the Cheyenne Indians and the eventual domination of the area by American settlers.

Sources:

Samuel P. Arnold, "William W. Bent," in *The Mountain Men and the Fur Trade of the Far West,* volume 4, edited by LeRoy R. Hafen (Glendale, Cal.: Arthur H. Clarke, 1968);

Dan L. Thrapp, *Encyclopedia of Frontier Biography,* volume 1 (Glendale, Cal.: Arthur H. Clarke, 1988), pp. 96–100.

ALBERT GALLATIN

1761-1849
ECONOMIST AND POLITICIAN

Visionary. As the third secretary of the treasury, Albert Gallatin faced many obstacles. Appointed by the new president, Thomas Jefferson, in 1801, he needed to ensure that the economy flourished while following the dictates of his party, which insisted on less control by the federal government and the country's financial elite. At the same time he had his own vision of the future of the United States, which included federal aid for the economic development of the Trans-Appalachian West.

Political Origins. Albert Gallatin was born on 12 January 1761 in the Swiss city of Geneva. After acquiring an education, Gallatin left for North America in the spring of 1780 and ended up in Pennsylvania, where he entered politics in 1788 as an Anti-Federalist (one who objected to certain features of the new Constitution). In 1790 he was elected to the Pennsylvania assembly. In 1793 this assembly elected him as one of their U.S. senators (which, at this time, were chosen by state legislatures). However, the Federalists, who felt threatened by

Gallatin's persistent and informed attacks on their agenda, managed to nullify his election to the Senate. Nevertheless, in 1795 Gallatin returned to Congress as a member of the U.S. House of Representatives from Pennsylvania.

Secretary of the Treasury. When Jefferson won the presidential election in 1801, he appointed Gallatin secretary of the treasury, a position he held for the next thirteen years. Gallatin helped finance the Louisiana Purchase while still managing to reduce the national debt. Gallatin recommended that the First Bank of the United States be rechartered. Although few people in his party supported the renewal of the national bank, he insisted that this institution, which had both public and private investors, could help stabilize the economy without harming the people of the United States.

Later Career. Because the Charter of the First Bank of the United States was not renewed, Gallatin had various problems funding the War of 1812. Before the war was over Gallatin resigned as secretary of the treasury and went to Europe as an American diplomat. Shortly after he returned in 1823 Gallatin was chosen to run as William Crawford's vice president in the 1824 election. Because his candidacy created so much controversy, he dropped out of the race. Gallatin spent his remaining years as a diplomat, banker, and ethnologist. He helped prevent a war with Great Britain over the Oregon Territory and, after retiring, studied the cultures of Native Americans. Gallatin died in 1849 in Astoria, New York. He was a close friend of the fur-trade magnate John Jacob Astor.

Need for Federal Programs. Gallatin remains an important part of U.S. history because of his work as a public official and his vision for the future of the American economy. He advocated economic diversity by insisting on federal support for agriculture, trade, and industry. Gallatin pushed for a level of equality of opportunity and a public land policy where the government helped all citizens, not just an elite group of merchants and speculators. Yet Gallatin also accepted his Federalist opponents' belief that the federal government needed to be involved in the economy. His fellow Jeffersonians often argued that the less government the better. Gallatin, by contrast, realized that in order for the U.S. economy to expand in a way that benefited the most people, some federal programs were necessary.

Transportation Visionary. Gallatin's vision included a nationwide transportation program, which he proposed to Congress in 1808, that was to be partially funded by the federal government. He hoped to connect all Americans to the market system while maintaining a national unity that would overcome local and sectional disputes. Gallatin pushed for roads and canals connecting the East to the newly settled West. He also suggested that certain roads be constructed to connect the new cities within the West. He asserted that canals should be built to join the Mississippi River valley to the Great Lakes and the Atlantic Ocean. He believed that all Americans would benefit from this program. Gallatin's specific plan was never carried out though the nation's transportation system did develop through partnerships between federal and state governments on the one hand and private firms on the other. This less organized program managed to link much of the United States together by 1860. Still, Gallatin's 1808 plan anticipated such aspects of the Transportation Revolution as the Erie Canal, which facilitated the economic development and American settlement of the Trans-Appalachian West.

Sources

L. B. Kuppenheimer, *Albert Gallatin's Vision of Democratic Stability: An Interpretive Profile* (Westport, Conn.: Praeger, 1996);

D. W. Meinig, *The Shaping of America: A Geographical Perspective on 500 Years of History, Volume 2: Continental America, 1800–1867* (New Haven: Yale University Press, 1993), pp. 311–352.

CYRUS McCORMICK

1809-1884

INVENTOR

Agricultural Efficiency. In the opening decades of the nineteenth century the amount of acreage a family could cultivate often depended on how many people they could get into the fields. As a result most farmers who produced for the market faced continual labor shortages, especially in the harvest season; but this would soon change. New machines cut the time required for harvesting grains roughly in half between 1800 and 1840, and half again by 1880. Farm production and efficiency grew rapidly, a crucial development for the economy of the West.

John Deere Plows. Iron and steel plows soon replaced those made of wood. In 1837 John Deere constructed his first iron plow with a steel edge. He annually manufactured one thousand plows by the mid 1840s and ten thousand a year the following decade. These new plows allowed the settler to slice into mile after mile of otherwise resilient Midwestern prairie, but even Deere's plows could not overcome the problem of finding sufficient labor at harvest time. Farmers growing small grains such as wheat still needed laborers to harvest with sickles, scythes, or larger hand implements called cradles.

McCormick Reapers. Cyrus Hall McCormick was born in Virginia in 1809; his father, Robert, was something of a tinkerer himself. Early mechanical reapers appeared in England around 1800, and inventors in Europe and the United States continued to explore new possibilities. Robert McCormick experimented with a reaper and gave it to his son, Cyrus, in 1831. After making improvements, the younger McCormick patented his new reaper in 1834. Although Cyrus McCormick left the farm machine business for a few years, his reaper, which would come to transform agriculture in the Trans-Appalachian West, hit the market in 1840. Between his own workshop in Virginia and some contractors in Cincinnati, Ohio, McCormick turned out 150 reapers in 1845. McCormick realized that a factory in the Midwest could significantly increase sales, so in 1847 he and a partner built a factory in Chicago. They manufactured 500 mechanical reapers there in 1848.

Competitors. It is important to realize that Cyrus McCormick was not the only inventor of the new reaper. In fact, Obed Hussey patented his first reaper a year before McCormick and remained his main competitor for years. There were other competitors as well, making McCormick's patents difficult to protect. McCormick repeatedly went to court to protect a variety of patents. Despite these legal obstacles, by 1850 McCormick had produced more than 1,600 reapers and had captured 50 percent of the American market. During the 1850s, while the number of reapers he produced increased as a result of continuous demand, his market share declined. By 1865 McCormick possessed only 5 percent of the reaper market. Indeed, new competitors were inventing and producing better machines more rapidly. Still, the McCormick Harvesting Machine Company continued to compete in the last half of the nineteenth century. When Cyrus died in 1884, his son Cyrus Jr. took charge of the business. In 1902 the McCormicks and other large producers of mechanical reapers merged to create a giant firm known as International Harvester.

Foreign Sales. Cyrus McCormick's success depended on a number of factors. As an early inventor he had a jump on the market, and he managed to obtain crucial patents. The cunning McCormick also employed ingenious methods for marketing his reapers. Early on, McCormick traveled to the countryside to see his machines at work during the harvest season. Later his agents and mechanics helped repair the reapers in the field. McCormick developed a warranty on his machines, and he sold them on credit. Like the competition, he also marketed his reapers at agricultural societies and fairs. In 1851 McCormick toured Europe to run trials on his reaper. He was so successful that he used his European praise for publicity back home. Soon his competitors went abroad to promote their own machines.

McCormick's Legacy. Vast changes in Western agriculture followed the development of the McCormick reaper and other new machines. Since the number of acres a farmer could harvest rose dramatically, farms in the West became increasingly larger. As with all technological change, some Americans were hurt by these developments. Poorer farming families often found they could not compete with wealthier commercial farmers. Less reliance on human hands pushed many agricultural laborers into the nation's urban factories. The ecological consequences eventually included soil erosion and the transformation of the American prairies into areas of comparatively little biodiversity. Before 1860 such concerns were not yet apparent to many Americans, and the nation instead celebrated the rise of seemingly efficient large-scale farming.

Sources:

Willard W. Cochrane, *The Development of American Agriculture: A Historical Analysis* (Minneapolis: University of Minnesota Press, 1993);

Esko Heikkonen, *Reaping the Bounty: McCormick Harvesting Machine Company Turns Abroad, 1878–1902* (Helsinki: Finnish Historical Society, 1995).

PUBLICATIONS

Nicholas Biddle, *History of the Expedition under the Command of Captains Lewis and Clark,* 2 volumes, edited by Paul Allen (Philadelphia: Bradford & Inskeep / New York: Abm. H. Inskeep, J. Maxwell, printer, 1814)—the journals of America's most famous Western explorers, who were to investigate possible U.S. participation in the fur trade. Among many other things, Meriwether Lewis and William Clark described features of the economies of the Native Americans of the Great Plains, Rocky Mountains, and Pacific Northwest;

Sir Richard Burton, *The City of the Saints and Across the Rocky Mountains to California* (London: Longman, Green, Longman & Roberts, 1861; New York: Harper, 1862)—this less than flattering portrait of the Far West in 1860 describes the bison, Native

Americans, landscapes, and trading posts Burton encountered between St. Joseph, Missouri, and Sacramento, California;

Mirriam Davis Colt, *Went to Kansas* (Watertown, N.Y.: Ingalls, 1862)—a published diary of a woman and her family from upstate New York who decided to homestead in southeastern Kansas in 1856. It describes the many difficulties facing early Kansas pioneers, including obtaining food and being unable to work because of malaria. It is an account of a family that failed to succeed in the West;

Josiah Gregg, *Commerce of the Prairies: or, The Journal of a Santa Fe Trader* (New York: H. G. Langley, 1844)—a description of the Santa Fe trade between Missouri and New Mexico. Gregg's popular work reports on the people, geography, plants, and animals of the Southwest and the Plains in the 1830s and 1840s;

James Ohio Pattie, *The Personal Narrative of James Ohio Pattie* (Cincinnati: John H. Wood, 1831)—an exciting, if not always accurate, tale of a trapper's six-year adventure in what was then Mexico's northern frontier. Pattie describes the difficulties faced by an American interloper in a region owned and controlled by Mexico and occupied by various native groups.

Gold miners, circa 1850 (Amon Carter Museum, Fort Worth, Texas)

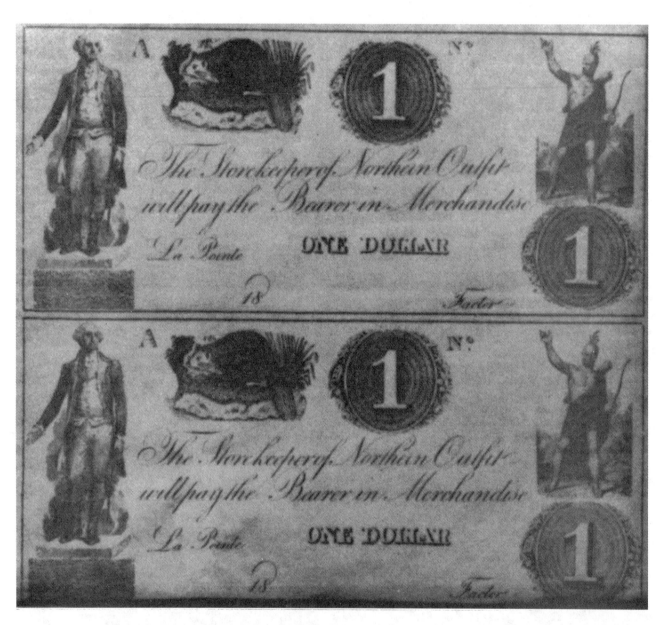

Paper currency meant for circulation among American Fur Company employees and their dependents in La Pointe, Wisconsin, circa 1840 (Minnesota Historical Society, St. Paul)

COMMUNICATIONS

by JOHN M. COWARD

CONTENTS

Sidebars and tables are listed in italics.

1800

- The secret treaty of San Ildefonso transfers control of the vast tract of North America known as Louisiana from Spain to France, a move that opens the way for its purchase by the United States.

1801

- The westernmost post office in the nation opens in Natchez, Mississippi.

1803

Jan. — *Medley, or Monthly Miscellany* publishes its first twenty-page issue in Lexington, Kentucky. It is the first general magazine west of Pittsburgh, and Lexington soon becomes home to several other Western periodicals.

1806

5 Nov. — News of Meriwether Lewis and William Clark's return to St. Louis from the Pacific is published in Boston's *Columbian Centinel*, more than six weeks after the actual event. The news travels through the mail from St. Louis to Baltimore and then to Boston.

1808

- The first newspaper published west of the Mississippi, *The Missouri Gazette*, begins operation in St. Louis.

1811

- *Niles' Weekly Register*, a magazine based in Baltimore and Washington that came to have nationwide circulation, is founded.

1815

- American troops under the command of Andrew Jackson repulse a British attack on New Orleans. Still in the pretelegraph era, however, both sides are unaware that the Treaty of Ghent, signed two weeks earlier, had ended the war.

1817

- The American Tract Society begins to circulate religious material on the frontier, promoting reading and educaiton in the West.

1819

Aug. — William Gibbes Hunt, a scholarly New Englander living in Lexington, Kentucky, issues the first volume of a new monthly, *Western Review and Miscellaneous Magazine*. The magazine publishes scientific articles, poetry, literary reviews, and political essays, reflecting the interests of its contributors, several of whom were professors at Lexington's Transylvania University, a leading school in the region.

1821
- *Western Review* suspends publication.

1823
- Photography pioneer Matthew Brady is born in Warren County, New York.

1825

26 Oct.
The Erie Canal officially opens and stretches for more than 350 miles between Lake Erie and the Hudson River at Albany, New York. The canal connects the Great Lakes and the Atlantic Ocean via the Hudson River.

1926
- Henry Rowe Schoolcraft begins publication of *The Muzzinyegun or Literary Voyager* in Sault St. Marie, Michigan, a weekly magazine devoted to Native American issues, Western topics, and poetry. Schoolcraft writes many of the entries himself, using information from Ojibwa sources, including his Native American wife, Jane, and her family.

1827

16 Mar.
Freedom's Journal, the first African American newspaper, is established in New York by John B. Russwurm (the first African American to graduate from a college in the United States) and the Reverend Samuel Cornish. The antislavery paper is founded in response to an attack on black leaders by the *New York Enquirer.* "We wish to plead our own cause," the editors of *Freedom's Journal* declare. "Too long have others spoken for us."

1828
- *The Cherokee Phoenix* begins publication in New Echota, Georgia. Editor Elias Boudinot prints the paper in English and Cherokee, using Sequoyah's eighty-six-symbol syllabary.

1829
- *Freedom's Journal* ceases publication.

1830

July
A new magazine for women, *Godey's Lady's Book,* appears. Publisher Louis A. Godey of Philadelphia increases the magazine's circulation to an impressive twenty-five thousand after nine years by printing sentimental, uplifting stories and verse, material thought suitable for "fair Ladies."

1831

1 Jan. William Lloyd Garrison begins publication of *The Liberator* in Boston. The newspaper soon becomes one of the most important weapons in the arsenal of abolitionists who aim to use "God's truth" to expose the evils of slavery in the United States.

1832

- After living and writing in Europe for years, Washington Irving joins a government expedition to the American West. Irving travels as far as present-day Norman, Oklahoma, before turning back.

1835

- Irving publishes *A Tour on the Prairies*.
- The first weekly newspaper, *El Crepusculo* (The Dawn), is published in Taos, a city once part of Spain's American territory. Only four issues are published.

Mar. Baptist missionaries in Shawnee Mission, Kansas, begin publication of *Siwinowe Kesibwi* (or *Shawnee Sun*), the first periodical published entirely in a Native American language. The newspaper uses a Shawnee orthography developed by the missionary and printer Jotham Meeker.

1837

- Sarah J. Hale becomes literary editor of *Godey's Lady's Book*. Hale improves the quality of the writing in the magazine and promotes the training of women as teachers, seminarians, and doctors.
- George Wilkins Kendall establishes the *New Orleans Picayune*. The *Picayune* is the city's first "penny paper," which helps the new paper thrive. Kendall goes on to become a leading supporter of Texas independence and a war reporter during the Mexican War.

1838

Oct. The Committee of the Oregon Provisional Emigration Society begins publication of *The Oregonian, and Indian's Advocate* in Lynn, Massachusetts. The editors intend for their publication to educate and assist Native Americans as their lands are settled by whites, but the magazine ceases publication the next year.

1839

- *Siwinowe Kesibwi* ceases publication.

1841

- *Siwinowe Kesibwi* resumes publication.
- The *New York Weekly Tribune* is founded by Horace Greeley and continues its pressrun until 1901.

1844

- Matthew Brady begins making daguerreotypes in New York City. Brady goes on to become one of the most important photographers of his day, documenting Civil War battlefields. Engravings based on his photographs become a regular feature of *Harper's Weekly,* an important nineteenth-century illustrated newspaper.

- Samuel F. B. Morse, painter and inventor, sends the first telegraph message on a line between Washington and Baltimore, launching a communication revolution.

- *The Cherokee Advocate,* a weekly newspaper published in English and Cherokee, begins operation in Tahlequah, Indian Territory. Editor William Potter Ross, a graduate of the College of New Jersey (now Princeton University), uses the paper to advance the intellectual and moral life of the Cherokees and to spread accurate information about the tribe to American readers.

1845

- The phrase *manifest destiny* is printed for the first time in the popular press. Commenting on the annexation of Texas, John Louis O'Sullivan, editor of the *United States Magazine and Democratic Review,* notes that the annexation defeated the European powers who had operated with the "avowed object of thwarting our policy and hampering our power, limiting our greatness and checking the fulfillment of our manifest destiny to overspread the continent allotted by Providence for the free development of our yearly multiplying millions."

- *The Californian* begins publication in Monterey, the first newspaper in California.

- Several popular Western guidebooks begin to appear, including *The Emigrants Guide to Oregon and California* by Lansford Warren Hastings.

3 June Cassius M. Clay establishes *The True American* in Lexington, Kentucky, a newspaper dedicated to the cause of abolishing slavery in the United States. Clay is attacked from the start, and he moves the paper to Louisville as the *Examiner,* where it ceases publication the next year.

1846

- Overton Johnson and William H. Winter publish *Route across the Rocky Mountains, with a Description of Oregon and California.*

1847

- The *Chicago Tribune* is founded.

- Frederick Douglass, the most famous former slave in antebellum America, begins *The North Star,* an antislavery newspaper in Rochester, New York. The first issue declares "Right is of no Sex—Truth is of no Color—God is the Father of us all, and we are all Brethren." However, Douglass's enemies disagree, burning his house and destroying his papers.

1848

- The *New York Herald* reports the discovery of gold at Sutter's Mill in California, helping promote "gold fever" around the nation.

May   David Hale of the *New York Journal of Commerce* calls a meeting of New York's most important publishers. His purpose is to form a cooperative news-gathering effort, saving each of the six newspapers represented the cost of expensive telegraphic news. The meeting leads to the organization of the New York Associated Press, which soon hires Alexander Jones, a physician-turned-reporter, as its first general agent. Eventually several regional news-gathering cooperatives are organized, including the Western Associated Press.

1850

- The Church of Jesus Christ of Latter-Day Saints (Mormons) begins Utah's first newspaper, *The Deseret News,* in Salt Lake City.

1851

- Frederick Douglass renames his paper *Frederick Douglass' Paper* and continues to publish it until 1860.

- The phrase, "Go West, Young Man. Go West!," originally written by editor John Soule of the *Terre Haute Express,* is popularized by *New York Tribune* editor Horace Greeley, one of the most enthusiastic promoters of Western expansion in the nineteenth century.

1852

- The *Columbian* newspaper is founded in Olympia, Washington.

1854

- The *Kansas Weekly Herald,* the first newspaper in Kansas, begins publication under an elm tree on the townsite of Leavenworth, before any buildings are erected. The paper continues under two other names until 1861.

3 Aug.   A ninety-page novel, *The Life and Adventures of Joaquin Murieta, the Celebrated California Bandit,* is published in San Francisco. The author is John Rollin Ridge, a Cherokee Indian from Arkansas who came West during the Gold Rush. Finding little gold, Ridge became a California journalist and one of the first Native American novelists.

1855

- *Frank Leslie's Illustrated Newspaper* begins publication in New York City. *Leslie's* and *Harper's Weekly* are pioneers of visual communication, turning artists' sketches and photographs into impressive and popular wood engravings. Both papers send artists west to document American expansion.

- Joseph Medill and Charles Ray purchase the *Chicago Tribune* and transform it into one of the most important newspapers in the United States.

1857

- Congress authorizes the postmaster general to secure bids for an overland stage service to carry mail and passengers from Missouri to San Francisco. The Brigham Young Carrying and Express Company, known as the XY Company, wins the contract. The first mail delivery from Independence, Missouri, to Salt Lake City takes twenty-six days. The federal government cancels the contract after only six months.

- A rail line between St. Louis and New York City is completed, inspiring dreams of a transcontinental railroad.

1858

17 Aug. England and America are connected for the first time by the Atlantic telegraph cable; it breaks within a few weeks.

1859

- William N. Byers launches *The Rocky Mountain News*, a modest newspaper that he uses to boost the fortunes of Denver.

- Horace Greeley begins a trip across the country, sending dispatches about his journey to the *New York Tribune*. Greeley attests to the rich land and resources in the West and scouts the best route for the transcontinental railroad. He is less impressed with the Indians he encounters along the way, calling them children.

Mar. Arizona's first newspaper, the *Weekly Arizonian*, is printed in Tumac. The paper's press was shipped around Cape Horn to California and then by wagon to the town.

1860

- *Godey's Lady's Book* reaches a national circulation of 150,000.

- Bret Hart, writer for the Union (now Arcata), California, *Northern Californian*, is forced to resign from the paper by angry citizens after writing an editorial criticizing white citizens for killing Native Americans.

- Publisher Irwin Beadle begins his series of dime novels with *Maleska: The Indian Wife of the White Hunter*, written by Ann Sophia Stevens.

Feb. *Frank Leslie's Illustrated Newspaper* claims a circulation of 164,000; that of *Harper's Weekly* is about 100,000.

3 Apr. A Pony Express rider heads west out of St. Joseph, Missouri, with forty-nine letters and a special newspaper edition in his saddlebag. Ten days later the last in a two-thousand-mile line of riders reaches Sacramento, California, where a boat takes the mail, rider, and horse on to San Francisco. The Pony Express captures the nation's imagination, but it is doomed from the start. The service closes on 26 October 1861, two days after Western Union opened its transcontinental telegraph line.

OVERVIEW

Facing West. The early national period was marked by a fascination with the West. Thomas Jefferson said in his first inaugural address in 1801 that Americans possess a "chosen country, with room enough for our descendants to the hundredth and thousandth generation." In pursuit of that vision, Jefferson created the Corps of Discovery, Meriwether Lewis and William Clark's amazing expedition up the Missouri River across the Rocky Mountains to the Pacific Ocean. This journey set the tone for the nationalist expansion of the first half of the century, offering white Americans the promise of new lands, vast wealth, and great opportunity for those brave and strong enough to move west and open up the territory. Walt Whitman, a former newspaperman and the first truly American poet, also saw hope and progress in the West. In one of his "songs" from *Leaves of Grass* (1855), Whitman imagined the satisfaction of the open range, a masculine vision of adventure and oneness with the land:

> Alone far in the wilds and mountains I hunt,
> Wandering amazed at my own lightness and glee,
> In the late afternoon choosing a safe spot to pass night,
> Kindling a fire and broiling the fresh killed game,
> Soundly falling asleep on the gathered leaves, my dog
> and gun by my side.

Romantic Visions. This romantic vision of the West imagined a place where Americans could live out their dreams, finding not paradise, perhaps, but fertile land and open spaces in which they could build a magnificent, new American civilization. The nature of this civilization—and its effects—was made clear in some of the nationalist paintings of the era. One such painting was *The Old House of Representatives*, completed in 1822 by Samuel F. B. Morse, the man who would later invent the telegraph. In Morse's painting, candles are being lit while Congress is assembling for an evening session. But the painting also includes an Indian named Petalasharoo peeking from the balcony, a reminder of the nation's Western gaze. "That very evening perhaps Congress will decide *his* destiny, and that of his people, as the nation turns to the West," the historian William Goetzmann wrote about this scene. By the 1840s the romantic idyll of Western expansion had given way to a harder, more

practical vision. A painting by John Gast, widely reproduced as a lithograph, was called *Westward Ho*. Gast showed Indians, buffalo, and bears fleeing progress, embodied by several hearty pioneers tramping west with tools and a plow. They were followed by a wagon, a stage, and two trains. Overhead was the white-robed Goddess of Liberty, flying west, with a book of laws in her arms, stringing the telegraph wire as she sailed along. Here were the elements of American progress in the early nineteenth century: the "sacred plow" of the farmer, the wood and steel of a transportation revolution, and the wires that would someday link Atlantic to Pacific, uniting America and making Manifest Destiny a reality.

Promoting Progress. American journalists were no exception to this movement. Indeed, many editors were leading proponents of expansion, using their papers to promote economic growth and advocate the conquest of western lands. Journalists promoted the West in at least two ways. First, explorers, newspapers, and travel writers advanced the ideology of Western expansion. From Horace Greeley of the *New York Tribune* to George Kendall of the *New Orleans Picayune* and William Byers of the *Rocky Mountain News*, American editors and their readers embraced the idea that the United States was entitled to a vast empire that would stretch from the Atlantic to the Pacific. Second, newspapers themselves spread rapidly in the new territories, each village and town providing a place for the local editor to promote. In Denver, for example, editor Byers started with few readers and even fewer advertisers. But every new strike in the mining districts—as well as agricultural and business successes—gave Byers more to crow about in the *Rocky Mountain News*. Denver grew and the publisher prospered, a pattern repeated throughout the West. The result of this journalistic drumbeat was a sustained ideology of growth and progress, constantly renewed by the dreams of new editors in new towns. Although there were some important exceptions, most antebellum editors were true believers in the gospel of expansionism.

"Uncle Horace" and the West. Horace Greeley was a native New Englander who lived most of his adult life in New York. As editor of the popular *New York Tribune* and an outspoken advocate of Western expansion, however, Greeley's influence on Western immigration was considerable. For one thing, "Uncle Horace" became a familiar figure around the nation, widely read by farmers and small-town folk in the *Tribune* weekly, semiweekly, and Pacific Coast editions. In the 1850s the *Tribune* weekly circulation grew steadily; by 1860 the pressrun topped three hundred thousand, and his readership was estimated at one million weekly. Greeley attracted readers by crusading. He spoke out boldly on many issues, including the spread of slavery into the Western territories, which he opposed. Greeley was also a tireless supporter of the Homestead Act, legislation he believed would give poor Eastern laborers an escape from the miseries of the city by allowing them to become landowners in the West. He is best known, however, for his advice to "Go West, Young Man. Go West!"—a slogan he did not coin. "Everyone knew the words were Greeley's," his biographer wrote, "although no one could remember just when he had first uttered them." The truth, biographer William Hale concluded, was that Greeley had given some form of this advice to hundreds of people over the years. In 1854, for example, Greeley received a letter from a young man named William H. Verity, who told Greeley that he was in love but had just learned that he was ill with consumption (tuberculosis). What should he do about the woman? Greeley answered: Marry her and go west. Verity did, settling in Illinois and living until 1930, when he died at the age of ninety-seven.

Greeley Goes West. Uncle Horace himself went west only once, in 1859, to see the country he had long imagined and to promote the transcontinental railroad. He used the trip to write letters to the *Tribune*, reporting firsthand on the tribulations of stagecoach travel and the natural wonders of the West. He wrote enthusiastically about the fertile land in Kansas and Colorado as well as the gold he saw in Central City. Greeley was less impressed by the Indians he encountered. Traveling across Kansas, Greeley saw Indians sitting when, in his opinion, they should have been farming. If the West was to be settled and improved, Greeley was certain, it would take ingenuity and hard work. To Greeley, son of a failed New England farmer, there was no excuse for the Indians' idleness. Indians, he decided, were simple but dangerous children, sorely in need of a work ethic and a progressive spirit. Greeley described Indian "braves" as unredeemable creatures. "Squalid and conceited, proud and worthless, lazy and lousy, they will strut out or drink out their miserable existence, and at length afford the world a sensible relief by dying out of it." If Indians could be saved, Greeley concluded, it would be up to Indian women who, unlike native men, were willing to work. They could be taught simple household, farming, and manufacturing skills, improving the condition of their people. Greeley's critique of Indians was harsh and paternalistic, but it reveals the contours of his expansionist ideology. Much of the West was productive country, Greeley concluded, ready for hard-working men and women to till and improve. For Indians, people in his view too lazy and dull to join the march of progress, there was little hope. Depressed by Indians, Greeley was cheered by the beauty and opportunity of California, and he traveled throughout the region examining its resources and peoples. He wrote glowing reports and sent the story East, first by Pony Express, then telegraph, to an anxious public. Greeley had taken his own advice, and he made sure that his readers knew that he had been right about the West all along.

TOPICS IN THE NEWS

A COMMUNICATIONS REVOLUTION

Transportation Revolution. American expansion was more than just talk. Locally and nationally, workers were busy building a transportation and communication infrastructure necessary to fulfill the transcontinental dream. The number of post offices, for example, grew from 903 in 1800 to 28,498 in 1860. The mileage of post roads needed to reach the new offices also expanded rapidly, from 20,817 miles in 1800 to 240,594 miles in 1860. The growth of the postal system facilitated expansion. Western immigrants used the mails to spread the word about their fortunes out West and to maintain links with their old lives in the East. In time, railroads made the expansion quicker and more convenient. Railroad mileage, a sign of the nation's growing industrial strength, grew from a mere twenty-three miles in 1830 to 30,626 miles in 1860. All of these developments helped Americans achieve the nationalist dream, linking together an increasingly scattered population across a growing number of towns, territories, and states.

Frederic Remington's 1900 painting *Coming and Going of the Pony Express* (Thomas Gilcrease Institute of American History and Art, Tulsa, Oklahoma)

Electric Communication. The first report on the telegraphic transmission of news appeared in the *Baltimore Sun* on 27 May 1844. "Some further experiments were conducted on the new telegraph on Saturday morning...," the paper reported. "Several messages were sent to and from [Washington] with almost incredible despatch, which, although unimportant in themselves, were most interesting from the novelty of the proceeding, forcing upon the mind the reality of complete annihilation of space. ...." The reporter for the *Baltimore Sun* got it right. The telegraph had indeed "annihilated" space, for the first time allowing news to be instantly and efficiently delivered wherever telegraph lines could be

strung. In a matter of months, in fact, a line was completed between Albany and Utica, New York, allowing the *Utica Daily Gazette* to run regular news bulletins from the state capitol. The Albany line was soon extended west, and by September 1846 the line was completed between New York City and Buffalo. New York State—and eventually the entire country—was now wired together in ways never before possible.

The Telegraph. From Samuel F. B. Morse's one experimental telegraph line in 1844, telegraph wires stretched across 16,735 miles by 1852. By 1860 the telegraph spanned 50,000 miles. The telegraph was, in a word, revolutionary. Using the power of electricity and the artificial alphabet known as Morse Code, the telegraph allowed—for the first time in human history—reliable and efficient transmission of messages faster than human locomotion. The telegraph broke the link between transportation and communication, putting a premium on speed and opening the way for the eventual centralization of communication. It emphasized the need for timely news and information, creating more competition among newspapers. The telegraph also created a new profession, the telegraphic reporter. These men made it their business to collect and send information to client newspapers, an arrangement that helped the papers get more news cheaper. Cooperative news-gathering was not new in the 1840s, but the new technology facilitated the cooperation between rival newspapers. After all, the telegraph was a capital-intensive system. Acquiring rights-of-way, stringing wires, and establishing a national system of telegraphic offices was not a task individual newspapers could manage. The

---

PONIES DELIVER THE MAIL

The Pony Express was a heroic undertaking, but the coming of the telegraph secured its fate. The young riders were fast, but electricity was instantaneous, and the express mail service closed two days after the transcontinental telegraph line began operations in October 1861. The following advertisement appeared in the 26 March 1860 issue of the *St. Louis Republic:*

To San Francisco in 8 days by the Central Overland California and Pike's Peak Express Company. The first courier of the Pony Express will leave the Missouri River on Tuesday April 3rd at 5 o'clock P.M. and will run regularly weekly thereafter, carrying a letter mail only. The point of departure ... will be in telegraphic connection with the East and will be announced in due time.

Thomas P. Rossiter's painting *Opening of the Wilderness,* circa 1846–1850 (M. and M. Karolik Collection, Museum of Fine Arts, Boston)

papers could cooperate for their mutual benefit, which is just what happened in New York in 1848, just four years after Morse's original experiment. The telegraph also fostered the growth of small-town dailies because these papers could now use the telegraph to overcome the handicap of distance. Thanks to Morse, they too could publish news from the important political and business centers of the nation.

Uneven Growth. The most important quality of the telegraph was its speed. Electricity reduced vast distances to insignificance, a change that had both psychological and physical consequences. On the psychological level the "annihilation of space" led to a change in national consciousness, allowing—in theory, at least—all Americans to hear the same news at about the same time. After the telegraph Americans spread across a vast landscape could respond quickly and simultaneously to national events. The wiring of the nation had more obvious consequences as well. The telegraph spread quickly, but it was not evenly distributed. Most of the early growth was in the East, of course, where cities were fairly close together and the need for instantaneous communication was greater. This left the vast spaces of the West unwired and isolated for a time from Morse's electric revolution.

Pony Express. In the 1850s mail to California traveled by boat and stage, a journey that could take nearly three weeks. Western Union, the telegraph company, was slowly but surely extending its lines, holding out the promise of a coast-to-coast telegraphic link. In the meantime the freighting firm of Russell, Majors, and Waddell organized and backed an express mail service, the Pony Express. This venture called on a cadre of young riders to change horses every ten or fifteen miles at

the 190 stations the service established. After about seventy-five miles a new rider took over. The route extended from St. Joseph, Missouri, the westernmost extension of any railroad line from the East, along the Platte River in Nebraska to Fort Bridger in present-day Wyoming, then south to Salt Lake City. Riders traveled south from Salt Lake across the desert to the Sierra Ne-

TRANSATLANTIC CABLE

The completion of the first transatlantic cable brought jubilant headlines in the United States, as published on the first page of *The New York Times* on 17 August 1858:

THE OCEAN TELEGRAPH.

VICTORY AT LAST!

THE FIRST MESSAGE.

ENGLAND GREETS AMERICA.

QUEEN VICTORIA TO PRESIDENT BUCHANAN.

THE PRESIDENT'S REPLY.

TRIUMPHANT COMPLETION OF THE GREAT WORK OF THE CENTURY.

THE OLD WORLD AND THE NEW UNITED.

GLORIA IN EXCELSIS!

he connection failed within a few weeks, and a permanent cable was not completed until 1866.

Richard Caton Woodville's 1848 oil painting *War News from Mexico* (National Academy of Design, New York)

The Press and the Public Good. The role of the newspapers in a democratic society was an important issue in the antebellum era, when the American experiment was new and the institutions of popular democracy were not yet fully formed. The press was one of these institutions, a private undertaking that had public responsibilities. How would the press use its power? Would it help or hinder the growth of democracy? No less than Alexis de Tocqueville, the French observer of early-nineteenth-century America, realized that newspapers did more than simply report the news. In Tocqueville's analysis the press was an effective instrument of democracy, providing individual citizens with a way to organize and make their voices heard. Thus newspapers, along with the voluntary associations Americans seemed so fond of organizing, worked together to address social problems and create a more responsive government. This was especially true in an expanding nation organized around local governments; a steady stream of newly organized towns, cities, and counties were both a challenge and an opportunity for enterprising journalists.

Tocqueville's View of the Press. Tocqueville was amazed at the zeal with which Americans organized themselves into voluntary, nongovernmental associations. "In the United States," he wrote, "associations are established to promote the public safety, commerce, industry, morality, and religion. There is no end which the human will despairs of attaining through the combined power of individuals united in a society. . . ." In a society without an aristocracy and where individual equality was the ideal, newspapers allowed private citizens to come

vada to Sacramento. Many of the two hundred riders employed by the Pony Express were teenagers, and the company gave them Bibles and made them promise not to drink or swear. The first run of the Pony Express in April 1860 proved successful, reaching California in only ten days. The service operated weekly at first, then twice weekly. In November 1860 the riders carried a telegraph report of Abraham Lincoln's election from Fort Kearny, Nebraska, to Fort Churchill, Nevada, in six days, their fastest ride yet. Fort Churchill was now linked by telegraph to San Francisco, a fact that foreshadowed the end of the Pony Express. By 1861, with tensions over Southern secession rising in the East, federal officials were more anxious than ever to have California connected to the rest of the nation. Just weeks after the Pony Express began, in fact, Congress had authorized a $40,000 annual subsidy to speed the completion of the telegraph line. Competing crews working east from Fort Churchill and west from Omaha completed its transcontinental line on 24 October 1861. The Pony Express closed two days later, a romantic venture that could not compete with the new technology. Russell, Majors, and Waddell lost more than $100,000 on the enterprise.

Sources:

Alfred M. Lee, *The Daily Newspaper in America* (New York: Macmillan, 1937);

Raymond W. Settle and Mary Lund Settle, *Saddles and Spurs: The Pony Express Saga* (Harrisburg, Pa.: The Stackpole Company, 1955).

NEW YORK TRIBUNE, 18 FEBRUARY 1854

Horace Greeley, popular editor of the *New York Tribune,* was a leading supporter of the Homestead Act (1862), which Greeley believed would offer land and hope for the urban poor:

Make the Public Lands free in quarter-sections to Actual Settlers and deny them to all others, and earth's landless millions will no longer be orphans and mendicants; they can work for the wealthy, relieved from the degrading terror of being turned adrift to starve. When employment fails or wages are inadequate, they may pack up and strike westward to enter upon the possession and culture of their own lands on the banks of the Wisconsin, the Des Moines, or the Platte, which have been patiently awaiting their advent since creation. Strikes to stand still will be glaringly absurd when every citizen is offered the alternative to work for others or for himself, as to him shall seem most advantageous. The mechanic or labor who works for another will do so only because he can thus secure a more liberal and satisfactory recompense than he could by working for himself.

The first page of the inaugural issue of William Lloyd Garrison's antislavery newspaper

together for the public good. "Newspapers make associations and associations make newspapers," Tocqueville wrote, recognizing the partisan and varied nature of the antebellum press. "A newspaper therefore always represents an association whose members are its regular readers. This association may be more or less strictly defined, more or less closed, more or less numerous, but there must at least be the seed of it in men's minds, or otherwise the paper would not survive," he wrote. In a new country, in an expanding nation, Tocqueville concluded, democracy needed newspapers: "We should underrate their importance if we thought they just guaranteed liberty; they maintain civilization."

Principles versus Profits. Tocqueville's view of the press was too idealistic. Newspapers did allow people to organize and act together to build an effective local democracy, but not all editors were as interested in democracy as Tocqueville; some were quite a bit more practical and self-serving, using their papers to boost their communities and enrich themselves even as they justified their profits in the name of high ideals. In short, antebellum journalism attracted both idealists and capitalists though these categories were often intermingled in the journalistic philosophy of individual editors. One such contradictory figure was James Gordon Bennett, the ambitious and controversial founder of the *New York Herald*. Bennett brought a new editorial energy to New York journalism in the 1830s, a drive for news that influenced many an enterprising editor. Bennett was outlandish and often crude—qualities that made the *New York Herald* sensational and enormously popular with readers—but his journalistic vision was lofty. "My ambition is to make the newspaper Press the great organ and pivot of government, society, commerce, finance, religion, and all human civilization." Following that philosophy, Bennett was an apostle of a greater America, using his editorial voice to push for Western expansion and the subjugation of Indians, Mexicans, and others who threatened the dominance of the United States in North America. For Bennett and many other nineteenth-century editors and readers, there was no contradiction between imperialism and democratic idealism. To these Americans, Western expansion meant the extension of liberty across the continent, the spread of Enlightenment values and progressive ideas to more primitive and less fortunate peoples. In this nation-building process American journalists believed they were serving the greater good by proclaiming the virtues of civilization and justifying the dispossession of those people and forces who stood in the path of progress. And if such positions attracted readers and helped the *New York Herald* prosper, so much the better. Bennett, far more than Tocqueville, made clear that journalism best served those people already committed to the dominant ideas of early-nineteenth-century America.

The Liberator. If Bennett was more interested in profit than principles, William Lloyd Garrison represented the other end of the journalistic spectrum. Garrison was a man with a mission—the abolition of slavery—and journalism was his weapon of choice. Garrison founded *The Liberator* in 1831, using the first issue to thank God for the ability "to speak his truth in its simplicity and power." Like Tocqueville, Garrison was idealistic about the role of journalism, believing that through discussion and debate the truth would conquer error, and slavery would fall. To this end Garrison opened the pages of *The Liberator* to his opponents, confident that God's ideas would triumph over falsity. For Garrison, then, the purpose of journalism extended well beyond the pursuit of profits and a superficial commitment to democratic ideals. Garrison believed that the public exchange of ideas was the essence of journalism. *The Liberator*, in fact, was at the center of an ongoing conversation among readers about abolition and slavery, including ideas Garrison himself found abominable. Yet Garrison never lost faith, publishing *The Liberator* for thirty-five years, long enough to see the end of slavery. In the end Garrison's career fulfilled Tocqueville's vision of democratic journalism. The core audience of *The Liberator* formed a loose association of like-minded individuals, people intent on ridding America of its most evil institution. In this noble calling, God's truth was the editor's goal, and it could be reached, Garrison believed, through free inquiry. Yet in the first half of the nineteenth century most journalists followed Bennett's path, not Garrison's. Perhaps the fact that they did so is not so surprising. After all, American newspapers operated in a free-market economy. They were businesses first, crusaders second. Moral crusades in newspapers, if they came at all, came when editors could please readers or turn a profit. In an industrializing market economy where growth and expansion were hallmarks of the age, even Garrison and other crusading editors could not eliminate widespread prejudice and discrimination.

Source:
David Paul Nord, "Tocqueville, Garrison and the Perfection of Journalism," *Journalism History,* 13 (Summer 1986): 56–63.

MAGAZINES MOVE WEST

The Kentucky Experience. Magazine publishing in America began in the East, especially in cities such as Philadelphia, Boston, and New York, where educational institutions and communities of scholars, journalists, and readers could support both general and specialized periodicals. As Americans moved west, building towns and cities, establishing schools and churches, they began to reproduce in the West some of the culture of the East. Once presses, paper, and type were available in the West, a variety of periodicals sprang up. One of the first was *Medley, or Monthly Miscellany,* a twenty-page monthly that lasted throughout 1803 in Lexington, Kentucky. In fact, Lexington became an early publishing center in the West, largely because of Transylvania University, a school that attracted several scholarly writers to its faculty. Another important Lexington-based magazine was the *Western Review and Miscellaneous Magazine,* a monthly started in 1819 by a New Englander named William Gibbes Hunt. Hunt called on Horace Holley, president of Transylvania, to write articles for the magazine. Another professor, Constantine S. Rafinesque, wrote articles on Kentucky botany and the fishes of the Ohio River. Hunt also published poetry, book reviews, political articles, and a series of stories about conflicts between whites and Indians. The *Western Review* ceased publication in June 1821 after several of its contributors died. Hunt launched another magazine almost immediately, the *Masonic Miscellany and Ladies' Literary Magazine,* which lasted until 1823.

Cincinnati's *Western Monthly Review.* Cincinnati was another early center of Western intellectual and publishing activity. By 1825 Ohio was home to various schools and colleges, two paper mills, a type foundry, and Cincinnati's own extensive printing industry. One of the city's most significant periodicals was the *Western Monthly Review,* founded in 1827. Its first issue reviewed the growth of intellectual and cultural life in the Ohio and Mississippi River valleys. Editor Timothy Flint, a Harvard-educated Congregational minister, praised Lexington, Memphis, Natchez, and New Orleans for "their distinguished literary circles." Flint was convinced that Western scholars were in every way equal to their Eastern kin. "In fact," Flint wrote, "there is nothing deep in science, or polished in literature, or pretending in learning, or long-winded in oratory, or full even to bursting in the inspiration of the muse, in the Atlantic country, which may not be found in the West." The *Western Monthly* published satire, criticism, translations of French and Spanish poetry, religious articles, and fiction. Flint was an energetic writer, supplying much of the content himself. Flint's praise of Western writers continued throughout the life of the magazine, prompting the *New York Evening Chronicle* to label him "the donkey of Cincinnati." The magazine attained a circulation of one thousand readers early in its existence but foundered because of delinquent subscribers. The last issue appeared in June 1830.

Source:

Frank Luther Mott, *A History of American Magazines, 1741–1850* (Cambridge, Mass.: Harvard University Press, 1939).

NATIVE AMERICAN JOURNALISM

Elias Boudinot's Vision. The power of the press to rally public support and advance a cause was used by a variety of Americans, not least by Native Americans and the Christian missionaries who sought to educate and convert them. Beginning in 1826 with Henry Rowe Schoolcraft's *The Muzzinyegun or Literary Voyager* in Sault Ste. Marie, Michigan, Native American media ranged from tribal and independent newspapers to religious and literary publications, most of which sought to civilize and educate Indian peoples. One of the most famous Native American papers was the *Cherokee Phoenix,*

The Cherokee syllabary devised by Sequoyah

founded in 1828 in response to Georgia's efforts to take control of tribal lands. The Cherokees, whose numbers included several educated and highly assimilated leaders, used the *Cherokee Phoenix* to publicize the state's actions and build sympathy for their cause in the East. The *Cherokee Phoenix* was also used as a means to educate the tribe about both Indian and non-Indian issues. In a prospectus for the paper published in 1827, editor Elias Boudinot listed four types of information he wanted to emphasize:

(1) The laws and public documents of the Nation.

(2) Account of the manners and customs of the Cherokees, and their progress in Education, Religion and the arts of civilized life; with such notices of other Indian tribes as our limited means of information will allow.

(3) The principal interesting news of the day.

(4) Miscellaneous articles, calculated to promote Literature, civilization, and Religion among the Cherokees.

The *Cherokee Phoenix.* The newspaper's content bore out this mission. The first issues of the *Cherokee Phoenix* published the tribal constitution in English and, using Sequoyah's syllabary, in Cherokee. Other editorial de-

An 1845 letter written in Cherokee by Oo-no-leh announcing the death of Sequoyah. It reads in part: "I met with Standing Rock who attended Sequoya during his last sickness and also witnessed his death and burial. Tsu-sa-le-tah, the son of Sequoya, remains on Red River. He is very sorry that the remains of his Father are buried so far from his own country. . . . As Sequoya was the object for which I had started in search and having learned the fact of his death, which I communicate to those who sent me, it will be useless for me to proceed any further. I will return toward home. He is dead without a doubt. . . ." (National Archives, Washington, D.C.)

partments included a letters section, news summaries of local, national, and international events, a poetry section, and religious stories. The paper also published educational material, including excerpts from William Hazlitt's *Life of Napoleon* (1828–1830). The paper ran regular moralistic articles that preached character development, temperance, and the like. However, the paper was always short of funds, and tribal infighting and increasing pressure from white Georgians caused the paper to fail in 1834.

The *Cherokee Advocate*. When the Cherokees were forced out of the South in 1838–1839 on the infamous Trail of Tears, Cherokee journalism moved west. The American Board of Foreign Missions, long active in Indian issues, helped the tribe secure a new press, type, and equipment in Boston, and in 1844 the Cherokees estab-

San Francisco Harbor in 1851 (California State Library, Sacramento)

lished the *Cherokee Advocate* in Tahlequah, capital of the Cherokee Nation, Indian Territory (now Oklahoma). Like the *Cherokee Phoenix*, the *Cherokee Advocate* was designed to educate and inspire Cherokee readers. Its editors aimed to provide accurate information about the Cherokees and other Indians for its white friends and allies, a way of combating the anti-Indian publicity of the mainstream press. The first editor of the *Cherokee Advocate* was William Potter Ross, a graduate of the College of New Jersey (now Princeton) and nephew of principal chief John Ross. The paper was a four-page weekly, and Ross filled its columns with general Indian news, laws and legal news, agents' reports, fiction, inspirational articles, and more. Most news was in English though the paper usually published three columns in Cherokee. The *Cherokee Advocate* published regularly through 1853, when financial problems caused its suspension until 1870.

Missionary Press. Early-nineteenth-century Christian missionaries recognized that print could be a useful way to spread their message among Indian people. The first such publication was a monthly newspaper established by the Baptists in Shawnee Mission, Kansas, in 1835. *Siwinowe Kesibwi* (or *Shawnee Sun*) was also the first periodical published entirely in a native language, using a Shawnee orthography developed by printer and missionary Jotham Meeker. Little is known about the contents of the paper, but apparently it was a four-page publication with articles by missionaries and several

Shawnee contributors. Though the paper ceased publication in 1844, other editors followed in its footsteps. In Lynn, Massachusetts, in 1838 one missionary group founded a paper called *The Oregonian, and Indian's Advocate*. The monthly was published by the Committee of the Oregon Provisional Emigration Society and carried this paternalistic motto: "Our Object the Elevation of the Indian Race—Our Means a Christian Settlement in Oregon." The first issue contained a statement that made clear the publisher's goals. Every political party and social movement has its organ, the editors noted. This publication, however, would serve a different cause, speaking for "an oppressed and afflicted race, fleeing away before the whites, as they fly from the fires of their own prairies. . . ." The editors continued, invoking the virtues they hoped to spread among the Oregon Indians: "We should cease our cruelty, treat them as men, and give them the blessings of civilization and religion. . . ." To achieve this goal the committee advocated living among the Indians, fulfilling the Christian duty "to educate them and elevate their moral and religious characters." The dream was never realized, of course, and *The Oregonian, and Indian's Advocate* stopped publication in 1839. Despite such failures, the missionary press continued. By 1860 twenty-five Native American periodicals had appeared, at least briefly, in the United States.

Source:
Daniel F. Littlefield Jr. and James W. Parins, *American Indian and Alaska Native Newspapers and Periodicals, 1826–1924* (Westport, Conn.: Greenwood Press, 1984).

CIRCULAR.

TO THE OREGON EMIGRANTS.

GENTLEMEN:

It being made my duty, as Superintendent of Indian affairs, by an Act passed by the Legislature of Oregon, "to give such instructions and directions to Emigrants to this Territory, in regard to their conduct towards the natives, by the observance of which, they will be most likely to maintain and promote peace and friendship between them and the Indian tribes through which they may pass," allow me to say in the first place, that the Indians on the old road to this country, are friendly to the whites. They should be treated with kindness on all occasions. As Indians are inclined to steal, keep them out of your camps. If one or two are admitted, watch them closely. Notwithstanding the Indians are friendly, it is best to keep in good sized companies while passing through their country. Small parties of two or three are sometimes stripped of their property while on their way to this Territory, perhaps because a preceding party promised to pay the Indians for something had of them, and failed to fulfil their promise. This will show you the necessity of keeping your word with them in all cases.

There is another subject upon which I would say a few words. A number of the emigrants of 1845 took a cut off, as it is called, to shorten the route, leaving the old road; the consequence was, they were later getting in, lost their property, and many lost their lives. Some of those who reached the settlements, were so broken down by sickness, that it was some months before they recovered sufficient strength to labor.

A portion of the emigrants of 1846 took a new route, called the southern route. This proved very disastrous to all those who took it. Some of the emigrants that kept on the old road, reached this place as early as the 13th of September, with their wagons, and all got in, in good season, with their wagons and property, I believe, except a few of the last party. While those that took the southern route, were very late in reaching the settlements—they all lost more or less of their property—many of them losing all they had and barely getting in with their lives; a few families were obliged to winter in the Umpqua mountains, not being able to reach the settlements.

I would therefore recommend you to keep the old road. A better way may be found, but it is not best for men with wagons and families to try the experiment.

My remarks are brief, but I hope may prove beneficial to you.

Dated at Oregon City, this 22d of April, 1847.

GEO. ABERNETHY,
GOVERNOR OF OREGON TERRITORY AND
SUPERINTENDENT OF INDIAN AFFAIRS.

An announcement to settlers advising them on preferred routes and trail conduct (Coe Collection, Yale University Library, New Haven, Connecticut)

News, Technology, and National Progress

Technology and Democracy. The technological development of American society in the first half of the nineteenth century inspired many newspapermen to idealize the role of communication and predict a new and glorious future for individuals as well as nations. New York editors such as James Gordon Bennett and Horace Greeley conceived of the newspaper as a force for good in America, promoting moral and civic virtue in its readers. In Massachusetts an idealistic editor also believed in the press, placing the newspaper and the rapid advancements in communication and transportation at the center of a new vision for humankind. Writing at the beginning of 1851, Samuel Bowles III, editor of the *Springfield Republican,* predicted a new community spirit based on new forms of human interaction. As Bowles put it, "The railroad car, the steamboat, and the magnetic telegraph, have made neighborhood among widely severed States, and the Eastern Continent is but a few days' journey away.—These active and almost miraculous agencies have brought the whole civilized world in contact. . . ."

Bowles's Vision. Bowles saw the powers of new communication and transportation as a liberalizing force promoting larger and more important issues over "the petty interests, fuels, gossips and strifes of families and neighborhoods." A result of the new technologies, Bowles argued, would be a grand sense of oneness among all humanity. "The wonderful extension of the field of vision; this compression of the human race into one great family, must tend to identify its interests, sympathies and motives." Not surprisingly for a newspaper editor, Bowles believed the newspaper was a chief instrument of this new, more humane vision of the world. His language was hyperbolic, but it was not unusual for a successful antebellum editor who had witnessed the ways electricity and steam power had transformed the American landscape. To Bowles and like-minded editors, newspapers were part of a more rational, more knowable world. "The brilliant mission of the newspaper is not yet, and perhaps may never be, perfectly understood," he wrote. "It is, and is to be, the high priest of History, the vitalizer of Society, the world's great informer, the earth's high censor, the medium of public thought and opinion, and the circulating life blood of the whole human mind." Echoing the libertarian ideology of European and American Enlightenment thinkers, Bowles also saw the press as a force for freedom and world peace. "[The newspaper] is the great enemy of tyrants, and the right arm of liberty, and is destined, more than any other agency, to melt and mould the jarring and contending nations of the world into that one great brotherhood which, through long centuries, has been the ideal of the Christian and the philanthropist."

Every Abode. Bowles predicted that the popular dissemination of information and ideas would transform the average American. "A few years more," he wrote, "and a great thought uttered within sight of the Atlantic, will rise with the morrow's sun and shine upon millions of minds by the side of the Pacific. The murmur of Asia's multitudes will be heard at our doors; and laden with the fruit of all human thought and actions, the newspaper will be in every abode, and daily nourishment of every mind." For Bowles and many other nineteenth-century journalists, communication was powerful indeed, the very heart of a new and better human existence.

Source:
Samuel Bowles, *Springfield Republican,* 4 January 1851, in *Voices of the Past: Key Documents in the History of American Journalism,* by Calder M. Pickett,(Columbus, Ohio: Grid, 1977), pp. 108–109.

Newspapers for a New Nation

The Newspaper Exchange System. In the early nineteenth century, editors developed an informal but useful system of newspaper exchanges to share news and information both regionally and nationally. To do so they relied, at least in part, on the postal service. Newspaper exchanges developed in part because they were free, a concession the press received over a sometimes reluctant post office. The press rationale was simple: the exchange of news promoted national identity and a sense of unity in the expanding nation. The exchange system allowed the news to travel both east and west. Frontier papers informed the urban dailies about events in the West, and the city papers gave rural editors news from Washington. Even after the spread of the telegraph, in the 1850s, the exchange system remained useful. It was cheaper than the telegraph, and it was not restricted to short, abbreviated messages common on the wires.

Competition and Cooperation. Well before the invention of the telegraph, timely news was an important goal in American journalism. An early advocate of "the latest intelligence" was A. S. Willington, owner of the *Charleston Gazette* in South Carolina. In 1813 Willington, rowed by two slaves, began boarding ships in Charleston Harbor in search of news from Europe, a practice that led Willington to publish the first reports of the Treaty of Ghent that ended the War of 1812. Soon the practice of meeting incoming ships became a regular practice of papers in Boston, New York, and other Eastern cities. In 1827 both the *New York Journal of Commerce* and *Morning Courier* launched speedy sailboats to meet incoming vessels, pick up European papers, and get them back to the newsroom first. The winner was rewarded with bragging rights and a profitable "Extra." By 1831 six news boats were operating in New York Harbor, along with a semaphoric telegraphic system used to alert boats to incoming ships and to notify publishers that their boats were returning with the news. One of the most aggressive New York journalists was James Gordon Bennett, the shrewd but outrageous editor of the *New York Herald.* Bennett went to extraordinary lengths to beat his rivals, employing faster boats, a network of riders, and, for a time, carrier pigeons, an idea first used by a

George Kendall of the *New Orleans Picayune* was an important war correspondent during the Mexican War. Kendall, who had been a Mexican prisoner, was an advocate of American expansion in the Southwest:

Another victory, glorious in its results and which has thrown additional luster upon the American arms, has been achieved today by the army under General Scott—the proud capital of Mexico has fallen into the power of a mere handful of men compared with the immense odds arrayed against them, and Santa Anna, instead of shedding his blood as he had promised, is wandering with the remnant of his army no one knows whither.

The apparently impregnable works on Chapultepec, after a desperate struggle, were triumphantly carried; Generals Bravo and Mouterde, besides a host of officers of different grades, taken prisoners; over 1000 noncommissioned officers and privates, all their cannon and ammunition, are in our hands; the fugitives were soon in full flight towards the different works which command the entrances to the city, and our men at once were in hot pursuit.

General Quitman, supported by General Smith's brigade, took the road by the Chapultepec aqueduct toward the Belén gate and the Ciudadela; General Worth, supported by General Cadwalader's brigade, advanced by the San Cosme aqueduct toward the garita of that name. Both routes were cut up by ditches and defended by breastworks, barricades, and strong works of every description known to military science. Yet the daring and impetuosity of our men overcame one defense after another, and by nightfall every work to the city's edge was carried. . . .

Boston editor. Not to be outdone, Bennett shipped his birds to Boston, where news reports were attached and the birds set free. At one point Bennett offered $500 an hour for each hour that a pigeon arrived ahead of his rivals. This kind of expense prompted more cooperation among New York papers. Even in the 1830s some editors began pooling their resources on news boats, trading a story for lower costs.

The Associated Press. With the emergence of the telegraph in the late 1840s, news-gathering costs quickly became intolerable for individual newspapers. In May 1848 David Hale of the *New York Journal of Commerce* arranged a meeting of six New York papers. Hale proposed that the rival publishers cooperate, reducing telegraph tolls and securing more-reliable news reports from around the nation. Not all the newsmen were enthusiastic; James Watson Webb of the *Courier and Enquirer* was Bennett's bitter enemy and at first resisted the plan, but even Webb could see that cooperation on the telegraph

offered advantages for all. The new group was called the New York Associated Press (NYAP). Dr. Alexander Jones, a physician with experience in journalism, was hired as the NYAP's first agent. One of Jones's first major assignments was the presidential election of 1848. Jones arranged for news from the Whig convention in Philadelphia to be telegraphed to Jersey City, where the line—because of the expanse of the Hudson River—ended. Jones devised a flag system to complete the transmission to the city. Unfortunately, the boy assigned to look for the flag saw a broker's signal flag and notified the papers that Zachary Taylor had been nominated. Fortunately for the NYAP, Taylor *was* nominated, but not until the following day. The success of the NYAP prompted other publishers to form similar organizations, and the Philadelphia Associated Press, the Southern Associated Press, and other companies soon began transmitting news to their member papers. During the Civil War years the Western Press Association challenged the dominance of the NYAP, leading to the eventual consolidation of the various cooperatives and the emergence of the modern Associated Press.

The Growth of Newspapers. National expansion meant the founding of new towns and cities, a process that involved the construction of roads, commercial and residential buildings, and other parts of a local economic and political structure. The need for immigrants and the growth of local economies also promoted the growth of newspapers. The press, after all, could be used to boost a town and stimulate the fortunes of its settlers. In short, as more Americans built more towns in the West, the number of newspapers grew as well. In 1800 Americans were publishing 178 weekly newspapers. Only ten years later the figure had doubled to 302. By 1840 there were 1,141 weeklies, and by 1860 the number of weeklies exploded to 3,173. Daily journalism showed similar growth. Only 24 dailies were being published in 1800; they reached 42 in 1820. In 1840, 138 daily papers were being published in American cities, and they tripled to 387 in 1860. Newspapers, it seems clear, were part and parcel of a robust, expanding America.

Journalism in the West. The newspaper became a standard feature of Western town building. Not every town had a railroad or a mine or a fort or a cattle pen, but virtually all of them had at least one newspaper. Newspapers served several functions in Western towns, some of them crucial to the town's hopes for success. Boosterism and self-promotion were certainly part of this function, and Western editors were fiercely partisan promoters of their own towns. Newspapers served other functions as well, including the social role of creating a local or ethnic identity for a particular community, helping knit together an otherwise loose association of people who happened to live in one place. The vigor of the journalistic urge flourished throughout the West, even in sparsely populated Mexican borderlands of the Southwest. The first newspaper published in present-day New Mexico was established in Taos in 1835, a dozen years before the Treaty of Guadalupe Hidalgo brought the territory under U.S. control. This paper, *El Crepusculo,* was published in Spanish, as were several other early papers. In the decade between 1840 and 1849, publishers started fifteen more papers in the territory. By the end of the nineteenth century an amazing 651 newspapers had been established in New Mexico, a testament to the power of print in the growth and Americanization of the Southwest.

Kansas. Journalism in Kansas started later, but like New Mexico, newspapers were an important asset in the frontier days. The first newspaper, the *Kansas Weekly Herald,* was published under an elm tree in 1854. "Only in Kansas could a newspaper be published before there was news to print," one Kansas scholar noted. More than 100 other newspapers were established during the state's turbulent territorial period from 1854 to 1861. Yet despite the chaos so seemingly endemic in what was called "Bleeding Kansas," each town still had at least one newspaper. Not surprising, many of these papers were booster publications that proclaimed the virtues of their town. By the end of the century no fewer than 733 newspapers were being published in the Jayhawk state, more papers per capita than any other state at the time.

Sources:

Eugene Decker, "Preface," in *Kansas Newspapers: A Director of Newspaper Holdings in Kansas,* edited by Aileen Anderson (Topeka: Kansas Library Network Board, 1984), pp. 3–4;

Oliver Gramling, *AP: The Story of News* (New York: Farrar and Rinehart, 1940);

Pearce S. Grove, Becky J. Barnett, and Sandra J. Hansen, eds., *New Mexico Newspapers: A Comprehensive Guide to Bibliographic Entries and Locations* (Albuquerque: University of New Mexico Press, 1975);

Alfred M. Lee, *The Daily Newspaper in America* (New York: Macmillan, 1937);

William H. Lyon, "The Significance of Newspapers on the American Frontier," *Journal of the West,* 19 (April 1980): 3–13.

HEADLINE MAKERS

CASSIUS MARCELLUS CLAY

1810-1903

ABOLITIONIST NEWSPAPER EDITOR

Journalism and Social Justice. The link between journalism and social justice has long been a feature of American life. This was certainly the case for the fiery Cassius Marcellus Clay, a wealthy Kentuckian who served as antislavery crusader, politician, journalist, soldier, and diplomat. Though his career in journalism was brief, Clay—like several other nineteenth-century journalists—founded a newspaper not to advance his fortunes but as a means to an end: the abolition of slavery.

Education. Born in 1810 to a large slaveholding family on a plantation near Lexington, Cassius Clay received an education including instruction in French at St. Joseph, a Jesuit school in Kentucky. In 1831 he traveled east, where he met President Andrew Jackson and other important men who were friends of his father. He soon enrolled at Yale College, where he was inspired by William Lloyd Garrison, the firebrand editor whose life and newspaper, *The Liberator,* were dedicated to abolition.

From Politics to Journalism. Back in Lexington, Clay began a political career, succeeding in a race for the state legislature when he was only twenty-five. His political career sputtered over the next decade, in large measure because of his increasingly outspoken opposition to slavery. In this hostile political climate, Clay's move to journalism was predictable, a way to extend his antislavery crusade. Clay's newspaper, the *True American,* established in Lexington in 1845, proved to be a financial disaster and a danger to its founder's life. Its mission was clear: "Devoted to Universal Liberty; Gradual Emancipation of Kentucky; Literature; Agriculture; the Elevation of Labor, Morally and Politically; . . . etc., etc."

The *True American*. The newspaper soon attracted enemies. More troubling to Clay, however, was finding like-minded writers to staff the paper. Clay's first choice as editor, a Frankfort man named T. B. Stevenson, was immediately intimidated and never moved to Lexington. Clay was not a man to dodge a fight. He fortified the paper's doors with sheet iron and installed two brass cannons loaded with shot and nails behind folding doors. "I furnished my office with Mexican lances, and a limited number of guns," Clay wrote. "There were six or eight persons who stood ready to defend me. If defeated, they were to escape by a trap-door in the roof; and I had placed a keg of powder, with a match, which I could set off and blow up the office and all my invaders; and this I should most certainly have done. . . ."

The Newspaper Fails. Among those who sought to stop Clay and his paper was a secret group known as the Committee of Sixty. Within weeks of the paper's founding, Clay came down with typhoid fever. While he was recovering, the Committee of Sixty broke into the office, where they packed up the type, presses, and other equipment and shipped it to Cincinnati. Clay continued to edit the paper from Lexington, though less effectively. The break-in hurt the paper, and it failed in 1846 after moving to Louisville. Clay used the incident to reinforce the fight for free expression in Kentucky. Having learned the identities of some of the Committee of Sixty, Clay filed suit and won, collecting $2,500 in damages. By prevailing, Clay demonstrated the importance and legitimacy of a free press in Kentucky and, by implication, in much of the Midwest.

Personal Tests. Clay went on to advance the antislavery cause as a passionate and effective orator. Like his stories in the *True American,* Clay's speeches frequently caused an uproar, involving him in several fights and at least one duel. Clay survived a duel in 1845 by dodging a bullet and then disfiguring his attacker, gouging out an eye, cutting off an ear, and splitting the man's face with his Bowie knife. Clay's courage was tested again when he led troops into battle in the Mexican War. He was captured in early 1847 and later freed in a prisoner exchange. Back in Lexington, Clay was honored as a war hero, even among his old proslavery foes. Clay entered politics again in 1849, running for governor under the banner of the Emancipation Party. He lost, but he attracted national attention for his efforts. In 1856 his abolitionist views led him to the new Republican Party, where he became a friend of Abraham Lincoln.

Ambassador to Russia. Following Lincoln's election, Clay hoped for a cabinet post. Instead Lincoln offered an ambassadorship. Clay turned down an ambassadorship in Spain in favor of Russia, a country Clay saw as important to the war-torn United States. After a year in St. Petersburg, Clay returned to Washington, where he urged Lincoln to sign the Emancipation Proclamation. Clay was ordered back to Russia in 1863, a move his wife protested. She and Clay's seven living children remained in the United States. He served in St. Petersburg until 1869, charming the Russian nobility and carrying on an affair with Anna Petrov, prima ballerina in the Russian Imperial Ballet.

The Lion of White Hall. Clay retired to the family plantation during the Ulysses S. Grant administration, an old man now known as the Lion of White Hall. He and his wife were finally divorced in 1878. Even in retirement, Clay was irascible. At age eighty-four he married a fifteen-year-old neighbor and held off the group of officials who had come to remove the girl. The marriage ended after three years, however, and Clay's finances ran low, prompting him to apply for and receive a pension for his service in the Mexican War. Clay died in 1903 during a violent thunderstorm, appropriate weather for the passing of a Southerner brave enough to carry on a lifelong crusade against slavery and racial injustice.

Source:

Ronald Truman Farrar, "Cassius Marcellus Clay," in *American Newspaper Journalists: 1690–1872, Dictionary of Literary Biography,* volume 43, edited by Perry J. Ashley (Columbia, S.C.: Bruccoli Clark / Detroit: Gale Research, 1985), pp. 98–102.

GEORGE KENDALL

1809–1867
EXPANSIONIST EDITOR

An Easterner Goes West. George Kendall was a native New Englander, but he made his mark as an editor and adventurer in the American Southwest, founding the *New Orleans Picayune,* promoting Texas independence, traveling to Santa Fe, suffering in Mexican jails, and reporting on the Mexican War. Though Kendall's adventures set him apart from most journalists, his achievements and ambitions nevertheless illustrate the ways that many nineteenth-century American newspapermen saw themselves and defined their paper's nationalist mission.

Youth. Born in 1809 to an old Massachusetts family, Kendall was a restless young man eager to make his way in the world. His education was haphazard, but he had a quick mind and enjoyed reading, music, painting, and theater. However, none of these were as meaningful to him as the world of action, a fact soon confirmed by his journeys west and south.

Apprenticeship. At age fifteen Kendall went to work as an apprentice in the print shop of his cousin's universalist newspaper, the *Amherst Herald.* Though the paper failed a few months later, Kendall liked the work and declared his intention to become a printer, a decision some family members discouraged. Kendall was undeterred and soon persuaded an uncle to take him to Boston, where he became an apprentice at the *Boston Statesman.* Within a year Kendall set his sights higher, moving to New York. He failed to find a job, however, and soon took a boat to Albany, where another uncle gave him fifty dollars, enough for him to head west in search of experience and adventure; he was seventeen.

Tramping About. Kendall traveled across New York to the Old Northwest, where he worked as a farmer, a traveling actor, and, sometimes, as a printer. He made his way as far west as Wisconsin and then tramped south through Tennessee to Natchez and on to New Orleans. New York beckoned, so he headed north, stopping off in North Carolina to work on a stage line. By 1832, when Kendall was twenty-three years old, he was making the rounds in New York again, seasoned by his travels and eager to succeed in journalism.

New Orleans. Success was to come in New Orleans. Kendall left New York in late 1833 for Washington, where he found a job at the *National Intelligencer* working next to a man named F. A. Lumsden. Kendall and Lumsden hit it off, and by 1835 both men turned up in New Orleans, working for rival papers. New Orleans in the mid 1830s was a bustling place filled with the adventurous spirit of the era. Eight new banks were chartered in 1836, and buildings, roads, canals, and railroads were under construction. An editor from *Niles' Weekly Register* wrote in late 1836 that he was "astonished to witness the great number of large and splendid edifices which were under way" in New Orleans. Carpenters and laborers poured into the city as it grew into a major Western entrepot.

Founding the *New Orleans Picayune*. By early 1837 Kendall and Lumsden were ready to launch their own paper, the *New Orleans Picayune,* named after a small Spanish coin and representing the paper's popular appeal. The *Picayune* was the first "penny press" paper in the South, and the paper's columns were filled with jokes, puns, and gossip as well as news from around the city. The penny press was designed to appeal to the common man with breezy, entertaining news and commentary. Thus the fatal outcome of a duel was fair game in the *Picayune:* "A duel took place yesterday afternoon which resulted in the death of the principals, each firing through the other's body. This is pretty sharp shooting, and, we think, very fair play—at least neither can say it was otherwise."

The Penny Press. Another feature of the penny press was its news-gathering enterprise. James Gordon Bennett became famous and rich in New York for aggressively searching for news. Unlike an earlier generation of newsmen, penny press editors were not content to wait on travelers and mail deliveries for the news; they began to search for stories, sending reporters to the police station, courthouse, and other places where interesting stories were likely to happen. In time Kendall and the *Picayune* became famous for their enterprise, especially in far-flung reports from the Southwest and Mexico.

Expansionist Politics. The *Picayune* had an expansionist view early on. About a year after the paper's founding, Kendall and Lumsden were successful enough to start a weekly edition aimed at Texas, newly independent from Mexico, but served only by a handful of papers. In the late 1830s and early 1840s the *Picayune* ran a popular series called "Prairie Sketches," stories widely reprinted in the Midwest and East. These articles, written by the brother of a *Picayune* staffer, included reports on a trip to Santa Fe and later to the headwaters of the Yellowstone. Kendall's interest in Western expansion was both personal and professional. The West represented adventure and opportunity, forces Kendall could not resist. Besides, general interest in the West in the 1840s was growing. More and more immigrants were traveling across the Great Plains to Santa Fe and California. The *Picayune* was eager to report Western news, promoting the nation's destiny and making a handsome profit along the way.

Travel to Santa Fe. In June 1841 Kendall joined an official Texas expedition to Santa Fe, a trip designed to secure the region as part of Texas and open a trade route between the Gulf of Mexico and Mexican territory in the West. Not surprising, Mexican officials viewed the Texans as a threat. To make matters worse, the expedition was poorly organized and equipped. Wagons overturned; supplies ran short; and the military escorts, some of them teenagers, were undisciplined. For the first six weeks of the journey Kendall rode in a wagon, unable to mount a horse because of a broken ankle suffered days before the trip began. "The worthy editor grumbles excessively, as well he might, over his annoyances and misfortunes," the *Picayune* told its readers.

Trouble in Texas. When Kendall and an advance party of about one hundred Texans finally reached Mexican territory, they were soon disarmed and arrested by Mexican soldiers who promptly executed two Texas officials. The remainder of the expedition eventually turned up in Mexican territory, beaten and hungry. Confronted by Mexican troops, they surrendered. The Texans' move on Santa Fe had been a fiasco. Rumors of the failure slowly drifted back to the press, but the *Picayune* remained optimistic that Kendall would prevail. In October, Kendall and other prisoners were ordered to Mexico City to meet Mexican president Antonio López de Santa Anna. The march to El Paso was difficult. Some prisoners died of exhaustion; others were killed by guards. The trip south from El Paso was easier, but smallpox and other illnesses broke out among the men. By early 1842 the prisoners were near Mexico City, but Kendall's partner at the *Picayune,* Lumsden, arranged for Kendall's release. By the time he was free Kendall had been imprisoned for months, some of the time in a leper hospital, other times in leg irons. The ordeal caused Kendall to hate Mexicans and the Mexican government, a fact that became clear in his coverage of the Mexican War.

Rising Success. The Texas prisoner controversy and the continuing dispute between Texas and Mexico reverberated in American papers. Kendall's imprisonment and reports of the prisoners' hardships led to editorial condemnation of Mexico and helped stir up public opinion against Santa Anna and the Mexicans. The *Picayune* prospered as a result of these conflicts. Kendall's captivity had become a public issue in New Orleans, inspiring more news-gathering activity in the West. As a major port and transportation hub, New Orleans was ideally situated as a news center for the Southwest and Mexico, a fact the *Picayune* exploited. Kendall placed correspondents in major Texas towns and in Mexican ports, and the reporters worked the wharves and hotels of New Orleans gathering the latest intelligence. Not surprising, stories from the *Picayune* were widely reprinted in the Eastern papers, sometimes well in advance of diplomatic dispatches.

Popularity. The reputation grew with the outbreak of the Mexican War in 1846. Kendall became more famous than ever. He reported on the successful attack on Monterrey, reports that helped propel Zachary Taylor to hero status and later to the presidency. The news carried across northern Mexico by riders and then by boat to New Orleans in eight days. This was no accident, the *Picayune* reports boasted, "but was due entirely to the foresight and prudence of our associate, now with the Army. Appreciating the vast importance of news. . . . Mr. Kendall determined to forward the despatches of our correspondents by express, cost what it would." Little wonder, then, that the *Picayune* was widely sought by the Eastern papers, which

had the paper carried by boat, rider, and rail across the Southeast. With luck, copies of the *Picayune* were in Baltimore, New York, and Boston in ten days. Kendall's reports from the Mexican front contributed to the popularity of the paper; compositors worked overtime to produce extras to meet the public demand.

Postwar Life. After the Mexican War the restless Kendall traveled to Europe, visiting the great cities and finding a wife and beginning a family. He was always writing letters, filling the pages of the *Picayune* with news from England and the Continent. Eventually he established his family on a ranch in his beloved Texas, raising sheep and a variety of crops. Always the optimist, he continued his letters to the *Picayune* and Eastern papers, praising the climate and the many opportunities of central Texas. Kendall died in Texas in 1867. His dream of owning a great and prosperous ranch never came true, but he remained an unabashed American expansionist who knew how to use a newspaper to advance his own causes.

Source:
Fayette Copeland, *Kendall of the* Picayune (Norman: University of Oklahoma Press, 1943).

PUBLICATIONS

Chicago Tribune—founded in 1847, the paper quickly became a major source of information about the Midwest; after Joseph Medill and Charles Ray purchased it in 1855, it became one of the most influential newspapers in the nation;

William Lloyd Garrison, *An Address. Delivered before the Free People of Color, in Philadelphia, New York, and Other Cities, during the Month of June, 1831* (Boston: Printed by S. Foster, 1831);

Horace Greeley, *An Overland Journey from New York to San Francisco in the Summer of 1859* (New York: C. M. Saxton, Barker, 1860)—Greeley's collected letters to the *Tribune* reveal popular nineteenth-century ideas about the need for American expansion in the West;

New Orleans Picayune—a "penny paper" founded in January 1837, this newspaper is a good source of news and opinions relating to the development of Texas and the Southwest in the 1840s and 1850s; the editor George Kendall's reports from the Mexican War were widely republished, establishing him as a pioneering

war correspondent and one of the most famous reporters of his era;

New York Weekly Tribune—published from 1841 to 1901, this newspaper circulated widely in the Midwest and the West, extending Horace Greeley's editorial crusades well beyond New York and making him one of the nineteenth century's most popular and influential journalists;

The Rocky Mountain News—founded in 1859 by William N. Byers, the paper is one of the best examples of the journalism common in the West in the mid nineteenth century; the newspaper's editors led a campaign to promote both Denver and the Colorado Territory, and they became increasingly hostile to American Indians during the 1860s;

United States Congress, House of Representatives, Committee of Commerce and Manufactures, *Electromagnetic Telegraphs . . .* (Washington, D.C.: Thomas Allen, 1838).

EDUCATION

by JACQUELINE S. REINIER

CONTENTS

Sidebars and tables are listed in italics.

1800
- The Massachusetts legislature gives local school districts the power to levy taxes.

1801
- Cane Ridge revivals in Kentucky initiate the Second Great Awakening.
- Moravian missionaries enter the lands of the Cherokees.

1802
- Cherokee chiefs urge Moravians to open a school.

1803
- Moravians found a school at Spring Place, Georgia.

1804
- Ohio University is founded in Athens, Ohio.

1805
- The New York Free School Society is organized.

1807
- East Tennessee College (present-day University of Tennessee) is founded in Knoxville.

1809
- Miami University is founded in Oxford, Ohio.

1814
- Emma Hart Willard organizes Middlebury Female Seminary in Vermont.

1815
- Gov. Pablo Vicente Sola urges that schools be established in California pueblos and presidios.

1816
- The Indiana constitution directs the legislature to establish a system of free education and recommends the establishment of township schools and a state university.

1817

- Transylvania University establishes a medical college in Kentucky.
- Plans leading to the founding of the University of Michigan at Ann Arbor are introduced to the state legislature.

1818

- Thomas Jefferson receives a legislative charter to establish the University of Virginia.
- The American Board of Commissioners for Foreign Missions establishes a school in the Cherokee nation.
- The Pennsylvania legislature provides for public schools.

1819

- A Supreme Court case (*Dartmouth College* v. *Woodward*) protects charters of privately organized colleges from government intervention.
- The University of Virginia is founded in Charlottesville.
- The University of Cincinnati is founded in Ohio.

1820

- Indiana University is founded in Bloomington.
- The University of Alabama is chartered.

1821

- The Ohio legislature establishes school districts.
- A medical department is founded at the University of Cincinnati.

1824

- The Indiana legislature establishes school districts.
- Robert Owen purchases New Harmony, Indiana.

1825

- Charles Grandison Finney conducts revivals in western New York.
- New York establishes public schools.
- Pestalozzian schools are founded in New Harmony, Indiana.
- The Illinois legislature establishes school districts.

1826
- The New York Free School Society becomes the Public School Society.
- Frances Wright establishes the Nashoba community in Tennessee.
- Case Western Reserve University is founded in Cleveland, Ohio.
- Episcopalians found Kenyon College in Ohio.

1828
- Indiana University is founded in Bloomington.

1829
- Baptists found Georgetown College in Kentucky.

1830
- The American Sunday School Union plans a campaign in the Mississippi River valley.
- A medical department is founded at Miami University in Ohio.

1831
- The Western Literary Institute and College of Professional Teachers is organized in Ohio.
- The University of Alabama is founded in Tuscaloosa.

1832
- Lyman Beecher moves to Cincinnati as president of Lane Seminary.
- Jesuits found St. Louis University in Missouri.

1833
- Catharine Beecher establishes the Western Female Institute in Cincinnati.
- Oberlin Collegiate Institute is founded in Ohio.

1834
- An antislavery controversy engulfs Lane Seminary in Cincinnati.
- Presbyterians found Wabash College in Crawfordsville, Indiana.
- Tulane University is founded in New Orleans.
- The University of the Ozarks is founded in Clarksville, Arkansas.
- William E. P. Hartnell opens a school for boys in Monterey, California.

1835

- Lane rebels enroll at Oberlin Collegiate Institute.
- Lyman Beecher publishes *Plea for the West*.
- Catharine Beecher publishes *An Essay on the Education of Female Teachers*.
- Congregationalists found Illinois College in Jacksonville.

1836

- The American Board of Commissioners for Foreign Missions sends Marcus and Narcissa Whitman to the Oregon country.

1837

- Horace Mann is appointed secretary of the Massachusetts State Board of Education.
- Bacon College (present-day University of Kentucky) is founded in Georgetown.
- Catholics found St. Mary's College in Kentucky.
- Methodists found Asbury College (present-day DePauw University) in Greencastle, Indiana.
- Calvin Stowe writes "Report on Elementary Instruction in Europe" for the Ohio legislature.
- State Superintendent of Public Instruction John D. Pierce writes a model school law in Michigan.

1839

- The state of Missouri passes school legislation.
- The University of Missouri is founded in Columbia.

1840

- Catholic bishop John Joseph Hughes, protesting the use of the King James Bible and the Protestant message of New York public schools, requests public funding for Catholic schools.
- Cincinnati, Ohio, provides bilingual education for children of German immigrants.

1841

- Catharine Beecher publishes *Treatise on Domestic Economy*.
- The U.S. Congress provides federal land grants to states in order to fund education.

1842

- The New York legislature denies public funds to sectarian schools.
- Catholics found the University of Notre Dame in Indiana.
- Methodists found Ohio Wesleyan University.

1843

- The Society for the Promotion of Collegiate and Theological Education in the West is founded in New York.
- The Sisters of Mercy enter the United States.

1844

- The University of Mississippi is founded in Oxford.
- California governor Manuel Micheltorena urges the establishment of schools in San Diego, Los Angeles, Santa Barbara, Monterey, San Jose, San Francisco, and Sonoma.

1845

- Lutherans found Wittenberg College in Springfield, Ohio.
- Baptists found Baylor University in Waco, Texas.

1846

- The Iowa constitution establishes free public education.
- Olive Mann Isbell opens a school for children of settlers from the East in Santa Clara and then Monterey, California.

1847

- The State Reform School for Boys is founded in Westborough, Massachusetts.
- Catharine Beecher's Central Committee for Promoting Female Education sends female missionary teachers to the West.
- The State University of Iowa is founded in Iowa City.
- Missionaries Marcus and Narcissa Whitman are murdered in Oregon by Cayuse Indians.

1848

- The Wisconsin constitution and legislature establish free public education.
- The University of Wisconsin is founded in Madison.

1849

- *Roberts* v. *City of Boston* protests segregation in Boston public schools.
- The United Brethren found Otterbein College in Westerville, Ohio.
- The city of San Francisco establishes free public schools.

1850

- Lutherans found Capital University in Columbus, Ohio.
- The Disciples of Christ found Butler University in Indianapolis.
- Quakers found Earlham College in Indiana.
- The University of Utah is founded in Salt Lake City.
- Oregon State University is founded in Corvallis.

1851

- German Reformed church members found Heidelberg College in Ohio.
- Northwestern University is founded in Evanston, Illinois.
- Universalists found Lombard College in Galesburg, Illinois.
- The University of Minnesota is founded in Minneapolis-St. Paul.
- Methodists found the College of the Pacific in Santa Clara, California, which later moved to Stockton.
- The Sisters of Notre Dame establish a boarding school for girls in San Jose, California.
- The California legislature provides school districts and apportions school funds to counties.

1852

- Antioch College is founded in Yellow Springs, Ohio.
- The Indiana legislature establishes free public education.
- Anna Peck founds Rockford Seminary for women in Illinois.
- Catharine Beecher founds Milwaukee Female College in Wisconsin.

1853

- Catharine Beecher lobbies for free normal schools.
- Louisiana State Seminary of Learning is founded in Alexandria.
- Unitarians found Washington University in St. Louis.
- Lindenwood College for women is founded in St. Charles, Missouri.

- Charles Loring Brace becomes urban missionary with the Children's Aid Society.
- John Swett becomes principal of Rincon Grammar School in San Francisco.

1854

- The Ohio legislature establishes free public education.
- Congregationalists found Pacific University in Oregon.

1855

- The Illinois legislature establishes free public education.
- Michigan State University is founded in East Lansing.
- California College (present-day University of California, Berkeley) is founded in Oakland.
- Jesuits found Santa Clara College in California.
- Sacramento City Council allows tax funds to support separate education for African American children.

1856

- Auburn University is founded in Alabama.

1857

- Illinois State Normal University is established in Normal, Illinois.
- The Ohio Reform School for boys is founded.
- Margarethe Meyer Schurz opens the first private kindergarten in America in Watertown, Wisconsin.
- The Children's Aid Society sends city boys to Western states.

1858

- The Minnesota constitution establishes free public education.
- Episcopalians found the University of the South in Tennessee.
- Iowa State University is founded in Ames.

1859

- Catholics found St. Ignatius College in San Francisco.

1860

- Louisiana State University and Agricultural and Mechanical College is founded in Baton Rouge.

OVERVIEW

Post-Revolutionary Plans. As citizens of the United States and immigrants migrated westward in the first half of the nineteenth century, they brought to new communities and states educational experiments and plans that had first taken shape in Europe and the Eastern states. While some individuals feared what they believed was an untamed land, many Americans who were influenced by ideas of the Enlightenment were convinced that the West would be civilized through the diffusion of knowledge. Others dared to hope for the regeneration of human nature in what they viewed as the blank slate of the West. In the early American republic the transmission of culture and work procedures still took place largely in home or workplace settings, outside of formal schools and colleges. The primary institution for educating children was the family. In the decades after the American Revolution, however, cultural leaders argued that schooling was essential in order to train citizens. According to the widely shared republican ideology, the stability of the nation would depend upon the virtue of its citizens, who would be capable of exercising sovereignty through their capacity for moral restraint. Those who were influenced by such thinkers of the Enlightenment as John Locke believed that human nature was malleable and formed by influences in the environment. For them, education would provide the means to form ordinary children into future citizens. In addition, in a large republic, diffusion of knowledge could shape a pluralistic population into a homogeneous body politic. Individuals from various parts of the British Isles and western Europe had flocked to America in the eighteenth century, settling in regions where they spoke in local dialects and identified with local folkways. Education could instill the common aspirations and behavior that would shape these colonial regional cultures into a uniform national polity. In the eighteenth century, religious establishments and denominations had assumed responsibility for moral and intellectual training. After state provisions and the First Amendment to the U.S. Constitution separated church and state, some individuals began to propose more-secular educational plans.

Jefferson and Rush. As early as 1779 Thomas Jefferson prepared his "Systematic Plan of General Education" for the House of Delegates in Virginia. Linked to his proposals to repeal the feudal practices of entail and primogeniture and to establish religious freedom, his plan aimed to eliminate aristocratic privilege and to create a republican society in which natural merit could be recognized and rewarded. According to the plan, in hundreds of wards in every county, state-supported elementary schools would teach reading, writing, and common arithmetic. In districts throughout the state, additional schools would offer the classics, grammar, geography, and higher arithmetic. The College of William and Mary would provide a scientific curriculum; elementary schools would teach the rudiments of education to ordinary citizens; district schools would develop reasoning skills and instill virtue in the more talented; and the university would form a select few into local leaders and national and international statesmen. In 1784 Benjamin Rush of Pennsylvania also was concerned with planning an education suitable for a republican society. Fearful that reason alone would not create binding social ties, Rush proposed a union of affection, in which an emotional patriotism would be reinforced in children through early associations in school. To instill the moral restraint essential for republican virtue, Rush believed that education should be grounded in Christianity, and he argued that the Bible should be the primary textbook. Boys who learned Christian principles and habitual obedience in early childhood would become adult citizens capable of submitting personal inclination to the rule of law and private interest to the public good. In 1787 Rush advocated a similar education for girls, who would learn to submit personal inclination to the demands of domestic life in preparation for their role as republican wives and mothers.

Early Educational Opportunities. Although legislatures in Virginia and Pennsylvania discussed these comprehensive plans for tax-supported schools in the 1790s, they enacted only limited provisions for charity education. The Massachusetts legislature in 1789 required towns of fifty or more families to provide "district" schools for at least six months of the year and towns of two hundred or more families to provide a grammar school. The state did not offer financial aid, however, and both initiative for and control over a school remained with local parents. The New York legislature in

1795 appropriated funds to local areas to support schools for five years, but they did not renew the legislation in 1800. Boston was the only city that supported a system of public schools. According to their provisions, an annually elected school committee supervised grammar schools for boys and girls ages seven to fourteen and a Latin school for boys over the age of ten. Children under the age of seven learned to read in dames' schools, private schools conducted in various homes by female teachers who were licensed by the city. Yet similar school systems were not enacted in other areas, largely because the United States was still a rural society where full-time schooling did not fit the needs of many families. Farmers and craftsmen relied on family more than hired labor and expected their large numbers of children to work. Education occurred in family or workplace settings, and schooling was only sporadic, fitted into hours of the day or seasons of the year that the rhythms of an agricultural society allowed. Revolutionary rhetoric inspired interest in education, but actual practice followed the rural intermittent model. Yet even under these conditions, enrollments increased in locally controlled district or subscription schools, and private academies throughout the nation proliferated, especially those that concentrated on the education of girls.

District and Subscription Schools. Following the American Revolution, New England farmers flooded into western New York, and yeomen from the Upper South and Carolina backcountry filtered into Kentucky and Tennessee. Under the Articles of Confederation of 1781, when states had relinquished their claims to western lands, congressional provisions initially drafted by Thomas Jefferson had provided for education in territories carved from this national domain. The Land Ordinance of 1785 required a survey of public lands to establish rectangular townships six miles square, consisting of thirty-six sections of 640 acres, one of which would be reserved for maintenance of public schools. The Northwest Ordinance of 1787 created the plan for carving out three to five states north of the Ohio and east of the Mississippi Rivers; it also outlawed slavery in the area, promised not to take lands from Indians without their consent, and earmarked support for education. Yet settlement did not follow these orderly plans. In many areas school lands went unsold and school funds went unused; where resources were available, differences in land quality and value led to rancorous disputes. Some states organized districts on the Massachusetts model, in which parents initiated and controlled a district school. In other areas parents took up a subscription, pledging support to erect a building and to hire and board a teacher.

Schools in New Communities. These district, or subscription, schools consisted of one-room log or clapboard buildings where children as young as two or three mingled with older pupils, each child memorizing and reciting his or her lessons under the direction of a more-or-less qualified teacher. Reflecting the post-Revolutionary concern with diffusion of knowledge, such schools dotted Western areas as soon as lands were settled. For example, Daniel Drake's family arrived in Mayslick, Kentucky, in 1788, when it was still Indian country. (Shawnees and their allies in the area would not be defeated until the Battle of Fallen Timbers in 1794.) Yet as early as 1790, when he was five, Drake attended a log cabin school with paper windows, a wooden chimney, and a puncheon floor, taught by an immigrant from Scotland named McQuitty. Later Drake poured over Dilworth's speller or the New Testament under the direction of Jacob Beaden, a teacher from Maryland's eastern shore who knew only reading, writing, and some arithmetic. Beaden had students of all ages recite the lesson aloud, gathering energy as they spoke. In later life Drake found that he could concentrate in almost any situation and thought it an advantage that he had learned to study in the midst of noise. He also learned to pay deference to adults; when someone came along the road, the children would take off their hats and try to bow or curtsey at the same time. Drake attended school only occasionally, though, for his father depended on his labor. When he was nine and the family moved to a larger farm, he left his lessons temporarily to help clear land. Six years later an injury to his father ended this schooling, and Drake worked the farm alone. Like many children in the early-nineteenth-century West, such would have been his fate had not his illiterate father been determined to have at least one educated child, sending Drake at the age of sixteen to Cincinnati to study medicine. After the War of 1812, as the United States acquired Indian lands through treaty or conquest, white families poured westward; shortly after their arrival in each new territory, local parents organized a district, or subscription, school. Planters and yeomen, who swarmed into Alabama and Mississippi from 1815 to 1819, arrived with not only their slaves but also schoolteachers seeking opportunity. Two years after Illinois became a state in 1818, settlers in Sangamon County founded a subscription school. By 1825 families in Blooming Grove, in central Illinois, subscribed their support to a log cabin school, which was soon followed by an academy.

Origins of Public Schools. From 1820 to 1840 commercial and industrial development transformed the economy of the Northeast, affecting not only urban areas but also rural families who began to rely on distant markets made available by improved transportation. As mechanized mills proliferated, textile production left the household. Merchants inserted themselves into patterns of exchange, engaging women and children in new kinds of outwork. Storekeepers tightened credit and preferred cash transactions, replacing older patterns of neighborly barter and local exchange. Mothers, perhaps influenced by evangelical religion, adopted domestic ideology and tried to curtail fertility. Fathers paid wages to hired workers, relying less on the labor of their children. As rural capitalism developed, children had more time to spend in school. In this economic context Horace Mann, who was the newly appointed secretary of the Massachusetts State Board of Education, worried about the urban poverty and crime accelerated by the financial panic of 1837. Fearing that the habits of adults were already established, he focused on forming moral character in malleable young children. Lecturing throughout the state and lobbying the legislature, Mann advocated a system of state-supervised and supported public schools. He urged that each school offer the same curriculum and conduct classes over a continuous ten-month term. He also argued for carefully designed school buildings and state-supported normal schools to train professional teachers. In 1838, when the Unitarian Mann was approached by managers of the American Sunday School Union and asked to adopt their line of evangelical children's literature, he refused, insisting instead on nonsectarian, yet Protestant, public schools, which would instill the values of republicanism and capitalism.

Public Schools in the Midwest. In the Northeast public schools received citizen support largely in areas where commercial development was well under way; their advocates tended to be Whigs who favored a positive role for the state rather than Democrats who usually opted for local control. Farmers in areas less affected by rural capitalism resisted the systems of state-supported education and fought to maintain local control over their district schools. As families moved to the Midwest, farmers there also opposed a general state tax for education and loss of their local control. Where subsistence farming and customs of barter and local exchange prevailed, families depended on their children's labor and preferred voluntary intermittent schooling that could mesh with agricultural work. Laws authorizing the creation of school districts and permitting settlers to support schools by taxing themselves were passed by Ohio in 1821, Indiana in 1824, Illinois in 1825, and Missouri in 1839. The Michigan law of 1837, written by the new state superintendent of public instruction, John D. Pierce, became a model for other states. Yet not until the 1850s, when railroads penetrated the Midwest, did speculators buy up land, tenant farming and hired labor become widespread, and state systems of free public schools characterized by strong district control take root. As rural capitalism transformed the Midwest, legislators established free public education in Indiana in 1852, Ohio in 1854, and Illinois in 1855. The Wisconsin Constitution of 1848 provided for free public education as did those of Iowa in 1846 and Minnesota in 1858. Yet in the Midwest, compromise prevailed between state supervision and local parental control. While states required the length of school terms and passed general rules licensing teachers, local district school boards elected by annual meetings managed the public schools.

Old Southwest. Alabama, Kentucky, and Louisiana in the old Southwest appointed state school superintendents in the 1850s. Yet slavery kept capitalistic relationships from penetrating the Southern rural household, preventing the development of an economic context in which parents and legislators advocated state-supported full-time schools. In Southwestern states slaves were denied schooling. Well-to-do planters hired a tutor to educate their children at home or sent youngsters to board at private academies. Yeoman families, which maintained the older patterns of barter and local exchange, high fertility, and patriarchal control of children's labor, continued to initiate and support subscription schools, where the intermittent lessons could mesh with agricultural work.

Mexican Cession. In the Spanish areas of the Southwest, Catholic priests had sought to form Indians into *gente de razon,* or people of reason, who would internalize self-restraint in order to contribute to the good of the community. Concentrating the natives into pueblos and missions, the friars had taught the Indians to engage in agriculture, use European tools, speak Spanish, and practice Catholicism. Focusing on children, whom they found more malleable than adults, the friars taught youngsters to sing and play musical instruments, to memorize and recite Catholic doctrine, and occasionally to read and write. In 1793 King Carlos IV ordered that schools be established in order to teach Indians to speak, read, and write Spanish, an early venture in public education. About the same time artisans arrived from Mexico to instruct neophyte boys in skilled trades and girls in cloth making and fine needlework. Although they fluctuated greatly in attendance and quality, some schools also were established for the children of settlers, who clustered in towns and settlements surrounding the presidios. After the missions were secularized during the period of Mexican rule from 1822 to 1848, Hispanic ranching families in New Mexico and California were eager to differentiate themselves as gente de razon from the Indian labor force. Although various governors promoted education, schooling was intermittent, and well-to-do families taught their children at home or hired private tutors. By 1844 seven or eight tax-supported schools for boys and for girls were established in California. As traders and immigrants from the United States filtered into the area, some individuals provided schooling for immigrant children. In 1848, after the Treaty of Guadalupe Hidalgo confirmed the conquest of the Southwest in the Mexican War and after gold was discovered in California, citizens of the eastern United States rushed into the area and advocated their concepts of state-supported public education. By 1849 the city of San Francisco supported a free public school, and the first California constitution included provisions similar to those in the 1837 Michigan law. In 1851 the legislature provided school districts and permitted citizens to tax themselves to support schools. Through the leadership of California State Superintendent of Public Instruction John Swett, a statewide system of free public schools was put into place in the 1860s.

Higher Education in the West. Influenced by revivals of the Second Great Awakening, which engulfed the eastern United States from 1800 through 1860, Protestant denominations competed in founding colleges in the West. Proposed to spread denominational doctrines and to train ministers, these small, often struggling, institutions proliferated. Simultaneously, Catholics founded many parochial institutions. Other educational reformers greatly admired the state-supported secular plan that Thomas Jefferson introduced in the University of Virginia in 1819. Funded by the state and directed by a board of visitors confirmed by the legislature, Jefferson's university was completely separated from religious influence and offered instruction in the ancient and modern languages, mathematics, natural history, moral philosophy, medicine, and law. In the 1820s this plan was greatly admired by individuals in Tennessee and Kentucky who hoped to build similar institutions. These and other plans were thwarted, however, when sectarian interests sought control over education and farmers resisted paying taxes for institutions they feared would create an elite upper class. Secular interests prevailed, however, in Michigan, where the state university, founded in 1837, closely followed the Jeffersonian ideal and became the model for other western states.

TOPICS IN THE NEWS

EDUCATION IN THE FAR WEST

Spanish California. After Upper California was settled in 1769, Franciscan friars established missions at San Diego and then San Carlos Borromeo near Monterey, where they taught Indians to cultivate the soil, build houses and churches, make clothing and tools, and practice Christianity. Indians stayed near the missions to obtain a steady supply of food, and the friars focused on their children, training them to live within the restraints of mission life. Some of the promising boys were taught to speak, read, and write in the Spanish language and to sing and play musical instruments; girls, who were protected under lock and key at night, learned to spin, weave, embroider, and engage in domestic tasks. In 1793 King Carlos IV ordered that the use of native languages be discouraged and that government schools be established to teach the Indians to speak, read, and write Spanish. Around the same time artisans were sent from Mexico—tailors, carpenters, masons, blacksmiths, potters, and leather workers—to instruct the neophyte youths in skilled trades. As the missions increased in number to eighteen, Gov. Diego de Borica levied a school tax on settlers in the surrounding towns and presidios, requiring that children of civilians and soldiers attend schools he established at San Diego, Los Angeles, Santa Barbara, Santa Cruz, Monterey, and San Jose. To meet the demand of parents that children have time for work, classes were held in early morning and late afternoon on alternate days. Although these schools lacked supplies and qualified teachers, by 1820 the four presidios and two towns in California each had primary schools.

Mexican Period. After the Mexican Revolution in 1822 the liberal government hoped to extend education in its states and territories. Governor of the California territory, Jose Maria Echeandia, emancipated Indians and offered them Mexican citizenship at the missions of San Diego, Santa Barbara, Monterey, and San Francisco, and urged compulsory education for all children, Indian and Mestizo as well as Hispanic. Yet disruption and conflict prevailed, and only a few schools existed in the 1820s. After the missions were secularized by the Mexican Congress in 1833, Indians became an agricultural labor force for the Hispanic ranching families, who taught their children at home or hired private tutors. Traders from Europe and the United States filtered into the area; some of them converted to Catholicism and married California women. In 1834 an English Catholic, William E. P. Hartnell, opened a boarding school for Indian and white boys, *El Collegio de San Jose* near Monterey, which offered instruction in the Spanish, French, English, and German languages as well as Latin grammar, mathematics, bookkeeping, philosophy, and religion. Although Hartnell continued to be active in California education, his school closed within two years. In 1842 Gov. Manuel Micheltorena arrived in California to instill order and deflect the influence of U.S. citizens entering the territory in ever larger numbers. Placing the missions once again under the care of the friars, he granted public funds to support a school in Los Angeles

When white citizens of the United States flocked to California during the Gold Rush, they brought with them the racial attitudes of Jacksonian America as well as the conviction that they had won land and resources through conquest in the Mexican War. Such attitudes prevailed in the 1850 Foreign Miners' Tax; aimed at Europeans, Indians, Mexicans, and Chinese, the act provided that only native or naturalized citizens of the United States could mine without a license, the cost of which was a prohibitive twenty dollars a month. Black Americans, slave and free, also had come or been brought to California, sometimes earning enough in the mines to purchase freedom or begin a business. The census of 1850 counted 962 African Americans in the state, 206 of whom lived near the northern mines in Sacramento City. After the Sacramento City Council levied a school tax in 1853, leaders of the black community, including the teacher Elizabeth Thorn Scott and the abolitionist Jeremiah B. Sanderson (newly arrived from Massachusetts in 1855), raised the issue of whether public funds would be available for the instruction of black children. Sanderson, who formed a Colored School Committee as soon as he arrived, must have been aware of the tumult in 1849 and 1850 concerning segregation in the Boston public schools, where black parents had sued the Boston School Committee in *Roberts* v. *City of Boston* and the future U.S. senator Charles Sumner had argued before the state supreme court that racially segregated schools did not recognize equality before the law. Boston public schools were not integrated until 1855, when the legislature mandated integration in the state. That same year, acting on its own, Sacramento's city council voted to allow tax funds to support separate education for black children, overcoming the argument that such provision would open schoolhouse doors to Indians, Hawaiians, and Chinese. Although Sanderson left the city a year later, the Colored School Committee continued his school, which received some security in 1860 when the Republican legislature authorized that public funds be allocated to segregated schools. During Reconstruction in 1866 legislators voted that school trustees could enroll non-Caucasians in white schools, a provision repealed in 1870.

Source: Susan Bragg, "Knowledge is Power: Sacramento Blacks and the Public Schools, 1854–1860," and Clarence Caesar, "The Historical Demographics of Sacramento's Black Community, 1848–1900," *California History*, 75 (Fall 1996): 198–221.

and established seven additional schools throughout the territory for children between the ages of six and eleven.

California under the United States. As immigrants from the United States increased in numbers by 1846, they improvised schooling for the education of their children. A widow, Olive Mann Isbell, opened a school in outbuildings of the Santa Clara mission. Initially she lacked supplies and was forced to teach the alphabet by drawing letters on children's hands. During the war between Mexico and the United States, Isbell moved her school to Monterey, where she taught fifty boys and girls, first in the Customs House and then in a schoolroom. In 1847 San Francisco citizens called a public meeting to elect school trustees, who hired Thomas Douglas, a Yale graduate, to provide a school. By 1849 the city supported a free public school in the Baptist chapel, where J. C. Pelton instructed more than one hundred students. After the war, when California became a territory of the United States, delegates to the 1849 Constitutional Convention adopted provisions of the 1837 Michigan school law. In addition the federal land grant of five hundred thousand acres for internal improvements, which had been enacted by the U.S. Congress in 1841, was added to the proceeds of the sale of land in two townships to constitute a school fund. Delegates also established the elective office of superintendent of public instruction and instructed the legislature to set up a system of common schools and allocate land for a university. Although these provisions would not be enacted fully until the 1860s, the California legislature provided for school districts in 1851 and a year later authorized a state property tax to support public schools.

A drawing of the first schoolhouse in San Francisco

Sources:

Laurence Murrell Childers, "Education in California under Spain and Mexico and under American Rule," dissertation, University of California, Berkeley, 1930;

Charles Toto Jr., "A History of Education in California, 1800–1850," dissertation, University of California, Berkeley, 1952.

EUROPEAN EXPERIMENTS

Lancasterian Schools. Educational trends emanating from Europe appeared in various experiments that flourished and ebbed in the unrestricted atmosphere of the West. In 1798 the British Quaker Joseph Lancaster, lacking funds yet eager to teach literacy to children in London's slums, devised an educational plan through which student monitors would aid a single teacher, enabling him to simultaneously instruct several hundred children. Arranging his school into small classes of equal ability, he placed each monitor in charge of about ten boys, teaching them letters of the alphabet and simple words, which they traced in dry sand. For more difficult lessons the students switched to slates, copying from cards that the monitors read aloud and passed from group to group. The bedlam that could have resulted from several hundred children in one room was avoided by Lancaster's insistence on uniform, drill-like behavior. Students were constantly marching, reciting, and responding to verbal commands. They also were motivated by emulation and were encouraged to compete with each other by earning and wearing a card indicating their rank in the class. Earning tickets similar to wages, they could purchase a toy to take home as a prize. Legislators and promoters in the United States extolled the Lancasterian system for its economy, efficiency, and machinelike replicability. During the urban depression following the War of 1812, the system was adopted by the Pennsylvania legislature for education of the children of the poor, and in 1818 it became the first public school system in the state. The New York legislature followed Pennsylvania's example in 1825 when they adopted as a public school system the city's existing Lancasterian primary schools and new monitorial high school. In the 1820s the New York teachers were called "operatives," and the machinelike replicability of the system was considered an educational panacea. Yet the schools were established not only in manufacturing areas but also throughout the nation. Children learned literacy, drill-like behavior, and the practices of a cash economy in more than 150 Lancasterian schools, not only in eastern states but also in such western locations as Cincinnati, Detroit, New Orleans, and Mexican Los Angeles.

New Harmony, Indiana. In the same decade different educational methods based on precepts of Heinrich Pestalozzi found expression in the West. As a young man in the 1770s at his farm near Bern, Switzerland, Pestalozzi had attempted to apply the principles of Jean-Jacques Rousseau's educational treatise *Emile* (1762) to destitute orphans. Drawing on that experience, he wrote *Leonard and Gertrude* in 1781, followed by *How Gertrude Teaches Her Children* in 1811, in which he explained how a child's nature could unfold through discovery of the environment and self-directed activity in an atmosphere of affection. From 1804 to 1825 Pestalozzi conducted a teacher's institute at Yverdon, Switzerland, training assistants and visitors who disseminated his ideas across the Continent and greatly influenced the state-supported school system of King Wilhelm III in Prussia. On a tour of Europe the English industrial reformer Robert Owen was so taken with these methods that he enrolled his sons Robert Dale and William in an academy directed by a follower of Pestalozzi, Philipp Emanuel von Fellenberg. After experience with his

---

SCHOOL REFORM

Legislation providing district schools on the New England model was enacted in Ohio in 1821, but school reform similar to that advocated by Horace Mann was promoted in the state in 1837 by Calvin Stowe, a professor at Lane Seminary who had married Harriet, a daughter of the seminary's president, Lyman Beecher. Stowe was a participant in Cincinnati's Western Literary Institute and College of Professional Teachers, which evolved from a conference in that city in 1831. Authors, teachers, clergymen, and other professionals met annually to deliver papers on Western education, which they published in the Institute's *Transactions*. Providing self-appointed leadership on such topics as female education and teacher training, the group sought to influence educational policy in the West. When Stowe embarked on a trip to Europe to purchase a library for Lane, he was asked by these individuals to observe the methods of Pestalozzi and the Prussian public schools. In the "Report on Elementary Public Instruction in Europe" he prepared for the Ohio legislature, Stowe argued that if monarchies could create affectionate patriotism through education, it was even more important for a republican government to awaken national spirit and develop and direct the talents of its citizens. Advocating republican education for immigrants and for girls who would be future wives and mothers, he called for dedicated teachers, supportive parents, and an eight-year continuously attended, gradually graded course for children. The report was printed and disseminated in ten thousand copies by the Ohio legislature, arousing the interest of educators in other states and influencing legislators throughout the antebellum period.

Sources: Edgar W. Knight, ed., *Reports on European Education* (New York: McGraw-Hill, 1930);

Milton Rugoff, *The Beechers: An American Family in the Nineteenth Century* (New York: Harper & Row, 1981).

---

model textile mill village at New Lanark, Scotland, Owen came to believe that education included all aspects of society. In 1817 he devised his "educational parallelogram," a planned community of family living quarters, children's dormitories, communal dining rooms, chapels, and schools, all supported by the community's stables, farms, and factories. Hoping to implement his ideas in America, in 1824 Owen purchased a religious community at New Harmony, Indiana. Since 1806 one of Pestalozzi's Yverdon assistants, Joseph Neef, had been joined by a Scottish scientist, William Maclure, in applying the master's principles in a Philadelphia school. Accompanied by other progressive teachers and scientists, Neef and Maclure came to New Harmony in 1825, where they conducted Pestalozzian boarding schools for infants and children and industrial training schools for adults. As the community deteriorated, these experiments were short-lived. Nevertheless, Robert Owen brought to the West a secular vision that education was the means to a perfect society.

Sources:

Lawrence A. Cremin, *American Education: The National Experience, 1783–1876* (New York: Harper & Row, 1980);

Robert B. Downs, *Heinrich Pestalozzi, Father of Modern Pedagogy* (Boston: Twayne, 1975);

Carl F. Kaestle, *Joseph Lancaster and the Monitorial School Movement* (New York: Teachers College Press, 1973);

Joseph Lancaster, *Improvements in Education as it Respects the Industrious Classes of the Community* (London: Darton & Harvey, 1805).

EVANGELICAL EDUCATION

Sunday Schools. The religious revivals sweeping the nation from 1800 through 1860, which historians have labeled the Second Great Awakening, had a direct and lasting impact on education in the West. In the great revival at Cane Ridge, Kentucky, in 1801, as many as twelve to twenty-five thousand settlers flocked to hear itinerant ministers. Converted in the revival, sixteen-year-old Peter Cartwright began his long career preaching on the Methodist circuit, culminating in the vigorous camp meetings he led in the new state of Illinois in the 1820s. Yet lay leaders of the Protestant Crusade in the East were fearful that rapid westward movement created a vacuum in civic order and moral restraint. One of the new national voluntary associations of the 1820s, the American Sunday School Union, gathered enough strength by 1830 to plan an operation in the Mississippi River valley, determined to plant a Sabbath school wherever there were settlers. Sunday school missionaries and materials disseminated evangelical values in the West, advocating Protestant nationalism and internalized restraints. As Sunday schools spread from Kentucky, Tennessee, and Ohio into Indiana, Illinois, and Missouri, teachers instructed children in reading and orderly self-regulated behavior. Yet they also sought to elicit conversion experiences in children as young as seven or eight, even four or five years of age. Initially the British tracts used in the schools sought to awaken children to religious instruction by evoking the emotions of pity and terror. By 1830, however, Eastern managers of the American Sunday School Union preferred instructional materials that followed the current pedagogical trends through teaching methods that emulated parental affection and evangelical children's literature that mingled its religious message with instruction in literacy, patriotism, and natural science.

Beecher. Evangelical education in the West also was influenced by the career of Lyman Beecher, a dynamic Congregational minister who graduated from Yale Divinity School in 1797 determined to fight religious infidelity and the declining status of the New England clergy. Although a Calvinist, Beecher responded to the democratic forces in post-Revolutionary society by allowing individuals enough free agency to choose to repent, a shift away from predestination and an arbitrary God. In 1832, after a career in the Northeast in which he conducted revivals, contested Unitarian doctrine, and advocated such evangelical causes as temperance, Beecher focused his energy on the West, accepting the positions of president of Lane Seminary and minister of the Second Presbyterian Church in Cincinnati. Two years later Lane was engulfed in controversy when students led by Theodore Weld held protracted meetings on

A SUNDAY SCHOOL PRIMER

In 1826 Joseph Dulles of Philadelphia, an active member of the Committee of Publications of the American Sunday School Union, prepared a primer that he hoped would be used to teach every American child to read. Its educational message combined literacy with moral instruction. For example, the children were taught the sentence, "Remember thy Creator in the days of thy youth." Each child was instructed to spell one word aloud while the teacher explained the meaning of the sentence and impressed the lesson on the hearts of the children. Stories in the primer contrasted tamed with untamed animal nature. An engraving of a sheep illustrated an animal useful and helpful to man. By contrast, an engraving of a fierce and shaggy bear depicted the destructive untamed animal. Yet the primer offered children the hope that animal nature could be tamed. It ended with an engraving of the lion lying down with the lamb, the millennial promise of the peaceable kingdom. And to help children tame their own animal natures, the schoolbook reminded them that God watched them all the time: "In every place, by night and day, *He* watches all you do and say."

Source: Joseph Dulles, *The Union Primer or First Book for Children, Compiled for the American Sunday School Union and Fitted for the Use of Schools in the United States* (Philadelphia: The American Sunday School Union, Revised by the Committee of Publications, 1826).

A drawing of a one-room schoolhouse, 1805. The boy at the right is forced to sit under the teacher's desk as a form of punishment. (Historical Society of York County, Pennsylvania)

slavery and sought to educate members of Cincinnati's free black community. Rebuffed by the response of the school's trustees, fifty-three students left Lane and joined the newly founded Oberlin Institute, where rival revivalist Charles Grandison Finney was on the faculty and blacks and women were admitted as students. Following this defeat Beecher traveled east to preach about the West, proclaiming the need for Protestant education. In his influential *Plea for the West,* published in 1835, he proclaimed his faith that the millennium could commence in America if only the nation understood its divine calling. According to Beecher, the battle would take place in the West. He called for institutions to train ministers who would distribute religious tracts, establish Sunday schools and public schools, and found churches and colleges to lead the region to true religion and republican values. For Beecher the adversary was the Catholic Church, which also was founding denominational institutions in the West. For him the solution was a Protestant education, which would cultivate the intellect, form the character, and regulate the affections of the potentially unruly Western population.

Sources:

Anne M. Boylan, *Sunday School: The Formation of an American Institution, 1790–1880* (New Haven: Yale University Press, 1988);

Lawrence A. Cremin, *American Education: The National Experience, 1783–1876* (New York: Harper & Row, 1980);

Milton Rugoff, *The Beechers: An American Family in the Nineteenth Century* (New York: Harper & Row, 1981).

HIGHER EDUCATION IN THE WEST

Denominational Colleges. Spurred by the revivals of the Second Great Awakening, Protestant denominations competed to establish colleges in the West, determined to spread their doctrines among Western settlers and to train ministers. Much of this impulse arose in Eastern colleges, such as Congregationalist Yale and Presbyterian Princeton, where revivals stimulated young missionaries to win the West from religious infidelity and Spanish Catholicism. Interest in the formation of denominational institutions also was encouraged by the U.S. Supreme Court in the Dartmouth case in 1819, which decided that privately organized colleges would be free from state intervention. Congregationalists and Presbyterians, who had joined forces in the Plan of Union in 1801, organized the Presbyterian Board of Education in

1819 and the American Home Missionary Society in 1826. After missionaries from the Connecticut Mission Society successfully founded Western Reserve University in Cleveland, Ohio, in 1826, Congregationalists and Presbyterians established Oberlin College in Ohio, Hanover and Wabash Colleges in Indiana, Illinois College and Knox College in Illinois, and Adrian College in Michigan in the 1830s. Rival denominations, which originally had relied on itinerant preachers, sought an educated and settled ministry by the 1830s. To combat Presbyterian influence, Methodists founded DePauw University in Indiana, and Baptists established Franklin College in that state and Denison University in Ohio. A strong motivation for this proliferation of Protestant institutions was the Catholic founding of St. Louis University in Missouri and St. Mary's College in Kentucky. By 1843 the Society for the Promotion of Collegiate and Theological Education in the West was organized in New York and began to act as a restraining influence on excessive denominational rivalry. Nevertheless, competing private institutions continued to proliferate in the Midwest and old Southwest, and the denominational impulse reached Oregon and California by the 1850s.

State Universities. The West also proved to be fertile ground for the establishment of secular state universities, based on the model of Thomas Jefferson's plans for the University of Virginia, established in 1819. In the late 1820s the Reverend Philip Lindsay sought to build a similar institution at the University of Nashville in Tennessee, as did Horace Holley at Transylvania University in Lexington, Kentucky. These liberal plans were dashed, however, as denominational interests sought control of higher education. Public lands had been granted by the United States for state universities since 1787, when members of the Ohio Company had refused to complete their purchase of lands in the public domain unless two townships in their tract be set aside as an endowment. After the state of Ohio took over these endowment lands in 1804, every new state west of the Appalachians was granted federal lands to support a university. States were required by enabling acts admitting them to the union to guarantee that these lands would be used for education. By 1857, when the Morrill Act providing federal land grants was first introduced in Congress, four million acres of public land in fifteen states already had been set aside for public universities. Yet the desire of denominational interests to influence higher education prevented state legislatures from enacting necessary taxes to produce permanent revenue. In Ohio, Illinois, and Indiana religious groups continued to dominate the state universities. In Michigan Territory in 1817 Judge Augustus B. Woodward worked out in consultation with Thomas Jefferson a secular plan he labeled the "Catholepistemiad," which was based on the French centralized system of education. Although the plan was not carried out, it was confirmed by the territorial legislature in 1821, which helped strengthen resistance to sectarian

THE FOUNDING OF OBERLIN COLLEGE

After Theodore Weld and other antislavery rebels left Lane Seminary in Cincinnati in 1834, they enrolled at Oberlin Collegiate Institute, which had recently been founded in northeastern Ohio by John Jay Shipherd, a Congregationalist minister, to advance the cause of Protestant Christianity in the West. Shipherd had designed the college as a manual-labor school, seeking to train the body and heart of each student as well as the intellect. According to his original plan, students would labor four hours a day; in addition to the Male Department, a Female Department already was contemplated, in which female students would engage in domestic tasks, the culture of silk, and the manufacture of clothing. Eliza Branch, the first female student, taught the infant school while she also was attending the academic course. In addition she helped Esther Shipherd care for the sixteen members of the tiny colony who boarded in the school's log cabin. Shipherd planned to finance the endeavor by producing iron cooking stoves, which he advertised in local newspapers. However, short of funds, he seized the opportunity offered when Weld and the other rebels left Lane, enticing them to relocate at his college and welcoming their one supporter on the Lane board of trustees, Asa Mahan, as Oberlin's new president. His coup was solidified when the renowned revivalist Charles Grandison Finney consented to join the faculty as professor of theology. Finney's participation prompted the wealthy New York philanthropist Arthur Tappan to offer ten thousand dollars to fund the institution, and other supporters agreed to supply the salaries of eight additional faculty members. Oberlin's board of trustees was then persuaded to consent to the demand of the Lane rebels and antislavery philanthropists that African Americans be admitted as students. In addition to thirty-two of the former Lane seminarians, young Protestant radicals flocked to Oberlin, eager to serve the cause of antislavery in the West. As the new college boomed, buildings and boarding houses were rapidly constructed, and preparatory manual-labor branches organized to ready students for the college curriculum. Religious revivals and radical causes continued to stimulate the students, and Oberlin College emerged as a flagship institution in the denominational effort to win the battle for Protestant Christianity in the West.

Source: Robert Samuel Fletcher, *A History of Oberlin College, from Its Foundation Through the Civil War* (New York: Arno Press, 1971).

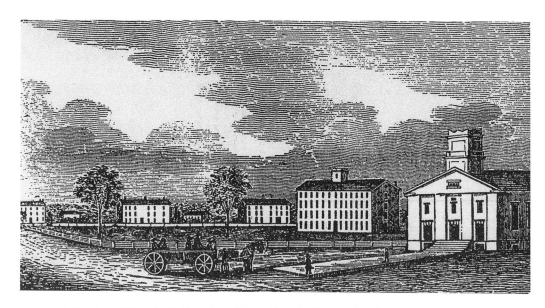

A drawing of Oberlin College from Henry Howe's *Historical Collections of Ohio* (1848)

influence when Michigan became a state. President Henry B. Tappan of the University of Michigan fought the battle with denominational interests in the 1850s, hoping to implement the Jeffersonian ideal of a secular state university. Seeking to create a great educational institution based on the model of the University of Berlin, Tappan worked for a public university that could pursue scientific knowledge free from sectarian control. The 1837 charter for the University of Michigan became a model for other states and was followed in the planning of the University of Wisconsin in 1848 and the University of Minnesota in 1851.

Sources:

John S. Brubacher and Willis Rudy, *Higher Education in Transition: A History of American Colleges and Universities, 1636–1976* (New York: Harper & Row, 1976);

Donald G. Tewksbury, *The Founding of American Colleges and Universities Before the Civil War* (New York: Arno Press, 1969).

IMMIGRANTS

Irish Catholics. Most Irish immigrants who came to the United States in the eighteenth and early nineteenth centuries were Scots-Irish Protestants, many of whom possessed education, skills, and some capital. As the population soared in southern and western Ireland and small holdings became increasingly subdivided, by the 1830s more Irish Catholics immigrated to the United States. Although these young men and women who traveled across the Atlantic may have hoped to become landowning farmers, most of them found work as day laborers and domestic servants. As a result of the great potato famine of the late 1840s 1.5 million people left Ireland for the United States; most were destitute farmers, cottiers, and laborers, and about half of them arrived in family groups including children. Famine immigrants were mostly Catholic, and one-fourth to one-third were Gaelic-speaking; unaccustomed to an urban industrial

society, they struggled to survive in Northeastern cities. About 85 percent of them were unskilled, and as a result, men found work mostly as laborers, driving carts, working in construction, or traveling to western areas to build railroads and dig canals. Women and children found work in small shops or joined the labor force in Eastern textile mills. In the 1840s Catholic priests began to protest the Protestant message taught in American public schools and nativist issues infused local politics. As the clergy struggled to church the famine immigrants in the context of inflamed nativism in the 1850s, Irish Americans began to create distinct ethnic communities and separate Catholic institutions. Much of this communitybuilding was done by women as nuns provided social services and founded parochial schools for girls. Parish schools for girls preceded those for boys and more girls attended them while boys attended public schools.

Catholic Schools in the West. By mid century Catholics began to create new schools in the West. Existing educational institutions, such as the eighteenth-century French Ursuline Convent in New Orleans and schools conducted by the Sisters of Charity in St. Louis, were joined by parochial and industrial schools taught by such groups as the Sisters of Notre Dame or the Sisters of Mercy. Arriving in the United States from Ireland in 1843, the Sisters of Mercy migrated from Eastern cities to Chicago, St. Louis, San Francisco, and Sacramento in the 1850s, where they provided community hospitals, social services, and protection for destitute women. The Sisters of Notre Dame conducted a boarding school for girls in San Jose, California, by 1851. Girls, who were taught reading, writing, and fine needlework by nuns, internalized a Catholic domesticity, which they, in turn, as mothers, transmitted to their children. Yet many Irish girls also learned middle-class values through their em-

In the American West, German immigrant families had varied options for the education of their children. Some families designated at least one child to become proficient in English. A tenant farmer named Wilhelm Stille emigrated from Lengerich in Westphalia with some of his siblings in 1833 and settled on an eighty-acre farm in Ohio. His sister Wilhelmina and her husband Wilhelm Krumme bought eighty additional acres across the Ohio River. Ten years later Stille had lost through death his firstborn child, his nineteen-year-old brother Rudolph, and his sister, Wilhelmina who left a three-year-old son, Johann. Wilhelm Krumme boarded his son with strangers and wrote to his in-laws in Wesphalia to send his wife's inheritance. When Johann was seven, his father reported: "[H]e now goes to the English school every day which costs 8 talers a year; he can already read pretty well, and I hope he'll take a shine to learning so he won't have to do any heavy work." Three years later he wrote of his ten-year-old son: "[H]e goes to school every day and he's a good pupil, that is in the English language since he can handle books fairly well but he doesn't know much German." Stille's sons would remain poor farmers, but Johann Krumme, assisted by money from his German relatives and his proficiency in English, assimilated into the American middle class. At the age of nineteen he clerked in a tobacco shop in Cincinnati; after marrying a native-born girl he advanced at the tobacco company to foreman and then to agent-salesman.

Source: "Letters from Wilhelm Stille and Wilhelm Krumme to relatives in Westphalia," in *News from the Land of Freedom: German Immigrants Write Home*, edited by Walter D. Kemphoefner, Wolfgang Helbich, and Ulrike Sommer; translated by Susan Carter Vogel (Ithaca, N.Y.: Cornell University Press, 1991).

ployment as domestic servants. Although Irish American community leaders considered service in Protestant homes a threat to Catholic religious life, these immigrant girls learned middle-class attitudes and behaviors that, in turn, also influenced their communities and eventually their children.

German Immigrants. As immigration rose to unprecedented levels in the 1840s and 1850s, 1.5 million Germans also entered the United States. Propelled in the 1830s by population growth and deterioration in crafts in home kingdoms, duchies, and provinces and by potato blight and the failed political revolution of 1848, German craftsmen, small proprietors, and laborers arrived alone or with their families. Although these immigrants settled in Northeastern cities from New York to Baltimore, many also traveled railroad lines, canals, and rivers to the Midwest, forming a "German-belt" that would eventually extend from Ohio to Nebraska and Missouri to Wisconsin. Most Germans brought with them a strong patriarchal tradition, yet many also espoused the liberal and democratic values of political movements fighting autocracy in Europe. Craftsmen and small-property owners who founded German organizations such as the *Turnvereine* expressed ideals of progressive democracy that were radical in mid-nineteenth-century America. Although German Catholics and both conservative and evangelical Lutherans favored parochial education, many of these immigrants were staunch supporters of American secular public schools. German Americans often advocated bilingual education, and they pressed for instruction in the German language. Legislatures passed laws permitting the teaching of German in public schools in Pennsylvania and Ohio before 1840, and in some remote areas in the West, such as rural Missouri, local school boards initiated German instruction in common schools without legal authorization.

Sources:

Hasia R. Diner, *Erin's Daughters in America: Irish Immigrant Women in the Nineteenth Century* (Baltimore: Johns Hopkins University Press, 1983);

Bruce Levine, *The Spirit of 1848: German Immigrants, Labor Conflict, and the Coming of the Civil War* (Urbana: University of Illinois Press, 1992);

Kerby A. Miller, *Emigrants and Exiles: Ireland and the Irish Exodus to North America* (New York: Oxford University Press, 1985).

JUVENILE DELINQUENCY

State Reform Schools. By the 1850s, as states increased their role in education and nativist attitudes toward immigrants became widespread, courts and legislatures increased intervention in families who deviated from prescribed domestic ideals. In the expansive early republic through individual decisions, judges had forged a liberal and contractual family law, decreasing patriarchy and extending the individual rights of wives and children. Expanding the doctrine of *parens patriae* to challenge paternal custody rights, they also used the argument of "the child's best interests" to enlarge judicial authority. As mothers assumed the central role in child rearing, women won an increasing number of custody cases. Yet new standards of child welfare and parental fitness also could reduce the rights of both parents as destitute or delinquent children who came before police courts were placed in more-acceptable domestic situations or in new institutions founded by the state. The first state reform school for boys was founded in Westborough, Massachusetts, in 1847; when the first compulsory attendance law was passed by that state's legislature in 1852, habitual truants could be sentenced to the state reformatory. School reformers, however—Horace

A circa 1820 painting of a teacher preparing to administer corporal punishment on a pupil
(Granger Collection, New York City)

Mann, Henry Barnard, and Samuel Gridley Howe—admired a new European model of a "family" reform school, charging that reformatories resembled prisons more than schools. This domestic model was followed in the Massachusetts Industrial School for Girls, founded in 1854. As the Midwest increasingly resembled the Northeast in the 1850s, legislatures in Ohio, Wisconsin, Illinois, and Indiana voted to establish similar state reform schools on the family model.

The Children's Aid Society. Reformers in Eastern cities came to believe that the West was an ideal environment for destitute or delinquent urban children. In the West, separated from the corrupting influences so rampant in Eastern cities, children could obtain physical and moral health as well as economic opportunity. One of these reformers was Charles Loring Brace, who became an urban missionary for the Children's Aid Society in 1853. Immersing himself in New York's most dangerous and notorious neighborhoods, where he founded industrial schools for girls and a Newsboys Lodging-house, Brace came to admire the self-reliant and resourceful urban children. Such children, he wrote, felt keenly "the profound forces of American life; the desire of equality, ambition to rise, the sense of self-respect and the passion

for education." Convinced that each child "ought to labor with a motive," with "something of the boundless hope which stimulates so wonderfully the American youth," he was critical of the state reform school, which he felt instilled its own habits and vices and did not prepare children to succeed in life. Concluding that "the best of all Asylums for the outcast child is the *farmer's home*," Brace determined to place city children with Western farmers, who would treat them like members of the family and would welcome extra labor. By 1857 the Children's Aid Society placed about six hundred city boys in Western states, transporting them by train to farmers who selected them at railroad stations in Michigan, Iowa, or Illinois. Catholic clergymen criticized the Protestant charity, charging that it kidnapped Catholic children, wrenching them from struggling immigrant families and weaning them from their faith. Other critics objected that the children sent west were exploited for their labor, that the charity failed to follow the fate of the boys, and that the plan benefited neither farmers nor the children. Nevertheless, placing its faith in time-honored patterns of children's work and the entrepreneurial energy of the children themselves, by 1860 the Children's

Aid Society sent to Western homes as many as 5,074 urban children.

Sources:

Charles Loring Brace, *The Dangerous Classes of New York and Twenty Years' Work Among Them* (New York: Wynkoop & Hallenbeck, 1872);

The Life Of Charles Loring Brace (London, 1894);

Robert Bremner, ed., *Children and Youth in America: A Documentary History*, 3 volumes (Cambridge, Mass.: Harvard University Press, 1970);

Michael Grossberg, *Governing the Hearth: Law and the Family in Nineteenth-Century America* (Chapel Hill: University of North Carolina Press, 1985);

Joseph M. Hawes, *Children in Urban Society: Juvenile Delinquency in Nineteenth-Century America* (New York: Oxford University Press, 1971);

Steven L. Schlossman, *Love & the American Delinquent: The Theory and Practice of Progressive Juvenile Justice, 1825–1920* (Chicago: University of Chicago Press, 1977).

NATIVE AMERICANS

A Moravian School. In the first decades of the new American republic, federal policy toward Indians sought to convert them into yeomen and eventually citizens through trading ties, intermarriage, and economic assistance. Thomas Jefferson as president in 1800 continued the policies of George Washington's administration, urging property ownership, obedience to law, and assimilation. Yet he also promised Georgia in 1802 that if the state ceded its Western claims (the territory that became Alabama and Mississippi) to the national domain, Indians within its borders eventually would be removed. The Louisiana Purchase in 1803 provided land across the Mississippi River for natives who wished to pursue their traditional ways. Although the federal government did not provide schools, its agents, such as Return J. Meigs among the Cherokees, encouraged admission of skilled whites into Indian lands to demonstrate development of resources and to promote trade. In a remarkable educational experiment characteristic of their faith, Moravian missionaries from Germany and eastern Europe entered the Cherokee nation in 1801, settling at Spring Place in northern Georgia. Although the missionaries came to preach, they were encouraged to begin a school by Upper Town chiefs, who favored acculturation and resisted removal and relinquishment of land. Chiefs who brought their children to the Moravian school expected them to learn English and become interpreters and intermediaries between old and new ways. By 1806 white farmers in the area also brought their children to the school; slaves would not be educated until they became converts, but African Americans attended the Moravian meeting. Pupils at the school learned to read the Bible, spell, and sing hymns. Required to work in the cornfields and peach orchards, they also learned to be farmers. In 1818 missionaries from the American Board of Commissioners of Foreign Missions (ABCFM) established another school in eastern Tennessee, and some of the original pupils of the Moravians traveled to Cornwall, Connecticut, to en-

The Cherokee scholar, Sequoyah

roll in the ABCFM's parent school. On their return to the Cherokee nation, where they were wealthy planters and slave owners, some of these children who began their education at the Moravian school—John Rollin Ridge, Elias Boudinot, David and John Vann, and Elijah Hicks—became leaders of the Cherokee "renascence" of the 1820s. In the following decade they worked with Northern missionaries and lawyers in the appeal to federal courts to save the lands and sovereignty of the Cherokee nation when President Andrew Jackson implemented the shift in federal policy toward Indian removal across the Mississippi River.

Missionaries in the Far West. Jackson's policy of Indian removal shifted the work of the ABCFM from Southern projects to the Trans-Mississippi West. In 1836 the newly married Marcus and Narcissa Whitman left their homes in western New York to travel as ABCFM missionaries to the Oregon country, territory far beyond the boundary of the Louisiana Purchase that still was claimed by Great Britain. Among the first white families to experience the Overland Trail, they journeyed with fur trappers and traders along the Platte River, across the Rocky Mountains at the South Pass, and down the Snake River and across the Blue Mountains to the Hudson Bay Company's Fort Walla Walla. Soon after, they established their mission there among the Cayuse Indians. Converted as a child in the evangelical revivals of western New York, Narcissa Whitman never doubted that her task was to bring Protestant Christianity and Anglo-American civilization to the Indians. The Cayuses and their neighbors the Nez Percés still were following an annual cycle of winter settlement and travel in

A painting of a women's school (circa 1840) by an unknown artist (M. and M. Karolik Collection, Museum of Fine Arts, Boston)

the other seasons to hunt, fish, and gather food. Although they welcomed the missionaries, they had little intention of living a settled life and relinquishing their cultural practices and beliefs. At the mission school she conducted in her kitchen, Narcissa Whitman instructed Cayuse children in English and the Nez Percés language, which she gradually learned. Her husband Marcus conducted services, tried to practice medicine, and struggled to persuade native men and boys to be farmers. Yet, in despair after the accidental drowning of her daughter, Narcissa was troubled by her lack of fitness for missionary life. When the Cayuses failed to accept the Protestant message, relations between the Indians and missionaries deteriorated. When prospective settlers from the United States entered the area in the mid 1840s, the Whitmans began to view their calling as the education of white children. In 1846, after the United States acquired the Oregon Territory through treaty with Great Britain and larger groups of emigrants entered the area, the Cayuses directed their resentment at the mission. Devastated by imported diseases, especially a lethal measles epidemic in 1847, Indians attacked the mission and killed the Whitmans and some of their associates. This disaster ended the work of the ABCFM in Oregon; Narcissa Whitman, who was greatly admired in the Eastern states, became a martyr.

Sources:

Julie Roy Jeffrey, *Converting the West* (Norman: University of Oklahoma Press, 1991);

William G. McLoughlin, *Cherokee Renascence in the New Republic* (Princeton, N.J.: Princeton University, 1986).

TEACHERS FOR THE WEST

Female Teachers. In the 1840s Calvin Stowe was persuaded by his sister-in-law, the educator Catharine Beecher, to head an organization raising funds to send young women to the West to serve as missionary teachers. Trained by Beecher in Albany, New York, and Hartford, Connecticut, seventy young women traveled in 1847 to Indiana, Illinois, Iowa, Wisconsin, Michigan, Kentucky, and Tennessee to teach in local district or subscription schools, establish Sunday schools, and serve as moral influences in their new communities. Eventually this Central Committee for Promoting National Education, renamed the National Board of Popular Education in the 1850s, sent 450 teachers to the West. Educated in academies inspired by Revolutionary rhetoric, most of the young women were converted in the evangelical revivals of the Second Great Awakening. They also sought independence in the West; although some returned home, others married and raised families in their new communities. In the 1840s women outnumbered men in the East and gradually were replacing them as teachers. In the new public school systems a hierarchy developed with female teachers directed by a male principal teacher. Communities in the West, however, were slower to employ women as teachers, perhaps because men still viewed teaching as short-term employment prior to a business career. Although female teachers often were better qualified than the men who held teaching positions, women were paid half the wage men received, a situation justified by the argument that women did not support a family and were working only until they married. Although Catharine Beecher defined teaching as an extension of domestic duties and emphasized the willingness of women to work for less money, she also lobbied Congress in 1853 for free normal schools that would provide both men and women with professional education and status.

Establishment of Normal Schools. As rural capitalism developed in the Midwest and new states established public school systems, demand arose for normal schools to train teachers. Such institutions were established by Whigs who advocated school reform, a commercial economy, and a positive role for the state. For example, Isaac Funk migrated westward with his parents and eight siblings from Kentucky through Ohio to Blooming Grove in McLean County, Illinois, in 1823. After attending a local subscription school in a log cabin, by the 1830s he was driving hogs and cattle purchased in Missouri to market in Chicago. Famous locally as the "beef king" in the 1850s, he owned twenty-five thousand acres of land farmed by tenants and hired labor, and he possessed one million dollars worth of livestock. As a Whig county supervisor Funk arranged the selling of county swamplands that would bring a new state normal school to the thriving agricultural area. Six male and three female scholars enrolled to study Horace Mann's lectures and the *American Journal of Education* (edited by Henry Barnard) when the Illinois State Normal University opened in 1857. "Our parents were sad-faced struggling pioneers of the prairies," one of them later recalled, "but we were cheery, resolute, and happy in our life and work."

Sources:

Polly Welts Kaufman, *Women Teachers on the Frontier* (New Haven: Yale University Press, 1984);

Semi-Centennial History of the Illinois State Normal University, 1857–1907 (Normal, Ill., 1907);

Kathryn Kish Sklar, *Catherine Beecher: A Study in American Domesticity* (New Haven: Yale University Press, 1973).

HEADLINE MAKERS

CATHARINE BEECHER

1800-1878

TEACHER

An Evangelical Childhood. Born in 1800 as the eldest child of Lyman Beecher, Catharine Beecher enjoyed a special relationship with her high-spirited father when he was a young, dynamic minister first on Long Island and then in Litchfield, Connecticut. Raised on a New England farm, Lyman Beecher played pranks on his eleven children, joined them in chopping wood and hoeing the garden, and participated with gusto in their rural tramps and games. He also taught them his robust Calvinism, badgering them with reminders of sin and a vividly imagined hell. Yet Catharine also was influenced by her genteel mother, Roxana Foote Beecher, as well as the education she received from age ten in the works of eighteenth-century British authors, admonitions to female virtue, and the genteel accomplishments at Sarah Pierce's Litchfield Female Academy. A lively and intelligent child, Catharine excelled in social situations and participated vigorously in school and community contests and games. On Roxana's death from consumption in 1816, she assumed full care of her seven younger siblings until her father's remarriage a year later. When in her early twenties she had not yet experienced conversion, her father pressed the issue until she fell ill. Catharine could not feel guilty enough to submit. Her religious crisis intensified when her fiancé, Alexander Metcalf Fisher, died in a shipwreck, and Lyman Beecher intimated that the young man may have been damned. Catharine's loss became a theological confrontation with her father and her God. Unable to accept eternal punishment for those who died without conversion, she immersed herself in intellectual study and did not join a church until she left the family home and moved to Hartford, Connecticut.

Becoming an Educator. In Hartford, Beecher achieved both personal and professional independence through the school she started in 1823, the Hartford Female Seminary. Living in a rented home with her siblings Mary, Harriet, and Henry, she appropriated for herself her father's cultural leadership in 1826 by initiating a revival in her school. She also became an educational reformer and entrepreneur, introducing an advanced curriculum for girls and raising funds for a building. As she worked out ideas she published in *The Elements of Moral Philosophy, Founded upon Experience, Reason, and the Bible* in 1831, she rejected the evangelical conversion experience and concluded that salvation could be achieved through a blameless life. Women, she believed, should submit their self-interest to the general good in order to act as moral guardians and shape the nation's standards. Merging her father's evangelical goals with her mother's refined gentility, Beecher turned her seminary to the training of teachers, who, she hoped, would exert a restraining moral influence on the democratic nation. When she accompanied her father on his move to Cincinnati in 1832, she planned to duplicate her Hartford success in the West, organizing within a year her Western Female Institute. This Cincinnati school soon resembled a conventional female academy and failed within four years. Beecher did not give up. In 1835 she joined Lyman Beecher's plea for education in the West, publishing an address she delivered to women in the East, *An Essay on the Education of Female Teachers.* Like her father, Beecher played on Eastern fears, urging the training of female teachers to civilize immigrants and the lower classes. One-third of Western children, she estimated, were unschooled; as men sought wealth in the market economy, the task of a national system of moral education would fall to energetic and benevolent women such as herself. Three years later, when she published *The Moral Instructor for Schools and Families* (1838), Beecher assumed the role that would bring her national acclaim; rejecting the individualized conversion experience of evangelical Calvinism, she focused on the family as a socializing force and the cultivated conscience as an agency of moral authority appropriate for the rapidly expanding democratic society.

Domestic Ideology. In 1841 Catharine Beecher wove these themes into her discussion of "The Peculiar Responsibilities of American Women," which introduced her *Treatise on Domestic Economy.* Urging women to support democratic institutions, she argued that to achieve social order hierarchical relationships also had to be maintained. Reiterating the responsible free agency she had learned from her father, she insisted that in democratic America, women could *choose* their superiors, submitting voluntarily to their husbands. American women would not participate in political life, yet they would mold the minds, morals, and manners of their children. Their reward would be participation in the providential plan as democratic equality spread throughout the world. As Beecher went on to instruct women in principles of domestic economy, she sought to transcend barriers of region and social class, creating national allegiance to a common culture. Democratizing the genteel values with which she had been raised, she argued that refinement was compatible with work. All was moving and changing in nineteenth-century America, she wrote: economic fortunes rose and fell; people in new settlements lived in log cabins; domestic servants were difficult to obtain; and individuals of all social classes mingled with and emulated those of larger means. According to Beecher, a democratic lady in her neat oilcloth apron need not forego gentility even as she performed her own domestic work. In a democracy, she argued, mothers should teach daughters, and teachers their pupils, that it was refined and ladylike to engage in domestic pursuits.

Teachers for the West. In the 1840s Beecher became the promoter and publicist of an organization ostensibly headed by her brother-in-law Calvin Stowe that proposed to raise funds to send young women as missionary teachers to the West. In 1847 she trained thirty-five young women in Albany, New York, and thirty-five more in Hartford to travel to Western states to teach district and subscription schools, found Sunday schools, and serve as moral influences in their communities. Eventually this Central Committee for Promoting National Education, which was moved to Cleveland by its general agent William Slade and renamed The National Board of Popular Education, sent out as many as 450 female teachers. After a confrontation with Slade, Beecher founded The American Women's Educational Association (AWEA) in 1852, seeking to replace the rural missionary teacher with women's colleges in urban settings. In the early 1850s she focused her attention on The Milwaukee Female College, where she hoped to prepare young women to be professional teachers and homemakers. By 1856, however, Beecher's plan to establish a home in Milwaukee had not materialized, and she withdrew from the college and resigned from the AWEA to end her career as an educator. Like her sister Harriet Beecher Stowe, she continued to ponder her heritage of New England Calvinism until she became an Episcopalian. Returning to Hartford, she briefly resumed her work at the still successful Hartford Female Seminary until she retired to her brother's home in Elmira, New York, shortly before her death in 1878.

Sources:

Catharine Beecher, *A Treatise on Domestic Economy* (Boston: T. H. Webb, 1841);

Milton Rugoff, *The Beechers: An American Family in the Nineteenth Century* (New York: Harper & Row, 1981);

Kathryn Kish Sklar, *Catharine Beecher: A Study in American Domesticity* (New Haven: Yale University Press, 1973).

DANIEL DRAKE

1785–1852

MEDICAL EDUCATOR

A Pioneer Childhood. Born in Essex County, New Jersey, in 1785, Daniel Drake was only two years old when his family migrated to Mayslick, Kentucky. His barely literate parents had been farm laborers and were able to buy only a thirty-eight-acre farm, where the family lived in a log cabin fitted into a hill over a sheep pen. In the early 1790s Kentucky was still Indian country, and the "children were told at night, 'lie still and go to sleep, or the Shawnees will catch you.'" Drake wrote later that nearly all his "troubled or vivid dreams included either Indians or snakes—the copper colored man & the copperheaded snake." Most of his neighbors still believed in "omens, ghosts, and even the self motion of dead men's bones." Yet Drake also was instructed from the age of six in the Calvinist catechism by an itinerant Baptist preacher, and among the family's few books were hymns by Isaac Watts that he recited from memory. From the age of five he attended a subscription school in a log cabin, alternating lessons with labor on the family farm, fetching the cow from the woods, grinding corn until his knuckles bled, and riding and guiding the horse while his father plowed. By the age of eight Drake was feeding and collecting the livestock and dropping corn in plowed furrows for his father to cover with the hoe. As the eldest child he also helped his mother, holding the ears of the cow while she milked, churning butter, and making cheese. On washing days he fetched water from the spring, watched the fire, and hung the clothes on fences. Helping with cloth production, he carded wool, walked backward and turned the rim of the big wheel while his mother spun, prepared dried flax for her to spin on the small wheel, and spread linen on the grass to bleach in the sun. When he was nine, the family purchased a two-hundred-acre farm, and Drake left school to help his father clear land. At ten he helped his father and a neighbor build fences, and at twelve he could lay rails himself, handle the plow alone and join his neighbors in the wheat harvest. "When I was thirteen, fourteen, and fifteen years old," he later wrote, "I was able to do half a man's work with the sickle and I may add (boastingly) with the scythe also. . . . In the harvest field my greatest ambition was to sweat so as to wet my shirt." After an injury to his father, fifteen-year-old Drake worked the farm alone. His barely literate father, however, was determined to have at least one educated child and sent him in 1801 to study medicine with William Goforth in the small community at Fort Washington, which would become Cincinnati.

The American Revolution in Medicine. In 1805 Drake fulfilled a dream when he traveled to Philadelphia to study medicine at the University of Pennsylvania with Benjamin Rush, one of the leading physicians of the young republic. Since the 1790s Rush had promoted innovations in therapy that he considered an American Revolution in medicine. Rush argued that all disease was caused by "indirect debility": excessive stimulation of vascular and nervous systems. During Philadelphia's devastating yellow fever epidemic in 1793 he had treated his patients with depleting measures, "copious" bloodletting, and calomel purges quickened with a dose of jalap. Other Philadelphia doctors were appalled by Rush's therapy, but he was adamant in defense of his theory, for it fit neatly into his search for an appropriate republican medicine. After the Revolution, just as he had sought educational plans suited to a republican nation, Rush had argued that disease varied in populations according to geography, climate, diet, and forms of government. Republics, he thought, were conducive to health, but only if citizens practiced industry, frugality, and sturdy virtue. Lingering loyalty to monarchy or a taste for aristocratic luxury, on the one hand, or liberty that became license, on the other, would have to be purged. Drawing on his early education in evangelical Presbyterianism, Rush viewed political and medical truths in terms of God's millennial plan. Disease had entered human life with the Fall, and nature alone could not be trusted to heal it; intervention by the physician was necessary to restore the human body to its original perfect state. Rush taught his theories to more than three thousand students at the University of Pennsylvania, who, fanning out to establish practices in Southern and Western states, recommended in almost all cases active intervention through extensive blood-letting and large doses of medicines. By 1800 this "heroic medicine" was defended as appropriate for the energetic and entrepreneurial population of the expanding democratic nation, and calomel, containing mercury, was the drug of choice.

Medical Education for the West. Although later in his life he would regret the reliance of his early practice on bleeding and the use of calomel, Drake was one of many students who disseminated Rush's therapy in the West when he returned to Kentucky in 1806 and to Cincinnati a year later. Keeping in touch with his medical mentors in Philadelphia, he contributed to *The Eclectic Repertory and Analytical Review* and then *The Philadelphia Journal of the Medical and Physical Sciences*. As physicians sought to fortify their profession and institutions of medical education mushroomed in nineteenth-century America, Drake was instrumental in establishing medical schools and networks in the West. After a year as a professor at Transylvania University in Lexington, Kentucky, in 1817, he returned to Cincinnati to teach at Lancaster Seminary, which became Cincinnati College in 1821. Continuing to teach at Transylvania and founding a medical department at Miami University (Ohio) in 1830, Drake assumed regional leadership as editor of *The Western Journal of Medical Sciences* from 1827 to 1836 and author of *Principal Diseases of the Interior Valley of North America* (1850). He also was a booster for Ohio, credited with naming it the Buckeye state. Considered the "Franklin" of Cincinnati, he held literary evenings in his home and joined Harriet and Catharine Beecher and Calvin Stowe in Cincinnati's Semi-Colon Club. Although he and James Hall, editor of the *Western Monthly Magazine,* took offense at Lyman Beecher's *Plea for the West* in 1835, Drake was a strong advocate of western education and a member of the circle that formed the Western Literary Institute and College of Professional Teachers. Shortly before his death in 1852, he recalled his Kentucky childhood in letters to his children.

Sources:

George W. Corner, *The Autobiography of Benjamin Rush, His "Travels through Life" together with his Commonplace Book for 1789–1813* (Princeton, N.J.: Princeton University Press, 1948);

Donald J. D'Elia, "Dr. Benjamin Rush and the American Medical Revolution," *Proceedings of the American Philosophical Society,* 110 (23 August 1966): 227–234;

Daniel Drake, *Pioneer Life in Kentucky, 1785–1800,* edited by Emmet Field Horine (New York: H. Schuman, 1948);

Dagobert D. Runes, ed., *The Selected Writings of Benjamin Rush* (New York: Philosophical Library, 1947).

CHARLES GRANDISON FINNEY

1792–1875

CLERGYMAN AND EDUCATOR

Revivals for the Middle Class. Charles Grandison Finney was born the seventh of eight children to a farming family in Litchfield County, Connecticut, in 1792. His parents named him after the model of gentility in the popular novel *Sir Charles Grandison* (1753) by Samuel Richardson. When he was two, his family joined the tide of migration into western New York, settling in Oneida County, where he attended a district school and probably the Hamilton Oneida Academy. When he was sixteen, the family relocated to remote Jefferson County on the shores of Lake Ontario, where Charles taught district school. In 1812 he returned to Connecticut and then taught district school in New Jersey before returning to western New York in 1818 to study law. There he met the young and energetic Presbyterian minister George W. Gale, whom Finney engaged in closely argued debate until he experienced a transforming conversion in 1821.

Scornful of formal theological training, Finney was licensed by the local Saint Lawrence Presbytery and began to inspire revivals in the new towns rapidly developing along the Erie Canal. Combining revival techniques of the itinerant Methodist preachers with blunt language and legalistic argument, from 1825 to 1830 Finney became a regional phenomenon. Wherever he went, he incited intense religious excitement among the entrepreneurs and wage earners along the canal, which had already become one of the most important transportation corridors of the market economy. Finney also elicited active participation by women, held informal and protracted spiritual meetings, singled out potential converts by naming names and listing their specific sins, and placed individuals on the "anxious bench" as objects of group prayer. Viewing sin as deep-seated self-interest one could choose to discard, he urged individuals to a life of disinterested benevolence and useful activism. Finney responded to democratic individualism, yet trimmed away revivalism's rough edges, energizing his middle-class audiences. In 1828 he was invited to bring his evangelical appeal to enlightened and Quaker Philadelphia. In 1830, at the height of his triumph, he and his followers stormed the bastion of wickedness in New York City. Two years later the wealthy merchants Arthur and Lewis Tappan financed renovation of the Chatham Street Theater to create a Broadway Tabernacle for Finney's ministry.

The Antislavery Rebels. One of Finney's early converts in Utica, New York, was a student at Hamilton College named Theodore Dwight Weld who initially resisted the revival impulse. Finney's meek response to Weld's hostility, however, melted the younger man in an emotional conversion, and Weld left college to join the evangelist's Holy Band. In 1827 Weld was encouraged by Charles Stuart, a Jamaican-born British officer and Utica schoolteacher, to enroll in the Oneida Institute founded by George W. Gale. Stuart was an activist in the British antislavery movement, and he converted and educated Weld, who brought his evangelical fervor to the cause. When Arthur and Lewis Tappan sought to promote evangelical higher education in the West, they sent Weld to locate a site for a manual labor seminary. Gathering a group of young men as he proceeded, in 1832 Weld selected Lane Seminary in Cincinnati, already chartered by the Ohio legislature. The Tappan brothers invited Lyman Beecher to be president of Lane, and young men converted by Finney and associated with Weld became the students. Although Beecher favored plans of the American Colonization Society to settle freed slaves outside the United States, other evangelicals simultaneously formed the New York Anti-Slavery Society, which adopted the British program of immediate emancipation and soon merged with William Lloyd Garrison's radical and secular New England group in the American Anti-Slavery Society.

Antislavery and Educational Reform. As the new national organization began its work in 1834, Lane Seminary was consumed by protracted meetings, in which the students rejected acceptance of the colonization option in favor of immediate emancipation. Turning to education of free blacks in Cincinnati, the students organized free reading rooms, lectures for adults, and Sunday schools for children. While fears of racial amalgamation rocked the city, protests reached Lyman Beecher, who was then on a fund-raising tour in the East. In Beecher's absence the board of trustees moved to abolish the seminary's antislavery society, expel its president William Allen and student leader Theodore Weld, and restrict further activity by the students among free blacks. In protest fifty-three students left Lane; supported by Arthur Tappan, several of them voted to move to the Oberlin Collegiate Institute, a manual-labor school initiated by John Jay Shipherd in northeastern Ohio. Reluctantly the new school's trustees were persuaded to meet demands of the Lane rebels that their one supporter at Lane, Asa Mahan, be appointed college president and that blacks be admitted as students. Pledging their generous support, the Tappan brothers invited Finney to join the faculty. In 1835 several of the Lane rebels trained by Weld became the core of agents of the American Anti-Slavery Society, embarking with evangelical zeal to convert the Midwest to abolitionism.

Oberlin Collegiate Institute. When the expanded institution began its course of instruction in 1835, buildings were still being constructed to accommodate the thirty-two Lane rebels and other students who enrolled. Gradually both Finney and Asa Mahan separated themselves from Weld's ardent abolitionism and concentrated on the cultivation of spiritual life, turning toward the doctrines of perfectionism for which the college would be known. Oberlin students were radical enough that Congregationalists and Presbyterians appointed committees in the 1840s to examine suspected beliefs of graduates, and two were rejected when they applied to become missionaries with the American Board of Commissioners of Foreign Missions. Drawn by Finney's reputation, students flocked to the school; in 1840 there were five hundred enrolled and by 1852, one thousand. In the 1850s an imposing chapel and four-story Tappan Hall dominated the college's quadrangle, surrounded by Oberlin Hall, Colonial Hall, and Ladies' Hall, which was built to accommodate the female students. Finney served as college minister and professor of theology. Although he maintained his concern with individual souls, he also was attentive to the physical health of students. As a result he supported the manual-labor system and advocated temperance and the Graham diet. The college became known as an abolitionist stronghold and produced students and graduates who aided fugitives on the Underground Railroad and conducted schools for free blacks. In 1850 Mahan was forced to resign from the presidency of the college, and Finney replaced him, holding the position until 1866. Serving as pastor of the community's First Congregational Church until he was almost eighty, Finney died at the age of eighty-three in 1875.

Sources:

Gilbert Hobbs Barnes, *The Anti-Slavery Impulse, 1830–1844* (New York: Harcourt, Brace & World, 1964);

Keith J. Hardman, *Charles Grandison Finney, 1792–1875, Revivalist and Reformer* (Syracuse, N.Y.: Syracuse University Press, 1987);

Nathan O. Hatch, *The Democratization of American Christianity* (New Haven: Yale University Press, 1989);

Memoirs of Rev. Charles G. Finney (New York: A. S. Barnes, 1876).

JOHN SWETT

1830-1913
EDUCATOR

A New England Childhood. Born in Pittsfield, New Hampshire, in 1830, John Swett was descended from New England farming families whose ancestors arrived in America as early as 1642. Like many children of his and the preceding generation, he combined intermittent lessons at district school with labor on the family farm. Able to attend Pittsfield Academy in the mid 1840s, at the age of seventeen he became a teacher, achieving immediate success and the nickname "Old Swett" because of his youth. Swett never attended college, but when he taught at Randolph, Massachusetts, he heard lectures by Ralph Waldo Emerson and Theodore Parker; during a short sojourn at Russell's Normal Institute on the Merrimac River he met William Russell, an associate of Horace Mann and the first editor of the *American Journal of Education* from 1826 to 1829. As a child and youth Swett was not influenced by evangelical religion; although a Congregationalist, he admired tracts by William Ellery Channing and later would consider himself a Unitarian. Like many young Northeastern men, he was excited in 1849 by news from California. Convincing himself that migrating westward would benefit his health, he embarked on a voyage around the horn of South America in 1852, arriving in San Francisco early in February the following year. Setting off immediately up the Sacramento River to Marysville, Swett prospected in the northern gold mines with little profit, returning to San Francisco after only five months.

Rincon School. After searching for a position as a schoolteacher Swett became principal of Rincon Grammar School, located in a small rented house on a sandbank. Throughout the 1850s he introduced New England traditions and the latest educational innovations until the Rincon School was admired as the finest in the city. Considering physical education essential to the curriculum, he offered daily calisthenics and gymnastics and made ball games and hikes to Protero Hill and the ocean regular activities. An advocate of coeducation of the sexes, he also supported education for African American children. A Unitarian and friend of the popular minister Thomas Starr King, Swett was a firm believer in secular public schools. Although the state board of education passed a resolution in 1851 that each school day begin with prayer and Bible reading, Swett considered the practice unwise policy in a city such as San Francisco, which had large Catholic and Jewish populations. Opposing support of parochial schools with public funds, he came under criticism in 1854 when Catholic schools for boys in the city merged with public schools. Swett attended state teachers' conventions and contributed to the liberal Congregational paper, the *Pacific,* and by 1860 he was recognized as a leading educator in the city as his students excelled in public examinations and a handsome new building was constructed for the Rincon School.

State Superintendent. In 1862 Swett was persuaded to run for the office of state superintendent of public instruction. Although roundly denounced for his Unitarian belief, he was elected along with the rest of the Republican ticket. Well aware of the need for funds for public schools, Swett soon drafted and lobbied for amendments to the school law, which were passed by the Republican legislature in 1862 and 1863. The amended school law provided for the levying and collecting of taxes based on a census of children in each school district, state control over the examination and certification of teachers, improved record keeping based on the example of the state of Illinois, and series of uniform textbooks. Aided by a graduate of the New York State Normal School, Swett also inaugurated a journal, the *California Teacher.* When Swett was reelected along with other Republicans in 1863, he proposed a new bill to secure a state school tax, to which the senate attached the amendment that school trustees could admit African American, Indian, and Chinese children to public schools. Although that provision was amended in 1870 to omit Chinese and specify separate schools for African American and Indian children, the new tax greatly increased public school revenue. Acting as secretary of both the assembly and senate education committees, Swett drafted the Revised School Law of 1866, summarizing existing statutes and providing for a state board of education and the introduction of school libraries. By 1867 a state-supervised and state-supported system of free schools existed throughout California, open for three months in smaller districts, five months in larger ones, and ten months in urban areas. Throughout his public career Swett sought to improve the status and professional education of teachers. He fought for higher salaries and for state support of teachers' institutes and the normal school founded in San Francisco in the 1850s, which would be moved to San Jose in 1871. Although renominated for his position on the Republican ticket in 1867, Swett was swept from office by a Democratic landslide. Returning to San Francisco as principal of the Denman Grammar School, he also taught evening classes for adults. In 1869 he was appointed deputy su-

perintendent of the city's schools until a Democratic victory once again caused his resignation and return to Denman. In 1876 he became principal of the Girls' High School and Normal Class of San Francisco, retiring briefly in 1889 to his Martinez farm until he was elected city superintendent of public schools in San Francisco in 1891. At his death in 1913, John Swett was eulogized as the father of free public education in California, one of the many individuals instrumental in the widespread transmission of eastern ideals and practices to the new states of the American West.

Source:
John Swett, *Public Education in California* (New York: American Books, 1911).

FRANCES WRIGHT

1795-1852

EDUCATIONAL REFORMER

Beginnings. Born in 1795, Frances Wright inherited a considerable fortune when she was orphaned at the age of two. Although a Scot, she and her younger sister, Camilla, were raised in England by a maternal aunt. As a teenager she became fascinated with America and was able to travel there with Camilla in 1818, a voyage she recounted in *Views of Society and Manners in America* in 1821. Renowned as an author, the tall and stately auburn-haired young woman corresponded with and then became attached to the sixty-four-year-old Marie-Joseph-Paul-Yves-Roch-Gilbert du Motier, Marquis de Lafayette, at whose family estate near Paris she and Camilla lived for two years. In 1824 the Wright sisters accompanied Lafayette on his triumphal tour of America, where they met James Madison, James Monroe, and Andrew Jackson, and Frances engaged in discussion with the elderly Thomas Jefferson at Monticello. As she traveled through the American South, Wright observed and became distressed with slavery. In the Northwest she visited a fellow Scot, the utopian industrialist Robert Owen, who was beginning to implement his ideals at New Harmony, Indiana. Determined to work for the benefit of slaves, Frances did not return to Europe with the marquis. In 1825 she published in the *Genius of Universal Emancipation,* Benjamin Lundy's antislavery journal, her own ambitious plan for gradual and compensated emancipation. Purchasing land in Tennessee with her own funds, she hoped to found an experimental community where slaves could work to earn their purchase price, learn skills, and then be resettled some place in the West. Central to her plan was a community boarding school, where enslaved children, separated from their parents, would receive an education in literature and the natural sciences.

The Community at Nashoba. In 1826 Frances and Camilla Wright were joined in Tennessee by Richeson Whitby, a Quaker from New Harmony; James Richardson, a fellow Scot and medical student; and George Flower, the one associate with a practical knowledge of farming, and his wife and three children. A South Carolina planter sent the slave Lucky and her five daughters, and Frances purchased eight additional slaves—five men and three women—with her own funds. Within a year the group built two log cabins; Camilla set up the school; and Frances and Whitby worked with the slaves in the vegetable garden, orchard, and corn and cotton fields. As thirty slaves, half of whom were children, were assembled on the tract, the community suffered from malaria and considerable disorder. Following a visit to New Harmony, Wright was inspired to reform Nashoba on Robert Owen's principles, relinquishing ownership to ten trustees, among them Lafayette, Owen, and his son Robert Dale Owen. When George Flower, unhappy with the new arrangements, left in 1827, Robert Dale Owen arrived, appalled at the poor quality of the land and primitive conditions. He and Frances immediately set off for Europe to enlist recruits, leaving management of the community to James Richardson and Camilla. Even with the nightly meetings Frances held to teach Owen's principles, enslaved parents failed to understand why they should be separated from their children at the boarding school; they were troubled as well by the Owenite concept of sexual emancipation, that individuals could mutually select sexual partners outside of marriage. When Richardson, who cohabited with an enslaved teenager, published his record of community activities in Lundy's journal, readers were shocked. Public outrage grew when Wright returned from Europe and defended the community's sexual practices; criticizing marriage and organized religion, she called for racial amalgamation and the equal education of white and black children. Yet the Nashoba experiment was defeated less by its ideals than by its finances; it failed to make a profit, and Wright's fortune and its supporters began to drift away. In 1828 Frances left for New Harmony, where she edited the *Free Inquirer* and planned a new career as a public reformer.

A Public Woman. In 1829 Wright moved to New York, joined by Camilla, Robert Dale Owen, and a New Harmony Pestalozzian teacher named Phiquepal D'Arusmont. Commencing a career as a lecturer, she bought a Baptist church and renamed it the Hall of Science, housing a lecture hall, a secular Sunday school, and a bookstore for free-thinkers. Wright's lectures challenged evolving concepts of domestic ideology when she explained the experience and ideals of Nashoba, criticized evangelical revivals, and advocated education and equal rights for women. Her favorite topic was educational reform. She proposed a "guardianship system" through which state government would establish district boarding schools, where Americans could be raised for social equality through a curriculum that instructed all children in free inquiry and the physical sciences. Wright found admirers in New York among the reformers and artisans who comprised the city's Workingmen's Party and who also advocated enlightened public education and such issues as the ten-hour workday, abolition of imprisonment for debt, and attacks on the privileges of banks and capitalists. In 1830, however, she returned to Nashoba, where she freed her slaves and escorted them by ship to a new life in Haiti. Traveling to Europe the following year, she and members of her entourage settled in Paris, where Camilla died and Frances married D'Arusmont, with whom she later had a daughter, Sylva. When Wright returned to the United States without her husband and daughter in 1835, she was too notorious to resume her public career. For the rest of her life she lived in Cincinnati, continuing to attack organized religion and advocate secular, state-supported public schools. Upon her death in 1852, the land in Tennessee was inherited by Sylva, who transformed Nashoba into a private estate, settled there and raised a family.

Sources:
Celia Morris Eckhardt, *Frances Wright: Rebel in America* (Cambridge, Mass.: Harvard University Press, 1984);

Richard Stiller, *Commune on the Frontier: The Story of Frances Wright* (New York: Crowell, 1972);

Nancy Woloch, "Frances Wright at Nashoba," in *Women and the American Experience*, by Woloch (New York: McGraw-Hill, 1994), pp. 154–169.

PUBLICATIONS

Catharine Beecher, *An Essay on the Education of Female Teachers* (New York: Van Nostrand, 1835);

Beecher, *The Moral Instructor for Schools and Families* (Cincinnati: Truman & Smith, 1838);

Beecher, *Suggestions Respecting Improvements in Education* (Hartford, Conn.: Packard & Butler, 1829);

Beecher, *A Treatise on Domestic Economy* (Boston: T. H. Webb, 1841)—a discussion of the educational role of American women and household tips for homemakers;

Daniel Drake, *An Introductory Discourse to a Course of Lectures on Clinical Medicine and Pathological Anatomy* (Louisville, Ky.: Printed by Prentice & Weissinger, 1840);

Joseph Lancaster, *Improvements in Education as it Respects the Industrious Classes of the Community* (London: Darton & Harvey, 1805)—Lancaster's system of education, which was implemented in various Western locations in the 1820s;

Delazon Smith, *A History of Oberlin or New Lights of the West* (Cleveland: S. Underhill, 1837).

A circa 1810 painting of the graduation ceremony at a women's seminary (Collection of Edgar William and Bernice Chrysler Garbisch)

CHAPTER SIX

GOVERNMENT AND POLITICS

by JONATHAN EARLE

CONTENTS

Sidebars and tables are listed in italics.

1800

- Thomas Jefferson and Aaron Burr tie in electoral college votes for president of the United States; both candidates are popular in Western districts.

1801

17 Feb. The House of Representatives selects Jefferson as president; Burr becomes vice president.

1802

6 Apr. All federal internal taxes are abolished.

1803

30 Apr. The Louisiana Purchase doubles the size of the United States.

1804

14 May Meriwether Lewis and William Clark set out to explore the Louisiana Territory.

1805

8 Nov. Lewis and Clark reach the Pacific Ocean.

1806

- The Burr conspiracy to establish an independent nation in the Southwest is revealed.

23 Sept. Lewis and Clark return to St. Louis.

1807

- Aaron Burr is captured and tried for high treason in the plot to "effect a separation of the Western Part of the United States." He is found not guilty.
- The Embargo Act is put into effect.

1808

1 Jan. The overseas slave trade is abolished; meanwhile, the internal slave trade from coastal to western states skyrockets.

1809

15 Mar. The Embargo Act is repealed, and Western farmers profit.

1810

27 Oct.   The United States annexes West Florida.

1811

7 Nov.   At the Battle of Tippecanoe, at the junction of the Wabash and Tippecanoe Rivers, Gov. William Henry Harrison of the Indiana Territory defeats the Shawnees under the Prophet Tenskwatawa and burn the nearby Indian village.

1812

30 Apr.   Louisiana is admitted into the Union, becoming the eighteenth state.

18 June   The United States declares war on Great Britain.

1813

5 Oct.   At the Battle of the Thames, Shawnee leader Tecumseh is killed, and his coalition of Native American warriors is dispersed.

1814

•   A British army burns Washington, D.C., but fails to take Baltimore.

1815

8 Jan.   At the Battle of New Orleans, U.S. forces under Gen. Andrew Jackson defeat a much larger British army.

1816

•   James Monroe is elected president.

1817

28 Apr.   The Rush-Bagot Treaty is signed between the United States and Great Britain, limiting the number and size of warships on the Great Lakes.

10 Dec.   Mississippi is admitted into the Union as the twentieth state.

1818

4 Apr.   Congress adopts the design of the U.S. flag still in use today.

30 Oct.   The Canadian-United States boundary is extended west along the Forty-ninth parallel.

1819

22 Feb. The United States and Spain sign the Transcontinental, or Adams-Onís, Treaty. The United States receives Florida and the western boundary of Louisiana is fixed along the Sabine, Red, and Arkansas rivers to the Continental Divide, and then to the Forty-second parallel and the Pacific Ocean.

1820

6 Mar. In the Missouri Compromise, Congress "forever prohibits" slavery in all parts of the Louisiana Purchase north of 36°30'.

1821

10 Aug. Missouri is admitted into the Union as a slave state.

1822

June The Denmark Vesey slave plot is thwarted in South Carolina.

1823

2 Dec. In his annual message to Congress, James Monroe enunciates the Monroe Doctrine, a foreign policy that declares the Western Hemisphere closed to further European colonization and interference.

1824

• John Quincy Adams wins the disputed presidential election.

1825

26 Oct. The Erie Canal is completed, connecting Western farmers and the Great Lakes to markets in New York.

1826

24 Jan. Creek Indians sign the Treaty of Washington, ceding territory to the federal government and gaining another year to remain on their lands.

4 July Thomas Jefferson and John Adams die on the fiftieth anniversary of the Declaration of Independence.

1827

6 Aug. The United States and Great Britain sign a treaty extending the 1818 agreement to continue joint occupation of the Oregon Territory.

1828

• Andrew Jackson is elected in a landslide, winning every Western state in the country.

1830

6 Apr.   Joseph Smith, author of *The Book of Mormon*, founds the Church of Jesus Christ of Latter-Day Saints at Fayette, New York.

27 May   Jackson vetoes the Maysville Road Bill, which would have provided federal monetary support for a sixty-mile road construction project entirely in Kentucky.

1831

•   Jackson forms a "kitchen cabinet," an informal group of advisors.

9 May   The Frenchmen Alexis de Tocqueville and William de Beaumont arrive in America.

1832

6 Apr.   Black Hawk surrenders, thus ending the Black Hawk War in the Northwest.

1833

2 Mar.   President Andrew Jackson signs the Force Act, authorizing the use of military force to collect tariff duties in South Carolina.

4 Dec.   The American Anti-Slavery Society is formed.

1834

30 June   The Indian Intercourse Act is passed.

1835

30 Jan.   Richard Lawrence tries to assassinate Andrew Jackson, the first attempt on the life of a U.S. president.

1836

6 Mar.   The Alamo falls to Mexican forces.

21 Apr.   At the Battle of San Jacinto, Sam Houston and a force of Texan militia defeat a Mexican army under Gen. Antonio López de Santa Anna. As a result of this battle, Texas wins its independence from Mexico.

1837

3 Mar.   The United States recognizes the Republic of Texas.

1838

Dec.   The forced removal of Southeastern Indians to Oklahoma, known as the Trail of Tears, begins.

1839

June   Slaves aboard the Spanish ship *Amistad* revolt and gain control of the vessel. They are captured off U.S. waters, but after a lengthy court battle the slaves are set free in 1841.

1840

•   William Henry Harrison wins the presidential election.

1841

•   John C. Frémont explores the headwaters of the Des Moines River in Iowa.

•   The Preemption Act grants "squatter's rights" to settlers.

1842

•   Frémont leads an expedition to explore the route to Oregon beyond the Mississippi River as far as the South Pass of the Continental Divide in Wyoming.

9 Aug.   In the Webster-Ashburton Treaty, the American and Canadian boundary is established between Lake Superior and Lake of the Woods.

1843

29 May   John C. Frémont leaves Kansas City for another exploratory journey of the West; the expedition yields an accurate survey of the immigrant route to Oregon.

1844

8 June   The U.S. Senate votes not to annex Texas.

27 June   Mormon leader Joseph Smith is murdered by a mob in Carthage, Illinois.

1845

23 June   Texas is annexed by the United States.

July   Magazine editor John L. O'Sullivan coins the phrase "Manifest Destiny."

1846

May   The Mexican War begins.

15 June   In the Oregon Treaty the boundary between the United States and Canada is set at the Forty-ninth parallel.

8 Aug.   The Wilmot Proviso passes the House of Representatives for the first time.

1847

24 July   Mormons arrive at the Great Salt Lake in Utah.

1848

24 Jan.   Gold is discovered at Sutter's Mill in California.

2 Feb.   The Treaty of Guadalupe Hidalgo ends the Mexican War.

1849

•   More than seventy thousand Americans, joined by eight thousand Mexicans and five thousand South Americans, head to the California gold fields.

1850

•   Congress grants land to the Illinois Central Railroad.

Sept.   Congress passes the Compromise of 1850.

1851

•   Northerners begin to resist the Fugitive Slave Act.

1852

•   Harriet Beecher Stowe's *Uncle Tom's Cabin* sells three hundred thousand copies and intensifies the controversy surrounding slavery.

1853

30 Dec.   In the Gadsden Purchase the United States receives twenty-nine thousand square miles of Mexican territory south of the Gila River for a southern railroad line.

1854

30 May   The Kansas-Nebraska Act repeals the Missouri Compromise of 1820.

1855

30 Mar.   Amid armed violence, Kansans choose legislators in the first territorial election. However, border ruffians from Missouri force the election of a proslavery legislature.

1856

21 May   Lawrence, Kansas, is sacked by proslavery forces.

22 May   South Carolina congressman Preston Brooks beats and severely injures Massachusetts senator Charles Sumner in the Capitol.

24 May   The Pottawatomie Massacre leaves five proslavery Kansans dead.

1857

6 Mar.   In *Dred Scott* v. *Sandford*, U.S. Supreme Court Chief Justice Roger Taney rules that the Missouri Compromise is unconstitutional and that blacks are not U.S. citizens.

1858

21 Aug.-
15 Oct.   Abraham Lincoln debates Stephen A. Douglas for an Illinois senate seat.

1859

16 Oct.   John Brown raids the federal arsenal at Harpers Ferry, Virginia.

1860

6 Nov.   Lincoln wins the presidential election with no support from Southern states.

20 Dec.   South Carolina secedes from the Union.

An 1829 map of the United States; the alligator represents the political followers of Andrew Jackson; the turtle represents the supporters of John Quincy Adams (New York Public Library)

OVERVIEW

A Princely Domain. On paper, the United States was an extremely large country at the close of the Revolutionary War. In the Treaty of Paris, which ended the war in 1783, the British ceded to the new nation all the territory between the Atlantic Ocean and the Mississippi River, except New Orleans and Spanish Florida. When George Washington took the oath of office as the nation's first president five years later, he became the leader of a country that stretched for more than a thousand miles in every direction—an impressive domain by any standard. However, with the exception of outposts along navigable inland rivers, most Americans lived along a tiny ribbon of settlement on the Atlantic seaboard at the close of the eighteenth century. The grand new maps rolling off American printing presses contained another fiction as well: they failed to account for the fact that tens of thousands of Indians still occupied their ancestral lands within U.S. territory. These Indian nations included the Cherokees, Creeks, Seminoles, Choctaws, and Chickasaws in the South and the Delawares, Potawatomies, Miamis, and Shawnees north of the Ohio River.

Western Settlement and Politics. The situation dramatically changed in the first half of the nineteenth century. Land-hungry European Americans quickly began spilling west across the Appalachians and into territory called the "Old Northwest" and north into Vermont, Maine, and upstate New York. This movement brought whites into conflict with the land's native inhabitants, and federal, state, and local governments worked to pave the way for continued white settlement. The federal government's methods ranged from outright warfare, practiced against native peoples during the War of 1812, for example, to a policy of forced removal of Indians to territory west of the Mississippi, the government's basic policy in the 1830s. Westward migration did not just happen in antebellum America—it was aided and facilitated by elected officials, politicians, and judges. The federal government used force to remove Indians from east of the Mississippi River and resources to foster economic development. Not surprisingly, the settlers of the West became an important constituency in American politics. By the 1840s the West also became the center of the most serious conflict facing the new republic: whether slavery would be allowed to spread into the western territories acquired from Mexico. The government's inability to solve the conflict over slavery in the 1850s led, ultimately, to the South's secession from the Union and the Civil War.

The Great Land Ordinances. From the beginning of the United States of America, the federal government was instrumental in setting out the terms for settling the West. Two major land laws, the Ordinance of 1785 and the Northwest Ordinance of 1787, set in place schemes for surveying, settling, and governing new territory. In a foretelling of major conflicts of the mid nineteenth century, Thomas Jefferson inserted a clause into the Northwest Ordinance forbidding slavery there.

The Louisiana Purchase. Jefferson also had a significant impact on Western settlement as president. In 1803 Napoleon Bonaparte afforded him the opportunity to purchase the vast lands from the Mississippi River to the Rocky Mountains. The Louisiana Purchase gave the new nation control of the entire Mississippi River valley, including the port of New Orleans, and doubled the size of the United States. Jefferson predicted that Louisiana would make the West an "empire of Liberty" for thousands of generations.

Lewis and Clark. To explore the new territory he purchased from France, Jefferson commissioned an expedition led by Meriwether Lewis and William Clark. In the spring of 1804 the two men, accompanied by forty-one other explorers, set out west from St. Louis. With the help of an Indian guide named Sacagawea, the expedition reached the Pacific Ocean in November 1805 and returned to St. Louis a year later. Along the way Lewis and Clark documented and took samples of the territory's flora and fauna and made contact with dozens of Indian nations. They also helped guarantee the wealth and promise Jefferson's purchase would have for the young republic.

Economic Development. After the War of 1812 the federal government became more closely involved with fostering the economic development of the West. The "American System" proposed in Congress by Henry Clay of Kentucky included provisions for internal improvements, protective tariffs to aid domestic manufacture, and a national bank to facilitate credit. Clay's plan, although controversial, helped usher in a market-driven economy that linked the West to older communities in the East. It also helped transform the frontier into an area dominated by commercial farmers eager to market their goods.

Missouri: Crisis and Compromise. The explosion of settlement and commercial growth in the West led to a conflict between North and South in the territory of Missouri over slavery. When Missouri petitioned for entry into the Union as a state in 1819, Northerners in Congress were wary of granting admission to an additional slave state. The issue of slavery's influence and expansion was already increasing tension within the government. The Missouri Compromise, passed by Congress in 1821, ended the crisis by admitting Maine as a free state and Missouri as a slave state and by prohibiting slavery north of 36° 30' north latitude. This compromise, which opened up the present-day states of Oklahoma and Arkansas to slavery while prohibiting it in territory that became Kansas, Nebraska, Colorado, Wisconsin, Minnesota, Iowa, Montana, Wyoming, and North and South Dakota, diffused the slavery issue in U.S. government for almost a quarter century.

The Battle for Texas. Citizens of the United States did not stop at the Mississippi, however. Thousands of Southerners, looking for new places to grow cotton and reap fantastic profits, began streaming into the Mexican state of Texas in the 1820s. The newly independent Mexican government offered settlers free land and generous tax breaks in Texas if they promised to speak Spanish, practice Catholicism, and adhere to Mexican laws, which included the prohibition of slavery. When it quickly became apparent that the American immigrants were not upholding their end of the bargain by speaking English, rejecting Catholicism, and bringing slaves into Texas, Mexico attempted to curtail further immigration. Instead the Texans began a war for independence in 1836, which they won later that year. After declaring themselves an independent republic, the Texans quickly applied for entry into the United States as a slave state. This provided government officials with a thorny issue. If President Andrew Jackson, a slaveholder and an expansionist, annexed Texas, he would split his party over the slavery issue and start a war with Mexico. So both Jackson and his successor, Martin Van Buren, virtually ignored Texas during their terms. It was not until Texas made overtures to Great Britain that the republic was annexed and made part of the United States in 1845.

War with Mexico. Just as Jackson had feared, annexation led directly to a war with Mexico. President James K. Polk, another expansionist Democrat, used the rapid victory of American troops to press Mexico for even more Western land. The Treaty of Guadelupe Hidalgo granted the United States virtually all of northern Mexico—as a result of the war the United States absorbed territory that eventually became the states of California, Nevada, Utah, Arizona, and parts of New Mexico, Colorado, and Wyoming.

Revival of the Slavery Issue. The acquisition of thousands of square miles of new territory only exacerbated the political crisis in Washington over whether slavery would be allowed there. A group of Northern Democrats attempted to prohibit the spread of slavery into the formerly Mexican lands but fell short of votes in the United States Senate. The issue of slavery's expansion was at the center of the presidential campaign of 1848, and the Free Soil Party, a new antislavery party, polled more than 9 percent of the vote. Politicians in Washington made a final attempt at a compromise in 1850, passing legislation that admitted California as a free state while at the same time enacting a stronger fugitive slave law to appease Southerners.

Toward Civil War. The Compromise of 1850 proved to be short-lived. Just four years later legislation to organize Nebraska Territory, part of the original Louisiana Purchase, reignited sectional tensions over slavery. The bill's author, Sen. Stephen Douglas of Illinois, planned to build a transcontinental railroad through Nebraska terminating in his hometown of Chicago. To placate Southerners he included a provision in the bill repealing the Missouri Compromise, which presumably would open the southern half of the territory, called Kansas, to slavery. "Anti-Nebraska" Northerners quickly coalesced into a new political party, the Republicans, and armed bands clashed in Kansas throughout the mid 1850s. The problem of slavery in the Western territories turned out to be one that could not be solved. While Western expansion added hundreds of thousands of square miles of territory to the United States, it also proved to be the Union's undoing.

TOPICS IN THE NEWS

AMERICAN EXPANSION: THE GREAT LAND ORDINANCES

Colonial Land Claims. While under British rule, the colonies of North America jealously guarded their paper claims to land north and west of the Ohio River. Of course the lands in question were already occupied by various tribes of American Indians, and until the Revolution the charter claims represented little more than the wishful thinking of would-be colonial developers, but the Revolutionary War and the waves of westward settlement launched by land-hungry pioneers forever changed the political economy of the Trans-Appalachian West. One of the new nation's earliest political battles was over whether the old Western land claims fell under state or federal control.

Virginia Cedes Western Lands. On paper the United States was a huge country. In the Treaty of Paris of 1783, which ended the Revolutionary War, Britain ignored the claims of its Indian allies and ceded all the land from the Atlantic to the Mississippi to the United States. After months of wrangling, Congress was able to persuade states with Western claims to cede them to the United States. Virginia's decision to cede its Western land claims in 1781 prompted other states to follow suit; this process turned Western lands—which once divided the states—into a force for national unity.

The Land Ordinance of 1785. Plans for the development of the Western lands were hotly debated by Congress. Some members of the new government favored letting individual settlers stake their own claims (mirroring historical patterns of development in colonies such as Virginia and the Carolinas); others wanted to carve the land into symmetrical townships resembling colonial New England towns. Legislators reached a compromise with the Land Ordinance of 1785. The legislation proposed surveying Western territories into six-mile-square townships before sale. Every other township was then to be further subdivided into 640-acre sections and sold for a minimum price of one dollar an acre. This law favored large land speculation companies over actual settlers since 640-acre farms were both too large and too expensive to be within the grasp of the typical pioneer family. Many politicians favored a national plan to survey, sell, and defend the Western lands from Indian attack. As a final measure, Congress set aside part of each township for schools.

The Northwest Ordinance. Far more significant was the Northwest Ordinance of 1787, which outlined how the West would be governed. In 1780 Congress resolved that all lands ceded to the Union should be "formed into distinct republican States," with the same rights of sovereignty, freedom, and independence as the original thirteen colonies. Congress instructed a committee chaired by Thomas Jefferson to formulate a plan for admitting future states. The result—enacted into law in 1787—provided for the following: first, the area bound by the Ohio, the Mississippi, and the Great Lakes (present-day Ohio, Michigan, Indiana, Illinois, and Wisconsin) would be divided into not less than three but no more than five territories; and second, the territories would immediately be governed by Congressionally appointed judges and a governor until the time when an individual territory's adult male population reached five thousand. When five thousand men of voting age had moved into one territory, they were authorized to elect a legislature, which had authority over that territory only. Finally, when the population reached sixty thousand the territory could apply to become a full-fledged state, with two restrictions: its government had to be "republican," and slavery would be prohibited.

A Farsighted Plan. Jefferson's ordinance was extremely farsighted. It provided a period for settlers to inhabit the new territory and encouraged them to create democratic local governments, and it specified an exact end date for territorial status. The ordinance also allowed Congress to take a stand against the moral evil of slavery, an institution challenged during the Revolution, without threatening the livelihood of Southern slave owners.

Source:
Frederick D. Williams, ed., *The Northwest Ordinance: Essays on its Formulation* (East Lansing: Michigan State University Press, 1989).

BURR AND JEFFERSON: ELECTION OF 1800

The West Chooses Jefferson. The election of Aaron Burr and Thomas Jefferson in 1800 was an early political victory for the West. The United States had experienced a dramatic rise in internal migration in the years after the

Revolution, with between 5 and 10 percent of the population moving each year. Not surprisingly, these major population shifts tended to be from East to West—from New England to western New York and Ohio, from New Jersey to western Pennsylvania, and from Virginia and the Carolinas into the new states of Kentucky and Tennessee. By contrast, there was little migration from North to South, or vice versa.

So Goes the Nation? The political significance of this internal migration was clear to both Federalists and their Democratic Republican opposition: the people who migrated West were among the strongest supporters of Thomas Jefferson and other Anti-Federalists. In fact, in the election of 1800 John Adams' Federalist supporters were clustered on the Atlantic coast between eastern North Carolina and Massachusetts' eastern counties. Jefferson won virtually every county west of central Pennsylvania.

Sources:

Lance Banning, *The Jeffersonian Persuasion: Evolution of a Party Ideology* (Ithaca, N.Y.: Cornell University Press, 1978);

James Roger Sharp, *American Politics in the Early Republic: The New Nation in Crisis* (New Haven: Yale University Press, 1993).

FORTUNATE ACCIDENT: THE LOUISIANA PURCHASE

Great Achievement. Jefferson's acquisition of the vast lands between the Mississippi River and the Rocky Mountains was by far the greatest achievement of his first term as president. Ironically, it came about as an accident. Jefferson had opined in his inaugural address that the United States already had enough land to provide "for a thousand generations," and he was not planning a major land purchase from European powers. However, the purchase of Louisiana, as the territory was called, made perfect political and geopolitical sense to Jefferson and his followers.

New Orleans. By 1801 nearly a half million Americans lived west of the Appalachian mountains. Federalists, many of them New England descendants of Puritans who had migrated to America in the seventeenth century, openly feared that the white residents of the frontier were illiterate barbarians. Jefferson's Republicans, on the other hand, saw Western expansion as the best hope for the survival of the Republic. As the nineteenth century began, settlers in the West remained under the political control of foreign powers who controlled the Mississippi River system. As a result these settlers depended on French and Spanish commercial systems to get their produce to markets—hardly a recipe for the continual renewal of the republican spirit. Jefferson understood that the key to securing permanent control of the West was to gain possession of New Orleans, located at the mouth of the Mississippi. "There is on the globe," Jefferson wrote, "one single spot, the possessor of which is our natural and habitual enemy. It is New Orleans."

Spain Threatens Commerce. In 1801 Spain owned New Orleans and under a treaty allowed Americans to transport produce from the interior. The year before, Spain had secretly ceded all of Louisiana to France, a move that allowed Napoleon to dream of creating a new French empire in America. In his scheme farmers in Louisiana would produce food for the immensely profitable French sugar-producing colonies based in Haiti. In late 1802 Spain closed New Orleans to American commerce, giving rise to panicked rumors that the city would soon be transferred to France. Such a move would have posed a serious threat to the existence of American settlements in the West.

Napoleon's Surprise. To avoid this potential debacle, Jefferson sent a high-level delegation to France with instructions to offer up to $10 million for New Orleans and West Florida (the southern portions of Mississippi and Alabama). By the time they got there, Napoleon's plans for a new French empire in America had cooled—thanks to the armed former slaves of Haiti, who rose up in 1793 and by 1801 had gained control of the entire island. At the same time, another war between France and England seemed imminent. When Jefferson's diplomats met with Napoleon on 11 April 1803, the French leader astonished them by offering to sell not only New Orleans but the entire territory of Louisiana for the bargain price of $15 million. The resulting treaty doubled the size of the United States and gave the new nation absolute control of the entire Mississippi River valley. Jefferson predicted Louisiana would make the West an "empire of liberty."

Source:

Robert W. Tucker and David C. Hendrickson, *Empire of Liberty: The Statecraft of Thomas Jefferson* (New York: Oxford University Press, 1990).

THE GREAT JOURNEY: LEWIS AND CLARK

Mapping the Louisiana Purchase. No one knew precisely how large Louisiana was or what it contained, so President Thomas Jefferson secured $2,500 from Congress in early 1803 to explore the territory. He appointed Meriwether Lewis, his private secretary and a former soldier, to command the expedition. To prepare for the mission, Lewis immersed himself in books on zoology, astronomy, and botany. For the expedition's coleader Lewis picked William Clark, another former soldier and an experienced mapmaker who had earned a reputation for canny negotiations with Indians.

Reaching the Pacific. In the spring 1804 Lewis, Clark and forty-one men started up the Missouri River from the village of St. Louis in two dugout canoes and a fifty-five-foot keelboat. During the summer and fall the team traveled one thousand six hundred miles through country inhabited by the Missouri, Pawnee, Crow, Sioux, and Mandan peoples. That winter the team, known as the "corps of discovery," built Fort Mandan in what is now North Dakota and sent Jefferson more than thirty boxes of minerals, plants, animals (including a live

William Clark, a soldier and explorer from Caroline County, Virginia, was asked in 1803 by Meriwether Lewis to join in leadership of an expedition to the Pacific Ocean across the newly acquired Louisiana Purchase and Rocky Mountains. He became the primary mapmaker and artist of the endeavor, as well as a gifted diarist. The following are excerpts from his journals:

Sunday May 13, 1804

River Dubois opposet [sic] the Mouth of the Missourie River

I dispatched an express this morning to Capt. Lewis at St. Louis, all our provisions goods and equipage on Board of a boat of 22 oars, a large Perogue of 71 oars, a second Perogue of 67 oars, Complete with sails &c. Men compd. With Powder Cartridges and 100 balls each, all in health and readiness to set out. Boats and everything Complete, with the necessary stores of provisions & such articles of merchandize as we though ourselves authorized to procure—tho' not as much as I think nessy. For the multitude of Indians thro which we just pass on our road across the Continent &c. &c.

20ᵗʰ August 1804

Sergeant Floyd [Charles Floyd, the only member of Lewis and Clark's expedition to die along the way] much weaker and no better. . . . We set out under a gentle breeze from the S.E. and proceeded on verry well. Sergeant Floyd as bad as he can be no pulse & nothing will Stay a moment on his Stomach or bowels. Passed two islands on the S.S. and at the first Bluff on the S.S. Serj. Floyd Died with a great deal of composure, before his death he Said to me, "I am going away" I want you to write me a letter." We buried him on the top of the bluff ½ a mile below a small river to which we Gave his name, he was buried with the Honors of War much lamented. . . . This Man at all times gave us proofs of his firmness and Determined resolution to doe Service to his Countrey and honor to himself after paying all the honor to our Decesed brother we camped in the Mouth of floyds River about 30 yards wide, a butifull evening.

30ᵗʰ of August 1804

A verry thick fog this morning after preparing some presnts for the Chiefs which we intended to make by giving Meadels, and finishing a Speech which we intended to give them. We sent Mr. Dorion in a Perogue for the Chiefs and Warriers to a Council un-der an Oak Tree near where we had a flag flying on a high flagstaff at 12 oCLock we met and Cap. L. delivered the Speach & then made one great Chief by giving him a Meadel & some clothes, one 2d chief and three Third chiefs the same way. . . . The Souex [Sioux] is a Sout bold looking people (the young men handsome) & well made, the greater part of them make use of Bows & arrows...they do not Shoot So Well as the Northern Indians the Warriers are Verry much deckerated with Paint Porcupine quils and feathers, large leagins and mockersons, all with buffalow roabs of different colors. The Squars wore Peticoats and a white buffalow roabe with the black hare tunred back over their necks and Sholders.

27ᵗʰ of October Saturday 1804

We set out early came too at the [Mandan Indian] Village on the L.S. this village is situated on an eminance of about 50 feet above the Water in a handsom plain it containes houses in a kind of Picket work, the houses are round and very large containing several families, as also their horses which is tied on one Side of the entrance. . . . I walked up & Smoked a pipe with the Chiefs of the village they were anxious that I would stay and eat with them, my indisposition prevented my eating which displeased them, untill a full explenation took place, I returned to the boat and Sent 2 Carrots of Tobacco for them to smoke, and proceeded on. . . .

Novr. 7ᵗʰ Thursday 1805

Great joy in camp we are in *view* of the *Ocian, (in the morning when fog cleared off just below last village of Warkiacum)* this great Pacific Octean which we been so long anxious to See. And the roreing or noise made by the waves braking on the rockey Shores (as I suppose) may be heard dinstinctly.

Sunday June 15ᵗʰ 1806

We passed through bad fallen timber and a high Mountain this evening. From the top of this mountain I had an extensive view of the rocky Mountains to the south and the Columbian plains for a great extent also the SW Mountains and a range of high Mountains which divides the waters of Lewis's & Clarks rivers and seems to termonate nearly a West course. Several high pts. To the N & N.E. covered with Snow. A remarkable high rugd. Mountain in the forks of Lewis's river nearly south and covered with snow. . . .

Source: Reuben Gold Thwaites, ed., *Original Journals of the Lewis and Clark Expedition 1804–1806* (New York: Arno, 1969).

Sauk and Fox warriors dancing and singing in demonstration of their support for Shawnee leader Tecumseh in 1808 (Library of Congress, Washington, D.C.)

prairie dog and two grizzly bear cubs), and Indian artifacts. In early 1805 they set out again, this time accompanied by a Shoshone woman, Sacagawea, who acted as an interpreter and guide. With her help, the team crossed the Rockies to the Snake and Columbia Rivers, which took them to the Pacific Ocean in November 1805. Their hopes to return by ship dashed, the group was forced to retrace its steps the following spring. The successful expedition arrived back in St. Louis in September 1806 with just one fatality. In addition to the volumes of journals, drawings, and notes they brought back, the corps of discovery provided valuable information on the territory's inhabitants (especially the increasingly powerful Sioux). They also returned with guarantees of the richness and promise of the "empire of liberty" purchased so cheaply from France.

Source:
Stephen E. Ambrose, *Undaunted Courage: Meriwether Lewis, Thomas Jefferson and the Opening of the American West* (New York: Simon & Schuster, 1996).

HOUR OF CRISIS: WAR OF 1812

A World War. The War of 1812 was fought in every region of the United States—from the Northern frontier to New Orleans to the edge of Western settlement. The war also held tremendous importance for the West. There were two major causes of the conflict. The first was international: the United States was caught up in the bitter Napoleonic wars ravaging Europe. Essentially, the federal government (under President James Madison, who was elected in 1808 and reelected in 1812) insisted that the United States be able to remain a neutral trading partner for both the British and the French. Neither Britain nor France wanted the United States to trade with the other warring party. Under pressure to stand up

for the new republic's rights on the high seas, Madison proclaimed that unless Great Britain overturned its policy barring French-American trade, the new republic would declare war on England.

Indians v. Settlers in the West. The second reason to fight involved the longstanding conflicts between Western settlers and Indians in the Great Lakes region. No government had been able to restrain the land-hungry white settlers flooding into the Ohio River valley, and Indians such as the Shawnees watched as, year after year, they were driven further west. To make matters worse, the Westerners complained that the British government in Canada was aiding the Indians in their raids on American settlements.

Tecumseh and the Prophet. Tecumseh, the Shawnee chief, and his brother Tenskwatawa, a holy man known as the Prophet, began working to unite the tribes east of the Mississippi into one confederation. The Prophet also insisted that Indians throw off the trappings of white culture, such as alcohol, and invigorate their own cultures. In November 1811 Gen. William Henry Harrison, the governor of Indiana Territory, led one thousand soldiers against the Prophet at Tippecanoe Creek. While the battle was essentially a draw, Harrison proved that the Native American followers of Tecumseh and his brother were far from invincible. The fledgling Indian confederation buckled.

Pioneers Cry for War. The settlers, unwilling to blame their own greed for land for the growing tensions, continued to blame the British in Canada. All along the frontier, American settlers cried for battle against Great Britain, with many fully expecting Canada to fall and be made part of the United States.

Hyacinthe Laclotte's 1815 painting of the Battle of New Orleans (Isaac Dolgado Museum of Art, New Orleans)

The "War Hawks." In Congress a group of talented young legislators took the lead in the movement for war against Great Britain. Known as the "War Hawks," nearly all of them were Madisonian Republicans from the South and West, including Henry Clay of Kentucky, John C. Calhoun of South Carolina, and George M. Troup of Georgia. Ardent nationalists, they favored war to protect American honor against repeated insults by the old mother country—to capitulate to Britain's demands, they argued, would amount to recolonization. During the winter and spring of 1811–1812, the War Hawks led Congress into a declaration of war. When it came on 18 June 1812, every Federalist and nearly every Northeastern Republican opposed the measure; Republicans of the South and West voted almost unanimously for war.

An Inauspicious Beginning. The war began badly for the United States. What the War Hawks had envisioned as a quick and welcome invasion of Canada turned out to be a costly disaster. Instead of sweeping gallantly through Canada, the British and their Indian allies, all of

whom formerly allied with Tecumseh, occupied most of the American garrisons in the Northwest, including Fort Michilimackinac in northern Michigan and Fort Dearborn (now Chicago). Creek Indians also drove American settlers out of western Tennessee.

The American Offensive. Americans fought back in 1813 by burning the Canadian capital of York (Toronto) and destroying the British fleet on Lake Erie. Richard M. Johnson, a Kentucky War Hawk on leave to command the state militia, killed Tecumseh in the Battle of the Thames River on 5 October 1813. Several officers built political careers on the battle: its participants included a future president (William Henry Harrison), vice president (Richard M. Johnson), four United States senators, almost twenty congressmen, and three governors of Kentucky. In the spring of 1814 Andrew Jackson, commanding the Tennessee militia and allied Chocktaws, Cherokees, and Creeks, defeated Indians allied with the British at Horseshoe Bend in Alabama. These battles dealt a final blow to Indian military power east of the Mississippi.

A Creek Indian leader surrendering to Gen. Andrew Jackson after the Battle of Horseshoe Bend (Bettmann Archive, New York)

The British Counterattack. Of course the British had other things to worry about before 1814, most notably Napoleon and the French, but after Napoleon's defeat at Waterloo in April of that year, the English were able finally to focus on the American war. During the summer of 1814 they raided the shores of Chesapeake Bay and burned the American capital in retaliation for setting York ablaze the previous year. An attack on the city of Baltimore proved less successful for the English. The most memorable legacy of that conflict was Francis Scott Key's poem "The Star-Spangled Banner," written to commemorate the British failure to advance past an American garrison guarding Baltimore Harbor at Fort McHenry.

The Battle of New Orleans. By late 1814 the British decided to seize the city of New Orleans and use it as a bargaining chip in peace negotiations, already under way in Europe. A large British force sailed up the Mississippi and clashed with an American army of Kentucky and Tennessee militiamen, New Orleans laborers and free blacks, and almost one thousand French pirates under the command of Andrew Jackson. On 8 January 1815, two weeks after a peace treaty that ended the war was signed at Ghent, six thousand British soldiers charged the well-entrenched American force of four thousand. After thirty minutes of horrific losses on the British side—two thousand one hundred redcoats were killed or wounded compared to just seventy-one Americans—the English halted the charge. Although the battle made no difference at all on the already concluded peace settlement, it made a national figure of Andrew Jackson, the "hero of New Orleans."

The Treaty of Ghent. After the war was over, the United States and Britain resolved many boundary difficulties and agreed to demilitarize the Great Lakes. As a result of this decision, British and American soldiers withdrew from the border between British Canada and the United States. In 1818 both sides agreed that the Forty-ninth parallel would be the northern boundary of the Louisiana Purchase between Lake of the Woods and the Rocky Mountains and that they would jointly control the rich Oregon Territory for the next ten years. With the threat of war and border skirmishes reduced by the treaties, settlers from both the United States and Great Britain began to occupy the upper Midwest and Oregon.

The Adams-Onís Treaty. Also as a result of the War of 1812, the United States acquired Florida from Spain and fixed the settlement of the western boundary of Louisiana. After Andrew Jackson led an invasion of Florida in 1818 to punish Seminole Indians for raiding American settlements, Spain decided it was too costly to defend its overseas possession. In the Adams-Onís Treaty (named for the American secretary of state John Quincy Adams and the Spanish foreign minister Luis de Onís), Spain ceded all of Florida to the United States and gave up all its possessions in the Pacific Northwest. In exchange the United States gave up its dubious claims to Texas. The future president John Quincy Adams, who had negotiated the treaty, wrote in his diary that "[t]he acquisition of a definite line of boundary to the [Pacific] forms a great epoch in our history."

Source:
J. C. A. Stagg, *Mr. Madison's War: Politics, Diplomacy and Warfare in the Early Republic, 1783–1830* (Princeton, N.J.: Princeton University Press, 1983).

A chromolithograph of a Baldwin Locomotive of the late 1850s

INTERNAL IMPROVEMENTS: THE AMERICAN SYSTEM

A Blueprint for Growth. The brainchild of former War Hawk and Speaker of the House Henry Clay, the American System was a neo-Federalist program of protective tariffs, a national bank, and internal improvements. Clay and his allies argued that it would foster economic growth and interdependence between geographical sections. Yet the system had its greatest impact in the West. In return for Western support of a tariff to aid domestic manufacturers, Eastern lawmakers backed federal aid for the construction of canals, roads, and turnpikes.

Impact. The largest effect of these internal improvements was to link rural farmers with markets. In 1816 a Senate report stated that nine dollars would move one ton of goods from Britain to the United States. Once on American soil, that same nine dollars covered the costs of moving the goods just thirty miles inland. To help remedy this crisis, Congress ordered construction of a federally funded national road to link the Chesapeake with the Trans-Appalachian West. Soon, the boom in canal and road construction led to a full-fledged transportation revolution, which drove the costs of moving people and goods down even further.

Second Bank of the United States. The chartering of a second Bank of the United States, another hallmark of the American System, greatly increased the frenzied sale of land in the West. The boom in land sales was fueled by the availability of easy credit to both settlers and speculators. Many of the politicians working to create the American System were also land speculators themselves, and they were often the most enthusiastic about

rechartering the bank. By federal law the bank's notes were accepted as payment for government land, so a land speculator could borrow the bank's money to buy thousands of acres of land in the new territories. This situation quickly injected capital into the West, but problems arose when speculators failed to pay back the generous loans. The nation's first severe depression—the Panic of 1819—was the result of these unsound financial practices.

Unity. Clay hoped that the federal government would create a market-driven economy that would help unify the nation's various regions. For example, stimulating the nation's infant industries would, in turn, create more demand for the West's raw materials. By the 1840s Western farmers and Northeastern businessmen fulfilled his dream; but the vast national market they created, which moved goods from place to place at a low cost, excluded Southerners. As a result much of the West's economy became increasingly tied to the energy of the North.

A Transportation Revolution. The American System was an attempt to put government power and money behind improvements such as roads, canals, and steamboats. While government projects such as the National Road made it easier for settlers and peddlers to move West, the cost of moving agricultural goods to markets in the East remained high. New York State funded the Erie Canal project to link the Hudson River with Lake Erie, opening a water route between the West and New York City and cutting New Orleans out of the market equation. The canal transformed sleepy western New York into a bustling grain-growing region and repaid the state's investment several times over.

Steamboats and Railroads. Steamboats and railroads completed the transportation revolution. When the entrepreneur Robert Fulton launched the *Clermont* upriver towards Albany, New York, in 1807, he began a new era of cheap transport. Within a decade new flat-bottomed steamboats made the trip up the Mississippi between New Orleans and Louisville in twenty-five days. Like the Erie Canal did in New York, the steamboat rapidly transformed the interior from rugged frontier into a busy commercial region. Railroads picked up where steamboats left off in the 1840s. By the eve of the Civil War most farmers in the North and West lived within a day's ride of a railroad, canal, or river that helped them move their goods to market.

Sources:

Charles Sellers, *The Market Revolution: Jacksonian America, 1815–1846* (New York: Oxford University Press, 1991);

George Rogers Taylor, *The Transportation Revolution, 1815–1860* (White Plains, N.Y.: M. E. Sharpe, 1951).

THE MISSOURI COMPROMISE

Slavery in Missouri. When Missouri applied for admission to the Union as a state in 1819, slavery was already a way of life there. Even before the United States acquired the Louisiana Territory (including the parts that became Missouri), Spanish and French settlers had owned slaves. As part of the agreement to purchase the territory in 1803, the Jefferson administration promised to safeguard the settlers' human property. By the time the population of Missouri (the name given to the territory encompassing the entire Louisiana Purchase besides the state of Louisiana, admitted to the Union in 1812) reached the sixty thousand people required to apply for citizenship, about ten thousand of those people were slaves. The application for statehood was far from routine: it precipitated an ominous sectional crisis that threatened the unity of the nation.

A Deadlock in Congress. When Congress received the application, James Tallmadge of New York added two amendments: one prohibiting the "further introduction of slavery" and another providing for the emancipation of all slaves in Missouri, who comprised 16 percent of the population, on their twenty-fifth birthday. In other words, Missouri would be admitted to the Union only if its residents agreed to create a state where slavery would eventually be prohibited. Tallmadge's move had more to do with longstanding Northern resentment about the South's added representation in Congress—under the Constitution's three-fifths rule, 60 percent of the South's slaves were counted in determining a state's representation in the House and the electoral college—than humanitarian objections to slavery or equal rights for blacks. Tallmadge's amendment passed the House, with the vote closely adhering to sectional lines, but the Senate defeated the measure. Unable to resolve the deadlock, Congress adjourned without passing the Missouri Enabling Act.

An Uneasy Compromise. The Missouri issue came up again early in the next Congress. As the votes the previous session had proven, the North controlled a bare majority in the House while the South, helped by the recent admissions of Alabama and Southern-oriented Illinois, controlled the Senate. A bitter debate raged for months in both chambers. Again, the argument turned on political influence rather than the rights of slaves or the morality of the institution. In 1820 Congress overcame its deadlock and hatched a compromise. This agreement, termed the Missouri Compromise, enabled Missouri to enter the Union as a slave state while the northernmost counties of Massachusetts became the free state of Maine. The scheme neutralized fears that the South would gain more influence in the Senate. Next, the South agreed to outlaw slavery north of 36° 30' latitude, a line extending west from Missouri's southern border. The compromise opened up the new territory of Arkansas (present-day Oklahoma and Arkansas) to slavery while barring the institution from the remainder of the Louisiana Purchase. As a result, Kansas, Nebraska, Colorado, Wisconsin, Minnesota, Iowa, Montana, Wyoming, and North and South Dakota all eventually joined the Union as free states. The plan satisfied Southern members of Congress, who viewed Arkansas as ideally suited for plantation slavery and the plains north and west of Missouri as little more than a treeless desert.

A "Fire-Bell in the Night." The Missouri Compromise made it plain that sectional issues were a political tinderbox. It brought the South's commitment to slavery and the North's resentment of Southern political power into direct confrontation, revealing what was becoming an unbridgeable gulf between slave and free states. Thomas Jefferson, in retirement at Monticello, was distraught by the Missouri Compromise: "a geographical line, coinciding with a marked principle, moral and political, once conceived and held up to the angry passions of men, will never be obliterated," Jefferson wrote. The dispute over Missouri, "like a fire-bell in the night, awakened and filled me with terror. I considered it at once the knell of the Union." A seemingly simple matter—admitting two new states to the Union—had bitterly divided a democratic government and staked out the West as the battleground over the rights and wrongs of slavery.

Sources:

Glover Moore, *The Missouri Controversy* (Lexington: University of Kentucky Press, 1953);

Charles Sellers, *The Market Revolution: Jacksonian America, 1815–1846* (New York: Oxford University Press, 1991).

NATIVE AMERICANS AND REMOVAL

Removal. Although the Constitution had excluded Native American Indians from the benefits of citizenship enjoyed by Americans of European descent, the federal government had not made a concerted effort to push Indians out of eastern North America. This changed in the

An 1843 painting of U.S. government officials and representatives of sixteen Native American tribes meeting at Tahlequah, Oklahoma (Bureau of American Ethnology, Smithsonian Institution, Washington, D.C.)

late 1820s, when the election of Andrew Jackson to the presidency combined with aggressive efforts of some Southern white farmers to gain control of lands owned by certain Indian groups. By the end of the decade, the federal government supported a policy of wholesale relocation for eastern Indians.

"Civilized" Tribes. Long before Jackson entered the White House in 1829, land-hungry whites—often with military backup—had encroached on the lands of the five so-called Civilized Tribes of the Southeast: the Cherokees, Choctaws, Chickasaws, Seminoles, and Creeks. Cherokee tribal holdings, for example, had dwindled from 50 million acres in 1802 to just 9 million in the early 1820s as a result of treaties, land sales, and blatant theft. And in 1814 the Creeks lost 22 million acres of tribal land in southern Georgia and central Alabama after they were defeated by Gen. Andrew Jackson at the Battle of Horseshoe Bend.

White Encroachment Worsens. In 1829 there were still approximately sixty thousand Seminoles, Choctaws, Creeks, Chickasaws, and Cherokees who remained on their ancestral lands. Legally, these Southeastern tribes' tenure on their land was secure; treaties signed by the federal government formally recognized them as sovereign nations. Congress had even passed legislation to provide the Indians with money for Bibles, tools, schools, and training in farming techniques; but federal Indian policy outraged many Southeastern whites, who believed that Indian-white relations should be left to the individual states and not the federal government. Some South-

erners even made claims that the federal government was antidemocratic since it seemed to ignore local white hunger for the Indians' fertile lands.

States' Rights and Land. One person who took this view was Georgia's governor, the former War Hawk George Troup. He forever linked the issues of states' rights and white greed for Indian land when in early 1829 he declared Cherokee lands to be under state, not federal, jurisdiction. He then transferred the lands to poor whites by way of a lottery. In response the Cherokees declared themselves an independent republic in 1827, complete with their own constitution, courts, government, and police force. The Cherokees had also sought to hold onto their land by adopting "white" ways of life, including sedentary farming and livestock raising; they had also developed a written language. However, the discovery of gold within the Cherokees' domain in late 1827 increased white lust for the land. Both the legislature and governor declared Cherokee laws null and void. Soon after, whites began surveying Indian lands for sale. Other states, including Mississippi and Alabama, which had large Creek, Chickasaw, and Choctaw populations, soon extended state authority over their Indian populations. All eyes focused on Washington to see what response President Jackson would have to the Southern states' actions.

Jackson. Declaring that the federal government lacked the authority to recognize Indian sovereignty within a state, Jackson chose to ignore Georgia's, Alabama's, and Mississippi's encroachments on Indian

The following is an excerpt from the journal of the French nobleman Alexis de Tocqueville, who, along with his companion Gustave de Beaumont, traveled through the United States in 1831–1832. Some of the journal's most moving passages concern Tocqueville's observations of Eastern Indians' removal west of the Mississippi:

The Chactas [Choctaws] were a powerful nation living on the frontiers of the States of Alabama and Georgia. After long negotiations [the U.S. government] finally, this year, succeeded in persuading them to leave their country and emigrate to the right bank of the Mississippi. Six to seven thousand Indians have already crossed the great river; those arriving in Memphis came there with the object of following their compatriots. The agent of the American government, who was accompanying them and was responsible for paying their passage, when he learned that a steamboat had just arrived, ran to the bank. The price that he offered for carrying the Indians sixty leagues further down was the final touch that made up the captain's unsettled mind; the signal for all aboard was given. The prow was turned south, and we gaily mounted the ladder down which sadly came the poor passengers who, instead of going to Louisville, saw themselves obliged to await the thaw at Memphis. Thus goes the world.

But we had not left yet: it was a question of embarking our exiled tribe, its horses and its dogs. Here began a scene which, in truth, had something lamentable about it. The Indians advanced mournfully toward the bank. First they had their horses go aboard; several of them, little accustomed to the forms of civilized life, took fright and plunged into the Mississippi, from which they could be pulled out only with difficulty. Then came the men who, according to ordinary habits, carried only their arms; then the women carrying their children attached to their backs or wrapped in the blankets they wore; they

were, be-sides, burdened down with loads containing their whole wealth. Finally the old people were led on. Among them was a woman 110 years old. I have never seen a more appalling shape. She was naked save for a covering which left visible, at a thousand places, the most emaciated figure imaginable. She was escorted by two or three generations of grandchildren. To leave one's country at that age to seek one's fortune in a foreign land, what misery! Among the old people there was a young girl who had broken her arm a week before; for want of care the arm had been frozen below the fracture. Yet she had to follow the common journey. When everything was on board the dogs approached the bank; but they refused to enter the vessel and began howling frightfully. Their masters had to bring them on by force.

In the whole scene there was an air of ruin and destruction, some-thing which betrayed a final and irrevocable adieu; one couldn't watch without feeling one's heart wrung. The Indians were tranquil, but somber and taciturn. There was one who could speak English and of whom I asked why the Chactas were leaving their country. "To be free," he answered. I could never get any other reason out of him. We will set them down tomorrow in the solitudes of Arkansas. One must confess that it is a singular fate that brought us to Memphis to watch the expulsion, one can say the dissolution, of one of the most celebrated and ancient American peoples.

The old are spared no more than the others. I have just seen on the boat deck an aged woman more than 120 years old. She is almost naked and carries on her only a miserable woollen covering scarcely protecting her shoulders from the cold. She seemed to me the perfect image of old age and decrepitude. This unhappy woman is obviously at deaths door, and she leaves the land where she has dwelt for 120 years to go into another country to begin a new life....

Source: George Wilson Pierson, *Tocqueville in America* (Garden City, N.Y.: Doubleday, 1959), pp. 597–598.

lands. Instead he decided to put the power of the federal government behind an effort to move eastern Indians to federal lands west of the Mississippi and temporarily out of the way of white settlement. This migration, he declared, would protect them from the "degradation and destruction to which they were rapidly hastening" in their own states. Put in writing, this *Act to provide for an exchange of lands with the Indians residing in any of the states or territories, and for their removal west of the river Mississippi*," became the basis for the policy known as Indian removal.

The Choice to Leave. Several native groups decided the time had come to give up and move West. Between 1831 and 1833 at least fifteen thousand Choctaws migrated from their tribal lands in Mississippi to loca-

tions west of Arkansas territory (now Oklahoma). Alexis de Tocqueville, a French nobleman traveling the country in the early 1830s, movingly described a group of Choctaws crossing the frozen Mississippi River:

The Indians had their families with them, and they brought in their train the wounded and the sick, with children newly born and old men on the verge of death... Never will that solemn spectacle fade from my remembrance. No cry, no sob, was heard among the assembled crowd; all were silent.

Black Hawk War. Other native groups chose not to move. Groups of Sac and Fox, who the federal government resettled west of the Mississippi, defiantly returned to Illinois in 1831 to occupy land vacated by other nations. White settlers, fearing an Indian war,

BLACK HAWK'S SURRENDER SPEECH

After the federal government resettled the Sac and Fox nations west of the Mississippi, some defiantly returned to Illinois in 1831 to occupy land vacated by other nations. Fearing war, settlers in Illinois petitioned the governor for troops to remove the Indians, who were led by a Sac warrior named Black Hawk. In the Black Hawk War, Illinois state troops forced the natives back across the Mississippi and killed most of the Indians that they caught. Black Hawk used his moving surrender speech in 1832 to shame the white occupiers of Indian lands:

You have taken me prisoner with all my warriors. I am much grieved, for I expected, if I did not defeat you, to hold out much longer, and give you more trouble before I surrendered. I tried hard to bring you into ambush, but your last general understands Indian fighting. The first one was not so wise. When I saw that I could not beat you by Indian fighting, I determined to rush on you, and fight you face to face. I fought hard. But your guns were well aimed. The bullets flew like birds in the air, and whizzed by our ears like the wind through the trees in winter. . . . [Black Hawk] is now prisoner of the white men; they will do with him as they wish. But he can stand torture, and is not afraid of death. He is no coward. Black Hawk is an Indian.

He has done nothing for which an Indian ought to be ashamed. He has fought for his countrymen, the squaws and papooses, against white men, who came, year after year, to cheat them and take away their lands. You know the cause of our making war. It is known to all white men. They ought to be ashamed of it. The white men despise the Indians, and drive them from their homes. But the Indians are not deceitful. The white men speak bad of the Indian, and look at him spitefully. But the Indian does not tell lies; Indians do not steal.

An Indian who is as bad as the white men, could not live in our nation; he would be put to death, and eat [sic] up by the wolves. The white men are bad school-masters; they carry false looks, and deal in false actions; they smile in the face of the poor Indian to cheat him; they shake them by the hand to gain their confidence, to make them drunk, to deceive them, and ruin our wives. We told them to let us alone; but they followed on and beset our paths, and they coiled themselves among us like the snake. They poisoned us by their touch. We were not safe. We lived in danger. We were becoming like them, hypocrites and liars, adulterers, lazy drones, all talkers, and no workers.

Source: Sean Wilentz, ed., *Major Problems in the Early Republic* (New York: Heath, 1991).

petitioned the governor to call for troops. Illinois state troops forced the natives back across the Mississippi and killed most of the Indians that were caught in a conflict later called the Black Hawk War. The surrender speech of the Sac leader Black Hawk in 1832 marked the end of the Northern Woodlands Indians' attempt to reclaim lands west of the Mississippi.

Cherokee Nation v. *Georgia.* The Cherokees tried another tactic: they took their claims to the Supreme Court. In *Cherokee Nation* v. *Georgia* (1831) Chief Justice John Marshall ruled that an Indian tribe did not constitute a foreign state, and therefore could not sue a state in federal court. A year after the Cherokees suffered that defeat, Marshall wrote in his decision *Worcester* v. *Georgia* (1832) that Georgia had no right to control the Cherokees or their territory. Further, in a third case, Marshall again declared Georgia's actions unconstitutional. In other words, though the Supreme Court limited the legal ability of Indians to seek redress in federal courts, Marshall and his colleagues also sought to limit any state's ability to impinge on a native group's territory.

The Trail of Tears. President Jackson ignored Marshall's rulings, reportedly remarking that "John Marshall has made his decision *now let him enforce it!*" Two years after Jackson left the White House, President Martin Van Buren sent the army to Georgia not to enforce the Supreme Court's decision, but to march the eighteen thousand remaining Cherokees to Oklahoma. During the forced march in the winter of 1838–1839—aptly called the "Trail of Tears"—four thousand Indians died of exposure, disease, and starvation.

Sources:
William G. McLoughlin, *Cherokee Renascence in the New Republic* (Princeton, N.J.: Princeton University Press, 1986);

Theda Perdue and Michael D. Green, *The Cherokee Removal* (New York: Bedford Books, 1995);

Michael Paul Rogin, *Fathers and Children: Andrew Jackson and the Subjugation of the American Indian* (New York: Knopf, 1975).

A NEW LAND: TEXAS AND ANNEXATION

"El Norte." During the months immediately following Mexico's independence from Spain in 1821, the nation's new rulers pondered ways to develop its sparsely populated northern states. A treaty signed by both Spain and the United States in February 1819 had drawn the American boundary so as to exclude the state of Texas, which was situated just west of the American tide of settlement. Nevertheless, within months of the treaty's ratification Americans began to settle in the eastern region of the Spanish (soon to be Mexican) state of Cuahuila-Texas. The new Mexican government quickly seized upon the idea of using American immigrants to develop their underpopulated Northern provinces.

Austin. Entrepreneurs and speculators such as Stephen F. Austin encouraged land-hungry farmers and planters to settle in easternmost Texas, far from the Mexican *tejano* settlements to the south and west. In

TEXAS FOREVER!!

The usurper of the South has failed in his efforts to enslave the freemen of Texas.

The wives and daughters of Texas will be saved from the brutality of Mexican soldiers.

Now is the time to emigrate to the Garden of America.

A free passage, and all found, is offered at New Orleans to all applicants. Every settler receives a location of

EIGHT HUNDRED ACRES OF LAND.

On the 23d of February, a force of 1000 Mexicans came in sight of San Antonio, and on the 25th Gen. St. Anna arrived at that place with 2500 more men, and demanded a surrender of the fort held by 150 Texians, and on the refusal, he attempted to storm the fort, twice, with his whole force, but was repelled with the loss of 500 men, and the Americans lost none. Many of his troops, the liberals of Zacatecas, are brought on to Texas in irons and are urged forward with the promise of the women and plunder of Texas.

The Texian forces were marching to relieve St. Antonio, March the 2d. The Government of Texas is supplied with plenty of arms, ammunition, provisions, &c. &c.

A recruitment poster misstating the facts of the Battle of the Alamo to attract volunteers for the Texan army (University of Texas at Austin)

order to gain title to their free land and qualify for Mexican tax breaks, the settlers had to agree to speak Spanish, convert to Catholicism, and adhere to Mexican laws—which included the abolition of slavery. However, the American settlers did not accede to these requests. Instead, they retained their own language, religion, allegiances, and institutions, including slavery. Moreover, they were coming in droves eager to plant cotton on the fertile plains of east Texas. By 1830 there were already twenty thousand white Americans and two thousand slaves in Texas; the number of Mexicans was less than five thousand.

Exertion of Power. Hoping to head off any conflict over the territory, President John Quincy Adams offered Mexico $1 million for Texas, and his successor Andrew Jackson was willing to pay $5 million. Although the Mexicans refused to sell, more than a few members of the government were beginning to rue the day they allowed the Americans into Texas. In 1830 the Mexican government decided to halt all further American immigration into the country. The Texans, chafing under the new restrictions, began talking about formally rejoining the United States.

Declaring Independence. Things got even worse for the Texans in 1835, when a conservative new government seized power in Mexico City, intent on establishing tighter authority in the north. For a time Anglo-Texans and *tejanos* (the Mexican residents of Texas) formed a political alliance in an attempt to protect their eroding political autonomy, but the new Mexican dictator, Antonio López de Santa Anna, responded in early 1836 by marching an army of six thousand men north into Texas. Just days after Santa Anna reached San Antonio, delegates from across Texas met in convention and, on 2 May, declared themselves an independent republic.

Siege at the Alamo. When Santa Anna's army arrived in San Antonio in late February 1836, a band of Texans took refuge in the Alamo, a former mission that they had already converted into a small fort. They withstood Santa Anna's frequent assaults and inflicted significant casualties on the Mexican army for ten days. Finally, on 6 March, Santa Anna captured the fort and killed all of its defenders, including frontier legends Jim Bowie and Davy Crockett. Responding to the cry "Remember the Alamo!" thousands of Texans and volunteers from

The Texan battle flag carried by troops under Sam Houston (Texas State Library, Austin)

Southern states flocked to the rebel army led by Sam Houston, a former Tennessee congressman and governor.

San Jacinto. Two weeks later the Mexican army slaughtered another band of Texans at Goliad, a town southeast of San Antonio, after they had surrendered. This seeming atrocity further galvanized Houston's men, who defeated a much larger Mexican force on 26 April at a battle on the San Jacinto River near present-day Houston. More significantly, Houston's forces captured Santa Anna in the battle and forced him to sign a treaty granting Texas's independence. The Texans almost immediately elected Houston president and petitioned for annexation to the United States as a slave state.

Annexation. In Washington, President Andrew Jackson found himself in a delicate position: if he annexed Texas, he would almost certainly provoke a war with Mexico and expose himself to charges that such a move would expand slavery. On his final day in office Jackson formally recognized the Texas republic, but he chose not to act on its request for annexation. His successor, Martin Van Buren, also refused to act on the Texas question. The Texans, for their part, spent their time securing their new republic and finding support from across the Atlantic. Both Great Britain and France recognized and signed trade treaties with Texas. An independent Texas perfectly suited the British, who hoped to free their thriving textile industry from dependence on American cotton. Politically savvy Texas diplomats also knew that their acceptance of British overtures would quickly catch the attention of the American government.

Sectionalism. The alliance between a newly independent Texas and the historic enemy of the United States sent shock waves across the American continent. Southern congressmen were especially alarmed. Fearing that a Texas dominated by Great Britain might abolish slavery, they urged action on annexation. When the sudden death of William Henry Harrison in 1841 made the states' rights advocate John Tyler president, the annexationists found an ally in the White House. The Virginian Tyler, spurned by the Whigs and hated by most Democrats, quickly seized upon Texas as an issue that could galvanize Southern support for his bid for reelection in 1844. Tyler named the proslavery South Carolinian John C. Calhoun secretary of state and charged him with negotiating a treaty of annexation with Texas. However, his strategy backfired. No one was more associated with slavery and its expansion than the outspoken Calhoun. In addition, Calhoun made the situation worse when he presented an annexation treaty to Congress in 1844 as if its only purpose was to extend slavery. Fearing a proslavery plot, Northern senators from both parties banded together to defeat the treaty, 36 votes to 16, in June 1844.

Polk. With a new presidential election in the offing, Texas became a hot political issue. Whig candidate Henry Clay openly opposed annexation, and in a surprise move so did the leading Democratic contender, Martin Van Buren. In the Democratic convention pro-Texas Southerners blocked Van Buren's nomination and threw the convention to their own "dark horse" candidate, former Tennessee

Gen. Antonio López de Santa Anna (New-York Historical Society)

congressman James K. Polk. Southerners were ecstatic. Polk was a slaveholder and an ardent expansionist, and his nomination at the expense of the Northerner Van Buren illustrated the extent to which Southerners dominated the Democratic Party.

Manifest Destiny. Democrats interpreted Polk's victory in the 1844 election as a mandate for annexation even though he won by less than 40,000 votes (he received 170 electoral votes to the Whig Henry Clay's 105). Before Polk even took office, President Tyler persuaded Congress to approve an annexation treaty in February 1845. Texas entered the Union as the fifteenth slave state the following December, bypassing the territorial stage. The drama surrounding Texas's annexation significantly altered the way the U.S. government viewed westward expansion until the Civil War. After the annexation of Texas, the issue of slavery's expansion would be forever intertwined with the political organization of the West.

Sources:

Marshall De Bruhl, *Sword of San Jacinto: A Life of Sam Houston* (New York: Random House, 1993);

Charles G. Sellers, *James K. Polk, Continentalist 1843–1846* (Princeton, N.J.: Princeton University Press, 1966).

RIVALRY ALONG THE RIO GRANDE: WAR WITH MEXICO

Tensions. After 1845 the fact that Texas was now part of the United States was beyond dispute. Yet annexation did not calm tensions since the Texas-Mexican border remained a subject of dispute. The Mexican government defined the south and west border of Texas at the Nueces River. The Texas government, now backed by the U.S. government, declared that the Rio Grande was its southern border, a claim that increased the size of Texas by almost 200 percent. Predictably, Mexico responded to the Texans' belligerent declaration by breaking off diplomatic ties with the United States. This move set in motion a series of events that changed the pattern of Western expansion, foreign relations with Mexico, and American politics.

The Oregon Question. In 1844 Democrat James K. Polk had run for president on a platform that called for the immediate annexation of Texas and a border for the Oregon Territory that reached north to 54°40', the boundary with Russia's settlements in Alaska. However, he secretly wished for more than Oregon and Texas: he coveted Mexican California and New Mexico as well. Texas annexation was accomplished even before Polk en-

PRESIDENT JAMES K. POLK'S WAR MESSAGE

Elected on a platform promising to expand the United States westward, James K. Polk of Tennessee wasted no time provoking a war with the Republic of Mexico over territory. With his eyes on California and New Mexico, Polk sent an envoy to Mexico City with an offer to purchase the territory. At the same time, he ordered American troops into disputed territory near the border, hoping to taunt Mexican soldiers into an attack. When the attack failed to materialize, Polk decided to declare war on Mexico anyway. On 9 May 1846, however, the day he planned to send his declaration to Congress, Polk learned that eleven U.S. soldiers had been killed by Mexicans in the disputed area. He quickly rewrote his declaration of war, excerpted here:

> The existing state of relations between the United States and Mexico renders it proper that I should bring the subject to the consideration of Congress. . . .

> The strong desire to establish peace with Mexico on liberal and honorable terms, and the readiness of this Government to regulate and adjust our boundary and other causes of difference with that power on such fair and equitable principles as would lead to permanent relations of the most friendly nature, induced me in September last to seek the reopening of diplomatic relations between the two countries. . . . The Mexican government not only refused to receive him or listen to his propositions, but after a long-continued series of menaces have at last in-

vaded our territory and shed the blood of our fellow-citizens on our own soil. . . .

> The grievous wrongs perpetrated by Mexico upon our citizens throughout a long period of years remain unredressed, and solemn treaties pledging her public faith for this redress have been disregarded. A government either unable or unwilling to enforce the execution of such treaties fails to perform one of its plainest duties. . . .

> Upon the pretext that Texas, a nation as independent as herself, though proper to unite its destinies with our own she has effected to believe that we have severed her rightful territory, and in official proclamations and manifestoes has repeatedly threatened to make war upon us for the purpose of re-conquering Texas. In the meantime we have tried every effort at reconciliation. The cup of forbearance had been exhausted even before the recent information from the frontier of the Rio Del Norte. But now, after reiterated menaces, Mexico has passed the boundary of the United States, has invaded our territory and shed American blood upon the American soil. She has proclaimed that hostilities have commenced, and that the two nations are now at war.

> As war exists, and, notwithstanding all our efforts to avoid it, exists by the act of Mexico herself, we are called upon by every consideration of duty and patriotism to vindicate with decision the honor, the rights, and the interests of our country.

Source: Sean Wilentz, ed., *Major Problems in the Early Republic* (New York: Heath, 1991).

An 1846 daguerreotype of American general John E. Wool and his staff in Saltillo, Mexico (Beinecke Library, Yale University, New Haven, Connecticut)

tered the White House; Oregon was another matter. Both England and the United States had agreed in 1818 to occupy the Oregon Country "jointly," with the understanding that a future treaty would decide what part of the territory would become American and what would become part of Canada. By 1845 there was talk of war by both Britain and the United States over the Oregon boundary. In fact, one of the catchiest Democratic slogans during the 1844 election was "Fifty-four forty or fight!" (a reference to the latitude where expansionists hoped to draw the northern boundary of the territory), suggesting that Oregon was worth a war with Great Britain.

Peaceful Resolution. President Polk, contrary to the bellicose promises of candidate Polk, was not willing to go to war with Britain over Oregon. Instead he accepted a treaty in 1846 that drew the territorial border at the Forty-ninth parallel, the current United States-Canadian boundary. Some Northern Democrats were upset that they had supported Polk's efforts to make the Rio Grande the Texas border, which expanded territory under control of slaveholders, and then signed away one-half of Oregon, territory they believed would have been for free farmers only.

Provoking a War. Polk, meanwhile, was busy plotting how to gain the rest of the Mexican northwest for the United States. His first move was to send an envoy to Mexico City with an offer to purchase California and New Mexico, an acquisition that would mean the loss of half of Mexico's territory, for $30 million. At the same time, he ordered American troops into the disputed ter-

ritory between the Nueces and Rio Grande, and he dispatched a naval squadron into the Gulf of Mexico. Polk also attempted to stir up pro-American sentiment among the settlers in central California by naming a popular businessman from Monterey American consul and starting talk about California becoming the thirty-first state. Then Polk sat back and waited for any of these forms of provocation to prompt the Mexicans to fight back. When they did not respond as he had anticipated, Polk decided to declare war on Mexico anyway. On 9 May 1846, however, before he took action on his own, Polk received word that Mexican soldiers had crossed the Rio Grande and killed eleven Americans patrolling the disputed area. He sent the official declaration of war to Congress two days later.

Conflict. The declaration of war ran into trouble in Congress, where Whigs, most of them from Northern states, tended to oppose both continued westward expansion and war with Mexico. Nevertheless, in the end most of them voted for the declaration rather than be branded unpatriotic. As a result the declaration of war passed the House by a vote of 174-14 and the Senate by 40-2. Many Whigs at the time remembered how the Federalist Party had openly opposed the War of 1812 and never recovered politically; despite their misgivings, they voted for war.

Slavery and Expansion. The American people were far from united on the subject of the war with Mexico. Many Northerners feared that slavery would spread into the fertile lands gained as a result of the war, reversing Mexico's abolition policy. Most Southerners, for their

This single paragraph, attached to an appropriations bill at the beginning of the war with Mexico, framed the tense national debate over slavery until the outbreak of the Civil War. Penned by a little-known Pennsylvania congressman named David Wilmot, the proviso united Northern Whigs and Democrats opposed to slavery's expansion in the West. Although it never became law, the Wilmot Proviso provided an ominous sign that the two-party system would not be able to contain the explosive issue of slavery expansion.

Provided, That, as an express and fundamental condition to the acquisition of any territory from the Republic of Mexico by the United States, by virtue of any treaty which may be negotiated between them, and to the use by the Executive of the moneys herein appropriated, neither slavery nor involuntary servitude shall ever exist in any part of said territory, except for crime, whereof the party shall first be duly convicted.

part, hoped that future American settlers would be able to take their slaves into the new Western lands. After all, a large majority of the soldiers fighting in the war came from the South. Besides, they reasoned, Americans were free to take their property wherever they wished.

Northern Fears. The slavery issue quickly became intertwined with war aims in the U.S. Congress. For years a small but growing number of concerned Northern congressmen had watched while proslavery Democrats invoked party unity to table antislavery petitions, bar abolitionist material from the mails, and expand the scope of the "peculiar institution" into the new state of Texas. To be sure, even those Northern Democrats who opposed slavery were often more than willing to repress abolitionism in order to maintain the Jacksonian coalition in both North and South. By the mid 1840s many of these politicians—including those with impeccable Democratic records—began to believe that Southern encroachment had outstripped the benefits of coalition.

Wilmot Proviso. In August 1846, during the early stages of the war with Mexico, President Polk requested $2 million from Congress to facilitate peace negotiations and, if possible, buy California and New Mexico. Northern Democrats saw the bill as an opportunity finally to thwart their Southern brethren, who appeared poised to snatch yet more territory for slavery. On 8 August, a first-term Pennsylvania representative named David Wilmot added a proviso to the bill that barred slavery from any territory acquired during the war. The amendment, known as the Wilmot Proviso, framed the national debate over slavery until the start of the Civil War.

Jeffersonian Precedent. Wilmot and his allies drew the language for the proviso directly from Jefferson's 1787 Northwest Ordinance. When it was his turn to speak, the freshman legislator endorsed the president's request for funds. The House of Representatives passed the measure 87-64. Nearly all Northern representatives, Democrats and Whigs, voted in favor of the proviso; Southern Democrats and Whigs voted almost unanimously against it. In the Senate, which was dominated by Southerners, the measure was defeated.

Southern Countermeasures. To counter the Wilmot Proviso, South Carolina senator John C. Calhoun introduced his own resolutions that argued Congress had no right to bar slavery from any territory. Calhoun reasoned that since territories belong to all the states, both slave and free states had an equal claim on them. In a reversal of the voting on the Wilmot Proviso, the Senate passed Calhoun's resolutions while the House defeated them. Northerners in Congress knew well that Calhoun's resolutions were but a small step from more-serious proslavery legislation: a demand that Congress guarantee the right to bring slaves into territories and enact federally backed slave codes there.

An Ominous Vote. The votes on the Wilmot Proviso and the Calhoun resolutions marked the beginning of an ominous new chapter in the fight over the future of slavery. Division over the slavery issue had become sectional. By the late 1840s it was far from clear that the Second Party System could handle the most explosive issue of the day.

American Victory. Mexico had a larger regular army than the United States, but that turned out to be their only advantage. The better-equipped and better-armed Americans won every battle in the eighteen-month war. While Gen. Stephen Watts Kearney and Capt. John C. Frémont occupied New Mexico and California, Gen. Zachary Taylor captured city after city in northern Mexico. Finally, Gen. Winfield Scott landed an invasion force at Vera Cruz and marched his army to Mexico City. After fierce hand-to-hand combat in the Battles of Chapultepec, Molino del Rey, and Contreras, Scott's army captured the capital. The war was over.

Manifest Destiny. Back in the United States, American expansionism was at high tide. Democratic journalist John L. O'Sullivan wrote in 1845 that it was "our manifest destiny to overspread and to possess the whole of the continent which Providence has given us for the development of the great experiment of liberty." Some Democrats spoke in favor of taking all of Mexico. Nevertheless, on the other side, many Americans, especially those from New England and those who opposed the extension of slavery, began voicing their doubts. In Washington antiwar sentiment was mostly confined to the Whig party, but even Northern Democrats had begun to worry about the future of all the Western territory that would be gained from the victory over Mexico.

Treaty of Guadelupe Hidalgo. Discussions with the United States took place even before the federal government had made peace with Mexico. President Polk had ordered Nicholas P. Trist, chief clerk of the state department, to accompany the American armies into Mexico City and to offer $15 million for the disputed territory in Texas, California, and New Mexico. On 2 February 1848 the Treaty of Guadelupe Hidalgo was passed by the Senate 38-14, with opposition split between Democrats who wanted more territory and Whigs who opposed any expansion at all. In the end the United States gained territory that eventually became the states of California, Nevada, Utah, Arizona, and parts of New Mexico, Colorado, and Wyoming.

Sources:

John S. D. Eisenhower, *So Far From God: The U.S. War with Mexico 1846–1848* (New York: Random House, 1989);

Robert W. Johannsen, *To the Halls of Montezumas: The Mexican War in the American Imagination* (New York: Oxford University Press, 1985).

THE SLAVERY ISSUE: THE ELECTION OF 1848

Crisis. Neither the Wilmot Proviso nor the Treaty of Guadelupe Hidalgo settled what was becoming the most convulsive political question of the day: whether slavery would spread into territory gained from Mexico. As the presidential election of 1848 approached, many Americans looked to the electoral system to decide the matter, and since President Polk decided not to seek reelection, the field was wide open.

The Liberty Party. First to make a formal nomination was the abolitionist Liberty Party. Although riven with strife over how radical a program to pursue, the political abolitionists of the Liberty Party agreed with the principle of the Wilmot Proviso. The party convention endorsed the Proviso and named John P. Hale, a former Democratic senator from New Hampshire, for president.

Calhoun and "Southern Rights." On the other side of the spectrum, John C. Calhoun staked out a firm "Southern rights" position based on his Senate resolutions. Calhoun articulated in 1848 what secessionists would repeat in 1860: that the Constitution itself protects the right of property and that no law passed by Congress can ever tell a man where he can or cannot take his property.

Democrats and "Popular Sovereignty." The Democratic Party tried to diffuse "Southern rights" and the slavery issue with a compromise called "popular sovereignty." Identified in 1848 with the candidacy of Lewis Cass of Michigan, popular sovereignty left it to a territory's settlers whether or not to allow slavery within its borders. However, Cass and the Democrats remained vague about the details; they never took an official position on precisely when or how settlers were to make the choice. Would it happen only after settlers had passed through the territorial stage and drawn up a state constitution? Or as soon as the territory was organized? The answers to

An 1848 daguerreotype of Martin Van Buren (Chicago Historical Society)

these questions were critical. In the first case settlers would presumably have been in the territory for some time, giving a new institution such as slavery time to take hold. For this reason Southerners tended to assume that this was what was meant by popular sovereignty. If the decision was made at the initial organizational stage, as many Northerners assumed it would be, there could be at most a few slaves and slave owners in a given territory since under Mexican law slavery had been abolished. When the Democratic convention met and nominated Cass, delegates from two state delegations walked out in protest: Alabama because slavery's future was not guaranteed in the platform, and New York because its favorite son, the former president Martin Van Buren, was passed over for the nomination.

Another Whig War Hero. The Whigs chose a more successful strategy: nominate a popular candidate and offer no platform whatsoever. The popular candidate was a hero of the Mexican War, Gen. Zachary Taylor, who was chosen despite his refusal to state an opinion on any contested topic. The Whigs were hoping to duplicate their success in 1840, when they nominated a popular general (William Henry Harrison), issued very few policy statements, and glided to victory. Another plus for the pro-Taylor faction, known as "Cotton" Whigs, was the fact that the candidate was a Louisiana planter who owned more than one hundred slaves. This situation no doubt promised to help the struggling party in the Southern states, but it was enough to drive antislavery partisans, who were known as "Conscience" Whigs, out of the party.

Free Soil Party. Almost immediately after the Whigs nominated Taylor, disgruntled Conscience Whigs such as Salmon P. Chase and Charles Sumner started talking about forming a new antislavery party with a broader political base than the abolitionist Liberty Party. The Van Buren wing of the Democratic party, many of whom had sponsored and supported the Wilmot Proviso, were extremely receptive to the idea. So members of all three groups—Conscience Whigs, Van Buren Democrats, and Liberty Men—held a convention in Buffalo in August 1848 to form the Free Soil Party. Pious abolitionists mingled with Democratic politicos, free blacks, and Whig Brahmins under the main tent while in the background a committee worked out the platform and candidates. The platform combined Liberty Party pronouncements ("No more Slave States and no more slave Territories") with popular Democratic planks such as a call for free homesteads. The organizers also unveiled a catchy slogan: "Free Soil, Free Speech, Free Labor, Free Men." For president, the party nominated former president Van Buren; for vice president, the Whig (and son and grandson of presidents) Charles Francis Adams.

Van Buren. Many seasoned abolitionists doubted whether Van Buren—who as president had supported purging the mails of abolitionist materials and automatically tabling antislavery petitions sent to Congress—was a changed man. Van Buren, however, had decided the time had come to take a stand against what free soilers called the Slave Power. "The minds of nearly all mankind," declared Van Buren, "have been penetrated by a conviction of the evils of slavery."

Southern Choice. The campaign itself was divided. In the North both the Whig and Democratic parties claimed to support the Wilmot Proviso; in the South, Democrats pointed to the thousands of square miles of new slave territory their party had delivered. The Whig war hero Taylor proved to be by far the strongest candidate in the South. "Will the people of [the South] vote for a Southern President or a Northern one?," asked Southern newspapers. In an ominous sequel to the votes on the Proviso, Southern Democratic voters jumped parties to vote for the slaveholder Taylor.

Another Victory for Taylor. When the votes were counted, Taylor carried eight of the fifteen slave states and seven of the fifteen free states. The Free Soil Party polled 290,000 votes (about 10 percent of the total, 14 percent in the North), enough to throw New York State and the election to Taylor. The new antislavery coalition also elected nine congressmen and two U.S. senators, the Ohioan Chase and Sumner of Massachusetts, who would carry the Free Soil message to Washington. No longer would the slavery issue be pushed to the political sidelines.

Sources:

Richard H. Sewell, *Ballots for Freedom: Antislavery Politics in the United States 1837–1860* (New York: Oxford University Press, 1976);

Arthur M. Schlesinger, ed., *History of American Presidential Elections, 1789–1968* (New York: Chelsea House, 1971).

THE SLAVERY ISSUE: WESTERN POLITICS AND THE COMPROMISE OF 1850

Growing Influence. Although less than three hundred thousand people voted for the Free Soil Party in 1848, these antislavery partisans exerted an influence on the national political agenda that far outpaced their numbers. Topping the list of priorities for Free Soilers, of course, was keeping slavery out of the western territories acquired from Mexico. Many Whigs and Democrats disagreed: they preferred to keep the explosive question of slavery in the territories on the political sidelines, but the discovery of gold near Sacramento, California, in 1848—causing the thousands of prospectors who headed west the following year—made postponing the issue impossible. The political crisis over whether the North or the South would control the settlement of the former Mexican lands almost tore the nation apart in 1850.

California Gold Rush. At first Easterners were skeptical about the gold-flecked rumors spreading from John Sutter's mill. After President Polk confirmed the "extraordinary character" of the strike in his annual message to Congress in December, gold fever engulfed the United States. More than eighty thousand gold seekers made it to San Francisco in 1849 alone—about twenty five thousand arriving by sea and fifty five thousand who crossed the continent by overland routes. And this was only the beginning: each year after 1849 thousands of people arrived in California hoping to strike it rich. Most people in the federal government agreed that the political future of the West had to be determined. The fate of California, now bustling with settlers, as well as the political destiny of New Mexico (inhabited by former Mexicans) and the Mormons at the Great Salt Lake, could no longer be postponed.

Washington in Disarray. Still, no one had come up with a solution to the slavery question. Congress, especially, was descending into anarchy over the matter. Fire-eating Southerners began to demand secession if Free Soilers' claims to abolish the slave trade ever became law; antislavery Whigs and Democrats in the House drafted a bill to organize California as a free state; and President Polk weighed in with a plan to extend the Missouri Compromise line (36° 30') to the Pacific. No compromise could take place before Zachary Taylor was sworn in as president.

Nationalist. Many Southerners expected (or at least hoped) that Zachary Taylor, the owner of more than one hundred slaves, would take their side on the extension issue. However, they were soon disappointed. Taylor proposed admitting California and New Mexico immediately into the Union as states, bypassing the territorial stage. Let the Californians decide for themselves whether to allow or prohibit slavery, the nationalist-minded president argued. This delighted Free Soilers: since slavery had been illegal under Mexican law, immediate admission of California and New Mexico—a huge territory containing the present-day states of New Mexico, Utah, Nevada, Arizona, and parts of Colorado—would bar slavery from ever taking root there. In addition, a large proportion of those who had migrated to California also opposed slavery.

A New Free State. These antislavery Californians quickly seized the initiative and in October 1849, with the Taylor administration's blessing, met in convention and applied for admission to the Union as a free state. Southern senators, who had long counted on their control of the Senate as a check to antislavery policies, were livid. "For the first time, we are about permanently to destroy the balance of power between the sections," seethed first-term Mississippi senator Jefferson Davis. He added that if California was admitted as the sixteenth free state, the fifteen states of the South would be reduced to permanent minority status within the Union. This was unacceptable to most Southerners, who feared that slavery confined to the South would quickly suffocate. The South, more and more of its representatives were saying, would either have to concede victory to the Free Soilers or leave the Union.

Compromiser. To most people, compromise on the slavery issue seemed impossible. However, the seventy-two-year-old Henry Clay insisted there was still room for an equitable solution, as there had been in 1820 in the Missouri crisis. In his long career Clay had helped broker several deals that alleviated sectional tensions, including the Missouri Compromise. If anyone in the government was able to ease the crisis over California in 1850, it was Clay. He began from the position that California should be admitted quickly to the Union as a free state and that the South should receive something in the bargain to avoid further talk of disunion. With this in mind, the Kentuckian worked out eight separate proposals "founded upon mutual forbearance" and introduced them to the Senate.

An Uneasy Bargain. Known as the Compromise of 1850, Clay's proposals became the source for the most famous congressional debate in U.S. history, and although the various speeches centered on different aspects of the slavery question, the debate was really about the political importance of the West and who would decide its future. Clay was the first to defend his proposals before the Senate. He grouped his first six proposals in pairs, each of which gave one concession to the North and one to the South. First, to offset the admittance of California as a free state, Clay suggested organizing the remaining Mexican cession without restrictions against slavery. Second, the long-disputed Texas-New Mexico border should be fixed well east of the Rio Grande, but in exchange the federal government should assume Texas's preannexation debt. The third proposal dealt with the slave trade in the District of Columbia, which particularly enraged abolitionists since it routinely split apart black families. The international slave trade was abolished by federal law in 1808, but the buying and selling of slaves between states was still legal and took place within shouting distance of the U.S. capitol. Clay proposed that the slave trade be abolished in the District of Columbia but that the continuance of slavery there should be guaranteed unless both neighboring Maryland and Virginia agreed to abolish it.

Too Many Concessions? Clay admitted that these three pairs of compromises seemed to favor the North: "[Y]ou have got what is worth more than a thousand Wilmot Provisos," Clay told the Northern senators. Nature, he said, would effectively bar slavery from even the neutral territory of New Mexico. To redress this imbalance, Clay offered two additional proposals to his Southern colleagues. The first stated, to Southerners' delight, that Congress had no jurisdiction over the lucrative interstate slave trade; the second called for a strong and strictly enforced fugitive slave law.

Calhoun's Rejection. The final version of the Compromise closely resembled Clay's original eight proposals, and debate over the bill provided some of the most famous political oratory in U.S. history. When Clay finished introducing the legislation, the Southern ideologue John C. Calhoun took the floor. Calhoun was in such failing health, dying within the month, that he sat wrapped in a blanket while a stand-in read his speech to a packed Senate chamber. He flatly rejected the compromise, insisting that the North should yield on every point of argument. If it refused, the South could never remain in the Union with its "honor and safety" intact. Instead of offering his own compromise, Calhoun offered what became known as "peaceable secession." "[L]et the States . . . agree to separate and part in peace," he argued. "If you are unwilling . . . tell us so, and we shall know what to do."

Webster. Calhoun's arguments offended the Unionist sentiments of the last of the "great triumvirate" of United States senators, Daniel Webster of Massachusetts. In words that would be memorized by millions of American schoolchildren, Webster urged the passage of the compromise: "I speak today for the preservation of the Union. Hear me for my cause." There could be no such thing as peaceful disunion, Webster insisted. The only way to head off the convulsion of secession was for the North to accept its constitutional obligation, "binding in honor and conscience," to return fugitive slaves.

Seward. The debate was not confined to the aging leadership: senatorial newcomer William Seward of New York also delivered what became a famous speech. Denouncing the Compromise (and his Whig colleague Webster), Seward declared that there was a "higher law than the Constitution"—God's law. This higher law stood firmly against evil and, as Seward noted, slavery and compromises with slaveholders. The speech instantly propelled Seward to the front ranks of antislavery politics in the North.

Douglas. As the senators made their speeches and debated higher and more temporal laws, legislators worked behind the scenes to construct the legislation of compromise. It was not an easy task. Clay's strategy was to lump all eight proposals in one untidy "omnibus" package—forcing legislators to vote either up or down. Yet senators on both sides worked to eliminate the parts they opposed by voting against the bill as a whole. Finally, President Taylor himself weighed in against the omnibus bill. Feeble and exhausted, the "Great Compromiser" Henry Clay departed the sultry capital, leaving the compromise in the hands of the young Illinois senator Stephen A. Douglas. Thus the Compromise of 1850 was, in many ways, a last gasp for the older generation of legislative giants such as Clay, Calhoun, and Webster (all three of whom would be dead by 1852). It was up to a new generation of legislators to decide the future of the Western territories.

Assembling the Majorities. If nothing else, Douglas proved to be a brilliant legislator. He broke up Clay's omnibus package into eight separate bills and marshaled majorities for each, usually by building on a core of support from Western Democrats from Illinois, Indiana, and Michigan and Whigs from Kentucky, Tennessee, and Virginia. To this "compromise core" he then arranged separate coalitions for each bill: antislavery Northerners for a free California, or proslavery Southerners for a fugitive slave law. Fortunately for Douglas and the compromisers, President Taylor died suddenly in July 1850—removing a certain obstacle to the eight compromise measures. His successor, Millard Fillmore of New York, was a conservative career politician and far more willing to support compromise than Taylor.

The Devil in the Details. One by one, Douglas's measures passed in Congress and received the President's signature, although just four senators and twenty-eight representatives voted for every one. California became the thirty-first state, and Congress carved New Mexico and Utah territories from the rest of the Mexican Cession, both to be admitted "with or without slavery as [its] constitution may prescribe." In a single stroke territory that became the states of Nevada, Utah, New Mexico, Arizona, and part of Colorado was added to the United States. Texas accepted a narrower boundary with New Mexico and received $10 million to pay off its pre-annexation debts. Congress also outlawed the slave trade in the District of Columbia after 1 January 1851. In a bitter blow for abolitionists, the federal government also strengthened the Fugitive Slave Act of 1793 by appointing federal commissioners—each of whom possessed the authority to issue arrest warrants, assemble posses, and compel private citizens for assistance—and charged them with returning runaway slaves to their owners. Fugitives would not be allowed to testify in their own defense, could not obtain a jury trial to air their views, and were to be returned to slavery on the mere submission of an affidavit from an aggrieved slaveowner. Moreover, a commissioner received a fee of ten dollars if he ruled in favor of a slaveowner, but only five dollars if he found for the fugitive. This was designed to account for the increased paperwork involved in returning a runaway to slavery, but it struck even some neutral observers as immoral. Antislavery partisans in the North and West vowed to resist the federal law.

Western Slavery? President Fillmore, stepping into the White House after Taylor's death in the summer of 1850, hailed the Compromise as a "final settlement" for each and every remaining sectional problem. For the moment, most Americans seemed ready to accept the Compromise. Only antislavery activists and Southern-rights ideologues came out publicly against the legislation in its early days. Ironically, the part of the Compromise that generated the most explosive opposition was the Fugitive Slave Law—not the predicted battle over the status of the territories of California and New Mexico. When the territorial legislatures of Utah and New Mexico voted to legalize slavery, few slave owners brought their property there, and California's U.S. senators in the 1850s quickly allied themselves with Southern, not Northern, interests. It would take the next showdown over slavery's expansion in the territories to dismantle the Second Party System and, eventually, the Union.

Sources:

John Ashworth, *Slavery, Capitalism and Politics in the Antebellum Republic* (New York: Cambridge University Press, 1995);

Holman Hamilton, *Prologue to Conflict: The Crisis and Compromise of 1850* (New York: Norton, 1964);

James M. McPherson, *Ordeal by Fire* (New York: Knopf, 1982).

TRANSPORTATION: PAYING FOR THE RAILROADS

Internal Improvements. One of the oldest political arguments in the United States was over the government's role in fostering commerce and building internal improvements in the West. As the territory called the West grew by leaps and bounds in the first half of the nineteenth century, the argument had enormous political and economic consequences. Henry Clay's American System represented one vision of cooperation between government legislation and privately owned capital in developing the West. Other politicians, notably those allied with Thomas Jefferson and Andrew Jackson, opposed any role for the federal government in promoting economic development. Some states, well aware of the political stalemate in Washington, threw the power of local governments into promoting growth. New York, for example, financed the building of the Erie Canal in the early 1820s without federal assistance. The canal was a stupendous success—by the early 1850s, the volume of Western commerce on the canal was twenty times what it had been in the mid 1830s—and areas of upstate New York and the Midwest were quickly transformed into regions that exported grain. More significant, the canal demonstrated the profit to be made when farmers and merchants could transport grains and other goods from the West to larger markets in the East, or even across the Atlantic. The price of moving goods over long distances dropped 95 percent between 1815 and 1860.

Railroad Boom in the Midwest. Canals were extremely expensive to dig and maintain. Railroads, on the other hand, were cheaper to build and moved goods at dizzying speeds. The first American railroads began service in the 1830s, but they did not constitute a true railroad system. Railroads still lacked links to one another; most simply connected one water route (rivers, lakes, and canals) to another. After 1840 railroads began to overtake canals and all other modes of transport in connecting the Northeast with the West. After the Mexican War an unprecedented burst of railroad construction revolutionized transportation. During the decade of the 1850s, builders in Illinois laid more than two thousand six hundred miles of track, those in Ohio more than two thousand three hundred, and in Wisconsin nearly nine hundred. Construction in the South was much slower. Mississippi, for example, laid just 800 miles of track during the decade.

Aid for Railroad Builders. The largest problem facing the railroads was how to finance the furious growth, especially of the longer lines linking the Midwest with the East. The answer, of course, was public aid. Of all the lines linking the two regions, only the prosperous New York Central required no government assistance. The others became mixed enterprises, receiving up to half their capital from state and local governments and raising the rest with bonds sold to individual investors. Federal aid, as with canals and turnpikes, was usually bogged down in Congress. This public assistance took various forms, including loans, government-bond purchases, tax exemptions, and even outright public ownership of rail lines.

Windfall for the Illinois Central. The federal government officially entered the railroad business in 1850, when a bill passed both houses of Congress granting federal land to the states to build a railroad connecting the Gulf of Mexico to Lake Michigan. The big winner in the deal was the Illinois Central Railroad, which received a staggering grant of 2.6 million acres of free land. The railroad was free to mortgage this land or, better yet, sell it to farmers. In effect, Congress gave the Illinois Central the entire $23.4 million it needed to construct the railroad. Other states and their railroad promoters quickly demanded the same arrangement, and by 1860 Congress granted more than 30 million acres for railroad construction to eleven different states. During the construction of the transcontinental railroad lines after the Civil War the

government was even more generous, offering companies free land and easy credit.

"Northernizing" the Midwest. The linking of East and West using government land and funds had enormous economic and political significance. As a result of federal grants to railroad companies, sparsely settled regions in Indiana, Illinois, and Wisconsin became prosperous farming centers connected to the world market. Farmers in the West, whose numbers swelled in the years before the Civil War, shared in the railroad promoters' prosperity. Finally, as the Mississippi River ceased to be a lifeline for farmers in Illinois, Indiana, and even Ohio (replaced, of course, by East-West railroads) citizens could afford to be hostile to slavery and its expansion. Cultural and economic ties made the region we now call the Midwest far more Northern than Southern.

Source:

George Rogers Taylor, *The Transportation Revolution* (White Plains, N.Y.: M. E. Sharpe, 1951).

UNION IN CRISIS: THE KANSAS-NEBRASKA ACT AND THE REPUBLICAN PARTY

A Brief Compromise. The political truce following the Compromise of 1850 lasted only four years, until the battle over slavery in the territories erupted again. This time the conflict centered on the Louisiana Purchase, where the slavery question had supposedly been settled in 1821 with the Missouri Compromise, which drew a northern boundary for slavery at 36°30'. Slavery re-emerged as a pivotal political issue in the West in 1853, when settlers in the Kansas, Platte, and Missouri River valleys petitioned for territorial status. Unlike during the previous crises over slavery in the territories, politicians failed to strike a compromise to diffuse the conflict.

Nebraska. With thousands of land-hungry settlers retracing Meriwether Lewis and William Clark's path up the Missouri River and entrepreneurs calling for a railroad connecting San Francisco to the East, many Americans favored organizing a territory north of Indian territory, present-day Oklahoma. Responding quickly, the House of Representatives passed a bill in 1853 creating Nebraska territory, encompassing the area north of Indian territory all the way to the Canadian border. Southern senators still smarting from the admission of free California in 1850 correctly foresaw that under the Missouri Compromise slavery would be prohibited in each state carved from Nebraska Territory. They desperately wanted to avoid the addition of new free states, which would further dilute their power in Congress.

Douglas's Motives. The sponsor of the Nebraska legislation was the Illinois senator Stephen A. Douglas, who had several aims in mind. First, he was an expansionist Democrat, and like others in his party, he believed that the time had come to organize the populous new territory of Nebraska. Second, he was a Northern senator who hoped to gain Southern support for a presidential run in 1856. Finally, Douglas was both a director of the Illinois Central Railroad and a land speculator who dreamed of building a rail line through Nebraska connecting California with his hometown of Chicago. Before construction could begin, however, Nebraska needed some form of government. Meanwhile, Southern railroad promoters began planning another transcontinental line emanating from either New Orleans or Memphis. To facilitate this plan James Gadsden, a Southern railroad executive and U.S. minister to Mexico, purchased twenty-nine thousand miles of Mexican desert south of the Gila River in 1853 to provide an easy train route through the mountains to California.

The Battle for Kansas. Southerners led by Sen. David R. Atchison, a Democrat from Missouri, opposed the organization of additional free territory, and they pressured the expansionist-minded Douglas to amend his Nebraska bill. In response Douglas proposed dividing the area into two separate territories called Kansas and Nebraska. Second, and more problematic, he proposed to repeal the part of the Missouri Compromise that prohibited slavery north of 36° 30'. Douglas argued that the principle of popular sovereignty dictated that each territory should be able to decide whether to be a free or slave state. To Northern observers such a strategy had obvious intent: to create a Nebraska that would be free while the southern territory of Kansas would be opened to slavery. By seeming to endorse introducing slavery to a territory that had been free for more than thirty years, Douglas alienated thousands of Northerners, many of whom viewed the Missouri Compromise as sacrosanct. It was a political miscalculation that would cost Douglas dearly.

"Anti-Nebraska" Feeling. Almost overnight, people who had never publicly opposed slavery's extension became energized. Antislavery congressmen fired off an "Appeal of the Independent Democrats," accusing Douglas of a "gross violation of a sacred pledge" and urging a popular campaign to repeal the act. The Northern public responded with enthusiasm. Abolitionists, Free Soilers, Northern Whigs, and many Northern Democrats quickly formed "anti-Nebraska" coalitions, which wrote petitions, held meetings, and staged rallies demanding the repeal of the Kansas-Nebraska Act. Abraham Lincoln, who had served one term as an Illinois congressman from 1847 to 1849, reemerged on the political stage as one of the fiercest critics of the Kansas-Nebraska bill. "The monstrous injustice of slavery," Lincoln wrote, "deprives our republican example of its just influence in the world—enables the enemies of free institutions, with plausibility, to taunt us as hypocrites."

The South Wins Round One. Opponents of the Kansas-Nebraska Act failed to prevent its passage in Congress. Southerners in both houses backed Douglas's plan, and President Franklin Pierce—an ardent expansionist unbothered by slavery as a moral issue—invoked every ounce of party discipline to ensure its success. The House, far less Southern-oriented than the Senate, passed the bill by a vote of 113-100.

Rise of the Republican Party. The political fallout from the Kansas-Nebraska Act was swift. First, the Whig Party in the South was all but destroyed, and it was fatally weakened in the North as well. Northern Whigs such as William Seward of New York had always hoped their party would one day absorb antislavery men from other parties, but Free Soilers and antislavery Democrats refused to become Whigs. They preferred a new party and a new name. The one that stuck was "Republican," the name adopted at an anti-Nebraska rally in Ripon, Wisconsin, in May 1854. It quickly became the banner under which all anti-Nebraska forces rallied in the 1854 elections.

Sources:

Eric Foner, *Free Soil, Free Labor, Free Men: The Ideology of the Republican Party Before the Civil War* (New York: Oxford University Press, 1970);

William E. Gienapp, *The Origins of the Republican Party, 1852–1856* (New York: Oxford University Press, 1986).

WAR ON THE BORDER: BLEEDING KANSAS

The Race for Kansas. Both Southerners and Northerners knew in 1854 that the bitter fight over slavery's extension would take place in the West, in the new territory of Kansas. Both proslavery Southerners and antislavery Northerners were determined to settle Kansas first and win the territory for their side. As soon as the Kansas-Nebraska Act passed in Congress, abolitionists formed the New England Emigrant Aid Society to bring settlers to eastern Kansas. The emigration of antislavery New Englanders to the territory incited proslavery Missourians to action. Led by Senator David Rice Atchison, the Missourians hoped to win Kansas back from Free Soilers attempting to settle it as a free state. "If we win we carry slavery to the Pacific ocean," declared Atchison. "[I]f we fail, we lose Missouri, Arkansas, Texas and all the territories."

Border Ruffians. The first battles in Kansas took place at the ballot box. In a November 1854 election to send a territorial delegate to Congress, bands of Missourians (labeled "border ruffians" by the antislavery press) crossed the border to vote—early and often, as it turns out, since more than one thousand seven hundred fraudulent ballots were counted—for a proslavery candidate. The following spring, after more Free Soilers had moved in, Atchison claimed in public that "there are eleven hundred coming over from Platte county [Missouri] to vote . . . and if that ain't enough, we can send five thousand." A later Congressional inquiry determined that, in fact, 6,307 votes had been cast in an election for a territorial legislature when there were only 2,905 eligible voters—making Atchison's claim eerily accurate. The new legislature promptly legalized slavery and adopted a rigid slave code to punish runaways and people who helped them.

Free Staters. Outraged Free Staters held their own elections, calling the elected legislature "bogus." More important, by the fall of 1855 the free staters constituted a majority of actual settlers in the territory. They called their own constitutional convention, adopted an antislavery constitution, and chose a governor. Thus there were two territorial governments in Kansas at the dawn of 1856—one fraudulent and proslavery (located in Lecompton) and the other, antislavery (located in nearby Lawrence), whose legality was questionable at best.

Violence Erupts. Fraud and extralegality soon begat violence. In the wake of President Franklin Pierce's statements denouncing the Free Staters, proslavery settlers sacked the antislavery town of Lawrence. A wild-eyed abolitionist named John Brown retaliated by murdering five proslavery settlers in Pottawatomie in May 1856. This episode led to still more civil strife in the territory, as armed bands on both sides began a guerrilla war. "Bleeding Kansas" became, for both Northerners and Southerners, a powerful symbol of sectional strife.

Sumner. Violence was hardly confined to Kansas Territory. After delivering a speech in the Senate titled "The Crime Against Kansas," the Republican Massachusetts senator Charles Sumner was beaten with a heavy cane by Preston Brooks, a South Carolina congressman who took offense to the speech's viciousness and slight to his uncle, Sen. Andrew Butler. So severe were Sumner's injuries that he was unable to return to the Senate for four years, a period during which his state refused to replace him. For his part, Brooks resigned after being censured by the House but returned to Congress after winning a special election for his own seat. Both Sumner and Brooks became symbols in their respective sections: Sumner as a martyr to the South's barbarism and Brooks as a hero for standing up to Yankee attacks. In addition, both served as evidence for how deep sectional antagonism ran over the issue of slavery in the West.

Sources:
David Donald, *Charles Sumner and the Coming of the Civil War* (New York: Knopf, 1960);

Paul W. Gates, *Fifty Million Acres: Conflicts over Kansas Land Policy* (Ithaca, N.Y.: Cornell University Press, 1954);

James A. Rawley, *Race and Politics: "Bleeding Kansas" and the Coming of the Civil War* (Philadelphia: Lippincott, 1969).

HEADLINE MAKERS

DANIEL BOONE

1734–1820

FRONTIERSMAN

Frontier Legend. The most famous of all American frontiersmen, the Kentucky pioneer Daniel Boone forever changed the history of westward settlement. He shocked his Eastern contemporaries with his Indian leggings and braided hair and disappeared for months at a time on "long hunts" for game and pelts. Boone helped create a backwoods culture that sharply contrasted that of the increasingly genteel seaboard communities and encouraged thousands of European Americans to settle the backcountry, pushing the frontier far west of the Appalachians.

Long Hunter and Soldier. Boone was born in Berks County, Pennsylvania, to Quaker parents, and he quickly discovered that he preferred hunting in the backwoods to attending school and learning a trade. He was therefore delighted when at age sixteen his family moved to northwest North Carolina. He became a legendary frontier long hunter, venturing for weeks at a time in search of game. During the 1750s he served on several military and road-building expeditions into the North American interior. He also journeyed to Spanish Florida in 1763.

Kentucky Paradise. It was in Kentucky that Boone found his true calling. He first journeyed there in 1767 and returned two years later with a small party of hunters. The group found some of the richest hunting grounds they had ever seen, thick with game. Boone was so taken with the place that he stayed behind when the party returned to North Carolina. He remained for two years.

The Career of a Frontiersman. The various native peoples who used Kentucky as a hunting ground were not pleased with the encroachment by whites, and when Boone returned in 1773, this time with forty settlers, they forced them to leave. Two years later Boone was back in the territory, marking and cutting the Wilderness Road. At its terminus he built Boonesboro, a small settlement. As a militia captain Boone spent much of the

1770s defending the settlements, and he was once captured by the Shawnees. His exploits as a pioneer and hunter won him many friends, and he served a term in the Virginia assembly (Kentucky was considered part of Virginia). He also owned vast tracts of land in Kentucky, but he lost them all with a combination of poor business skills and ruthless competitors. In 1799, commenting that Kentucky had become too civilized, Boone joined one of his sons in Missouri. There he continued to roam and hunt until he died in 1820.

Sources:

Stephen Aron, *How the West Was Lost: The Transformation of Kentucky from Daniel Boone to Henry Clay* (Baltimore: Johns Hopkins University Press, 1996);

John Mack Faragher, *Daniel Boone: The Life and Legend of an American Pioneer* (New York: Holt, 1992).

THOMAS HART BENTON

1782-1858
STATESMAN

A Western Jeffersonian. Thomas Hart Benton's rise as a political leader mirrored that of the West. Born near Hillsboro, North Carolina, Benton spent some time at the state university before being expelled for stealing. To escape the controversy, he moved west to Franklin, Tennessee, in 1801 and became a farmer. Benton read law and entered politics, winning election to the state senate in 1809.

Missouri. During the War of 1812 Benton served as Andrew Jackson's aide-de-camp; the two men had a competitive and often violent relationship despite their common political principles. Partly to remove himself from Jackson's circle, he moved to St. Louis in 1815 to practice law and edit a newspaper. When Missouri became a state, Benton was elected to the U.S. Senate, where he served until 1851—he was the first senator to serve three decades in the chamber.

Transition to Nationalism. At the dawn of his political career, Benton was a booster for his region. He spoke of the Pacific Northwest as if it belonged to the United States by right, and he chided John Quincy Adams for failing to include Texas in the 1819 treaty that decided the nation's southern border. He also tirelessly supported (and was rewarded by) business interests of American fur traders and their "rights" to harvest pelts west of the Rockies. As his years of service multiplied, Benton's politics and policies became more national in scope. For example, he spoke frequently of using the Missouri and Columbia Rivers as potential trade routes for Pacific nations, and he introduced legislation to protect traders on the Santa Fe and Oregon Trails from criminals. He also became a leading advocate

for offering government lands to actual settlers: as early as 1824 Benton offered a bill to provide for the gradual reduction of the price of unsold public land. Benton's advocacy of "graduation" and "preemption" rights both pointed to his support of popular democracy and Jeffersonian notions of a nation of freeholders.

Issues. Benton achieved his greatest fame in his pitched battles against the Second Bank of the United States and paper money. His attacks against the "Monster" bank in favor of hard currency earned him his nickname of "Old Bullion." Finally, although a slaveholder himself (and a representative of a slave state), Benton came to oppose the expansion of slavery into new Western territories. He continued to oppose abolitionism, but wanted new territory to be reserved for freehold farmers. Slavery's extension, he said in 1848, would only divide the Union. After he was defeated for reelection in 1850, Benton went on to oppose the Compromise of 1850, the Kansas-Nebraska Act, and the presidency of fellow Democrat James Buchanan.

Source:

William N. Chambers, *Old Bullion Benton: Senator from the New West, 1782–1858* (Boston: Little, Brown, 1956).

HENRY CLAY

1777-1852
STATESMAN

An Enduring Career. Despite losing five presidential races, Henry Clay played a central role in Western—and national—politics for more than four decades. As Speaker of the House of Representatives from 1811 to 1820 and from 1823 to 1825, longer than anyone else in the nineteenth century, Clay emerged as the outstanding Western leader of the period. He also served as John Quincy Adams's secretary of state from 1825 to 1829 and was regarded as the most influential senator of his era.

A Pioneer Nationalist. Although one of the most prominent leaders to come out of the West, Clay was first and foremost a nationalist. As Speaker of the House in 1812, Clay advocated war against Great Britain to preserve the overseas markets of the nation's producers. After the War of 1812 Clay introduced plans for an integrated system of protective tariffs, a national bank, and subsidized internal improvements known as the American System. Although Clay intended this program to foster economic development and integrate the regions of the United States politically, many of its provisions joined the North and West, yet isolated the South.

The American System. The American System had direct bearing on westward expansion. Under this scheme the federal government sold public land in the West rather than give it away to settlers, with the proceeds benefiting transportation projects and schools. The plan's supporters in Congress expected these projects, in turn, to benefit all sections of the nation and tie them together economically. The American System became central to the political beliefs of Whigs, who arose in opposition to Andrew Jackson and the Democratic Party.

A Great Compromiser. Clay was also known as the Great Compromiser for his leading role in two watershed legislative compromises: the Missouri Compromise of 1820 and the Compromise of 1850. Though Clay intended these compromises to relieve sectional tensions, neither was able to prevent Southern secession and Civil War.

Sources:

Daniel Walker Howe, *The Political Culture of American Whigs* (Chicago: University of Chicago Press, 1979);

M. D. Peterson, *The Great Triumvirate: Webster, Clay and Calhoun* (New York: Oxford University Press, 1987);

Robert V. Remini, *Henry Clay: Statesman for the Union* (New York: Norton, 1991).

DAVID (DAVY) CROCKETT

1786-1836

FRONTIERSMAN AND CONGRESSMAN

Hero. David Crockett was a respected, if less-than-successful, frontier politician in the 1820s and 1830s. However, as a result of a series of tall tales published about "Davy" Crockett, a backwoods superhero who wrestled alligators and could wade the Mississippi River, he became a central character in American folklore.

Origins. Unlike Daniel Boone, Crockett was born on the frontier, in a cabin along the Nolichucky River in Tennessee. Following a familiar pattern of frontier life, the Crocketts moved often. As a young man Crockett finally settled in the extreme northwest corner of the state, near the Missouri border.

Alamo. He enlisted twice with the Tennessee militia commanded by Andrew Jackson but was not present at either of that group's two most famous battles, Horseshoe Bend (27 March 1814) and New Orleans (8 January 1815). Back home, Crockett began a career in politics. He served as a justice of the peace and state legislator before winning a congressional seat as a Democrat in 1827. He lost his seat in 1831 after he broke with his party's president, Andrew Jackson, but returned two years later as a Whig. After losing his battle for reelection in 1835, Crockett moved to east Texas in search of a new home. He participated in the defense of the Alamo, a mission

converted to a fort in Texas's war of Independence, and died when it fell to Mexican troops on 6 March 1836.

Significance. Although he died in the siege at the Alamo and had a respectable career as a politician, Crockett's fame can be attributed to the media in Jacksonian America. Crockett's frontier drawl and penchant for folksy stories had always drawn the attention of journalists, and in the 1830s dozens of Davy Crockett books and almanacs flooded the market. Many of them, filled with coarse language and virulent racism as well as remarkable exploits, became best-sellers. These tall tales were later rediscovered by Hollywood in the 1940s and 1950s—the same actor, Fess Parker, played both Crockett and Daniel Boone in popular movies and television shows—and his fame continues to this day.

Source:

Michael A. Lofaro and Joe Cummings, eds., *Crockett at Two Hundred: New Perspectives on the Man and the Myth* (Knoxville: University of Tennessee Press, 1989).

STEPHEN A. DOUGLAS

1813-1861

POLITICIAN

A New Generation in Politics. During his long political career Stephen A. Douglas was deeply involved in every major issue to come before the nation. He is most famous as Abraham Lincoln's Democratic opponent for the Senate in 1858 and the presidency in 1860, but his time in Congress also had a lasting impact on the politics of the West. Douglas's career marked a changing of the guard in U.S. politics, from the era of compromisers and nationalist leaders such as Henry Clay and Daniel Webster to one dominated by men with sectional interests such as Jefferson Davis of Mississippi, Abraham Lincoln of Illinois, and William Seward of New York.

Rising Democratic Star. Douglas grew up in Vermont and upstate New York before moving to Illinois in 1833. Captivated by Andrew Jackson, he helped build the Democratic Party in that state and rose rapidly in political circles. Just one year after arriving in his adopted home he became state's attorney; one year later he was a member of the state legislature. After a failed bid for the United States Congress in 1837, Douglas acted as Illinois secretary of state and as a judge on the Illinois Supreme Court. He finally won election to Congress in 1843, and he spent the rest of his life as a member of that body, after 1847 as United States senator.

The "Little Giant." Douglas served as chair of the powerful Committee on Territories, and he developed a strong interest in political issues involving the West. He acted quickly to propose legislation encouraging territorial expansion, the organization of territorial governments, a homestead policy, and the construction of a transcontinental railroad. These policies in turn led him to back the annexation of Texas in 1845, the acquisition of all of Oregon, and the war with Mexico. Standing just 5'4" tall, Douglas was dubbed the "Little Giant" for his legislative and oratorical prowess.

Popular Sovereignty. When the slavery issue emerged as a threat to the Union in the late 1840s, Douglas fastened onto the idea of "popular sovereignty" (the idea that the people of a state or territory should decide on the slavery issue themselves) as a concept that could avert sectional strife. He led the fight in Congress for the Compromise of 1850 after Henry Clay was forced by ill health to leave Washington, and the version of the accord that passed in the fall of that year was his creation. Four years later Douglas made popular sovereignty the centerpiece of the Kansas-Nebraska Act, which repealed the Missouri Compromise of 1820 by opening the territories to slavery. Douglas saw the immediate need to form governments in that part of the Louisiana Purchase to promote economic growth, especially railroad construction, in which he had a personal interest as a director of the Illinois Central Railroad. Douglas severely miscalculated that the American people would accept the repeal of the Missouri Compromise. Instead, the Kansas-Nebraska controversy ignited bitter opposition and sparked the formation of the Republican Party as well as violence in the new territory of Kansas.

Middle Ground. By 1854 the once-popular Douglas was suddenly a controversial figure in Democratic politics. However, such attention only fed his hunger for political power. In 1856 he ran unsuccessfully for his party's nomination for president, losing to Pennsylvania's James Buchanan, who was conveniently out of the country on a diplomatic mission during the Kansas-Nebraska crisis. The next year, Douglas broke publicly with President Buchanan's Kansas policy, which was decidedly proslavery. In 1858 he engaged in series of heated debates with Abraham Lincoln in a successful effort to defend his Illinois senate seat. Throughout the debates and in his presidential campaign in 1860, Douglas attempted to tread a middle ground on the slavery issue, blaming Northern abolitionists for fueling political flames and Southern disunionists for threatening the nation's future, but slavery was not an issue that could be viewed impartially by either side.

Freeport Doctrine. In the famous Freeport Doctrine, named by the press for the Illinois town in which he unveiled it, Douglas claimed that the Supreme Court's 1857 Dred Scott decision, which guaranteed the right of slaveholders to bring their human property into any federal territory, was meaningless. Under popular sovereignty, he argued, local settlers could keep slavery out by refusing to enact the police legislation necessary to protect it. Douglas's position was well received in Illinois (and helped him regain his Senate seat), but it forever lost him support in the South. Thus Douglas's 1860 presidential nomination by the Democrats caused Southern members of the party to bolt and select their own candidate, John C. Breckinridge. His party split, and Douglas won electors only in Missouri and New Jersey despite receiving 1,383,000 votes. Lincoln won the election without a single Southern electoral vote. Douglas's last legislative act was a desperate attempt to forge another sectional compromise in 1860 to head off secession, which failed miserably. Broken in spirit and worsening in health (Douglas was a heavy drinker), he died in June 1861.

Sources:
Paul Angle and David Zerefsky, eds. *The Complete Lincoln-Douglas Debates of 1858* (Chicago: University of Chicago Press, 1991);
Robert W. Johannsen, *Stephen A. Douglas* (Urbana: University of Illinois Press, 1997).

ANDREW JACKSON

1767–1845

GENERAL, GOVERNOR, AND PRESIDENT OF THE UNITED STATES

Symbol. Even before he became the nation's seventh president, Andrew Jackson was a living, breathing symbol of the West. As a youth fighting in the Revolutionary War, a frontier lawyer and jurist, a plantation parvenu, a military leader, and, finally, as president, Jackson's life had a tremendous effect on the nation's Westward expansion.

Planter-Politician. Born in the North Carolina backcountry to a family of Irish immigrants, Jackson's childhood was interrupted by the American Revolution. Although he was only thirteen, he was captured and imprisoned by the British; all but one member of his immediate family died from war-related causes. With no family to turn to, the ambitious and troubled Jackson decided to study law and move to North Carolina's western district (now Tennessee). The rough-hewn lawyer made friends quickly and began a political career as a delegate to Tennessee's constitutional convention and the new state's first elected congressman. He even served for a few months as a U.S. senator before returning home to take a seat on the state supreme court. By 1800 the young jurist had purchased several slaves and a plantation near the bustling town of Nashville.

Military Career. Jackson's true calling was the military. As commander of a group of Tennessee volunteers in the war of 1812, he decimated the Creek Indians in Mississippi. Promoted into the regular army, Jackson led a much larger force against the British at the Battle of New Orleans in 1815, an engagement fought after a peace treaty was signed in Europe. Jackson emerged as the war's greatest hero. Three years later he invaded Florida to chastise the Seminoles. Despite significant controversy over his actions there—he ordered the execution of two British subjects suspected of aiding the Indians—President James Monroe named Jackson military governor of Florida in 1821.

"Old Hickory." The governor's reputation as an opponent of British tyranny and as a soldier who helped open millions of acres of Indian lands to white settlement made him a popular man (to many whites) in the West, a region of growing political importance in the 1820s. After a brief return to the Senate, Jackson, known as "Old Hickory," ran for president in 1824. With tremendous Western support, he won a popular plurality but fell short of the majority necessary to claim victory. As mandated by the Constitution, the election was thrown into the House of Representatives, where Jackson lost the election to John Quincy Adams. Claiming publicly that the election was stolen from him as the result of a "corrupt bargain," Jackson and his supporters built a massive coalition of Western expansionists, Southern slaveholders and Northern farmers and artisans. He won the election of 1828 in a landslide.

An Eventful Presidency. As president, Jackson held himself up as an opponent of established wealth, federally backed internal improvements, and moral reforms such as abolitionism. He also pursued a program that ruthlessly forced removal of Indians from east of the Mississippi to less-fertile land the federal government labeled Indian territory. Although Jackson refused to annex the Republic of Texas in 1836 for fear of igniting the slavery issue, he squarely set the nation on a course of geographic expansion. His career and rise to power in many ways exemplified and gave shape to the history of westward expansion in the United States.

Sources:

Robert V. Remini, *Andrew Jackson and the Course of American Democracy, 1833–1845* (New York: Harper & Row, 1984);

Remini, *Andrew Jackson and the Course of American Freedom, 1822–1832* (New York: Harper & Row, 1981);

Remini, *Andrew Jackson and the Course of Empire, 1767–1821* (New York: Harper & Row, 1977).

SACAGAWEA

1788?–1884?
INTERPRETER

An Opportune Encounter. Fortunately for the explorers Meriwether Lewis and William Clark, their expedition through the Louisiana Purchase brought them into contact with the Shoshone woman Sacagawea. Her skills as an interpreter and guide were instrumental to the expedition's success; it is difficult to imagine such an outcome without her language skills and help.

An Invaluable Guide. As a girl of about fourteen, Sacagawea was captured by a rival tribe (probably Crow) and won in a gambling match by the French fur trader Toissant Charbonneau. Lewis and Clark hired Charbonneau in 1805 to guide them to the Pacific after meeting him in the Mandan villages at the big bend of the Missouri River in Dakota country. Sacagawea and her infant son Jean Baptiste (or "Pomp") accompanied the expedition west up the Missouri. The Shoshone woman quickly demonstrated that she was far more indispensable as a guide and interpreter than her rather useless husband.

The Return Trip. The first band of Indians the expedition encountered west of the Mandan villages was headed by a chief named Cameahwait, who turned out to be Sacagawea's brother. Instead of a tense first meeting, Lewis and Clark were able to trade for horses and supplies necessary to cross the Rockies. The expedition reached the Pacific in November 1805 and spent the winter on the coast of what is now Oregon. After retracing their steps the following spring, Sacagawea remained at the Mandan villages with her family until 1809. That year they visited Clark in St. Louis, and according to one historian, they left their son behind to be educated. There are conflicting accounts as to what happened to Sacagawea after this visit. One version states that, in 1812, Charbonneau's wife died of fever. However, since Charbonneau had at least three wives, Clark reportedly never believed Sacagawea to be dead. Another more probable version suggests that Sacagawea remained in St. Louis for a time, then went to live with the Commanche tribe. Eventually she rejoined her relatives on the Wind River Reservation of Wyoming, where she died of natural causes in April 1884.

Sources:

Ella E. Clark, *Sacagawea of the Lewis and Clark Expedition* (Berkeley: University of California Press, 1979);

Harold P. Howard, *Sacajawea* (Norman: University of Oklahoma Press, 1971).

PUBLICATIONS

George Bancroft, *The History of the United States from the Discovery of the Continent* (Boston: Little, Brown, 1834)—the first of a ten-volume history by Bancroft, a Jacksonian Democrat and one of the first Americans to obtain a doctoral degree; the last volume appeared in 1875;

Nicholas Biddle, *History of the Expedition under the Command of Captains Lewis and Clark*, 2 volumes, edited by Paul Allen (Philadelphia: Bradford & Inskeep / New York: Abm. H. Inskeep, J. Maxwell, printer, 1814)—the genuine published version of the journals kept by Meriwether Lewis and William Clark on their three-year exploration of the Louisiana Purchase in 1804–1806;

David Crockett, *A Narrative of the Life of David Crockett, of the State of Tennessee* (Philadelphia: E. L. Cary & A. Hart, 1834)—an assortment of episodes about the frontier adventurer Davy Crockett. Spawned numerous almanacs and books that spun even taller tales about the larger-than-life frontiersman;

James Russell Lowell, *The Bigelow Papers* (Cambridge, Mass.: Nichols/New York: Putnam's, 1848)—the philosophical doggerel of a rustic Yankee invented by Lowell, an abolitionist poet, to chastise the Mexican War and slavery's expansion;

Harriet Beecher Stowe, *Uncle Tom's Cabin; or, Life Among the Lowly*, 2 volumes (Boston: Jewett / Cleveland: Jewett, Proctor, & Worthington, 1852)—a popular sentimental novel about the cruelties of slavery that had a profound impact on public opinion in the North and West;

Alexis de Tocqueville, *De la démocratie en Amérique*, 2 volumes (London: Saunders & Otley, 1835–1840)—observations written by a French nobleman who, with his friend Gustave de Beaumont, traveled in the United States in 1831–1832. It has important firsthand accounts of Indian removal, slavery, and Western life.

LAW AND JUSTICE

by ERIC T. L. LOVE

CONTENTS

Sidebars and tables are listed in italics.

1800

13 Feb.   Congress provides for six circuit courts to be established to cover the thirteen original colonies, Kentucky, Tennessee, and Vermont, and the districts of Maine and Ohio. Congress repeals this act in 1802 but then passes a new act that contains many of the same elements.

3 Mar.   President John Adams appoints last-minute "midnight judges."

1802

24 Apr.   Georgia cedes lands along the Yazoo River to the United States in an attempt to dodge responsibility for the state legislature's fraudulent land-grant practices in 1795.

1803

24 Feb.   In *Marbury* v. *Madison* Supreme Court Chief Justice John Marshall rules that under the doctrine of judicial review the Supreme Court has the authority to declare acts of Congress unconstitutional.

1 Mar.   Ohio enters the Union as a free state as a result of the Northwest Ordinance of 1787, which prohibited slavery in the Northwest Territory.

3 Mar.   Congress provides for the sale of all uncommitted public lands in Mississippi.

2 May   The United States purchases the Louisiana Territory from France. From this land will arise thirteen new states: Arkansas, Colorado, Kansas, Iowa, Louisiana, Minnesota, Missouri, Montana, Nebraska, North Dakota, Oklahoma, South Dakota, and Wyoming.

7 June   In Indiana Territory the United States signs a treaty with nine tribes along the Wabash River.

1804

•   In reaction to Spanish expansion into their grazing land, Navajo warriors attack the town of Cebolleta in the present-day Four Corners area of the Southwest (where the boundaries of Colorado, New Mexico, Arizona, and Utah meet). In turn the Spanish massacre Navajo women, children, and old men at Canyon de Chelly.

26 Mar.   Congress passes the Land Act of 1804, reducing the price of public lands and making it available in 160-acre parcels. Congress also creates the Territory of Orleans, which includes a portion of present-day Louisiana. The region retains the Napoleonic Code of Law originally established there by the French.

3 Nov.   William Henry Harrison, governor of Indiana Territory, negotiates a five-million-acre land cession from the Sauk and Fox tribes.

1805

11 Jan.   Congress creates the Mississippi Territory out of the Indiana Territory.

1806

29 Mar.   Congress authorizes the federally financed Cumberland Road. It will extend from Cumberland, Maryland, to Wheeling, Virginia, and provide a better route for pioneers heading west.

30 May	Andrew Jackson, former Tennessee Supreme Court judge and future president of the United States, kills a lawyer named Charles Dickinson in a duel.
27 Nov.	Gen. James Wilkinson reveals the Burr conspiracy, a plan by former vice president Aaron Burr to encourage a rebellion and independence movement in the American Southwest and Mexico.

1807

•	Congress passes an act creating a seventh circuit to the federal courts.
19 Feb.	Aaron Burr is captured in present-day Alabama.
1 Sept.	The Supreme Court acquits Burr of treason on the grounds of insufficient evidence.

1808

1 Jan.	Congress bans the importation of African slaves into the United States.
10 Nov.	The Osages sign a treaty with the United States, ceding lands in Missouri and Arkansas, and move to a reservation in present-day Oklahoma.

1809

20 Feb.	In *United States* v. *Peters* the Supreme Court rules that the national government has powers superior to those of the states.
1 Mar.	Congress establishes the Illinois Territory, carved out of western Indiana Territory.
2 July	Tecumseh, a Shawnee tribal leader and prophet, begins a confederacy of Indian tribes in order to defend against the increasing encroachment of American settlers on Native American lands.

1810

•	In *Fletcher* v. *Peck* Supreme Court Chief Justice John Marshall declares that Georgia violated the contract clause of the Constitution in ceding disputed lands along the Yazoo River to the United States. This land grant conflict is one of many problems that arise from unrestrained speculation in Western lands.
26 Sept.	American settlers in Spanish West Florida rebel against the Spanish government, seize the Fort of Baton Rouge, and seek annexation by the United States.

1811

26 Sept.	Indiana Territory governor William Henry Harrison leads a large military force against the confederacy of Tecumseh, who is now seeking allies among the Creeks.
7 Nov.	Tecumseh's forces nearly defeat the forces of William Henry Harrison at the Battle of Tippecanoe, but Harrison rallies and destroys the local Indian village.

1812

Apr.   Indians loosely allied under Tecumseh's confederacy begin raids again in the Northwest.

14 May   Congress incorporates Spanish West Florida into the Mississippi Territory.

1813

Nov.   In the Creek War, generals John Coffee and Andrew Jackson raid and destroy Indian villages in the Mississippi River valley and Alabama.

1814

9 Aug.   The Creeks sign the Treaty of Fort Jackson, which cedes more than twenty million acres of land in south Georgia and eastern Mississippi Territory to the federal government.

1815

July–Sept.   With the signing of the Treaties of Portage de Sioux the United States puts a virtual end to organized, armed Indian resistance in the Old Northwest.

1816

•   Vigilantism is on the rise in Illinois.

June   The Indiana Territory holds a convention to draft a state constitution in Corydon, Indiana.

11 Dec.   Congress admits Indiana to the Union as a free state.

1817

27 Sept.   Native Americans cede four million acres to the United States in northwestern Ohio.

10 Dec.   Congress admits Mississippi to the Union as a slave state.

1818

19 Oct.   In a treaty with the United States, Chickasaw Indians cede lands between the Mississippi River and the northern Tennessee River.

3 Dec.   Congress admits Illinois as a free state.

1819

13 Feb.   Congress deliberates the Missouri Bill, which would allow Missouri to apply for statehood. Against the context of rapidly proceeding westward expansion, the debate is whether Missouri will enter the Union as a free or slave state.

14 Dec.   Alabama enters the Union as a slave state.

1820

- Indiana experiences an outbreak of vigilantism.

3 Mar. The Missouri Compromise passes Congress, admitting Missouri as a slave state and Maine as a free state and declaring that no slavery will be allowed in the Louisiana Purchase north of 36°30'.

24 Apr. Congress passes the Public Lands Act, further lowering the prices of public lands and decreasing the minimum acreage of purchase to eighty acres.

1821

- After the opening of the Santa Fe Trail the booming market in horse and mules encourages theft. Ute Indians and white mountain men are the primary participants of the illegal trade.

3 Mar. In *Cohen* v. *Virginia* the Supreme Court maintains that a higher federal court can review state court decisions.

1822

3 Sept. The United States signs a treaty with the Sauk and Fox Indians, allowing them to live on lands in Wisconsin Territory and Illinois already ceded to the federal government.

1823

- In *Johnson* v. *M'Intosh* Supreme Court Chief Justice John Marshall hands down the Court's opinion that Indians did not hold adequate title to their lands compared to that of Euro-Americans, earned through the "right of discovery" of the North American continent.

18 Feb. Emperor Augustin de Iturbide of Mexico confirms the land grant title transfer to Stephen Austin of land in present-day Texas. Within two years Austin will move three hundred American families to these lands along the Brazos River.

1824

- In *Gibbons* v. *Ogden* the Supreme Court broadly defines Congress's power to regulate interstate commerce by declaring that New York State cannot grant a monopoly on steamboat navigation.

Feb. President James Monroe decides to institute a policy of removing Indians east of the Mississippi into the American West.

17 June Congress establishes the Bureau of Indian Affairs within the War Department.

Dec. Indiana passes a fugitive slave act, giving both claimant and accused the right to a jury trial. The federal Fugitive Slave Law of 1850 will invalidate this act.

1825

- Stephen Austin forms the first group of local vigilantes, the precursor of the Texas Rangers, to protect Anglo interests in Texas.

12 Feb.	After Creek Indian chief William McIntosh signs a treaty ceding all Creek lands in Georgia to the United States, other Creek Indians repudiate it and kill him.
19 Aug.	The federal government arranges an intertribal pact between the Chippewa, Iowa, Potawatomi, Sauk, Fox, Sioux, and Winnebago tribes.

1830

- Alabama and Mississippi experience outbreaks of vigilantism.
- The Indian Removal Act is passed by Congress.

1831

- In *Cherokee Nation* v. *Georgia* Supreme Court Chief Justice John Marshall defines the Cherokee tribe as a "domestic, dependent nation" and a ward of the federal government.

1832

- In *Worcester* v. *Georgia* the Supreme Court finds for missionaries Samuel Worcester and Elizur Butler, establishing the doctrine of Indian sovereignty by recognizing that state laws had no force in Indian country. Furious, President Andrew Jackson refuses to enforce the verdict and decides to proceed with Indian removal.

1833

- In *United States* v. *Percheron* the Supreme Court gives a liberal interpretation of the land grant rights preserved under a Florida treaty between Spain and the United States. It also holds that both the Spanish and English translation of a treaty must be considered in order to determine its meaning. Later cases would substantially narrow this ruling, especially to the benefit of Anglo-Americans in California and New Mexico.

1835

- In Georgia a few unauthorized members of the Cherokee tribe sign a treaty ceding all tribal lands to the state. Several thousand Cherokees protest the treaty, and the United States ignores it. Georgia sells the lands to whites in a state lottery. Many Cherokees refuse to move to the lands in present-day Oklahoma offered in exchange.

24 Nov.	Texas creates the first official group of Texas Rangers.

1837

- The landmark case of *Charles River Bridge* v. *Warren Bridge* indicates that in the ongoing struggles over state versus federal government sovereignty the limitation of the commerce clause in the federal constitution signifies an increase in the power of states to regulate interstate commerce.

- Congress passes the Act of 1837, which expands the jurisdiction of the Supreme Court to include appeals from incoming new territories and states.

- Texas passes the first antimiscegenation law in the West.

1838

- Federal troops begin the forced removal of the Cherokees from Georgia to present-day Oklahoma. Nearly a quarter of the Cherokees die en route from starvation and exposure. The U.S. Army removes thousands of Creeks, Choctaws, Chickasaws, and the few remaining Seminoles to Oklahoma.

1839

- Vigilantism breaks out in Arkansas.

1841

16 Dec.   In order to encourage immigration to Oregon, Sen. Lewis Lim of Missouri introduces a bill providing military protection along the Oregon Trail between St. Louis and Oregon. The bill will not pass, but this same year a substantial group consisting of forty-eight wagons passes over the trail and ends their journey in Sacramento, California.

1842

- Vigilantism breaks out in Missouri.

1843

3 Feb.   The U.S. Senate finally passes Sen. Lewis Lim's Oregon bill, originally proposed in 1841, but the bill fails to pass the House of Representatives.

2 May   Oregon settlers at Champoeg decide to form their own government.

17 June   The settlers at Champoeg adopt their own constitution.

1844

18 Mar.   The Martinez Treaty is signed at Jemez Pueblo, requiring the Navajos to return their slaves but asking no such concession from the New Mexicans. At the time an estimated 75 percent of the three to six thousand slaves in New Mexico are Navajos. The treaty quickly breaks down.

12 Apr.   John C. Calhoun, secretary of state, negotiates a treaty for the annexation of Texas. The antislavery forces in the Senate eventually force its rejection, fearing the admission of Texas into the Union as a slave state.

1845

3 Mar.   Florida joins the Union as a slave state.

| 29 Dec. | Texas joins the Union as a slave state. |

1846

•	As a result of the Mexican War, California, Texas, Arizona, and New Mexico experience a great increase in racial strife.
27 Mar.	The House of Representatives defeats a bill providing free homesteading in the West.
14 June	Anglo-American settlers in California throw off the Mexican government and form the short-lived Bear Flag Republic.
28 Dec.	Iowa joins the Union as a free state.

1847

| • | In present-day Washington State, Cayuse Indians kill missionaries Marcus and Narcissa Whitman as well as other settlers. |
| • | In Missouri, Dred Scott's first legal battle to define himself as a free man ends when his case is dismissed on a technicality. |

1848

•	The United States and Mexico ratify the Treaty of Guadalupe Hidalgo, ending the Mexican War. The harsh provisions of the treaty, in particular the federal courts' subsequent and widely varying interpretations of controversial Articles 8 and 10, cause considerable confusion and injustice in preserving native Mexicans' property rights.
29 May	Wisconsin joins the Union as a free state.
14 Aug.	The U.S. Senate agrees to organize Oregon as a free state.

1849

| • | Over the course of the next fifty-three years an estimated 210 vigilante movements "hand out justice" in the West, especially in California after the Gold Rush. Many vigilante incidents are a cover for white supremacist attacks on local minorities. |
| 9 Sept. | The U.S. signs a treaty annexing Navajo lands and requiring the return of captives. Most Navajos repudiate the treaty. |

1850

•	The gunfighter Benjamin F. Thompson establishes a reputation for himself by participating in at least fourteen shoot-outs over the next three decades.
•	California passes the Foreign Miners' Tax.
•	As a result of the population explosion after the Gold Rush, a wave of violence hits California. In one fifteen-month period in Los Angeles County forty-four homicides occur.

1851

9–12 Sept.   As part of the Compromise of 1850, Congress passes the Fugitive Slave Act.

23 July   Members of the Sioux nation sign the Treaty of Traverse des Sioux, ceding to the U.S. government much of their land in Iowa and Minnesota.

1853

30 Dec.   The U.S. and Mexico negotiate the Gadsden Purchase, whereby the former receives 29,644 square miles of territory (the southernmost areas of present-day Arizona and New Mexico) for $15 million. The purchase establishes the final boundaries of the continental U.S. and provides the needed land for a railroad route. The U.S. Senate approves the purchase in June 1854.

1854

- In *People* v. *Hall* the California Supreme Court holds that no Chinese witnesses can give testimony against a white man.
- In Clarke County, Missouri, David McKee organizes the Anti-Horse Thief Association.

1855

- California counts 370 homicides in the first eight months of the year.

1856

- The Committee of Vigilance holds sway in San Francisco. Led by the wealthy and powerful William Tell Coleman, its objective is attacking Irish Catholics, Chinese, and Mexican Americans as well as "punishing criminals."
- The Apaches kill the U.S. Indian agent Henry Dodge. Because of the efforts of Dodge, Navajo-U.S. relations had been fairly peaceful for the last six years.

1857

- The decision of the Supreme Court in the *Dred Scott* case in effect rules that slaves are property and cannot be considered citizens under the Constitution.

1858

- Kansas repeals its antimiscegenation law.

1860

- Navajo warriors attack Fort Defiance, and in retaliation New Mexico volunteers invade Canyon de Chelly. The subsequent period of warfare, in the language of the Dineh (the Navajo peoples), is called *Nahondzhod,* or the Fearing Time.

OVERVIEW

Land Law. The migration of hundreds of thousands of Americans into the Trans-Appalachian West gave birth to a multitude of legal problems regarding land. States were anxious that the land be settled and developed by their citizens. As a result state legislators sponsored internal improvements such as roads and canals, which raised the value of the land since then it could be developed more profitably. Further, state politicians wanted land under their control because land held by the federal government generated no income for the state. Movements that favored land reform and settlement gained support on a number of levels as a result. For example, Illinois passed laws that favored profitable settlement. The Preemption Act of 1830 helped the squatters who had moved to, occupied, and developed land held in the public domain without ownership. Under the act these illegal settlers could purchase up to 160 acres for a minimum price of $1.25 per acre. The Preemption Act further encouraged westward movement even though it seemed to condone the ongoing criminal activity of settling land without a legal title. Congress continued to authorize preemption acts throughout the 1830s, further evidence that migration into the public domain was a constant and active process.

Economic Development. Government on the local, state, and national levels worked increasingly to facilitate westward expansion through land grants for railroad construction and internal improvements such as the building of roads and canals. Between 1850 and 1855 more than 2,200 miles of track were laid, terminating in Chicago and linking more than 150,000 square miles of territory to that city. Legal questions relating to patents, contracts, charters, land rights, franchises, and lawsuits accompanied all these developments. Courts faced a growing number of cases dealing with the rights and demands of businesses and corporations in the West. Demands on the legal system attracted an impressive group of highly trained and polished lawyers. It was not uncommon to find the most lucrative practices dealing with issues of transportation in service to the railroads. The role of the law in the process of westward expansion was enormous.

Indian Removal. In 1828 approximately one hundred thousand Native Americans occupied large territories throughout the Southern and Eastern territories of the United States. Westward migration and land greed placed greater and greater pressure on these tribes to leave, opening the land for white settlement. The Five Civilized Tribes—Creeks, Choctaws, Seminoles, Chickasaws, and Cherokees—occupied ancestral lands that whites wanted to use in order to expand their commercial agriculture. Justifying their demands on the foundations of white supremacy and states' rights, white settlers appealed to the states to evict the tribes. Some of the natives fought while others surrendered their ancestral lands peacefully and retreated further to the West. A few resisted through legal means. The Cherokees, acting as a sovereign nation, established a constitution, legal system, and representative government. When Georgia's legislature declared the Cherokee's constitution and laws void and attempted to expel the Native Americans, the nation appealed its case to the Supreme Court. In *Cherokee Nation* v. *Georgia* (1831) Chief Justice John Marshall determined that the Cherokees constituted a "domestic dependent nation" and not a sovereign nation, and as such the natives could not sue the state of Georgia. In *Worcester* v. *Georgia* (1832) the Court declared that Georgia's laws could not be enforced against the Cherokees. According to Marshall, only the national government could determine Indian affairs. President Andrew Jackson—whose enmity toward Native Americans and sympathy for the white Georgians and states' rights were both well established—ignored the Court's decision. He supposedly challenged the chief justice with the declaration: "John Marshall has made his decision: *now let him enforce it!*" Passed by Congress in 1830, the Indian Removal Act facilitated the eviction of tens of thousands of Cherokees and other Native Americans along the infamous Trail of Tears to the Oklahoma Territory.

Slavery in the Territories. Differing interpretations of the Constitution dramatically effected political conflicts over the expansion of slavery into the Western territories. The case of *Dred Scott* v. *Sandford* (1857) represented the most critical moment of this controversy. Scott, a slave, sued for both his and his family's freedom based on the fact that he had spent several years in free territories in the West. The case moved slowly through Missouri's court system until Scott finally appealed to the Supreme Court. In presenting the majority opinion, Chief Justice Roger Taney attempted both to render a judgment on Scott and to settle the legal controversy surrounding slavery in the West. Taney declared that regardless of their status—free or slave—blacks could not be citizens of the United States. The Court rejected Scott's claim that his residence in free territory made him a free man. More important for the West, Taney declared that the Missouri Compromise of 1820 was unconstitutional because Congress did not have the power to ban slavery in the Western territories. The decision exacerbated the sectional conflict dividing the North and South over the future of the West and quickened the nation's descent into the Civil War.

Frontier Justice. Somewhat unfairly, the frontier is frequently associated with unconstrained lawlessness. Although it was often crude, frontier justice quickly assumed recognizable forms—judges presided in courtrooms and over juries, and lawyers, plaintiffs, and defendants followed established legal practices. Recent scholarship demonstrates that learned jurists entered the westward movement and effectively brought order to the territories, but their impact was uneven. Often in distant or isolated regions, individuals and groups attempted to maintain the rule of law within a framework characterized by an absence of established and strong civil authority. Here there were incidents of local people taking the law into their own hands. Dueling provides the most dramatic example. Andrew Jackson was involved in several famous duels, including one in 1813 in which the future president exchanged shots with Thomas Hart Benton, a future senator, and his brother. Jackson carried bullets in his shoulder and chest that plagued him for much of his life. A debate in Kentucky's legislature in 1809 led to a duel with pistols between Henry Clay and Humphrey Marshall. Although they fired three rounds at each other, neither man was seriously injured. An unlawful act in much of the nation during this period, efforts to discourage the practice proved to be futile, especially where civil authority was weak. Vigilante movements enforced local laws in the West through extralegal means. In San Francisco in the 1850s mobs punished criminals by staging public trials, corporal punishment, and executions. They also upheld more-loosely defined codes of morality, evicting from the city people whom the vigilance committees considered to be morally suspect.

TOPICS IN THE NEWS

THE AARON BURR CONSPIRACY

Imperial Scheme. Soon after resigning the vice presidency in 1805, Aaron Burr began a journey throughout the West. Following his departure, President Thomas Jefferson received an anonymous warning that Burr was "meditating the overthrow of your Administration," "conspiring against the State," and acting as an agent of Great Britain. Other rumors of political instability in the West added to suspicions surrounding Burr's activities. Reliable sources reported that Burr was actively recruiting men for an army and officers to lead them in an effort to separate the Western territories from the United States. Combined with territories to be taken from Spain, it was alleged that Burr intended to create a new empire in the West.

The Conspiracy. One of Burr's allies was Gen. James Wilkinson, the governor of Upper Louisiana. Wilkinson was known to be corrupt, but few at the time considered him to be capable of treason. (It was later discovered that he had been a paid agent of the Spanish.) Identified as a suspect early on, Wilkinson became convinced that the plan was doomed. The general betrayed his alleged coconspirator by sending incriminating letters directly to Jefferson. The papers described the planned movements of thousands of armed men through Ohio, Kentucky, and Mississippi, all of whom would be under Burr's leadership. Attempting to direct suspicion away from himself, Wilkinson claimed ignorance: "I am not only uninformed of the prime mover and ultimate objects of this daring enterprize, but am ignorant of the foundation on which it rests." He nevertheless speculated that these activities were probably connected to rumors of revolt in the Orleans Territory and part of a plan to invade and seize parts of Mexico.

The Arrest. Jefferson responded by issuing directions to military commanders and civil authorities in the West, ordering them to watch for any evidence of suspicious activities. In January 1807 the president informed the Senate and House of Representatives of what he called "an illegal combination of private individuals against the

John Marshall (1828); portrait by Chester Harding
(Boston Athenaeum)

peace and safety of the Union, and a military expedition planned by them against the territories of a power [Spain] in amity with the United States." Jefferson named Burr as the leader and added that his "guilt is . . . beyond question." Burr was in the Mississippi Territory when he received word that Wilkinson had betrayed him and that orders had been issued for his arrest. He quickly surrendered to local authorities, but the Territorial Supreme Court was comprised of sympathetic Federalists. The judges decided not to indict Burr, but they divided over the terms of his arrest. During these deliberations Burr fled but was soon captured, arrested, and taken to Richmond, Virginia, where the trial would be heard by John Marshall, chief justice of the Supreme Court.

Jefferson and the Court. While organizing his defense Burr asked the Court to subpoena Jefferson, which would have required the president both to appear in court in person and to provide papers that the defendant insisted were essential to his case. Jefferson replied that, "independent of all other authority," it was the president's right to decide "what papers coming to him as President, the public interests permit to be communicated [and] to whom." The president believed at this point that he had made available all of the papers and correspondence relevant to the case. Jefferson was no obstructionist, but he was deeply concerned with the independence of the executive and sought to uphold it. He would not come to Richmond to testify because it would establish a significant and undesirable precedent and at some future time compel the chief executive to attend trials in Ohio or the Mississippi Territory. Second, Jefferson asked, "Would the Executive be independent of the judiciary, if he were subject to the *commands* of the latter, and to imprisonment for disobedience?" The president's main concern was to maintain the Constitution's rule that guaranteed the executive's independence from the judicial branch of government.

The Trial. A toast given at the time of the trial represented, in general, the public's enmity toward Burr: "Aaron Burr—may his treachery to his country exhalt him to the scaffold, and hemp be his escort to the republic of Dust and ashes." In court the former vice president was tried on two charges: first, treason for allegedly "assembling an armed force" in order to take New Orleans and "separate the western from the Atlantic states," and second, "a high misdemeanor" for sending a military expedition against territories belonging to Spain. Burr's lawyers argued that the defendant had committed no treasonous act. The case turned on whether simple intent—in the absence of overt action—was enough to convict a man of the high crime of treason. The prosecution rested the weight of its case on the part Burr played in organizing a meeting of armed men and alleged traitors in Ohio in 1806. They insisted that although he was not present, Burr was a principle agent in bringing the meeting together and that this should be enough to convict him. The defense countered with a strenuous argument that unless an act of war had been committed—and all agreed that it had not—the prosecution's case should fail and Burr should go free.

Marshall's Decision. Marshall's opinion was delivered on 31 August 1807. It covered forty-four printed pages and took three hours to read. Its length and breadth indicated a purpose that transcended Burr specifically as Marshall sought to define the meaning of treason. Marshall sided with the defense regarding the gathering of alleged conspirators and traitors. He declared that the prosecution had failed to provide an adequate number of witnesses in order to support its case. More significant was the narrow definition that Marshall applied to the charge of treason, a construction that would make prosecution for this crime a difficult task thereafter. Treason did not require the accused to take up arms, but the chief justice insisted that merely suggesting war or engaging in a conspiracy was not enough to require a conviction. Those accused of the crime, Marshall declared, must have committed an overt and provable act of participation. He concluded that the prosecution had failed to provide such proof in the Burr case. The jury deliberated for less than one half-hour and then announced that it had found the defendant not guilty. Jefferson responded angrily to the verdict and suggested that it was "equivalent to a proclamation of impunity to every traitorous combination which may be formed to destroy the Union." A free man, Burr spent the next five years in Europe. He returned to the United States in 1812, practicing law and engaging in various business schemes until his death in 1836.

Sources:

Nobel E. Cunningham Jr., *In Pursuit of Reason: The Life of Thomas Jefferson* (Baton Rouge: Louisiana State University Press, 1987);

Milton Lomask, *Aaron Burr, The Conspiracy and Years of Exile, 1805–1836* (New York: Farrar, Straus & Giroux, 1982);

Herbert S. Parmet and Marie B. Hecht, *Aaron Burr: Portrait of an Ambitious Man* (New York: Macmillan, 1967).

THE DRED SCOTT CASE

The Plaintiff. Dred Scott was born a slave in Virginia around 1802. In 1830 his owner took him west to St. Louis, Missouri, where he was sold to Dr. John Emerson, an army surgeon. Emerson carried Scott with him as he would any other piece of property, first to Fort Armstrong, Illinois, from 1833 to 1836, then to Fort Snelling

in the Wisconsin Territory from 1836 to 1838. The latter sojourn brought Scott into territory where slavery had been explicitly prohibited under the Northwest Ordinance of 1787, the Missouri Compromise of 1820 (which excluded slavery in the land acquired by the Louisiana Purchase north of latitude 36°30'), and the Wisconsin Enabling Act. This last piece of legislation stated that the Wisconsin Territory would be subject to the same laws that governed Michigan. Since Michigan prohibited slavery, the institution became illegal in Wisconsin as well. While in Wisconsin, Scott married another slave, Harriet Robinson, in a ceremony performed by her owner. However, because marriage was, in the eyes of the law, a contract and slaves lacked the legal right to make contracts, observers wondered about the intent of Scott's and Robinson's owners as well as the legal implications of allowing the marriage in the first place. Did the fact of their marriage mean that Scott and Robinson were recognized as free? When Emerson died suddenly in December 1843, ownership of Scott, Robinson, and their daughter Eliza passed to the doctor's widow. In 1846 Scott attempted to purchase freedom for himself and his family. Irene Emerson refused, and in April, Scott sued for his freedom.

The Missouri Courts. The Scott case spent six years in the Missouri court system. The first trial, held in 1847, was dismissed on a technicality. Three years later a circuit court in St. Louis determined that Scott's long term of residence in a free territory made him and his family free. Emerson appealed, and the case moved to the Missouri Supreme Court. In 1852, in the case of *Scott* v. *Emerson*, the state supreme court overturned the lower court's ruling and determined that Scott was still a slave. In making this decision the state's jurists ignored legal precedent and made concessions to proslavery politics and ideology. With new lawyers, Scott's case moved to the federal court system. The new suit was made against John Sanford of New York, the brother of Irene Emerson who managed his sister's estate. The case came to trial in May 1854. Scott sued in diversity—a reference used when the plaintiff and defendant in a suit are citizens of different states. In other words, Scott claimed that he was a citizen of Missouri and Sanford a citizen of New York. Sanford's lawyers responded with a plea in abatement, or a call to stop the suit and throw it out. They argued that no court had jurisdiction over the case. Scott, they declared, was "not a citizen of the state of Missouri, as alleged in his declaration, because he is a negro of African descent." Sanford argued that no black could be a citizen of the state of Missouri whether his or her status was slave or free. Therefore, no black, per se, could legally execute a suit in a federal court since this right was reserved exclusively for citizens. The federal court upheld the state supreme court's ruling, and Scott remained a slave.

The Supreme Court. Scott appealed to the U.S. Supreme Court in 1854, and after long delays the case was

Missouri Courtroom (1852); oil painting by William Josiah Brickey (National Museum of American Art, Smithsonian Institution, Washington, D.C.)

finally heard in February 1856. The heart of the case rested on three crucial issues. First, could people of African descent, slave or free, be citizens of the United States? Second, did the federal government have the power to ban slavery in the Western territories? Third, was the Missouri Compromise and its geographical limitations on slavery constitutional? Scott's chances at winning freedom for himself and his family were small since a majority of the Supreme Court justices were either Southerners, who had themselves held slaves, or Southern sympathizers. Chief Justice Roger B. Taney, a former slave owner, openly supported the South and its "peculiar institution."

Taney's Decision. Writing for the 7–2 majority in *Dred Scott* v. *Sandford* (the name Sandford was the result of a record-keeping error), Taney handed down three rulings. First, he wrote that African Americans were "beings of an inferior order . . . altogether unfit to associate with the white race." They were, he continued, members of a group that "had no rights which white men were bound to respect." He then determined that Scott was not a citizen and therefore had no right to sue in a federal court. Second, Taney maintained that moving in and out of free states and residing for long periods in those states had no effect on Scott's status. Despite their migrations, Scott and his family remained slaves. Finally and most significant, Taney and the Court's majority ruled that the Missouri Compromise was unconstitutional since

Congress did not have the power to prohibit slavery in any territory (as opposed to a state).

Conclusions. In rendering his judgment Taney had reached beyond the mere application of legal and constitutional principles. He attempted to settle the most critical and divisive issue in American politics and society in a single stroke: the slavery question. Ultimately the results led to disaster. The decision that the remaining territories, including a significant portion of the lands taken as a result of the Mexican War, were open to the expansion of slavery gave the sectional conflict a new and dangerous urgency. The South's defenders hailed the decision as a monumental victory. The future of that section's agricultural economy depended not only on its primary system of labor but also on its expansion into the fertile Western territories that had previously banned slavery. The Supreme Court had given the South's distinct culture, power structure, and economy new life in part by interpreting the Constitution in such a way that it favored property rights over natural rights. Opponents of slavery claimed that this decision was the work of a vast conspiracy masterminded by "the slave power." The *Dred Scott* decision revealed that freedom was in jeopardy everywhere, they warned. Campaigning for the U.S. Senate in 1858, Abraham Lincoln warned his audience of the logical outcome of this ruling: "We shall lie down pleasantly dreaming that the people of Missouri are on the verge of making their state free; and we shall awake to the reality,

During much of the nineteenth century Frederick Douglass was recognized as "the Representative Colored Man of the United States." Born a slave in Tuckahoe, Maryland, he escaped and began one of the most extraordinary public careers in U.S. history. Although Douglass was many things over the course of his long and eventful life—orator, reformer, editor, publisher, and diplomat—he was known first as a leader in the abolitionist movement and one of its most passionate and eloquent champions.

The following speech, a response to the *Dred Scott* decision, was delivered to the American Anti-Slavery Society on 11 May 1857. Douglass refuted Judge Roger B. Taney's assertion that the Constitution did not apply to African Americans and that it was a proslavery document.

The argument here is, that the Constitution comes down to us from a slaveholding period and a slaveholding people; and that, therefore, we are bound to suppose that the Constitution recognizes colored people of African descent, the victims of slavery at that time, as debarred forever from all participation in the benefit of the Constitution and the Declaration of Independence, although the plain reading of both includes them in their beneficent range.

As a man, an American, a citizen, a colored man of both Anglo-Saxon and African descent, I denounce this representation as a most scandalous and devilish perversion of the Constitution, and a brazen misstatement of the facts of history. . . .

Washington and Jefferson, and Adams, and Jay, and Franklin, and Rush, and Hamilton, and a host of others, held no such degrading views on the subject as are imputed by Judge Taney to the Fathers of the Republic. . . . All at that time, looked for the gradual but certain abolition of slavery, and shaped the Constitution with a view to this grand result. . . .

It may, however, be asked, if the Constitution were so framed that the rights of all the people were naturally protected by it, how happens it that a large part of the people have been held in slavery ever since its adoption? Have the people mistaken the requirements of their own Constitution?

The answer is ready. The Constitution is one thing, its administration is another, and, in this instance, a very different and opposite thing. I am here to vindicate the law, not the administration of the law. It is the written Constitution, not the unwritten Constitution, that is now before us. If, in the whole range of the Constitution, you can find no warrant for slavery, then we may properly claim it for liberty.

Good and wholesome laws are often found dead on the statute book. We may condemn the practice under them and against them, but never the law itself. To condemn the good law with the wicked practice is to weaken, not to strengthen out testimony. . . .

The American people have made void our Constitution by just such traditions as Judge Taney . . . [has] been giving the world of late, as the true light in which to view the Constitution of the United States.

It may be said that it is quite true that the Constitution was designed to secure the blessings of liberty and justice to the people who made it, and to the posterity of the people who made it, but was never designed to do any such thing for the colored people of African descent.

This is Judge Taney's argument . . . but it is not the argument of the Constitution. The Constitution imposes no such mean and satanic limitations upon its own beneficent operation. And, if the Constitution makes none, I beg to know what right has any body, outside of the Constitution, for the special accommodation of slaveholding villainy, to impose such a construction upon the Constitution?

The Constitution knows all the human inhabitants of this country as 'the people.' It makes, as I have said before, no discrimination in favor of, or against, any class of the people, but is fitted to protect and preserve the rights of all, without reference to color, size, or any physical peculiarities. Besides, it has been shown by William Goodell and others, that in eleven out of the old thirteen States, colored men were legal voters at the time of the adoption of the Constitution.

In conclusion, let me say, all I ask of the American people is, that they live up to the Constitution, adopt its principles, imbibe its spirit and enforce its provisions.

When this is done, the wounds of my bleeding people will be healed, the chain will no longer rust on their ankles, their backs will no longer be torn by the bloody lash, and liberty, the glorious birthright of our common humanity, will become the inheritance of all the inhabitants of this highly favored country.

Source: Paul Finkelman, ed., Dred Scott *v.* Sandford: *A Brief History with Documents* (Boston: Bedford Books, 1997), pp. 169–182.

instead, that the Supreme Court has made Illinois a *slave state*."

Sources:

Don Fehrenbacher, The Dred Scott *Case: Its Significance in American Law and Politics* (New York: Oxford University Press, 1978);

Paul Finkelman, ed., Dred Scott v. Sandford: *A Brief History With Documents* (Boston: Bedford Books, 1997);

William Freehling, *The Road to Disunion: Secessionists at Bay, 1776–1864* (New York: Oxford University Press, 1990);

William Wiecek, "Slavery and Abolition before the United States Supreme Court, 1820–1860," *Journal of American History,* 65 (January 1979): 34–59.

GIBBONS V. OGDEN

Fulton's Steamboat. In August 1807 Robert Fulton's steam-powered ship, the *Clermont,* traveled up the Hudson River from New York City to Albany in thirty-two hours. Fulton's success proved that steamships traveling through inland waterways could be an efficient and profitable means of transporting passengers and commodities. Steamboats were faster and more reliable than wind-powered vessels, and their services proved to be far less expensive than hauling goods by wagon over primitive road networks. Political leaders in New York envisioned their state becoming a vital passage for both migration and trade to the West, and they worked aggressively to capitalize on the revolution represented in Fulton's success. As early as 1800 some enterprising New Yorkers hoped to open a canal through upstate New York, linking the Hudson River to Lake Erie. In 1815 DeWitt Clinton, former mayor of New York City, became the canal's leading advocate, and in 1817 New York's legislature agreed to finance the project. The Erie Canal was completed in 1825 at a cost of $7 million. Travel and trade along this and ancillary water routes (many inspired by the Erie project) quickened the movement of people and commerce into the Trans-Appalachian West. Shipping costs between New York City and Lake Erie dropped from one hundred dollars to nine dollars per ton. The western periphery of New York, and thus the Great Lakes, now could be incorporated into the economy of the eastern United States.

State-Sanctioned Monopoly. The great success of the Erie Canal demonstrated the efficacy of governmental efforts to support commerce and migration through the creation of a permanent transportation system. States supported businesses and protected their competitive advantage with regard to other states through other means as well. New York State awarded Fulton and his partner, Robert R. Livingston, the exclusive rights to navigate "all the waters within the jurisdiction of that State, with boats moved by fire or steam." In other words, Fulton and Livingston received a monopoly. Hoping to make a profit in the shipping business, the steamship operator Aaron Ogden purchased a license from Livingston that allowed his company to operate in New York waters. Thomas Gibbons, owner of a license under the Federal Coasting Act, ran a competing line that ran between New York City and New Jersey. To defend his business against a rival Ogden filed an injunction against Gibbons. In 1820 the New York courts upheld Fulton and Livingston's monopoly, and by extension Ogden prevailed in his suit. Gibbons appealed his case to the Supreme Court.

Commercial Nationalism. *Gibbons* v. *Ogden* reached the U.S. Supreme Court in 1824. The critical issue that emerged was not over the legitimacy of the virtual monopoly New York State awarded to a few businesses but rather whether states could pass such laws, which, in operation, restrained trade. Chief Justice John Marshall, speaking for the Court in a 6–0 decision on 2 March, overturned the act passed by the New York legislature. Taking a nationalist position, Marshall referred to the power that the Constitution gave Congress to regulate interstate commerce. The Court defined trade and commerce broadly and in such a way as to embrace the transportation of people as well as goods. In this light, acts passed by Congress (such as granting navigation rights to commercial ships engaged in coastal trade) superseded state laws, many of which overlapped or conflicted with one another. Marshall was careful to articulate a narrow interpretation and avoided claiming that the federal government had exclusive rights in matters of interstate commerce. In the end the decision discouraged states from pursuing independent policies on trade.

Sources:

Lawrence M. Friedman, *A History of American Law* (New York: Simon & Schuster, 1985);

Charles Sellers, *The Market Revolution: Jacksonian America, 1815–1846* (New York: Oxford University Press, 1991).

GOVERNMENT TREATIES WITH NATIVE AMERICANS

Background. Since the first Europeans landed in the Western Hemisphere, they and the indigenous peoples they called Indians have made many agreements, often known as treaties. In theory these treaties set out the guidelines for how these different cultures would get along and share resources and lands. In practice, however, treaties between American Indians and Euro-Americans often caused as much conflict as they resolved. Over time both groups, but especially the U.S. government, abridged the terms of these treaties. Particularly during the era of Western expansion, controversies over treaty interpretation and enforcement led to conflict between indigenous and American peoples.

Conflicts. There are several reasons these conflicts occurred. When the colonists first began negotiating treaties with Native Americans, they were relatively powerless against the more numerous Indians. Therefore, colonial treaty makers often took pains to placate the Indians; normally these diplomats recognized distinctions between Native American nations. However, over time this balance of power began to shift. The numbers of European settlers in the New World grew, and

An 1838 presidential declaration by Martin Van Buren affirming Cherokee rights to 14 million acres in Arkansas (Cherokee National Historical Society, Tahlequah, Oklahoma)

they also brought new diseases with them, so-called virgin soil epidemics to which Indian populations had no acquired immunities. As time passed indigenous populations decreased drastically. Eventually the devastation wrought by the Revolutionary War weakened Eastern Indian communities as well as their negotiating power at the bargaining table.

Negotiations. After it formed, the U.S. government repeatedly negotiated with Indian communities. In nearly every instance the government's basic goal was to gain more land to open it for westward-moving Americans, most of them of European origin. Over time the federal government became increasingly rigid in its tactics, a policy that made it difficult for Indian communities to get what they wanted. Further, negotiators for the federal government typically identified selected native leaders and dealt exclusively with them. For example, in the controversy over Indian removal in Georgia, Andrew Jackson stubbornly negotiated only with the "Treaty Party" of Cherokees, who in the nation were outnumbered 17 to 1. Still, Jackson maintained that the treaty signed by the Treaty Party was binding on the rest of the tribe.

Trouble in the West. Prior to the Civil War the strong Western Indian nations still held an upper hand in treaty negotiations. At the Treaty of Fort Laramie in 1851 the Sioux, Cheyenne, Arapaho, Crow, Assiniboine, Gros Ventre, and Arikara peoples agreed to allow pioneers to safely cross the plains in exchange for annuities from the federal government. However, promises such as this often proved hollow, especially after the United States descended into the Civil War. The federal government could not afford to pay the annuities in the agreed-upon gold coin, let alone provide the promised rations, education, and health care. Also, the federal government was often unable or unwilling to enforce restrictions on white settlers, such as land boundaries, or regulate the alcohol trade. As a result many Indian peoples renounced the treaties and at times turned to violence against settlers and the U.S. Army as the only way left to assert their rights.

Conclusion. Indigenous peoples suffered from the United States's often egregious abridgment of the treaties. Yet even this fact does not lessen the initiative that Indians took in asserting their demands and destinies as white Western expansion transformed Indian country.

Sources:

Patricia Nelson Limerick, *The Legacy of Conquest: The Unbroken Past of the American West* (New York: Norton, 1987);

Richard White, *"It's Your Misfortune and None of My Own": A New History of the American West* (Norman: University of Oklahoma Press, 1991).

JOHNSON V. M'INTOSH

The Law and Land Cessions. *Johnson* v. *M'Intosh* (1823) was the first in a crucial line of nineteenth-century Supreme Court cases to delineate the extent and limitations of American Indian sovereignty. Chief Justice John Marshall wrote the opinion and later elaborated many of the same principles in *Cherokee Nation* v. *Georgia* (1831) and *Worcester* v. *Georgia* (1832). In *Johnson* v. *M'Intosh* Marshall tried to describe the limits of Indian sovereignty (indigenous peoples' political rights to self-determination and self-government) in order to sort out the legal position of American Indians in the rapidly expanding United States. During the early nineteenth century U.S. citizens had made substantial encroachments on American Indian lands, and there was little sign that this movement would end on its own. The federal government, eager to get lands for white settlers and to avoid conflict with Indians, tried to negotiate land cessions from Indian communities through treaties. Despite such efforts, white settlers often illegally entered Indian lands. As a result confusion often arose over what property belonged to whom.

The Issue. *Johnson* v. *M'Intosh* resulted from one such controversy over title. The plaintiff in the case traced his title to a direct cession that the local leaders of the Illinois and Piankeshaw tribes had made to a private citizen. The defendant contended that his title, traced through a later Indian cession to the federal government, was the one that was valid. The issue that *Johnson* v. *M'Intosh* turned on, then, was whether the Illinois and Piankeshaw leaders could grant a more valid title than the federal government. If so, then M'Intosh's title would be invalid.

The Decision. The Supreme Court held that Johnson's title was not valid. That decision rested on the Court's definition of Indian land rights as limited by the

doctrine of Indian sovereignty. According to this idea, tribes did not have the ability to cede "absolute title" (apparently with the exception of the federal government in treaties). Marshall reasoned that Indians' "rights to complete sovereignty, as independent nations, were necessarily diminished." As a result of the European discovery and conquest of America, the U.S. government had "extinguished" absolute Indian title in land. Marshall asserted this conclusion reluctantly, but the way he saw it, to decide otherwise was to invalidate U.S. title to all lands in America and indeed question the legitimacy of the very government: "these claims have been maintained and established as far west as the river Mississippi, by the sword . . . it is not for the courts of this country to question the validity of this title."

A Reluctant Opinion. The significance of this case was far-reaching. For the first time there were now explicit limitations on Indian sovereignty in the law of the land. Yet while limiting tribal sovereignty, Marshall took pains to protect it. As he admitted, "conquest gives a title which the court of the conqueror cannot deny," but Marshall also stressed that the "conquered shall not be wantonly oppressed." If the Indian peoples coexisted with their conquerors in peace, he wrote, then the Indians and their rights to occupy the land should be protected. From the language of the opinion, Marshall demonstrated his ambivalence about the United States' conquest of native peoples and wanted to offer American Indians protection through the courts. Indeed, Marshall's later opinion in *Worcester* v. *Georgia*, holding that Indian sovereignty was not subject to state laws, reinforced these protections.

Indian History. Marshall's legal reasoning also depended on several complicated and conflicting cultural assumptions of his time. First, Marshall assumed that America was one vast wilderness before Europeans came and that the original inhabitants, the Indians, had done nothing to properly "use" the land. He did not recognize that through farming, hunting, fishing, and other subsistence activities Indian peoples did have long-standing effects on and relationships with their environment. Marshall's vision of proper land use was an inherently European vision of tidy, controlled farms producing agricultural commodities for trade. Therefore, he did not recognize Indian subsistence activities as valid interactions with the land, much less as permanent enough to give Indians absolute title. Second, Marshall's opinion also held ambivalent, typically nineteenth-century ideas about how these "conquered" indigenous peoples would integrate into American society. On the one hand he considered Indians to be "fierce savages" while on the other he hoped they could peacefully assimilate into the larger society. Marshall's views toward both proper land use and Indian assimilation foreshadowed late-nineteenth-century efforts, such as the Dawes Act of 1887, to assimilate Indians into white society by turning them into farmers. Therefore, *Johnson* v. *M'Intosh* held not only political and legal but also social consequences for American Indian sovereignty and Indian-white relations.

Sources:

Johnson v. *M'Intosh*, 21 U.S. (8 Wheat) 543 (1823);

Carol Rose, "Possession as the Origin of Property," in *Property and Persuasion, Essays on the History, Theory, and Rhetoric of Ownership* (Boulder, Colo.: Westview Press, 1994), pp. 11–23.

PEOPLE V. HALL

Foreign Miners Tax. As a result of the Gold Rush in 1849, people from all over the world flocked to California. In part as a result of the fierce competition in the gold fields, the state legislature and court system structured the law to socially and financially benefit Anglo-Americans. One example was the Foreign Miners Tax of 1850, which forced nonwhites—usually varying Hispanic groups (local *californios* as well as Mexicans) and Chinese immigrants—to pay sixteen dollars per month on their mining claims. Racist violence of Anglo-American miners against nonwhite miners was also common.

The Case. *People* v. *Hall* (1854) reflected the racist climate of California's early settlement. A white defendant was convicted on the basis of the testimony from a Chinese witness. On appeal the defendant's lawyer argued that a nonwhite witness could not testify against a white person. The legal basis for this claim was a California law that stated that blacks, mulattos, and Indians could not testify in any case against a white person. This law did not specifically mention the Chinese. However, in *People* v. *Hall* California Supreme Court justice John Murray decided that since all nonwhite peoples were similarly "degraded," no one of nonwhite blood, including the Chinese, could ever testify against a white. Such a court decision mirrored the prejudice, especially anti-Chinese racism, prevalent in California well into the twentieth century.

Sources:

Patricia Nelson Limerick, *Legacy of Conquest: The Unbroken Past of the American West* (New York: Norton, 1987);

Cheng-Tsu Wu, ed., *"Chink!" A Documentary History of Anti-Chinese Prejudice in America* (New York: World, 1972).

THE REMOVAL CASES

Expansion and Conflict. The relentless pressure of westward expansion in the first quarter of the nineteenth century brought Euro-Americans and Native Americans into a conflict over who would control territory east of the Mississippi River that had, since long before the colonial period, been controlled by Indians. White Americans were eager to seize land from Native Americans in the Southeast, hoping to transform Indian towns into cotton farms to produce a crop that was then perhaps the most desirable in the Atlantic world. By the late 1820s the contest over land was particularly evident in Georgia, where the discovery of gold in 1828 only heightened whites' desire to push Indians out of the state.

The Civilized Tribes. For much of the colonial and early republican periods Americans of European descent had argued that Indians needed the benefits that European culture could provide. Indians, so Europeans had argued as early as the sixteenth century, needed to be converted to Christianity and to live like Europeans; they needed to learn to read and write and thus lessen their reliance on oral customs and histories; and they needed to become farmers and not act like nomads forever wandering in a primeval forest. In the early nineteenth century, however, many American citizens recognized that the Indians who lived in the Southeast—the Cherokees, Creeks, Choctaws, Chickasaws, and Seminoles—were already living much like their white neighbors. Whites thus labeled these Indians the Five Civilized Tribes. According to whites' perspective, perhaps the most "civilized" of these native peoples were the Cherokees, a group who had a written language (based on a syllabary devised by Sequoyah in 1821), had allowed Baptist missionaries to live in their nation, and possessed a written plan of government for their nation and even, in 1827, a constitution in which they called themselves a "sovereign and independent nation." Various treaties with the U.S. government protected the Cherokee land from intrusion by non-Cherokees.

Georgians' Desires. Although many Americans might have agreed that the Cherokees were living much like Europeans had always wanted Indians to live, residents of Georgia were nonetheless eager to find a reason to expel the Cherokees and other Indians from the state. To do so they argued that the parts of the Cherokee nation that fell within the boundaries of the state were under Georgia's jurisdiction and that the federal government's claim that it alone had power to deal with Indian nations violated the state's sovereignty. Since Georgia was in fact a sovereign state before 1789, the year the U.S. Constitution came into effect, lawyers for the state argued that Georgia's prior sovereignty meant that the United States could not eliminate Georgia's controlling interest. In other words, though Georgians' desires for Cherokee lands were self-serving, the state's attorneys nonetheless articulated their views by asserting their understanding of the U.S. Constitution and its relations to specific states. Once framed in that way the issue became an ideal case for the Supreme Court, a body that (since the case of *Marbury* v. *Madison* in 1803) defined itself as the ultimate interpreter of the Constitution. The legal issue, however, evident as early as 1828, did not become significant until Congress passed the Indian Removal Act on 28 May 1830, a statute that provided "for an exchange of lands with the Indians residing in any of the states or territories, and for their removal west of the river Mississippi."

Jackson's Support. Andrew Jackson, elected to the presidency in 1828, was among the most eager support-

The Trail of Tears (1838–1839) by Robert Lindneux (Woolaroc Museum, Bartlesville, Oklahoma)

ers of removal. His first comments to Congress on the subject came on 8 December 1829—his first address to the governing body—in which he outlined what he perceived were the failures of previous government policies toward American Indians and his belief that Eastern Indians would benefit if they were forced to leave their homelands and move west of the Mississippi River. When Jackson delivered his State of the Union Address in early December 1830, only seven months after passage of the act, he spent much of his time expressing his keen support for removal. Jackson, a longtime foe of various native groups, reveled in what he perceived as the triumph of Europeans in North America. "What good man would prefer a country covered with forests and ranged by a few thousand savages," he asked, "to our extensive Republic, studded with cities, towns, and prosperous farms, embellished with all the improvements which art can devise or industry execute, occupied by more than 12,000,000 happy people, and filled with all the blessings of liberty, civilization, and religion?" Responding to critics who pointed out that forced removal of Eastern Indians was unjust, Jackson declared that the policy sprang from benevolent aspirations on the part of whites. In Jackson's mind removal was the proper policy. "Rightly

considered," he concluded, "the policy of the General Government toward the red man is not only liberal, but generous. He is unwilling to submit to the laws of the States and mingle with their population. To save him from this alternative, or perhaps utter annihilation, the General Government kindly offers him a new home, and proposes to pay the whole expense of his removal and settlement."

Indians and the Constitution. Jackson's logic had little impact on the thousands of Indians who had no desire to leave their homeland. As many Cherokees pointed out, the lands that their nation inhabited not only were theirs historically but also were protected by treaties with the United States. Since the U.S. Constitution defined treaties as part of fundamental law (that is, superior to the acts passed by state or federal legislators), the Cherokees' position seemed to many more valid than the position of the federal government, but what rights did natives have under the U.S. Constitution? The Founders, in Article 1, Section 8, had granted Congress the power to "regulate commerce with foreign nations, and among the several States, and with the Indian tribes." In other words, the rebels who had fought a war to free themselves from what they perceived to be a despotic foreign power had defined the native peoples of North America as non-Americans, lumping them together with citizens of foreign states and thus implicitly denying them the rights that citizens of the United States retained. Further, under this clause in the Constitution, Indians were members of corporate bodies, "tribes," and could not be treated as individuals in courts.

Cherokee Nation v. *Georgia.* The exact constitutional status of American Indians at the time of the Removal Act was in many ways ambiguous. However, a murder case on Cherokee land gave the Supreme Court in 1831 the opportunity to clarify the place of Indians in American law. In the case a Cherokee man named George Tassel was accused of murdering another Cherokee, with all parties agreeing that the murder took place on Cherokee territory. In response the state of Georgia ordered Tassel arrested; he was convicted at his trial, held in a Georgia courthouse, and imprisoned. The state seized jurisdiction on the grounds that the crime had taken place within the state of Georgia. The Cherokees protested, claiming that land on their reservation was under their exclusive jurisdiction. They hired William Wirt to argue their case in federal court, the only venue the Cherokees believed that they had in such an instance. As the case was moving forward, authorities in Georgia executed Tassel. Still, the Cherokees and Wirt pressed their case, with Wirt, a former attorney general for James Monroe and John Quincy Adams, articulating the fundamental constitutional issue: did the state of Georgia have jurisdiction over Cherokee territory and the citizens of the Cherokee nations? In *Cherokee Nation* v. *Georgia,* one of the most important decisions ever rendered by the Supreme Court, Chief Justice John Marshall argued that it could not decide who had jurisdiction because the Cherokee nation had no standing in an American court. In other words, the definition of Indian nations as "foreign nations" in the Constitution deprived natives of any recourse to the courts. Rather than having the right to sue another party for an alleged grievance, the Cherokees (and by extension all Indians who lived on reservations) were, in Marshall's phrasing, a "domestic dependent nation."

Worcester v. *Georgia.* In his decision in the *Cherokee Nation* case Marshall focused his majority opinion only on the question of whether a citizen of the Cherokee nation had standing in a U.S. court; he did not address the related issue of whether a white person—a citizen of the United States—who lived in an Indian nation had standing in a U.S. court. That issue surfaced in 1832, when Samuel Worcester and Elizur Butler, missionaries working for the American Board of Commissioners for Foreign Missions, sued the state of Georgia for refusing to sign an oath demanded by the state for every white who lived in an Indian nation. Though the state had arrested eleven missionaries who had initially refused to sign the oath, by the time the case moved forward nine had been released (either by promising to leave the state or acceding to the state's law), and the cases of Butler and Worcester were combined as *Worcester* v. *Georgia.* In this case Marshall agreed with Worcester's position; by doing so the

There was no American more eager to move the Cherokee Indians from their homeland than President Andrew Jackson. In his State of the Union Address on 6 December 1830 Jackson enumerated the many reasons, in his opinion, removal was in the best interest of all Americans—the Cherokees as well as citizens of the United States:

The waves of population and civilization are rolling to the westward, and we now propose to acquire countries occupied by the red men of the South and West by a fair exchange, and, at the expense of the United States, to send them to a land where their existence may be prolonged and perhaps made perpetual. . . . Our children by thousands yearly leave the land of their birth to seek new homes in distant regions. Does Humanity weep at these painful separations from everything, animate and inanimate, with which the young heart has become entwined? Far from it. It is rather a source of joy that our country affords scope where our young population may range unconstrained in body or in mind, developing the power and faculties of man in their highest perfection. These remove hundreds and almost thousands of miles at their own expense, purchase the lands they occupy, and support themselves at their new homes from the moment of their arrival. Can it be cruel in this Government when, by events which it can not control, the Indian is made discontented in his ancient home to purchase his lands, to give him a new and extensive territory, to pay the expense of his removal, and support him a year in his new abode? How many thousands of our own people would gladly embrace the opportunity of removing to the West on such conditions! If the offers made to the Indians were extended to them, they would be hailed with gratitude and joy.

Source: Andrew Jackson, "State of the Union Address, December 6, 1830," in *The Cherokee Removal: A Brief History with Documents,* edited by Theda Perdue and Michael D. Green (Boston: Bedford Books, 1995), pp. 119–120.

Supreme Court made clear that state laws can have no effect on individuals residing in an Indian nation. In other words, after 1832, in the opinion of the Supreme Court, the ultimate arbiter of constitutional law in the United States, it was impermissible for any state to try to impose its laws on the citizens of any Indian nation, even when the members of that nation had no standing as individuals in a U.S. court.

Cherokee Protest. The two cases handed down by Marshall's court had a mixed legacy for the Cherokees. On the one hand, they were denied the right to have standing in a U.S. court, which meant that their ability to defend themselves in court against the actions of an external state was thereafter limited. On the other hand, the state of Georgia had no jurisdiction over affairs in the Cherokee nation. Al-

In 1831, in the case of *Cherokee Nation* v. *Georgia*, Chief Justice John Marshall had written that the Cherokee nation had no standing in U.S. courts because the Cherokees were a "domestic dependent nation" who had been (along with other Indians) defined by the Constitution as foreign nationals. The following year Marshall clarified his views about the power that a state had in an Indian nation in the case of *Worcester* v. *Georgia*, which sprang initially from the plaintiffs' refusal to sign an oath that the state of Georgia required for all whites who lived in Indian nations. Marshall's ruling in this case had a fundamental impact on American law, particularly his determination that states lacked jurisdiction over matters that took place in Indian nations. In his opinion he argued that states lacked this jurisdiction because historically Indian nations had been separate sovereign entities.

The Cherokee nation, then, is a distinct community, occupying its own territory, with boundaries accurately described, in which the laws of Georgia can have no force, and which the citizens of Georgia have no right to enter, but with the assent of the Cherokees themselves, or in conformity with treaties, and with the acts of Congress. The whole intercourse between the United States and this nation, is, by our Constitution and laws, vested in the government of the United States.

The act of the state of Georgia, under which the plaintiff in error was prosecuted, is consequently void, and the judgment a nullity. Can this Court revise and reverse it?

It is the opinion of this Court that the judgment of the Superior Court for the county of Gwinnett, in the state of Georgia, condemning Samuel A. Worcester to hard labour in the penitentiary of the state of Georga, for four years, was pronounced by that Court under colour of a law which is void, as being repugnant to the Constitution, treaties, and laws of the United States, and ought, therefore, to be reversed and annulled.

Source: United States Supreme Court, "*Worcester* v. *Georgia*, March 1832," in *The Cherokee Removal: A Brief History with Documents*, edited by Theda Perdue and Michael D. Green (Boston: Bedford Books, 1995), pp. 70–75.

moval. Their declaration, like many protests made by or on behalf of the Cherokees during the 1830s rested on the argument that the Cherokees' right to their nation was legal under the U.S. Constitution.

The Trail of Tears. The Cherokees, as their memorial protest of 1836 put it, had "a correct knowledge of their own rights, and they well know the illegality of those oppressive measures which have been adopted for their expulsion, by State authority." Though many Americans—Indians and non-Indians alike—agreed with the legitimacy of the Cherokees' stance against removal, the lesson of the 1830s was nonetheless clear and overpowering. As a result of the *Cherokee Nation* case Indians had no standing in U.S. courts; even though specific states could not pass laws governing the lives of people in Indian nations (the legacy of the *Worcester* case), Indians were powerless to battle the force of the federal government. More significant, though Marshall's decision in the *Worcester* case limited any state's ability to govern Indians in their own nations, Jackson did nothing to prevent the state of Georgia's continued efforts to drive Cherokees off their lands. When the federal government in the late 1830s decided to use armed troops to force thirteen thousand Cherokees westward, there was little that the protesters could do. The rule of law in the United States had no impact on the behavior of those troops or their commanders, whose tactics during the Trail of Tears led to the death of an estimated four thousand Cherokee men, women, and children, many of whom perished for lack of food or adequate clothing. The tragedy of the Trail of Tears went beyond the horrors that the marchers endured. The fact that the federal government could force the Cherokees off their homeland, protected by a treaty with the United States, suggested the limits of any court in the antebellum period to find justice for nonwhites.

Sources:

Joseph C. Burke, "The Cherokee Cases: A Study in Law, Politics, and Morality," *Stanford Law Review*, 21 (1969): 500–531;

Theda Perdue and Michael D. Green, *The Cherokee Removal: A Brief History with Documents* (Boston: Bedford Books, 1995);

Anthony F. C. Wallace, *The Long, Bitter Trail: Andrew Jackson and the Indians* (New York: Hill & Wang, 1993);

Charles F. Wilkinson, *American Indians, Time, and the Law* (New Haven: Yale University Press, 1987).

SQUATTERS' RIGHTS

Land for the Taking. In the 1820s and 1830s thousands of American citizens moved west to find a new life. Many of the emigrants dreamed of owning their own farms, but even though the federal government had gained control of massive parcels of land, thousands of the would-be farmers did not have the money to purchase land when it became available. Faced with the choice of remaining in the East or moving west and taking possession of land without paying for it, many Americans chose the latter course and became squatters. They knew that they would be able to farm their land until the individual who had obtained the title arrived to

though some Cherokees might have celebrated Worcester's victory in 1832, neither of these decisions undermined Congress's Removal Act of 1830. Further, division within the Cherokees over the issue of removal made it more difficult to protest this action of the federal government. During the early 1830s perhaps two thousand Cherokees decided to move west. Others, however, remained and were willing to fight for the right to retain their homeland. Among those who resisted was a group who in June 1836 issued a protest against the tide of re-

dispossess them. To the emigrants the West was vast. Many no doubt believed it was unlikely that the legitimate property owners would arrive at any time in the near future. Often with little more than a dream of owning land, many settlers took their chances and moved to the prairie. When they did so, they broke the law, which defined their actions as trespassing on private property.

Pike Creek. In February 1836 Jason Lothrop, a man with many talents—he was a schoolteacher and Baptist minister among other things—emerged as the leader of a group of squatters in Pike Creek, Wisconsin, a small community on the banks of Lake Michigan. The settlers apparently wanted to apply for a title to sections of the land in the area, but the legal infrastructure was not yet in place for them to do so. Fearing that they might lose their lands and the labor that they put into clearing forests, planting fields, and building houses and fences, the settlers decided to organize themselves. They were responding to the difficulties that they confronted in trying to lay a claim to land in parts of the West. "Some were greedy in securing at least one section of 640 acres for themselves," Lothrop later recalled, "and some as much for all their friends whom they expected to settle in the country."

Pike River Claimants Union. On 13 February 1846 the settlers gathered at a local store and signed a document written by Lothrop. Their treatise, "The Pike River Claimants Union . . . for the attainment and security of titles to claims on Government lands," attempted to establish the legality of the squatters' actions. They began by noting the importance of bonding together since "a union and co-operation of all the inhabitants" of the region would be "indispensably necessary, in case the pre-emption law should not pass, for the securing and protecting" of their claims. In essence the squatters wanted to make sure that their claim to the land was as valid in law as the claims destined to be made by land speculators. The squatters knew that the speculators would have used all of the weapons in their legal arsenals to gain title to this territory as soon as the federal government had completed its survey and a local land office opened to accept applications. The trespassers were not lawless. They based their attempted seizure of the land on the notion that, as their manifesto claimed, the federal "Government has heretofore encouraged emigration by granting pre-emption to actual settlers," which meant that they were "assured that our settling and cultivating the public lands is in accordance with the best wishes of Government."

Rationale. The squatters of Pike Creek were not obeying the law, but at the same time they were doing all they could to make sure that the land, when it became legally available, would be theirs to own. In other words, their actions were extralegal rather than illegal. The Pike Creek squatters' actions mirrored those of many members of the Revolutionary generation who had declared their independence from Britain in order to preserve

rights they believed they possessed under British constitutional law. It is perhaps not surprising, then, that the squatters in this community in southeastern Wisconsin invoked the language of the Revolution when they tried to establish their claim to land there. "We, therefore, as well meaning inhabitants, having in view the promotion of the interest of our settlement," they declared, "and knowing the many advantages derived from unity of feeling and action, do come forward this day, and solemnly pledge ourselves to render each other our mutual assistance, in the protection of our just rights."

Rights of Squatters. Everywhere in the West in the early nineteenth century, white settlers arrived on newly available land before local, state, or federal officials opened it for legal settlement. In some ways those who

CHEROKEE PROTEST

Among the protests offered by members of the Cherokee nation and their allies during the 1830s, few were as effective as those remonstrances that pointed out that many Cherokees' determination to retain their homeland was justified under American law, particularly the U. S. Constitution. That point was clear on 22 June 1836, when a group of Cherokees protested the federal government's continuing efforts to pressure them to move to Indian country:

The Cherokee delegation have thus considered it their duty to exhibit before your honorable body a brief view of the Cherokee case, by a short statement of facts. A detailed narrative would form a history too voluminous to be presented, in a memorial and protest. They have, therefore, contented themselves with a brief recital, and will add, that in reviewing the past, they have done it alone for the purpose of showing what glaring oppressions and sufferings the peaceful and unoffending Cherokees have been doomed to witness and endure. Also, to tell your honorable body, in sincerity, that owing to the intelligence of the Cherokee people, they have a correct knowledge of their own rights, and they well know the illegality of those oppressive measures which have been adopted for their expulsion, by State authority. Their devoted attachment to their native country has not been, nor ever can be, eradicated from their breast. This, together with the implicit confidence, they have been taught to cherish, in the *justice, good faith, and magnamity of the United States*, also, their firm reliance on the generosity and friendship of the American people, have formed the anchor of their hope and upon which alone they have been induced and influenced to shape their peaceful and manly course, under some of the most trying circumstances any people ever have been called to witness and endure.

Source: "Memorial of Protest of the Cherokee Nation, June 22, 1836," in *The Cherokee Removal: A Brief History with Documents*, edited by Theda Perdue and Michael D. Green (Boston: Bedford Books, 1995), pp. 78–82.

moved West into such lands in the nineteenth century were doing something that had been done for generations during the colonial period: moving west to create a farmstead. In colonial times these westward-moving settlers often lived in or near communities of Native American Indians. By the 1820s and 1830s, after the federal government had gained access to territory once owned by Indians, either by treaty or through warfare, white settlers thought that they had a right as citizens of the United States to stake out their tract. Although many were eventually disappointed when surveyors and government officials favored the rights of land speculators over those of squatters, these settlers nonetheless demonstrated two crucial features of life in the West. First, they believed, as the Pike Creek squatters declared, that they had a legal right to gain possession of land in the West even if the federal government did not deed the land to them. Second, though their action was beyond the boundaries of the law, the effort to articulate their beliefs in 1836 demonstrated that westward-moving Americans wanted their own land, but they did not want to inhabit lawless communities. In nascent communities across the plains and the far West, citizens of the United States believed it was necessary to establish the rule of law if they were going to enjoy the rights to property that they so desperately wanted to hold.

Source:
James Willard Hurst, *Law and the Conditions of Freedom in the Nineteenth-Century United States* (Madison: University of Wisconsin Press, 1956).

A circa 1848 daguerreotype of an unknown Texas Ranger in battle dress (Beinecke Rare Book and Manuscript Library, Yale University, New Haven, Connecticut)

VIGILANTE JUSTICE

Crisis and Response. Before civil and judicial institutions could be firmly established, frontier law was often enforced by vigilantes who, without legal authorization, took the law into their own hands. In San Francisco in the 1850s these bodies were known as vigilance committees. The city was a rough-hewn little settlement prior to the discovery of gold in January 1848. Over the course of the next year the Gold Rush drew eighty thousand people to the territory. With them came a wave of competition, greed, overcrowding, fear, violence, and crime that local authorities could not control.

The Public Court. A store robbery in San Francisco's business district in February 1851 left the proprietor, C. J. Jansen, badly beaten. Besides the assault the robbers stole $2,000. The police arrested two Australians for the crime, and an angry crowd quickly gathered. One of the men present, a merchant named William Coleman, led the crowd in demanding the immediate organization of a people's court. Three judges and a twelve-member jury were selected from the crowd, and Coleman acted as prosecutor. Jansen, however, could not positively identify the alleged attackers, and the jury deadlocked. Over the course of the deliberations the crowd's anger diminished. The prisoners were returned to the proper authorities, where they were tried for the crime a second time and convicted in a normal court, but in the aftermath of the original assault and extralegal trial the first vigilance committee remained active for about a month. During that time it carried out four hangings; one man was executed after he was found guilty of attempting to steal a safe. For various other crimes the committee forced twenty-eight men to leave the city and never return.

Mob Justice. Later vigilance committees were just as direct and violent in their methods. By 1855 many San Franciscans had come to believe that an atmosphere of lawlessness had overwhelmed the city, a fearful development helped along by the ineffectiveness of the existing legal system. In November of that year Charles Cora, uncharitably described as an "Italian gambler," murdered a U.S. marshal. Attentive citizens grew increasingly angry when efforts to convict Cora failed. Not long afterward a newspaper editor, known for his attacks on the city's criminal element, was shot to death. Police arrested James Casey for the crime, but the public was not satisfied. The vigilance committee's signal, an engine bell, was rung, attracting a large and formidable mob. Cora and Casey were taken from their cells and hanged in public from the roof of a building.

Vigilante headquarters in San Francisco in 1856 (Society of California Pioneers, San Francisco)

TEXAS RANGERS

The law enforcement group known as the Texas Rangers plays a prominent part in many myths about the West. While Stephen Austin first formed this group in 1823 to organize retaliation against local Indians, not until 24 November 1835 did Texas create the first official group of Texas Rangers. At first, since the Indian policy of Texas president Samuel Austin was friendly, the Rangers did not do much. After the more aggressive reign of Texas president Mirabeau Lamar, during which the Texas Rangers fought many battles with local Mexicans and American Indians, the role of the Rangers shifted toward that of a guerrilla fighting force. When Austin regained the presidency of Texas in 1841, he decided to use the Rangers to protect the Texas frontier.

By his definition, however, the "frontier" in Texas was represented by the incoming Anglo-Americans that Austin had recruited for settlement. Understandably, the indigenous Indians and long-time Mexican residents did not welcome either this encroachment on their lands or the Rangers' often ruthless enforcement of pro-American policies. The Rangers also aroused hostility when they participated in the Mexican War and in their perpetual harassment of non-whites in Texas. In essence the Rangers in these years saw their primary job as defending white ranchers. In this sense the Texas Rangers as a law enforcement unit often caused as many problems as they defused.

Source: Julian Samora, *Gunpowder Justice: A Reassessment of the Texas Rangers* (Notre Dame, Ind.: University of Notre Dame Press, 1979).

The Second Vigilance Committee. The second vigilance committee distinguished itself from the first by being significantly larger (it reportedly had more than six thousand members) and for carrying out part of its agenda by using electoral politics as a weapon. Besides punishing criminals with the rope, the committee dedicated itself to smashing a corrupt political machine led by Democrat David Broderick. Candidates supported by the vigilance committee defeated Broderick's men at the polls. Despite such actions, however, vigilante groups focused most of their attention and energies toward discharging the law whenever and wherever they believed civil and judicial authorities had failed to protect the community. In some places their deliberateness and adherence to legal precedence overturned the simplistic no-

tion that a vigilance committee was nothing more than a euphemism to describe what was in reality a lawless mob. In Payette, Idaho, the committee gave the accused the right to a trial by jury: a body comprised of seven members whose majority decision was final. Their bylaws allowed for only three forms of punishment: banishment, public whipping, and execution. The apparent benefits of such a system, devised for simplicity and efficiency, were undermined by episodes of retribution, which no doubt punished the innocent as well as the guilty.

Sources:

Lawrence M. Friedman, *Crime and Punishment in American History* (New York: Basic Books, 1993);

Richard White, *"It's Your Misfortune and None of My Own": A New History of the American West* (Norman: University of Oklahoma Press, 1991).

HEADLINE MAKERS

ABRAHAM LINCOLN

1809-1865

LAWYER AND PRESIDENT OF THE UNITED STATES

Rails and the West. Before Abraham Lincoln decided to enter electoral politics, a decision that ultimately led to his election as the sixteenth president of the United States in 1860 and his assassination in Ford's Theater in 1865, he rose to prominence as a Western lawyer. During that phase of his life he recognized that railroads were the principle engine of internal development and improvement in the West, a notion that was on the mark. Between 1830 and 1860 railroads provided the most dependable, efficient, and least expensive means of transporting agricultural products, commercial goods, information, and people. Their routes determined whether towns flourished or died. Chicago, Illinois, provided the prime example of the former. As late as 1850 the city had practically no rail lines. Within five years the construction of more than two thousand miles of rail transformed the city into a vital center of transportation, industry, agriculture, and commercial development.

Lucrative Practice. Railroad development placed growing demands on legal institutions. Before routes could be constructed, many legal problems demanded solutions: issues of land and resource rights, franchises and charters, taxation, rights of passengers, finance, consolidation, and incorporation. In Illinois, Lincoln's practice benefited greatly in the mid to late 1850s. All of his political life Lincoln belonged to parties—the Whigs and then the Republicans—that championed national development with federal and state support of internal improvements. Demand for his services, sympathetic political ideology, great legal skill, and personal ambition placed Lincoln among the most important attorneys in the West.

First Railroad Case. Lincoln's first important case for the railroads occurred in 1851, when the Alton and Sangamon Railroad sued James A. Barrett, a landowner and one of the railroad's original stockholders. The company's original plan would have carried the rail line close to Barrett's property, driving up the value of his four thousand acres significantly. A new plan was designed to shorten the route by twelve miles, moving it far away from Barrett's land. To protest this change Barrett refused to pay money owed on the thirty original shares that he purchased. Alton and Sangamon sued for payment and hired Lincoln to represent the company in court. Lincoln was convinced that this railroad was crucial to development in the West, a vital part "in the great chain of railroad communication" uniting the Atlantic coast "with the Mississippi." He argued that a decision for the defendant "might encourage others to stop payments" on their stock subscriptions, stunting the growth of economic development. The Illinois Supreme Court decided in the company's favor. Following the logic of Lincoln's case, Chief Justice Samuel Treat declared that "a few obstinate stockholders should not be permitted to deprive the public and the company of the advantages that will result from a superior and less expensive route." This case established a legal precedent cited in twenty-five subsequent cases throughout the United States.

Illinois Central Cases. In 1852, following his success with the Alton and Sangamon case, Lincoln began taking cases for the Illinois Central Railroad, a company that hoped to lay tracks that would give Chicago quick and reliable transportation to the Gulf of Mexico. The state of Illinois granted the railroad an exemption for all state taxes on the condition that it pay an annual "charter tax." Representatives of McLean County, protested that the state had no right to exempt a company from paying county taxes. The Illinois Central declared that payment of both county taxes and the charter tax would force it into bankruptcy. Lincoln, working for the railroad in the case of *Illinois Central Railroad* v. *the County of McLean,* argued that the exemption was constitutional and should be upheld. The court decided in favor of the Illinois Central in January 1856.

Lincoln Sues the Railroad. Lincoln charged the company $2,000 for his services in this case, a substantial fee at the time. The Illinois Central balked at paying this extraordinary sum to a man it considered to be an obscure frontier lawyer. "This is as much as Daniel Webster himself would have charged," they declared. Lincoln reconsidered his position, then increased his fee to $5,000. When the railroad still refused to fulfill its obligation, he sued. In court Lincoln defended the amount he charged, arguing that the Illinois Central would have paid nearly one hundred times his fees had McLean County won the case. The court decided in Lincoln's favor. Lincoln continued to represent the Illinois Central Railroad over the years that followed.

Land of Rivers. Although working for the railroad companies was lucrative, Lincoln provided services for steamship companies as well. In 1851 he argued a case in which a riverboat sunk after colliding with a bridge on the Illinois River. The defendant, the company that built the bridge, denied responsibility because construction had been authorized by the state of Illinois. Lincoln turned his argument against the state, denying that it had the right "to authorize a total obstruction of a navigable stream" vital to commerce. While the court agreed with Lincoln that the Illinois River should "remain free, clear and uninterrupted," the trial ended in a hung jury. The case was finally settled out of court. In an 1857 case in which another riverboat, the *Effie Afton,* struck a bridge pier and burned, Lincoln tried to reconcile competing interests of the railroad and waterway transportation in-

dustries. Working then for the railroad, Lincoln determined that the accident resulted from a malfunction in one of the steamship's paddle wheels, not because the bridge presented a significant obstruction. While giving the railroads credit for the "astonishing growth of Illinois," Lincoln maintained the importance of the waterways. The jury deadlocked over the decision, and the case was eventually thrown out of court.

Conclusions. Lincoln's biographer David Herbert Donald has stated that Lincoln had "no consistent legal philosophy," nor did he "leave behind him a record of cases that made a major contribution to the development of American legal thought." Quoting Lincoln's law partner, William Herndon, Donald concluded that Lincoln was "purely and entirely a case lawyer." Lincoln's willingness to work for whoever requested his services and contemporary opinion lends substance to this observation. However, the significance of Lincoln's career as a lawyer in service to railroad companies is best understood within the context of national development. In that arena Lincoln's application of legal principles made him a representative agent of Western expansion.

Source:
David Herbert Donald, *Lincoln* (New York: Simon & Schuster, 1995).

ROGER BROOKE TANEY

1777-1864
CHIEF JUSTICE OF THE U.S. SUPREME COURT

Taney in History. Roger Brooke Taney is remembered generally for having authored the majority decision in *Dred Scott* v. *Sandford* (1857), perhaps the single worst decision in the history of the Supreme Court—a "ghastly error" by the reckoning of one important legal scholar. According to a later chief justice, Charles Evans Hughes, *Dred Scott* became one clear example where "the Court . . . suffered severely from self-inflicted wounds." Yet regardless of that notorious decision, a small but formidable body of judicial scholars in the late twentieth century consider Taney to be one of the great justices of the Supreme Court, ranked alongside John Marshall, Louis Brandeis, and Oliver Wendell Holmes.

Background and Early Career. Taney was born in Calvert County, Maryland, in 1777 to an aristocratic planter family. He was educated in rural schools and by a private tutor before attending Dickinson College, where he graduated in 1795. Taney began to practice law in 1799. He was a staunch Federalist, serving first in the Maryland legislature as a member of the House of Delegates, then as a state senator. He broke with his party during the War of 1812 and eventually switched his allegiance to the Democratic Party, led by Andrew Jackson. By the mid 1820s Taney's politics were Jacksonian in nature. He supported states' rights, opposed monopolies, and was the author of Jackson's veto of the act that would have extended the charter of the Bank of the United States. After serving as Jackson's attorney general and briefly as secretary of war, Taney became chief justice of the Supreme Court in 1835.

Chief Justice. Taney was attacked by anti-Jacksonians as a "political hack" who was appointed on partisan grounds rather than merit. Others saw him as an unworthy successor to the great John Marshall, who died in July 1835. Taney's decisions conformed to the Jacksonian vision of the West, including its philosophy of state sovereignty, belief in the sanctity of private property, and defense of slavery. Taney heard a broad spectrum of cases over the course of his tenure, and some of the most significant reflected the controversial movements affecting the nation during a period of national expansion. In *Charles River Bridge* v. *Warren Bridge* (1837) Taney confronted a conflict arising out of the rapid growth of corporations and the impact of such commercial growth on the rights of communities. "While the rights of private property are sacredly guarded," he wrote in the majority decision, "we must not forget that the community also have rights, and that the happiness and well being of every citizen depends on their faithful preservation." The chief justice sought to protect the rights of states to regulate commerce by interpreting the Constitution's commerce clause—which empowered Congress to regulate interstate trade—narrowly. He was a staunch believer that the states were best suited to respond to the great questions that faced the nation.

Slavery. No doubt Taney believed in the fundamental inequality of races and that whites deserved to be dominant over blacks. To Taney's mind African and European Americans could never peacefully coexist in a nation in which both were free and equal. Such a view placed Taney alongside other white Southerners of his age. Yet however racist he might seem in retrospect, Taney freed his own slaves, which he had inherited; though he purchased others, he allowed them to earn manumission through work. He also supported repatriation efforts designed to send blacks back to Africa.

***Dred Scott* Decision.** Taney's decision in *Dred Scott* v. *Sandford* can be traced to his convictions regarding the inherent inferiority of people of color, his previous record as a jurist dealing with the issue of slavery, and his adherence to the doctrines of state rights and limited federal power. Slavery was the single most explosive issue in the nation in 1857, and Taney's intent in drafting the Court's opinion was to settle the matter once and for all. He ruled that African Americans could not be citizens of the United States regardless of whether they were slaves or free people and, further, that under the Constitution slaves were property and like all other property could be transported without restriction. Perhaps most significant, Taney struck down the Missouri Compromise and declared that Congress did not have the power to restrict slavery in the Western territories (on the grounds that territories were not yet states). In the wake of Taney's opinion, which also had the effect of reinforcing the Fugitive Slave Act, legislators in some Northern and Western states passed personal liberty laws to demonstrate their continued belief that any slaves who made it to such areas could remain free.

Later Career. For what remained of his life, Taney could not escape the consequences of *Dred Scott*. Sen. Charles Sumner declared that Taney's name would be "hooted down the page of history." His influence on the Court diminished considerably after 1861. He remained with the Union during the Civil War and attempted, mostly in vain, to uphold the Constitution against some of President Abraham Lincoln's actions. When Lincoln suspended the writ of habeas corpus in April 1861, Taney ruled that the president had acted unlawfully, reminding him of his oath of office and the executive's constitutional duty to faithfully execute the laws. Indicative of both the enormity of the secession crisis and Taney's waning power, Lincoln ignored the bitter and ineffective chief justice. Taney also privately opposed the legality of both the Emancipation Proclamation and conscription. Taney died in Washington, D.C., on 12 December 1864.

Sources:

Paul Finkelman, Dred Scott v. Sandford: *A Brief History with Documents* (Boston: Bedford Books, 1997);

Charles W. Smith, *Roger B. Taney: Jacksonian Jurist* (Chapel Hill: University of North Carolina Press, 1936).

PUBLICATIONS

Joseph Angell, *A Treatise on the Common Law in Relation to Water-courses Intended More Particularly as an Illustration of the Rights and Duties of the Owners and Occupants of Water Privileges: To Which is Added an Appendix, Containing the Principal Adjudged Cases* (Boston: Wells & Lilly, 1824)—an effort to assert the common law on riparian development, but the argument had little power in industrializing America;

Thomas Hart Benton, *Historical and Legal Examination of That Part of the Decision of the Supreme Court of the United States in the* Dred Scott *Case: Which Declares the Unconstitutionality of the Missouri Compromise Act, and the Self-extension of the Constitution to Territories, Carrying Slavery Along with It* (New York: D. Appleton, 1857)—a view of the *Dred Scott* case by one of the most prominent politicians of the antebellum period;

Montgomery Blair, Dred Scott *(a Colored Man) vs.* John F. A. Sandford. *Argument of Montgomery Blair, of Counsel for the Plaintiff in Error* (Washington, D.C.: Gideon, 1857)—the views of one of the principal players in the *Dred Scott* decision;

George Caines, *An Enquiry Into the Law Merchant of the United States, or,* Lex mercatoria americana: *On Several Heads of Commercial Importance: Dedicated by Permission to Thomas Jefferson, President of the United States,* 2 volumes (New York: Isaac Collins & Son, 1802)—the first book published in the United States dealing with commercial law;

The Case of Dred Scott in the United States Supreme Court. The Full Opinions of Chief Justice Taney and Justice Curtis, and Abstracts of the Opinions of the Other Judges; With an Analysis of the Points Ruled, and Some Concluding Observations (New York: H. Greeley, 1860);

Daniel Chipman, *An Essay on the Law of Contracts for the Payment of Specific Articles; With a Supplement by D. B. Eaton* (Burlington, Vt.: C. Goodrich, 1852)—the author argued for the importance of the market in determining the value of goods in a contract: "Let money be the sole standard in making all contracts.";

Thomas Cooper, *An Introductory Lecture to a Course of Law* (Columbia, S.C.: Telescope Office, 1834)—a pamphlet by a prominent political theorist;

Nathan Dane, *A General Abridgement and Digest of American Law,* 9 volumes (Boston: Cummings & Hilliard, 1823–1829);

Stephen A. Douglas, *Kansas—Utah—Dred Scott Decision: A Speech of the Hon. S. A. Douglas Delivered at Springfield, Illinois, June 12, 1857* (Springfield, Ill.: Lanphier & Walker, 1857)—an excellent example of a political speech delivered by a leading politician that dealt with the West and was published and distributed in that region;

E. N. Elliott, *Cotton Is King, and Pro-slavery Arguments: Comprising the Writings of Hammond, Harper, Christy, Stringfellow, Hodge, Bledsoe, and Cartwright, on This Important Subject* (Augusta, Ga.: Pritchard, Abbott & Loomis, 1860)—one of several political pamphlets issued by Southerners in the late antebellum period dealing with issues fundamental to the economy of the South and the Southwest. Sen. James Henry Hammond, one of the authors, was among the most famous Southern politicians of the age and in a speech to the Senate on 4 March 1858, issued the famous declaration: "You dare not make war on cotton—no power on earth dares make war upon it. Cotton is king.";

David Hoffman, *A Course of Legal Study,* 2 volumes (Baltimore: J. Neal, 1836);

Benjamin C. Howard, *Report of the Decision of the Supreme Court of the United States, and the Opinions of the Judges Thereof, in the Case of Dred Scott versus John F. A. Sandford, December Term, 1856* (Washington, D.C.: C. Wendell, 1857)—a version of the original opinions in one of the most famous cases ever handed down by the U.S. Supreme Court;

James Kent, *Commentaries on American Law,* 4 volumes (New York: O. Halsted, 1826–1830)—a summary of the principles of a former chief judge of the New York Supreme Court, with much attention to commercial law;

Laws of the Cherokee Nation Adopted by the Council at Various Periods: Printed for the Benefit of the Nation (Talequah, Cherokee Nation: Cherokee Advocate Office, 1852);

Laws of the Cherokee Nation, Passed during the Years 1838–1867 (St. Louis: Democrat Print, 1868)—the Indian nation's laws enacted in the period of removal and in Oklahoma;

Theophilus Parsons, *The Law of Contracts,* 2 volumes (Boston: Little, Brown, 1853–1855)—one of the central texts from the mid nineteenth century dealing with the importance of contracts in American society, by the younger Parsons (his father, with the same name, had been chief justice of the Massachusetts Supreme Court), who also wrote *Maritime Law* (1859) and *Outlines of the Religion and Philosophy of Swedenborg* (1875);

Joseph Story, *Commentaries on the Constitution of the United States,* 2 volumes (Boston: Little, Brown, 1858)—the views of one of the preeminent American jurists of his age who served as associate justice on the U.S. Supreme Court from 1811 to 1845, during which time he was also teaching a generation of lawyers at Harvard Law School;

Story, *Commentaries on Equity Jurisprudence as Administered in England and America* (Boston: Hilliard, Gray, 1836)—a central text in the evolving law of contracts in the United States;

Story, *Life and Letters of Joseph Story, Associate Justice of the Supreme Court of the United States, and Dane Professor of Law at Harvard University, Edited by His Son William W. Story,* 2 volumes (Boston: Little, Brown, 1851);

William Wetmore Story, *A Treatise on the Law of Contracts,* 2 volumes (Boston: Little, Brown, 1856)—the repeated publication of this book by the son of Joseph Story (the first edition had appeared in 1844) signaled the wide acceptance within the United States of the modern form of contract law; the younger Story, for his part, eventually settled in Rome, where he studied sculpture and became a close friend of many nineteenth-century luminaries including Nathaniel Hawthorne and Robert and Elizabeth Barrett Browning;

Zephaniah Swift, *A Digest of the Law of Evidence in Civil and Criminal Cases. And a Treatise on Bills of Exchange and Promissory Notes* (Hartford: Oliver D. Cooke, 1810)—a tract by the former chief justice of Connecticut that argued that business was "governed by the customs and usages of nations, and not by municipal law";

Roger Brooke Taney, *Opinions of the Judges of the Supreme Court of the United States in the Case of the* Proprietors of Charles River Bridge *vs.* the Proprietors of Bridge and Others, *at the January Term of the Court, 1837* (Boston, 1837)—opinions in a case that had far-reaching implications for the economic development of much of the United States, including the West;

St. George Tucker, *Blackstone's Commentaries: With Notes of Reference to the Constitution and Laws of the Federal Government of the United States and of the Commonwealth of Virginia: In Five Volumes: With an Appendix to Each Volume Containing Short Tracts Upon Such Subjects as Appeared Necessary to Form a Connected View of the Laws of Virginia,* 5 volumes (Philadelphia: W. Y. Birch & A. Small, 1803)—an American version of the famous English jurist's views on the law;

Gulian C. Verplanck, *An Essay on the Doctrine of Contracts* (New York: G. & C. Carvill, 1825)—one of the most original and significant new interpretations of the law of contracts in antebellum America.

LIFESTYLES, SOCIAL TRENDS, FASHION, SPORTS, & RECREATION

by MARTHA K. ROBINSON

CONTENTS

Sidebars and tables are listed in italics.

1800

- The sport of gouging is at its peak of popularity in the Ohio River valley.

- The population of North America reaches an estimated thirteen million.

1 May — Congress creates the Indiana and Ohio Territories.

1 Oct. — Spain cedes the Louisiana Territory to France in the secret Treaty of San Ildefonso.

1801

- Through the efforts of Thomas Jefferson some Native Americans receive a smallpox vaccine.

1802

- The Spanish colonial administrator of New Orleans prohibits American use of the port.

1803

1 Mar. — Ohio is admitted as the seventeenth state in the Union.

30 Apr. — The United States pays approximately $15 million for the Louisiana Purchase.

1805

- Tenskwatawa, the Shawnee Prophet, awakes from a trance and begins to prophesy.
- Congress creates the Michigan Territory from part of the Old Northwest Territory.

1806

- The fur trade between the United States and China is worth more than $5 million annually. The United States exchanges ginseng and furs for tea, spices, china, and other goods.

1807

- The *Clermont* begins regular steamboat service on the Hudson River.

1809

- Sequoyah begins work on a syllabary to create a written form of the Cherokee language.

1810

- The American Board of Commissioners for Foreign Missions is created.

23 June   Wilson Price Hunt and a band of fur traders establish the first permanent U.S. settlement on the Pacific Coast, at Fort Astoria in modern Oregon.

1811

- Steamboats begin to travel on the Mississippi River.
- The Cumberland Road opens from Cumberland, Maryland, to Wheeling, West Virginia. It will eventually extend to St. Louis, Missouri, becoming the major westward road for settlers.

1813

5 Oct.   Tecumseh dies at the Battle of the Thames.

1814

- The journals of Meriwether Lewis and William Clark are published.

1816

11 Dec.   Indiana joins the Union as the nineteenth state.

1817

4 July   Construction begins on the Erie Canal.

10 Dec.   Mississippi joins the Union as the twentieth state.

1818

3 Dec.   Illinois joins the Union as the twenty-first state.

1819

- Congress organizes the Arkansas Territory from areas of the Missouri Territory.

1820

- Cherokees create a republican government with a principal chief, a senate, and a house of representatives.

1821

- Mexico becomes independent from Spain.
- William Becknell opens the Santa Fe Trail.

10 Aug.   Missouri enters the Union as the twenty-fourth state.

1822

- Stephen Austin founds the first American community in Texas.

1824

- Jedediah Smith, an American mountain man, and Thomas Fitzpatrick, a fur trapper, cross the Rocky Mountains through the South Pass. Their crossing initiates regular use of the Oregon Trail.
- The Bureau of Indian Affairs is created by the federal government.

1825

- William Ashley organizes the Green River Rendezvous for fur trappers.

26 Oct. The Erie Canal opens.

1826

5 Feb. Led by Robert Owen, a utopian socialist community at New Harmony, Indiana, draws up a constitution.

1827

- Cherokees draw up a written constitution.

15 Nov. Creek Indians cede their remaining lands to the U.S. government.

1829

- Mexico abolishes slavery.

1830

- Over the next decade, artists George Catlin, Carl Bodmer, and Alfred Jacob Miller travel in the West.
- Mexico closes Texas to further American immigration.

30 June Congress passes the Indian Removal Act.

1831

- The Supreme Court rules in *Cherokee Nation* v. *Georgia* that the Cherokees have a legal right to their own lands.
- Catharine Beecher publishes *A Course of Calisthenics for Young Ladies*, encouraging exercise for women to prepare them for their roles as wives and mothers.

1832

- A cholera epidemic strikes the United States, killing some six thousand in New Orleans and unknown numbers among the Plains tribes.
- In *Worcester* v. *Georgia* the Supreme Court holds that the Cherokee nation has not given up its right to control its own territory.

1833

- John Deere invents the first American steel plow.

1834

- A Protestant mission opens in Oregon's Willamette Valley.
- Cyrus McCormick patents the mechanical reaper.

1835

- Western wheat crops fail.

1836

- Congress organizes the Wisconsin Territory.

2 Mar.   Texas declares independence from Mexico and adopts a constitution.

15 June   Arkansas joins the Union as the twenty-fifth state.

22 Oct.   Sam Houston becomes the first president of the Republic of Texas.

Nov.   The Shawnee Prophet, Tenskwatawa, dies in Kansas.

1837

- Epidemic diseases strike the Plains tribes.

26 Jan.   Michigan joins the Union as the twenty-sixth state.

1838

1 Oct.   The removal of the Cherokees begins. By the time they reach their destination in the Indian Territory, some four thousand will have died.

1839

- *The Boy's and Girl's Book of Sports* is published in Providence, Rhode Island. It includes rules for games such as tag, jump rope, and "base," or "goal ball."

1840

- Birling, in which contestants on a floating log try to keep their balance while spinning the log with their feet, is a popular sport in lumber camps in Canada and the Northern states.

- Over the next twenty years Norwegian immigrants introduce skiing to the United States.

1841

- The Preemption Law recognizes squatters' rights to land.

- *Schreiner's Sporting Manual: A Complete Treatise on Fishing, Fowling, and Hunting, as Applicable to the Country* is published in Philadelphia.

1843

12 July   Joseph Smith announces that he has had a divine revelation sanctioning polygamy.

1844

- A mob in Illinois kills Joseph Smith and his brother Hiram.

1845

- Congress votes to annex Texas, which joins the Union as a slave state.

1846

- Mormon migration to Utah begins.

- John C. Frémont proclaims the Bear Flag Republic in California.

- Congress ends joint occupation of Oregon.

13 May   Congress declares war on Mexico.

10 Sept.   Elias Howe receives a patent for his sewing machine.

Dec.   A winter storm traps a group of settlers led by Jacob and George Donner in the Sierra Nevada mountain range of California. By the following February only 45 of the original 87 members are alive. The survivors had practiced cannibalism on those who had died.

28 Dec.   Iowa joins the Union as the twenty-ninth state.

1847

- Cayuse Indians kill Marcus and Narcissa Whitman.

- Mormons arrive in Utah and found Salt Lake City.

1848

- The Treaty of Guadalupe Hidalgo is signed, ending the Mexican War and adding 1.2 million square miles of land to the United States.
- Friedrich Hecker founds the first American Turnverein, a gymnastic and social club, in Cincinnati.

24 Jan.   James Wilson Marshall discovers gold at Sutter's Mill, about forty-five miles northeast of Sacramento, California.

2 Feb.   California becomes a U.S. territory.

29 May   Wisconsin joins the Union as the thirtieth state.

1849

- A major cholera epidemic strikes the United States.
- California applies for admission to the Union as a free state.

1850

- Scandinavian gold miners in California form the first ski clubs in the United States.

2 June   A series of fires destroys several million dollars worth of property in San Francisco.

1851

- Cornelius Vanderbilt establishes a steamship route from New York City to California.

1852

- Congress establishes the Oregon Territory.

1853

- A San Francisco club introduces the Irish sport of hurling to the United States.
- A yellow-fever epidemic kills more than five thousand in New Orleans.

1854

- The Kansas-Nebraska Act opens the Kansas and Nebraska territories to popular sovereignty on the issue of slavery.

1855

- Violence erupts over the expansion of slavery in "Bleeding Kansas."

1856

•	Mormon leaders furnish handcarts to immigrants who intend to cross the plains.
24 May	John Brown and his sons kill five proslavery men at Pottawatomie Creek in Kansas.

1857

•	U.S. troops are sent to Utah to put down a Mormon rebellion.
•	An expedition led by Albert Sidney Johnston and guided by James Bridger explores the Yellowstone River valley.

1858

•	John Butterfield opens an overland stage route.
2 May	Marathon horse riding is the craze in California. John Powers rides 150 miles on a racetrack in 6 hours, 43 minutes, and 31 seconds. He uses twenty-five mustangs and wins a $5,000 bet.
11 May	Minnesota enters the United States as the thirty-second state.

1859

•	Mining operations increase in Nevada and Colorado.
•	Painter Albert Bierstadt travels through the Rocky Mountains.
14 Feb.	Oregon enters the Union as the thirty-third state.

1860

22 Feb.	The first known organized baseball game is played in San Francisco.
3 Apr.	William F. Cody (Buffalo Bill) leaves St. Joseph, Missouri, carrying mail on the Pony Express.
6 May	San Franciscans found The Olympic Club of San Francisco, the oldest American club dedicated to athletics.

OVERVIEW

The Old West. For white Americans in the early nineteenth century the West represented many things. For some it offered adventure or a chance to get rich quick; for others, the opportunity to own land. The stock figures of the Old West remain in American memory: the mountain man, the hardy pioneer, the immigrant on the Overland Trail, the gambler, and the gold miner. However, when Americans advanced into what they thought of as wilderness, they were entering a land with a long history. For uncounted generations Native American peoples had created their own cultures and told their own stories about the land on which they lived. Whites and Native Americans sometimes met peacefully, but more often disease and warfare took a heavy toll on the original inhabitants of the West. The West was also home to Spanish and Mexican settlers. Texas, New Mexico, Arizona, and California would become states of the Union, but in 1800 they were claimed by Spain. They would in turn pass to Mexico, which gained its independence in 1821. Conflicts between expansionist Americans and Mexicans would eventually lead to war.

Travel. Americans who sought to go west expected the trip to be difficult. By 1860 railroads extended from the East to Chicago, Cincinnati, St. Joseph, St. Louis, and Memphis, but travel was still time-consuming. Rail gauges were not standardized, requiring the loading and unloading of cargo. Delays were common, and rail travel was still too expensive for many Americans. The first transcontinental railroad would be completed in 1869, but until then Americans who wanted to go from the East to the Rocky Mountains or Pacific relied on human and animal power. The 250,000 to 500,000 individuals who traveled on the overland trails anxiously watched the health of their horses and livestock as they crossed the plains and mountains.

Hardships. Life was often precarious for the peoples of the West. Native Americans feared disease, enemy attacks, drought, and hunger. They also faced the pressing problem of white immigration into the West. Trade, diplomacy, and warfare all seemed unable to slow the influx of Americans onto the plains. The Mexican and Spanish residents of the Southwest faced some of the same problems. Americans who moved into Texas brought an assumption of superiority with them, and tensions sometimes flared into violence. Americans in the West, like other peoples, faced hardships. Western farmers suffered through drought and dust storms while cholera epidemics devastated the wagon trains. Miners found cold and poverty more often than they found gold. Settlers in the West also suffered from loneliness and missing friends and family left behind.

Social Life and Sport. The inhabitants of the West faced hardships, but they also enjoyed social gatherings and sports. Observers commented on the wide variety of games played by Native Americans. Native Americans enjoyed lacrosse, shinny, and games of chance. White settlers seldom played the team sports that were gaining popularity in the East. Rather than baseball, for example, Westerners favored rough-and-tumble sports such as wrestling and gouging. Shooting contests were also popular as men sought to prove their skills. Women found fewer opportunities for sport although they were sometimes able to socialize in bees and "frolics."

Diversity. The daily life of the peoples of the West reflected their diversity. A Native American in the West might belong to a people who followed the buffalo herds on the plains and praised the virtues of warriors. On the other hand, he or she might live in a relatively peaceful community in California or the Southwest. A Tlingit from the coast of what is now Alaska would have little in common with an Apache from the Southwest or a Crow from the plains. The cultures of Native Americans were not static. Members of various communities traded, fought, and intermarried with others despite vast differences in language and culture. The descendants of Europeans who came west had more similarities, but their cultures were also diverse. Recent emigrants from Germany and Ireland mingled with Kentuckians and residents of Santa Fe. For the white Americans who went west in great numbers, however, diversity was not a goal. They envisioned a West transformed by Euro-American hands, one that had little room for Native Americans or Mexicans.

TOPICS IN THE NEWS

EVERYDAY LIFE: AMERICAN SETTLERS

Fur Trappers. In the early nineteenth century, beaver hats were at the height of fashion for men. To obtain beaver pelts, trappers traveled into the mountains in small parties during the spring and fall. A typical trapper carried about half a dozen traps, seldom more, for the traps were heavy. The traps, which were forged by hand, cost the fur companies $2.00 to $2.50 each but were sold to trappers at $12.00 apiece. To catch a beaver, the trapper set traps in a stream and baited them with castor, an oily substance derived from beaver glands. Great care was taken to ensure that the beaver would not be able to detect human scent. If the trap was set properly, the beaver would drown, although escaped beavers and lost traps were not uncommon. Once dead, the beaver could be skinned on the spot or taken to camp. The trapper cut off the head, feet, and tail of the animal and then skinned it. The skin was stretched into a circle to dry by one of two methods. The first method was to lace the skin within a circular hoop, although learning how to make such a hoop took practice. Alternatively, the skin might be stretched on pegs driven into the ground. After two to five days of drying, the skins were ready to be marked and packed for sale.

The Prairie. In the early nineteenth century Sugar Creek, Illinois, was a typical Western community. Most of the area residents had moved from Southern states, including Kentucky, Tennessee, Virginia, and the Carolinas. They came hoping to acquire land and establish self-sufficient farms. These settlers valued individualism, but they also relied on a network of kin and neighbors and shared a sense of community obligation. Individuals who owned scarce tools or materials were expected to allow others to use them. Farmers hunted in woodlands owned by other settlers, and hogs roamed freely. The settlers recognized the rights of squatters to land they had cleared and planted and prevented challenges to such customarily accepted rights. If, for example, a land speculator tried to bid for a squatter's land, he was liable to be physically knocked down by local settlers. Settlers also gathered together, combining work and play in bees and frolics. An English visitor to Illinois in

A photograph of an Iowa log house in the 1850s (Iowa State Historical Museum, Des Moines, Iowa)

1819–1820 recorded that the Americans he met did much of their work together. The men, he wrote, "have husking, reaping [and] rolling frolics" while the women met "to pick cotton from the seeds, make clothes, or quilt quilts." Regardless of the kind of frolic, whiskey and dancing were always popular at the end of the day. One early settler, Elizabeth McDowell Hill, recalled a "spinning frolic" in which two young ladies competed for the affections of a young man. "They began at six in the morning and spun until six in the evening," she recalled. "At six o'clock Nancy was thirty rounds ahead. Forever afterward the fair Sarah had to look elsewhere for her swain."

Marriage and Women's Work. Folk songs and poems of the early nineteenth century sometimes reflected a view of marriage as less a romantic tie than an economic partnership. The happy marriage, according to folk wisdom, had to be founded on the practical and reciprocal skills of husband and wife. A part of a doggerel from Illinois suggests that romantic love was not always expected to last long in a marriage:

> First month, honey month,
> Next month like pie;
> Third month, you dirty bitch,
> Get out and work like I.

Women had few conveniences in Western settlements, but their labor was indispensable for maintaining a successful farm. Women were responsible for child care, meals, and cleaning. They carded, spun, wove cloth, and made nearly all of the family clothing. In addition they kept gardens; made towels, soap, candles and other necessities; and cared for cattle. The women of Sugar Creek also had large families: those born before 1810 who lived past age forty-five raised on average more than eight children. Of these children, one or two would probably die before reaching adulthood.

Sources:

John Mack Faragher, *Sugar Creek: Life on the Illinois Prairie* (New Haven: Yale University Press, 1986);

Faragher, *Women and Men on the Overland Trail* (New Haven: Yale University Press, 1979);

Daniel D. Muldoon, "Daily Life of the Mountain Trapper," *Journal of the West*, 26 (October 1987): 14–20;

John Woods, "Two Years' Residence in the Settlement on the English Prairie, in the Illinois Country, United States," in *Early Western Travels, 1748–1846*, volume 10, edited by Reuben Gold Thwaites (Cleveland: Arthur H. Clark, 1904), p. 300.

EVERYDAY LIFE: NATIVE AMERICANS

Diversity. In 1800 the United States contained only sixteen states. Vermont, Kentucky, and Tennessee had joined the original thirteen in the 1790s, but the young nation was still bounded on the west by the Mississippi River and on the south by Spanish Florida. Both within the United States and in the lands that it would acquire lived indigenous people who called the land their own. Americans called these people Indians, but the name concealed the diversity of the native peoples. Native Americans were not politically united and did not view themselves as one people. They had created many cultures and spoke hundreds of languages. These cultures were not static. Rather they were constantly changing as native peoples traded and fought with each other, mi-

WATERLILY

Waterlily is Ella Cara Deloria's fictional portrayal of a Sioux family in the middle of the nineteenth century, in the years before sustained contact with whites. After Waterlily, the protagonist, suffered a serious illness as a child, her stepfather, Rainbow, promised to hold a *hunka*, or "child-beloved," ceremony for her. In this passage Deloria describes the dress of a child-beloved.

When enough elk teeth were on hand . . . Dream Woman made the gown; and it was something to behold. . . . As usual, Dream Woman had dreamed an original design. It was worked into the wide border of embroidery that topped the heavy fringe around the bottom of the skirt and of the loose, open sleeves. The matched teeth, which had been painstakingly polished to a high luster by the grandfather . . . were appliqued in pleasing groups all over the upper half of the gown, above the belt and down over the sleeves. The gown was exactly alike both front and back.

Two whole years were spent in getting ready for the ceremony. . . . But at last the great day arrived. At dawn Gloku [Waterlily's grandmother] began to prepare special foods for the *hunka* candidate and fed her as the sun appeared. Then Blue Bird [her mother] bathed her at the stream and washed and oiled her long hair until it shone. She braided it in two long braids in the usual style and tied on the new hair ties that were part of the special outfit. They were fragrant, for Dream Woman had made colorfully embroidered balls and stuffed them with perfume leaf, and these were attached to the ties.

The new gown and the necklace and belt and bracelet were put on Waterlily, and some long, wide pendants of tiny shells were hung from her ears. Though they were so heavy that they pulled the small lobes down, elongating them, Waterlily knew they must be endured for beauty's sake. Last of all, the new moccasins of solid red quillwork with matching leggings went on. A detail of the dreamed design on the gown was here skillfully repeated, making of the entire costume a charming harmony. And not only the tops but also the soles of the moccasins were covered with quillwork. This seemed extravagant and unnecessary, and Waterlily ventured to say so. "When I walk, I shall quickly break the quills and ruin the soles." Her aunt Dream Woman replied, "But you will not walk." Then she told the girl that child-beloved moccasins for the *hunka* were always decorated so, and that one did not walk to the ceremonial tipi; one was carried.

Source: Ella Cara Deloria, *Waterlily* (Lincoln: University of Nebraska Press, 1988), pp. 74–75.

A carved Tlingit pipe, circa 1800 (Museum of the American Indian, Heye Foundation, New York)

grated into lands new to them, and assimilated foreigners and captives into their worlds.

The Pueblos. By the 1500s, when the Spanish first encountered them in what is now the U.S. Southwest, the Pueblo Indians had been settled in farming communities for hundreds of years. Pueblos grew corn, beans, and squash in irrigated fields, made pottery in various

A Tlingit coat, woven from goat hair (Portland Art Museum, Oregon)

styles, and traded for ornaments made of copper and shell. Men wore shirts, kilts, and loincloths made of deerskin or cotton. They also wore sandals or leather moccasins. Women wore a kind of wraparound dress, belted at the waist and fastened over the right shoulder, leaving the left arm bare. They also wore a square piece of cloth that tied under the chin and hung down the back. Women sometimes went barefoot and sometimes wore high boots made of whitened deerskin. Both men and women wore their hair long. Travelers frequently commented on the distinctive hairstyle worn by unmarried Pueblo women, in which they gathered their hair into large whorls on either side of the head. Despite cultural similarities among the various Pueblo towns, there were considerable differences. The Pueblo towns were not politically united, and the languages of many towns were mutually unintelligible. The Tanoans, for example, spoke a language related to Kiowa while the members of some western Pueblos spoke a language related to those spoken in the Great Basin. The Keresans' language was apparently unrelated to any known language.

The Spanish. By 1800 the Pueblo Indians had a long history of contact with Europeans. During the late sixteenth and seventeenth centuries the Spanish had colonized the region. Spanish priests and friars tried to eradicate the native religion of the Pueblos while both religious and secular leaders exploited Pueblo labor. In the Pueblo Revolt of 1680 the Indians expelled the Spanish. They would remain independent for the next twelve years only, but when the Spanish returned, they tempered their demands on the Indians' labor and beliefs. By 1800 most Pueblo Indians outwardly conformed to the religious demands of the friars, but older religious traditions remained strong.

The Mandans. When the nineteenth century began, the Mandans were farmers, hunters, and traders. Their

Members of the Mandan White Buffalo Cow sorority, circa 1834 (American Museum of Natural History, New York)

villages along the upper Missouri River valley were at the center of a trade network that extended from Mexico to Canada and as far west as the Pacific Ocean. Among the Mandans men hunted, fought, and were responsible for most religious ceremonies. Women tilled the fields, produced food and clothing, and built and owned the earth lodges in which the people lived. Meriwether Lewis and William Clark spent the winter of 1804–1805 with the Mandans, and Americans and Mandans remained on good terms until a smallpox epidemic in 1837 killed 90 percent of the tribe.

Clothing. Mandan clothing resembled that of other plains tribes. Men commonly wore a buffalo robe, sometimes with a leather tunic and loincloth. They also wore moccasins and deerskin leggings. These clothes were often plain, but on ceremonial occasions Mandan men wore clothing decorated with porcupine quills, beads, and fur. Women wore long dresses with fringes or scalloping at the hem. They also wore moccasins with leggings that reached from ankle to knee. Like the men, women wore more-highly decorated clothing on special occasions. Both men and women wore their hair long. Men usually braided their hair, which might be worn in various styles, and often added brown or red clay to it. Women wore their hair loose or braided and parted it in the center; they painted the part red with vermillion.

Religious Beliefs. The Mandans, like members of other tribes, tried to live in a relationship of respect with the land and with nonhuman life. Daily life and special occasions required rituals meant to create a correct relationship with the supernatural. Men and women fasted and offered sacrifices to gain the protection of super-

natural protectors. In the Okipa ceremony, for example, young men endured torture to help ensure the return of the buffalo and the welfare of the people. In this ritual young men's backs or chests were slit open, and wooden skewers were inserted beneath the skin. Thongs were attached to the skewers, and the young men were suspended from tall poles by the thongs until they fainted. Certain tribal members also held sacred bundles, which might belong either to an individual or to the tribe as a whole. These sacred bundles held items of symbolic significance. Maintaining and caring for a bundle was a complicated process, and children who might expect to inherit one someday began learning how to maintain the bundle at a young age. Although the Mandans belonged to matrilineal clans, the bundles were passed down to the eldest male heirs of these clans.

The Tlingits. The Tlingits lived on the mainland and islands of what is now British Columbia and the southeastern Alaska panhandle. They did not have a central political body, such as a council or chief. Instead local communities were composed of members of several clans. These clans were matrilineal and divided into two larger moieties, Raven and Wolf. With the exception of foreign slaves, every member of Tlingit society belonged to one moiety or the other.

Social Organization. Tlingit society was hierarchical. Each clan had a nobility, made up of the headmen of clans or lineages and their families. More-distant relations were commoners; slaves, sometimes taken in warfare, were outside the social system. The clan, not the Tlingits as a whole or the moiety, held rights to land, and clan headmen had considerable authority. They could,

George Catlin's 1837–1839 oil painting *Bird's-eye View of the Mandan Village, Eighteen Hundred Miles above Saint Louis* (National Museum of American Art, Smithsonian Institution, Washington, D.C.)

for example, have trespassers killed, make rules regarding hunting and fishing, and hold elaborate ceremonies in honor of deceased family members. Clans and lineages possessed crests that represented their totems. These crests, which might portray (among other things) animals, birds, or heroes, appeared on graves, dishes, totem poles, blankets, and other objects.

Childhood and Puberty. Young boys among the Tlingits began training for adult life at the age of seven or eight. At that point a boy went to live with his maternal uncle, who began teaching him to endure hardships of various kinds. The uncle also taught him hunting, magic, and the traditions of his clan and lineage. Girls endured a difficult passage to adulthood. A girl's conduct during her first menstruation was considered particularly important since it had implications for her future. She endured an eight-day fast and was confined to a dark cellar or room for a time after her first menstruation. The ideal time for this confinement was two years although its length varied depending on rank. During this time her father's sister and other female relatives taught her the traditions of the clan.

Villages. Tlingit villages were usually occupied only in the summer. In the winter families left the village to hunt and fish independently. A good village site included a sheltered bay, a beach, and access to water, timber, and other resources. A village contained large houses, each of which held roughly forty to fifty people. Each house had a central fire, and families within the house occupied positions of more or less honor. The highest-ranking family held the rooms at the back of the house while slaves slept near the front door. A clan crest might be painted on the front of the house.

Sources:

Frederica De Laguna, "Tlingit," in *Handbook of North American Indians*, volume 7, *Northwest Coast*, edited by Wayne Suttles (Washington, D.C.: Smithsonian Institution, 1990), pp. 203–228;

Edward P. Dozier, *The Pueblo Indians of North America* (New York: Holt, Rinehart & Winston, 1970);

Dayton Duncan and Ken Burns, *Lewis and Clark* (New York: Knopf, 1997);

Fred Eggan, "Pueblos: Introduction," in *Handbook of North American Indians*, volume 9, *Southwest*, edited by Alfonso Ortiz (Washington, D.C.: Smithsonian Institution, 1979), pp. 224–235;

Roy W. Meyer, *The Village Indians of the Upper Missouri: The Mandans, Hidatsas, and Arikaras* (Lincoln: University of Nebraska Press, 1977);

Virginia Bergman Peters, *Women of the Earth Lodges: Tribal Life on the Plains* (New Haven: Archon, 1995);

Virginia More Roediger, *Ceremonial Costumes of the Pueblo Indians: Their Evolution, Fabrication, and Significance in the Prayer Drama* (Berkeley: University of California Press, 1961);

Marc Simmons, "History of Pueblo-Spanish Relations to 1821," in *Handbook of North American Indians*, volume 9, *Southwest*, edited by Ortiz (Washington, D.C.: Smithsonian Institution, 1979), pp. 178–193.

An 1849 sketch of the Laguna Pueblo, forty-five miles west of Albuquerque, New Mexico (Peabody Museum, Harvard University, Cambridge, Massachusetts)

EVERYDAY LIFE: SPANISH AND MEXICAN SETTLERS

Spanish America. When Americans headed west in the nineteenth century, they were not entering "virgin land." Native Americans, of course, had lived in the West for thousands of years, but Spanish settlers and their descendants had also lived there for two centuries. Much of the area that would become the American West was part of the viceroyalty of New Spain when the nineteenth century opened. Although Indians had inhabited the territory for countless generations, the area was not densely populated. Many colonists regarded the region as a distant backwater of an empire centered in Spain. In 1800 a Spanish mining engineer commented that the people of central Mexico "speak with as much ignorance about the regions immediately to the north as they might about Constantinople." Despite their relatively small numbers, colonists in California, New Mexico, and Texas created a distinctive culture marked by social hierarchy and patterns of deference.

Stereotypes. Citizens of the United States and Spanish and Mexican settlers often regarded each other with hostility. Americans regarded the Spanish and Mexican inhabitants of the region as ignorant, lazy, and superstitious. Spanish observers, for their part, commented unfavorably on the Americans who entered the region. After Mexico ceded California, New Mexico, and Texas to the United States in the Treaty of Guadalupe Hidalgo in 1848, these stereotypes did not disappear, and hostility remained. In later years some Americans would reverse the value judgment of the stereotype. Rather than condemning the Spanish and Mexican colonists of California as lazy, they would look back on an imagined golden era of carefree, gracious, and welcoming Spanish settlers.

Women's Fashions. In the early nineteenth century, women's dress in colonial New Mexico varied according to status. In 1832 a Missouri trader commented that the "female peasantry" wore simple, handmade clothing, of-

NEGATIVE STEREOTYPE

Albert Pike, an American who passed through the Southwest in 1831, presented his view of a dance in New Mexico. His description suggests the negative stereotypes held by Americans:

On the evening after my arrival in the village, I went to a fandango. I saw the men and women dancing waltzes, and drinking whiskey together. . . . It is a strange sight—a Spanish fandango. Well dressed women—(they call them ladies)—harlots, priests, thieves, half-breed Indians—all spinning round together in the waltz. Here a filthy, ragged fellow with a half shirt, a pair of leather breeches, and long, dirty woolen stockings, and Apache moccasins, was hanging and whirling round with the pretty wife of Pedro Vigil; and there, the priest was dancing with La Altegracia, who paid her husband a regular sum to keep out of the way, and so lived with an American. I was soon disgusted; but among the graceless shapes and more graceless dresses at the fandango, I saw one young woman who appeared to me exceedingly pretty. She was under the middle size, slightly formed; and besides the delicate foot and ancle [*sic*] and the keen black eye, common to all the women in that country, she possessed a clear and beautiful complexion, and a modest, downcast look, not often to be met with among the New Mexican females.

Source: Albert Pike, *Prose Sketches and Poems Written in the Western Country*, edited by David J. Weber (Albuquerque: Calvin Horn, 1967), pp. 148–149.

ten in blue or scarlet, while women of rank more commonly wore fashionable European dress. Fashionable Spanish clothing included the mantilla, or lace head covering held up by a tall comb. The comb, or *peineta*, might be made of ivory, gold, silver, or other metal. Both common and elite women wore shawls that covered the head and body. An expensive shawl might be made of fine wool and fringed with silk. After the establishment of the Santa Fe Trail in 1821, trade with the United States increased, and American goods became more widely available. As the influence of the United States increased and as New Mexico passed into American hands, women's fashions gradually came to reflect these changes.

Dances. Various forms of dance were popular among Spanish and Mexican settlers in California. Dances might be events that any member of the community could attend or formal balls open only to members of the elite. One early settler recalled that at informal dances the elderly people danced the *contradanza* while younger people waltzed and performed Spanish folk dances. Formal balls, known as fandangos in early years, were one of the few places where unmarried young men and women could meet, under the watchful eye of their elders. At such balls men and women sat apart from each other, and young people were expected to behave respectfully toward their elders. As the population of Spanish California grew, formal balls were increasingly restricted to the elite. These events came to be called *bailes* rather than fandangos, and the term *fandango* began to be used to refer to the dances of the lower classes.

Sources:

Carmen Espinosa, *Shawls, Crinolines, Filigree: The Dress and Adornment of the Women of New Mexico, 1739 to 1900* (El Paso: Texas Western Press, 1970);

David J. Langum, "From Condemnation to Praise: Shifting Perspectives on Hispanic California," *California History*, 61 (Winter 1983): 282–291;

Anthony Shay, "Fandangoes and Bailes: Dancing and Dance Events in Early California," *Southern California Quarterly*, 64 (Summer 1982): 99–113;

David J. Weber, ed., *Foreigners in Their Native Land: Historical Roots of the Mexican-Americans* (Albuquerque: University of New Mexico Press, 1973);

Weber, "The Spanish-Mexican Rim," in *The Oxford History of the American West*, edited by Clyde A. Milner II, Carol A. O'Connor, and Martha A. Sandweiss (Oxford: Oxford University Press, 1994), pp. 45–77.

MINING CAMPS

Life in the Mines. Few gold rushers went to California intending to stay. Most hoped to become rich and return home to family and friends. Both those who came to stay and those who hoped to return found the mining camps to be lonely places. In some parts of the West there were more than a hundred men for every white woman, and children were nearly as scarce. A

A RARE SIGHT

Women were a rare sight in the mining camps. In *Pen Knife Sketches; or, Chips of the Old Block* (1853) Alonzo Delano recalled the excitement in a mining camp caused by the arrival of a woman:

We knew that delays were dangerous, so shouldering our picks and shovels, pistols and rifles, and taking a bottle or two of *guardiente*, we marched to the new tent, in file, our leader whistling "Come haste to the wedding," and gave three cheers and a discharge of firearms. The alarmed occupants rushed to the door to see what was up. Our captain mounted a rock, and addressed the amazed husband in something like this strain:

"Stranger, we have been shut up here so long that we don't know what is going on in the world, and we have already forgotten what it is made of. We have understood that our mothers were women, but it is so long since we have seen them, that we have forgotten how a woman looks, and being told that you have caught one, we are prospecting to get a glimpse." The man, a sensible fellow, by the way, entering into the humor of the joke, produced the *animal*, when the nine cheers, a drink all around, and a few good natured jokes, we quietly dispersed.

California author recorded a song that expressed the miners' loneliness:

Our friends all so kind we have left far behind,
Our wives and our little ones too,
And those who have not any little [ones] got
Have sweethearts or wives, most true.
We see the gold shine in the damp, cold mine;
It cheers and rejoices our eyes,
For with it we mean at home to be seen
'Neath our own native sun and skies.

Seeking Entertainment. Mining was difficult and dangerous work, and when the week was over, miners sought entertainment. Like other men of the time, they enjoyed drinking, gambling, bull- and bearbaiting, and horse races. Diarists and travelers commented on the dances of the miners. Because women were rare in the camps, dances might be nearly all-male affairs. Men danced with each other in couples, with one man wearing a scarf or patch pinned to his clothes to indicate that he was, temporarily, a "lady." The few white women in California recalled that their scarcity made them popular. Luzena S. Wilson recalled that "the feminine portion of the population was so small that there was no rivalry in dress or fashion, and *every man thought every woman in that day a beauty*. Even I have had men come forty miles over the mountains, just to look at me, and I never was

A painting of a fandango in a miners' camp; men designated as "ladies" are indicated by a patch on their pants or a handkerchief on their sleeves

called a handsome woman, in my best days, even by my most ardent admirers."

Sources:

Gretchen Adel Schneider, "Pigeon Wings and Polkas: The Dance of the California Miners," *Dance Perspectives,* 39 (Winter 1969): 4–57;

Elliott West, *Growing Up With the Country: Childhood on the Far Western Frontier* (Albuquerque: University of New Mexico Press, 1989).

NATIVE AMERICAN SPORTS

Popular Games. Despite the diversity of Native American cultures, some games were widespread. The rules of a game might vary, but several games were popular in large regions of the West. Native Americans occasionally incorporated games into religious ceremonies. Heavy betting was common with most games.

Lacrosse. The best known of Indian games is lacrosse. It was most common among the tribes of the Atlantic seaboard and around the Great Lakes, but it was also played in the South, on the plains, in California, and in the Pacific Northwest. It was played with a ball made either of wood or of buckskin, which was caught with curved rackets with a net on one end. The goal was usually marked with two poles although in some areas only one was used. In 1860 J. G. Kohl, a white traveler in Wisconsin, examined some lacrosse equipment. He admired the fine carving of crosses, circles, and stars on the white willow ball and praised lacrosse as "the finest and grandest" sport of the Indians. Although he was unable to see a game, he claimed that the Indians "often play village against village or tribe against tribe. Hundreds of players assemble, and the wares and goods offered as prizes often reach a value of a thousand dollars and more."

Shinny. A kind of field hockey known as shinny was among the most popular Native American games. It was usually played by women, but sometimes, especially on the plains, might also be played by men. Among the Sauk, Foxes, and Assiniboine Indians, men and women played the game together, and among the Crows, teams of men played against teams of women. Native Americans in the East, on the plains, in the Southwest, and on the Pacific Coast played shinny. It was played with a ball or bag, often made of buckskin, which was hit with sticks curved at one end. The ball and sticks might be decorated with paint or beads. The length of the field varied from two hundred yards (among the Miwok Indians) to a mile or more (among the Navajos). The object of the game was to hit the ball through the opponent's goal. The ball could be kicked or hit with the stick but not touched with the hands.

Lacrosse Playing Among the Sioux Indians; 1851 oil painting by Seth Eastman (Corcoran Gallery of Art, Washington, D.C.)

AMONG THE APACHES

In the 1860s Col. John C. Cremony described a Mescalero Apache game as follows:

There are some games to which women are never allowed access. Among these is one played with the poles and a hoop. The former are generally about 10 feet in length, smooth and gradually tapering like a lance. It is marked with divisions throughout its whole length, and these divisions are stained in different colors. The hoop is of wood, about 6 inches in diameter, and divided like the poles, of which each player has one. Only two persons can engage in this game at one time. A level place is selected, from which the grass is removed a foot in width, and for 25 or 30 feet in length, and the earth trodden down firmly and smoothly. One of the players rolls the hoop forward, and after it reaches a certain distance, both dart their poles after it, overtaking and throwing it down. The graduation of values is from the point of the pole toward the butt, which ranks highest, and the object is to make the hoop fall on the pole as near the butt as possible, at the same time noting the value of the part which touches the hoop. The two values are then added and placed to the credit of the player. The game usually runs up to a hundred, but the extent is arbitrary among the players. While it is going on no woman is permitted to approach within a hundred yards, and each person present is compelled to leave all his arms behind.

Source: Stewart Culin, *Games of the North American Indians,* volume 2, *Games of Skill,* Twenty-fourth Annual Report of the Bureau of American Ethnology (Lincoln: University of Nebraska Press, 1992), pp. 449–450.

Snow-Snake. In regions of the West cold enough to have snow and ice in the winter, snow-snake was played. Its rules varied even more than those of lacrosse or shinny, but in general the game involved sliding darts or poles along snow or ice as far as possible. The projectile could be only a few inches long or might be a javelin up to ten feet long. The game was usually, but not always, played by men. Among the Crees, who played a variant of the game in which the dart had to pass through barriers of snow, only men played the game. Among the Arapahos, on the other hand, snow-snake might be played by adults or children but was most commonly played by girls.

Hoop and Pole. Hoop and pole was another widespread game with varying rules. In general a hoop was rolled along the ground while men tried to knock it over with spears or arrows. The hoop was usually relatively small, from three inches to a foot in diameter. The hoop might be open, but often the players stretched cords or a net across it. The hoop itself was often of wood but might be made of corn husks, stone, or iron. It was sometimes decorated with paint or beads. The score was determined by the way the hoop fell when hit by the pole. The game was most frequently played by two men although in some cases more participated.

Source:
Stewart Culin, *Games of the North American Indians,* volume 2, *Games of Skill,* Twenty-fourth Annual Report of the Bureau of American Ethnology (Lincoln: University of Nebraska Press, 1992).

A circa 1860 photograph of a Mormon family on a westward trail (Utah State Historical Society, Salt Lake City)

THE OVERLAND TRAILS

Traveling West. From the 1830s to the 1860s between 250,000 and 500,000 individuals traveled to California and Oregon on the overland trails. The trip from the Missouri River to the West Coast was nearly two thousand miles. Emigrants came from many backgrounds, but about six in ten male heads of households were farmers who hoped to find better farmland in the West. Other men worked as artisans or professionals, but many of them also took up farming in Oregon or California. The men and women who made this journey expected it to be long and dangerous, and most prepared carefully for its rigors.

Limitation. The people who traveled on the overland trails, like most Americans in their day, had limited wardrobes of largely handmade clothing. Little girls began learning to sew early, and by the time they married, women knew how to make clothing for themselves and their families. Women who were preparing to take the overland journey found their workload increased, for there would be few opportunities to make or mend clothing on the trail. Before departing, then, all the clothing needed for the trip had to be made.

Making Clothes. Making clothes was a time-consuming process. In much of the West settlers bought raw wool and cotton and grew flax for linen. Women spun and wove their own cloth. A popular cloth was linsey-woolsey, made by weaving linen and wool together. This cloth was less expensive than pure wool but still warm and strong. Women also dyed the clothing they produced. They used some local materials, such as alder bark and black oak bark, to produce browns and yellows. Imported woad and indigo (both for blues) and madder (for reds) were also popular. Women made much of the family's clothing from these homemade fabrics although they might also buy calico or gingham cloth for special occasions. In the winter Westerners wore knitted socks, mittens, and caps, but in the summer no one wore socks, and children usually went barefoot.

What They Wore. Generally, families tried to bring two or three changes of clothing for each person. Men wore loose, full shirts, often open at the neck, and loose trousers. They also wore heavy boots and hats made of straw, fur, or felted wool and brought heavy coats of jean fustian. Women almost always wore long dresses. According to the historian John Mack Faragher, women

Catherine Haun was a young bride when she and her husband "decided to follow the path of the gold rush." In later years she dictated an account of the 1849 journey to her daughter:

It was the fourth of July when we reached the beautiful Laramie River. Its sparkling, pure waters were full of myriads of fish that could be caught with scarcely an effort. . . . After dinner that night it was proposed that we celebrate the day and we all heartily join[ed] in. America West was the Goddess of Liberty, Charles Wheeler was orator and Ralph Cushing acted as master of ceremonies. We sang patriotic songs, repeated what little we could of the Declaration of Independence, fired off a gun or two, and gave three cheers for the United States and California Territory in particular! The young folks decorated themselves in all manner of fanciful and grotesque costumes—Indian characters being most popular. To the rollicking music of violin and Jew's harp we danced until midnight. There were Indian spectators, all bewildered by the (to them) weird war dance of the Pale Face and possibly they deemed it advisable to sharpen up their arrowheads.

Source: Catherine Haun, "A Woman's Trip Across the Plains in 1849," reprinted in *Women's Diaries of the Westward Journey*, edited by Lillian Schlissel (New York: Schocken, 1982), pp. 180–181.

"required two or three dresses, usually of dark gingham, calico, or heavy wool, with perhaps one or two petticoats of linen, aprons, and shoulder kerchiefs, a warm shawl, and perhaps a coat." These clothes were simply tailored. Unlike fashionable Eastern women, Western women wore simple, slip-on dresses. Dresses might be made in one piece or might consist of a sacque and overskirt. The sacque was a long dress with a full skirt that hung loosely to the floor or the ankle. Over it, women wore a long skirt. Women also wore sunbonnets, often of colorful calico stretched on wire or wooden frames. Men wore the loose shirts and trousers common in Western settlements. They used knit or leather suspenders or a leather belt. Men usually also wore a hat of straw or felted wool although fur was sometimes used. Both men and women wore heavy boots to protect their feet on the trail. Children above the age of six or seven dressed like their parents, but younger children of both sexes wore a loose linen dress called a wannis.

Bloomers and Dress Reform. Women's long dresses were not well suited to the trail. They dragged on the ground, tore frequently, and made cooking over an open fire hazardous. A few women hemmed their skirts up or wore wash-day dresses, designed not to drag on wet ground, but most preferred to wear the clothing to which they were accustomed. A few women in the 1850s made the trip wearing bloomers, full skirts that reached to the knee or below, with full pantaloons. Bloomers were associated with female radicals, and so many women rejected them. Furthermore, women who had only two or three dresses were unlikely to make an entirely new suit of clothes that they would use only on the trail. Finally, women were badly outnumbered on the trail. In a culture that highly valued female modesty women's long skirts

George Caleb Bingham's 1857 oil painting *The Jolly Flatboatmen in Port* (St. Louis Art Museum, Missouri)

were useful as curtains. As the historian Lillian Schlissel observed, for these women, "So simple a matter as bodily functions on a terrain that provided no shelter could make daily life an agony of embarrassment when there was no other woman to make of her extended skirt a curtain."

Recreation. In the settlements of Ohio, Indiana, and Illinois women had fewer opportunities for leisure than men, and the same was true on the trail. Indeed, women were often lonelier on the trail than they had been at home. Away from the ties of family and friends, women on the Overland Trail felt isolated. Until 1849 women made up only 15 to 20 percent of immigrants, and women's diaries show that they missed female companionship. When traveling parties stopped, women were responsible for cooking, child care, and washing while men were able to rest and play. The most popular sport for men was hunting, and they thought little of stopping the journey for a chance to kill buffalo. Little of this hunting was done to feed the travelers. One traveler recalled that he and his companions had killed enough buffalo for forty thousand pounds of meat, but as

they "had neither the time, the equipment, nor the inclination for butchering," they left nearly all of it to rot on the plains. Children also enjoyed sports and play on the Overland Trail. Adults on the trail noted their energetic play, sometimes with some irritation. One traveler's diary noted that the children were "grumbling and crying and laughing and hollowing and playing all around." Children occasionally invented sports of their own as well. In the summer of 1841 boys in a party on the Oregon Trail discovered the bloated body of an ox. Somehow, the historian Elliott West wrote, "they discovered that if they jumped against the animal's bloat, it would fling them vigorously back. Champions rose and fell as boys ran faster, jumped harder, and bounced farther. Finally, Andy, a long-necked redhead, backed off a great distance, lowered his head, sprinted, leaped—and plunged deep into the rotting carcass. His friends pulled him out, though with some difficulty, and the contestants went on their way. . . ." Children's sports on the trail were usually simple. Girls and boys played variants of hide-and-seek and tag as well as simple ball games.

Sources:

John Mack Faragher, *Women and Men on the Overland Trail* (New Haven: Yale University Press, 1979);

Lillian Schlissel, ed., *Women's Diaries of the Westward Journey* (New York: Schocken, 1982);

Elliott West, *Growing Up With the Country: Childhood on the Far Western Frontier* (Albuquerque: University of New Mexico Press, 1989).

POLYGAMY

Polygamy among the Mormons. The Church of Jesus Christ of Latter-Day Saints was among the most distinctive American religious communities of the nineteenth century. The founder of Mormonism, Joseph Smith, claimed that an angel had revealed golden plates to him on which a religious history was written. These plates, Smith said, told the story of the appearance of Christ in the New World after his crucifixion. The church grew rapidly, both within the United States and in Europe. Between 1837 and 1846, for example, Mormon missionaries baptized nearly eighteen thousand people in England, of whom nearly five thousand immigrated to Nauvoo, Illinois, to join the Mormon community there. Smith was killed by a mob in 1844. His role as leader was taken by Brigham Young. Driven from Missouri, Ohio, and Illinois by hostile neighbors, the Mormons set out in 1846 for the West. In 1847 they established Salt Lake City, the new headquarters of the Mormon Church. In the forty years after 1846 some one hundred thousand converts moved to Mormon communities in the West.

Family and Marriage. Between the mid 1840s and 1890 polygamy was the ideal form of Mormon marriage, but even during this time fewer than one-fifth of Mormons lived in polygamous households. Even dedicated Mormons initially found the idea of plural marriage troubling. According to the historians Leonard J. Arrington and Davis Bitton, when Brigham Young heard of Smith's revelation allowing plural marriage, he said "it

A nineteenth-century engraving of a settler plying a Native American with alcohol (American Antiquarian Society, Worcester, Massachusetts)

was the first time in my life that I desired the grave." Later, however, both men and women defended the practice as a command of God that was also "a practical, honorable means of providing marriage and motherhood for thousands of deserving women who would otherwise be condemned to a life of spinsterhood." Mormons claimed that polygamous families offered distinct advantages. Women with several children might find another woman's assistance invaluable, and the presence of another adult could ease loneliness. Older women, without means of support, might find a polygamous marriage promised a secure old age. Still, polygamy remained controversial and difficult even for believers. Men might find it hard to support more than one wife while women struggled with jealousy.

Sources:
Leonard J. Arrington and Davis Bitton, *The Mormon Experience: A History of the Latter-Day Saints* (New York: Knopf, 1979);

Jessie L. Embry, *Mormon Polygamous Families: Life in the Principle* (Salt Lake City: University of Utah Press, 1987).

RECREATION IN WESTERN COMMUNITIES

A Man's Domain. Men had more frequent opportunities for sport in the West than women did. Women might participate in frolics and dances, but most men and women believed that a woman should spend her time on domestic duties. This ideology suggested that women belonged at home and limited their contact with others. Their work was done alone more often than men's, and women were seldom encouraged to display strength or athleticism. Men, who had more opportunities to work in company with other men, also had more opportunities to play sports.

Hunting and Shooting Contests. In these contests men sought to prove their skill with weapons. In the late eighteenth century competitive squirrel hunts were a popular form of recreation. In one such contest two teams of four men each spent a day hunting squirrels. When they returned, one team had killed 152 squirrels, the other 141. In another example a Kentucky newspaper reported that a group of hunters killed more than 7,000 squirrels in a single day. Shooting at targets was also popular. The winner in such contests might receive a prize of a cow or a barrel of whiskey. The noted painter John James Audubon reported that he observed a nighttime contest in Kentucky in which the goal was to extinguish a lit candle fifty yards away. In this contest one marksman "was very fortunate, and snuffed the candle three times out of seven," a record that no other was able to match. "Shooting the tin cup," played in the western Carolinas, was a more dangerous game of marksmanship. In this contest the hunter attempted to shoot a tin cup off another man's head.

Wrestling and Fighting. Wrestling and fighting contests were popular among men in the West. One brutal form of this sport, popular in the Ohio River valley in the late eighteenth and early nineteenth centuries, was known as gouging. Unlike wrestling or boxing, gouging had few rules to prevent injury to one man or the other. Contemporary observers commented that the goal was to grab the

A painting of an Indian buffalo hunt, by George Catlin, circa 1830 (British Museum, London)

opponent's hair at the temple and gouge out his eyes. Biting, kicking, and kneeing were permitted. Timothy Flint, a New Englander who spent ten years in the Mississippi River valley in the early nineteenth century, was disgusted by the sport. He reported seeing men who had lost an eye and overheard fighters speaking with a "disgusting familiarity about mutilation." Spectators of such matches also enjoyed watching animals fight. Cockfights and dogfights were both popular throughout the West.

Horse Racing. Horse races of all kinds were found throughout the West. The most famous and widely advertised contests took place in the cities of the eastern sea-

---

DOGFIGHTS

A 23 January 1859 *New York Clipper* newspaper account of a dogfight held in New Orleans in 1858:

One of the great features of Christmas Day in New Orleans was a contest between a Kentucky coon and a famous terrier dog, known as "Fighting Bob," which came off . . . before a refined, fashionable, and aristocratic audience. . . . At the hour appointed . . . the two animals were brought into the arena and pitted after the most approved style. The first attack was tremendous, the dog going in confident, while the coon backed to his side of the ropes, and stood on the defensive. The terms of the fight were, that the dog should kill the coon, or that the coon should cause the dog to run and throw him out of time, which, in this instance, was two minutes. The betting at the start was two to one on the dog, a large number of which bets were taken. After the fury of the first attack was over, the dog evidently found that he had an enemy to deal with worthy of his steel, and began to scan more closely the vulnerable parts of his country cousin, and came up to scratch with less haste than at the lead. . . . [the dog] darted at the coon and seized hold of him, and was seemingly about to finish his mortal career, when his sly old antagonist, by an agile movement, threw his quarters out of reach, and while the dog lay down a moment for wind, seized hold of a paw and led him a three-legged dance around the ring. The backers of the coon shouted, while those of Fighting Bob looked wise and said that the terrier would soon recover himself. But alas! for the vanity of knowing ones, and the short-sightedness of dog fanciers; the coon continued his advantage, threw his opponent about easily, mauled him most incontinently, and finally threw him down and out of time. The excitement in the crowd at this unexpected denouement was intense. . . .

Source: Kirsch, George B., ed., *Sports in North America: A Documentary History,* volume 3, *The Rise of Modern Sports, 1840–1860* (Gulf Breeze, Fla.: Academic International, 1992).

---

board, but there were also race tracks in New Orleans, Cincinnati, Louisville, and San Francisco. Western settlers in smaller communities also set up informal matches of their own. The sport, which was found in every part of the West, was also one of the few sports open to women in the early nineteenth century. While critics worried that horseback riding was indelicate and might even injure women, some women still took part in horse racing and other displays of equestrian skill. Supporters of women's riding hastened to reassure their readers that such women were still ladies. The competitors in one 1858 contest, according to a reporter, showed a "graceful and queenly bearing," and the winner of the race finished the course "without disturbing her own or the horse's serenity in the least."

Sources:

John James Audubon, *Delineations of American Scenery and Character* (New York: G. A. Baker, 1926);

John Bernard, *Retrospections of America* (New York: Harper, 1887);

Foster Rhea Dulles, *A History of Recreation: America Learns to Play* (New York: Appleton-Century-Crofts, 1965);

John Durant and Otto Bettman, *Pictorial History of American Sports: From Colonial Times to the Present* (Cranbury, N.J.: A. S. Burns, 1973);

Timothy Flint, *Recollections of the Last Ten Years, Passed in Occasional Residences and Journeyings in the Valley of the Mississippi* (New York: Da Capo, 1968);

George B. Kirsch, ed., *Sports in North America: A Documentary History*, volume 3, *The Rise of Modern Sports, 1840–1860* (Gulf Breeze, Fla.: Academic International, 1992);

Earle F. Zeigler, *History of Physical Education and Sport* (Champaign, Ill.: Stipes, 1988).

HEADLINE MAKERS

DOÑA GERTRUDIS BARCELÓ

1800-1852
PROFESSIONAL GAMBLER

Santa Fe Stakes. In the 1830s and 1840s Doña Gertrudis Barceló, known as La Tules, owned and ran the most fashionable gambling parlor in Santa Fe (then part of Mexico). Born into an elite family, La Tules married at age twenty-three and chose a career as a professional gambler. She specialized in dealing monte, a card game. According to one traveler, she was regarded as the best monte dealer in Santa Fe.

Fashion. When dealing cards, Barceló dressed simply, but on other occasions she favored expensive silk fashions. She also wore gold rings and heavy gold necklaces. When she chose to wear the long gowns popular in the United States, American traders claimed that her influence led other women to adopt the same styles.

Status. To the surprise of American visitors, La Tules's career as a gambler did not hurt her social position. She was a close friend of Gov. Manuel Armijo, who held a financial interest in her business. Although she was married, Barceló "claimed the rather unusual privileges of entertaining whatever friends she pleased, male or female, in whatever degree of intimacy she chose, and of conducting her business any time and any place that suited her." By the time of her death Barceló's gambling had made her wealthy. She owned a nine-room home on 160 acres of land and two other houses. In her will she left land, jewelry, silver plate, clothing, and furniture. According to contemporary accounts, nearly all the people of Santa Fe attended Barceló's elaborate funeral.

Source:

Janet Lecompte, "La Tules and the Americans," *Arizona and the West*, 20 (Autumn 1978): 215–230.

SIR ST. GEORGE GORE

1811-1878
HUNTER

Sportsman. Sir St. George Gore was a wealthy Irish nobleman, baronet of Gore Manor in County Donegal. He loved hunting and fishing, and in the 1850s he decided to visit the American West. His expedition lasted nearly three years, from 1854 to 1857, taking him to Colorado, Wyoming, Montana, and the Dakotas, and cost some $500,000. The exact number of animals killed by Gore for sport is unknown. He himself claimed to have killed 2,000 buffalo, 1,600 deer and elk, and 105 bears.

Expedition. As a member of the aristocracy, Gore saw no need to rough it in the wilderness. His chief guide was the famous mountain man Jim Bridger, and his company included twenty-seven vehicles, more than one hundred horses, eighteen oxen, and three cows. Gore also had a wagon loaded with weapons, including pistols, shotguns, and about seventy-five rifles. He had a "large striped green and white linen tent," a brass bedstead, a rug, and a portable table. Gore hired at least forty men for a variety of jobs, including cooking, hunting, and tending greyhounds and staghounds.

Difficulties. Gore and his expedition traveled through lands held by various Indian tribes, some of whom resented the slaughter of animals in their lands. At one point a band of Piegans stole twenty-one horses, and in another incident Blood Indians tried to capture more horses. On the other hand, the company traded peacefully with a band of Crows, acquiring fresh horses

from them. Officials of the United States also found Gore's hunting excessive. Superintendent of Indian Affairs Alfred Cumming protested that Gore was killing game that the Indians needed to survive. Another observer, M. C. Meiggs, wrote to the secretary of the interior to complain. Observing that Gore had killed thousands of buffalo, he commented, "We punish an Indian for killing a settler's cow for food. . . . How can such destruction of their game be permitted by their friends in the Government of the United States?" The government, however, took no action against Gore, who returned to Ireland in 1857.

Source:

Clark C. Spence, "A Celtic Nimrod in the Old West," *Montana*, 9 (April 1959): 56–66.

PUBLICATIONS

Henry Marie Brackenridge, *Views of Louisiana: Together With a Journal of a Voyage Up the Missouri River, in 1811* (Pittsburgh: Cramer, Spear & Eichbaum, 1814)—a traveler's account of a trip through the Louisiana Territory;

William Faux, *Memorable Days in America* (London: W. Simpkin & R. Marshall, 1823)—the author describes his journey to Illinois, undertaken to determine the agricultural prospects for British immigrants;

Edmund Flagg, *The Far West: or a Tour beyond the Mountains* (New York: Harper, 1838)—Flagg studies the geography of the Mississippi River valley, St. Louis, and Illinois and criticizes the religious enthusiasm of Westerners;

Frederick Gerstaecker, *Wild Sports in the Far West* (London: Geo. Routledge, 1856)—a German tourist describes hunting and the hardships of travel in Ohio, Indiana, Illinois, Missouri, and Arkansas;

Harriet Martineau, *Retrospect of Western Travel* (London: Saunders & Otley, 1838)—Martineau describes her travels in the United States, including a voyage on the Mississippi and a view of Cincinnati;

William Partridge, *A Practical Treatise on Dyeing Woolen, Cotton, and Silk* (New York: William Partridge & Sons, 1847)—a manual describing various dyes and their uses;

Pierre Jean de Smet, *Letters and Sketches, with a Narrative of a Year's Residence Among the Indian Tribes of the Rocky Mountains* (Philadelphia: M. Eathian, 1843)—a Jesuit's description of his journeys among the Native Americans of the West, including the Flatheads, Shoshones, and Sioux.

Trappers' Rendezvous, by Alfred Jacob Miller, circa 1837, depicting Shoshoni Indians arriving at the Green River Rendezvous, Wyoming (Thomas Gilcrease Institute of American History and Art, Tulsa, Oklahoma)

Interior of a Mandan Earth Lodge; painting by Carl Bodmer, circa 1834 (Joslyn Art Museum, Omaha, Nebraska)

RELIGION

by CYNTHIA JO INGHAM

CONTENTS

Sidebars and tables are listed in italics.

1800

- Spokane prophet Yurareechen (the Circling Raven) predicts that "soon there will come from the rising sun a different kind of man from any you have yet seen, who will bring with him a book and will teach you everything, and after that the world will fall to pieces."

1801

- The Cane Ridge, Kentucky, camp meeting revival becomes the symbol and standard of evangelical religion in the early republic.

- The Plan of Union between the Congregationalists and Presbyterians allows the creation of "presbygational" churches in order to facilitate missionary work along the frontier.

1803

- Barton Stone and associates publish "Last Will and Testament of the Presbytery of Springfield," secede from the denomination, and call themselves simply "Christians."

1805

- Shawnee Lalawethika falls into a coma and awakens to proclaim a vision given by the Master of Life, instructing the Indians on what must be done to restore Indian power. The Shawnees acknowledge him as a prophet, and his name becomes Tenskwatawa, "the one that opens the door."

1806

- Inspired by the Shawnee Prophet, the Delawares begin a witch hunt to root out those who would undermine the new religion. Those singled out are Christian converts or Indians with ties to the white world; four are burned at the stake.

1808

- Tenskwatawa leaves Greenville, in western Ohio, and moves with his followers to Prophetstown, or Tippecanoe, a site offered to him by the Kickapoos and Potawatomis.

1809

- Thomas Campbell withdraws from the Presbyterians and forms the nondenominational Christian Association of Washington (Pennsylvania).

- Under the provisions of the Treaty of Fort Wayne, the federal government buys 2.5 million acres from the tribes in the Old Northwest. The unfairness of the treaty enhances the appeal of the Shawnee Prophet and the pan-Indianism of his brother Tecumseh.

1810

- The American Board of Commissioners for Foreign Missions (ABCFM) forms as an interdenominational agency to coordinate missionary endeavors.

1811

- Tecumseh takes his first journey to the Southern tribes to gain allies against white encroachment.

7 Nov. The Shawnee Prophet's forces are routed at the Battle of Tippecanoe.

1813

5 Oct. Tecumseh is killed at the Battle of the Thames, Ontario.

1814

- Baptists begin foreign missions under the authority of their Triennial Convention.

1815

- German pietist George Rapp moves his communitarian experiment to New Harmony, Indiana.

1816

- Cumberland Presbyterian Church splits from the main Presbyterian Church over issues of ordination and deviations from the Westminster Confession. Its alterations are a direct response to the religious needs of westward-expanding settlements.

1819

- Congress establishes a "civilization fund" to be distributed among the missionary societies operating Indian schools. Although the money is a small portion of the private contributions, the alliance provides an important psychological boost to the missionary endeavor, linking it with a vision of national destiny in Christian terms.

1820

- Two dozen Iroquois Catholics from a mission near Montreal settle among the Flatheads in the Columbia Plateau. After introducing them to rudimentary Catholicism, the Iroquois leader, Ignace La Mousse, urges the Flatheads to seek further religious instruction.

1823
- Joseph Smith is first visited by the angel Moroni, who tells him of ancient gold plates buried in a hill near Palmyra, New York.

1827
- The Campbellites sever ties with the Baptists and begin calling themselves Disciples of Christ.

1828
- Alexander Campbell defends Christianity against Robert Owen's charge that "religion was founded on ignorance and was the chief source of human misery."

1830
- *The Book of Mormon: Another Testament of Jesus Christ* is published.
- The Church of the Jesus Christ of Latter-Day Saints forms, with Joseph Smith and five others as elders.

1831
- Four Nez Percé and Flathead Indians arrive in St. Louis, seeking the "white man's book of heaven." This so-called Macedonian cry prompts a new stage in the missionary drive in the West.

1832
- The Disciples of Christ and the Christians unite in Kentucky.
- The Black Hawk War, given religious definition by the Winnebago Prophet, Wabokieshiek, becomes the last Indian conflict in the Old Northwest.

1834
- Jason Lee and his nephew head west with three other Methodist missionaries with the intention of serving the Flathead Indians in present-day southwestern Montana. They instead settle in the Willamette River valley of Oregon.

1835
- Alexander Campbell publishes *The Christian System in reference to the Union of Christians, and a Restoration of Primitive Christianity, as Plead in the Current Reformation* to clarify the Christian movement.
- Lyman Beecher, head of Lane Seminary in Cincinnati, publishes *Plea for the West*, which summarizes the Protestant establishment's aspirations for the West and warns of a Catholic plot to take over the region.

1836

- Under the auspices of the ABCFM, the Whitmans and the Spaldings cross the Rockies to set up a mission among the Columbia Plateau Indians. Narcissa Whitman and Eliza Spalding are the first Euro-American women to make the journey across the Rocky Mountains.

1837

- The first of five smallpox epidemics among the Western Indians over the next thirty years nearly wipes out the Mandans.

- In the Presbyterian General Assembly, moderates and conservatives band together to void the Plan of Union, striking more than five hundred churches and between sixty thousand and one hundred thousand members off the rolls.

1838

- A struggle between New School and Old School factions within Presbyterianism leads to a division of the denomination.

1840

- Fifty-one recruits arrive at the Methodist mission in the Willamette River valley.

- Massive immigration of Irish and German Catholics makes the Catholic Church the largest denomination in the nation by 1850.

- Jesuit priest Pierre-Jean De Smet makes a grand tour of Western tribes.

1843

- Jason Lee becomes involved in the creation of the Oregon Provisional Government, and the Missionary Society recalls him for being overly engaged in secular activities.

- Marcus Whitman returns from the East, bringing the largest contingent of settlers and wagons to date along the Oregon Trail.

1844

- The Methodist Episcopal Church divides into Northern and Southern branches over the issue of slavery.

27 June   Joseph Smith and his brother Hiram are murdered in a Carthage, Missouri, jail by a mob.

22 Oct.   William Miller and his followers await the end of the world. When it fails to materialize, the prediction's date is changed. The movement evolves into the Seventh-Day Adventists.

1845

- The Baptists split into Northern and Southern branches; the Southern Baptist Convention remains a separate body to this day.

1846

- The Mormons begin to evacuate Nauvoo.

1847

- The first Mormon settlers reach the Salt Lake basin.

28 Nov.   In the Whitman Massacre, Cayuse Indians kill fourteen white adults at the Waiilatpu Mission in Oregon.

1848

- Under the Treaty of Guadalupe Hidalgo the United States acquires a large tract of Southwestern territory, which brings into the nation indigenous peoples and a Hispanic population of nominal Catholics.

1849

- Disciples of Christ/Christians hold their first national convention in Cincinnati, primarily to mount evangelism efforts, despite the resistance of many members to any institutional organization beyond the congregation.

1852

- The First Plenary Council of the Roman Catholic Church in the United States is held.
- Brigham Young publicly announces that plural marriage is a holy practice incumbent on Saints deemed worthy of the privilege.

1857

- Fearing the invasion of a federal army, Mormons and their Ute allies attack a wagon train and kill 120 California-bound settlers.

1858

- President James Buchanan orders an expedition of 2,500 soldiers to Utah in order to assert federal authority over the Mormons. The force camps outside Salt Lake City until recalled at the outbreak of the Civil War. Meanwhile, Buchanan pardons the Mormons.

OVERVIEW

Churches in the Expanding West. To Anglo-Americans in the nineteenth century the "West" was a migratory concept, continually being relocated as the next geographical region beyond white settlement. At the turn of the century the "uninhabited" frontier—though home to some 120,000 Native Americans—was the area between the Appalachian Mountains and the Mississippi River. Waves of migration swept into the region from two primary directions: settlers from the Upper South and Middle Atlantic states streamed across the mountains into Kentucky, Tennessee, and southern Ohio, and impoverished New Englanders pushed into western New York and northern Ohio, Indiana, and Illinois territories. Migrants carried their religious background with them to their new homes, but settlement had to reach a certain density before pious inclinations could be expressed corporately. Although the rudiments of survival distracted from institution building, churches often took priority because they served multiple functions as vital centers for secular fellowship as well as for spiritual comfort. Communities, however dispersed, could use the churches as reference points for the assertion of behavioral norms. Denominational leaders were well aware of the potential for either good or ill in the areas of expanding settlement and reached out to the West with evangelizing programs. Without the civilizing presence of churches and the consolations of religion, the vulnerable communities might become hotbeds of immorality and lawlessness. A Christian West, however, promised not only a harvest of souls but also a pristine environment in which virtue and godliness might become a beacon to the jaded, older states. Whatever future awaited, one thing seemed certain as the nineteenth century opened: religious developments in the West were pivotal to the religious destiny of the nation overall.

Presbyterians. Religious freedom, enshrined as a revolutionary principle, meant that the denominations entered the West as equal competitors. Of the three major groups in the early republic—the Presbyterians, the Methodists, and the Baptists—the Presbyterian Church was the oldest and most established, and those attributes often made it attractive to people seeking stability in the midst of very uncertain conditions. The Scots-Irish, who formed a large bloc of the Presbyterian membership, had

tended to migrate to the fringes of settlement in the eighteenth century. Strategically located in the Southern backcountry and the Ohio River valley after the American Revolution, they were among the first to move westward, and they carried their native faith with them to new communities. The structure of the church allowed local control through the elders, who handled the daily affairs of the congregation, while the regional presbyteries and synods ensured that the scattered flocks maintained order and orthodoxy. The Calvinist theology of Presbyterianism, spelled out in the Westminster Confession, declared that the salvation of the elect was achieved by grace alone, not by any effort on the part of the individual. Doctrinal conformity required the guidance of properly educated ministers and catechistic instruction, both of which were in short supply in the West. Given time, these disadvantages might have lessened, with accommodation in the interim to the practical realities of the sparse settlement, but the Presbyterian Church, still shaken by a schism in the eighteenth century, remained fearful that any compromise in polity or doctrine opened the floodgates to ungodliness.

Plan of Union. Presbyterian and Congregationalist churches dominated New England at the turn of the century, and one characteristic they shared was that they held ministerial aspirants to strict standards of education and experience. Consequently, both denominations suffered a dearth of ministers, and both were hamstrung in their ability to serve the communities quickly forming in western New York and the Ohio River valley. Under the Plan of Union in 1801, the two groups allowed the creation of joint churches, with the minister and polity to be chosen by the majority. This "presbygational" hybrid was an innovative strategy for evangelizing the West, yet it had long-range consequences for both churches. In institutional terms the Presbyterians' more aggressive structure tended to absorb the Congregational churches, but in doctrine the Congregational infusion served to weaken Presbyterianism's Calvinist orthodoxy. Fears of corruption led conservative Presbyterians to question the benefits of all interdenominational programs and set the stage for a later division.

Methodists. Methodism had originated as a reform movement within the Church of England, but with

American independence, the Methodist Episcopal Church had ventured out as a distinct denomination. By the early nineteenth century Methodism was enjoying explosive growth, especially in the West. Its key innovation—the circuit rider, or itinerant preacher—seemed admirably suited to the needs of far-flung settlements. The circuit rider would journey into the wilds, close on the heels of the pioneers. Evangelizing wherever there were people, he would gather converts into classes to meet, read the Bible, and keep one another out of sin's reach until his return. Long circuits covering hundreds of miles gradually divided and contracted as more people moved into the area, increasing the number of local societies. To ensure connection with the larger Methodist fellowship, the circuit membership assembled quarterly for a "refreshing" time of communion and witness. In its organization the church was fundamentally hierarchical. Authority flowed downward from the bishops to the itinerant preachers, who met in annual conferences and laid out standards of belief and practice for the members. Yet in other respects the church displayed democratic elements. The Methodist preacher was an ordinary person who had been raised up from a class and had proven his dedication and abilities before a conference of fellow itinerants. Equality of opportunity was the rule for lay leadership as well. In theology Methodism repudiated the exclusivity of Calvinist election. Instead, salvation, offered by the grace of God, was open to all, and human beings could choose to accept or refuse the gift. Free will thus supplanted predestination. (This religious stance was popularly known as Arminian, in reference to the sixteenth-century theologian Jacobus Arminius.) By deciding to accept God's invitation, the convert set out on a rigorous journey of "sanctification," which could lead the faithful toward the ultimate Methodist goal of perfection—perfect in love and perfect in understanding. Methodism, then, seemed to respond to the two conflicting needs of religion in the West. Its celebration of free will and open opportunity meshed with the independent image of the pioneer, yet its structure and discipline provided cohesion and behavioral boundaries. The numbers substantiated Methodism's appeal, and competing churches ruefully acknowledged the legendary speed with which Methodism advanced into every new territory. By 1820 Methodist membership had reached 250,000, and by 1844 the Methodist Episcopal Church was the largest denomination in the nation.

Baptists. The spontaneous emergence of Baptist churches in newly settled areas distinguished the denomination from other groups. The farmer-preacher simply felt a calling that, if acknowledged by his peers, could lead to the gathering of a congregation. This liberated concept of the ministry was one of the Baptists' three defining principles—the other two being adult baptism by immersion and intense congregationalism. The absence of organizational controls beyond the local church gave the Baptists flexibility as they planted new

congregations, but they submitted to voluntary discipline and oversight through regional associations. The theological alignments of the Baptists paralleled their institutional focus on autonomy. Although Baptists in the Northern states often claimed a Calvinist heritage, confirmed by subscription to a shared confession, many Baptists in the Upper South had emerged from the revolutionary fires with less patience for binding creeds or Calvinist uniformity. Distinctly Arminian principles of free will and general redemption were among the traditions carried to the Trans-Appalachian West by Virginia and North Carolina Baptists.

Cane Ridge Camp Meeting. The nineteenth century awakened to scattered signs of revival in New England, but it was a camp meeting in Cane Ridge, Kentucky, in 1801 that became the symbol and standard of religion in the early republic. Cane Ridge was the climax to a series of gradually expanding revivals, spearheaded by Presbyterian minister James McGready. During prolonged church services filled with impassioned sermons and prayers, McGready encouraged an emotional response from his listeners. His success among his churches in Logan County, Kentucky, enthused fellow minister Barton W. Stone in neighboring Bourbon County. Stone announced that a camp meeting would be held in early August. Rumors of a miraculous work astir had already generated a considerable amount of curiosity, and this meeting, publicized for more than a month, was set closer to the center of Kentucky's population. When the day arrived, Elder David Purviance remembered that "the roads were literally crowded with wagons, carriages, horsemen, and people on foot, all pressing to the appointed place." More than ten thousand people from all walks of life gathered at Cane Ridge, convincing participants that a divine hand was indeed guiding events. The revival continued for five emotion-charged days. Baptist, Methodist, and Presbyterian ministers joined forces to evangelize the masses, and the air was filled with exhortation, hymn singing, and wailing. The spectacular experience was the stuff of legends. Stone carefully detailed in his memoirs the sights and sounds, especially the various "exercises" that struck the people as they wrestled with sin and then discovered their salvation: bodily jerks, dancing, singing, laughing, barking, and falling down. Col. Robert Paterson also described the scene: "in the woods, ministers preaching day and night; the camp illuminated with candles, on trees, at wagons, and at the tent; persons falling down, and carried out of the crowd, by those next to them, and taken to some convenient place, where prayer is made for them; some Psalm or Hymn, suitable to the occasion sung." Another contemporary wrote that "there were present, besides 18 Presbyterian ministers, and a number of Baptist and Methodist preachers, the Governor of the State, each of whom was personally and busily engaged, either in preaching, praying, or exhorting!"

Reaction to Cane Ridge. News of the Cane Ridge camp meeting spread to the East, becoming the butt of jokes to critics but evidence of a second Pentecostal outpouring of the Holy Spirit for others. Opponents explained the reports of the participants' behavior as evidence of nervous troubles, feeblemindedness among frontier people, or susceptibility to mass delusion. Sympathetic observers pointed to altered behavior as proof of the meeting's benefits. The *Washington Intelligencer* published George Baxter's favorable account in 1802:

> On my way to Kentucky, I was informed by settlers on the road, that the character of Kentucky travellers was entirely changed; and that they were now as remarkable for sobriety as they had formerly been for dissoluteness and immorality. And indeed I found Kentucky, to appearance, the most moral place I have ever seen . . . [The revival's] influence was not less visible in promoting a friendly temper among the people . . . It has confounded infidelity, awed vice into silence, and brought numbers beyond calculation under serious impressions.

Coming as it did at the cusp of a new century, Cane Ridge offered seemingly indisputable evidence that God was sending a "new dispensation" to regulate human affairs. As a result it nourished the millennial hopes of the early nineteenth century, and its location in Kentucky seemed to indicate a special role for the West in bringing about Christ's anticipated reign of peace and holiness. The Cane Ridge camp meeting inspired a chain reaction not only along the frontier of Kentucky, Tennessee, and southern Ohio but also among the Eastern churches, until the entire nation seemed on fire. The organized revival became the means to congregational growth, especially among Baptists and Methodists. The number of Baptists in Kentucky grew from 4,700 to 13,500 within a year of Cane Ridge, and from 1801 to 1806 the Methodist membership in Kentucky and Tennessee increased from 3,000 to 10,000. The Methodists in particular embraced the camp meeting and, in their usual methodical way, stylized it until it was a carefully structured event by the 1830s. As the decades passed, some came to view Cane Ridge as an uncontrolled explosion. Writing in his 1856 autobiography, Peter Cartwright had to acknowledge its power though he was not so complimentary of its aftershocks:

> I suppose since the day of Pentecost, there was hardly ever a greater revival of religion than at Cane Ridge; and if there had been steady, Christian ministers, settled in gospel doctrine and Church discipline, thousands might have been saved to the Church that wandered off in the mazes of vain, speculative divinity, and finally made shipwreck of the faith, fell back, turned infidel, and lost their religion and their souls forever. But evidently a new impetus was given to the work of God, and many, very many, will have cause to bless God forever for this revival of religion throughout the length and breadth of our Zion.

From both vantage points Cane Ridge remained a symbol of the age: looking forward in anticipation of the "new dispensation" and looking backward at the wreckage caused by human frailty.

Second Great Awakening. The wave of renewed interest in spiritual concerns crested in what historians refer to as the Second Great Awakening, forever changing American religion. In confronting colonial Calvinism an evangelical sensibility emerged that extolled free will in claiming redemption and human agency in effecting change. For the first three decades of the nineteenth century, its distinctive characteristics included a consuming zeal to reform the world and a millennial conviction that the United States was singularly poised to realize, as Alexander Campbell wrote, "that ultimate amelioration of society proposed in the Christian Scriptures." The feverish burst of religiously motivated activity was the product of hope as well as fear. Harmony best characterized the godly society, yet from the beginning the nation had experienced discord, and the new century boded more instability and conflict. The generation coming of age in the early republic felt keenly the burden of the revolutionary legacy, and the uncertainty expressed in the common reference to "the American experiment" was no euphemism. The evangelical persuasion was thus simultaneously optimistic and apprehensive, fearing that unless every Christian shouldered the cross, the experiment would crash. Inspired and prodded by widespread humanitarian campaigns in Great Britain, an "evangelical united front" of voluntary associations sprang up to tackle such issues as temperance, prostitution, prison conditions, slavery, and women's rights. Shared dedication to a cause took precedence over denominational differences, which again seemed to augur the idealistic possibilities for the nation's future under Christian influence. The coalition behind this "benevolent empire" lasted until the late 1830s, when it was battered and overwhelmed by economic and political forces.

Missionary Impulse. The missionizing push by benevolent societies to the unchurched and unconverted in the Western settlements was a key development for religion in the West in the nineteenth century. Andover student Samuel Mills toured west of the Alleghenies from 1812 to 1814 and galvanized concerned Christians with his stories of distressed frontier communities lacking ministers, churches, or Bibles. In the territorial capital of Illinois, for example, Mills could not find a single complete copy of the Bible. These "fact-finding" expeditions were extremely influential in an age of limited communication, and they inspired local churches and regional organizations to engage in mission projects. The urgency of the problem seemed to demand wider cooperation, so national groups formed to address the problem of the Western settlements. Their objectives were two-fold: to prevent barbarism from overtaking the new and unchurched communities and to bring the Native Americans into the protecting fold of Christian civilization.

Although achieving the second goal would facilitate the first, it was the particular concern with Indian "uplift" that initially drew missionaries into the field. The evangelical thrust to Native America was an important manifestation of religious aspirations for the West in the first half of the nineteenth century. It occurred in two stages. Interdenominational associations, such as the American Board of Commissioners for Foreign Missions (ABCFM), at first concentrated on the Indian groups nearest to white centers of population: in the areas of the Old Northwest, the Southeast, and just beyond the Mississippi. The second push began in 1831, after four Indians from the Columbia Plateau arrived in St. Louis seeking "the white man's book of heaven." Methodists, Presbyterians, and Jesuits turned their attention to the distant lands beyond the Continental Divide until 1847, when the massacre of eleven people at an Oregon mission brought a dramatic halt to missionary projects in the region. The confrontation between the belief systems of indigenous peoples and Euro-Americans was a clash of sacred worlds: an encounter not initially of conquest and domination but of interaction and eventual alienation. Indians responded variously to religious representatives: utilitarian curiosity over a potential new source of power, theological critique, adaptation, conversion, and/or nativist countermovement. The most universal consequence of the missionary impulse for native peoples was factionalism within communities, as Indians individually and corporately struggled to comprehend within a religious framework the changes provoked by westward-expanding settlements.

Cumberland Schism. After the Cane Ridge camp meeting, denominational leaders had rejoiced that revivals in the West had encouraged the spread of churches, but they soon discovered that such an intense release of religious energy was hard to contain. The Presbyterians, the first to enjoy the harvest of the camp meeting, were also the first to suffer schism. Exhilarated by the revivals, the Kentucky Presbyterians sought to keep the momentum going, but that required ministerial leadership. To supply their own needs in the face of a denomination-wide shortage, the revivalists took a practical approach and borrowed a leaf from the Methodist manual: they sent unordained licentiates to the scattered settlements to preach the gospel. Nor were they as strict about how closely new converts adhered to the Westminster Confession. These tactics reopened old wounds within the denomination. Facing opposition from more-traditional Presbyterians, the revivalists affiliated as the Cumberland Presbytery, but the Synod of Kentucky refused recognition. Upon appeal to the General Assembly, the highest governing body, the synod declared that its objective "was to suppress the growing irregularities in the west, and yet save one of her Presbyteries from disruption and final ruin." The assembly reprimanded the dissidents, so they declared their independence from the synod in 1810 and finally severed ties in 1816. The emer-

gence of the Cumberland Presbyterian Church was a direct response to the circumstances and needs of the frontier in the wake of Cane Ridge. The church adopted revival methods and a version of the Westminster Confession that was more amenable to free will. Its ministers were also subject to less-rigid educational demands. The Cumberland church grew rapidly in the Trans-Appalachian states, from Mississippi to Indiana, where its membership numbered approximately seventy-five thousand by 1850.

Unity and the Christian Movement. The pride of the Cane Ridge camp meeting had been the unusual spirit of cooperation displayed among the ministers, who set aside their denominational differences for the higher goal of bringing salvation to the wayward. Many believers regarded such disinterested behavior as a sign that unity within Christendom—an essential if elusive prerequisite for the ultimate triumph of the universal Church—was at last within reach. The call to unity was a strong current in the religious aspirations of the early republic, but as seen in the Cumberland division, the desire for harmony among churches confronted the reality of competing claims to religious truth. The "Christian" movement was the most radical response to sectarian rivalry and was especially prominent in the religious landscape of the Trans-Appalachian West. Ironically, its institutional form emerged as the result of two rifts. In 1803 Barton Stone and other revivalists separated from the Presbyterians, called themselves simply "Christians," and declared their allegiance to the New Testament as their sole guide. Spreading from Kentucky to Ohio to other states bordering the Mississippi, the number of Stone's followers grew to more than twelve thousand by the late 1820s. Meanwhile, in 1809 Thomas Campbell withdrew from his Seceder Presbyterian Church in Western Pennsylvania and formed a nondenominational "Christian Association." His son Alexander gave the movement a clearer theological identity, and in 1827 the churches formed by their followers adopted the name "Disciples of Christ." Five years later the Stone and Campbell churches were loosely affiliated, though congregations continued to call themselves Christians or Disciples of Christ, according to preference. By 1860 membership in the combined churches totaled two hundred thousand and was concentrated west of the Appalachian Mountains.

Mormonism. The Church of Jesus Christ of Latter-Day Saints, known as the Mormons, originated in Western New York in April 1830 under the leadership of Joseph Smith. Hailed by his followers as God's new prophet, Smith provided the Latter-Day Saints with an indigenous scripture: the Book of Mormon, which he allegedly had translated from ancient plates hidden in a hill near Palmyra, New York. Pushed relentlessly from place to place by opponents, the church attracted increasing numbers of adherents, apparently answering the longings of many for reassurance and purpose in troubled times. In 1840 Mormons began to construct an impressive "New Jerusalem" in Illinois, but success did not bring acceptance from nonbelievers. On 27 June 1844 a mob descended on the Carthage jail where Joseph Smith was awaiting trial on charges of inciting a riot. He and his brother Hiram were murdered. Brigham Young assumed the leadership of the official church, and from 1846 to 1848 he guided some twelve thousand Latter-Day Saints across Iowa and then a thousand miles to the Salt Lake valley. Isolated, the Mormons prospered and expanded, at the same time outraging the East by the practice of polygamy and by claiming a vast "empire" under their control. In an attempt to secure their position, the Mormons created a state they called "Deseret." The federal government instead designated the area a territory in the Compromise of 1850. The conditions were ripe for conflict. In 1857 President James Buchanan decided to dispatch federal troops to the region to assert federal authority over the rebellious Mormons. Enthusiasm for the half-hearted Utah expedition quickly waned, and the so-called Mormon War had the unintended consequence of confirming the practical autonomy of the Mormon monolith. A towering presence in the religious history of the West, the Church of Jesus Christ of Latter-Day Saints challenged the nineteenth-century Protestant establishment with a faith that both reflected and refracted the culture in which it flourished.

New Harmony. In the early nineteenth century the United States became home to a number of communitarian experiments, utopian as well as millenarian. The most famous communities—such as Brook Farm and Oneida—were located in the East or had a minor role in the religion of the Trans-Appalachian West. An exception was New Harmony, a religious community in Indiana Territory founded by German pietist George Rapp. Fleeing persecution for refusing to worship in the state church, Rapp and three hundred of his followers had arrived in the United States in 1803 and started a community in Western Pennsylvania. In search of better agricultural land, the group decided in 1814 to move to a tract on the Wabash River in Indiana Territory. The Rappite community, now numbering about seven hundred, quickly became the largest and most impressive town in the territory. New Harmony was a model of agricultural and manufacturing productivity, with woolen and saw mills and flourishing vineyards and orchards. The community owned twenty thousand acres of land and 180 brick, frame, and log buildings—churches, shops, granaries, mills, factories, barns, stables, and houses. Visitors from the East and from Europe came to New Harmony and extolled its neat appearance and the industry of its people; reformers looked to it as an economic model. Yet the primary purpose of New Harmony was to accumulate wealth for Christ's use when He returned, and Rapp considered his congregation to be the bride of Christ, as described in Revelation. Since the Second Coming was thought to be quickly approaching, the Harmonists re-

mained celibate, held all property in common, and submitted to the paternal guidance of their founder, who served as religious leader and confessor. Despite the visible accomplishments of New Harmony, within a decade the leaders decided to return to Pennsylvania, disheartened at the toll taken by malaria and missing the advantages of residing in a state amenable to people of German ancestry. In 1825 they sold all holdings to Robert Owen, who transformed New Harmony into a socialist experiment. The Rappites' third settlement in Economy, Pennsylvania, became renowned for its woolen manufacture, but after the death of Father Rapp in 1847 the spiritual character of the communitarian project faded. Linkages to the outside world increased interest in secular affairs, dampening chiliasm, or millenarianism, and the drive for sinless perfection. In that respect, the evolution of New Harmony was somewhat analogous to the drift of antebellum religion overall.

Searching for Order. During the 1830s the centrifuge of religious ferment slowed, and the impetus shifted away from the disorder of creative experimentation in matters of faith toward a desire for respectability. In the East a new wave of revivals addressed urban anxieties in particular: the doubts and fears accompanying rapid economic growth, changing work patterns, widening gaps within society based on wealth, and incredible immigration. The area around Rochester, New York, was so inflamed by revivals that it became known as the "burned-over district." Once again, revived Easterners turned their eyes to the West in missionary zeal, but with altered perception. Observing the settled areas beyond the Appalachians, it now seemed apparent that simply building churches would not "civilize" the behavior and manners of the Western communities. Cultivation of the character through formal education had to go hand in hand with care of the soul. (In fact, this shift in attitude echoed the debate over "Christianization or civilization" of the Native Americans.) In response the nondenominational American Sunday School Union vastly expanded the work it had begun in 1824 and for the rest of the century provided rudimentary education for many children in both the East and the West. The religious influence of the Union was formidable since its teachers were essentially missionaries and its instructional materials were mostly Bible stories. Especially in Western areas newly opened to white settlement, Sunday school missionaries often arrived before churches had been organized, and they provided a bridge to civilization with religious instruction that instilled such moral virtues as punctuality, cleanliness, and industry. The domestic mission drive was spearheaded primarily by the American Home Missionary Society (AMHS), founded in 1826. Representing Presbyterians and Congregationalists, the AMHS supplied much of the personnel for the West: college-age men from New England and the Middle Atlantic who shrank from the challenge of the slave South and so directed their ardor westward. Asa Turner was one of seven Yale theological students to form the "Illinois Band," pledging himself to missionary and educational work in 1829. Ten years later, as the first AMHS minister in Iowa, he wrote to the society asking for more helpers. In 1843 Turner received a reply from a group of students at Andover Seminary. This Iowa Band offered to come to the territory and help establish churches. The seasoned Turner doubted that their youthful idealism could withstand the rigors of pioneer life, but in fact ten of the Andover group did found Congregational churches in Iowa. They complemented their long ministerial service with the establishment of Iowa College in 1848. Through the AMHS, New England religious and cultural influences reached beyond the Mississippi to Western settlements.

Sectional Prejudice. Since Easterners tended to regard Westerners as perfectly content in their barbarism, missionaries were often contemptuous of those whom they served. Missionary John Parsons, stationed in southern Indiana in 1833, railed at the "universal dearth of intellect" and the lack of interest in self-improvement. "Need I stop to remind you of the host of loathsome reptiles such a stagnant pool is fitted to breed! Croaking jealousy; blotted bigottry; coiling suspicion; wormish blindness; crocodile malice!" Other prejudices came to the fore in the less conciliatory mood of the 1830s. The AMHS persisted in calling areas "destitute of both religious and moral principles" even when Baptists or Methodists were firmly entrenched there. A Presbyterian missionary reported to the society that "Campbellism is the great curse of the West—more destructive and more injurious to the cause of religion than avowed Infidelity itself." Church adherence may best illustrate the reaction of the West to being civilized by the East. Although the Presbyterians led in the educational invasion of the Old Northwest states, they could claim less than 250,000 members in 1840. Meanwhile, the Methodists had 850,000 and Baptists more than 570,000. The Eastern denominations may have supplied the educators, but Western people signed up with other communions. As expressed in the familiar slogan "no creed but the Bible," Protestants in the Trans-Appalachian West required basic literacy skills in order to decide religious matters for themselves, but they disdained intellectual pretense. The popularity of religious journals spoke to their commitments despite the scorn of New Englanders. For example, during 1831–1832 the post office in Jacksonville, Illinois, received 133 periodicals, 42 of which were religious journals.

Charles Grandison Finney. Charles Grandison Finney, one of the most important religious figures to emerge from the antebellum era, made Oberlin College in Ohio his professional home beginning in 1835. A schoolteacher then a lawyer in New York, Finney abandoned both and turned to evangelism in the 1820s. He came under the influence of New Haven theology, developed in the late 1820s at Yale Divinity School by Congregational minister Nathaniel Taylor. Taylor furnished an intellectual foundation for revivalism by softening Calvinist orthodoxy in order to place more emphasis on free will and thus human instrumentality. By the early 1830s Finney's fame and powerful preaching had swept urban centers in the East. Oberlin then became the focus for his "new measures" in revivalism, which included carefully planned methods to win converts and a postconversion commitment to Christian reform. Finney's conviction that people chose the way of Christ and the way of holy living—that "perfection" meant the potential for unlimited moral improvement—had both sacred and secular implications. Consequently, though Finney's theology emerged from an urban landscape that was alien to the West, his prescriptions harmonized with a Western milieu. His was a familiar language of activism (especially regarding temperance reform), of pragmatism, and of millennialism. As Finney declared, "If the church will do her duty, the millennium may come in this country in three years." However, Finney's new measures were also a telling sign of the religious change since Cane Ridge. Then the revivalists had seen the hand of Providence at work, heralding a divine dispensation. In Finney's view revivals were not miraculous but only the purely calculated result "of the right use of the constituted means." The advent of a new age certainly required God's blessing, but it would come about as the intentional product of human endeavor.

Lyman Beecher. In 1832 Lyman Beecher, famed New England Presbyterian minister, became head of Lane Seminary in Cincinnati—a physical separation from his roots that was paralleled in theological distance. Although he was more conservative than Finney, Beecher also favored New Haven theological modifications. In fact, in Ohio a trustee of the seminary made a formal complaint to the synod about Beecher's doctrinal deviation, and though he was acquitted of heresy, the event drew the church one step closer to schism. Beecher's denomination was not the one sweeping the West, yet he emerged as the spokesman for the West's role in the nation's destiny, and, given his own profession, he visualized both the role and the destiny in religious terms. Beecher published *Plea for the West* in 1835, and the work was widely reprinted and cited. To Beecher, the driving question of the age was whether republican institutions could be reconciled with universal suffrage. The danger, he declared, was that "our intelligence and virtue will falter and fall back into a dark minded, vicious populace—a poor, uneducated reckless mass of infuriated animalism." The remedy was Bibles, schools, and seminaries—strong institutions infused with religious purpose that would apply "needed intellectual and moral power." Not only the nation was at risk but also the entire world. "If this work be done, and well done, our country is safe, and the world's hope is secure . . . nation after nation, cheered by our example, will follow in our footsteps, till the whole earth is free." The West had become the testing ground for the entire American experiment. In hindsight, the irony of Beecher's dramatic appeal was his perception that mobocracy posed the major threat to the republic. Meanwhile, in 1834 an alarming number of Lane Seminary students, including future abolitionist-firebrand Theodore Weld, decided to attend Oberlin because there they would be able to take a stronger stance against slavery.

The Denominations Divide. At the turn of the century the strength of revival currents had fostered interdenominational cooperation. Churches were means to the greater end of realizing God's special plan for the nation. During the late 1830s and 1840s the religious mood began to change, and denominational lines hardened under the discipline of orthodoxy. Controversies, especially slavery, became the points on which faith turned. The Methodist church, for example, split into Northern and Southern branches in 1844, over the issue of excluding slaveholders from the ranks of preachers. Western Methodists thus had to take sides as they formed their own societies. For the Presbyterians and Baptists, policies directly related to the West triggered division. Over the years conservative Presbyterians, known as the Old School, had protested the liberal policies of the New School majority, but to no avail. The key grievances of the Old School were, first, that the New School had been lax in enforcing doctrinal conformity; and, second, that the support of interdenominational societies had weakened the Presbyterian mission. Finally, New School boldness pushed conservatives and moderates together, and the General Assembly of 1837 took decisive action. The delegates voided the Plan of Union of 1801, which nullified the four Western synods organized during the life of the Union. The assembly removed more than 500 churches and between 60,000 and 100,000 members from the Presbyterian rolls in one swoop. The Old School majority created the Board of Foreign Missions (BFM) with explicit instructions to pursue a strict Presbyterian line and informed other mission groups to stay clear of BFM stations. The struggle between new and old schools continued as tensions heightened over slavery, and the denomination split in 1838. Missions were also the bane of Baptist unity, but while the Presbyterians had been primarily concerned about heterodoxy, the Baptists chafed at external efforts to contravene the will of congregations. Combined with different opinions over slavery, the result was explosive. At first Baptist evangelization of the West had occurred under the auspices of regional associations, but in 1814 representatives of Baptist churches met to develop a more comprehensive mission thrust. Over the next twenty years the General Missionary Convention of the Baptist Denomination in the United States for Missions, known as the Triennial Convention, sent out more than one hundred missionaries, across the continent and abroad. This extracongregational body did not have the support of many Baptists, who declared their resistance by calling themselves Primitive, Hard-shell, or Anti-mission. Particularly in the Trans-Appalachian West, Baptists remained committed to local control. The issue that brought matters to a head was the evangelization of the slaveholding Cherokees in the Indian Territory. In 1844 antislavery Baptists withdrew from the Triennial Convention to form their own missionary group. In answer to a direct query from the Alabama Baptists, the convention's executive committee replied that it would never certify a slave owner as a missionary. In 1845 the Baptists split into Northern and Southern branches, and the Southern Baptist Convention remains a separate body today.

Roman Catholicism. By the 1830s many Protestant leaders regarded Roman Catholicism as a clear threat to the American republic. The Catholic Church had quickly added an institutional branch to its hierarchy to cover the new nation, but the number of communicants was modest until the 1830s. That decade marked the beginning of large-scale Irish Catholic immigration. The potato blight of the early 1840s turned the Irish departure from their homeland into panicked flight. By 1850 the census recorded 961,000 Irish in the United States, with 200,000 immigrating in that year alone. Meanwhile the arrival of nearly 1.5 million Germans in the 1840s and 1850s also boosted the number of Catholics in the United States. The results were staggering. From 1830 to 1860 the nation's population grew from 13 million to 31.5 million (two and one half times). The Catholic population burgeoned from 300,000 to over 3 million. Consequently, by the middle of the century there were more Catholics in the United States than any other denomination—though they remained a minority in a nation dominated by varieties of Protestantism. Moreover, a severe shortage of priests kept the church at a competitive disadvantage. At the Catholic Church's first American plenary council in 1852, the record revealed 1.6 million Catholics but only 1,800 priests to serve its 1,600 churches and mission stations. Before the Civil War the Catholic population beyond the Mississippi was relatively modest and was concentrated in the Southwestern region. Given its minimal presence, the primary role played by Catholicism in the West was in the fertile imagination of Protestant leaders. Lyman Beecher's *Plea for the West,* in fact, appended a long exposé of the great Catholic conspiracy to conquer the Western region. Despite his hysteria, anti-Catholicism and nativism did not seem to be a significant factor in the religious life of the West as it was in other regions, though the efficient advance of the Jesuits in Western missions did put the Protestant missionaries on the defensive. In any event, neither the Jesuits nor the Catholic Church lived up to their nefarious image as an "evil empire."

Catholicism in the Southwest. In the Treaty of Guadalupe Hidalgo of 1848, the United States purchased California and New Mexico as the spoils of the Mexican War. These acquisitions, combined with Texas statehood in 1845, presented the Catholic Church with a Southwestern population of nominal Catholics, possibly 25,000 in New Mexico and 10,000 in Texas, as well as the remnants of the Franciscan mission system in California. Since the mid eighteenth century the attentions of Iberian Catholicism had wandered away from New Spain. Over the years, then, Hispanic settlers had developed a unique folk Catholicism, which was characterized by an abundance of local patron saints and religious holidays, an emphasis on the Virgin Mary, and lay religious brotherhoods. In New Mexico, for example, Los Hermanos de Nuestro Padre Jesus Nazareno, or the Penitentes, assumed much of the burden for worship and parish ministrations, though Catholic authorities looked askance at their use of physical penance and their autonomy. Under the umbrella of United States possession, the Catholic hierarchy embraced the region but could do little more than assert administrative control, given the dearth of priests. Jean Marie Odin was named bishop of Galveston in 1847, and six years later Jean-Baptiste Lamy became bishop of Santa Fe. Odin's multinational constituency included Hispanics as well as Germans and Silesian Poles. Such diverse ethnicities, and the linguistic hurdles they posed, placed an even greater strain on American Catholicism in this period. Technically the Catholic Church did not have exclusive control over the Southwest, but Protestants found that determined opposition from the bishop was enough to empty their schools and bring their evangelism to a screeching halt. In New Mexico, Baptist, Methodist, and Presbyterian representatives charged into the territory soon after its acquisition, and one by one they abandoned their efforts to convert the Hispanic-Catholic population, not to return until after the Civil War.

California. The discovery of gold in California in 1848 prompted a vast migration that affected the state's religious environment: the population rose from 14,000 in 1848 to 200,000 four years later to 380,000 in 1860. The sudden emergence of a makeshift society exclusively devoted to the accumulation of wealth captured the attention of the nation. One common image of gold-rush California depicted it as a breeding ground of a creeping corruption that could infect the rest of the country. By the 1850s the Protestant establishment became absorbed with California as the bellwether for the evangelical impulse; that preoccupation now displaced the earlier enthusiasm for the conversion of the Native Americans. In the words of historian Kevin Starr, the state's religious significance came down to a struggle between "California as Babylon, as hopelessly flawed, and California as Eden of the West, as continual recipient of special grace." Entangled within the debate was California's position as the jumping-off point for the Orient and thus as a vital hub for the westward march of American Protestantism—perhaps even giving it new life, since large areas and many people of the West had proven impervious to its summons. Although contemporary accounts be-

moaned California's unchurched wasteland, there were a few stalwart clergymen accompanying the Forty-Niners, and they industriously established at least fifty small churches within a short time. In the early years of the gold rush, the letters and reports of the overworked ministers tell of the endless round of duties—marriages, funerals, care of sick and dying—interspersed with street-corner and saloon evangelism. Methodist minister William Taylor exhorted daily on San Francisco's wharf, to ensure that the first words heard by arrivals would be the gospel.

The Lessons of California. The state's dramatic religious diversity discomfited evangelical Protestants, for their faith represented merely one option among many. The multiplicity of ethnic groups in California stretched the idea of religious competition to unheard-of lengths. Besides the major denominations there were Unitarians, Mormons, Jews, Spiritualists, Theosophists, Russian Orthodox, and, from the 45,000 Chinese laborers who arrived in California between 1849 and 1854, Buddhism, Taoism, and Confucianism. Blacks had also responded to California's siren call, as fortune seekers and as slaves accompanying masters. Their churches quickly emerged as focal points for the black community, paralleling the importance and multiple functions of the black church in other regions. In 1853 Catholicism officially extended from shore to shore with the organization of the archdiocese of San Francisco. Yet many Hispanics found themselves marginalized as the church tried to respond to a wide range of immigrants. In southern California, Hispano-Catholicism did not surrender so easily, though communicants had to battle the disciplinary bent of their bishop, who tried to weed out folk practices and "corrupt Catholicism." In the view of recent historians, adopting a Pacific Coast vantage point in American religious history can suggest an alternative to the usual model of a Westward march of religious institutions and beliefs from the Atlantic seaboard. California's extreme pluralism was therefore an integral part of antebellum religion rather than an aberration. Moreover, after a decade of labors amid the bewildering religious variety in California, evangelical missionaries were forced to admit that the tried-and-true strategies of revivalism had failed to work. Church attendance and membership remained discouraging, and the situation seemed to call into question the efficacy of revivalism itself. By challenging the universality of the evangelical appeal, the California experience set the stage for theological shifts later in the century.

Western Judaism. The corporate life of American Jews in the West took shape with the gold-rush immigrations in the 1850s. Before the Civil War, Jews were a recognizable presence in Portland, Denver, and other Western towns, but it was California that became home to the largest Jewish communities. In 1860 the census recorded about 5,000 Jews in San Francisco, 500 in Sacramento, and 150 in Los Angeles. The commercial needs of booming areas opened the door to Jewish bankers and merchants, and they often became a stable center amid rapid change. Pioneer Jews served as community founders and organizers alongside gentiles, and they frequently held public office, though not significantly represented in the electorate. Anti-Semitism thus was less apparent in the West than in other regions, perhaps because, as the historian Moses Rischin has suggested, the lack of structure made all outsiders potential insiders. Indeed, in contrast to other religious outsiders in California, including the Chinese Buddhists and the Mormon polygamists, Jewish religious differences seemed tame, placing them from the start on a better footing in relation to the Protestant majority.

The Iowa Example. At midcentury the "West," defined for these purposes in terms of Euro-American population density, barely extended beyond the Mississippi. Each type of Western society—the boom towns of the Gold Rush, the gradually expanding territorial settlements, the maturing communities in older regions—had its own religious character. Even so, by the close of the antebellum age, pluralism had emerged as a distinguishing trait of religion in the Trans-Appalachian West. While California may have represented one extreme on the spectrum, Iowa, which became a state in 1846 and shared with California the attentions of evangelists, serves as an example of the quintessential Middle West. According to the 1860 census there were 90,000 Methodists, twice as many as any other group. The Presbyterians, Baptists, Congregationalists, and Catholics each claimed 20,000 members or more. Diversity sprang from the soil of religious freedom: the state was home to Dutch Reformed, Quakers, Swedenborgians, and Mennonites. The Community of True Inspiration, a movement originating in Germany, moved westward from New York in 1855 and established the Amana Colonies in east-central Iowa, practicing a form of communal theocracy. Despite the proliferation of options, the census recorded the "unchurched" population (meaning those who did not indicate a denominational preference) at about 60 percent. Even so, it is likely that membership numbers did not tell the complete story of either churchgoing or patterns of belief. Iowa boasted a church for every 711 residents; by comparison, the national high was Ohio, with one for every 449 people, while California bottomed out with one church for every 1,103 people (Euro-Americans). Iowans, in common with residents of other states, would have considered themselves "religious" as long as they could individually define what that meant.

Conclusion. In denominational terms, the significant events of the period from 1800 to 1860 in the religion of the West were the ascendancy of the Methodists and Baptists and the emergence of the Christians and Disciples of Christ and the Church of Jesus Christ of Latter-Day Saints. In terms of religious expression, the common language was evangelical Protestantism, operating within a voluntarist and pluralist framework. Yet the diversity of dialects within evangelicalism in the West exposed contradictory currents within antebellum society as a whole: interdenominationalism and schism, individualism and communitarianism, postmillennial optimism and premillennial pessimism. Overall, what dominated in the Protestant West was the "democratization" of American Christianity. According to the historian Nathan Hatch, the religious terrain was populist, not because church polity or doctrine were intrinsically democratic but because religion responded to the spiritual needs and life circumstances of ordinary people. They claimed the privilege of interpreting Scripture and organizing churches for themselves. The result was not necessarily libertarian, since sometimes thinking for oneself meant choosing to submit to authority. The right to define one's own faith was empowering, if not liberating. The Western religious experience during the first decades of the nineteenth century was thus an addendum to the revolutionary story, as Euro-Americans tested certain radical implications of freedom in matters of faith—such as the extent of tolerance in a regimen of religious liberty and the proper means to a harmonious society. Gradually, a Romantic worldview began to transform perception and change what people asked of their faith. In the words of the historian William McLoughlin, rather than adopting an inclusive religious vision, "Americans discovered who they were by deciding who they were not." That sense of the religious "other" emerged in divisions among denominations, between Protestants and Catholics, and along racial lines, as Euro-Americans gradually displaced Native Americans from the physical and sacral landscape of the West. By the Civil War, religion in the Trans-Appalachian West had assumed many features of its Eastern fountainhead and was affected by the same trends, but it was never a replica. The relationship in matters of faith remained symbiotic, for there was a persistent sense that the West, in its ever-shifting definition, represented the potential redemption of the East and of the nation.

TOPICS IN THE NEWS

THE CHRISTIANS AND DISCIPLES OF CHRIST

The Christian Movement. As the new nation ventured into the unknown territory of religious pluralism, many Protestant leaders decried the appearance of sectarian rivalry, which they saw as counterproductive to larger evangelical goals and as contrary to the ecumenical ideal of the apostolic church. The "Christian" movement answered sectarianism with a call to unity, to be achieved by shedding denominational tags and restoring the church on primitive, New Testament grounds. Christian groups emerged in New England and in the Southern backcountry, but the movement's appeal was particularly concentrated in the Trans-Appalachian West.

Barton Stone. Shortly after the Cane Ridge camp meeting, Barton Stone and other Kentucky revivalists began to chafe under the rigidity of Presbyterian doctrine and polity, so they devised an alternative system that was radically congregational in form and decidedly Arminian in theology. In 1803 they organized into a separate presbytery, but a year later even that institutional tie became unbearable. Publishing the "Last Will and Testament of the Presbytery of Springfield," the group called themselves simply Christians and rejected all contrived creeds in favor of the New Testament as the only guide. Within a short time it was apparent that individual interpretation of biblical truths could lead to anarchy. As Stone wrote, "Some of us were verging on fanaticism; some were so disgusted at the spirit of opposition against us, and the evils of division, that they were almost led to doubt the truth of religion in toto; and some were earnestly breathing after perfection in holiness." A few of the latter group drifted off into the Shakers, while others returned to the safety of traditional denominations. Under Stone's leadership, the remainder formed the core of an influential movement. As related in his periodical *The Christian Messenger*, Stone preached the rational means by which an individual comes to believe in the testimony of the gospel, has faith in the promise of salvation, and is thereby reconciled to God. In his theology, reason was full partner to evangelical Protestantism, and the church was a voluntary association of autonomous individuals. The message struck a responsive chord among settlers in the states bordering the Mississippi River, and by the late 1820s the Christians numbered more than twelve thousand.

Thomas and Alexander Campbell. The Stonites were not alone in their emphasis on Christian unity through restorationism. In 1809 Thomas Campbell, a Seceder Presbyterian minister in Western Pennsylvania, withdrew from his church and formed a nondenominational "Christian Association of Washington (Pennsylvania)." In the association's "Declaration and Address" Campbell expressed a simple maxim of the movement: "Where the Scriptures speak, we speak; where the Scriptures are silent, we are silent." Since "the church of Christ upon earth is essentially, intentionally, and constitutionally one," all that was necessary to achieve the brotherhood intended by the New Testament was to remove human innovations from the churches. That same year Campbell's son Alexander arrived from studies at the University of Glasgow. The Christian Association constituted itself into Brush Run Church and licensed Alexander Campbell as preacher. Because the congregation affirmed believer's baptism, it aligned with the Baptists until 1827 (though under the rubric of "Reformers").

Religious Populism. In their ministry the Campbells stressed the reclamation of "the ancient order of things," as prescribed by the New Testament. According to their investigation, the Scriptures enjoined the observance of weekly communion, local congregational autonomy, equality between laity and minister, and baptism by immersion. Although the Stonites may have differed in their priorities, a first principle among all the "Christians" was the exaltation of the individual's authority to interpret the New Testament. No institution or collectivity could mediate gospel truths since it was the individual who would be held accountable on the day of judgement. As the historian Nathan Hatch has written, "A remarkable number of people awoke one morning to find it self-evident that the priesthood of all believers meant just that—religion of, by, and for the people." This religious populism was the most widespread legacy of the Christian movement, becoming part of the ethos of the age rather than simply a denominational trait.

Disciples of Christ. Alexander Campbell's ideas continued to claim adherents and churches in northeastern

A painting of a frontier camp meeting by Jacques Gerard Milbert, circa 1830 (New-York Historical Society)

Ohio and Western Pennsylvania under the auspices of the Mahoning Baptist Association. In 1827 those affiliated with Campbell severed ties with the Baptists and called themselves Disciples of Christ. (Opponents referred to the group as Campbellites to belittle them as merely a personality cult.) The followers of Campbell and Stone might never have merged, nor their movement taken shape, had it not been for Walter Scott. Scott, a schoolteacher, had migrated to the United States from Scotland in 1818. Embracing restorationism, he became an evangelist for Campbell in 1821. Six years later he had a vision of his own. Scott took Campbell's theology and distilled it to six points: faith, repentance, baptism, remission of sins, gift of the Holy Spirit, and eternal life. The first three were what an individual does upon conversion; the last three were what God does in response. No longer did salvation entail a subjective experience of conversion, related before a congregation or minister and then evaluated by them as to its validity. Instead, the gospel offered an objective plan of salvation, requiring obedience to simple tenets. Combining the final two elements, Scott preached the "five-finger exercise" with great success in northeastern Ohio. Scott's ministry spanned three decades, during which time he estimated that he had won a thousand converts a year.

Union Achieved. Union between the two groups had been broached in each of their publications. In 1832 Disciples and Christians in Kentucky began worshiping together and later united by a handshake. Other congregations followed suit, but there was no compulsion. The adherence to different names was symbolic of the radically voluntarist temper of the Christian movement, yet it was also a portent that "the ancient order of things" was itself subject to varied interpretation. Thomas Campbell, Walter Scott, and Barton Stone all favored the plain name of Christians, but Alexander would not be moved from his conviction that Disciples of Christ had the strongest biblical precedent. Consequently, congregations employed both names until the twentieth century. Regardless, there was much common ground between the followers of Stone and Campbell. Both groups rejected creeds as a bar to fellowship, and the slogan "no creed but the Bible" was a familiar expression of this commitment. Both recognized only two ordinances, the Lord's supper and adult baptism by immersion. Both opposed "partyism" and advocated the New Testament church as the basis for the union of all Christians. Both rested their fellowship and their attitude toward diversity on the principle of unity in essentials, liberty in nonessentials, and charity in all things. The movement was simple, direct, and inclusive. There were differences in tone—after all, the Stonites had emerged from the fires of the Western revivals, while Campbell was building a theology of Christian rationalism. The Stonites contributed about 10,000 members to the merger, and the Campbellites, another 12,000. The movement spread to other parts of the nation, but its strength continued to be west of the Appalachians. By 1860 the membership had increased to 200,000, putting it in the top five of American denominations.

The quintessential Methodist itinerant in the Trans-Appalachian West was Peter Cartwright, who began riding the circuit in the rough areas of Kentucky, Tennessee, Ohio, and Indiana in 1802, at the age of 17. This burly, rugged preacher was famous for his homespun sermons and for his ability to handle every situation that arose in the course of his journeys. Converted at a Kentucky camp meeting and later licensed as a Methodist exhorter, he traveled circuits for twenty-two years. As he later wrote, many of the Methodist preachers in those years could not "conjugate a verb or parse a sentence, and murdered the king's English almost every lick. But there was a Divine unction attended the word preached, and thousands fell under the mighty power of God, and thus the Methodist Episcopal Church was planted firmly in this Western wilderness." Unlike many of the early itinerants who were bachelors by necessity, Cartwright was married and had nine children. In fact, his decision to move to Illinois in 1823 was prompted by family concerns, especially a desire to raise his seven daughters and two sons in a free state and to be able to purchase land for their future inheritance. He continued to farm and itinerate for another quarter century. Looking back, Cartwright remembered that his first Illinois district in 1826 "commenced at the mouth of the Ohio river, and extended north hundreds of miles, and was not limited by the white settlements, but extended among the great, unbroken tribes of uncivilized and unchristianized Indians; but now in 1851 how changed was the whole face of the country!" In time-honored fashion, Cartwright contrasted the zeal of former times to the complacency of the present: "When I consider the insurmountable disadvantages and difficulties that the early pioneer Methodist preachers labored under in spreading the gospel in these Western wilds in the great valley of the Mississippi and contrast the disabilities which surrounded them on every hand, with the glorious human advantages that are enjoyed by their present successors, it is confoundingly miraculous to me that our modern preachers cannot preach better, and do more good than they do." Twice elected to the Illinois legislature, he lost in his bid to the U.S. Congress to Abraham Lincoln. Cartwright's autobiography, written in 1856 and published a decade later, appeared at a time when Methodism's dominance in the Trans-Applachian West was unquestioned, despite the fact that controversies over slavery had riven the membership and divided the church. His memories helped to rally Methodists around their early history, which was closely identified with westward expansion, and his portrayal of the "backwoods preacher" in the old frontier contributed to the cultural romanticization of the West. Perhaps his most lasting contribution was to mythologize the vanishing figure of the frontier Methodist circuit rider:

A Methodist preacher in those days, when he felt that God had called him to preach, instead of hunting up a college or Biblical institute, hunted up a hardy pony or a horse, and some traveling apparatus, and with his library always at hand, namely, Bible, Hymn-book, and Discipline, he started. . . . He went through storms of wind, hail, snow and rain; climbed hills and mountains, traversed valleys, plunged through swamps, swam swollen streams, lay out all night, wet, weary, and hungry, held his horse by the bridle all night, or tied him to a limb, slept with his saddle blanket for a bed, his saddle or saddle-bags for his pillow, and his old big coat or blanket, if he had any, for a covering. Often he slept in dirty cabins, on earthen floors, before the fire; ate roasting ears for bread, drank butter-milk for coffee, or sage tea for imperial; took, with a hearty zest, deer or bear meat, or wild turkey, for breakfast, dinner, and supper if he could get it. . . . This was old fashioned Methodist fare and fortune.

Source: Peter Cartwright, *Autobiography of Peter Cartwright, the Backwoods Preacher,* edited by W. P. Strickland (Cincinnati: Hitchcock & Walden, 1868).

Expounding the Christian System. The Christians and Disciples of Christ contended that sectarian discord was a choice, not an inevitability. However, their shared conviction that restoration entailed certain fundamental truths ultimately turned unity into a secondary goal. In fact, Alexander Campbell became renowned for his theological debates, which served a publicity function but did not foster a spirit of amity. In 1828 Campbell defended Christianity against Robert Owen's charge that "religion was founded on ignorance and was the chief source of human misery"; his concluding speech at the end of the eight-day debate lasted twelve hours. Campbell's 1832 pamphlet, titled *Delusions: An Analysis of the Book of Mormon,* was widely reprinted, and his scathing but insightful explanation of the new church is still quoted by historians today. He also "exposed" Roman Catholic doctrines in a weeklong debate with the Catholic archbishop of Cincinnati in 1837 and critiqued presbyterianism at length in 1843. Campbell himself was meticulous in elucidating his ideas, which he synthesized in 1835 as *The Christian System, in reference to the Union of Christians, and a Restoration of Primitive Christianity, as Plead in the Current Reformation.* The text covered a range of theological topics and history and illustrated his allegiance to the Enlightenment philosophy of John Locke, combined with "the Bible, the whole Bible, and nothing but the Bible, as the foundation of all Christian union and communion." Although detractors accused him of producing exactly what he abhorred—a creed—Campbell replied that a personal statement of faith was a proper exercise of responsible Christianity, as long as the statement was not held up as a condition of union or fellowship. Protests notwithstanding, *The Christian System* was designed to winnow out error, even in the absence of coercion. The determination of the Campbell-Stone movement to communicate its ideas was demonstrated in its chartering of colleges and its prolific publications—in 1859 three weeklies, twelve monthlies, and one quarterly. Despite the Eastern prejudice that the West reveled in ignorance, the Christian movement revealed a more subtle dynamic at work. Westerners tended to be anti-intellectual in contesting the idea that certain castes had exclusive possession of special knowledge, yet people sought the "uplift" of education and honored biblical scholarship. As Campbell and Stone declared in their writings, just as theological fineries should never stand in the way of Christian union, so learning was the handmaiden of faith, not its superior. In fact, when Campbell organized Bethany College, he instructed that it should not have a professorship of theology since that would imply some had greater access to biblical truths than others.

Sect or Church? After the union, the Christians and Disciples of Christ began to establish "connections" beyond the individual congregations, but the linkage implied no assertion of authority over local churches. Part of the appeal of the movement had been its radical break with previous organizational forms. The members referred to the union of churches as a brotherhood rather than a denomination; they regarded joint efforts between congregations as cooperative rather than associative. Yet Campbell favored an extracongregational network in order to mount projects on a broader scale, especially evangelization. In the 1840s Campbell pressed forward on this theme, and in 1849 the first national convention of the Disciples was held in Cincinnati, though not without dissent. As with other denominations, foreign mission had served as the catalyst for larger institutional imperatives and for eventual division. Given the decentralized basis of authority, the Christians and Disciples of Christ moved cautiously in their efforts to define themselves corporately. Critics took this as a sign of the movement's weakness, proving that Campbellism was a sect, not an authentic church. Yet the emphasis on voluntarism was a consensual organizational strategy for gathering a community without resorting to dogmatism or authoritarianism. The Christian movement seemed to represent something fresh and unfettered, yet it harkened back to an "ancient order"—and to revolutionary principles. Alexander Campbell wrote that 4 July 1776 was comparable to the Jewish Passover because God had preserved the American people for a special destiny: "This Revolution, taken in all its influences, will make men free indeed."

That is, if the nation lived up to its ideals, its institutions and way of life would be pleasing in the sight of God. Restorationism in a religious context thus meshed with millennial hopes for the secular development of the nation.

Antebellum Religious Tensions. Issues that energized the Christian/Disciples of Christ movement revealed tensions within antebellum Protestantism in general. These included finding the proper balance between authority and freedom in religious matters, searching for harmony in the midst of difference, merging the claims of individual conscience with the need for Christian community, and reconciling evangelical sentiment to common sense, or reason. In its early stages the Christian movement imagined the possibilities of sovereign individuals united in fellowship by their own volition, of theological chaos tamed by people determining their faith for themselves. In the end slavery would capsize its call to unity, just as it did the national Union.

Sources:

John Boles, *The Great Revival 1787–1805* (Lexington: University Press of Kentucky, 1972);

Nathan Hatch, *The Democratization of American Christianity* (New Haven: Yale University Press, 1989);

Lester G. McAllister and William E. Tucker, *Journey in Faith: A History of the Christian Church (Disciples of Christ)* (St. Louis: Bethany Press, 1975);

Ralph E. Morrow, "The Great Revival, the West, and the Crisis of the Church," in *The Frontier Re-examined*, edited by John F. McDermott (Urbana: University of Illinois Press, 1967).

THE MORMONS

Mormonism. The Church of Jesus Christ of Latter-Day Saints, popularly known as the Mormons, initially seemed just another odd outcropping on the sacred topography of the period. By the Civil War it was clearly much more—to some, a true faith; to others, a powerful delusion. The growth of the church, alarming to non-Mormons, meant that it could not be easily dismissed, and Mormonism became an integral chapter in Western religious history. Opponents railed at the church's sanction of polygamy and at its union of religion and politics: the former defiled the Christian family while the latter sullied the ideals of the American republican experiment. Yet the American religious establishment realized that, somehow, Mormonism spoke to the unmet yearnings of thousands; it ran both with and against the grain of religion in the antebellum age.

Origins. For Mormons the spiritual beginnings of the church can be traced to September 1823, when Joseph Smith, their founder and leader, experienced his first prophetic vision. The eighteen-year-old Smith was visited three times by the angel Moroni, who told him of golden plates hidden in a nearby hill that contained the lost history of the Americas. Once translated, this new scripture would provide the basis for the restoration of the true church. Joseph discovered the plates at the site foretold, but his heart was not yet right with God, and so he had to wait four years until the angel Moroni at last permitted him to remove the treasures and begin the translation. Within eighteen months *The Book of Mormon* (1830) was ready for publication.

Organization. Because the present churches were all corrupted and condemned by God, a fresh bestowal of authority was necessary in order for Smith to recapture the purity of the primitive church. Although believers hailed *The Book of Mormon* as proof that God spoke in the here and now, the basis for the restoration of the church was firmly grounded in Smith himself and in his role as the prophet and revelator. According to tradition, in May 1829 John the Baptist appeared to Smith and to his scribe Oliver Cowdery and endowed them with the Aaronic priesthood, or the power to baptize for the remission of sins. Later that summer the Apostles Peter, James, and John conferred upon them the Melchizedek priesthood, or the power to ordain and to organize the true church. In April 1830, at a gathering of about sixty people, the Church of the Latter-Day Saints, as it was soon called, was formed, with Smith and five others as elders. Outwardly, the structure of the church was ordinary: a pyramid topped by elders, who ordained priests, teachers, and deacons. However, what connected all the parts was Smith's claim to charismatic leadership, that is, that he had been endowed with divine power. In one of his numerous revelations that informed the doctrine of the church, Smith declared that he was God's prophet, whose authority to decide for the Latter-Day Saints was not to be questioned. He alone held the keys to the mysteries, for as another revelation disclosed, "No one shall be appointed to received commandments and revelations in this church excepting my servant Joseph Smith, jun."

Mormon Beliefs. In the 1830s and early 1840s the message of Mormonism was simple: God was speaking through his prophet Joseph Smith. There were three sources for the church's doctrine: the Bible, *The Book of Mormon,* and the incontestible revelations of Joseph Smith, which were eventually compiled as *Doctrines and Covenants* (1835). Since *The Book of Mormon* had come directly from God, there was no possibility of error. On the other hand, the Bible was susceptible to mistakes in translation, which accounted for any inconsistencies between the two texts. The "articles and covenants" of 1830 contained such familiar theological tenets as faith in Christ, repentance, baptism by immersion, and the laying on of hands for the Holy Spirit. However, these ordinances were only valid if performed by those to whom the dispensation to act in the name of God had been restored, that is, those ordained by Joseph Smith. Membership in the Latter-Day Saints required re-baptism, as an affirmation that the church was the only one favored by God. Everyone else was lost. Other Mormon precepts dispatched the puzzles of the Trinity (how could there be one God divided into three parts?) and the Eucharist (was Christ physically or metaphorically present in the communion elements?)—debates that still divided Christendom. Smith's answer was to posit an anthropomorphic conception of God and Jesus Christ, who were separate personages of material substance. In his view the idea of a nonmaterial deity was nonsense. Even the Holy Spirit possessed a body, though made of purer stuff than human beings and only discernible by pure eyes.

Kirtland, Ohio. Early members of the church came primarily from the relatives of Smith's small circle. In 1830 Smith sent missionaries westward to scout for a site for the new Zion. Stopping in Kirtland, in northeastern Ohio, they converted Sidney Rigdon, a former Campbellite minister. Rigdon became one of Smith's counselors and substantially increased Mormon numbers when he brought his flock of more than one hundred into the fold. Harassed by neighbors in Western New York, the Saints community around Smith moved to join Rigdon in Kirtland in 1831, whereupon they continued to expand and organize. By 1835 nearly two thousand Mormons had gravitated to the area. Although the later success of the church has given its development an aura of inevitability, for many years it seemed entirely possible that the Church of Latter-Day Saints would follow the pattern of other sects in the antebellum era and become a footnote in American religious history. Their sojourn in Ohio came to an abrupt end when a Mormon banking venture collapsed in the financial Panic of 1837. Smith declared Independence as the site of the New Jerusalem, and the Mormons migrated to Missouri. The state was already something of a maelstrom because of slavery, and hostility against the Mormons reached a fever pitch. Smith delivered a Fourth of July oration in 1838 in which he promised vengeance on any who persecuted the Saints. Open warfare broke out; Smith was arrested on charges of treason; and the governor of Missouri declared the Mormons a blight to be exterminated. After six months in jail, Smith escaped. The wearing process of founding a community and then abandoning it continued as the Mormons headed northeast to Illinois.

Nauvoo. On a peninsula jutting out into the Mississippi, the Saints began once more to build Zion, which they called Nauvoo. The elections of 1840 offered an opportunity for the Mormons to achieve some measure of security. Utilizing the weapon of the ballot box, Smith pledged and delivered Mormon support for a gubernatorial candidate in exchange for a city charter, which guaranteed their autonomy. The Mormons promptly began to transform Nauvoo, and by 1844 it was the second largest city in Illinois, with a population of 10,000, not counting outlying Mormon communities. The infusion came partly from immigration. In a daring gamble at a low point in Mormon fortunes, Smith had sent to England seven Apostles from the elite Quorum of Twelve. They had an immediate impact, especially in urban areas, and from 1837 to 1846 about 18,000 Saints were baptized; 4,700 of them journeyed to Nauvoo. Migration compensated for the inevitable falling away of converts after the first blush of excitement. Some of Smith's earli-

The Book of Mormon (1830) is a long and extraordinarily complex story, a retelling of God's plan of salvation with North America at its center. The bulk of the narrative deals with the descendants of an Israelite named Lephi, who received a vision in the sixth century B.C., before the Babylonian captivity, that he was to lead a band out of the desert. Eventually reaching the Indian Ocean, the Israelites constructed a boat and sailed to the west coast of the North American continent. Soon the people divided into warring factions, allied with either Nephi or Laman, the sons of Lephi. The conflict continued for centuries. In the meantime the Nephites met favor in the sight of God, building a flourishing civilization with temples and cities. The Lamanites turned away from God and reverted to warring and hunting. The Lamanites were the ancestors of the Native Americans, cursed by God because of their disobedience. "Wherefore, as they were white, and exceeding fair and delightsome," the "sin of blackness" was placed upon them. After his resurrection, Jesus Christ appeared to the descendants of Lephi, and for two hundred years all the people lived in idyllic harmony. They strayed again into unrighteousness, and the peace was shattered by internecine war. By the close of the fourth century, the Lamanites were on the verge of eradicating the last of the Nephites, so Mormon, a Nephite prophet-historian, gathered together the ancient records of his people and wrote an abridged account of their history. Mormon instructed his son Moroni to bury the plates on which this scripture was written in a hill called Cumorah (near Palmyra, New York) after the final battle between the Lamanites and the Nephites. Moroni, the only Nephite survivor, added an epitaph on the extermination of his people and then followed his father's instructions. The plates lay hidden until uncovered by the one who would restore the ancient church: Joseph Smith. Mormon detractors were hard-pressed to account for this six-hundred-page opus, written by a semiliterate man at a pace of three thousand words a day and imitating the style of the King James Bible. For many years opponents attributed the work to one of Smith's counselors. Sidney Rigdon was an acknowledged biblical scholar, and many non-Mormons thought that he adapted *The Book of Mormon* from a contemporary fictional tale whose central plot was that one of the lost tribes of Israel had found its way to the American continent. The timing of events discredited this explanation, and what has persisted is an "environmentalist" critique, first proposed by Alexander Campbell and expanded by modern-day analysts. As Campbell expressed it in the *Millennial Harbinger* of February 1831, *The Book of Mormon* contained "every error and almost every truth discussed in N. York for the last ten years." Some of the book's appeal did draw from its familiarity with great controversies of the day: the origin of the Indians, Free Masonry, anti-Catholicism, national destiny, and, in religion, free will over predestination. Woven throughout its histories of ancient peoples were simple object lessons on why civilizations rose and fell, and their repetition has led the historian Nathan Hatch to characterize *The Book of Mormon* as a "populist manifesto." The wrath of God repeatedly struck down proud people who flaunted their wealth and defined success by riches and status, or who claimed authority based on secular learning rather than knowledge of God. Divinely inspired or not, *The Book of Mormon* was never intended to be a theological tract, nor was it used in an exegetical sense. A companion to the Bible rather than its replacement, the mere existence of a new scripture became the basis for faith. *The Book of Mormon* was, in a sense, Joseph Smith's license to serve as Prophet of the Church of Jesus Christ of Latter-Day Saints.

Sources: *The Book of Mormon: Another Testament of Jesus Christ*, translated by Joseph Smith (Nauvoo, Ill.: Printed by J. Smith, 1842);

Nathan Hatch, *The Democratization of American Christianity* (New Haven: Yale University Press, 1989).

est followers, including Oliver Cowdery, were excommunicated, often for opposing the Prophet, and former elders, such as John Bennett, became determined enemies. The doctrines revealed by Smith during this time were a key source of division, for Nauvoo marked a new stage in Mormon theology. The Saints became less identifiably Christian and more sui generis. Among the most controversial revelations were baptism for the dead (a vicarious offer of salvation to the deceased); the potential divinity of man, which implied a plurality of gods (though only God the Father was the proper object of human worship); and polygamy (a practice kept secret until 1852).

Appeal. In several key ways Mormonism drew from broader sentiments running through antebellum religion. First, American denominationalism had produced what seemed to many as a cacophony of competing churches. Religious freedom may have offered a surfeit of choices for people, with no guarantee except individual conviction that the choice made was the right one. The result was a longing for certainty through the reclamation of the one true church. The Christians and the

Disciples of Christ, another movement that blossomed in the West, also sought to reclaim spiritual authority in an age of doctrinal rivalry. Their answer was "no creed but Christ," giving priority to the individual conscience seeking knowledge and faith through contemplation of the Bible. In contrast to this spiritual restoration of the New Testament church, Mormons believed in a literal restoration. Simply put, God had withdrawn from the churches until the moment when Joseph Smith received his new dispensation. Now only the Mormons possessed the authority to baptize in the name of Christ and to carry out God's will for humankind. This exclusive claim was joined to a universal appeal—that is, every person was endowed with the free will to decide to become a Saint. For those who searched for religious authority, there was no greater comfort than the belief in the direct revelation of God to the Prophet Joseph. Second, the evangelical thrust of the Second Great Awakening had congealed in a massive reform movement. Mormonism again spoke to the urgent twin concerns of the religious: what must I do to be saved? and, what must I do next? Once embraced by the Latter-Day Saints, a convert immediately set to work on the practical tasks of building the new kingdom of God here and now. Belief followed by action was a common thread in antebellum religion, yet Mormon enterprises offered a structure and direction that was sometimes lacking in the disputatious evangelical united front. Third, *The Book of Mormon* had "mythic potency," in the words of the theologian Mircea Eliade, and tantalized those drawn more to the supernatural than the rational. The story that unfolded in this new scripture also provided a biblical history for the Americas, an immensely satisfying account that literally made the West (near Independence, Missouri) the site of Eden and therefore the location of God's restored kingdom. Given this interpretation, the "new world" now asserted a prior claim over the "old" in God's great plan of salvation. No other doctrine, secular or religious, had placed American destiny in such a spectacular historical context. Mormons believed that from the moment Columbus set foot on the New World, events had been unfolding to prepare the way for the recovery of the church. Even independence from Great Britain had occurred so that Joseph Smith would be able to claim his mantle as Prophet. For those uncertain of the future of the American experiment within the great sweep of human history, here was a religious assurance of its necessary continuance. Finally, Mormonism was a religious expression of the Jacksonian credo of the common man. Anyone could be granted the gift of revelation within their sphere of relations (individuals for themselves, fathers for their households, and bishops for their wards), though only the Prophet could speak for the whole church. All worthy males, except for blacks, who bore the "mark of Cain," could be ordained to the lay priesthood. The prerequisite for advancement was unquestioned loyalty to Smith and demonstrated merit of some kind. Ordinary people who had been denied access to upward mobility may have found that "sainthood" offered better opportunities for empowerment. Further, as expounded by Smith in Nauvoo, Mormonism asserted that all beings evolved, including God. By following the pathways of righteousness, true Saints could advance after death to a celestial stage and continue to grow in the faith until they themselves attained godhood. This celebration of the infinite potential of man was captured in Smith's maxim: "As man is, God once was; as God is, man may become."

Death of the Prophet. In 1844 visitors to Nauvoo would have seen a neat, bustling town, with sawmills, flour mills, a tool factory, a foundry, a chinaware factory, and, in the center, an unfinished yet clearly ambitious temple. However, jealousies again began to mount, as non-Mormon merchants and developers in the surrounding areas saw themselves shut out from the benefits of Nauvoo growth. Illinois politicians had been willing to use Mormon bloc voting, but suddenly they perceived it as a dangerous corruption of democratic politics. Residents felt threatened by Mormon expansion, and rumors of the Saints' bizarre beliefs exacerbated public hostility. Especially in the communities surrounding Nauvoo, there were several instances of petty violence, theft of property, and harassment. Given the various sources of public antagonism, it is questionable whether the persecution can be considered strictly religious. Mormons were not passive victims, and the violence between Mormons and non-Mormons was typical of the antebellum West. The Danites, formed in 1838, were a formidable group of avenging Mormons who followed the dictum of an eye for an eye. The Nauvoo Whittling and Whistling Brigade, created for Mormon youth in 1844 also engaged in retributive activities. The Nauvoo Legion consisted of two thousand troops, which Smith enjoyed parading in formation as a not-too-subtle reminder of strength. Both sides justified the use of force, creating a volatile situation even under normal circumstances. During 1844 Smith sent some of his Apostles to the East to construct a foundation for a presidential bid—an alarming suggestion of combined religious and political ambitions. Meanwhile, in Nauvoo a group of disaffected Mormons published an anti-Mormon newspaper, whereupon Smith sent representatives to confiscate all copies and destroy the printing office. The dissidents swore out a complaint against Smith at the county seat of Carthage. Smith submitted to a trial in Nauvoo before a sympathetic, if non-Mormon, judge, and the court declared him innocent. Enraged, the adversaries of the Saints appealed to the governor, who ordered Smith to comply with the original warrant. Smith declared martial law and mobilized the legion. Illinois militia groups, empowered by the governor, advanced on the town, so Smith, his brother Hiram, and two other Mormon leaders placed themselves in custody. At Carthage the governor did nothing to quench the rising anti-Mormon hysteria, and in fact left the town and the Mormons to the mercy of state militia. On the evening of 27 June 1844, a group calling themselves the Carthage Greys stormed the jail, shot Hiram and Joseph Smith to death, and then beat a hasty retreat.

Succession. The Saints mourned the loss of the Prophet and faced a crucial turning point in their restoration of the Church of Jesus Christ. No provision had been made for succession. However, Brigham Young's unflagging loyalty to Joseph Smith had made him first among the Apostles. Raised in a strict Methodist family in Vermont, Young was also among the disenchanted of the Second Great Awakening, drawn to Mormonism by his devotion to Joseph Smith and by the practical orientation of the faith. His conversion to Mormonism brought to the Saints a man of incredible organizational skill. While Joseph had the ability to inspire, Young had a gift for putting ideas into action. A remarkable individual in his own right, he asserted himself only as the divine designee of Joseph Smith. When Young offered his leadership to the assembled Saints in August 1844, many there swore that his "form, size, countenance, and voice" were that of Smith. The Prophet had passed the scepter to Young directly. (After Young's death in 1877, succession became a matter of seniority rather than a manifestation of prophecy.) The emergence of ten or so splinter groups, each claiming to have inherited Smith's authority, belied the seeming ease of the transfer of power. Only the Reorganized Church of Latter-Day Saints constituted a permanent alternative to "Brighamism." Among its members were Emma, Joseph's wife, and her son Joseph III, who became the church's leader when he came of age. Centered in the Midwest, the reorganized church eventually rejected all of the Nauvoo teachings, including the exclusion of blacks from the priesthood.

Westward Immigration. For a time after the death of Smith, Young turned the attention of the Saints to the completion of the temple, for it was only there that the sacred rites enjoined by the Prophet could be performed. In 1845 the Illinois legislature revoked the Nauvoo charter. Young and the Twelve Apostles recognized that the time had come to seek the protection of an isolated setting, a project that Smith had begun investigating several years before. After examining the report of the explorer John C. Fremont, Young decided that the arid Salt Lake valley, a neglected possession of the independent Mexican state, would not be a pearl coveted by other settlers. Although Young had hoped for an orderly departure, stepped-up harassment prompted a more precipitated evacuation, which occurred in waves from February 1846 until the fall. The Mormons had to leave many possessions behind and sold land and goods for well below market value. As 12,000 Saints straggled across 120 miles of Iowa, Young halted the migratory stream near present-day Omaha to wait out the winter. Meanwhile, he prepared the Mormons for the thousand-mile journey ahead to the Salt Lake valley. It was an organizational tour de force. Young divided the emigrant families into groups

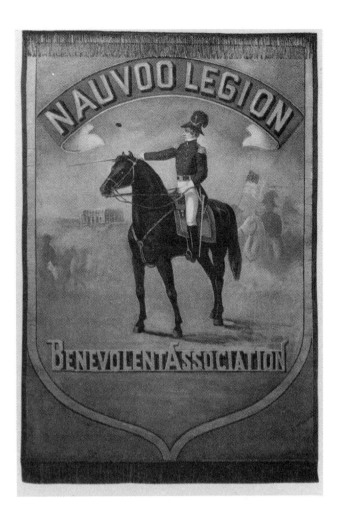

The banner for Joseph Smith's 2,000-man militia force (Church of Jesus Christ of Latter-Day Saints Museum of Church History and Art, Salt Lake City, Utah)

of tens, fifties, and hundreds, assigned leaders to each unit, and ensured that each company had the necessary supplies and survival skills. In April 1847 a pioneer contingent, streamlined for speed, traversed the little-known territory to the Salt Lake valley in three months. Young left instructions on settlement and headed back to guide ten more companies to the new Zion. In the analysis of the historian Jan Shipps, the rigorous trek forged the Mormons into a people, imbued with a self-conscious identity that set them apart from the Gentiles, or non-Mormons. With Young's encouragement, the exodus and its trials became a transformative Exodus event in Mormon consciousness. Thereafter, the Saints commemorated the parallels between their journey and that of the ancient Hebrews: like them, the Mormons had been led by a Moses through a wilderness to a promised land.

Salt Lake Valley. In contrast to the gradual and often haphazard gathering of other Western settlements, the entire community of Mormons was transplanted and nearly operational within months of their arrival in the Great Basin. The precise layout of Salt Lake City mirrored the comprehensiveness of the church's control over everyday affairs. At the center of the city was the site for the temple (not completed until the end of the century), and from it streets radiated out in graphlike fashion. The area was divided into ten-acre blocks, which in turn were partitioned into eight lots of one-and-one-quarter acre each. Sidewalks were laid twenty feet from the street, and houses had to be set back another twenty feet from the sidewalk. The migration had reinforced the mandate of obedience upon the Saints, and everyone had a role in the building of the kingdom. The Council of Fifty, now the de facto governing body, organized the settlement into wards, or congregations, of seventy to one hundred families. The "bishop" in charge, appointed by the church hierarchy, was often the same leader who had brought the group across the desert. The bishop's functions were both temporal and spiritual and included oversight of schools, worship, provisions for the poor, and public works. Through his office the council regulated the disparate communities. The Mormons had experimented with communal ownership in Kirtland, following precepts in the Book of Enoch. Since then the leadership had pursued a course of directed growth through cooperative enterprise. Brigham Young was less interested in promoting a particular economic system than in shielding the Saints from the speculation and commercial preoccupations that had distracted them in the past. Yet the environment encouraged central planning in the management of the scarce resources of water and timber. At the ward level, the mandatory tithe continued the communal ideal. Each family had to contribute one-tenth of its livestock, grain, flour, butter, eggs, vegetables, and commodities to a storehouse for distribution to the poor or for times of shortage.

Polygamy. In 1852 Brigham Young publicly announced the revelation that had been kept secret since 1843: plural marriage (the "Order of Jacob") was a holy rite incumbent on the Saints whom the leaders deemed worthy of the privilege. Elder Heber C. Kimball was the most dedicated practitioner in Mormon history, with more than forty wives, and Young himself had more than twenty wives. Such numbers were the exception. During the fifty years that the Order of Jacob was in force, the vast majority of Mormons were monogamous, and plural unions frequently involved no more than two wives. Despite the relatively small percentage of participants, polygamy was a continued source of outrage to non-Mormons. Critics pointed to it as proof that Smith was a false prophet—that he indulged his lust under the guise of religious commandment. The high divorce rate during Young's leadership in Utah, as well as the lower birth rates in plural marriages, testified to the strains of polygamous unions, especially for first wives. Regardless, women not only acquiesced to the practice but defended it, convinced that their demonstration of piety would yield the highest exaltation in the next life. Certainly polygamy strengthened the Mormon sense of difference from surrounding society. However, the reaction of Emma, Joseph's wife, may be taken as an indication of its controversial nature for even the firmest believer. Smith was apparently "sealed" in marriage to as many as forty-eight women, though only a handful of these may have been physical relationships. Emma allegedly burned the first record of the revelation on plural marriage. Not only did she never accept it, she initially counseled women against it and later denied that Joseph had had other wives.

Native Americans. As Mormon colonists began to move into areas contiguous to Salt Lake City, they encroached further on tribal lands, especially those of the Utes. The result was periodic armed conflict, until the U.S. Army solved the problem by forcing the indigenous peoples of the region onto reservations in the late 1850s. In Mormon eschatology, the conversion of the Native Americans was an essential prerequisite to the Second Coming, but the construction of Zion preoccupied the Saints more than the conversion of the Indians. Despite the inclusion of the Indians in the Mormon worldview, Mormon missionaries expressed the same mandate as their Protestant counterparts: to educate the "despised and degraded sons of the forest" in "the arts of civil life . . . principles and practice of virtue, modesty, temperance, cleanliness, industry, mechanical arts, manners, customs, dress, music." The Mormon appeal included the notion that the Indians' acceptance of *The Book of Mormon* was the means by which they would once again become great, "and have plenty to eat and good clothes to wear, and should be in favor with the Great Spirit." Young pragmatically decided that it was easier to feed and clothe the Indians than to eradicate them, but benevolence gave way before the priority of protecting the Saints. Ultimately, therefore, there was little noticeable difference in the Indian policies of Mormons and non-Mormons.

Prosperity and Growth. Migration had stripped the Mormons of much of the wealth accumulated at Nauvoo, but the Mexican War provided an opportunity to recoup some losses. President James Polk had welcomed a force of 500 Mormons who volunteered for Col. Stephen Kearny's expedition to California. Although they saw no action, the wages of the recruits added nearly $70,000 to the church's coffers. Since the death of the Prophet Joseph, competing factions had whittled away at the membership of the official church; after migration, the forbidding Utah Basin and the lure of California gold drove others to seek more hospitable climes. Once again, strong missionary drives overseas replenished the Saints. By 1845 nearly 2,000 young men had set out as proselytes. The church established a Perpetual Emigrating Fund to provide loans to emigrants. Between 1852 and 1855, 10,000 migrants received its assistance. Of the 22,000 converts traveling to the Salt Lake valley through 1855, 19,500 were from Great Britain, 2,000 were Scandinavians, and the rest were French, Italians, and Germans. Brigham Young acknowledged in 1855 that many of the newcomers were "actuated by no other motive than to have the privilege of being removed from their oppressed condition to where they will not suffer." Even so, the practical prophet instructed church agents to recruit skilled workers, especially in the iron and textile industries, for the voyage to the United States. By the mid 1850s the burgeoning flock had become somewhat unruly. Young's counselor called for a Reformation to wake up the Saints and exhort them to keep their covenants. Bishops went from house to house to remind ward members that their personal cleanliness and the tidiness of their homes were necessary for spiritual purity. Missionaries also visited the congregations and, in revival fashion, roused the people with impassioned sermons. To some the reports of visions and speaking in tongues seemed evidence of success, but one bishop preferred to define "reformation" as "good fences, clean streets, debts paid, tithing receipts."

Deseret. In 1849 the Council of Fifty converted the Mormon colony into the State of Deseret, complete with a ratified constitution and currency. Deseret encompassed 210,000 square miles at the farthest communities and included present-day Nevada, Western Utah, southern parts of Wyoming, Idaho, and Oregon, and most of southern California. The Mormons lobbied the federal government to accept Deseret as a new state, but instead, in the Compromise of 1850, the United States Congress delineated the area as Utah Territory. This meant federal governance, but Mormons were relieved when President Millard Fillmore named Brigham Young as the first territorial governor. For several years there was little outside intervention in Mormon affairs, though relations with federal appointees were often bitter. Then in 1856 the Republican Party platform declared opposition to "twin relics of barbarism—slavery and polygamy." Because of the public outcry President James Buchanan felt pressured to replace Young as governor and tame Mormon resistance to federal authority. In 1857 he mustered a force of 2,500 men, but the Utah expedition was something of a fiasco from the start. Regardless, the Mormons reacted to federal intervention as a hostile invasion, and by the fall they had fortified the mountain passes and burned their supply forts. Their exaggerated fears led to the Mountain Meadows Massacre in August 1857, in which a combined force of 54 Mormons and 300 Ute allies attacked and killed 120 members of a wagon train of California-bound settlers. The massacre was a rallying cry for Mormon opposition throughout the century since it seemed to prove the callous disdain Mormons felt for Gentiles. While winter storms halted the expedition in the Rocky Mountains, Young recognized that it was counterproductive to take on the U.S. government, so he indicated his willingness to negotiate. Buchanan was receptive, given the mounting opposition to the campaign's costs and its ominous implications for states' rights. In 1858 the president granted the Mormons a full pardon; the new territorial governor was installed without incident; and the army set up camp forty

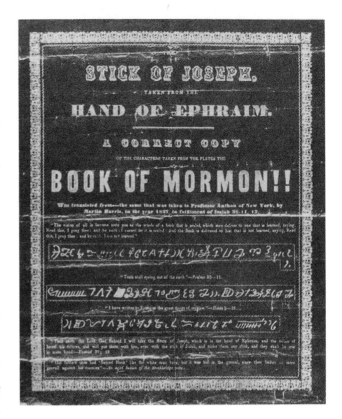

An early advertisement for Joseph Smith's book translated from tablets he claimed to have found buried in upstate New York (National Portrait Gallery, Washington, D.C.)

miles outside of Salt Lake City to ensure the peace. When they left in 1861, with the outbreak of the Civil War, the Mormons could claim to have gotten the best of the deal in the profits they made from trade with the army. Moreover, in the initial panic over rumors of invasion, Young had responded by gathering in all the outlying settlements. The episode thus served as a timely and compelling reminder for the Mormons of their unified identity in the face of an unfriendly world.

Conclusion. The Church of Jesus Christ of Latter-Day Saints was a recognizable product of the nineteenth-century milieu from which it emerged. As the New England poet John Greenleaf Whittier wrote in 1845, "They speak a language of hope and promise to weak, weary hearts, tossed and troubled, who have wandered from sect to sect, seeking in vain for the primal manifestation of the divine power." Nor could the Mormons ultimately escape the economic and intellectual influences of the surrounding culture. As the historian Sidney Ahlstrom has observed, by the end of the nineteenth century "a strait-laced kind of prosperity and stability had replaced enthusiasm and millennial expectation as the leitmotiv of Mormon life." Yet the Mormons were also something completely original. In their secular organization they seemed to assail the separation of church and state enshrined in American religious liberty, creating instead a political, theological, and economic nexus of unprecedented scale. In their beliefs they tested the boundaries of the new nation's commitment to religious toleration. The Mormon challenge to antebellum orthodoxy was vigorous and successful, suggesting to the Christian establishment that neither reason nor providence could eradicate human delusion.

Sources:

Leonard Arrington and Davis Bitton, *The Mormon Experience: A History of the Latter-Day Saints* (New York: Knopf, 1979);

John L. Brooke, *The Refiner's Fire: The Making of Mormon Cosmology, 1644–1844* (Cambridge: Cambridge University Press, 1994);

Mario S. De Pillis, "The Quest for Religious Authority and the Rise of Mormonism," *Dialogue*, 1 (Fall 1966): 68–88;

Klaus I. Hansen, *Mormonism and the American Experience* (Chicago: University of Chicago Press, 1981);

Jan Shipps, *Mormonism: The Story of a New Religious Tradition* (Urbana: University of Illinois Press, 1985).

NATIVE AMERICANS: RELIGIOUS PRACTICES IN THE WEST

Confrontation. By the early nineteenth century all Native Americans had been touched to various degrees by contact with Europeans. Historians often analyze the social, political, and economic challenges presented by white culture, yet to most Native Americans contact and its consequences had to be grasped first in religious terms. From the perspective of the Native American "West," religion in the first half of the nineteenth century was characterized by the struggle to reconfigure sacred worlds in light of shifting circumstances. Unfortunately, most of the available information concerning nineteenth-century Indian religions comes not from the Indians themselves but from the observations of whites, whose cultural and individual biases influenced what they saw and recorded. Euro-Americans and Native Americans had to fit their experience of the other into their own framework. The European understanding of different religions was generally based on a model of progress, with Christianity as the pinnacle. Yet each observer's own opinion also came into play in the process of interpretation: to whites, Indian religiosity could represent either the darkness of heathenism, the primitive ways of an unenlightened culture, or the clear evidence of universal truths embedded in the Indian heart in common with the rest of humanity. In 1839 George Catlin published his famous journal of his travels among the Western tribes, and he responded to the different currents of opinion at that time:

> I have heard it said by some very good men, and some who have even been preaching the Christian religion amongst them, that they have no religion—that all their zeal in their worship of the Great Spirit was but the foolish excess of ignorant superstition—that their humble devotions and supplications to the Sun and the Moon, where many of them suppose that the Great Spirit resides, were but the absurd rantings of idolatry.... I fearlessly assert to the world, (and I defy contradiction) that the North American Indian is everywhere, in his native state, a highly moral and religious being, endowed by his Maker, with an intuitive knowledge of some great Author of his being, and the Universe; in dread of whose displeasure he constantly lives, with the apprehension before him, of a future state, where he expects to be rewarded or punished according to the merits he has gained or forfeited in this world.... Of their extraordinary modes and sincerity of worship, I speak with equal confidence; and although I am compelled to pity them for their ignorance, I am bound to say that I never saw any other people of any colour, who spend so much of their lives in humbling themselves before, and worshipping the Great Spirit, as some of these tribes do.

Clash of Worldviews. Regardless, white observers, no matter how sympathetic, were incapable of apprehending certain crucial aspects of how Native Americans viewed reality—in particular, the spatial orientation that was very different from the temporal anchoring of European culture. This clash of perspectives was probably the most fundamental difference between the way whites and Indians considered their worlds. The Indians possessed a sense of place that was generally alien to Euro-Americans, who regarded land as a commodity. Native religion entailed a "sacred geography," which was reflected in cosmology as well as in ceremony. The context of religious observance was therefore vital, for tribal traditions, events, and revelations were linked to specific sites. These connections were not transferable, and abandoning the ancestral places meant severing spiritual ties. By contrast Europeans saw themselves grounded in time and therefore in history. The past was a record that had to be scrutinized for its lessons, then hammered into a better future. Without this discipline civilizations would slide back into darkness. To the Indians such a linear, temporal progression made little sense, and the image of a circle captured better the "movement" of their sacred

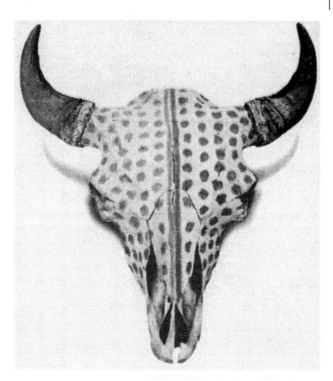

A painted buffalo skull used in Sun Dance ceremonies, circa 1850 (Royal Ontario Museum, Toronto)

Sioux Chief Short Bull's hide paintings of Sun Dance worshipers, circa 1850 (American Museum of Natural History, New York)

history. As might be expected, then, Indian religions were not absorbed with promulgating moral precepts or points of doctrine against which the advance or decline of a person or group could be measured. Instead of emphasizing a past historical event (such as the resurrection of Jesus Christ), with its theological implications, the focus of native belief tended to be experiential, centered in ritual practice and the power gained thereby.

Diversity and Adaptability. The multiplicity of indigenous belief systems makes it difficult to do more than generalize about common features of Native American religion. Groups that shared linguistic ties also often shared religious traditions, but there were always local variations. Moreover, tribal rites and ceremonies were generally not static but assimilative. Indian religions continually merged ancient traditions with new introductions that seemed to offer another way of approaching the sacred. As the historian James Axtell has observed, in religious matters "purposeful change and adjustment was the only norm," and the process of borrowing extended to myths, heroes, artifacts, ceremonies, and beliefs. Turned outward, this inclusive approach meant that other religious systems were regarded as different rather than wrong. Many groups, including the Cherokees, the Nez Percés, and the Navajos, considered themselves as "the real people," but their special relationship with their Creator was not framed in opposition to another group's similar claim.

A Holistic Sensibility. Even before contact, then, Indian religions were diverse, adaptable, and holistic. A religious awareness permeated every activity, and there was no compartmentalization of religion from the rest of life. The physical world was so filled with potent spiritual energy that the supernatural and the natural merged. The kinship with nature arose from its spiritual animation: animals, plants, rocks, mountains, rivers, and weather phenomena all possessed power and personality. Consequently, religious goals were focused on the search for and renewal of spiritual allies, who conferred power and favor when treated with respect (and removed favor when snubbed). Native Americans courted disaster in every aspect of life if they failed to honor all variety of sacred beings through the correct performance of ritual. Ceremonies and rites thus formed, in the phrase of the anthropologist Ruth Underhill, "the very fabric of life," nourishing harmonious relationships with the spirit world and keeping the universe orderly.

Indigenous Ceremonies. There were common ceremonial themes throughout Native America, such as acknowledgment of the firstfruits of the hunt or the harvest, but each group shaped the exact form of a ritual, combining ancient usages with new elements to create a unique amalgam. To nineteenth-century white observers, two of the best-known indigenous ceremonies represented opposite sides of Indian religiosity. The Green Corn Dance, or Busk, was celebrated by some Eastern Woodlands cultures, usually in July or August, when ears of corn had grown to the roasting stage. The ceremony commemorated the renewal of connections between all parts of creation, and by extension, within the tribal community. Among the Creeks, for example, it served a healing function, for every infraction except murder could be absolved and the transgressors be reinstated into the tribe. Fire furnished the symbol of a fresh beginning, as all hearth fires were extinguished, then relit by drawing from a newly kindled community fire. To Anglo-Americans, such observances had a familiar, if primitive, ring, fulfilling the same function as a day of thanksgiving. Not so among the Plains Indians, who held a major ceremony at the conclusion of the hunting season. A dance lasting several days provided an opportunity to pay respect to all of creation and to seek its renewed favor, especially with regard to the buffalo. The ceremony was vital to the well-being of the tribe as well as to the prestige of the participants. Although each group had its own traditions and name for the event, the Lakota (Sioux) Sun Dance became famous through descriptions in travelers' accounts. Among the Oglalas of the Teton Sioux, self-torture was a part of the dance and was undertaken as proof of the individual's intense commitment to seek a vision through pain. George Catlin visited the Mandans and the Lakotas in the 1830s and observed their inclusion of "privation and torture" in this communal ceremony. In both instances, splints were inserted into the body through strategic muscles in the chest, arms, and legs, and the individual was suspended from the center pole in the lodge, sometimes with additional weights applied. The Mandan boys were soon released, whereupon they willed themselves to resist exhaustion and join the dance outside the lodge. The Lakota adults, on the other hand, remained suspended and bleeding from sunrise to sunset, which put their chances of survival in doubt. Voluntarily participating in such a practice was so alien to Anglo-American concepts of civilized behavior that the Sun Dance was outlawed after the Civil War.

Vision Quests. The most intensely personal religious experience for Indians was achieved through the vision quest, which was the individual's acknowledgment of dependency on the spirit world. In general the vision quest was a rite of passage for all males reaching puberty, but in the Columbia Plateau both boys and girls could seek out a spirit guide. The person often spent several nights alone, fasting, praying constantly for a spiritual guide or contact, and perhaps even punishing his or her body by mutilation or by plunging into icy water. The goal was to have a tutelary or guardian spirit show itself in dream or vision, which would signify its unique spiritual linkage to that person throughout life. The spirit would offer instruction on what activities would bring success and what would lead to harm or failure. As a commemoration of their bond, the spirit might tell the individual to carry a specific token or to gather certain items and keep them in a sacred bundle, or might teach the person a special song that would call out the supernatural power. The more spirit helpers one obtained, the better, but only the exceptional seeker went beyond the initial vision quest.

Organization and Ritual. Religious organization varied throughout Native America, but it often influenced a group's ritualistic emphasis. For example, personal visions were not as important in the Puebloan culture of the Southwest, where religious activity was carefully structured around societies and priesthoods. There the priest candidate became qualified for his office by learning prescribed rituals and songs from a mentor. For less organized tribal religions, such as those in the Plains and the Columbia Plateau, direct interaction with the spirits through visions, dreams, or possession was highly valued. Those who achieved the status of shaman or medicine man were set apart not by training but because they demonstrated superior communication with the spirit world or with more powerful spirits. The proof was their ability to locate game, control the weather, cure illness, identify spirit guides, and perhaps even prophesy.

The Great Spirit. Although some indigenous belief systems (such as those on the Columbia Plateau) tended toward pantheism, others seemed to establish a hierarchy, topped by a single Great Spirit. This mysterious power animated the physical universe and could be employed for good as well as evil ends, which helped to explain the occurrence of misfortune and calamity. There were different interpretations of the Great Spirit, but the description of an Osage Indian in 1925 is suggestive: "All life is wakan. So also is everything which exhibits power, whether in action, as the winds and drifting clouds, or in passive endurance, as the boulder by the wayside. For even the commonest sticks and stones have a spiritual essence which must be reverenced as a manifestation of the all-pervading mysterious power that fills the universe." The Oglalas, linguistic kin of the Osages, spoke of Wakonda, or Great Wakan, in the sense of "supreme being," which encouraged the missionaries to adopt the word as a translation for the Christian God.

Religion and the Natural World. The Great Spirit, which differed in substance from the power connected with individual nature spirits, was not conceived in anthropomorphic terms. Because relations with nature were on an equal level with human relations, other parts of nature, from birds to fish to rocks, were in some sense people. In their ancestral form they behaved in human ways, and their activities explained a wide range of natural phenomena: from how night and day were divided (Creeks) to why dogs have long tongues (Caddos). Many tribal religions included a "trickster," such as the coyote in the Plains, the blue jay or raven in the Northwest, and the rabbit in the Woodlands. Whether the trickster's activities benefitted or hurt human beings was a matter of chance. The rich traditions of myth and legend, which were an essential part of indigenous religious ceremony and of a particular group's history, often celebrated the exploits of these man-animals while simultaneously offering moral lessons on pride, greed, or folly to all who would listen. The stories that were so much a part of religious observance demonstrated the connection of native religions to experiences in the physical world, rather than to theological abstractions.

Sources:

James Axtell, *The Invasion Within: The Contest of Cultures in Colonial North America* (New York: Oxford University Press, 1985);

John Bierhorst, *The Mythology of North America* (New York: William Morrow, 1985);

Vine Deloria, *God Is Red: A Native View of Religion* (Golden, Colo.: Fulcrum, 1994);

Ruth Underhill, *Red Man's Religion: Beliefs and Practices of the Indians North of Mexico* (Chicago: University of Chicago Press, 1965).

NATIVE AMERICANS: RESPONSE TO CHRISTIANIZATION

On the Defensive. Despite the differences between the religious worlds of Euro- and Native Americans, there was no avoiding interaction. By the early nineteenth century the dynamic of religious contact was both aggressive and defensive, for the encroachment of white civilization coincided with a receding native confidence in the incontestible power of indigenous belief systems. Dispossession and removal had gradually undercut the ability of many native groups to assimilate change; involvement in trade and the consumption of alcohol, once seen as means to power, became corrosive cultural forces. Defeat in battle also opened the door to religious reexamination, leading to doubt in the efficacy of the old rituals, or to reproach for their neglect. Finally, disease often furnished the most devastating attack on Indian equilibrium. The advance guard of white settlement was often microbial, and waves of epidemics continued to ravage native populations throughout the nineteenth century. In 1837 smallpox nearly wiped out the Mandans entirely. In the next decade migration along the Oregon Trail carried cholera to the Great Plains, decimating the Lakotas and Cheyennes in particular.

Encounter with Christianity. Into this disordered universe came nineteenth-century Christianity. The Indians' response to the "white man's medicine" was varied and often depended on local factors—how a certain tribe experienced disease, defeat, or removal, for instance, or how long a group was able to maintain autonomous relations with whites and therefore to resist unwanted elements of Euro-American culture. Many groups evinced

an initial interest in the secrets of the Bible, or Great Book, and were willing to "convert" to learn about this new potential source of power. If the expected benefits did not materialize, one response was to reject the missionaries and turn hostile. In other cases the coincidence of a Christian representative with victory in battle, prophetic fulfillment, or healing was sufficient to win allegiance. However, this type of assimilation did not represent a shift in indigenous perception. The more substantive reactions to Christianity can be summarized as theological criticism, syncretism, and/or revitalization. All three might occur within a single group, generating community conflict as different factions arrived at different solutions for coping with disaster and change.

Theological Criticism. One criticism leveled against the exponents of Christianity decried the gap between how Christians behaved and what they preached. Writing in his 1833 autobiography, Sauk leader Black Hawk was embittered by his life-long experience with white deception and disparaged their standard of conduct: "The whites may do bad all their lives, and then, if they are sorry for it when about to die, all is well! But with us it is different: we must continue throughout our lives to do what we conceive to be good." In a famous speech in 1828 Red Jacket of the Iroquois touched a sore point among Protestants in his comment on denominational divisions: "You say there is but one way to worship and serve the Great Spirit. If there is but one religion, why do you white people differ so much about it? Why do you not all agree, as you can all read the book? . . . We also have a religion which was given to our forefathers, and has been handed down to us their children. We worship that way. It teaches us to be thankful for all the favors we receive, to love each other, and to be united. We never quarrel about religion." To counter the dogmatic certitude of the missionaries, several native spokesmen argued for a kind of "cultural dualism," in which whites and Indians were intended to pursue their separate ways. As Black Hawk wrote, "If the Great and Good Spirit wished us to believe and do as the whites, he could easily change our opinions, so that we would see, and think, and act as they do." Petalesharo, principal chief of the Pawnee Indians, registered these sentiments at a conference in Washington, D.C., in 1822, at which President James Monroe was present. "The Great Spirit made us all—he made my skin red, and yours white; he placed us on this earth, and intended that we should live differently from each other. He made the whites to cultivate the earth, and feed on domestic animals; but he made us, red skins, to rove through the uncultivated woods and plains. . . . We worship [the Great Spirit], but we worship him not as you do. . . . We differ from you in our religion . . . but still, my Great Father, we love the Great Spirit—we acknowledge his supreme power—our peace, our health, and our happiness depend upon him, and our lives belong to him—he made us and he can destroy us." If there was a purposeful design behind the divergent

Kennekuk was a Kickapoo leader in the early nineteenth century whose band lived along the Vermilion River in present-day Illinois. Regarded as a prophet by his people, his religious teachings focused on reform through abstention from liquor and public whippings for backsliders. Kennekuk's following drew from several neighboring groups, especially the Potawatomis. As many Native Americans succumbed to pressure to move voluntarily to an Indian territory beginning in the 1820s, Kennekuk managed to stave off removal for a decade. His strategy was a form of passive resistance, presenting himself as in agreement with relocation but unable to comply because of various practical obstacles. This adroit management of disadvantageous circumstances was also expressed in religious matters. Kennekuk evinced an interest in missionary overtures and asked Baptist Isaac McCoy to establish a school among his people. The Methodists eventually licensed the Kickapoo as a preacher. Finally, under the treaty of 1833, Kennekuk's intertribal group had to move to a reserve in Indian Territory, as did most of the remaining indigenous peoples in the Old Northwest. At this new location Roman Catholics, Baptists, and Presbyterians all came to call, competing for rights to mission work. Kennekuk assisted the Methodist missionary, and together they baptized about four hundred members of his community. As stipulated in the removal treaty, Kennekuk had

his own church built in Indian Territory. Once it was completed, however, he allowed no one else to preach there, no doubt to the dismay of the missionaries. Kennekuk designed and conducted his own brand of Christian worship. McCoy visited in 1833 and reported that it was "less christian than ideas inherent in the religion of common wild Indians." On this occasion Kennekuk spoke for nearly three hours, pausing at specific points for set congregational chants. Flagellation continued to serve a penitential role in his religion. Later, the itinerant preacher Jane Livermore added a millennial edge to Kennekuk's system: she declared that the end of the world was nigh because Napoleon Bonaparte was the Antichrist, but both she and the Kickapoos would be taken into heaven. Eventually Kennekuk proclaimed that he was the Indian Christ, just as Jesus had been the Son of God sent to the whites. In so doing, Kennekuk continued his unique brand of syncretism by merging Christianity with the theology of the "two ways": that is, that Native and Euro-Americans each had to follow their own spiritual path.

Sources: Robert A. Brightman, "Toward a History of Indian Religion: Religious Changes in Native Societies," in *New Directions in American Indian History*, edited by Colin G. Calloway (Norman: University of Oklahoma Press, 1988);

George A. Schultz, *An Indian Canaan: Isaac McCoy and the Vision of an Indian State* (Norman: University of Oklahoma Press, 1972).

customs, then crossing over to another's path would be contrary to the will of the Great Spirit. Although this stance seemed to offer a shield against insistent missionary overtures, its premise of polygenesis—of separate origins for whites and Indians—had some dramatic implications. On the one hand it could serve as an argument for pan-Indianism: for setting aside tribal affiliations in favor of a unified Indian identity. On the other hand, by the Civil War polygenesis was also a position used by white racists to rationalize Indian oppression or extinction.

Syncretism. When tenacious adherence to the ancient ways seemed insufficient, some Indians chose to incorporate Christian rites and beliefs into their own framework. Syncretism did not indicate capitulation as much as an attempt to shore up Indian traditions with new materials. Religious incorporation became part of a stabilizing process of readjustment as a means to survival. Before the Civil War indigenous-Christian fusion was a silent partner of the missionary endeavor because the missionaries for the most part lacked the coercive power to root out native beliefs. For example, in the Columbia Plateau

the Coeur d'Alenes took to Jesuit instruction during the 1840s and honored the new medicine by building an impressive Renaissance-style church, without nails, in present-day Idaho. Yet their Catholicism suited their own traditions. The Coeur d'Alenes developed a Christian war ethic, which prescribed prayer before battle, proscribed scalping and warfare on Sundays, and enlarged the meaning of charity to include killing in defense of the community. They also emphasized ritualistic elements that had a familiar ring, such as physical penitence, which paralleled a precontact tradition of voluntary whipping as punishment. Perhaps the quintessential example of successful syncretism occurred among the Eastern Pueblos in the Southwest. By the mid eighteenth century the Puebloan groups had already been missionized, had rebelled, and had made a separate peace with Iberian Catholicism. For nearly one hundred years from 1750, the Southwestern Indians were left alone to reject or assimilate what the Franciscans and Jesuits had planted among them during the century of conquest. While the Hopi, Zuni, Navajos, and some Puebloan peoples took advantage of their relative isolation and simply ignored Christianity, other groups called them-

Louis Choris's 1816 painting of Native American dancers at a San Francisco mission
(Oakland Art Museum, California)

selves Catholic yet were less than orthodox. Bereft of priests, they adapted the Christian rituals and prayers under their own interpretation, deciding that the way to preserve their traditions was by grafting Catholic belief and practice onto them. In the late eighteenth century, when the Catholic hierarchy renewed its attention to the region, it confronted a religious weaving of Puebloan-Catholic practice and belief whose threads were no longer separable.

Revitalization. Christianity could stimulate religious revitalization in two ways: first, as a negative reaction, by inspiring nativist movements; second, by offering a source of strength to Indian converts whose faith in the efficacy of their traditions had faltered. Nativist movements were often led by prophets who called for Indians to reject corrupting aspects of white culture as a first step toward purification and winning back the protection of the spirit world. What differentiated these holy men from other shamans was that their dreams or special knowledge of the Great Spirit attempted to provide a larger vision of meaning and direction for disordered Indian lives. Most prophets sought to usurp the sacred power of Christianity by transforming its rituals rather than dismissing them. Although prophets commonly depicted an Indian utopia that was premised on the destruction of white people and the restoration of Indian lands, their advocacy of new sacred symbols and behavioral norms indicated that the future had to be more than just a retreat to the past if Native America was to survive.

Native Conversions. Perhaps the most controversial reaction to the sacred encounter between white and Indian peoples was native conversion to Christianity. The passage of time makes it impossible to determine whether an individual's conversion was in earnest, was simply surrender to the seeming inevitability, or was a utilitarian move to gain a competitive edge. Certainly it would be condescending to native Christians themselves to insist, as some opponents have, that all were deluded, succumbing to the victimization of their oppressors. Whether Indians decided to resist, to adapt, or to convert, the choices made were their own; to suggest otherwise is to deny the agency of the people themselves. Few generalizations apply with regard to native Christians: individuals of both mixed ancestry and native parents adopted Christianity, and adherents could be found among nomadic as well as sedentary groups. Those who called themselves Christian often chose a lonely path, for they were frequently harassed and persecuted by their own people and betrayed by their white "brothers." The dilemma for native Christians was evident in an anecdote attributed to the Fox tribe:

> Once there was an Indian who became a Christian. He became a very good Christian; he went to church, and he didn't smoke or drink, and he was good to everyone. He was a very good man. Then he died. First he went to the Indian hereafter, but they wouldn't take him because he was a Christian. Then he went to heaven, but they wouldn't let him in—because he was an Indian. Then he went to Hell, but they wouldn't admit him there either, because he was so good. So he came alive again, and he went to the Buffalo Dance and other dances and taught his children to do the same thing.

Regardless, some Indians found in their understanding of Christianity a source of empowerment, though they had to sever Christian tenets from the actions of the "Christian" white race. For example, William Apess, a Pequot from New England and an ordained Methodist minister, published his autobiography in 1829, *A Son of the Forest*. He condemned the hypocrisy of Christian practitioners but declared his confidence in Christian teachings as the repository of certain universal truths, including the rationale for a social order in which "age, sect, color, country, or situation made no difference." Despite the prejudice of white Christians, egalitarianism was embedded in the fact that "the Spirit of Divine Truth in the boundless diversity of its operations, visits the mind of every intelligent being born into the world."

Legacy of Religious Encounters. In the first half of the nineteenth century the decisive changes taking place in the physical world of Native America put the Indian sacred world in flux as well. In such a context, Christianity offered a benchmark for religious inquiry. Was it this that gave the whites so much power—or had the Indians merely abandoned their own spiritual resources? For a time, despite the stridency of missionary voices, the sacred encounters engaged the Indians as agents in their own religious reconstruction. After the Civil War the Protestant establishment and the government, formerly allies in the enlightened civilizing of the Indians, became actual partners in the deliberate destruction of Indian culture. Christianity became an instrument of oppression. Despite this shameful association the phenomenal religious leader Quanah Parker was able to construct the Native American Church at the turn of the twentieth century, combining the "peyote road" with liturgy to make Christianity serve Indian religious needs. As in so much of American and religious history, ideals battled their misuse by human actors and survived with enough energy to provide the spark for a later fire. It is this human story, often tragic but also triumphant, that forms the essence of religious encounters in the expanding West.

Sources:

Robert A. Brightman, "Toward a History of Indian Religion: Religious Changes in Native Societies," in *New Directions in American Indian History*, edited by Colin G. Calloway (Norman: University of Oklahoma Press, 1988);

Peter Nabokov, ed., *Native American Testimony: A Chronicle of Indian-White Relations from Prophecy to the Present* (New York: Penguin, 1991);

James P. Ronda and James Axtell, *Indian Missions: A Critical Bibliography* (Bloomington: Indiana University Press, 1978);

James Treat, "Native Christian Narrative Discourse," in *Native and Christian: Indigenous Voices on Religious Identity in the United States and Canada*, edited by James Treat (New York: Routledge, 1996).

THE RELIGIOUS CRISIS OF REMOVAL

The Cherokees and Accommodation. By the late eighteenth century the Cherokees, like other indigenous peoples in the Southeast, had made a tactical decision to adjust to the encroachment of settlers on their lands by relying less on hunting and moving toward sedentary, agriculture-based communities. One influential faction within the Cherokees advocated additional accommodation. Adopting the English language and Anglo-American dress, this group also welcomed offers from Protestant missionary societies to open schools for Indian children; in 1828 there were five different denominations working among the Cherokees. Despite the appearance of rapid acculturation, the civilizing mission triggered stress within the Cherokee communities. The first religious tensions appeared in 1811, when several minor prophets called for a reconciliation between old and new ways. In general, the *adonisgi*, or holy men, did not advocate complete repudiation of white civilization but a middle ground of accommodation that respected the traditions of the past while adopting whatever was useful to the Cherokee people. The movement was under way when the Shawnee leader Tecumseh made his tour of the Southeastern nations in 1811, and the news that other groups were experiencing prophetic awakenings probably lent strength to the Cherokee revival—as did the spectacular comet and the New Madrid earthquake of that tumultuous year. The War of 1812 halted any further religious ground swell, but thereafter traditional rites and ceremonies continued in tandem with the "Christianization" of the tribe.

Removal Policy. Even so, by the late 1820s the missionaries regarded the Cherokees as the very model of what could be accomplished among the "sons of the forest." The annual reports of the societies proudly pointed to the Cherokees' Christian, English-speaking leadership; their written constitution, which paid homage to the U.S. compact; and their farming economy. However, a troubling current endangered this success story: the impetus for removal—that is, for relocating all native peoples to an Indian territory west of the Mississippi River—had been gaining speed throughout the decade. Andrew Jackson, a determined advocate of the policy, became president in 1828, and at his behest Congress passed the Indian Removal Act in 1830 by a slim margin. In the meantime the state of Georgia had already asserted title to the Cherokee lands and declared that the autonomous polity of the Cherokee Nation was dissolved. The American Board of Commissioners for Foreign Missions (ABCFM) sponsored a lawsuit on behalf of the Cherokees. Although the U.S. Supreme Court upheld the Cherokees' claims against Georgia, President Jackson refused to enforce the decision. Holding out for several years, the Cherokees were betrayed in 1835 when several chiefs signed a treaty with Jackson's commissioner and thereby agreed to removal. Although the action violated Cherokee law, which dictated that only treaties ratified by the council were valid, the federal government claimed it was legitimate. Soon some villages began to move westward voluntarily, but the recalcitrant majority stood fast. In 1838 the U.S. Army forcibly evicted sixteen thousand Cherokees from their homelands and then drove them to what is now northeastern Oklahoma on a poorly planned and executed expedition that became known as the Trail of Tears. About four thousand Cherokees died on the journey, and another thousand perished soon after arrival.

Missionary Turmoil. The responses of the missionary societies to the removal crisis were mixed. The ABCFM stood staunchly behind the Cherokees, and its corresponding secretary, Jeremiah Evarts, became a leading opponent of removal on moral grounds. To Congress and to the public, Evarts's opposite in the debate was Baptist minister Isaac McCoy. Working primarily among the melting pot of remnant indigenous peoples in Michigan, Indiana, and Illinois, McCoy had long lobbied for a large expanse to be set aside in the West as a self-governing Indian "colony." Only by isolating natives from the corrupting influence of disreputable traders and their liquor could the Indians as a whole be civilized and Christianized. McCoy soon realized that his Indian "Canaan" provided an altruistic veneer to the land greed of frontier congressmen, but he continued to believe that the plan could work to the benefit of the Indians (especially if he were at the helm). Within the missionary community, removal caused ruptures between individuals and institutions and engendered quandaries of conscience. James Trott, a Methodist missionary, was so disgusted at his church's proremoval stance that he switched his affiliation to the Disciples of Christ. The Baptist board and most of its missionaries had followed McCoy in supporting removal as early as 1823. Yet two of its preachers among the Cherokees refused to counsel their members to vacate their lands. Two ABCFM missionaries, the Reverend Samuel Worcester and Dr. Elizur Butler, became heroes to the Cherokees when they went to jail in 1831 in defense of the Indians' possessory rights. In 1832 the ABCFM, now under new leadership with the untimely death of Evarts, gave up its opposition when the Senate ratified the fraudulent Cherokee treaty and the government threatened to cut its annual appropriation ($2,500). The imprisoned missionaries sought pardon from the Georgia court, and the ABCFM advised the Cherokees to accede to the inevitable.

Religious Crisis. As the historian William McLoughlin has noted, though removal was a political and social crisis for the Cherokees, it was an even more profound spiritual shock, for both Christians and traditionalists. In the wake of the capitulation of their missionary allies, the Christian Cherokees regarded the religion of the white majority to be as false as their treaty promises, and there was an inevitable decline in conversions and church membership. The disillusionment with Christianity, however, could not be remedied simply by a return to traditional religion, since that too was in disarray. Severed from the sacred lands of their ancestors, the adonisgi lost their connection to the spiritual world, as well as access to the herbs that were the source of their medicinal powers. For the Cherokees, dispossession, death, and internal conflict demanded a fresh religious synthesis to provide order and meaning to confused and disordered lives. In the Trans-Mississippi West, Christianity ultimately contributed to that process because the Cherokees were able to mold it into a viable faith for themselves. No longer passive recipients of "Christianization," the Cherokees discovered a passageway between sacred worlds that offered a means to renewal on their terms.

In Indian Territory. Differences among the denominations significantly affected the Cherokee experience of Protestantism after removal. In the early nineteenth century, during the first period of missionary intervention among the Southeastern Indians, the ABCFM workers had dominated. In Indian Territory, from 1840 to 1860, it was the Baptists and Methodists who increasingly made converts while the mission stations of the ABCFM declined. The theology and practice of such evangelicals offered flexibility in contrast to the rigidity that characterized the Congregationalism and Presbyterianism of the ABCFM. For example, the Baptists and Methodists itinerated, going to the people instead of establishing settled missions and requiring people to come to them. This popularized their appeal—a different approach from the ABCFM strategy of cultivating a leadership core. The evangelical missionaries among the Cherokees tended to encourage parallels between Christian and traditional rites, such as baptism and the Cherokee purification ceremony, in which community harmony was reasserted by a "washing away" of the past. The stress in Arminian theology on "growing in grace" (celebrated by both Methodists and Baptists) allowed for more leniency in behavioral lapses, in contrast to the Calvinist tendency to regard backsliding as possible evidence of an unregenerate soul. Finally, the Baptist concept of the ministry as individuals raised by the choice of the people allowed for the emergence of a native ministry. Ironically, the missionaries in the Southeast had targeted and achieved success among Cherokees of mixed Indian-white ancestry; after removal the Cherokee "full-bloods" redefined and legitimized what it meant to be a native Christian. Once the door was open to native interpretation of Christian beliefs, the result was a syncretic mixture. The Christian Cherokees conflated the Christian God with the Great Spirit, gave traditional ceremonies and dances (and therefore the adonisgi) a role in worship, and focused on what was familiar in Christian practice and teachings over what was alien.

The Reverend Evan Jones. The revitalization of Christianity among the Cherokees in Indian Territory was also due to the example of a few stalwart missionaries who had remained true to their convictions during the removal crisis. Of particular importance was the Reverend Evan Jones, a Baptist who served as missionary to the Cherokees from 1821 to 1872. He resisted removal to the last alongside his Cherokee church members despite the rebuke of his denomination. Before their forced departure he and his four hundred congregants voted to refuse fellowship to any of the signatories to the Cherokee treaty. Jones walked the Trail of Tears with his Cherokee colleague, the Reverend Jesse Bushyhead. Missionary strategy in general favored the use of the vernacular by the 1830s, but Jones was unique in his ability to write, speak, and read the Cherokee language. He spearheaded the effort to translate the Bible into Cherokee, which offered traditionalists their first opportunity to read and interpret for themselves. Jones was later adopted into the tribe, and his son joined him in laboring among the Cherokees as a Baptist minister. The acceptance of the Joneses illustrated that the Indians judged the value of Euro-American religion by the behavior of the individual exponent, not by doctrinal abstraction. Therein lay the tragedy of many of the sacred encounters in the West.

Aftermath of Removal. For the missionary community, Indian removal was a turning point. In the millennial enthusiasm that propelled the missionary organizations in the 1810s and 1820s, it seemed natural to hope that evangelical religion could guide the unfolding identity of the nation, ushering in a glorious new age of Christian harmony and republican liberty. When the removal legislation passed, a disheartened Evarts said to a congressman, "My hope is, that when the people of the United States come to understand the subject, there will be a redeeming spirit arise; for I will not believe that the nation is yet lost to truth and honor." The plain fact was that the best efforts of the ABCFM leadership had made no impact on the course of events. As one of its committees queried in 1838, why bother to "detain men in the field only to have their efforts paralyzed, and for all the labor, property, and life expended, to reap little else than disappointment?" The deepest irony for the evangelicals was their inability to protect or to intercede for these particular Indians, who, by all outward appearances had become both Christianized and civilized and had, in fact, become the representative of national and denominational aspirations for the savage. The redemption of both the Indians and the nation suddenly seemed more of a far-off ideal than a postmillenial likelihood. Instead of creating a permanent Indian Canaan, removal "out of sight" became "out of mind." In 1841 the Baptist General Convention still blithely extolled the policy: the Indians "have at last found a settled home in the regions of the far west, where they have a country guaranteed to them by the faith of the nation. . . . Here by the fostering care of the government, and the holy influence of religious institutions, they are acquiring those habits which are essential to their comfort and usefulness on earth, and to their happiness beyond the grave." In fact, removal had emptied not just the Southeast but the Western Reserve and the first Indian territory in Arkansas. Previous Indian occupants, such as the Osage, were displaced, and the result was a hodgepodge of oddly drawn grants, some of them quite small, to various tribes. As Kansas and Nebraska became states, these holdings "in perpetuity" were further adjusted. There was to be no impenetrable protective barrier, only constant encroachment. After 1859 the Southeastern Indians collectively became known as the Five Civilized Tribes, indicating their continuing association with "progress" in the white

mind. Yet the Cherokees could no longer serve as the showpiece for the Protestant missionary effort, given the issue of slaveholding in their midst as well as the "impure" syncretic elements in their Christianity. Almost in spite of the missionaries, the Christian Cherokees had taken the religion of the white majority and made it respond to their religious needs, creating a means to cohesion and therefore a defense against their absorption into Euro-American society.

Sources:

John Andrew III, *From Revivals to Removal: Jeremiah Evarts, the Cherokee Nation, and the Search for the Soul of America* (Athens: University of Georgia Press, 1992);

William G. McLoughlin, *Champions of the Cherokees: Evan and John B. Jones* (Princeton, N.J.: Princeton University Press, 1990);

McLoughlin, *The Cherokees and Christianity, 1794–1870: Essays on Acculturation and Cultural Persistence* (Athens: University of Georgia Press, 1994);

George A. Schultz, *An Indian Canaan: Isaac McCoy and the Vision of an Indian State* (Norman: University of Oklahoma Press, 1972).

SACRED ENCOUNTERS: MISSIONARY IMPULSE TO NATIVE AMERICA

Call to Mission. The missions established among Native Americans were sites of sacred encounters in the West. The experience of contact varied from one encounter to the next, not only because of the differences between the missionaries but also because the native peoples whom they engaged were embroiled in their own dynamic histories. By 1820 more than a dozen organizations around the country sponsored missionary work, but a few dominated the scene. The American Board of Commissioners for Foreign Missions (ABCFM), founded in 1810, was primarily supported by Presbyterian, Dutch Reformed, and Congregationalist churches. As an interdenominational coalition, this group typified the irenic spirit of the early-nineteenth-century reform movements. In 1814 the Baptists entered the foreign mission field under the authority of their denomination's Triennial Convention. Two years later conservative Presbyterian and Reformed leaders formed the United Foreign Missionary Society, but the group later merged with the ABCFM. That the work was dubbed a "foreign" mission reflected the evangelicals' ultimate goal of spreading Christianity throughout the world. However, American religious leaders were sensitive to charges from their English counterparts that they had abandoned indigenous peoples "for the distant heathen in India." In 1805 the Reverend Edward Griffin delivered a widely reprinted sermon before the Presbyterian General Assembly that set the tone for mission work among the American Indians: "We are living in prosperity on the very lands from which the wretched pagans have been ejected; from the recesses of whose wilderness a moving cry is heard, 'When it is well with you, think of [the] poor Indians.'" Twenty-four years later the Baptist mission board again called for "a sense of the obligations which we are under to this injured people, whose home and country we possess, [to] redress the wrongs we have com-

HAZELWOOD REPUBLIC

For forty years from 1837, Presbyterian missionaries Stephen Return Riggs and his wife, Mary, labored among the Wahpetons, a band of the Santee Lakotas (Sioux) in Minnesota. At first intent on studying the Lakota language as a means to evangelism, Riggs eventually came to see in the use of the native tongue an enlargement of the gospel rather than its degradation. With the help of several influential Indians who saw the benefits of communication, the mission published a Lakota grammar and dictionary in 1852 and later in the decade a Lakota hymnbook and selections from the New Testament. Over the years a core of interested Wahpetons kept up the missionaries' hopes for widespread conversions despite indifference and opposition from many others. The plight and the struggle of the native Christian was poignantly illustrated by Simon Anawangmane, the first full-blooded Lakota man to declare himself a Christian. When he decided to "renounce all for Christ," as Mary wrote in her diary in 1841, he put on "white man's clothing" and began to plant a field of corn and potatoes. He severed connections with the past by returning his war club, spear, pipe, and medicine bag to the man who made them. For this behavior he was ridiculed as "the man who has made himself a woman," but because he had been a respected warrior in his youth, he suffered none of the vandalism that often expressed Lakota disapproval. After a few years Simon developed a passion for drink, returned to native dress, and tried to obtain horses by trading in liquor. That life, however, brought him no peace either. In 1847 he reconsecrated himself to the church, was eventually reinstated, and became a ruling elder in the Presbyterian church and a licensed exhorter. In the meantime, by about 1850, the constancy of the Riggs' presence among the Wahpetons made their lifestyle seem an appealing alternative, especially among the rising generation. A group of young people removed themselves from the village, built cabins, changed their style of clothing, and adopted agriculture. As a result, when the Eastern Lakotas ceded most of their lands and moved to a reservation, Stephen Riggs established in 1854 a separate community, Hazelwood, for Christian Indians. Their distinctive identity continued to develop, and in 1857 eighteen Wahpetons declared themselves a separate band and sought the recognition of the Indian agent, which was necessary in order to receive a portion of the government annuity. The group produced a constitution for their new Hazelwood Republic that illustrated how closely Christianization and civilization had become linked in their perception. "We consider that we are in vastly different circumstances from those in which we were before the Word of the Great Spirit was brought into the country. . . . We hope to make progress and teach our brethren progress. . . . It has been for the purpose of instructing according to our ability our own relations and the whole Dakota people in regard to dress and manners, and indeed in regard to every thing that pertains to their well-being in this present life, and in the life to come, that we have formed ourselves into a government." The Hazelwood Republic elected a president, asked for private allotments of land, and pledged obedience to the U.S. government. Riggs worked for several years to obtain citizenship for nine of the Hazelwood band, given a provision in the state constitution whereby Indians could become citizens if they demonstrated progress in civilization. Finally, a judge ruled in 1861 that being literate in the Lakota language did not constitute "civilized" progress. Only English competency met that standard, and thus only one Hazelwood member qualified. This episode tragically symbolized the dilemma of Christian Indians, who were still not acceptable despite their cropped hair, their non-Indian dress, and their professed faith. Yet as events continued to favor the Anglo-American majority, the non-Christian Lakotas confronted the possibility that a superior power backed their enemies. In 1862 Little Crow led the Santees in an uprising against surrounding settlements and trading posts. The army rounded up three hundred Lakotas, including Christians who now faced guilt by association, and sentenced all to be hanged. In the largest mass execution in United States history, thirty-eight Santee Sioux were hanged at one time on 26 December 1862. The illustration of greater "wakan" was not lost on the remaining imprisoned warriors. At the request of the Lakotas themselves, missionaries, including Riggs, conducted Bible study sessions and held mass baptisms over the three years of the Indians' incarceration. President Abraham Lincoln eventually reviewed the proceedings and commuted the sentences of most of the condemned.

Sources: Robert Berkhofer Jr., *Salvation and the Savage: An Analysis of Protestant Missions and American Indian Response, 1787–1862* (Lexington: University of Kentucky Press, 1965);

Stephen Return Riggs, *Mary and I: Forty Years with the Sioux* (Minneapolis: Ross & Haines, 1969).

mitted." Guilt over the fate of the Indians, and the evangelical's responsibility to uplift the "sons of the forest" and thereby save them from extinction, were recurring themes of the missionary impulse in its early history.

Government Policy. The federal government's position toward the missionary endeavor remained fairly consistent until Andrew Jackson's presidency. As Henry Knox, secretary of war under George Washington, had stated, the most effective and least expensive way to handle the Indian problem along the Western frontier was to turn the natives into citizens, a task for which "missionaries of excellent character" seemed admirably suited. After the War of 1812 Anglo-American settlers began to fill the area between the Appalachian Mountains and the Mississippi River, which was still occupied by more than 120,000 Native Americans. The civilizing mission was no longer an academic exercise but was expounded as one solution to an urgent problem; the other options were removal of the Indians beyond the Mississippi or their extermination. In 1819 Congress instituted a permanent civilization fund with an annual appropriation of $10,000 to be distributed among the societies that were operating Indian schools. The grants provided more of a psychological than financial boost to the missionary program. In 1825, for example, the various societies received $13,600 from the government, $11,750 from Indian annuities, and $177,000 from private contributions (in-kind and cash). Even so, the government imprimatur was an important stimulus because it convinced the evangelical leadership that the nation was indeed committed to a Christian destiny. From the Indian side of the fence, the partnership between church and state, however loose, ultimately undermined the reform character of the missionary societies and made them agents of the government rather than of God.

Western Removal. From the first, the removal of native peoples from the path of white expansion forced missionaries to choose between conflicting loyalties. Displacing the Indians by purchasing their title and by outright coercion may have seemed a prudent course to politicians, but it undercut the civilizing mission by eliminating at a stroke all progress made as well as hard-won trust. The Wyandots of Ohio provided an early example of the issues that removal raised. Despite treaty guarantees, the Wyandots had been continuously pushed westward since the late eighteenth century. In the mid 1820s federal officials were again promising that if the tribe would submit to relocation one more time, that site would be a permanent home. The Wyandots sent a letter to the War Department declaring that they were "making progress in religion, and in the cultivation of their lands." Methodist missionary James Finley wrote that the Wyandots should be left undisturbed, given that they had kept faith with the government and had received its pledge that they would never again be moved. "Little doubt can be entertained but, in a short time, these people will be well prepared to be admitted as citizens of the

state of Ohio, and to remove them just at this time, contrary to their wishes, would be . . . a most cruel act. It would be undoing what has been done, and throw them again into a savage state." Finley faced a powerful opponent in Baptist Isaac McCoy. This influential missionary argued that, to protect the Indians from pernicious white influence, the native peoples should be relocated and isolated on a large grant of land that would be theirs "in perpetuity." McCoy's position became a useful rationalization for a policy of removal as in the Indians' "best interests." Finley, meanwhile, was transferred by the Methodist conference from Indian work shortly after this episode.

The Missionaries. Although the denominations and societies offered guidelines for their volunteers in the field, the missionaries brought to the task their distinct personalities, abilities, sentiments, and beliefs. Missionaries were chosen on the basis of availability rather than aptitude, and screening was minimal, generally requiring the recommendation of the person's minister or church elder as to character, piety, and commitment. A retired sailor who applied to the Methodists listed the fact that he had "given chase to pirates" as part of his qualifications for mission work. The missionary societies preferred married couples, not only to prevent moral mischief but also to serve as examples to the natives of God's intentions for the human family. Men and women who were determined to follow the calling of their hearts sometimes underwent whirlwind courtships in order to marry a missionary partner. The individuals drawn to the vocation were undoubtedly motivated by both selfish and selfless reasons and by idealistic and practical considerations. Regardless, their common perception of sacrificing for compassion's sake, of having an unshirkable obligation to heed the Great Commission, is undeniable. Indeed, given the repeated declarations of officials and unsympathetic writers that the Indians were a doomed race, the missionaries often regarded themselves as the last line of defense. This gave their crusade an urgency that at times made them blind to the lives and needs of the people to whom they were assigned.

Civilized or Christianized? Congress' creation of the civilization fund intensified a long-running debate as to whether the Indians should first be civilized or Christianized. Would giving them the Bible or offering them the plow best achieve the goal of uplift? Although much ink was spilled over this question, in practice it was difficult to separate the two, especially when the object was the same. As the United Foreign Missionary Society declared in 1823, by conveying

the benefits of civilization and the blessings of Christianity" to the Indians, the day may come "when the savage shall be converted into the citizen; when the hunter shall be transformed into the mechanic; . . . when throughout the vast range of country from the Mississippi to the Pacific, the red man and the white man shall everywhere be found, mingling in the same benevolent and friendly feelings, fellow citizens of the same civil and religious community, and fellow-heirs to a glorious inheritance in the kingdom of Immanuel.

In 1824 Congress considered repealing the civilization fund, but the house committee recommended its continuance. They were influenced especially by the report of Jedediah Morse, a New England Congregational minister and renowned geographer. Touring Western Indian villages and mission sites, Morse praised the combination of Christian education with agricultural instruction and concluded that evangelizing alone would not reform the "sons of the forest."

Image of the Indian. Although the missionaries as a group carried cultural baggage with them into the West, mainstream culture was itself in flux in the antebellum period, especially before the 1840s. There were, however, certain philosophical and theological preconceptions that affected the way the missionaries approached their calling. Both white and Indian peoples had to account for one another in their cosmology. To Christians the most important biblical truth relative to the Indians was that all races originated in a single creative act by God. Monogenesis meant that Indians were human beings like any other, possessing an immortal soul and capable of receiving salvation. Enlightenment thought bolstered this understanding in its assertion of universal natural laws and the essential oneness of human nature. The evangelical persuasion emerging from the Second Great Awakening had taken an Arminian direction, declaring that redemption was offered to everyone, not simply the elect. Even among Calvinists the door remained open, for in God's plan all human beings were capable of regeneration, even if only a few were chosen. The operative theology of the early nineteenth century was thus based on the essential equality of humanity in the sight of God. The missionaries might have displayed extreme intolerance or suffocating ethnocentrism, but had they denied a belief in the redemptive potential of the Indian, the basis for their own salvation would have been thrown into question. Given these premises, Euro-Americans typically explained differences between societies as stages in human progress, with each society on the same path but at distinct points in development. To the evangelicals the values and ideals of the United States represented an advance in human history, though they believed the nation's aspirations were more praiseworthy than its reality. People caught on a lower rung of the ladder of progress only needed knowledge to move up because environment rather than biology was the key. As Isaac McCoy declared in 1841: "If the habits are formed by circumstances surrounding [the Indian], as they are formed by those which surround us, then the point can be established that a change in circumstances would be followed by a change of habits. Let this change be favorable to civilization and religion." "Culture" as a web of traditions and institutions unique to a particular group of people was not a concept recognized until the twentieth century. Consequently, the missionaries' attitudes toward Indian were informed by the perception that, given proper education, Indians could become like whites. Although such logic seems racist today, it was for antebellum evangelicals the only way of including the Indians in the human family—and the alternative (in both theological and practical terms) seemed too terrible to contemplate. If there had been no conversions, or no adoption of the "civilized" ways of the whites, then the missionaries might have faced a critical challenge to their perception of the Indians' temporary differentness. As it was, the occasional success confirmed that God would gather the Indians one by one, just as He had called the missionaries in their individual conversions.

Mission Strategy. As the historian Robert Berkhofer has observed, all mission activities attended in varying degrees to three goals: piety, learning, and industry. The general strategy was to obtain a group's permission to establish a mission on or near their settlement, then to begin a school, hold church services, and start agricultural production. Meanwhile the missionaries would enlist the Indians in the tasks of building and farming as the means of teaching them. Because of the emphasis on reforming customs or habits, missionaries frequently spoke of the rising generation as the salvation of the Indian, but their ability to override parental influence on Indian children was limited until boarding schools became federal policy after the Civil War. Exactly what transpired between the missionaries and the Indians in worship can only be imagined, but unless there was some form of communication, either by translators or by the missionaries learning native tongues, the encounters must have had a farcical quality. Some Protestant leaders had opposed perpetuating the "dying Indian tongues," until Sequoyah's Cherokee syllabary proved its usefulness to the missionary endeavor. Even so, the missionary corps overall lacked the level of competency required for translation and bilingual comprehension. Considering the problems with language, the missionaries discovered that the easiest approach to religious instruction was through behavior: defining sin as alcohol consumption, idleness, warfare, and marital infidelity. Although this strategy paralleled the evangelical effort to make Euro-American society more godly, the attack on certain traditional aspects of native life could serve to weaken tribal cohesion, especially for a group that was already in crisis. The missionaries soon realized that persuading Indians to adopt white clothing was an extremely important symbolic step. As Stephen Riggs, missionary to the Eastern Lakotas, observed in the 1850s, "It is true that a change of dress does not change their hearts, but in their estimation it does change their relations to the Dakota religion and customs." Yet if missionaries became too preoccupied with externals, more-elusive spiritual goals could suffer—until conversion became a matter of form rather than substance.

The Jesuits. The involvement of the Jesuits in Western mission work provided a spur to Protestant efforts as well as a contrast for the native peoples. Known as the Black Robes to the Indians, the Jesuits differed from Protestant missionaries in ways that seemed to confer advantages. First, because they came from a variety of nationalities, they appeared less like agents of the U.S. government. The Jesuits' perspective with regard to other races tended to embrace an element of cultural relativism, which meant that they were generally more open to similarities between the sacred worlds of Catholics and Indians. In theological terms the Jesuits adopted an incarnational stance that considered all human good as potentially Christian. Catholicism, with its sacramental focus, also appealed to Indian groups whose religion was based on ceremony and ritual. Unlike the Protestant missionaries, who arrived with wives and children and were quickly absorbed in the concerns of settlement, the Jesuits came as single men. This gave them flexibility and substantiated their claim that they were solely devoted to the Indians' welfare—perhaps offsetting the Indians' bewilderment at priestly celibacy. Although the Jesuits managed to dot the Northwest with mission stations, the duration of their efforts was no more remarkable than that of the Protestants before the Civil War.

Chastened Expectations. By the 1840s the missionary impulse, along with other reforming projects, was becoming more chastened in its expectations and more sensitive to internal disagreements. The Removal Crisis in the Southeast, which culminated in the late 1830s, seemed to strike a blow at the earlier hopes for a harmonious society and the potential for an "awakened" nation. As expansion pushed forward to the Pacific Coast, the West became a home (not foreign) mission field, catering to the needs of the settlers. Perhaps a sobering recognition of their own limits helped turn missionary attention increasingly overseas: keeping their eyes fixed on the high standard of Christianizing the world made it easier to ignore the seemingly insoluble problems on their own continent. When a newspaperman coined the phrase "Manifest Destiny" during the Mexican War, it added another element to the religious controversies of the antebellum age, especially in regard to the missionary drive. Consider the statement of Indian Commissioner Luke Lea in 1853, not atypical for the times: "When civilization and barbarism are brought in such relation that they cannot coexist together, it is right that the superiority of the former should be asserted and the latter compelled to give way. It is, therefore, no matter of regret or reproach that so large a portion of our territory has been wrested from its aboriginal inhabitants and made the happy abode of an enlightened and Christian people." Such an official posture caused conflict for evangelicals, as is evident in the experience of two Methodist missionaries who journeyed to the Northwest in the 1850s. The pair came to completely opposite conclusions about the efficacy of their work among indigenous peoples. The

Blaines, in Puget Sound, took an immediate dislike to the natives. "The Indians are at best but a poor degraded race, far inferior to even the lowest of those among us. . . . However, they are fast passing away and will soon disappear." Kate Blaine wrote home: "You talk about the stupidity and awkwardness of the Irish. You ought to have do with our Indians and then you would know what these words mean." In glaring contrast, John Beeson took his family to the Rogue River valley of Oregon. He became an advocate for the Indian cause although he found few allies among the local Methodist societies. The fault for the Indians' rejection of Christianity, he believed, lay with the missionaries, who offered a religion that "insult[ed] their common sense, by presenting itself with Whisky and Creeds in one hand, and Bibles and Bowieknives in the other." Beeson's faith in the Indians' capacity arose from his religious convictions: "It is true that their creed is not written in a book. . . . But they have, on their own mountains and valleys, the same Presence that dwelt with Moses. . . . [With] the babbling brook, the sighing zepher, and singing birds . . . they unite, in adoration of the Great Spirit, whose informing presence animates the whole and in whom the Indian, as well as the Christian, lives, moves, and has his being."

Antebellum Changes. By 1860 the ABCFM, a leader in the evangelization of the Indians, had sent out 472 men and women to Indians across the continent, including the Cherokees, Choctaws, Chickasaws, Osages, Ojibwas, Creeks, Pawnees, Nez Percés, Flatheads, Lakotas, Abenakis, and groups in Ohio and Michigan. Often oblivious and unprepared, these stalwart individuals marched out into the unknown, at great risk and with little expectation of worldly reward, to bring the gospel to the natives. The task required more time, effort, and skill than many had anticipated; evangelical optimism proved to be an inadequate qualification. Without quick success, the entire missionary enterprise faltered, casting doubt on the ability of the godly to transform even a little corner of the world. Given this opening of diminished hopes, a burgeoning mood of romantic nationalism began to change the tone of American society in the two decades before the Civil War. Woven into this new intellectual tapestry was a greater willingness to define what it meant to be an American in terms of racial otherness. Instead of perceiving the white-Indian relationship as "us" and "not-yet-us," the lines became drawn between "us" and "them." Nineteenth-century scientists had already begun to explore the idea of polygenesis, or separate origins for the races, which would make racial differences ineradicable and encourage a hierarchical ranking. This postulate remained a minority opinion among Protestants until late in the century, but new science was trickling into mass consciousness. Discrimination against the Irish and other races deemed inferior by Anglo-Americans, justification of African slavery, and carte blanche for action against the so-called doomed Indians—such furies were the heralds of another age, another vision for the nation born in the retreat of the evangelical-Enlightenment ethos.

Sources:

R. Pierce Beaver, *Church, State, and the American Indians: Two and a Half Centuries of Partnership in Missions between Protestant Churches and Government* (St. Louis: Concordia, 1966);

Robert Berkhofer Jr., *Salvation and the Savage: An Analysis of Protestant Missions and American Indian Response, 1787–1862* (Lexington: University of Kentucky Press, 1965);

Henry Warner Bowden, *American Indians and Christian Missions: Studies in Cultural Conflict* (Chicago: University of Chicago Press, 1981);

Michael Coleman, *Presbyterian Missionary Attitudes toward American Indians, 1837–1893* (Jackson: University Press of Mississippi, 1985);

Clifton J. Phillips, *Protestant America and the Pagan World: The First Half Century of the American Board of Commissioners for Foreign Missions, 1810–1860* (Cambridge, Mass.: Harvard University Press, 1969).

SPREADING THE FAITH: THE "MACEDONIAN CRY" FROM THE COLUMBIA PLATEAU

The "Macedonian Cry." In 1831 four Flathead (Salish) and Nez Percé Indians made an unprecedented journey to St. Louis from their homelands in the Columbia Plateau in the Northwest. They were unable to speak English, but officials interpreted their religious purpose in their signs of the cross and the gestures that suggested baptism rites. When presented with a cross, they kissed it, so William Clark, commissioner of Indian Affairs in St. Louis, sent them to the Jesuit mission, where they were baptized. This event, pivotal in Native and Anglo-American history, became known in evangelical folklore as the Macedonian cry—a reference to the spread of the early Christian church to Asia Minor upon the appeal of the Macedonians to the Apostle Paul. Although both native and white traditions agreed that the Indians came seeking "the white man's book of heaven," the reasons for the search were poles apart.

Prophetic Impulse. The journey of the Indian delegation to St. Louis had begun in prophecy. About 1800 the Spokane prophet Yurareechen (the Circling Raven) revealed a vision that was passed down as follows: "Soon there will come from the rising sun a different kind of man from any you have yet seen, who will bring with him a book and will teach you everything, and after that the world will fall to pieces." Renewal and the resurrection of the dead would follow destruction. Another prophecy circulated among the Flatheads. The medicine man Shining Shirt had foretold that white men wearing long black robes would arrive to teach the Indians new prayers and a new moral law that would radically change their lives. The intertribal wars would cease, but it would be the beginning of the end, for a flood of white people would come in the wake of the Black Robes.

The Columbia Plateau. The region between the Cascade Mountains and the Rocky Mountains was home to about two dozen distinct groups, most of them organized loosely around the band or village. Predominantly members of the Salishan and Sahaptian linguistic families, the Plateau Indians included the Nez Percés, the Cayuses, the Spokanes, the Kutenais, the Coeur d'Alenes, and the Flatheads (a misnomer, since it was actually the Chinooks along the Northwest Coast who flattened the heads of their children). The native peoples of the Columbia Plateau were ready for a prophetic message, given the changes of the past century. The introduction of the horse, guns, and the fur trade had pushed many groups from their semisedentary lifestyle into hunting, which exposed them to disease and created competition and conflict with such Plains neighbors as the Blackfeet. In 1805 Meriwether Lewis and William Clark traveled among the Plateau Indians, the first whites known to do so. Although Lewis and Clark represented "a different kind of man," as in the prophecy, they brought no book. So the people waited. In 1820 two dozen Iroquois Catholics from a mission near Montreal settled among the Flatheads. Their leader, Ignace La Mousse, related the fundamentals of Catholicism to the Flatheads but urged them to seek further instruction. The conjunction of Iroquois influence and the eagerness of the Plateau Indians to pursue the prophecy encouraged native adoption of Christian devotional practices. By the end of the decade traders and explorers commented on how the Indians of that region engaged in morning and evening prayers, spoke grace at meals, and observed the Sabbath. Seeking to discover more about white medicine, a Kutenai man and Spokan Garry, the son of a Spokane chief, attended an Anglican mission school near modern-day Winnipeg. When they returned in 1829, they introduced rudimentary Christian worship and Bible reading to their people. This in turn coincided with, and may have augmented, a general religious awakening throughout the Plateau as a "prophet dance" spread from the Flatheads to the Nez Percés and other neighboring groups. Impatient to learn more about the book that was a prerequisite to the promised restoration of Indian power, the Flatheads and Nez Percés decided to send representatives to connect with the annual trade rendezvous and possibly find their friend William Clark. They reached St. Louis in 1831.

The East Hears the Cry. Within two years of the delegation's appearance, Methodist William Walker had immortalized the event. His account was published in a denominational journal and picked up by Eastern newspapers. Perhaps more striking than his dramatic narrative was the accompanying drawing of the profile of an Indian with a flattened head, a poignant image of barbarism that horrified Anglo-American sensibilities. The renown of the "Indian lament" spread throughout the religious community and sparked a new stage in the missionary endeavor. The appeal originated in a distant location far to the West, stretching the evangelical imagination to envision a continental Christendom and a new scope for the nation's destiny. A fresh goal had become all the more urgent by the 1830s because the Protestant expectations arising from the awakening at the turn of the century had faltered in the face of quarrels and unresolvable differences of opinion. Perhaps the hope for a unified church and a Christian nation lay farther to the West, with the conversion of these imploring Indians and the establishment of harmonious settlements that would be a beacon (and a chastisement) to the East. Consequently, with the Macedonian cry, the millennial visions of both Indians and whites met and, for a time, found they needed one another for their consummation.

The Methodists Respond. In 1833 the Methodist Missionary Society declared in its *Christian Advocate and Journal:*

> Hear! Hear! Who will respond to the call from beyond the Rocky Mountains?. . . The subject of the deputation of the Flat-head Indians to Gen. Clarke, has excited in many in this section intense interest. And to be short about it, we are for having a mission established there at once. . . . Let two sutable [*sic*] men, unencumbered with families, and possessing the spirit of martyrs, throw themselves into the nation. Live with them—learn their language—teach Christ to them—and, as the ways open, introduce schools, agriculture, and the arts of civilized life."

Jason Lee and his nephew were the first to snap to attention, and they headed out with three other Methodist missionaries in 1834 with the intention of serving the Flathead Indians in present-day southwestern Montana. They instead ended up in the Willamette River valley of Oregon, a development that passed without comment in official circles but that boded ill for the accomplishment of missionary goals. The effort reflected the character of Methodism: its personnel was the stalwart bachelor itinerant; its trust was in Providence over preparation; and its methodology regarded both Christianizing and civilizing as procedural problems that only required the orderly application of systems. The expectation that the Indians would be won over with dispatch met with disappointment. Lee decided to return to the East to raise additional funds and bring more people. In 1840 fifty-one recruits arrived in the valley; this time they were primarily families who were supposed to serve as role models of piety and industry to the indigenous peoples. The requirements of community settlement began to overtake the evangelical thrust, and the site seemed more akin to a colony than a mission. Against the wishes of the Missionary Society, Lee established different centers for the functions of Christianizing and civilizing. The main settlement was oriented to industry and family life, and its ostensible missionizing purpose was to edify the Indians by example. The Dalles, a northern station isolated from white settlement, was the only place given over to Christianization. There the spiritual focus included sharing worship with the Indians and making an effort to learn their languages.

From Mission to Colony. In 1843 Lee became involved in the creation of the Oregon Provisional Government, and the Missionary Society censured him for being overly engaged in secular activities. After ten years in Oregon, Lee was recalled, leaving a legacy of a land claim in the Willamette River valley and a school for children of white settlers. Not a single Indian convert could be counted. Some observers took the moral of the story as a reflection on the natives themselves. One Methodist preacher left the region in 1841 declaring that "extinction appears to be their inevitable doom . . . . They will never be reached by the Voice of the gospel." Lee acknowledged the lack of progress among the Plateau Indians, and by the end of his missionary service he agreed that some special "unction" of the Holy Spirit would have to move the hearts of the Indians before they would respond to the evangelical call. Yet he also recognized that Methodism could not repudiate a belief in the conversion potential of the Indian without jeopardizing its very essence. In fact, the denomination had recently reasserted its conviction that "the gospel was universally adaptable," and thus the whole world was the proper scope of evangelization. The most ominous lesson of the Methodist experience was that the missionary endeavor had been instrumental in establishing a toehold for American occupation of the Northwest. Especially in this region and in this stage of missionizing, political and economic objectives were often advanced by the actions of the religious. In the process the evangelical dream of converting the nation and then the world became the captive of a secular blueprint.

The ABCFM Responds. When the Macedonian cry first reached an Eastern audience, New England was aflame with revival fires, and evangelists used the plight of these "poor savages" to demonstrate the urgent need for the redeemed to act on their faith. As the Reverend Samuel Parker declared, "The heathen themselves are chiding Christians for their negligence in not obeying the commandment 'go ye into all the world and preach the gospel to every creature.'" Under the auspices of the American Board of Commissioners for Foreign Missions (ABCFM), Parker and an associate, Dr. Marcus Whitman, volunteered to explore the possibility of a mission in the Northwest. At the annual trade rendezvous in 1835 they received such an enthusiastic welcome from the Plateau Indians represented there that Whitman returned East to assemble the necessaries for the project. The ABCFM preferred married couples, so Whitman found a spouse to be a "fellow laborer in the Lord's vineyard." Another couple, Henry and Eliza Spalding, were also given an Oregon commission by the ABCFM. The fact that these were the first Anglo-American women to cross the Rockies demonstrates the significance of this adventure as well as the motivating power of evangelical commitment in the nineteenth century. Reverend Parker had been instrumental in convincing the ABCFM that women would be in no more danger travelling over land to the Northwest than by sea around Cape Horn. In 1836 the missionaries set out on their three-thousand-mile journey, taking a wagon to Pittsburgh, riverboat to Liberty, Missouri, horseback (with women riding side-saddle, or in a light wagon) to Fort Walla Walla on the Columbia River, and then boat down the Columbia. The journey took seven months. After making the trip, Spalding wrote to the board, "Never send another mission over these mountains if you value life and money." Whitman, by contrast, declared, "I see no reason to regret our choice of a journey by land." In the end their decision to cross the Rockies with women and wagons opened the door to family migration and so furnished a crucial impetus to the coming invasion of the region.

Mission Life. In 1838 reinforcements arrived from the ABCFM so that two couples could be placed at each of the three stations. The Whitmans and Smiths settled among the Cayuses at Waiilatpu; the Walkers and the Eells went north to the Spokanes at Tshimakain; and the Spaldings and the Grays were stationed at Lapwai among the Nez Percés. Initially mission life was an exercise in basic survival, and the group was dependent on the fort and the Hudson's Bay Company for supplies. As with most missionaries in this period, none of the ABCFM appointees had any relevant training, though several of the women had been teachers. The New Englanders were isolated among a non-English-speaking people, and their likelihood of success was hamstrung from the start. Internally, personality conflicts sundered the fragile stability of the Oregon mission, which drove the Grays and Smiths to leave by 1842.

Relations with the Indians. For the Plateau Indians the most apparent outcome of the missionary intrusion was to create divisions between "praying" and "non-praying" Indians. Some ignored the mission presence; others were curious or perceived some advantage in allying themselves with the missionaries. The Spaldings had a more receptive audience at Lapwai than the Whitmans did at Waiilatpu, for the Nez Percés were determined to learn what they could about the white medicine. As Spalding declared in 1837, "We might as well hold back the Sun in his march through the heavens, as hold back the minds of this people from religious inquiries." Two Nez Percé men, Joseph and Timothy, were received into the church in 1839. Although Joseph became disillusioned and drifted away from the mission, Timothy continued to identify himself as a Christian. At Tshimakain, Spokan Garry made occasional visits, but he preferred the Anglican ritual to Presbyterian practice. By 1841 his enthusiasm for the new religion had waned, especially after some of his own people had harassed him. Though he sometimes acted as interpreter for the missionaries, he would as often refuse. Overall, communication was hit or miss. The Walkers had the valuable help of Mungo Mevway, a half-Hawaiian, half-Native American youth who could speak English, and the Spaldings were also assisted by an interpreter. Elkanah Walker hoped to translate the Gospel of Matthew into Salish, but the only book printed for the benefit of the Plateau Indians was a Spokane Primer. As time passed, the missionaries, convinced that heathenism was a lifestyle choice, became increasingly disdainful of their charges, which dampened their zeal. Walker declared that "if anyone doubts the doctrines of total + native depravity, one year's sojourn among them, I think, would remove all his doubts." Spalding believed that forcing Anglo-American agricultural habits onto Indians was a prerequisite to Christianization, and a published photo showed him standing with a hoe in one hand and a Bible in the other. As one historian has noted, the Indians of the Plateau had their own agenda. Their willingness to endure the intolerance and encroachments of the missionaries demonstrated the degree to which they were invested in their prophecy's hopes. Other cultural presumptions that affected the missionary endeavor were not religious. In 1843 the Indian agent for Oregon "organized" the Nez Percés into a tribe led by an elected chief. Although this fit the white perception of proper structure and representation, it destabilized the Nez Percés, who had operated for centuries around loosely affiliated bands. New factions generated animosity that was often directed against the missionaries. Again, a variety of Anglo-American interests—economic, diplomatic, political, and religious—had begun to merge to the detriment of the Plateau Indians.

Catholic Competition. In the Northwest, for the first time the sacred encounter between Indian and white religious worlds involved competing claims of Protestants and Catholics. As a teaching tool the Jesuits had developed a pictorial "ladder" of significant events in Christian history, interpreted through a Catholic lens. The Presbyterian Spaldings retaliated with a "Protestant ladder." Both were paper charts, approximately six feet by two feet, marked with lines to indicate the passage of time. Pictures beside the markings indicated key moments in biblical or Christian history. In the Roman Catholic version Protestants had wandered off the path of salvation and now followed a doomed course. On the Spaldings' ladder the Catholics were the ones on the wrong road, and at its terminus the Pope fell off into a fiery pit. One can only guess how the Indians themselves interpreted the exclusivity and intolerance of these rival sacred worlds.

Whitman Massacre. By the mid 1840s the Whitmans at Waiilatpu had become the focus of Indian suspicions about Anglo-American intentions in the region. Tensions came to a head on 28 November 1847. The Cayuses attacked the mission and, over a two-day period, killed Marcus and Narcissa Whitman and twelve other whites. News of the massacre spread to the other stations, and eventually the missionaries congregated in the forts while volunteer militia went out in search of the perpetrators. What was dubbed the "Cayuse War" was actually an unsuccessful attempt by the Cayuses to rally the Nez Percés, Flatheads, and other Plateau peoples to go on the offensive against the white invasion. Not even all the Cayuses were in favor of this solution, so they ceased hostilities, and five men surrendered for their part in the violence. They were hanged by the army in June 1850. Whether it was an intentional comment on the Presbyterian Whitmans or merely circumstance, they chose to die under Catholic unction.

The Legacy. The Columbia Plateau had been a crucible of Indian-white religious relations, and the Whitman massacre served as notice that the millennial visions of both whites and Indians had failed to flower. The Plateau people had pursued the prophecy, but the "different man" had offered nothing that might trigger the restoration of Indian power, though there was ample evidence that their world might indeed end. As with the pan-Indian movement in the Old Northwest, the disintegration of a shared prophetic vision among the Plateau people also shattered other alliances. An informal defensive coalition broke down as each group grabbed for whatever it could get from subsequent treaties. As a result, by 1855 the Plateau Indians had bargained away 174 million acres for dubious gains and were confined to reserved tracts. Religious factions also consolidated, and the Plateau Indians remained divided in their response to the sacred encounter with Christianity. After the Civil War another prophet arose on the Columbia Plateau (Smoholla) who preached a return to the old ways in order to appease the anger of the Great Chief Above; at the same time both Catholic and Protestant missionaries (including Henry Spalding) returned to the region and found some who welcomed their ministrations. From the Anglo-American perspective the massacre had dashed evangelical expectations for the easy conversion of the continent, sealing the priority of white occupation over the goal of harmonious coexistence. When territorial authorities closed the region to missionaries in 1848, it was an official declaration that the Plateau Indians had lost their favored position in the millennial program and had thus forfeited even the minimal protection of Christianization.

Sources:

Clifford Drury, *Marcus and Narcissa Whitman and the Opening of Old Oregon,* 2 volumes (Glendale, Cal.: Arthur Clark, 1973);

Robert J. Loewenberg, *Equality on the Oregon Frontier: Jason Lee and the Methodist Mission, 1834–43* (Seattle: University of Washington Press, 1976);

Christopher Miller, *Prophetic Worlds: Indians and Whites on the Columbia Plateau* (New Brunswick, N.J.: Rutgers University Press, 1985);

Robert Ruby and John Brown, *Dreamer-Prophets of the Columbia Plateau: Smohalla and Skolaskin* (Norman: University of Oklahoma Press, 1989).

THE WAIILATPU MISSION AND THE WHITMANS

A Historic Journey. In 1836 Narcissa Whitman and Eliza Spalding accompanied their husbands, Marcus and Henry, respectively, on a momentous journey to the Pacific Northwest in order to set up missions among the indigenous peoples of the region. They were the first Euro-American women to cross the Rocky Mountains,

and their evangelical motivation seemed to ennoble Westward expansion to the Eastern establishment. Similarly, the murder of the Whitmans eleven years later marked the severance of any lingering connection between Indian evangelization and national destiny. The Whitmans' role in the opening of the West and Northwest to white settlement gave them a place in history, yet it is their personal story that offers closer insight into the nature of sacred encounters in the Columbia Plateau.

The Whitmans and Spaldings. Narcissa Prentiss had been swept up in the revivals of Western New York during the 1830s, and her parents' home had been a center for the young people in her Presbyterian church. Narcissa had heard a visiting preacher tell of the Indians who had come to St. Louis in search of the Bible. With her family's approval, she had determined to dedicate herself to missionary work among the heathen. However, the sponsoring agency, the American Board of Commissioners for Foreign Missions (ABCFM), informed her that single women were not being accepted into the foreign mission field. Meanwhile, at a neighboring church Dr. Marcus Whitman had made a similar commitment to mission service and soon learned of Narcissa's application. After an exchange of letters and a brief meeting, Marcus obtained Narcissa's pledge of marriage, after which he immediately set out with the Reverend Samuel Parker to explore the prospects for a mission. Henry and Eliza Spalding had been living in Cincinnati, attending Lane Seminary, and had already accepted a mission assignment with the Osages. When that plan proved abortive, Henry agreed to go instead to the Oregon Territory, albeit reluctantly, because he had once proposed to Narcissa and been rejected. This sensitive issue often resurfaced in conjunction with other disputes between the two couples.

At Waiilatpu Mission. For several years Narcissa's letters to her sister and parents spoke of her evangelical aspirations and her desire to teach Indian children. Since she had little knowledge of the language, and since the Cayuses were on the move during their hunting season, however, there were few indications that she found her efforts rewarding. Marcus's duties were extensive: farming, raising stock, producing the planks and adobe bricks for construction, and practicing medicine, which often required him to travel long distances in response to a call for assistance. Neither of the Whitmans had the time or skill to uncover the secrets of the native tongue. The pair taught the Cayuses songs as part of their religious instruction, and the image of the Indians repeating the words with no knowledge of their meaning was perhaps symbolic of the mission's overall impact on the spiritual life of the natives.

Reinforcements. In 1837 Narcissa gave birth to her only child, Alice, and the Cayuses seemed charmed by the sight of a white baby in their midst. When Alice drowned before her second birthday, Narcissa fell into a depression. She was thus overjoyed to learn that four

A sketch of the Waiilatpu Mission, Oregon Territory, drawn by Nancy Osborn, circa 1847 (Oregon Historical Society, Portland)

couples were being sent as reinforcements for the Oregon mission, and she anticipated the companionship of other women. The Walkers, Grays, Eells, and Smiths arrived in 1838, but they soon wore out their welcome in the cramped quarters of Waiilatpu. Though all the missionaries were either Presbyterian or Congregational, differences in religious practice caused tensions. In Narcissa's church women were encouraged to pray in public, but for most of the men this was regarded as unbecoming. The Whitmans favored grape juice in communion while the others preferred fermented wine. As Narcissa wrote to her sister, "Now how do you think I have lived with such folks right in my kitchen for the whole winter? If you can imagine my feelings you will do more than I can describe it." Mary Walker, wife of Elkanah, presented another side to the experience, which revealed much about Narcissa's personality. Still grieving the loss of her daughter, Narcissa criticized Mary for not nursing her own infant as frequently as Narcissa thought she should, adding that Mary must not love the child much. When she was upset, Narcissa would closet herself in her room and remain there all day, leaving her guests at a loss as to what to do, or she would find some secluded spot outside where she would weep openly. One day Mary confronted her, but she reported that Narcissa "was disposed to justify her conduct in every particular. She said we did not know her heart. That we thought her out of humor when it was anxiety for the salvation of sinners caused her to appear as she did. . . . This rather stumbled us & we almost felt that she designed to make a cloak of Religion. Can it be, we thought, that anxiety for sinners can cause one to appear so petulant, morose & crabbed?" Mary was glad to be sent with Cushing and Myra Eells to the Spokanes at Tshimakain.

Tensions Mount. The arrival of the 1838 contingent seemed to generate more conflict than Christian zeal, and the missionaries sent many letters to the ABCFM detailing their grievances against one another. In 1842 Marcus received the board's response, which was to reorganize the Oregon stations. Yet circumstances had changed in the year it had taken to obtain that communication. The Grays had become settlers in the Willamette River valley while the Smiths had begun an independent station at Kamiah among the Nez Percés. (The Indians apparently disliked them so much that they demanded their removal; the ABCFM transferred the couple to a Hawaii mission.) To salvage the situation Marcus sped to Boston to intercede directly with the board. When he returned in 1843, he came with two hundred wagons and one thousand settlers, the largest contingent of immigrants to date and a clear sign to the Indians of an unfavorable wind. It was only the beginning, for more than ten thousand settlers moved along the Oregon Trail during the 1840s. As Narcissa Whitman wrote to her mother, "The poor Indians are amazed at the overwhelming numbers of Americans coming into the country. They seem not to know what to make of it."

The Whitman Household. The diaries of several of the missionary women indicated the competing demands of mission work and family life. While some balanced the two or found their interest in the welfare of the Indians overwhelmed by the preoccupations of managing a mission household, Narcissa seemed to develop a real feeling of repugnance toward the Indians. Lack of privacy was the bane of her existence, especially because the Indians were always wandering in and out of the house. Though they tried to persuade the Cayuses to build a place of worship, the Indi-

Elkanah and Mary Walker, missionaries of the American Board for the Commissioners of Foreign Missions (ABCFM), worked for nine years among the Spokanes at Tshimakain in the Oregon Territory. Through her extensive diary Mary offered a portrait of the antebellum woman caught in the tides of evangelicalism. Born in Maine in 1811, Mary attended a Congregational church but had her conversion experience during a Methodist revival. She came from an educated family and was ambitious for greater adventure than the dull prospect of life as a New England farmer's wife. In her missionary application, one of her teachers offered the following recommendation:

> Her intellectual acquirements are more than respectable. She has a strong love for natural science and mathematics, in which her attainments are valuable. She is a chemist and practical botanist . . . . The powers of her mind are strong and masculine, quick for observation and fond of investigation. Her moral courage is conspicuous from which has grown out real independence of character, which combined with energy, perseverance, industry and a robust physical constitution admirably qualify her to meet the exigencies and bear the trials and privations of a missionary life.

Mary, however, was turned down by the ABCFM because she was single. In 1837 a mutual acquaintance wrote privately to Mary about Elkanah Walker, who was seeking a missionary post in South Africa. "I think you can love the man. But you must judge for yourself. A husband is a husband notwithstanding the fact he may be a missionary." Their courtship involved arranged meetings over a forty-eight hour period, at the conclusion of which Mary accepted Elkanah's proposal. Though in appearance an odd couple—Mary could stand beneath Elkanah's outstretched arm—theirs was a story of growing affection. Because of the financial crisis of 1837 and a tribal war in South Africa, the board decided to send the Walkers to the Oregon mission in 1838. Once settled among the Spokanes, Mary's writings re-

corded a continual round of household activities, especially as her family grew. Elkanah held regular worship with the Indians, and they seemed interested in following the outward forms, but, as Mary reported: "They are very anxious to devise some way to get to heaven without repenting and renouncing their sins." By 1839 she was already aware that for her the adventure had taken on a life of its own. "I have desired to become a missionary and why? Perhaps only to avoid duties at home. If I felt a sincere interest in the salvation of the heathen, should I not be more engaged in acquiring the language that I might be able to instruct them? But instead of engaging with interest in its acquisition, I am more ready to engage in almost anything else . . . . May I realize now the awful responsibility that rests on me. I have great reason to fear that the object of pursuit with me is not to glorify God but to please myself and my husband." Mary's candor was perhaps verified in the impact of their efforts on the Indians since by 1846 it seemed apparent that the Indians had returned to the medicine men and their "superstitions." With the massacre of their fellow missionaries Marcus and Narcissa Whitman in 1847, the Walkers chose to devote themselves to family rather than the salvation of Indians. They left the isolation of Tshimakain with their six children in tow and settled in the populated Willamette River valley, where they lived comfortably by farming and preaching. Mary survived Elkanah by twenty years, and in their marriage she remained her own person to the end, refusing her husband's deathbed plea that she promise not to remarry. Mary Walker, matriarch, lived to the age of eighty-six.

Sources: Clifford Drury, *First White Women over the Rockies: Diaries, Letters, and Biographical Sketches of the Six Women of the Oregon Mission Who Made the Overland Journey in 1836 and 1838*, volume 2 (Glendale, Cal.: Arthur Clark, 1963);

Drury, *Nine Years with the Spokane Indians: The Diary, 1838–1848, of Elkanah Walker* (Glendale, Cal.: Arthur Clark, 1976).

ans insisted on using the Whitman house. Narcissa wrote to her mother,

> The greatest trial to a woman's feelings is to have her cooking and eating room always filled with four or five or more Indians—men—especially at meal time—but we hope this trial is nearly done, for when we get into our other house we have a room there we devote to them especially, and shall not permit them to go into the other part of the house at all. They are so filthy they make a great deal of cleaning wherever they go, and this wears out a woman very fast. We must clean after them, for we have come to elevate them

and not to suffer ourselves to sink down to their standard. I hardly know how to describe my feelings at the prospect of a clean, comfortable house, and one large enough so that I can find a closet to pray in.

A new house was finished in June 1840, and the separate Indian room made Narcissa happy. However, the Cayuses were insulted and began increasingly to refer to her as haughty. The contents of the Whitman house showed a comfortable lifestyle for that time and place, leading the Indians to suspect that the missionaries prospered at their expense. Narcissa wrote, "It is difficult for them to feel but that we are rich and getting richer by the houses we dwell in and the clothes we wear and hang out to dry after washing from week to week, and the grain we consume in our families." By 1845 the mission complex included a blacksmith shop, "mansion house," mission building, sawmill, and surrounding Indian lodges. Immigrant families camped around the station, trying to recover from the overland journey before continuing westward. By the fall of 1847 Narcissa had found a new purpose for her life in caring for a large family of foster children. Left at their door were seven children whose parents had died along the trail. The mission also became a repository for five children of Indian and white parentage, including Jim Bridger's daughter. As a result Narcissa's time was consumed by household and maternal chores, and the conversion and education of the Indians receded further into the background.

The Massacre. By November 1847 many Indians around Waiilatpu were showing signs of hostility to the missionaries, as developments over several years reached a crescendo. The mission had become a rest stop for settlers traveling the Oregon Trail, and more attention was given over to their needs than to the Indians. The winter of 1846-1847 had been unusually severe, killing possibly one-half of the area's cattle and horses. Immigrants brought a virulent form of measles to the Plateau, and more Indians were affected than whites, which lent credence to the rumor that Dr. Whitman was deliberately poisoning the Indians to get their land and horses. Animosity came to a head on 28 November. A group of Cayuses forced their way into the main house, fatally attacked the doctor, and began shooting others as they fled. As the fury subsided, the Indians gathered about fifty hostages into the Indian room and contemplated what to do next. It was finally decided that there would be no further killings, with the exception of Narcissa, who was taken outside and hacked to death. The hostages were eventually released unharmed, but the violence escalated as militia troops determined to punish all Cayuses, regardless of their involvement in the massacre. The so-called Cayuse War dragged on for two years.

Understanding the Attack. In 1849 the Reverend H. K. W. Perkins, a Methodist missionary in Oregon, provided a moving epitaph on the Whitman story. Jane, Narcissa's sister, had written him to ask why the Indians had killed people "who had done so much for them." Perkins replied as kindly as honesty would permit:

The truth is Miss Prentiss your lamented sister was far from happy in the situation she had chosen to occupy. . . . I should say, unhesitatingly that both herself and husband were out of their proper sphere. They were not adapted to their work. They could not possibly interest and gain the affections of the natives. I know for a long time before the tragedy that closed their final career that many of the natives around them looked upon them suspiciously. Though they *feared* the Doctor they did not *love* him. They did not

love your sister. They appreciated neither the one nor the other.

Marcus, said Perkins, had "never identified himself with the natives as to make their interests paramount" and instead had been overly attentive to the needs of the white settlers. Narcissa, continued the Methodist preacher,

was not adapted to savage but civilized life. She would have done honor to her sex in a polished and exalted sphere. The natives esteemed her as proud, haughty, as far above them. No doubt she really seemed so. It was her misfortune, not her fault. . . . She wanted something exalted—communion with mind. She longed for society, refined society. She was intellectually and by association fitted to do good only in such a sphere. . . . She loved company, society, excitement and ought always to have enjoyed it. The self-denial that took her away from it was suicidal. . . . Certain it is that we needed such minds to keep us in love with civilized life, to remind us occasionally of home. As for myself, I could as easily have become an Indian as not . . . I could gladly have made the wigwam my home for life if duty had called. But it was not so with Mrs. W. She had nothing apparently with them in common. She kept in her original sphere to the last. She was not a missionary but a woman, an American highly gifted, polished American lady. And such she died.

Legacy of Waiilatpu. After the massacre the remaining ABCFM missionaries gave up their evangelical aspirations and melded into immigrant communities. The missions to the Northwest had been motivated by evangelical ideals, but it turned out to be easier to mourn the fate of the heathen from a distance than to care for them as people. What role denominational background played in the failure of the Oregon missions is unknown, but it seems a fair statement that New England Presbyterians were, as a group, singularly out of place among the Plateau Indians. Add to the mix an abrasive personality, and the outcome could be disastrous. On both sides the expectation of a signal sacred encounter had been disappointed, and relations between Indians and whites on the Columbia plateau reverted to the sad and familiar course of betrayal, hostility, retribution, and dispossession.

Sources:

Clifford Drury, *First White Women over the Rockies: Diaries, Letters, and Biographical Sketches of the Six Women of the Oregon Mission Who Made the Overland Journey in 1836 and 1838*, 3 volumes (Glendale, Cal.: Arthur Clark, 1963);

Drury, *Marcus and Narcissa Whitman and the Opening of Old Oregon*, 2 volumes (Glendale, Cal.: Arthur Clark, 1973).

WESTERN JESUITS

"Black Robes." During the 1830s four delegations of Plateau Indians made the long journey to St. Louis, generally seeking religious instruction and assistance. The representatives of the Flatheads, influenced by the Catholic Iroquois who had settled among them, directed their appeals specifically to the Jesuit "Black Robes." In 1839 one group found Jesuit priest Pierre-Jean De Smet, who had been making little headway among the Osages

A nineteenth-century engraving of Jesuit missionaries proselytizing among the Native Americans

and was elated at the prospect of an enthusiastic audience. With the approval of his superiors, De Smet embarked in 1840 on a grand tour of the Western tribes. Among those he visited were the Cheyennes, Mandans, Kansas, Lakotas, Crows, Blackfeet, Snakes, Bannocks, Kalispels, Nez Percés, Flatheads, Kutenais, and Coeur d'Alenes. The Belgian priest cut an imposing figure in his black cassock, and word spread among the Native Americans about this new spiritual leader. In the Pierre Hole Valley of present-day Wyoming, De Smet conducted an open-air mass among nearly fifteen hundred Plateau Indians, whose curiosity had drawn them from the fall hunt. The Belgian priest who spoke the "Great Prayer" (the Catholic Mass) also presented each headman with a medal bearing the likeness of Pope Pius IX—the Great Chief of all the Black Robes. De Smet capitalized on the mystique that surrounded his tour, turning extraneous developments to his advantage. An Oglala leader asked him to intercede on behalf of his daughter, who had been taken prisoner by the Crows. De Smet wrote that when the child escaped, "the report flew quickly from village to village, and this coincidence, that Divine Providence permitted for the good of the Ogallallahs, was to them certain proof of the great power of Christian prayer."

Jesuit Plans. Since Secretary of State John C. Calhoun had first invited the Jesuits to minister to the indigenous peoples beyond the Mississippi in the 1820s, the Society of Jesus had nurtured the hope that it could replicate in North America the *reducciones* (or reductions) organized among the Guarani Indians in Paraguay. The Jesuit plan of reduction gathered the Indians into self-sustaining towns, where, isolated and protected from outside influences, their economic, social, and religious development could be closely monitored. De Smet was convinced that an Oregon reduction was not only possible but would be even more successful than those in Paraguay. Appointed as head of the project, he set out for the Northwest in 1841 with a small group of fellow priests to establish a mission to the Flatheads. For several years St. Mary's (in the Bitterroot Valley of what is now northwestern Montana) was the showpiece for Catholic efforts among the North American Indians.

The Mission at St. Mary's. At St. Mary's the Jesuits applied time-tested strategies for work among the heathen. Father Gregory Mengarini immediately began to prepare a Salish grammar, and Father Nicholas Point relied on sketches to breach the language barrier. To the Plateau Indians, Catholic sacramentalism offered a familiar form of religious expression. The cross, the saints, and the rote prayers found parallels in the medicine bundles, the ancestral spirits, and the chants. To the drums and whistles used in ceremonies the Flatheads added the musical instruments brought by Father Gregory Mengarini across the Plains—accordian, clarinet, and piccolo. And no radical change was involved when the Feast of Corpus Christi was celebrated at St. Mary's, since it fell in line with other community rituals and processions. Given their limited personnel and resources in the Northwest, the Jesuits were unable to prevent syncretic adaptation, though they recognized that the Indian understanding of Catholic rites was superficial. As Father Nicholas Point wrote during his time among the Flatheads, "with the Indians particularly, 'tis better to graft than to fell." Because of their own engagement with prophecy, the Flatheads were eager to gather for prayers, hymns, and the catechism. Catholic practices supplemented rather than replaced their traditional ways. As the Jesuit fathers observed, the prayers of the Flatheads "consisted in asking to live a long time, to kill plenty of animals and enemies, and to steal the greatest number of horses possible." The Jesuits pushed their influence as far as it would go; for example, they admonished those who sought their "medicine" to refrain from scalping.

The Limits of Success. At their peak in the early 1840s, the Jesuits had four central missions (among the Kalispels, the Flatheads, the Okanagans, and the Coeur d'Alenes) and possibly five outlying stations, although sites might open and close with the migration of the tribes whom they served. The reaction of the Plateau Indians was fairly consistent: adopting the outward forms of Catholicism did not necessarily involve any alteration of their underlying religious perspective. Some Indians did choose to withdraw from polygamous unions and have their vows to one spouse consecrated by the priest. Across the board, however, the Indians resisted Jesuit efforts to turn them into farmers, and the priests had to ac-

A photograph of the Jesuit missionary Pierre-Jean De Smet and Native American converts
(private collection)

company them on their hunting migrations if they hoped to continue their instruction. Perhaps more disturbing to the Jesuits than the persistence of seasonal nomadism was their inability to bring peace to the region. In fact, their presence seemed to make matters worse, given that success in battle against adversaries was one of the primary reasons many groups sought out white medicine. Jesuit policies actually promoted this association since St. Mary's kept a supply of gunpowder on hand to ensure that "their" Indians could defend themselves against warring neighbors. The Flatheads seemed to gain such bellicose confidence after the Jesuits arrived that their historic enemies, the Blackfeet, extended their own invitation to the Black Robes.

The Blackfeet. The Blackfeet, the undisputed masters of the northern plains, centered their existence around the buffalo. Although traditional ways had been modified by the adoption of horses and European tools and weapons, the Blackfeet had remained autonomous, selectively incorporating change rather than capitulating to it. Content with their own medicine, then, the Blackfeet had generally remained aloof from Jesuit overtures and continued their raids on the Flatheads after the establishment of St. Mary's. Yet one band of Blackfoot Indians, the Piegans, had developed a trading relationship with the Flatheads. The Piegans apparently witnessed a victory of the Flatheads over the Crows: "While the battle lasted, we [the Blackfeet] saw their old men, their women and children, on their knees, imploring the aid of heaven; the Flatheads did not lose a single man—one only fell, a young Nez Percé, and another mortally wounded. But the Nez Percé did not pray." They were so impressed that they allowed the priests to baptize eighty

of their children, and they served as intermediaries to the other Blackfeet, relaying their belief that the Black Robes had powerful medicine available for the asking. In 1846, encouraged by the success among the Piegans, De Smet and Point went in search of the main body of Blackfeet, hoping to effect a truce between them and the Flatheads so that a mission could be started. Satisfied when the Blackfeet presented the calumet to a Flathead representative, De Smet decided that Father Point would remain among the Indians for a season. His was the longest missionary sojourn with the Blackfeet until after the Civil War. Point's report contained much that was promotional rather than factual, but he claimed that as a result of his efforts, "there is scarcely any camp among the Black-Feet in which the sign of the cross is not held in veneration." The Jesuit declared that the various camps argued among themselves as to which would be patrons of the priest and the mission, because "they think that all other imaginable blessing will come with them; not only courage to fight, but also every species of remedy to enable them to enjoy corporeal health." The Blackfeet considered the Flathead adoption of prayer over the "medicine-sack" as the possible explanation for their increased bravery and protection from disease. Point followed the Blackfeet on the hunt and baptized more than six hundred children, but he would not baptize the adults, who sought the ceremony because they believed "that when they have received baptism they can conquer any enemy whatsoever."

Conflict within the Society. In the late 1840s conflict within the Society of Jesus began to affect its activities. In 1848 De Smet was relieved of his position as superior general of the Oregon mission. From the first, it was clear that De Smet was less a missionary than a promoter. He never lived among the Indians for any length of time and never mastered any native language. Instead he was continually on the move, writing reports of his travels and experiences in order to raise funds from European patrons and raise interest among the Catholic hierarchy, which was reluctant to enlarge its commitment to the Indian missions. Other Jesuits complained about De Smet's wanderings and his expansion of the reduction program against their advice. Father Point disagreed so strongly with De Smet about the viability of a reduction among seminomadic tribes that he transferred to a Canadian station. De Smet's ambitious goal of a huge Western reserve under Jesuit control came at a time when anti-Catholic nativism was rising in the East. His reassignment to an administrative post in St. Louis was intended to offset Protestant fears of the papacy's greedy intentions. Meanwhile, Jesuit associates in the field warned that their work had already been undermined by De Smet's actions. At St. Mary's one priest wrote, "We are expecting other distressing things to occur very soon by reason of the lavish promises which Father De Smet scattered about him everywhere in his journey, and which neither he nor others will be able to keep." The alienation of the Flatheads had actually begun as a consequence of the peace with the Blackfeet in the fall of 1846. The idea that the Jesuits would share their medicine with enemies was taken as a betrayal. As a consequence of the Whitman massacre, there was a general estrangement between the Plateau Indians and all missionaries. As time passed, the Flatheads refused to protect the Jesuit stations against raids. St. Mary's was abandoned in 1850, and the superior general reported to Rome that "the idea of renewing the miracle of Paraguay" among the Rocky Mountains appeared hopeless.

De Smet's Legend. By the late 1850s De Smet had essentially become a government functionary. Because of his high profile among the Plains Indians, officials asked him to sit in on treaty negotiations, including the Fort Laramie treaties, hoping that his mere presence would reassure the tribes of the government's fidelity. He achieved renown at this task and remained loyal to federal policies as the best hope for the Indians despite the betrayal of treaty promises. De Smet's journal of his earlier Western travels was published in English in 1863, but by then his primary purpose of depicting the natives' need for Jesuit missions was moot. Instead his descriptions of idolatry and savagery may have added fuel to the suspicion that the Indians were beyond the pale of voluntary conversion, leaving coercion and extermination as the next logical strategies.

Jesuit Legacy in the West. The encounters of the Jesuits with the Blackfeet and Flatheads suggest the variable impact of white religion among Western indigenous peoples. Searching for the fulfillment of prophecy, the Flatheads were willing to entertain Catholic introductions for a time, but they then rejected the Jesuits when their expectations were unmet. By its end, St. Mary's had a sawmill, twelve frame houses, a flour mill, and fertile fields, but like the Indian embrace of Catholicism, it was something of a false front. Jesuit power was limited to persuasion, and the Indians participated in their medicine but never to such an extent that they forsook their traditional ways. The Blackfeet were interested observers of the passing parade, yet they felt no urgency to participate unless it presented some advantage, some access to heretofore untapped religious power. Jesuit logs carefully counted baptisms as a record of their success, but until the 1850s the resilience of Plateau culture limited the penetration of Catholicism to form over substance. Yet the work of the Jesuits in the 1840s laid the foundation for the reinvigorated mission thrust of the Catholic Church after the Civil War, when external factors weakened the Indians' ancient tethers and created an opening for a more intrusive sacred encounter. By then even Blackfoot autonomy had begun to shudder under the impact of devastating epidemics, the extermination of the buffalo, and unstoppable white immigration.

Sources:

Robert Ignatius Burns, *The Jesuits and the Indian Wars of the Northwest* (New Haven: Yale University Press, 1966);

Pierre-Jean De Smet, *Western Missions and Missionaries: A Series of Letters* (Shannon: Irish University Press, 1972);

Howard Harrod, *Mission among the Blackfeet* (Norman: University of Oklahoma Press, 1971).

HEADLINE MAKERS

JOSEPH SMITH

1805–1844

MORMON PROPHET

Family Background. Crafty charlatan, brilliant psychopath, inspired prophet—such were the varied conclusions drawn by contemporaries and later writers about the person of Joseph Smith. He was born in Western New York to Joseph Smith Sr. and Lucy Mack Smith, the third of eight children. The recollections of his mother are the primary source for his early family life, but they were written after her son's death and so contain the inevitable distortion of hindsight. By all accounts the family was a closely knit circle whose bonds were strengthened by repeated disappointments. Lucy had come from wealthy New England stock, but her own parents had struggled on the edge of poverty. Although she and Joseph Smith Sr. began their marriage in comfortable circumstances, with a small farm and store in Vermont, Joseph was cheated in a speculative venture. Overwhelmed by debt, the couple became tenants in 1803. From that time until the founding of Nauvoo, the Smith family lived in the midst of economic uncertainty, with periods of brief prosperity sabotaged by unexpected setbacks. Driven by changing circumstances, the family moved frequently; the children thus grew up painfully aware of the insecurity facing those on the margins of the market economy. In 1825, at last on the verge of landownership, Lucy and Joseph found themselves at the mercy of an unscrupulous land agent and were once more reduced to tenancy. From her reminiscences it is apparent that Lucy bore these misfortunes with long-suffering indignation, believing the family deserved better for all their industry and virtuous living.

A Family of Seekers. In their religious inclinations both Joseph and Lucy were "seekers," concerned with matters of faith but unchurched because of their disdain for denominational strife and discord. Lucy would get swept up in revival preaching but then find no merit in the churches themselves. She eventually joined a Presbyterian church in Palmyra and took some of the younger children on occasion, but for the most part the family worshiped together by means of Bible reading and family prayers. Joseph Sr. had at least seven visions (inspirational dreams) during his adult life, which he reported to his wife. All of them expressed his search for a religious home and confirmed his belief that he would find no solace in contemporary churches. Their spiritual journeys reflected the negative side of revivalism, when raised expectations evaporated for lack of sustenance.

Early Life. Joseph Jr., born 23 December 1805, received basic schooling at home from his parents and participated in the family economy at an early age. However, when he was 7, he fell victim to the typhoid epidemic raging through the region. The infection (osteomyelitis) invaded his shin bone, and he had to undergo painful surgery to remove diseased sections. Joseph was so weak that his mother had to carry him from place to place, and for three years he was more or less an invalid. When he was about fifteen, he evinced a serious concern for the state of his soul. As with his father, Joseph's religious inquiry gravitated to the revelations imparted in visions. While deep in prayer one night, he believed that God and Jesus Christ appeared before him, assuring him that his sins were forgiven and that his dissatisfaction with the contemporary churches was well-placed since all were false. The apparitions also hinted at his future role in the restoration of the true church. Like his parents, the young Joseph had rejected the churches around Palmyra, but his vision suggested a deeper critique: all churches had turned away from God, and therefore none possessed religious authority. The emotionalism of the revivals had simply masked the emptiness of their claims of truth. Several years passed. Then, on the night of 21 September 1823, as Smith again sought divine guidance through prayer, the angel Moroni visited him and told him of ancient gold plates buried nearby that contained a previously unknown religious history. Following Moroni's directions, Smith uncovered a box with the plates and two stones, Urim and Thummim, to be used in translation, though he was not permitted to remove them from their hiding place. According to his mother's later narrative the family rejoiced when Smith related what had transpired, having now found "something upon which we could stay our minds."

Between Visitations. In his youth Joseph had found that, with the help of a seerstone, he could locate items not visible to the naked eye. A local farmer heard of this reputation and contracted Joseph in 1825 to search for a Spanish treasure that he believed was buried on his property in northeastern Pennsylvania. This stint as a money digger was to dog Smith all his life, as was his arrest on a charge of disturbing the peace in connection with a treasure hunt. During 1826, as he waited for the angel Moroni to allow him to remove the plates, he worked on the farm of Isaac Hale in Harmony, Pennsylvania, and he fell in love with Hale's daughter Emma. Isaac disapproved of the match, questioning Joseph's prospects, but the pair eloped anyway in January 1827. Then, on 22 September, Joseph took possession of the golden plates and began their translation. His first assistants were Emma and Martin Harris, a local farmer and benefactor of the young seer in this early period. Progress was slow until Oliver Cowdery, a Palmyra schoolteacher, became involved. From April to July 1829 the bulk of the work was transcribed.

Witnesses to the Translation. According to David Whitmer, one of his first converts, as Joseph held the sacred stones Urim and Thummim to his eyes, a symbol would appear on the plate with the English translation below it. Joseph would dictate the translation, the scribe would read it back for verification, and then another symbol would replace the one translated. That Joseph was more than a lens in this work was demonstrated when Cowdery became insistent about attempting a translation. Joseph finally relented, but Oliver was unable to fathom the markings. Emma also was convinced of the divine inspiration behind the translation, telling of the steady stream of dictation that always began where it left off without any prompting from the scribe. She declared that "for one so ignorant and unlearned as he was, it was simply impossible." *The Book of Mormon* included a statement from Smith's three associates in the work of translation—Oliver Cowdery, Martin Harris, and David Whitmer—as to the reality of the engraved plates and the veracity of the translation. Smith had acquiesced to their entreaties and led them in prayer one day until the angel Moroni appeared. Moroni allowed the trio to see what Smith had seen on the plates. The three were ecstatic, though when pressed, Harris could simply report that the engravings were discernible only "with the eye of faith." Smith then returned the plates and sacred stones to Moroni. Although Cowdery, Harris, and Whitmer all eventually left the church, they never recanted their witness to the divine origin of *The Book of Mormon.*

Joseph Becomes the Prophet. Historians have scrutinized Joseph Smith's early origins for clues to the man, the movement, and the times because, with the publication of *The Book of Mormon* in 1830, Joseph's personal life became inseparable from his role as the prophet of God. By all accounts the role came to him naturally. Whether he was hated or loved, one fact is apparent from the historical record: Joseph Smith was a man of remarkable magnetism and persuasive power. He recognized talent and surrounded himself with trusted apostles and counselors, but he never doubted his authority as prophet and freely excommunicated any who questioned him. The currents surrounding his early life doubtless influenced the type of religious movement he created, in which order, certainty, structure, and divine charisma replaced the chaos of the times. From the standpoint of biography rather than hagiography, his martyr's death at the hands of a Carthage mob on 27 June 1844 turned him from religious leader to insoluble enigma. Whatever one's verdict on Joseph Smith personally, the testimony of Mormonism's growth made him impossible to dismiss lightly.

Sources:

Leonard Arrington and Davis Bitton, *The Mormon Experience: A History of the Latter-Day Saints* (New York: Knopf, 1979);

Richard L. Bushman, *Joseph Smith and the Beginnings of Mormonism* (Urbana: University of Illinois Press, 1984).

TENSKWATAWA, THE SHAWNEE PROPHET

1775?-1836
RELIGIOUS MYSTIC

The Old Northwest. By the end of the eighteenth century the Old Northwest, defined as the Great Lakes region west of Pittsburgh and north of the Ohio River, was home to a number of Eastern Woodland tribes, many of whom had already been decimated by disease and warfare and displaced by colonial land cessions. For a time the Miamis, Shawnees, Delawares, and Ottawas, among others, successfully held off the federal government's campaign to pacify the region, but they met defeat at the Battle of Fallen Timbers in 1794. The treaty signed the following year ceded present-day Ohio and a large part of Indiana to the United States. Consequently, as the new century opened, Native Americans of the Old Northwest felt keenly that their power was diminishing in comparison to that of the white Americans. Not only defeat in battle but also the continual loss of land, the accelerating disappearance of game, the continued social trauma caused by alcohol abuse, and the tidal wave of white settlers signaled that something had gone terribly amiss since the days of their ancestors. This disturbing realization triggered a variety of religious responses, one of which was the emergence of prophets throughout the eighteenth and nineteenth centuries. Though the vision and message of these religious leaders differed in particulars, their ability to gather a following illustrated the widespread perception that the Indians' loss of power was fundamentally linked to disrupted relations with the spirit world.

Lalawethika. Against the background of uncertainty and disruption in the Old Northwest, a shaman arose from the Shawnees, and his teachings struck a responsive chord within many tribes. The early years of Lalawethika were certainly not auspicious. He was an awkward and unattractive youth, disfigured from a childhood accident that left him with only one eye. As an adult he failed to achieve acclaim in battle or display hunting skills, and in fact there were rumors of cowardice. He turned to drinking, but alcohol made him a braggart and led him into further disgrace. Married and with children, Lalawethika sought a role for himself within the tribe by learning from its medicine man, Penagashea. When the elderly Shawnee died in the winter of 1804, Lalawethika tried to replace him, but the tribe rejected him when his remedies had little impact on a raging influenza epidemic. One evening in April 1805 Lalawethika fell into a coma and, by morning, was taken for dead. As funeral arrangements were being made, he suddenly awoke and declared that he had received a vision. At a village meeting the former reprobate related at length what had transpired and the instructions given to him by the Master of Life about what must be done to restore his favor. The Shawnees acknowledged Lalawethika as a prophet, and his name became Tenskwatawa, meaning "the one that opens the door." Among whites he became known as the Shawnee Prophet.

The Vision and the Message. In his vision Tenskwatawa had been shown a paradise that awaited the virtuous Indian but was closed to the sinful, who were instead subjected to various degrees of fiery torture. The path to virtue required renunciation of all that the whites had introduced into the Indian world: whiskey, European-style clothing and weapons, flour bread, and domestic animals. Instead the "red men" should return to the bow and arrow in hunting, to the breechcloth, to the cultivation of corn, and to the sustenance provided by the animals of the forest and stream. There could be trade and contact with the whites, but never should Indians relinquish their independence. Thus he condemned government annuities and the acceptance of white missions as corrupting influences. Trade was permissible, but the goal should not be the accumulation of goods, which again lulled Indians into false desires and put them under the control of others. There should be no intermarriage with whites; wives should be obedient to husbands; and polygamy should be curtailed. Some of the Prophet's admonitions reaffirmed traditional moral standards: cease quarreling; show respect to elders; and care for the injured within the village. His movement, however, was not regressive. The Prophet's followers were to discard the old medicine bundles, which now represented a tainted past. A new set of rituals would henceforth mark the restored covenant between the Master of Life and his favored ones. Symbolic of this fresh start, the Prophet enjoined his followers to kindle a fire, without using the flint and steel of the whites, and keep it burning continuously in their lodges. As his teachings clarified over the coming months, Tenskwatawa instructed the people on new dances and chants to express their piety and distributed prayer sticks to remind them of the need to observe faithfully the rituals and pray frequently to the Master of Life. The whites had only succeeded because the Indians had neglected the source of their power. That error would now be corrected. Within Tenskwatawa's precepts there was evidence of Christian influence. The process of becoming a follower involved a public confession before the Prophet or his representative, then a pledge of obedience to the Prophet's instruction. Followers confirmed their loyalty by the rite of "shaking hands with the Prophet," symbolized by running one's hand down a string of beans (reminiscent of a rosary). In Native American belief systems, punishment in the afterlife had typically taken the form of isolation. Tenskwatawa's vision of fiery torment for misdeeds was probably an image taken from Christianity. The incorporation of "white" magic demonstrated the vision's strength, reinforced by the apocalyptic message, which was for Indians only. If the Indians heeded the instruction of the Master of Life, the whites would eventually be swept from the land. The Prophet's theory of genesis supported this development. As told to him in his vision, whites were not created by the Master of Life. In fact their origin was completely different—they were the offspring of an evil spirit. As such, the Prophet urged Indians to avoid all unnecessary contact.

The Message Spreads. As other tribes heard rumors of a holy man who had risen from the dead, they sent delegations to learn about the vision. In late November representatives from the Delawares, Ottawas, Wyandots, and Senecas visited Tenskwatawa's camp at Greenville in Western Ohio, affirmed his prophethood, and returned home as evangelists for his message of renewal. The religious upsurge became regional, with a widening circle of conversions adding substance to Tenskwatawa's stature as visionary. Although Tenskwatawa preached a message of intertribal peace, he also warned of witches who would try to undermine the new religion. In the spring 1806 the Delawares who had taken his words to heart began to accuse about a dozen people, singling out Christian converts or Indians with ties to the white world. They burned four at the stake before the witch-hunt fever subsided. The grisly dedication of the Prophet's followers caught the attention of William Henry Harrison, governor of Indiana Territory at Fort Vincennes, and he challenged the Delawares to test Tenskwatawa by demanding a miracle: "Ask of him to cause the sun to stand still—the moon to alter its course. . . . If he does these things, you may then believe that he has been sent from God." Harrison was to regret his boldness. Tenskwatawa responded by announcing that on 16 June he would in fact cause the sun to darken and then would restore its light. Thousands of Indians gathered on the appointed day at Greenville and found their faith confirmed at the onset of an eclipse. The Prophet's fame spread to the Kickapoos, Potawatomis, Ottawas, and Winnebagos, from Illinois to Wisconsin. As before, a few emissaries would journey to hear the Prophet, become convinced that his "open door" was the way to Indian deliverance, and then carry their new faith back to their own people. An Ottawa Indian known as "the Trout" became the Prophet's special emissary to the Great Lakes region, though his own message opposed even trade with whites and contained a stronger apocalyptic warning. Main Poc, a powerful medicine man from the Potawatomis, stayed with Tenskwatawa for two months. He was willing to be an ally but not a convert, for he believed that giving up alcohol would make him ordinary. The prophethood of Main Poc contrasted with Tenskwatawa's in other ways, in that his social injunctions were more conventional and less far-reaching than the Shawnee's. Main Poc was a traditional shaman, earning respect for his medicine because it gave him power against the Osages. Nor would he abandon the Potawatomis' long-running animosity against the Osages on behalf of a pan-Indian ephemera.

To Prophetstown. Like a perpetual camp meeting, Greenville became the center for religious seekers in the Old Northwest during 1806 and 1807, and there were reports that the roads were sometimes crowded with Indians heading to or from the site. Officials became alarmed at the activity, especially fearing that the British might take advantage of the situation to "manipulate" the Indians. Meanwhile tensions were increasing within the Eastern Woodland tribes over the continued cession of lands. Millions of acres passed out of Indian control from 1804 to 1807, sometimes through barely disguised fraud, as so-called Indian representatives signed treaties and became the recipients of government annuities. The Indians of the Old Northwest were divided over how to respond to white encroachment, and factions on this question often affected the response to Tenskwatawa's spiritual movement. Even among the Shawnees, Black Hoof resented the upstart prophet and his condemnation of those who parleyed with white officials. In 1809 Harrison managed to find signatories to the Treaty of Fort Wayne, and at one stroke two-and-one-half million acres were sold to the United States for about two cents an acre. Fifteen years of relative peace now broke out in violence on outlying settlements. In the spring of 1808 Tenskwatawa left Greenville and moved to Prophetstown, or Tippecanoe, a site offered to him by the Kickapoos and Potawatomis. Later that summer the Prophet visited Vincennes with a large contingent of followers, supposedly to assure Harrison of his pacific intentions. Harrison observed his preaching and concluded, "The celebrated Shawneese Prophet is rather possessed of considerable talent . . . he frequently harangued his followers in my presence and the evils attendant upon war and the use of ardent spirits was his constant theme."

Tecumseh. In most histories the Prophet's more famous brother, Tecumseh, takes center stage as a canny strategist who used the religious revival to achieve his political goal: uniting all the Indians along the Western border against the Anglo-American advance. In fact there was no separation between the sacred and the profane in the movement. Tecumseh was also a shaman and, according to oral tradition, had a gift of prophecy. He established the authority of his political message by demonstrating certain powers, especially his empathy with nature. Moreover, the basis for pan-Indianism was firmly religious: if whites and Indians were children of different Spirits, then it was right for them to live separately—and right that tribal allegiances should be subsumed under a pan-Indian identity in order to defeat a common enemy. In 1811 Tecumseh took his first journey to the South to seek the support of the Chickasaws, Choctaws, Creeks, and Cherokees. Tenskwatawa remained behind to continue his preaching to Northern delegations while another prophet, Seekaboo, accompanied Tecumseh. Among the Creeks, Tecumseh gathered a group of dedicated supporters known as the Red Sticks, a name derived from the colored wands they received. Prepared with proper ceremony and used correctly, the red sticks would reveal the location of enemies. Tecumseh also distributed a bundle of thirty red sticks to bands of his Creek followers, with one stick to be thrown each night into the fire. After the bundle was gone, they were to watch the sky for a meteor (a celestial sign of his name, "panther passing across"). Tecumseh promised that thirty days after the meteor, he would stamp his foot and cause the earth to shake. In a stunning demonstration of his shamanistic authority, this coincided with the New Madrid earthquake of 16 December 1811.

Tippecanoe. While Tecumseh was negotiating with Southern nations, Tenskwatawa was supposed to keep the unofficial truce between Harrison and the Northern coalition of Indians. Harrison, however, began to claim that individuals at Tippecanoe were involved in frontier raids and had to be turned over to white authorities. In September and October, he built a new fort one hundred miles south of Tippecanoe, called Fort Harrison, and assembled about one thousand men from the militia and army. For several weeks messages and threats passed between the Indian camp and Harrison, and military forces advanced to within two miles of Prophetstown. Tenskwatawa became convinced that the Great Spirit would guarantee an Indian victory by covering the battlefield with a magical fog, which would blind the white soldiers but not his warriors. His followers accepted the pronouncement as a true vision. Before dawn on 7 November 1811 the warriors engaged in an aggressive charge, abandoning their usual stealth in their conviction of inevitable triumph. Tenskwatawa was perched on a promontory, beating a drum and chanting to motivate the warriors. As the morning waned, it was clear that the Battle of Tippecanoe was a disaster for the Indians. Only fifty whites were killed, but Indian losses were much heavier. The Indians were forced to evacuate

Prophetstown, which Harrison then burned. More than lives were lost, however, for with defeat the mystical foundation of pan-Indianism evaporated. Many in the coalition returned to their homes declaring Tenskwatawa a false prophet. Some remained allies, persuaded by Tecumseh's powerful leadership. After Tippecanoe not even Tenskwatawa put any stock in his claim that he had been chosen by the Master of Life. Within a year the Shawnee Prophet's fires were extinguished. Although his brother attempted to hold the confederacy together, sometimes by sheer willpower, he was defeated in 1813. On 5 October Tecumseh earned a mythic death during a battle with the U.S. Army on the Thames River in Ontario. Tenskwatawa later moved to Kansas with the rest of his people, where he remained until his death in 1836.

The Historical Verdict. Historians debate Tenskwatawa's role in the attempt to create a pan-Indian, nativist response to white encroachment, and many favor the idea that he was the tool of his more astute and charismatic brother, Tecumseh, whose carefully planned strategy was dashed by the precipitate action of the Prophet. Epitomizing the noble savage fighting for his country, Tecumseh appealed, then and now, to many Anglo-Americans, who could fit him in the mold of a brave, if tragic, freedom fighter. To the evangelical mind, Tecumseh demonstrated the heroic potential of all Indians if they were given the needed corrective of civilization and Christianity while Tenskwatawa illustrated the opposite. The Prophet's superstitious heathenism was what kept Indians in ignorance and darkness, kept them from realizing their "true" selves. The brothers represented two sides of the Anglo-American debate over the Indian question, and both stirred the pious zeal of evangelical Protestants. However historians may assess the actual nature of Tecumseh's rebellion, the Indians themselves responded to its religious claims. The defeat of pan-Indianism was also a defeat for a pan-Indian religious revival, at least until the Ghost Dance of the late nineteenth century. Even in resistance the encounters between Anglo- and Native Americans in the expanding West occurred on a sacred plane.

Epilogue. To many Indians of the Old Northwest, the inability of the Shawnee Prophet to restore their power was counted as an individual failure—as a severed connection between Tenskwatawa and the Master of Life, not as disproof of the underlying perception that their alienation from the spirit world was the source of their malaise. From Tenskwatawa the spark of that conviction was carried on by the Winnebago Prophet, who played a role in the Black Hawk War of 1832. Again the effort to grapple with the advance of the whites assumed a religious character. Since 1804 the Sauk and Fox had contended that the cession of their lands around Rock River in Illinois had not been legitimate. By 1830 resistance had coalesced around Black Hawk's band. Meanwhile the Winnebago Prophet, Wabokieshiek, who was half Sauk and half Winnebago, accepted an invitation from the Sauk to settle on their lands with his band of about two hundred tribesmen. Like Tenskwatawa, his influence was broad-based, spreading to other tribes, including some members of the Kickapoo and Potawatomi tribes. His message was also familiar: by rejecting white ways and returning to moral purity, there would be a rebirth among the Indians. Added to this was the vision that if the Indians made a stand on their lands, the British and other tribes, including all the Potawatomis, Winnebagos, Osages, and even Southern tribes, would come to their aid and assure their success. Such religious assurances doubtless bolstered the hopes of the group gathered around Black Hawk. The actual war centered on the attempt of Black Hawk's band to cross the Mississippi and settle in their ancestral village on the Rock River. Officials decided to regard the action as an invasion. The outnumbered and starving Indians initially defeated a group of American militia, but after nearly three months of pursuit federal troops caught up with them as they attempted to ford the river at another point. Several hundred of Black Hawk's band, including women and children, were killed. The Prophet's influence faded, though Black Hawk, through his autobiography, became one of the most famous spokesmen for the plight of Indians. This so-called war was the last Indian conflict in the Old Northwest. The region had furnished some of the most compelling personalities of the age as reference points for the Anglo-American view of Indianness, especially the warrior legends of Tecumseh and Black Hawk. That nineteenth-century whites failed to grasp the religious motivation behind resistance was not surprising. The prophets' message of indigenous cultural integrity, with its presumption of white people as agents of evil, was less comprehensible to the Anglo-American worldview than the romantic notion of the noble savage.

Sources:

Gregory Evans Dowd, *A Spirited Resistance: The North American Indian Struggle for Unity, 1745–1815* (Baltimore: Johns Hopkins University Press, 1992);

R. David Edmunds, *The Shawnee Prophet* (Lincoln: University of Nebraska Press, 1983);

Carl Waldman, *Atlas of the North American Indian* (New York: Facts on File, 1985);

Anthony F. C. Wallace, *Prelude to Disaster: The Course of Indian-White Relations Which led to the Black Hawk War of 1832* (Springfield: Illinois State Historical Library, 1970).

PUBLICATIONS

Robert Baird, *Religion in America, Or an Account of the Origin, Progress, Relation to the State, and Present Condition of the Evangelical Churches in the United States, with Notices of the Unevangelical Denominations* (New York: Harper & Row, 1844)—a classic analysis of American religious history that emphasized the West's impact on religious developments;

Lyman Beecher, *A Plea for the West*, second edition (Cincinnati: Truman & Smith, 1835)—a widely read tract on the role of the West in the nation's destiny, to which is appended a lengthy exposé of a supposed Catholic conspiracy to take over the Western regions;

Black Hawk, *Life of Ma-Ka-Tai-Me-She-Kia-Kiak, or, Black Hawk* (Boston: Russell, Odiorne, & Metcalf, 1833)—the reminiscences of this Sauk leader concerning the mistreatment and betrayal of the Indians in the antebellum period made him a native spokesman for all time;

Alexander Campbell, *The Christian System, in Reference to the Union of Christians and a Restoration of Primitive Christianity, as Plead in the Current Reformation* (Bethany, Va.: 1839)—Campbell's synthesis of the theology behind the Christian movement, which served as a guide for believers for many decades;

Peter Cartwright, *Autobiography of Peter Cartwright, the Backwoods Preacher*, edited by W. P. Strickland (Cincinnati: Hitchcock & Walden, 1868)—the experiences of a Methodist preacher who itinerated for more than fifty years in Kentucky, Tennessee, Ohio, Indiana, and Illinois;

George Catlin, *Letters and Notes on the Manners, Customs, and Conditions of the North American Indians; Written During Eight Years' Travel Amongst the Wildest Tribes of Indians of North America*, 2 volumes (London: The author, 1841)—a record of the Plains Indians by a sympathetic observer during his travels from 1832 to 1839;

Pierre-Jean De Smet, *Oregon Missions and Travels Over the Rocky Mountains in 1845–1846* (New York: E. Dunigan, 1847)—a famous Jesuit's reports to his superiors on his Western travels during the 1830s and 1840s;

Charles Grandison Finney, *Lectures on Revivals of Religion* (New York: Leavitt, Lord / Boston: Crocker & Brewster, 1835)—readable explanations of Finney's new measures, which effectually institutionalized revival techniques;

Barton Stone, *The Biography of Eld. Barton Warren Stone, Written by Himself* (Cincinnati: Published for the author by J. A. & U. P. James, 1847)—the memoirs of a leader in the Kentucky revivals, including the Cane Ridge camp meeting, and a founder of the Christian movement;

John Greenleaf Whittier, *The Stranger in Lowell* (Boston: Waite, Peirce, 1845)—this poet's description of "a Mormon Conventicle" offers a New England perspective on the appeal of the Latter-Day Saints.

CHAPTER TEN

SCIENCE
AND
MEDICINE

by JAMES N. LEIKER

CONTENTS

Sidebars and tables are listed in italics.

1801

- A smallpox pandemic begins to ravage Indian peoples in Central and North-western regions, particularly along the Missouri River.

1802

Sept. Thomas Jefferson initiates plans for an American expedition to the Pacific Ocean.

1804

14 May The U.S. Corps of Discovery, headed by Meriwether Lewis and William Clark, leaves St. Louis.

1805

8 Nov. Lewis and Clark reach the Pacific Ocean.

1806

- Cartographer John Cary publishes a map of the Pacific coastline.
15 July Zebulon Pike starts an exploratory expedition west of the Mississippi River into northern New Spain and eventually crosses the Great Plains.
23 Sept. Lewis and Clark return to St. Louis after exploring the Upper Missouri River and the northwestern region of the present-day United States.

1807

- The North West Company explorers spend the next four years on the Upper Columbia River searching for a route to the Pacific.
- John Colter journeys through the Bighorn Basin into present-day Yellowstone National Park.
Mar. Manuel Lisa's fur-trading party begins to explore tributaries of the Upper Missouri River.

1811

- A second American overland expedition, financed by John Jacob Astor, travels through the Northwest and reaches the Pacific Ocean by April 1813.

1814

- The journals of Lewis and Clark's expedition are published.

1819

- Stephen Long's expedition crosses the plains to the Rocky Mountains and explores the Mississippi and Missouri River valleys.

1820
- Henry Schoolcraft's party locates the source of the Mississippi River.

1824
- Over the course of the next six years the Hudson's Bay Company explorers travel through present-day Montana, Idaho, Oregon, Utah, and California.
- A party of trappers employed by the Rocky Mountain Fur Company, among them James Bridger, become the first Euro-Americans to reach the Great Salt Lake.

1826
- Henry Schoolcraft's map of the Upper Mississippi River is published.
- Albert Gallatin publishes *A Table of Indian Languages of the United States*.

1831
- Henry Schoolcraft leads a second expedition to the mouth of the Mississippi River.

1832
- Artist George Catlin journeys up the Missouri River.

1836
- Albert Gallatin compiles a map of the Great Basin and the Colorado River.
- A smallpox epidemic begins to sweep the Northern Plains tribes and by 1840 kills thousands of Blackfeet, Pawnees, Mandans, and others.

1837
- A map drawn by Benjamin Louis Eulalie de Bonneville depicts the major river systems west of the Rocky Mountains.

1838
- The U.S. Army Corps of Topographical Engineers begins to conduct the first geological explorations of the Trans-Mississippi West.

1842
- Albert Gallatin and others begin the American Ethnological Society.

1843

Apr.–Aug. John James Audubon travels to the mouth of the Yellowstone River, examining natural flora and fauna along the way.

16 June John C. Frémont leads an expedition from Independence, Missouri, along the Kansas River, over the Rocky Mountains, and eventually to the Columbia River and California.

1845

• John C. Frémont's account of his expedition to the Rockies, Oregon, and California is published.

1847

• Henry Schoolcraft receives a government commission to assemble information on history and culture of North American Indians.

1849

• Native American and Anglo travelers along the overland trails suffer from cholera epidemics.

July The U.S. Topographical Corps begins its survey of the Rio Grande.

1851

• Lewis Henry Morgan's study of the Iroquois is published.

1852

• Audubon begins publishing *The Vivaparous Quadrapeds of North America*.

1853

• The Pacific Railroad and the U.S. Army Corps of Topographical Engineers conduct a series of expeditionary surveys in the Northwest until 1855.

1854

• G. K. Warren compiles all known geographic information into a map of the United States from the Mississippi River to the Pacific Ocean.

June–Dec. John Boardman Trask's geological report on the agricultural and mineral resources of the coastal mountains is presented to the state legislature of California.

OVERVIEW

A Collision of Worlds. At the time of the founding of the United States diverse peoples with varying languages, religions, and levels of technology lived across the breadth of North America. On the Eastern seaboard, the former English colonists struggled with their new republic; west of the Appalachian Mountains hundreds of indigenous groups farmed, hunted, and traded for subsistence, and in the Southwest, Spanish missionaries and ranchers occupied the northern reaches of New Spain's frontier, living in a tenuous balance with nomadic raiding tribes. Though already linked through continental trade networks by 1800, Americans often had only vague knowledge of each other and the land itself. The process of American expansion from 1800 to 1860 that extended the United States's political boundaries west to the Pacific Ocean and south to the Rio Grande brought these peoples together in a maelstrom of scientific discovery: mapping mountains and rivers, documenting newfound animal and plant forms, adapting technology for new Western cities, and utilizing the fruits of the land to fight illness and produce food. Yet these collisions also raised important questions about the people themselves, about the origins of Indian society and their relationship to Europeans, and how all fit into "the Great Chain of Being." The answers that naturalists, explorers, and healers suggested to these questions did more than contribute to scientific learning; these hypotheses also repudiated, or in some cases justified, military expansion and cultural warfare. As in all cases throughout history, science and medicine in the American West influenced and was influenced by the diplomatic, economic, and social interactions of the people who met there.

New Lands and Peoples. People, of course, did not "discover" the West in the nineteenth century. Native Americans had traversed its regions for centuries and created elaborate civilizations that rose and fell long before European contact. Indigenous peoples understood the land intimately since they depended on it for survival; predicting weather, watching animal movements, and knowing the location of vital water holes and mountain passes proved crucial for existence. Though many twentieth-century observers might hesitate to call it "science," Indians possessed a working understanding of geography, zoology, and meteorology that preceded the

formation of those same disciplines among Europeans. Yet beyond the confines of specific natural territories Indians lacked knowledge of other continents and civilizations. Americans of European descent, by contrast, knew the broad contours of the world since the voyages of Christopher Columbus, Ferdinand Magellan, and James Cook but understood few details about the North American landscape beyond territory they had traveled prior to 1800. Westward expansion, then, proved a process of mutual learning. White explorers' efforts in cataloguing the Rocky Mountains, Great Salt Lake, Missouri River, and many other natural wonders could not have occurred without the assistance and teaching of Indian guides. Indians too came to understand through white contact the existence of a larger universe that challenged their traditional beliefs. Historians often focus on the violence that shaped collisions between these peoples but overlook the countless episodes of cooperation and learning that stimulated for both a New World perspective.

The Great Chain of Being. During the eighteenth century Anglo-Americans and Europeans gained new perspectives from the Enlightenment, an intellectual movement that taught the value of reason and observation in understanding the natural world. Scientists believed that animals, plants, minerals, and even governments and ideas sprang from some common source and were thus interrelated. Carolus Linnaeus, the Swedish botanist who established a system of classifying and naming life-forms, helped to establish this notion of "the Great Chain of Being." In contrast to previous theories that had asserted separate creations or claimed that life could emerge from nonliving things, Enlightenment philosophers held to the theory of biogenesis, that life originated only from other life. "New science" attempted to document all forms on earth and classify them into their respective places in the chain of life. Anglo-Americans and Europeans sought to place the people and creatures of North America into this structure, studying the rattlesnake, the grizzly bear, and the bison and trying to decipher their relationships to similar Old World animals. One of the most daunting questions involved the origins of Native Americans. From what branch of humanity did they descend? Or did they stem from a separate origin, refuting the very notion of a single human race? In time such speculations encouraged the formation of racial theory, the thesis that humans are divisible into population groups and evolve at different speeds. Most contemporary biologists now dispute the idea of race. However, in the early 1800s the concept held potential for explaining the great diversity of peoples and cultures encountered by Europeans in North America.

New Diseases and Medicines. Human beings, however, seldom passively observe nature; they alter it by their presence. European descendants had brought to the Western Hemisphere plants such as wheat and peach trees as well as livestock, mostly cattle, horses, sheep, and hogs. They unwittingly transported disease-bearing microbes previously unknown in the Americas. Europeans often carried acquired immunities to diseases such as smallpox and measles that Indians lacked, and the intro-

duction of these new organisms wrought horrific epidemics in Native American communities, killing thousands. Most major epidemics raged through the West prior to the nineteenth century, before natives encountered European colonists through war. Yet even after 1800 Western migration remained an unhealthy endeavor that affected whites as well as Indians. Poor diet, inadequate sanitation, an overabundance of alcohol, and the scarcity of trained physicians made sickness on the frontier much more dangerous than elsewhere. Like the Indians whom they encountered, pioneers discovered ways to cope. They employed herbal medicines and other native treatments to deal with a variety of ailments. Westerners became their own doctors. Through this accommodation they contributed to later generations' knowledge of medicine and healing in ways that rivaled the great geographic and anthropological discoveries that characterized the age.

TOPICS IN THE NEWS

ANTHROPOLOGY AND ETHNOLOGY

Beginnings of Anthropology. Western imperialism of the nineteenth century brought Americans and Europeans into contact with a diverse array of global cultures, all with varying social systems and levels of technology. While few whites at the time questioned their "superiority" over other peoples, they nonetheless approached the nonindustrialized world with immense curiosity. In the United States constant warfare with Western tribes over land rights accompanied a nearly carnivalistic fascination with Native Americans. Some hoped that by studying indigenous societies whites could find evidence that supported the progress of their own culture. Thus, though missionaries and government agents who worked most closely with Indians encouraged natives to abandon ancestral ways and to dress, work, and behave like Euro-Americans, some natural scientists wondered if such assimilationist strategies destroyed valuable components of traditional Indian cultures. American anthropology emerged in the mid nineteenth century from an effort to observe and record the cultural practices of societies in danger of extinction. Many early anthropologists depended heavily on the cooperation of Native Americans. For example, Lewis Henry Morgan, one of the founders of anthropology in the United States, relied on the col-

laboration of Ely S. Parker, a Tonawanda Seneca who acquainted Morgan with the history and structure of the Iroquois League.

Anthropological Museums. During the eighteenth and nineteenth centuries many Americans of European descent collected Indian artifacts for private museums. Thomas Jefferson's collection at Monticello became one of the largest in the country. In time anthropological museums became a venue for documenting the artistic and technological activities of specific cultures in contrast to libraries and archives that preserved their written past. However, museums alone did not satisfy the intellectual curiosity of many Americans. Distressed by the changes wrought by urbanization and industrialization, the first anthropologists turned westward to understand the lessons of nonliterate and nontechnological peoples who shared the continent.

Ohio and Mississippi Civilizations. Scientists had long been fascinated with the archaeological evidence of the mound-building societies that flourished in the Eastern woodlands. Contemporary archaeologists date this civilization, centered along the Mississippi River's banks from the Gulf of Mexico to Minnesota, from about A.D. 700 to 1500. Reports from travelers and military men excited scholars as early as the 1790s, raising the possibility

Men of the Mandan Buffalo Bull Society; watercolor and pencil sketch by
Carl Bodmer, circa 1834 (InterNorth Art Foundation, Joslyn Art
Museum, Omaha, Nebraska)

of an earlier civilization with elaborate agriculture and political systems that preceded the Indians. Some nineteenth-century antiquarians believed the mounds to be constructed by ancient Toltecs who later migrated south to Mexico and founded the Aztec Empire. Others asserted an Asian origin, pointing to similarities with Hindu artifacts. Nearly all believed the Mound Builders' sophistication indicated they could not have been related to contemporary Indians. However, that conclusion raised the question about how this mysterious race became extinct. Had barbarous, warlike tribes annihilated a superior culture, and if so, could a similar feat be repeated, thereby justifying government warfare against Indians? These questions of science influenced decisions about public policy and raised further speculation about the origins of native peoples themselves.

Gallatin and Environmental Theory. Albert Gallatin, who had served as secretary of the treasury under Thomas Jefferson, became one of the United States's leading ethnologists. A staunch nationalist, Gallatin welcomed the opening of Western lands to American settlers but main-

tained that Indians' land claims must be evaluated and understood from their own respective cultures. His *A Table of Indian Languages of the United States,* published in 1826, was the first philological attempt to classify Indian tribes by language. Gallatin subsequently tried to determine the ancestral origins of native groups. By the 1830s evidence unearthed from the mound civilizations caused many ethnologists to conclude that Native Americans had somehow degenerated in their development. The finding encouraged scientists to explain Indians' history as an example of racial decline. Gallatin resisted this trend, claiming that environment, not race, proved more important. Gallatin compared North American tribes to Aztec and Mayan peoples in Central America, pointing out that several factors such as climate, soil, and availability of game encouraged some societies to continue hunting and gathering while others practiced agriculture. These latter groups developed specialized labor and elaborate political systems out of necessity, eventually forming what Europeans recognized as "civilization." Several decades later Franz Boas, a pioneer in the disci-

As ethnologists sought to understand indigenous cultures during the early nineteenth century, they increasingly employed linguistic analysis—the study of language and its construction—to comprehend natives' cosmological view of the universe. In the process some such as Henry Rowe Schoolcraft discovered that these differences in speech represented deeper, more fundamental differences in whites' and Indian's conceptual understandings of nature, creating a barrier to effective communication:

It has been remarked that the distinction of words into animates and inanimates, is a principle intimately interwoven throughout the structure of the language. . . . For the origin of the principle itself, we need look only to nature, which endows animate bodies with animate properties and qualities, and vice versa. But it is due to the tribes who speak this language, to have invented one set of adjective symbols to express the ideas peculiarly appropriate to the former, and another set applicable, exclusively, to the latter. . . . In giving anything like the spirit of the original, much greater deviations, in the written forms, must appear. And in fact, not only the structure of the language, but the mode and order of thought of the Indians is so essentially different, that any attempts to preserve the English idiom—to give letter for letter, and word for word, must go far to render the translation pure nonsense.

While he remained optimistic that Indian concepts might eventually be translated into English terms, Schoolcraft preceded by more than a century a school of postmodern literary scholars who assert that culture remains inextricably bound with language and that the cultural intricacies from which language emerges may create problems in communication between various peoples.

Source: Henry R. Schoolcraft, *The American Indians, Their History, Condition and Prospects* (Buffalo: George H. Denby, 1851).

pline of anthropology, affirmed many of Gallatin's conclusions. Nevertheless, in Gallatin's own day his emphasis on environmental adaptation received little attention compared to the majority of scientists who argued that racial differences alone explained cultural differences among disparate peoples.

Racial Thought. Gallatin represented an earlier Enlightenment tradition that taught the universality of humankind. However, in the first half of the nineteenth century intellectuals began to speak of the "races" of man, claiming that certain peoples carried a natural disposition toward progress while others would degenerate and become extinct. Racial theorists built on the writings of Georges Louis Leclerc, Count de Buffon, a French naturalist. Buffon claimed that on the scale of geologic time America's life-forms were relatively young, having just emerged from the primordial sea. As a result native groups remained primitive in comparison to European societies. Racial theories rested on the notion that human beings descended from separate origins, a departure from Judeo-Christian teachings that advocated a single creation. Many scientists' deistic beliefs caused them to reject the biblical, creationist explanation of man's origins and to adopt a polygenic view that humans descended from multiple lineages. Known as polygenesis, this new view encouraged the notion of racial differences as fixed and essential. The concept found a receptive audience in a nation struggling with the ethical dimensions of African slavery and Indian dispossession. Josiah Nott, a Southern physician, employed zoological studies and phrenology (the study of the cranium) to justify slavery as an institution that allowed "inferior" blacks to reach their full potential under the white man's guidance. According to Nott, since Indians did not enjoy the same benefits of slavery, they would eventually recede and become extinct. Strengthened by Charles Darwin's theories relating to evolution, "scientific racism" emerged as a justification for conquest during westward expansion.

Lewis Henry Morgan, like many educated people of his time, held ethnocentric views of native cultures as barbaric even though his anthropological works helped to advance understanding of Indian ways. Yet Morgan proved to be exceptional for how he advocated intermarriage between whites and Indians:

I think an amalgamation with the Indians by the white race, or the absorption of the best blood of their race into our own is destined to take place. . . . Hitherto the lowest and basest whites have been the fathers of the half breeds. Now we are to see respectable white people marry the daughters of wealthy and respectable Indians and bring up their children with the advantages of education, Christianity, and wealth, and these half breeds will again intermarry respectably with the whites. Our race, I think, will be toughened physically by the intermixture and without any doubt will be benefitted intellectually.

For Morgan, whites and Indians would advance only when "the best" from both sides recognized their common interests and decided to amalgamate. His disdain for the lower classes resembles the bias that many ethnologists had for dark-skinned people as well as poor whites. Nevertheless, his hope for cooperation and union between the races placed him at odds with many scientific thinkers who taught the values of racial purity.

Source: Lewis Henry Morgan, *The Indian Journals, 1859–62*, edited by Leslie A. White (New York: Dover, 1993), pp. 46–47.

Detail from an 1850 schematic panorama depicting the excavation of a Native American burial mound in Louisiana. The painting was commissioned by Dr. Montroville Dickeson, who supervised the excavation. (St. Louis Art Museum)

American Ethnological Society. Although whites used the concept of race to justify a variety of atrocities, racism itself actually emerged from a long attempt to reconcile the existence of blacks and Indians with Western scientists' view of the world. The geological and geographic discoveries about the Western part of North America in the early nineteenth century attracted scientists to new fields such as ethnology, anthropology, and archaeology. In 1842 Gallatin helped to found the American Ethnological Society in New York. Although other organizations such as the American Antiquarian Society and the American Philosophical Society had funded ethnological research, many anthropologists felt the need for an exclusive organization. Gallatin held most of the meetings at his home in New York City, where members presented and discussed books, maps, and artifacts from leading Western explorers and scientists. The society provided a network of communication for specialists in the burgeoning new field and developed a prestigious reputation, providing panels of experts to the newly formed Smithsonian Institution for its ethnological manuscripts. Gallatin, however, tended to recruit only members who shared his environmentalist, or monogenist, views. After Gallatin's death in 1849, the society's membership declined, partly because of its avoidance of the race question and its growing alienation from physical anthropology and the study of Western North America.

Sources:

Robert E. Bieder, *Science Encounters the Indian, 1820–1880: The Early Years of American Ethnology* (Norman: University of Oklahoma Press, 1986);

Brian W. Dippie, *The Vanishing American: White Attitudes and U.S. Indian Policy* (Lawrence: University Press of Kansas, 1982);

Anthony Pagden, *The Fall of Natural Man: The American Indian and the Origins of Comparative Ethnology* (Cambridge: Cambridge University Press, 1982).

DISEASE AND WESTWARD EXPANSION

Health. Immigrants who entered the Trans-Appalachian region in the early nineteenth century hoped to leave behind the disease and contamination that seemed so characteristic of Eastern cities. They expected to find in the West an environment of clean air and water, with limitless opportunities for health and material advancement. However, the process of settling the West changed the environment itself. Migrants brought more than their culture; they also transported bacteria and viruses, and with those came epidemics that wrought turmoil in both white and Native American communities. The fact that most people lived far from medical care in primitive, makeshift conditions added to the dangers of disease. When students think of the American West, they often think of gunfights and ambushes even though more persons died from illness than from violence. Thousands of anonymous, unmarked graves along the great trails and in small, deserted towns remain today as a testimony to the unhealthy nature of life in the era of westward expansion.

Indian Depopulation. Disease took its greatest toll on Native Americans. As contact with whites grew more frequent, Indians became exposed to germs and pathogens for which they had no immunity, and as a result they suffered sickness and mortality rates much higher than whites. Scholars estimate that the American Indian population (within contemporary U.S. boundaries) declined from about 600,000 in 1800 to a mere 250,000 by 1900. Besides leaving tribes numerically ill prepared to resist white encroachment, imported diseases struck hardest at elders who filled important leadership roles in Indian societies. Native Americans increasingly blamed these losses on white intrusion while many whites believed that Indians were a dying race destined for extinction. Thus disease exacerbated tensions between whites and natives and made peaceful co-existence far more difficult.

Smallpox. No other disease ravaged Indian peoples more than the dreaded smallpox. The first major pandemic in the nineteenth-century West occurred in 1801–1802 among tribes in the Central and Northwestern regions of the continent. This epidemic devastated people along the Missouri River with particular ferocity. Between 1836 and 1840 another epidemic swept the Northern plains, killing many, including thousands of Blackfeet, Pawnees, and Mandans. The artist George Catlin described a tragic scene among the Mandans in 1837: Chief Four Bears, who always had advocated peace with outside traders, witnessed the deaths of his family and tribal members to smallpox. Surviving the disease himself, Four Bears denounced the White Dogs who brought disease to his people and rather than witness their further destruction, starved himself to death over a period of nine days. Smallpox continued its widespread devastation until the late nineteenth century though not with the same intensity as before 1840. Government officials from both the United States and Mexico attempted to vaccinate certain Indian groups, yet such actions had little effect because of sporadic implementation and many Indians' suspicion that vaccination was another white plan to kill them.

Cholera. Medical science had no vaccination for the other great scourge of the nineteenth century: cholera. Merchants and sailors transported the disease, believed to have emanated from India, to the United States in 1832, where the poor sanitary facilities of Eastern cities allowed it to thrive. During the 1849 California Gold Rush, travelers carried the bacterium along the Santa Fe Trail and other overland routes. Migrants' notoriously filthy hygienic habits caused them to eat spoiled meat and to drink and bathe in waste water. These conditions proved ideal for the spread of cholera. Yet unlike the contagious smallpox virus, cholera's danger lay less in its actual spread than in how it struck at undernourished populations. Prospective gold seekers often suffered from overwork and poor diet, leaving their bodies susceptible to cholera infection. Nomadic Indian tribes suffered the same conditions; as many as one-half of the Pawnees and two-thirds of the Southern Cheyennes died of cholera between 1849 and 1852. Reports among the Comanches state that survivors lacked the strength to bury their hundreds of dead while Arapaho legends tell of several people who committed suicide rather than face the dreaded sickness. Medical practitioners could do little for cholera patients other than administer tinctures such as laudanum, which relieved the horrifying abdominal cramps suffered by the afflicted.

Other Diseases. Westerners contended with many other ailments as well. Malaria, tuberculosis, measles, scarlet fever, mumps, influenza, and whooping cough were common. If settlers had the luck of living in the vicinity of a military base, they could seek help from the post surgeon. Military doctors frequently prescribed mercury and calomel (a laxative) in the hope of purging infectious matter. Yet since trained physicians rarely traveled to remote areas (and since many of these diseases were untreatable at the time), pioneers learned to fashion home remedies. In mining camps or wagon crews any person with a meager knowledge of animal birthing or bone setting could be called on to render medical advice. Many Western diseases conferred long-term immunity to survivors, an advantage that Native Americans did not share. The transfer of dangerous organisms from one people to another became a decidedly one-way process that worked against Indians. Venereal disease also appeared common. Miners, fur trappers, and traders engaged frequently in sexual relations with natives, increasing the possibility of both sides becoming infected with syphilis and gonorrhea. Nearly every man on Meriwether Lewis and William Clark's famous expedition received treatment for syphilis, which at the time consisted of a heavy dose of mercury.

Sources:

Ramon Powers and James N. Leiker, "Cholera among the Plains Indians: Perceptions, Causes, Consequences," *Western Historical Quarterly,* 29 (Autumn 1998): 317–340;

Powers and Gene Younger, "Cholera on the Overland Trails, 1832–1869," *Kansas Historical Quarterly,* 5 (Spring 1973): 32–49;

Russell Thornton, *American Indian Holocaust and Survival: A Population History Since 1492* (Norman: University of Oklahoma Press, 1987).

DRINKING AND ALCOHOLISM

Alcohol Consumption. The poor health of most nineteenth-century Americans cannot be separated from their overwhelming consumption of alcoholic beverages. From 1790 to 1840 adult males drank nearly one-half pint of hard liquor each day, more than at any other time in American history. Because of the poor quality of water and milk, and the inordinate expense of tea and coffee, settlers in the West consumed mostly whiskey and cider. They drank these beverages in small amounts with family meals or in communal binge drinking, which generally led to public drunkenness. Settlers transported their drinking habits with them when they moved west of the Appalachians. Far removed from Eastern markets, settlers often used jugs of locally distilled liquor as the standard medium of exchange. Given the scarce opportunities for entertainment on the frontier, practically any occasion where two or three men gathered provided a reason for drinking. Soldiers, traders, fur trappers, and miners all imbibed to excess, and often suffered harsh physical consequences such as nausea, vomiting, and even death as a result. Drinking, it seems, became an integral part of Westerners' daily activities, leading to gambling, fighting, and, not infrequently, murder. Today, twentieth-century Americans comprehend a little better the psychological effects of alcoholism. However, few understand or even acknowledge how Western settlement occurred in the context not only of constant sickness and disease but in an almost continual state of intoxication.

Whiskey. By 1800 whiskey replaced rum as Americans' favorite beverage for a variety of reasons. The use of imported sugar in the distilling process made rum, like wine, more expensive than whiskey. During the late eighteenth century Scots-Irish settlers, who had long known how to distill grain, migrated into the western reaches of British America and produced their own whis-

key. The opening of agricultural lands in the Upper Midwest during the early nineteenth century created a corn surplus that could then be used to make alcohol. Whiskey, unlike most agricultural products, could be hauled without fear of spoilage. Since settlers in the West were limited to local ingredients in their manufacture of medicines, locally grown foods dominated their diets. As a result they had a rather monotonous diet of pork and corn supplemented by distilled whiskey. Many adhered to the popular notion that alcohol served as an efficient preventive to disease; Westerners sometimes distributed free liquor during cholera and smallpox epidemics because of the belief that alcohol had curative power. Western pioneers also lived in isolation, far from towns and sometimes even far from family. The exhaustive work, loneliness, danger, worry, and even boredom that haunted their lives encouraged many to seek refuge in a whiskey jug, causing the West to develop a reputation for drunkenness that surpassed every other region of the country.

Indian Drinking. Native Americans in Mexico and the Southwest had fermented local plants to make alcohol long before European contact, which they used almost exclusively in religious rituals. However, most natives in North America first obtained alcohol through exchange with white traders. Some of the natives perhaps learned the joys and trials of liquor consumption from some of the heaviest drinkers in the world. Because of its imperishability, liquor became more valuable on the frontier than money, providing a medium of exchange between disparate cultures. Many Indians enjoyed the sense of power and liberation that accompanied drunkenness, even integrating its use into their ceremonies and rituals. At times, when natives experienced the devastation of epidemics, food shortages, and warfare, drinking habits increased, a characteristic response of cultures undergoing rapid transformation. Especially after the 1830s, when federal officials paid Indians in cash for lands they ceded to the government, some natives often bought alcohol rather than invest in agricultural improvements. Natives such as the Kansa even became regular suppliers to other Indians, providing alcohol to their neighbors the Osages and to nomadic bands along the Arkansas River. The image of Indians inebriated on government annuity payments stirred the resentment of whites, fueling the stereotype of "the drunken Indian" that had started during the colonial period.

Temperance Movements. Consumption of spirituous liquor peaked in the 1820s and then plummeted the following decade, reflecting the partial successes of temperance and other reform organizations. Originating in New England, antiliquor crusaders depicted drink as an agent of the devil. Clergymen and civic leaders held monthly meetings where they urged drunkards to "take the pledge" and become abstinent. These reformers cast drunkenness as a family problem since men under the influence often engaged in domestic violence or deprived their families of basic needs after squandering their resources on drink. On the frontier a wave of religious revivalism brought Methodist and Baptist missionaries to the West who exhorted the evils of "Demon Rum" at every opportunity. When more settlers entered the region and began establishing communities, the sense of isolation that had led to alcohol abuse faded amid a new popular movement for abstinence, reinforced by regular camp meetings and temperance sermons. Obviously such efforts never completely succeeded. As a result many reformers campaigned long and hard to convince state and federal legislators to enact prohibition laws. Overall, as churches, schools, and other institutions followed pioneers westward, alcohol use and its accompanying destructive effects tended to decrease.

Indian Prohibition. At the same time that voluntary temperance spread among white Americans, reformers, government officials, and tribal leaders preferred to prohibit alcohol availability altogether in order to combat Indian drinking. Many tribes passed their own legislation to prohibit alcohol use. The nineteenth century also had several federal laws that aimed to eliminate the liquor trade on reservations. An act of 1834 prohibited the introduction of alcohol into Indian country, and an 1847 revision mandated imprisonment for any person providing alcohol to Indians in Indian Territory and denied annuities to any tribe that failed to pledge themselves to abstinence. Yet such laws had power only on federal lands, not in areas under territorial or state governance. Further, these acts proved virtually impossible to enforce, and by maintaining the image of the drunken Indian, federal prohibition policies helped to sour Euro-American/Native American relations. As long as Indians desired drink, suppliers could always be located to sell them liquor, a lesson that Americans learned much more painfully a century later during the era of federal prohibition.

Sources:

Peter C. Mancall, "Men, Women, and Alcohol in Indian Villages in the Great Lakes Region in the Early Republic," *Journal of the Early Republic*, 15 (1995): 425–448;

Robert J. Miller and Maril Hazlett, "The 'Drunken Indian': Myth Distilled into Reality Through Federal Indian Alcohol Policy," *Arizona State Law Journal*, 28 (1996): 223–298;

W. J. Rorabaugh, *The Alcoholic Republic: An American Tradition* (Oxford: Oxford University Press, 1979);

William E. Unrau, *White Man's Wicked Water: The Alcohol Trade and Prohibition in Indian Country, 1802–1892* (Lawrence: University Press of Kansas, 1996).

FRONTIER HEALING

Traveling Doctors. Prior to the establishment of licensing laws and other legal regulations of medical practice, Americans tried in various ways to fill the gaps created by the absence of college-trained physicians. Especially in the West, self-styled "doctors" wandered from place to place offering cures or peddling remedies for various ailments. Some were honest people who thought themselves to be human benefactors, but many others were quacks and charlatans who worked the circuits in search of profit. White pioneers' deep fascination with Native American lore led many of them to consult so-called Indian doctors for treatment. Most white men who toted saddlebags of herb and root medicines to frontier communities claimed to have learned their knowledge from Indian healers, but most of their prescriptions included ingredients unused by most tribes: cayenne pepper, snake root, sage, skunk cabbage, and other combinations that supposedly cured croup, loosened bowels, and prevented smallpox and cholera. Though they became more popular after the Civil War, traveling medicine shows

A Tlingit shaman's rattle used to call up guardian spirits (American Museum of Natural History, New York City)

toured the country during westward expansion, offering entertainment as well as patent remedies to isolated frontier people. Indians occasionally accompanied such troupes, performing war dances and other spectacles to ward off sinister forces known to cause bad health. Difficult to comprehend from a modern perspective, some nineteenth-century Americans adhered to ancient beliefs that disease emanated from otherworldly forces and therefore could be combated more by magic and ritual than by reason and experimentation.

Folk Medicine. Settlers who pushed west of the Appalachian Mountains came to rely on home remedies acceptable on the frontier long before marketed pharmaceuticals. One such remedy for dysentery involved concocting a sweetened tea from red pepper and sumac leaves, which was to be digested while breathing heavy steam. This treatment apparently helped to control diarrheal ailments in the West, usually caused by poor food preservation. Other folk cures had less success: red onions as a poultice for cancer and baldness, or mixed with oil of roasted almonds to cure deafness, or fried and mixed with olive oil to ensure easy childbirth. Pioneers had little choice but to attempt remedies with ingredients immediately available, making home experimentation common. By the late 1800s the use of botanical remedies gradually declined, although historians note that many twentieth-century pharmaceutical companies rely on the same indigenous plants for ingredients that pioneers employed a century earlier.

Indian Cosmology. Though whites learned many such cures from interaction with Native Americans, they rarely made sincere efforts to understand the role of traditional Indian beliefs concerning health and spirituality. Most Indian groups in the West perceived the individual's state in holistic terms, believing that physical well-being depended on harmony between the body, mind, spirit, and universe. Healing ceremonies—regarded as superstitious by Anglo science—focused less on curing than on restoring balance within the community. Called medicine men or shamans by whites, aboriginal healers thus served as religious and social leaders as well. In contrast to the Anglo view of linear progressive time, natives perceived life as a circle, a series of cycles that people experience on their journey back to nature. Since natives tended to view certain illnesses as natural, most cures involved treatment with herbs or rituals, but as outside contact grew, Indians encountered foreign diseases such as smallpox and cholera that remained outside the power of native healers.

Native Treatments. Indian medicine varied considerably depending on tribal culture and the illness itself. Healing rituals could be conducted in the intimate surroundings of the patient's home, or they could be public affairs that lasted for months. Southern Plains tribes met every one or two years for the Sun Dance, a ceremony that required participation of musicians, dancers, politi-

INDIAN TREATMENT OF SNAKEBITE

Whites learned from Native Americans a variety of remedies for treating poisonous wounds. Indians of Lower California used tight bindings between the bite and the heart while the San Carlos Apaches practiced sucking the poison out of snakebites and scorpion stings. The Flathead Indians employed this same technique in dealing with wounds from poisoned arrows, as described by Nathaniel Wyeth in 1832:

I had an opportunity of seeing a specimen of Indian surgery in treating a wound. An Indian squaw first sucked the wound perfectly dry, so that it appeared white as chalk; . . . [which] taught the savage Indian that a person may take poison into his mouth without any risk, as the poison of a rattlesnake without harm, provided there be no scratch or wound in the mouth, so as to admit it into the blood?

Many Americans of European descent grudgingly came to respect Indians' remedies and their familiarity with indigenous mendicants. Often, roots from certain plants, which could be ingested or applied externally, proved effective in treating snakebites. Some tribes learned these treatments through their experience with handling snakes in religious rituals. For instance, the Hopis held live rattlesnakes in their mouths during certain dances. A white doctor remarked that there had never been "a case of fatal snake bite among those tribes to whom the snake is sacred, . . ." possibly because the snakes had been rendered docile or that their poison glands had been emptied prior to their use in rituals.

Source: Virgil J. Vogel, *American Indian Medicine* (Norman: University of Oklahoma Press, 1970), pp. 221–224.

cal elders, and many other specialists. Indian healers sought not to cure a person's ailment but to provide the proper environment for the natural healing process. This included wearing special garments or masks and body paint with symbolic images that aided deities in their work. Natives constructed sweat lodges to purify the individual for the arrival of healing spirits. Not all such remedies worked when dealing with imported diseases; "doing a sweat," followed by a plunge in cold water, often induced hypothermia, which worsened the resistance of cholera and smallpox victims. However, nineteenth-century Indian medicine rested on many assumptions that twentieth-century practitioners are beginning to discover, especially the link between a person's physical state and his or her mental and spiritual condition. Modern psychiatry's use of group therapy, for example, bears a strong resemblance to the "talking circles" long practiced by North American tribal groups.

Indigenous Drugs. Modern medicine's use of substances has many interesting parallels to pioneer and indigenous therapeutic remedies. The use of the cactus peyote (*Lophophora williamsii*) originated among natives in the American Southwest and spread across the United States through the nineteenth century. Employed mostly in rituals, peyote also could be applied as a poultice for wounds or as a muscular lotion and could be used in a drink for fevers. U.S. Army surgeons noted its effectiveness and frequently employed peyote as a pain killer. Many Western tribes used smoke treatment to fight respiratory or rheumatic illnesses. Accompanied by song and ritual, natives burned fumigant substances such as cedar branches, sage, or prickly pear cactus over live coals for ingestion by patients.

Hygiene and Sanitation. White settlers gradually learned from Indians an appreciation for frequent bathing, both as a sanitary precaution and as a treatment for ailments. When a member of Meriwether Lewis and William Clark's expedition developed rheumatic stiffness, Lewis tried a sweat-bath by pouring water over hot stones to produce steam. Combined with a strong tea of horsemint, the procedure led the patient to a full recovery. Sulfurous warm springs alleviated skin and breathing disorders. In other ways, however, Westerners proved painfully slow in developing proper hygiene, especially with regard to food supplies. Given the scarcity of fruits and vegetables, nutritional deficiencies became a common problem. Meat, the basic staple, spoiled quickly and attracted insects and parasites. After a successful buffalo hunt, Comanche and Cheyenne hunters pitched their lodges in the vicinity of the slaughtering area. U.S. military forts often gave little attention to proper disposal of animal remains and human waste, leading to localized epidemics. In all, Westerners of the early nineteenth century struggled to compensate for the absence of institutionalized medicine in a variety of improvisational ways. However, as with so many other matters, preventive health care received little priority in the rush to open new lands or in the fight to maintain old ones.

Sources:

Jennie R. Joe, "Health and Healers," in *Encyclopedia of North American Indians*, edited by Frederick Hoxie (New York: Houghton Mifflin, 1996), pp. 237–240;

Virgil J. Vogel, *American Indian Medicine* (Norman: University of Oklahoma Press, 1970).

GEOLOGY AND GEOGRAPHY

The Fur Trade. Fur trappers, or mountain men as some people called them, while not scientific or government explorers, gathered empirical information that aided the soldiers and naturalists who followed them. Either learning from Indians or on their own, trappers discovered the courses of river systems and the locations of critical passes as well as the scarcity or abundance of game in particular regions. Manuel Lisa launched an expedition in 1807 that explored the tributaries of the Up-

---

FIRST VIEW OF THE ROCKIES

On 15 November 1806 Zebulon Pike recorded his first observation of the Rocky Mountains near the present-day site of Lamar, Colorado. Pike's description indicates both his natural appreciation for their grandeur and his curiosity about the Rockies' hydrological and even political importance.

At two o'clock in the afternoon I thought I could distinguish a mountain to our right, which appeared like a small blue cloud. Viewed it with the spy glass and was still more confirmed in my conjecture, yet only communicated it to Doctor Robinson, who was in front with me, but in half an hour they appeared in full view before us. When our small party arrived on the hill they with one accord gave three cheers to the Mexican mountains. Their appearance can easily be imagined by those who have crossed the Alleghanies; but their sides were whiter, as if covered with snow or a white stone. Those were a spur of the grand western chain of mountains which divides the waters of the Pacific from those of the Atlantic Ocean, and it divided the waters which empty into the bay of the Holy Spirit from those of the Mississippi as the Alleghanies do those which discharge themselves into the latter river and the Atlantic. They appear to present a natural boundary between the provinces of Louisiana and New Mexico, and would be a defined and natural boundary.

Source: Zebulon Montgomery Pike, *The Southwestern Expedition of Zebulon M. Pike*, edited by Milo Milton Quaife (Freeport, N.Y.: Books for Libraries Press, 1970), pp. 70–71.

---

per Missouri River, seeking a mountain route to the Spanish settlements of Taos and Santa Fe. One of Lisa's employees, John Colter, a former member of Meriwether Lewis and William Clark's Corps of Discovery, delivered reports of a beautiful area known today as Yellowstone National Park. Following Mexican independence from Spain in 1821, American traders explored the mountains of the Southwest, seeking alternative trade routes. A party led by Etienne Provost in 1825 crossed the Uinta mountain range in northeastern Utah and located the Great Salt Lake, never before seen by whites. The following year Jedediah Smith directed an expedition that left Utah and followed the Adams River to the Colorado below the Grand Canyon. From there Smith's party followed an ancient Indian trail into the Mohave Desert, becoming the first citizens of the United States to cross the Southwest into the Spanish settlements of California. Traders such as Smith, while pursuing profit more than science, nevertheless shared their findings with government agents, sending a steady flow of knowledge eastward that excited ethnographers and naturalists.

Maps. At the beginning of the nineteenth century the most accurate picture of Western North America derived from a 1795 map that mistakenly showed several inland

A photograph of a hydraulic mining crew, circa 1860 (Denver Public
Library, Colorado)

lakes, considerably larger than the Great Salt Lake, that cartographers probably included from vague reports they had received from Indians. In 1806 John Cary produced a map that accurately depicted the Pacific coastline, but he wisely refrained from presenting undocumented inland features. As a result he left blank almost the entire region west of the Mississippi. The expeditions of Lewis and Clark and Henry Schoolcraft, who explored the Upper Mississippi in 1820, produced two new maps in 1818 and 1826 respectively, but neither of these new maps accurately represented the country west of the Rockies with any real precision. In 1836 Albert Gallatin compiled a superior map—based on the findings of Smith and others—that depicted the Great Basin, the waterways of California, and the course of the Colorado River. The popularity of Gallatin's work, however, paled beside a map published the following year by Capt. Benjamin Louis Eulalie de Bonneville. Advertised extensively by Washington Irving, Bonneville's map depicted the complete hydrography of the region west of the Rockies. He determined the extent, direction, and sources of several major rivers including the Sacramento and San Joaquin. Until the Frémont-Preuss map of the 1840s, Bonneville's map remained dominant, even though he repeated many findings already located in Gallatin's map. In 1854 G. K. Warren compiled all known research from the previous half-century to produce an exhaustive map of the United States from the Mississippi to the Pacific. Geog-

raphers concur that Warren's publication marked the official end of geographic exploration and the beginning of a new research stage: the detailed survey, which John Wesley Powell pioneered in the 1870s.

Topographical Engineering. During the War of 1812 the federal government created a unit of topographical engineers to survey and make plans for all military positions and routes. After 1816 the unit reconnoitered several routes in the Old Northwest, surveyed the Santa Fe Trail, and supervised many internal improvements such as the Chesapeake and Ohio canal and the Cumberland Road. Their successes led to the official establishment of the U.S. Army Corps of Topographical Engineers in 1838, which conducted the first geological explorations of the American West. For instance, Howard Stansbury surveyed the Great Salt Lake, finding evidence of an ancient shoreline that indicated a formerly more extensive lake at least eight hundred feet above the modern one. In the 1850s the Pacific Railroad conducted several surveys in the far Northwest. Pursuing Lewis and Clark's observations that Mount St. Helens in present-day Washington State had erupted in 1802, railroad geologists studied the effects of ancient volcanic processes on shaping the Northwestern terrain. In 1857 J. S. Newberry, a geologist for the Pacific Railroad, investigated shell beds and alluvial plains on the West Coast and inferred that the Oregon Cascades once had been covered by an ice cap. The findings of geologists and engineers in this early period, built on the reports of earlier explorers and Indian tribes, launched an ongoing study into the geological origins of North America.

Theoretical Challenges. Beginning in the late eighteenth century naturalists turned considerable attention to the New World and hoped, through the growing knowledge of geophysical sciences, to complete an inventory of the entire planet. Decades later natural scientists and surveyors pursued these goals with renewed vigor following the United States's conquest of the Southwest. In the 1850s the U.S. Coast Survey undertook a thorough exploration of the Pacific coast, while scores of private agencies located and identified the major plant and animal species of California. This work influenced scientists' thinking on a number of issues. Many had studied under Louis Agassiz, noted for his studies of glaciation and his rejection of Charles Darwin's evolution theory. Therefore North American scholars often agreed with Agassiz in rejecting Darwinian views about natural selection. Yet surrounded by fossil evidence of a prehistoric past, others did come to believe in a "subtle" form of evolution theory where species transmute gradually. They supported their views by pointing to the diversity of ecosystems in California, asserting that the ocean once had extended to the Sierra Nevada mountain range and that prehistoric seas had shaped the land's major contours.

Trask and Condon. John Boardman Trask, a San Francisco physician, conducted several geological and agricultural excursions into the Sierra Nevada, gaining a reputation as California's first unofficial state geologist. Arriving in California in 1849, Trask collected and catalogued numerous plants, rocks, and fossils and produced an extensive mineral district map that outlined the state's agricultural and mining potential. Several of his mid-1850s reports suggest that the Pacific Ocean had once extended far inland and then receded. These theories encouraged later paleontological surveys. In Oregon the geologist Thomas Condon, best known for exploring the John Day Fossil Beds, collected a variety of Cretaceous and Tertiary fossils, which led him to support the Development Theory (as evolution was then known). In doing so Condon, who also served as a congregational minister, supported a theory quite radical for its time. Condon also located evidence of a three-toed horse, strengthening theories of animal evolution. He made geologic observations of the Columbia River gorge. Trask and Condon are only two examples of the many Western scientists who, isolated from the institutions and financial support of the Atlantic Coast, turned to the vast outdoor laboratory around them. Like the government surveyors who accompanied them, they learned the importance of firsthand field observation and pushed American science forward.

Sources:

E. W. Gilbert, *The Exploration of Western America, 1800–1850: An Historical Geography* (New York: Cooper Square, 1966);

Alan E. Leviton, Peter U. Rodda, Ellis Yochelson, and Michele L. Aldrich, eds., *Frontiers of Geological Exploration of Western North America* (San Francisco: Pacific Division of the American Association for the Advancement of Science, 1982);

Michael L. Smith, *Pacific Visions: California Scientists and the Environment, 1850–1915* (New Haven: Yale University Press, 1987).

MILITARY EXPLORATIONS

Jefferson and the West. By 1800 Europeans and Americans understood the basic geography of the world's continents, with the exception of the western two-thirds of North America as well as the interior of Africa, the Arctic, and Antarctica. France, England, Russia, Spain, and the United States all eyed the region beyond the Mississippi River in North America for its commercial potential but never had explored it sufficiently. Even Indian communities knew only the terrain of specific subregions that they hunted or cultivated regularly. They too lacked a continental perspective. Thomas Jefferson, obsessed with cartography and natural history, understood the necessity of exploring and mapping the vast region west of the Mississippi. Through the 1790s he tried in vain to obtain funding for a scientific journey to the Pacific Ocean. At the time of his inauguration in 1801, Jefferson—one of the early republic's most learned men—believed the Blue Grass Mountains of Virginia to be the tallest peaks in North America; the woolly mammoth and other prehistoric creatures might yet live in the Dakotas; the Great Plains held volcanoes and a mountain of pure salt; the Rio Grande, Missouri, and Columbia rivers all rose from a single source; and a navigable water route connected the Atlantic and Pacific Oceans. While Jefferson turned out to be wrong on all of these points, his ignorance reveals the primitive state of scientific knowledge about the territory that became the West. However, his intense curiosity provided incentive for the initial outlay of government funds that set in motion a half-century of continental explorations and geographic advances.

Lewis and Clark. The expedition of the Corps of Discovery from 1804 to 1806 represented the importance of Enlightenment science in future nation building. Jefferson charged Meriwether Lewis with taking measurements; obtaining geological samples; describing the flora, fauna, and people he would encounter; and studying the soil for its agricultural potential. In preparation Lewis spent several weeks in Philadelphia consulting with members of the American Philosophical Society, one of the most distinguished learned associations in the world at that time. From its members he learned botany, astronomy, and other necessary disciplines. During his journey Lewis sent Jefferson boxes of natural specimens and described others in his journals. His writings describe animals previously unknown to whites, such as hares, coyotes, rattlesnakes, and grizzly bears. During the winters of 1804–1805 and 1805–1806 he wrote about approximately one hundred Western creatures (mammals, birds, reptiles, and fish), more than two dozen of which had never before been seen by people of European descent. Lewis considered himself a better zoologist than

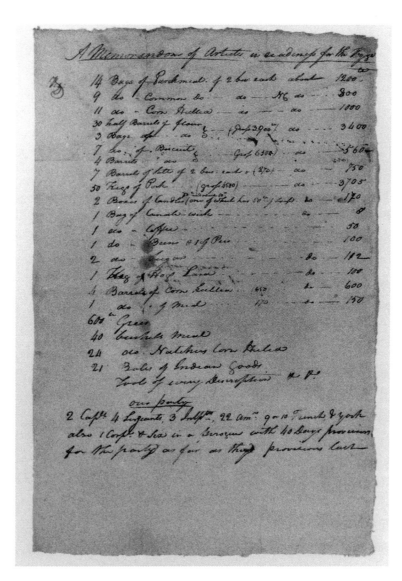

William Clark's list of necessary items for the journey of the Corps of
Discovery in 1804 (Beinecke Rare Book and Manuscript Library,
Yale University, New Haven)

botanist, yet he also described dozens of unfamiliar plants. Historians have long criticized Jefferson for not sending scientific specialists on the expedition, but many now agree that his choice of commander fulfilled the expedition's scientific purpose. For his day, Lewis became a remarkable naturalist, and his sample gathering and written descriptions (published several years after his return to the East) made an invaluable contribution to nineteenth-century understanding of the North American continent.

Pike and Long. Lewis and Clark's mission proved to be only the first expedition to chronicle nature in the West. In 1806–1807 Zebulon Pike led an expedition west of the Mississippi that extended into northern New Spain. Perhaps Pike's most notable observations included his widely circulated report on the Rio Grande, his description of the Great Plains as a desert, and his discovery of the mountain peak that now bears his name in Colorado. In 1819–1820 Stephen Long's expedition led soldiers and scientists west across the central Plains to the Rocky Mountains, also exploring vast portions of the Mississippi and Missouri River valleys. Naturalists on this trip collected and reported new information about plants, animals, soil, climate, and geology. By the mid 1820s Long's journey had prompted a series of books, maps, and scientific articles that aided the later investigations of men such as John C. Frémont and John Wesley Powell. Long affirmed Pike's assessment of the Plains as an unsuitable region for agriculture and domesticated livestock despite the fact that its grasses supported thousands of buffalo. In the process Pike and Long helped to establish the stereotype of the Great Plains as a "Great American Desert." While contemporary Plains agrarians and ranchers never have forgiven them for this depiction, some agronomists and environmentalists have affirmed Pike and Long's assertions about the region and its ability for sustaining long-term agriculture and ranching.

A painting by C. M. Russell of the Lewis and Clark expedition encountering Chinook Indians at Gray's Bay on the Columbia River, 8 November 1805. Sacagawea (standing in the canoe at right) uses sign language to communicate with the Chinooks. (Amon Carter Museum, Fort Worth, Texas)

Frémont. Lt. John C. Frémont, known as "the Pathfinder," led an expedition from Independence, Missouri, in 1843 that followed the Kansas River west, crossed the Rocky Mountains, and trekked over the Laramie Plain through South Pass. Frémont's description of the Salt Lake Valley inspired Brigham Young and his Mormon followers to settle there a decade later. Frémont's party eventually reached the Columbia River north of what he called the Great Basin. From there Frémont followed the Sierra Nevada range south into California. The expedition endured a brutal winter season before finally arriving at Sutter's ranch, a site that in 1849 would be overwhelmed by prospective gold seekers. Like most military explorers, the potential for increasing American territory motivated many of Frémont's explorations. However, his findings proved significant for subsequent geographical research. With the aid of Charles Preuss, a Prussian cartographer, Frémont produced the first accurate map of the overall Trans-Mississippi West as well as a special emigrant map of the Oregon and California trails with precise information on distances, landmarks, and river crossings.

Other Explorations. During the Mexican War of 1846–1848 and the increasing hostilities between the federal government and Plains Indians, the U.S. Army

mapped large portions of the West for reconnaissance purposes. Scouts produced maps that identified the locations of water holes and mountain passes, which permitted them to deduce enemy movements. Following the Treaty of Guadalupe Hidalgo, which established the official border between the United States and Mexico, the U.S. Topographical Corps surveyed the length of the Rio Grande, producing studies that proved valuable in later railroad development. At individual military posts, army surgeons wrote descriptive reports of the local terrain and flora and fauna as well as detailed accounts of health and sanitation levels of the troops and neighboring civilian communities. Government employees—engineers, soldiers, and topographers—also prospected for water, mapped rivers and harbors, built dams, and supervised road construction. These early efforts represented an alliance between science and government that continues to the present day.

Sources:

Daniel B. Botkin, *Our Natural History: The Lessons of Lewis and Clark* (New York: Putnam, 1995);

William H. Goetzmann, *Army Exploration in the American West, 1803–1863* (Lincoln: University of Nebraska Press, 1959);

Roger L. Nichols and Patrick L. Halley, *Stephen Long and American Frontier Exploration* (Newark, N.J.: Associated University Presses, 1980).

HEADLINE MAKERS

JOHN JAMES AUDUBON

1785-1851
NATURALIST AND ARTIST

Background. After his death John James Audubon's descendants claimed him to be the lost dauphin (prince) of France. In actuality, although his ancestry included no royalty, he did descend from French origins, the son of a sea captain and a Creole mother on the island of Santo Domingo (now Haiti). Audubon grew up near Philadelphia and developed an early interest in ornithology. After moving to Kentucky and failing in several business ventures, Audubon wandered the countryside, studying and sketching birds in their natural surroundings. When his business career ended in 1819 following bankruptcy and a brief imprisonment for debt, Audubon decided to publish a collection of paintings of North American birds. Eventually he settled in Louisiana, working as an instructor of music and drawing.

Travels and Works. Audubon's drawings attracted the notice of publishers in England and Scotland, where his collection *Birds of America* (1826–1838), consisting of eighty-seven parts containing more than four hundred life-sized engravings made from his watercolors, achieved recognition as a masterpiece of natural study. With the Scottish naturalist William MacGillivray, Audubon authored an accompanying text, *Ornithological Biography* (1831–1839), a work that made him well known in the United States. Following his success, Audubon extended his zoological curiosity to other animals. He collaborated with the naturalist John Bachman to prepare a collection on quadrapeds, for which he traveled and researched extensively. In 1843 Audubon journeyed from St. Louis up the Missouri River to the mouth of the Yellowstone, where he examined and recorded natural flora and fauna. His logs formed the basis for *The Vivaparous Quadrapeds of North America* (1852–1854).

Legacy. Audubon's colorful, lifelike drawings reflect his artistic talent in the naturalist school, which sought to depict panoramic landscapes and minute details of animals in their pristine states. American artists who followed Audubon's style tried to combine the artist's skill of visual assessment with the scientist's knowledge of anatomy and botany in order to replicate nature onto a canvas. Audubon's work lent itself in subsequent decades to the conservation movement. Founded in 1905, the National Audubon Society tries to advance public understanding about water, soil, and wildlife conservation. Environmentalists today recognize Audubon as an early precursor to John Muir, Aldo Leopold, and other Westerners who taught intelligent use of nature by trying to understand nature's limits.

Source:
John Francis McDermott, ed., *Audubon in the West* (Norman: University of Oklahoma Press, 1965).

MERIWETHER LEWIS AND WILLIAM CLARK

1774-1809 AND 1770-1838
SOLDIERS AND EXPLORERS

Early Years. The names of Meriwether Lewis and William Clark survive as perhaps the most famous pair in American history. Yet beneath the legacy surrounding their 1804–1806 expedition and the partnership that directed it lay a friendship between the two men whose names have become indissolubly linked. Although Lewis and Clark both descended from prominent Virginia families, they did not meet until adulthood. Clark's family (which included his brother,

George Rogers Clark, a famed Revolutionary War general) had moved to Kentucky in the 1770s. Following their formal education, Lewis and Clark enlisted for military service. While campaigning with Gen. Anthony Wayne in 1795, they served in the same unit and became friends. Both developed reputations as efficient commanders and hardened outdoorsmen although Clark's skills in surveying and water navigation outpaced those of Lewis. Their mutual acquaintance with Thomas Jefferson aided them in subsequent years. Following Jefferson's inauguration in 1801, Lewis became the president's personal secretary. While planning the Corps of Discovery expedition, Jefferson endorsed Lewis's choice of Clark as cocommander; even though Clark served officially as the second in command, Lewis regarded Clark as his equal, and the two made all decisions jointly during the expedition.

Trip to the Pacific. While Lewis supervised material preparations, Clark recruited and trained most of the men who served on the expedition. Departing in May 1804, the party ascended the Missouri River and, after five months, reached the Mandan Indian country, where they camped for the winter. With the crucial help of Native American guides and interpreters, the most significant of whom was Sacagawea, a Shoshoni woman, Lewis and Clark crossed the Rocky and Bitterroot Mountains. The tortuous terrain often required them to travel on foot, using horses they had obtained from natives as pack animals. Reaching the tributaries of the Columbia River, the party built boats that carried them to the mouth of the Columbia and to the Pacific Ocean. Lewis spent much of his time recording natural observations and ministering to the men's health while Clark oversaw physical operations and mapped mountains and rivers, trying to deduce navigable routes. Following their winter in present-day Oregon in 1805–1806, the team began their return journey, splitting up along the way to explore the Continental Divide and the Upper Missouri River. Arriving in St. Louis in September 1806, Lewis and Clark set to work in preparing their journals, which would assist later explorers in constructing an accurate geographical portrait of North America.

Territorial Governors. The expedition proved to be the high point of their careers. In 1807 Jefferson appointed Lewis as governor of the Louisiana Territory, a position that would sustain him while he prepared his papers. Always prone to melancholy, Lewis had badly managed his financial affairs and went into debt, increasing his depression and proclivity toward excessive drinking. In 1809 Lewis, only thirty-five years old, died from a gunshot wound while staying at an inn in central Tennessee. Some researchers claim a conspiracy in his death, but most of the available evidence supports the conclusion that Lewis took his own life. Clark became superintendent of Indian affairs in 1807 and six years later was appointed as governor of the

Missouri Territory. After Lewis's death, Clark assumed the task of preparing his journals for publication, obtaining the assistance of the banker Nicholas Biddle, who edited the papers for their 1814 printing. Biddle focused mostly on the expedition's geographical discoveries, including few of Lewis's meticulous notes on flora and fauna, but the journals' release did stimulate curiosity about the West for its information on Indian tribes and its descriptions of natural wealth, proving extremely valuable to the geologists, surveyors, and anthropologists who followed in Lewis and Clark's wake.

Sources:

Stephen E. Ambrose, *Undaunted Courage: Meriwether Lewis, Thomas Jefferson, and the Opening of the American West* (New York: Simon & Schuster, 1996);

James Ronda, *Lewis and Clark among the Indians* (Lincoln: University of Nebraska Press, 1984).

LEWIS HENRY MORGAN

1818-1881
ANTHROPOLOGIST

Background. Scholars consider Lewis Henry Morgan, who was born in a well-to-do family in western New York, to be the father of American anthropology. Educated at Union College, Morgan studied ancient history, mathematics, and comparative political economy. He combined his studies with a romantic optimism in American democracy and institutions, beliefs that somewhat colored his nationalistic view of American westward expansion. Yet unlike many historians of his day, Morgan believed that a society's progression and decline depended less on key individuals than on its laws, customs, political culture, religion, and civil institutions. Heavily influenced by the Romantic movement, Morgan grew fascinated with Native American cultures. His work provided a theoretical framework for the burgeoning field of ethnology and even informed federal policies toward Indians.

Collaboration with Ely Parker. Morgan's *League of the Ho-de-no-saunee, or Iroquois* (1851) remains one of the premiere anthropological studies, a work he completed with the aid of Ely S. Parker. A Seneca Indian who met Morgan as a teenager, Parker provided him with information on the structure and history of the Iroquois League. The book focused primarily on Iroquois political organization, as well as subsistence patterns, laws, and material culture. Morgan's emphasis on politics, perhaps a result of his legal training, caused him to slight discussion of religious and family life even though he spent considerable time attending Iroquois ceremonies and rituals at many reservations in western New York. His collaboration with Parker established a model for later anthropological studies. The two men's partnership proved mutually beneficial; Parker's reputation enabled him to serve as a spokesman for his own people on the Tonawanda reserve. In the 1860s Parker became military secretary to Ulysses S. Grant. During Grant's presidency Parker also became the first Native American to hold the office of commissioner of Indian Affairs.

"Social Evolution." Morgan's research into the Iroquois and other North American tribes led him to a monogenic (one origin) hypothesis that claimed Indians and whites descended from the same branch of humanity. Morgan explained cultural differences in a manner similar to Gallatin, relying less on the assumption of inherent characteristics than on how societal organizations and institutions affected a people's development. By positing the importance of hunting as a means of subsistence, Morgan tried to explain the Indian lack of both literacy and the need for money, features crucial for the advancement of any civilization. He believed that once Indians abandoned their traditional patterns, they would easily assimilate to American norms and become indistinguishable from any other group. Following a trip to Kansas and Nebraska in 1859, Morgan even encouraged intermarriage as a way of hastening the civilizing process. By this time he had immersed himself in kinship studies, trying to accumulate evidence in support of an Asian origin for Native Americans. He published a full account of his progress theory in *Ancient Society; or, Researches in the Lines of Human Progress from Savagery through Barbarism to Civilization* (1877). Most scientists of the time considered this work too specialized. They preferred the grander evolutionary scheme established by Charles Darwin. Morgan's rather rigid paradigm of societal transitions now appears outdated. However, at the time, his theories lent support to missionaries and government agents who hoped that Indians and whites could live together peaceably. In his later years he turned to studying architecture and archaeological ruins to discover the pasts of preliterate societies. He remains famous today among scientists for his assertions of evolutionary anthropology. Eventually the Senecas called Morgan "One Lying Across," signifying his role as a bridge between North American peoples.

Sources:

Robert E. Bieder, *Science Encounters the Indian, 1820–1880: The Early Years of American Ethnology* (Norman: University of Oklahoma Press, 1986);

Brian W. Dippie, *The Vanishing American: White Attitudes and U.S. Indian Policy* (Lawrence: University Press of Kansas, 1982).

HENRY ROWE SCHOOLCRAFT

1793–1864
ETHNOLOGIST AND GEOLOGIST

Travels. Born in Watervliet, New York, and educated as a mineralogist and glassmaker, Henry Rowe Schoolcraft originally intended to become a federal superintendent of mines for the Missouri Territory. However, like many natural scientists who journeyed West, he developed an interest in North American geography and ethnology. Schoolcraft eventually received an appointment as an Indian agent on the northwestern frontier, a position that gave him extensive contact with Western lands and peoples. In 1820 he toured with a party that located the source of the Mississippi River. In 1831–1832 Schoolcraft led a second expedition there. Geographers regarded his account of this trip, published two years later, as one of the major geographic works of the decade. Schoolcraft also recorded examples of Indian folklore, which provided material for fiction writers such as Henry Wadsworth Longfellow.

Ethnological Work. Schoolcraft's observations of Indian life lacked the systematic approach of early anthropologists such as Lewis Henry Morgan. His eclectic interests proved useful for how he collected massive amounts of information. However, unwilling to venture into more theoretical approaches, Schoolcraft never suggested how his findings could be integrated into some larger purpose. His weaknesses became more evident following his 1847 commission by the U.S. government to collect materials relating to the history, present conditions, and future prospects of Indian tribes. Schoolcraft confronted an awesome task with this project, which demanded the better part of a decade to compile. Some reviewers praised his six-volume work for its research but criticized Schoolcraft for how he provided little overall guidance for policymakers. To his credit, any attempt to generalize about all of North America's indigenous peoples and recommend policy measures would have been flawed, revealing whites' meager understanding of Indian heterogeneity. Yet Schoolcraft's array of data marked one of the first holistic efforts to comprehend Indian cultures, one often utilized by later scholars and historians.

Source:

Richard G. Bremer, *Indian Agent and Wilderness Scholar: The Life of Henry Rowe Schoolcraft* (Mt. Pleasant: Clarke Historical Library, Central Michigan University, 1987).

PUBLICATIONS

Louis Agassiz, "Prof. Agassiz on the Origin of Species," *American Journal of Science and Arts*, 80 (1860): 142–154—Agassiz's rebuttal to Charles Darwin's proposed theory of evolution and natural selection;

"Annual Reports of the Chief of Topographical Engineers," in *The Annual Reports of the Secretary of War, 1839–1861* (Washington, D.C.: U.S. Government Printing Office, 1861)—contains geographical and surveying information on selected sites for topographical study;

John James Audubon, *Ornithological Biography, or An Account of the Habits of the Birds of the United States of America,* 5 volumes (Edinburgh: A. Black, 1831–1839);

Audubon, *The Vivaparous Quadrapeds of North America,* 3 volumes (New York: V. G. Audubon, 1852–1854)—a collection of observations from his 1843 trip to the mouth of the Yellowstone River;

Georges-Louis Leclerc, Count de Buffon, *Natural History: General and Particular,* translated by William Smellie (London: A. Straham & T. Cadell, 1791)—one of the first arguments for both the polygenic thesis of separate creations of man and the idea that disparate groups emerged at different times and evolved at varying speeds;

James E. DeKay, *Anniversary Address on the Progress of the Natural Sciences in the United States: Delivered before the Lyceum of Natural History of New York* (New York: G & G Carwell, 1826)—a useful discussion about research in the United States, although it includes little discussion of science in the Trans-Mississippi West;

John C. Frémont, *Report on an Exploration of the Country Lying between the Missouri River and the Rocky Mountains on the Line of the Kansas and Great Platte Rivers* (Washington, D.C.: Printed by order of the U.S. Senate, 1843);

Frémont, *Report of the Exploring Expedition to the Rocky Mountains in the year 1842, and to Oregon and North California in the Years 1843–44* (Washington, D.C.: Gales & Seaton, 1845);

Albert Gallatin, *A Table of Indian Languages of the United States, East of the Stony Mountains, Arranged According to Languages and Dialects* (N.p., 1826)—the first philological attempt to classify Indian groups by language;

Asa Gray, "Review of Darwin's Theory on the Origin of Species by Means of Natural Selection," *American Journal of Science and Arts,* 79 (1860): 153–184;

Meriwether Lewis and William Clark, *The Journals of the Expedition Under the Command of Capts. Lewis and Clark to the Sources of the Missouri, thence Across the Rocky Mountains and Down the River Columbia to the Pacific Ocean. Performed During the Years 1804–5–6,* 2 volumes, edited by Nicholas Biddle (Philadelphia: Bradford & Inskeep, 1814)—a popular account of the major expedition that prompted curiosity in Western exploration;

Samuel G. Morton, *An Inquiry into the Distinctive Characteristics of the Aboriginal Race of America* (Boston: Tuttle & Dennett, 1842)—the book builds on Morton's earlier studies of the comparative crania of North American peoples, asserting essential inequalities that strengthened racial theorists;

Henry R. Schoolcraft, *Narrative Journal of Travels Through the Northwestern Regions of the United States, Extending from Detroit Through the Great Chain of American Lakes; to the Source of the Mississippi River* (Albany: E. & E. Hosford, 1821);

Benjamin Silliman, "Expedition of Major Long and Party, to the Rocky Mountains," *American Journal of Science and Arts,* 6 (1823): 374–375—a brief synopsis of Long's expedition across the Central Plains and reports on climate, agricultural potential, and indigenous plants and animals;

Jared Sparks, "Major Long's Second Expedition," *North American Review,* 21 (July 1825): 178–189.

GENERAL REFERENCES

GENERAL

Ray Allen Billington and Martin Ridge, *Westward Expansion: A History of the American Frontier,* fifth edition (New York: Macmillan, 1982);

Lisbeth Haas, *Conquests and Historical Identities in California, 1769–1936* (Berkeley: University of California Press, 1995);

Howard Lamar, *The Readers Encyclopedia of the American West* (New York: Crowell, 1977);

Patricia Nelson Limerick, *The Legacy of Conquest: The Unbroken Past of the American West* (New York: Norton, 1987);

D. W. Meinig, *The Shaping of America: A Geographical Perspective on 500 Years of History,* volume 2, *Continental America, 1800–1867* (New Haven: Yale University Press, 1993);

Clyde Milner and others, eds., *The Oxford History of the American West* (New York: Oxford University Press, 1994);

Charles Sellers, *The Market Revolution: Jacksonian America, 1815–1846* (New York: Oxford University Press, 1991);

Henry Nash Smith, *Virgin Land: The American West as Symbol and Myth* (Cambridge, Mass.: Harvard University Press, 1950);

Richard White, *"It's Your Misfortune and None of My Own": A New History of the American West* (Norman: University of Oklahoma Press, 1991).

ARTS

Mary Bywater Cross, *Treasures in the Trunk: Quilts of the Oregon Trail* (Nashville, Tenn.: Rutledge Hill Press, 1993);

David Dary, *Seeking Pleasure in the Old West* (New York: Knopf, 1995);

Ronald L. Davis, *A History of Music in American Life,* volume 1, *The Formative Years, 1620–1865* (Malabar, Fla.: Robert Krieger, 1982);

John C. Ewers, *Artists of the Old West* (Garden City, N.Y.: Doubleday, 1965);

Carol Fairbanks, *Prairie Women: Images in American and Canadian Fiction* (New Haven: Yale University Press, 1986);

Dawn Glanz, *How the West Was Drawn: American Art and the Settling of the Frontier* (Ann Arbor: UMI Research, 1978);

William H. Goetzmann and William N. Goetzmann, *The West of the Imagination* (New York: Norton, 1986);

Ann Hyde, *An American Vision: Far Western Landscape and National Culture, 1820–1920* (New York: New York University Press, 1990);

Richard E. Lingenfelter, Richard A. Dwyer, and David Cohen, *Songs of the American West* (Berkeley: University of California Press, 1968);

Thomas J. Lyon and others, *Updating the Literary West* (Fort Worth: Texas Christian University Press, 1997);

Angela Miller, *Empire of the Eye: Landscape, Representation and American Cultural Politics, 1825–1875* (Ithaca, N.Y.: Cornell University Press, 1993);

Jules David Prown, *Discovered Lands, Invented Pasts: Transforming Visions of the American West* (New Haven: Yale University Press, 1992);

A. LaVonne Brown Ruoff, *American Indian Literatures* (New York: Modern Language Association, 1990);

Richard Slotkin, *The Fatal Environment: The Myth of the Frontier in the Age of Industrialization, 1800–1860* (New York: Atheneum, 1985);

Slotkin, *Regeneration Through Violence: The Mythology of the American Frontier, 1600–1860* (Middletown, Conn.: Wesleyan University Press, 1973);

Robert E. Spiller and others, *Literary History of the United States,* third edition (New York: Macmillan, 1973);

Jeanne Van Nostrand, *The First Hundred Years of Painting in California, 1775–1875* (San Francisco: John Howell, 1980);

Franklin Walker, *San Francisco's Literary Frontier* (New York: Knopf, 1939);

Andrew Wiget, *Native American Literature* (Boston: Twayne, 1985);

John Wilmerding, *American Art* (New York: Penguin, 1976).

BUSINESS AND THE ECONOMY

John O. Baxter, *Las Carneradas: Sheep Trade in New Mexico, 1700–1860* (Albuquerque: University of New Mexico Press, 1987);

William Cronon, *Nature's Metropolis: Chicago and the Great West* (New York: Norton, 1992);

William DeBuys, *Enchantment and Exploitation: The Life and Times of a New Mexico Mountain Range* (Albuquerque: University of New Mexico Press, 1985);

John Mack Farragher, *Sugar Creek: Life on the Illinois Prairie* (New Haven: Yale University Press, 1986);

Paul Gates, *The Jeffersonian Dream: Studies in the History of American Land Policy and Development,* edited by Allan G. Bogue and Margaret B. Bogue (Albuquerque: University of New Mexico Press, 1996);

R. Douglas Hurt, *Indian Agriculture in America: Prehistory to the Present* (Lawrence: University Press of Kansas, 1987);

David Rich Lewis, *Neither Wolf Nor Dog: American Indians, Environment, and Agrarian Change* (New York: Oxford University Press, 1994);

Carolyn Merchant, ed., *Major Problems in American Environmental History* (Lexington, Mass.: D. C. Heath, 1993);

Malcolm J. Rohrbough, *Days of Gold: The California Gold Rush and the American Nation* (Berkeley: University of California Press, 1997);

George Rogers Taylor, *The Transportation Revolution, 1815–1860* (White Plains, N.Y.: M. E. Sharpe, 1951);

David Weber, *The Spanish Frontier in North America* (New Haven: Yale University Press, 1992);

Richard White, *Roots of Dependency: Subsistence, Economy, and Social Change among the Choctaws, Pawnees, and Navajos* (Lincoln: University of Nebraska Press, 1983);

David J. Wishart, *The Fur Trade of the American West, 1807–1840* (Lincoln: University of Nebraska Press, 1979).

COMMUNICATIONS

Oliver Gramling, *AP: The Story of News* (New York: Farrar & Rinehart, 1940);

William Harlan Hale, *Horace Greeley: Voice of the People* (New York: Collier, 1951);

William Huntzicker, "The Frontier Press, 1800–1900," in *The Media in America,* edited by William D. Sloan

and others (Worthington, Ohio: Publishing Horizons, 1989), pp. 165–190;

Richard John, *Spreading the News: The American Postal System from Franklin to Morse* (Cambridge, Mass.: Harvard University Press, 1995);

Richard B. Kielbowicz, *News in the Mail: The Press, Post Office, and Public Information, 1700–1860s* (Westport, Conn.: Greenwood Press, 1989);

Alfred M. Lee, *The Daily Newspaper in America: The Evolution of a Social Instrument* (New York: Macmillan, 1937);

Daniel F. Littlefield Jr. and James W. Parins, *American Indian and Alaska Native Newspapers and Periodicals, 1826–1924* (Westport, Conn.: Greenwood Press, 1984);

William H. Lyon, "The Significance of Newspapers on the American Frontier," *Journal of the West,* 19 (April 1980): 3–13;

Frank Luther Mott, *A History of American Magazines, 1741–1850* (Cambridge, Mass.: Harvard University Press, 1939);

David Paul Nord, "Tocqueville, Garrison, and the Perfection of Journalism," *Journalism History,* 13 (Summer 1986): 56–63;

Calder M. Pickett, ed., *Voices of the Past: Key Documents in the History of American Journalism* (Columbus, Ohio: Grid, 1977);

Raymond W. Settle and Mary L. Settle, *Saddles and Spurs: The Pony Express Saga* (Harrisburg, Pa.: Stackpole, 1955).

EDUCATION

Anne M. Boylan, *Sunday School: The Formation of an American Institution* (New Haven: Yale University Press, 1988);

John S. Brubacher and Willis Rudy, *Higher Education in Transition: A History of American Colleges and Universities, 1636–1975,* third edition (New York: Harper & Row, 1976);

Lawrence A. Cremin, *American Education: The National Experience, 1783–1876* (New York: Harper & Row, 1980);

Celia Morris Eckhardt, *Frances Wright: Rebel in America* (Cambridge, Mass.: Harvard University Press, 1984);

Wayne E. Fuller, *The Old Country School: The Story of Rural Education in the Middle West* (Chicago: University of Chicago Press, 1982);

Julie Roy Jeffrey, *Converting the West* (Norman: University of Oklahoma Press, 1991);

Carl F. Kaestle, *Pillars of the Republic: Common Schools and American Society, 1780–1800* (New York: Hill & Wang, 1983);

Polly Welts Kaufman, *Women Teachers on the Frontier* (New Haven: Yale University Press, 1984);

Jonathan Messerli, *Horace Mann* (New York: Knopf, 1972);

Jacqueline S. Reinier, *From Virtue to Character: American Childhood, 1775–1850* (New York: Twayne, 1996);

Frederick Rudolph, ed., *Essays on Education in the Early Republic* (Cambridge, Mass.: Harvard University Press, 1965);

Donald G. Tewksbury, *The Founding of American Colleges and Universities Before the Civil War* (New York: Teachers College of Columbia University, 1932).

GOVERNMENT AND POLITICS

Stephen E. Ambrose, *Undaunted Courage: Meriwether Lewis, Thomas Jefferson and the Opening of the American West* (New York: Simon & Schuster, 1996);

Stephen Aron, *How The West Was Lost: The Transformation of Kentucky from Daniel Boone to Henry Clay* (Baltimore: Johns Hopkins University Press, 1996);

John Ashworth, *Slavery, Capitalism and Politics in the Antebellum Republic* (New York: Cambridge University Press, 1995);

John S. D. Eisenhower, *So Far From God: The U.S. War with Mexico, 1846–1848* (New York: Random House, 1989);

John Mack Farragher, *Daniel Boone: The Life and Legend of an American Pioneer* (New York: Holt, 1992);

Eric Foner, *Free Soil, Free Labor, Free Men: The Ideology of the Republican Party Before the Civil War* (New York: Oxford University Press, 1970);

Paul W. Gates, *Fifty Million Acres: Conflicts over Kansas Land Policy* (Ithaca, N.Y.: Cornell University Press, 1954);

William E. Gienapp, *The Origins of the Republican Party, 1852–1856* (New York: Oxford University Press, 1986);

Holman Hamilton, *Prologue to Conflict: The Crisis and Compromise of 1850* (New York: Norton, 1964);

Daniel Walker Howe, *The Political Culture of the American Whigs* (Chicago: University of Chicago Press, 1979);

Robert W. Johannsen, *To the Halls of Montezumas: The Mexican War in the American Imagination* (New York: Oxford University Press, 1985);

William G. McLouglin, *Cherokee Renascence in the New Republic* (Princeton, N.J.: Princeton University Press, 1986);

Robert V. Remini, *Andrew Jackson and the Course of American Democracy, 1833–1845* (New York: Harper & Row, 1984);

Remini, *Andrew Jackson and the Course of American Freedom, 1822–1832* (New York: Harper & Row, 1981);

Remini, *Andrew Jackson and the Course of Empire, 1767–1821* (New York: Harper & Row, 1977);

Michael Paul Rogin, *Fathers and Children: Andrew Jackson and the Subjugation of the American Indian* (New York: Knopf, 1975);

Richard H. Sewell, *Ballots for Freedom: Antislavery Politics in the United States, 1837–1860* (New York: Oxford University Press, 1976);

J. C. A. Stagg, *Mr. Madison's War: Politics, Diplomacy and Warfare in the Early Republic, 1783–1830* (Princeton, N.J.: Princeton University Press, 1983); .

Robert C. Tucker and David C. Hendrickson, *Empire of Liberty: The Statecraft of Thomas Jefferson* (New York: Oxford University Press, 1990);

Frederick D. Williams, ed., *The Northwest Ordinance: Essays on its Formulation* (East Lansing: Michigan State University Press, 1989).

LAW AND JUSTICE

Joseph C. Burke, "The Cherokee Cases: A Study in Law, Politics, and Morality," *Stanford Law Review,* 21 (1969): 500–531;

Nobel E. Cunningham Jr., *In Pursuit of Reason: The Life of Thomas Jefferson* (Baton Rouge: Louisiana State University Press, 1987);

Don Fehrenbacher, *The Dredd Scott Case: Its Significance in American Law and Politics* (New York: Oxford University Press, 1978);

Paul Finkelman, ed., *Dred Scott vs. Sandford: A Brief History with Documents* (Boston: Bedford Books of St. Martin's Press, 1997);

Lawrence M. Friedman, *Crime and Punishment in American History* (New York: Basic Books, 1993);

Friedman, *A History of American Law* (New York: Simon & Schuster, 1985);

Morton J. Horwitz, *The Transformation of American Law, 1780–1860* (Cambridge, Mass.: Harvard University Press, 1977);

James Willard Hurst, *Law and the Conditions of Freedom in the Nineteenth-Century United States* (Madison: University of Wisconsin Press, 1956);

Milton Lomask, *Aaron Burr: The Conspiracy and Years of Exile, 1805–1836* (New York: Farrar, Strauss, & Giroux, 1982);

Herbert S. Parmet and Marie B. Hecht, *Aaron Burr: Portrait of an Ambitious Man* (New York: Macmillan, 1967);

Theda Perdue and Michael D. Green, *The Cherokee Removal: A Brief History with Documents* (Boston: Bedford Books of St. Martin's Press, 1995);

Carol Rose, *Property and Persuasion: Essays on the History, Theory, and Rhetoric of Ownership* (Boulder, Colo.: Westview Press, 1994);

Anthony F. C. Wallace, *The Long, Bitter Trail: Andrew Jackson and the Indians* (New York: Hill & Wang, 1993);

Charles F. Wilkinson, *American Indians, Time, and the Law* (New Haven: Yale University Press, 1987).

LIFESTYLES, SOCIAL TRENDS, FASHION, SPORTS, AND RECREATION

Edward P. Dozier, *The Pueblo Indians of North America* (New York: Holt, Rinehart, & Winston, 1970);

Foster Rhea Dulles, *A History of Recreation: America Learns to Play,* second edition (New York: Appleton-Century-Crofts, 1965);

Dayton Duncan and Ken Burns, *Lewis and Clark* (New York: Knopf, 1997);

John Durant and Otto Bettman, *Pictorial History of American Sports: From Colonial Times to the Present,* third edition (Cranbury, N.J.: A. S. Burns, 1973);

John Mack Farragher, *Women and Men on the Overland Trail* (New Haven: Yale University Press, 1979);

Roy Meyer, *The Village Indians of the Upper Missouri: The Mandans, Hidatsas, and Arikaras* (Lincoln: University of Nebraska Press, 1977);

Virginia Bergman Peters, *Women of the Earth Lodges: Tribal Life on the Plains* (North Haven, Conn.: Archon, 1995);

Virginia More Roediger, *Ceremonial Costumes of the Pueblo Indians: Their Evolution, Fabrication, and Significance in the Prayer Drama* (Berkeley: University of California Press, 1961);

Lillian Schlissel, *Women's Diaries of the Westward Journey* (New York: Schocken, 1982);

Anthony Shay, "Fandangoes and Bailes: Dancing and Dance Events in Early California," *Southern California Quarterly,* 64 (Summer 1982): 99–113;

David Weber, ed., *Foreigners in Their Native Land: Historical Roots of the Mexican-Americans* (Albuquerque: University of New Mexico Press, 1973);

Elliott West, *Growing Up With The Country: Childhood on the Far Western Frontier* (Albuquerque: University of New Mexico Press, 1989).

RELIGION

John Andrew III, *From Revivals to Removal: Jeremiah Evarts, the Cherokee Nation, and the Search for the Soul of America* (Athens: University of Georgia Press, 1992);

Leonard Arrington and Davis Bitton, *The Mormon Experience: A History of the Latter-Day Saints* (New York: Knopf, 1979);

R. Pierce Beaver, *Church, State, and the American Indians: Two and a Half Centuries of Partnership in Missions Between Protestant Churches and Government* (St. Louis: Concordia Publishing House, 1966);

Robert Berkhofer Jr., *Salvation and the Savage: An Analysis of Protestant Missions and American Indian Response, 1787–1862* (Lexington: University of Kentucky Press, 1965);

John Boles, *The Great Revival, 1787–1805* (Lexington: University of Kentucky Press, 1972);

Henry W. Bowden, *American Indians and Christian Missions: Studies in Cultural Conflict* (Chicago: University of Chicago Press, 1981);

John L. Brooke, *The Refiner's Fire: The Making of Mormon Cosmology, 1644–1844* (Cambridge: Cambridge University Press, 1994);

Robert Ignatius Burns, *The Jesuits and the Indian Wars of the Northwest* (New Haven: Yale University Press, 1966);

Richard Bushman, *Joseph Smith and the Beginnings of Mormonism* (Urbana: University of Illinois Press, 1984);

Michael Coleman, *Presbyterian Missionary Attitudes toward American Indians, 1837–1893* (Jackson: University Press of Mississippi, 1985);

Vine Deloria, *God Is Red: A Native View of Religion* (Golden, Colo.: Fulcrum Press, 1994);

Gregory E. Dowd, *A Spirited Resistance: The North American Indian Struggle for Unity, 1745–1815* (Baltimore: Johns Hopkins University Press, 1992);

R. David Edmunds, *The Shawnee Prophet* (Lincoln: University of Nebraska Press, 1983);

Klaus I. Hansen, *Mormonism and the American Experience* (Chicago: University of Chicago Press, 1981);

Howard Harrod, *Mission Among the Blackfeet* (Norman: University of Oklahoma Press, 1971);

Nathan Hatch, *The Democratization of American Christianity* (New Haven: Yale University Press, 1989);

Robert J. Loewenberg, *Equality on the Oregon Frontier: Jason Lee and the Methodist Mission, 1834–43* (Seattle: University of Washington Press, 1976);

Lester G. McAllister and William E. Tucker, *Journey in Faith: A History of the Christian Church (Disciples of Christ)* (St. Louis: Bethany Press, 1975);

William G. McLoughlin, *Champions of the Cherokees: Evan and John B. Jones* (Princeton, N.J.: Princeton University Press, 1990);

McLoughlin, *The Cherokees and Christianity, 1794–1870: Essays on Acculturation and Cultural Persistence* (Athens: University of Georgia Press, 1994);

Christopher Miller, *Prophetic Worlds: Indians and Whites on the Columbia Plateau* (New Brunswick, N.J.: Rutgers University Press, 1985);

Clifton J. Phillips, *Protestant America and the Pagan World: The First Half Century of the American Board of*

Commissioners for Foreign Missions, 1810–1860 (Cambridge, Mass.: Harvard University Press, 1969);

James P. Ronda and James Axtell, *Indian Missions: A Critical Bibliography* (Bloomington: Indiana University Press, 1978);

Robert Ruby and John Brown, *Dreamer-Prophets of the Columbia Plateau: Smohalla and Skolaskin* (Norman: University of Oklahoma Press, 1989);

George A. Schultz, *An Indian Canaan: Isaac McCoy and the Vision of an Indian State* (Norman: University of Oklahoma Press, 1972);

Jan Shipps, *Mormonism: The Story of a New Religious Tradition* (Urbana: University of Illinois Press, 1985);

James Treat, ed., *Native and Christian: Indigenous Voices on Religious Identity in the United States and Canada* (New York: Routledge, 1996);

Ruth Underhill, *Red Man's Religion: Beliefs and Practices of the Indians North of Mexico* (Chicago: University of Chicago Press, 1965);

Anthony F. C. Wallace, *Prelude to Disaster: The Course of Indian-White Relations Which Led to the Black Hawk War of 1832* (Springfield: Illinois State Historical Library, 1970).

SCIENCE AND MEDICINE

Robert E. Bieder, *Science Encounters the Indian, 1820–1880: The Early Years of American Ethnology* (Norman: University of Oklahoma Press, 1986);

Daniel B. Botkin, *Our Natural History: The Lessons of Lewis and Clark* (New York: Putnam, 1995);

Brian W. Dippie, *The Vanishing American: White Attitudes and U.S. Indian Policy* (Lawrence: University Press of Kansas, 1982);

E. W. Gilbert, *The Exploration of Western America, 1800–1850: An Historical Geography* (New York: Cooper Square, 1966);

William H. Goetzmann, *Army Exploration in the American West, 1803–1863* (Lincoln: University of Nebraska Press, 1959);

Alan E. Leviton and others, eds., *Frontiers of Geological Exploration of Western North America* (San Francisco: Pacific Division of the American Association for the Advancement of Science, 1982);

Peter C. Mancall, "Men, Women, and Alcohol in Indian Villages in the Great Lakes Region in the Early Republic," *Journal of the Early Republic,* 15 (1995): 425–448;

John Francis McDermott, ed., *Audubon in the West* (Norman: University of Oklahoma Press, 1965);

Robert J. Miller and Maril Hazlett, "The 'Drunken Indian': Myth Distilled into Reality Through Federal Indian Alcohol Policy," *Arizona State Law Journal,* 28 (1996): 223–298;

Roger L. Nichols and Patrick L. Halley, *Stephen Long and American Frontier Exploration* (Newark, N.J.: Associated University Presses, 1980);

Anthony Pagden, *The Fall of Natural Man: The American Indian and the Origins of Comparative Ethnology* (Cambridge: Cambridge University Press, 1982);

James Ronda, *Lewis and Clark Among the Indians* (Lincoln: University of Nebraska Press, 1984);

Michael L. Smith, *Pacific Visions: California Scientists and the Environment, 1850–1915* (New Haven: Yale University Press, 1987);

Russell Thornton, *American Indian Holocaust and Survival: A Population History Since 1492* (Norman: University of Oklahoma Press, 1987);

William E. Unrau, *White Man's Wicked Water: The Alcohol Trade and Prohibition in Indian Country, 1802–1892* (Lawrence: University Press of Kansas, 1996);

Virgil J. Vogel, *American Indian Medicine* (Norman: University of Oklahoma Press, 1970).

CONTRIBUTORS

WORLD CHRONOLOGY

MARIL HAZLETT
University of Kansas

THE ARTS

JAMES MANCALL
Harvard University

BUSINESS & THE ECONOMY

MARK C. FREDERICK
University of Kansas

COMMUNICATIONS

JOHN M. COWARD
University of Tulsa

EDUCATION

JACQUELINE S. REINIER
California State University, Sacramento

GOVERNMENT & POLITICS

JONATHAN EARLE
University of Kansas

LAW & JUSTICE

ERIC T. L. LOVE
University of Kansas

LIFESTYLES, SOCIAL TRENDS,
FASHION, SPORTS, & RECREATION

MARTHA K. ROBINSON
University of Kansas

RELIGION

CYNTHIA JO INGHAM
Van Buren, Arkansas

SCIENCE & MEDICINE

JAMES N. LEIKER
University of Kansas

GENERAL INDEX

A

Abenaki tribe   300
Abolition   49, 75–76, 118–119, 128, 135, 165, 190, 194, 221
An Account of an Expedition from Pittsburgh to the Rocky Mountains (James)   34
Adams, Charles Francis   196
Adams, John   172, 180
Adams, John Quincy   172, 184, 190, 202, 205, 227
Addison, Joseph   64
Adrian College   155
The Adventures of Captain Bonneville (Irving)   36, 45, 50, 54, 134, 173, 190, 203
Adventures of Huckleberry Finn (Twain)   74
African American education   155
African American newspapers   117
Agassiz, Louis   332
Agriculture   92, 111, 273, 297
Ahlstrom, Sidney   287
Alcohol consumption   58, 327
Allen, William   47, 165
Alta   51
Alta California   53
Alton & Sangamon Railroad   232
American Antiquarian Society   325
American Anti-Slavery Society   164–165, 173, 221
American Board of Commissioners for Foreign Missions (ABCFM)   130, 141, 143, 159–160, 165, 227, 239, 265, 267, 272, 294–296, 300, 302, 304, 306
American Colonization Society   164
American Ethnological Society   319, 325
American Farmer   83
American Fur Company   64, 72, 81, 84, 106, 109–110
American Home Missionary Society (AMHS)   155, 273
American Journal of Education   161, 165
American Museum   37
American Philosophical Society   325, 332
American Sunday School Union   142, 149, 153, 273

American System   185, 198, 202
American Tract Society   116
American Turnverein   243
American Women's Educational Association (AWEA)   162
Americans as They Are (Sealsfield)   34
Amherst *Herald*   136
Amistad (ship)   174
An Essay on the Education of Female Teachers (Beecher)   143
Anawangmane, Simon   297
Ancient Society or, Researches in the Lines of Human Progress from Savagery through Barbarism to Civilization (Morgan)   337
Andover Seminary   274
Annexation   87, 119, 174, 178, 191–192, 204–205, 209, 242
Anthropology   325, 336–337
Anti–Horse Thief Association   215
Anti-miscegenation laws   213, 215
Antioch College   145
Anti-Semitism   277
Apache tribe   57, 215, 245, 254
Apess, William   58, 293
"Appeal of the Independent Democrats"   200
Arapaho tribe   223, 254, 326
Archaeology   325
Arikara tribe   223
Arkansas Territory   239
Armijo, Manuel   260
Arrington, Leonard J.   257
Articles of Confederation   148
The Arts   31–78
Asbury College   143, 155
Ashley, William   83, 107, 240
Assiniboine tribe   35, 64, 223, 253
Assiniboine Medicine Sign (painting)   64
Assiniboine-Cree Attack (painting)   35
Associated Press   134
Astor, John Jacob   36, 80–81, 91, 106, 109–111, 318
Astoria trading post   81–82, 109, 111
Astoria (Irving)   36
Atala (painting)   32
Atchison, David Rice   200
The Atlantic   68
Auburn University   146
Audubon, John James   36, 39, 62, 258, 320, 335

Austin, Samuel   231
Austin, Stephen   189, 211, 231, 240
Averill, Charles   38, 41, 43
Avery, Hiram   86
Axtell, James   289
Aztec culture   323

B

Bachman, John   335
Bacon College   143
Bailes (formal balls)   252
Bailey, Margaret Jewell   39, 49
Baker, George Holbrook   52
Baldwin, Joseph B.   68
Baltimore and Ohio Railroad   84, 88, 104
Baltimore Sun   124
Bancroft, Hubert Howe   49, 60
Bankruptcy laws   80, 87
Banks   82, 87
Bannock tribe   308
Banvard, John   55
Baptist Church   118, 142, 144, 163, 225, 229, 265, 268–270, 277, 292, 296
Baptist General Convention   296
Barceló, Doña Gertrudis (La Tules)   260
Barili-Thorn, Clotilda   53
Barker, Robert   54
Barnard, Henry   158, 161
Barnum, P. T.   37
Barrett, James A.   232
Baseball   244
Battles—
—Alamo (1836)   36, 68
—Chapultepec (1847)   194
—Contreras (1847)   194
—Fallen Timbers (1794)   148, 312
—Goliad (1836)   191
—Horseshoe Bend (1814)   187, 203
—Molino del Rey (1847)   194
—New Orleans (1815)   171, 184, 203, 205
—San Jacinto (1836)   173
—Thames River (1813)   171, 183, 239, 265
—Tippecanoe (1811)   171, 209, 265, 314

Fur trade   42, 44, 80–81, 83–84, 86, 91, 100–101, 106–109, 111, 202, 238, 246, 301, 318, 330
Fur Traders Descending the Missouri (painting)   37, 50

G

Gadsden Purchase (1853)   89, 175, 215
Gadsden, James   200
Gale, George W.   164
Gallatin, Albert   81, 103, 110, 319, 323, 331, 337
Gambling   252, 260, 327
Garrard, Lewis H.   42
Garrison, William Lloyd   118, 128, 135, 164
Garry, Spokan   301, 303
Gast, John   122
Gates, Paul   97
Gateway cities   100
General Missionary Convention of the Baptist Denomination in the United States for Missions. *See* Triennial Convention.
Genius of Universal Emancipation   166
Genre painting   49
Georgetown College   142
Georgia Scenes (Longstreet)   35, 68
German Reformed Church   145
Gerstacker, Friedrich   45
Gibbons v. *Ogden* (1824)   84, 211, 222
Gibbons, Thomas   222
Gilbert, Edward   51
Glover, Sarah Koontz   66
Godey, Louis A.   117
Godey's Lady's Book   117–118, 121
Goetzmann, William   122
Goforth, William   163
Gold camps   51, 66
Gold Mines of California, Voyage to California and Return (painting)   55
Gold Rush (California)   38, 42, 50, 52, 55, 59, 65, 71, 88–89, 93–94, 106, 120, 151, 175, 196, 214, 225, 230, 256, 326
Gold Rush (Pikes Peak)   89
Golden Eagle Bakery   52
Golden Era   39, 51, 59, 76
Goodell, William   221
Gore, Sir St. George   260–261
Gouging   238, 245, 258
Gould, Charles   39, 54
Government and Politics   169–206
Graduation Act (1854)   89
Grain production   89, 101–102
The Grains (Bailey)   39, 49, 65
Grand Medicine Society   58
Grant, Ulysses S.   136, 337
Greeley, Horace   40, 51, 120–123, 126, 133
Green Corn Dance (Busk)   290
Green River Rendezvous   240
Gregg, Josiah   37–38, 69, 105
Gridley, Samuel   158
Griffin, Reverend Edward   296

Gros Ventre tribe   223
Guarani tribe   308
Guidebooks   119
Gymnasiums   243

H

Hale, David   120, 134
Hale, Isaac   312
Hale, John P.   195
Hale, Sarah J.   118
Hale, William   123
Hall, James   34, 47, 62, 65, 164
Hamilton College   74, 164
Hamilton Oneida Academy   164
Hamilton, Alexander   81
"Hangtown Gals" (song)   66
Harding, Chester   34, 47, 50
Harper's Weekly   119–121
Harris, George Washington   42, 68
Harris, Martin   312
Harrison, William Henry   171, 174, 182–183, 191, 195, 208–209, 313
Harte, Bret   42, 52, 74, 121
Hartford Female Seminary   162
Hartnell, William E. P.   142, 150
Harvard University   69
Hastings, Lansford Warren   119
Hatch, Nathan   277–278, 283
Haun, Catherine   256
Hawthorne, Nathaniel   46, 68
Hayes, Catherine   53
Hazelwood   297
Hazlitt, William   130
Heath, John   88
Hecker, Friedrich   243
Heidelberg College   145
Hemingway, Ernest   74
Herndon, William   233
Hesperian   51, 59
Hicks, Elijah   159
Hill, Elizabeth McDowell   247
Hill, Walter   67
History of New York (Irving)   33
History of the Indian Tribes of North America (McKenney and Hall)   62
History of the Ojibway Indians (Jones)   59
History of the Ojibway, Based Upon Traditions and Oral Statements (Warren)   59
History, Condition and Prospects of the Indian Tribes of the United States (Schoolcraft)   38
Holley, Dr. Horace   129, 155
Holly, Mary   35, 49
Holmes, Oliver Wendall   233
Home as Found (Cooper)   74
Homer   49
Homestead Act of 1862   96, 126, 204
Homicide rates   214–215
Hoop and pole game   254
Hooper, Johnson Jones   37, 68
Hopi tribe   58, 292
Horse racing   252, 259–260
Horse trade   301
Hosack, David   32
Houston, Sam   173, 191, 241

How Gertrude Teaches Her Children (Pestalozzi)   152
Howard, George   46
Howe, Elias   242
Hudson River School   38, 42, 47, 53
Hudson's Bay Company   106, 159, 303, 319
Hughes, Charles Evans   233
Hughes, John Joseph   143
Hunt, William Gibbes   33, 65, 116, 129
Hunt, Wilson Price   239
Hunting   65, 224, 250, 257–258, 260, 301, 337
Hupa tribe   98
Huron tribe   59
Hussey, Obed   112
Hydraulic mining   94
The Hyperion   65, 74

I

The Indian Princess, or La Belle Sauvage (play)   33
Ignace La Mousse, Iroquois chief   265
Il trovatore (Verdi)   53
Illinois Central Railroad   89, 175, 199–200, 204, 233
Illinois Central Railroad v. *the Country of McLean*   233
Illinois College at Jacksonville   143
The Illinois Monthly Magazine   65
Illinois State Normal University   146, 161
Illinois Supreme Court   203, 233
Illinois Territory   209
Illinois tribe   224
Indian Gallery (paintings)   36, 72
Indian Intercourse Act (1834)   173
Indian Removal Act (1830)   75, 85, 212, 216, 240, 294
Indiana Territory   140, 209, 273
Indiana University   141–142
Inez, A Tale of the Alamo (Evans)   39, 49
Influenza   326
Interracial marriage   36, 44
Iowa College   274
Iowa State University   146
Iowa tribe   212
Irish potato famine   156
Iron production   101, 287
Iroquois tribes   59, 265, 291, 301, 307, 320, 322, 336–337
Irving, Washington   33, 35–36, 40, 49, 69, 118, 331
Isbell, Olive Mann   144, 151
Iturbide, Augustin de   211
Ives, James Merrit   45

J

Jackson, Andrew   68, 84–86, 116, 135, 159, 166, 171–173, 178, 183–184, 187, 190–191, 198, 202–204, 209, 210, 212, 216–217, 223, 225, 227, 234, 294, 298

INDEX OF PHOTOGRAPHS